MW01289583

Buffalo Bayou

An Echo of Houston's
Wilderness Beginnings

Books by Louis F. Aulbach

The Devils River
The Great Unknown of the Rio Grande
The Lower Canyons of the Rio Grande
The Lower Pecos River
The Upper Canyons of the Rio Grande

Front cover: Photo by Linda Gorski. Natalie Wiest and daughter Ellen paddle Buffalo Bayou in Memorial Park with the Houston Canoe Club.

Back cover: The founding of Houston dates from the advertisement placed in the Telegraph and Texas Register *on August 30, 1836 by Augustus C. Allen and John Kirby Allen.*

Buffalo Bayou

An Echo of Houston's
Wilderness Beginnings

by

Louis F. Aulbach

[signature]

12/11/13

Louis F. Aulbach, Publisher
Houston, Texas
2012

Copyright © 2012 by Louis F. Aulbach

ISBN 978-1468101997

All rights reserved. No part of this book may be used or reproduced in any form
or by any means, or stored in a database or retrieval system, without prior written
permission of the publisher except in the case of brief quotations embodied in
critical articles and reviews.

Third printing

To Rachel, Laurence, Luther, Stephen and Matthew -
the next generation

Contents

.

Acknowledgements

An endeavor like this is not something that one can do alone. Many people are a part of the process, whether they realize it or not, so I would like to recognize a few of those who shared the experiences along the way and contributed to the making of this book.

From the beginning, Linda Gorski was there to explore the banks of the bayou on foot and in canoes. She also was tenacious in her pursuit of research into the facts which became the building blocks of the many stories. Many members of the Houston Canoe Club, including Linda Gorski, Dana Enos, John Rich and Natalie Wiest, paddled up and down the bayou to locate ruins and remnants of the city's past lying on the lower banks and in the water.

Kirk Farris introduced me to Frost Town and its significant role in early Houston. In addition, he sent me to the late Jim Glass who was an important source of information about Houston and a source of inspiration for the telling of the stories.

Von Maszewski, besides providing encouragement and enthusiasm for the local history, showed me the importance of the Germans immigrants to Houston and Texas in the nineteenth century.

When the Buffalo Bayou Partnership initiated their pontoon boat tours on Buffalo Bayou, Anne Olson and Trudi Smith asked me to provide the historical commentary. Their confidence allowed me to develop many of the narratives that have been included in this book. Captain Robby Robinson handled the boat in perfect timing to each story.

Robbie Morin's postcards and documents made story of Camp Logan come alive after all these years.

To all of these individuals and to anyone I have forgotten or neglected to mention, I offer my sincere gratitude for the help you have given me. Thank you.

Introduction

The idea for this book came in early 2000 as a few of us were talking about the bayou, and Linda Gorski suggested that I write a river guide to Buffalo Bayou, just as I have done for the rivers in West Texas. With that, a remarkable journey of over twelve years began. Initially, it was conceived of as a regular river guide, showing access points to the bayou, mileages along the bayou and suggested day trips. A little of history would be thrown in, too.

That was a slight miscalculation. There was a lot more history than I had imagined. The focus of the guide then turned to the stories of people and places along the bayou, and the book blossomed from a standard one hundred page guidebook into a full tome totaling nearly eight hundred pages. Even as a native Houstonian, there was much more to the story of Buffalo Bayou than I had ever realized. I learned a lot in this exercise, and I hope that you may, too.

Although there are maps for each chapter of the book, space considerations have limited the production of maps large enough to provide the detail necessary to follow the journey downstream. I recommend that you use a more detailed map as you read the book and follow the stories of Buffalo Bayou from Katy to Harrisburg. One easy way might be to use an online map service such as Google Maps (http://maps.google.com) or Open Street Maps (http://www.openstreetmap.org) so that you can zoom in closely to the area of interest.

The stories of early Houston display the same richness and diversity of cultures and experiences that we know of Houston today. I hope you enjoy the stories that I have written.

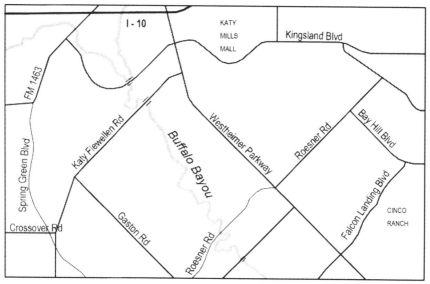

Map by Rachel A. Garcia

Buffalo Bayou begins at the junction of the Willow Fork and Cane Island Branch that is located on the north side of the Kingsland Boulevard crossing of the bayou (see map above). From there, Buffalo Bayou flows through the former farm and ranch land that has become the residential subdivisions of Katy and Cinco Ranch (below).

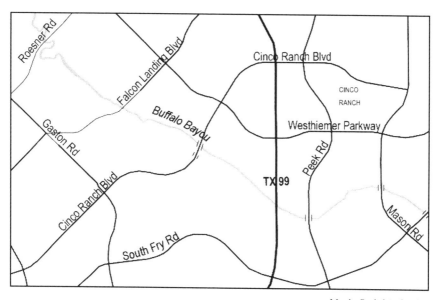

Map by Rachel A. Garcia

Chapter 1
The Headwaters of Buffalo Bayou

Buffalo Bayou begins near the city of Katy. Just below Interstate 10, about a mile and a half southwest of the town, two small creeks, Willow Fork and Cane Island Branch, join to form Buffalo Bayou. Yet, because there is no significant geographic or topographic feature to mark it, you would not be aware of the bayou's headwaters unless someone pointed the spot out to you[1].

Driving west from Houston on Interstate 10, the town of old Katy is visible from the highway to the right. On the left is the vast sprawl of the Katy Mills Mall. Long before the town of Katy was incorporated in 1945, the community existed as a stagecoach stop on the San Felipe Road. Colonists traveling between San Felipe de Austin and the port of Harrisburg often rested at Cane Island, the name of the settlement in the 1830's. The present Fifth Street in Katy follows the course of the San Felipe Road[2].

Although the village of San Felipe has faded from significance and today's traffic patterns make the San Felipe Road a historical curiosity, it is worth noting the stories this area can tell. Santa Anna followed the route from San Felipe through Cane Island on his march to San Jacinto in 1836. Texas independence brought streams of immigrants along this road as they traveled from Houston to San Antonio. During the period of the Republic, Prince Carl of Solms-Braunfels, returning from his travels to the German settlements in central Texas, followed this route in 1845. In his journal, he noted that he could leave Cane Island at sunrise and arrive in Houston in the evening[3].

Anglo settlers moved into the area around present-day Katy in the 1850's. The early settlement of the area, known as Cane Island until 1894, proceeded rapidly because people were attracted to the rich farm land. The Karankawa Indians who hunted in the area began moving out, making it even more desirable for the settlers.

Ample grazing land and free-roaming herds of longhorn cattle encouraged the first settlers in Cane Island (Katy) to combine cattle-raising with farming. Typical of these settlers were Thomas and Mary Robinson who acquired 200 acres in 1872 on the Cane Island Branch of Buffalo Bayou.

A new group of settlers began to arrive in the area in December, 1894 and the influx continued into 1895. James Oliver Thomas, who came from Mississippi, bought 320 acres of land and laid out the town site, which he named Katy for the MKT Railroad. The Missouri, Kansas & Texas Railroad reached the region by that time and enabled farmers to get their products to the markets of Houston.

The hurricane of 1900, which made landfall on September 8, destroyed most of the buildings in Katy, but the town was quickly rebuilt. William Eule introduced rice farming to Katy in 1901. Rice soon replaced corn, wheat, sorghum, peanuts and cotton as the main crop.

A gas field was discovered in 1934 just west of town, adding gas refining to the local economy[4].

During the decades of the 1980's and 1990's, the urban growth of Houston has changed the agricultural nature of Katy into a residential community serving the large city to the east. Suburban developments along the I-10 corridor extend in a continuous and unbroken mosaic of new homes and shopping centers from downtown Houston to downtown Katy.

Interstate 10 curves around Katy in a southwesterly sweep. Immediately past the Pin Oak Road interchange just beyond Katy Mills Mall, a small creek exits the wooded area on the north side of the highway. The creek goes almost unnoticed through a couple of culverts under I-10 and re-enters the woods on the south. This is the Cane Island Branch of Buffalo Bayou.

About a mile or so downstream, the Cane Island Branch joins with the Willow Fork. That is where Buffalo Bayou officially begins at 29 degrees, 46 minutes North and 95 degrees, 50 minutes West. The bayou flows sixty-five miles in an easterly direction to its mouth on the San Jacinto River at Lynchburg. The fascinating story of the city of Houston is found along the way.

Photo credit: Louis F. Aulbach

Near the headwaters, Buffalo Bayou has been channelized to improve drainage for the new developments in Katy.

Wood Creek Reserve

If you take the Pin Oak Road exit and turn south across the freeway continuing on to the Katy Flewellen Road, you will come to a bridge across Buffalo Bayou. At this point, you are approximately one mile below the confluence of the two forks that form the origin of the bayou.

Upstream of the bridge, the bayou has been politely channelized resulting in a finely sculptured stream in manicured, grassy banks with the trees and brush neatly set back some 30 feet from the water on each side. The channelization of the Willow Fork and the main channel of the bayou was done in the mid-1980's as an improvement to the Barker Reservoir flood control project. A locked gate indicates that the greenbelt is private property.

Although the width of the bayou would indicate that it is technically navigable at this point, the recreational use of the bayou is certainly not encouraged.

The bayou's origin lies between Katy Flewellen Road and the next road to the west, Farm Road 1463. On the Willow Fork, above the origin, there is a new residential development called the Wood Creek Reserve. The Wood Creek Reserve property was purchased from the Elizabeth Poorman-Moore family in 1996. The family had owned the property known as the Poorman Family Ranch which was used as a family retreat.

The Wood Creek Reserve incorporates a 100 acre nature park, nestled along the north bank of the Willow Fork of Buffalo Bayou, that combines nature preservation with residential amenities. The developers plan to place sports fields, nature trails, tennis courts, picnic areas in a green belted reserve[5].

Grayson Lakes

The downstream side of the Katy Flewellen bridge is less developed at this time. Trees line the north bank while the south side of the bayou is largely open fields. Although it is not immediately adjacent to the bayou, there is a housing development planned for the tract of land along the bayou. Newland Communities, a San Diego-based developer of master-planned communities, is developing the 325 acre community called Grayson Lakes.

The development is located at the intersection of Katy Flewellen and Katy Gaston Roads. Grayson Lakes will have over about 524 single family, detached homes, multiple lakes covering over 30 acres, a recreation center with pool, tennis courts and picnic areas.

Home prices in Grayson Lakes, whose grand opening was July 13, 2002, range from $200,000 to $750,000. Each home will be wired for high speed, state of the art Internet access. Promoted with the idea that there is access to Houston via the Westpark Tollway, this development continues the trend to build residential neighborhoods as an extension of the suburban growth of Houston. The farmland west of the city is systematically being replaced by homes, golf courses and other structures of urban growth[6].

The effect of this development on the nature and quality of Buffalo Bayou is yet to be seen. The Grayson Lakes development is connected to Buffalo Bayou through a small creek drainage that cuts across the southern corner of the Grayson Lakes property. Storm runoff will be channeled into the bayou via this waterway. The effect of residential runoff on the bayou will undoubtedly be negative due to trash, oil and other pollutants that typically are washed into the waterways during times of high rainfall. Wastewater treatment facilities appear to be located on this tributary as well.

Fulshear Oil Field

Immediately downstream of the Grayson Lakes development, the Fulshear Oil Field extends across both sides of the bayou, while a pipeline, which may or may not be associated with the field, crosses the bayou about three miles from the bayou's headwaters. The Fulshear Oil Field produces gas from the Hillebrenner formation. According to the July, 2002 report from the Texas Railroad Commission, the field has ten injection/disposal wells operated by Aquila Storage and Transportation.

Katy Prairie

Between Green Bush Road and the Grand Parkway, Buffalo Bayou flows across the farm land and fields without much evidence of development. The flat, open prairie is the southernmost extent of the coastal grasslands that has become known as the Katy Prairie.

In 1832, German writer Charles Sealsfield described this prairie as a confettied sea that stretched to the horizons. Obviously traveling in the Texas springtime, he wrote of the prairie as a variegated carpet of flowers of every color. The Katy Prairie extends from near the Brazos River on the south, through Interstate 10 to Highway 290 and the area around Cypress Creek and Spring Creek on the north. The prairie stretches in a broad sweep from just beyond the Houston city limits west to Brookshire and northwest to Hempstead[7].

Millions of migratory birds, especially waterfowl, winter in Katy Prairie until March before returning to nesting areas in the Upper Midwest and Canada. In the period 1977 to 1994, 196 avian species were recorded during Christmas bird counts on the Katy Prairie. The original Katy Prairie covered a half million acres. Today it is about 200,000 acres.

Suburban development accelerated after World War II along major highways. Substantial growth between 1950 and 1966 took the city as far as Dairy Ashford, only 5 miles from the Katy Prairie.

Enormous growth occurred to the west and northwest in the late 1960's and 1970's. By 1978 approximately 32,000 acres of the Katy Prairie had been converted to urban uses. By 1993, that figure had quadrupled to 134,000 acres.

The Katy Prairie Conservancy, founded in 1992, is dedicated to the preservation of this valuable natural resource. However, the task before them is overwhelming considering the sustained momentum of urban development. The Conservancy believes that protecting 30,000 to 50,000 acres in the heart of the region is a realistic goal.

Along the Buffalo Bayou drainage, the situation is even more bleak for the open prairie. In July, 2002, Terrabrook Development, the developer of Cinco Ranch, bought 1,828 acres west of Grand Parkway for 4,000 home expansion of Cinco Ranch[8]. This large tract of land is located west of the Grand Parkway and west of Katy-Gaston Road, north of FM 1093, and east of FM 1463. The few miles of vacant land between Green Bush Road and the Grand Parkway is surely on some developer's drawing board.

Cinco Ranch

Improvements to the drainage capacity of Buffalo Bayou up-stream of Barker Reservoir were made in the mid-1980's. The channelization of the bayou is visually evident in the straightened stream course. Although two oxbows are found immediately below Katy Flewellen Road, the straightening of the natural meanders is more apparent below Green Bush Road. At least eight cut off segments of the old stream bed can be found between Green Bush Road and Fry Road.

About three miles downstream of Green Bush Road is State Highway 99, known locally as the Grand Parkway. The Grand Parkway was opened in the mid-1990's as a major thoroughfare connecting the Katy Freeway on the north and US 59 on the south. The growth of development, both in the west Houston suburbs and in the Sugar Land and Richmond-Rosenberg areas of Fort Bend County, has necessitated the highway. And, in some ways, the Parkway itself has contributed to the increased development of the area as new subdivisions are being built along its access roads.

As the bayou flows under the Grand Parkway, it enters the residential development of the Cinco Ranch, once a large ranching operation that has now become the major residential community along the bayou on the west side of Barker Reservoir. The land has historical roots that extend back to the earliest settlement of Texas and, under the ownership of Bassett Blakely, it was a significant participant in the rise of the Texas cattle industry during the last quarter of the nineteenth century.

Bassett Blakely was the grandson of Randolph Foster, one of Stephen F. Austin's Old Three Hundred colonists. Arriving in Texas in 1822, Foster received title to a league of land, about 4,400 acres, in what is now Waller and Fort Bend Counties in 1824. Foster's daughter Mary married Thomas Blakely, a pioneer cattleman in Fort Bend County. Bassett, their son, subsequently operated the combined family ranches of over 15,000 acres with over 14,000 head of cattle. Blakely's cowhands were well known for cattle drives of 10,000 head of cattle to the rail lines in Kansas. The property near Katy was called the Blakely Ranch.

In 1937, Bassett Blakely sold the ranch to William M. Wheless, Jr. who brought in four of his friends as partners. The joint venture of these five ('cinco' in Spanish) partners became the Cinco Ranch. The Wheless family lived on the ranch and raised cattle, grew rice, soybeans and peanuts for over 40 years[9].

The American General Investment Corporation bought the 5,000 acre Cinco Ranch land in a venture with the Mischer Corporation and Homecraft Development (called the Cinco Ranch Ventures) in February, 1984. The first homes in the master-planned development were built in 1991. American General sold its interests in the Cinco Ranch development to Westbrook Partners in 1997[10].

Cinco Ranch has seven subdivisions: Fountain View, Greenway Village, Meadow Green, North Lake Village, South Lake Village, South Park and Summer Pointe. By 2001, after 10 years of homebuilding, Cinco Ranch included 5,000 homes and nearly 41,000 people. The development, completed in 2006, has a total of 8,300 homes[11].

Little Prong Creek

Little Prong Creek enters Buffalo Bayou at the Grand Parkway, coming in from the southwest. In a scene that is common in many of the new residential developments, golf courses are an important amenity. The first tee of the Meadowbrook Farms Golf Club crosses Little Prong Creek.

Yet, in a trend that is becoming more common, golf courses are attempting to coexist with the natural environment. Meadowbrook Farms Golf Club's environmental goal is to restore the surrounding grasslands to their original condition before the land was settled.

Meadowbrook Farms Golf Club was designed by Greg Norman and developed by Landmark National. It is Greg Norman's first project in Texas. In case you are thinking of playing a round at the course, be forewarned. Green fees at Meadowbrook Farms Golf Club are among the highest in the state at $90[12].

Diversion Channel

From the Peek Road bridge over Buffalo Bayou, about one quarter mile downstream of the Grand Parkway, you can see a fork in the stream bed. Large homes fill the land beyond an eight to ten foot concrete bulkhead, while the bayou goes off to the left and to the right. Although the stream bed is fairly wide here, there is usually little water and the channel is mostly grass.

The flood control program that was approved in 1940 and resulted in the building of Barker Reservoir included plans for retention and diversion of floodwaters from Buffalo Bayou. The construction of a high flow diversion canal was completed in the late 1980's. This diversion channel, along with the channelization and widening of the bayou upstream, is designed to funnel flood waters directly into Barker Reservoir and to prevent the flooding of the upper watershed which is now largely residential neighborhoods[13].

Access along the bayou and the diversion channel is open and it appears that the developers will improve the facilities for recreational use of the easement. Parking near the road crossings, however, is generally non-existent, and the hiking and biking trails along easement are undeveloped. However, the potential is there.

Photo credit: Louis F. Aulbach

As Buffalo Bayou leaves Cinco Ranch and enters the western edge of Barker Reservoir, a diversion canal takes flood waters south of the housing developments.

From the point where the diversion channel separates from the main channel of Buffalo Bayou to the point where the two branches rejoin in Barker Reservoir, a three and one half mile long "island" of land lies between the waterways. The western half of this island is residential development. The eastern half is within the boundaries of Barker Reservoir and is known as Cinco Ranch Park. An extension of the Katy YMCA facility is in the Cinco Ranch Park adjacent to the Diversion Channel off South Mason Road in Fort Bend County. The Katy YMCA Trailblazers use this facility. The rest of Cinco Ranch Park in Barker Reservoir is heavily wooded and undeveloped for recreational use.

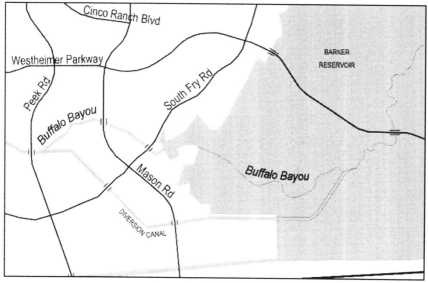

Map by Rachel A. Garcia

Beyond Mason Road and South Fry Road, Buffalo Bayou enters the wild landscape of Barker Reservoir (above). The southern part of the reservoir offers recreational opportunities, but soon the bayou makes a course through a dense and overgrown riparian forest (below).

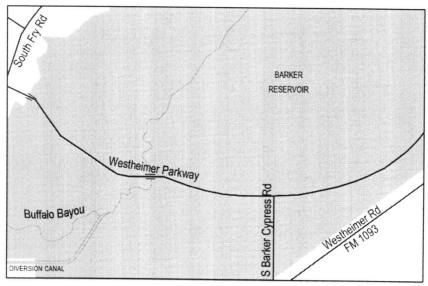

Map by Rachel A. Garcia

Chapter 2
Barker Reservoir

On the left bank of Buffalo Bayou, about a quarter of a mile downstream of the South Mason Road bridge and before you get to the Fry Road bridge, is a short segment of the Willow Fork Country Club that borders the bayou. Most of the property for the club and the golf course is to the north along Fry Road. Willow Fork Country Club is a typical neighborhood country club and golf course whose claim to fame is that 12 of the 18 holes have water hazards.

Immediately beyond Fry Road, the bayou passes a pipeline right of way and enters the boundary of the Barker Reservoir. The western boundary of Barker Reservoir is a very irregular line that follows the elevation contour of the reservoir level. The Cinco Ranch development hovers along the boundary giving it an unconventional neighborhood pattern not often found in modern planned communities.

The greenbelt along the north bank of the bayou from Fry Road to Westheimer Parkway is maintained and provides an excellent opportunity for hiking and biking. The trails are undeveloped, but they are clear of the trees and brush that are the predominant feature of the riparian woodland. The remnants of oil and gas wells can be seen within a few yards of the easement along the north side of the bayou. Abandoned storage tanks, well heads and miscellaneous oil field equipment litter the sites of these old wells. Be careful when inspecting them and respect the "no trespassing" signs!

Within a half mile of Westheimer Parkway, the Diversion Channel enters the main channel of Buffalo Bayou from the southwest. A sturdy, single lane bridge just downstream of the junction, probably used to service the oil wells on the north bank, provides access to the south bank of the bayou and the south side of the Diversion

Channel. Bike riders and hikers who want to do the loop back to Mason Road can cross here and return back along the south side.

The Harris County-Fort Bend County line crosses within a quarter mile of Westheimer Parkway. On the north bank is a small park with benches and opportunities for picnicking and fishing. Access to this park is through a gate at Westheimer Parkway where there is a small parking area off the roadway. Although you may be tempted to put a canoe or kayak in to the water here, kayaking and canoeing is prohibited in Barker Reservoir due to restrictions imposed by the Corps of Engineers.

Beyond Westheimer Parkway, Buffalo Bayou enters the wildest, most remote and inaccessible sections of its course. Protected from development and allowed to remain in a mostly natural state, the land in the interior of Barker Reservoir is a wild and untamed place within a stone's throw of urban civilization. The 13,000 acres of the reservoir teem with raccoons, bobcats, deer, coyotes and other wildlife. As late as 1967, Harris County paid bounties for dead wolves and coyotes because they attacked livestock. Not surprisingly, Barker Reservoir is ideal habitat for these predatory canines.

The county discontinued the bounty programs in the 1970's. When food becomes scarce in winter, coyotes, often weighing 60 to 80 pounds, can be seen hunting in packs and prowling the adjacent subdivisions, such as the Briar Hills Subdivision. They leave their undeveloped woodlands habitat in pursuit of food when their natural prey, such as rodents, rabbits and quail, cannot be found[1].

In some sense, the use of the land for a reservoir was to utilize the land for its best purposes. Historically, land use in Barker Reservoir has been primarily agricultural. The poor drainage and the general low, wet nature of the terrain was the main reason that the area was so sparsely settled. For those who did try to cultivate the land, cotton farming was of prime importance between 1870 and 1930. Mechanical farming techniques allowed the previously unproductive land in Barker Reservoir to produce rice crops around 1900, and livestock raising increased in importance and value after 1900[2].

However, the events of nature destined the land for another purpose. Torrential rains during the first week of December, 1935, produced the worst flood in the city of Houston's history. Several blocks of downtown were flooded and damage was extensive. The gauge at Shepherd Drive registered 40,000 cubic feet per second (cfs) on December 9, 1935. This flood can be compared to the flood caused by Tropical Storm Allison in June, 2001, when the gauge at Shepherd Drive read a mere 14,000 cfs on June 9. More importantly, the 1935 flood followed a similar flood in 1929 when the gauge reading was 19,000 cfs on May 31[3].

The outcry from the 1935 flood led to the creation of Barker Reservoir to provide flood control on the Buffalo Bayou watershed. In 1945, the US Army Corps of Engineers claimed 450 acres of the prominent LH7 Ranch along with over 12,500 additional acres for a reservoir that is bounded on three sides by a rolled earth dam that is 72,900 feet long and 112.5 feet high. Construction on the dam for Barker Reservoir was completed in 1946[4].

George Bush Park

Many areas of Barker Reservoir do not see flooding very often. Although heavy rains turn much of the reservoir along the course of the bayou into a shallow lake, there are large areas that remain high and dry even during the rainy periods. These areas have been made into parks and recreational facilities, the largest of which is George Bush Park. Activities in the park include a shooting range, fishing, baseball and softball fields, a model airplane facility, soccer fields, an exercise station, and birding trails.

George Bush Park is located along Westheimer Parkway in Barker Reservoir. The park extends from just west of the Westheimer Road-Westheimer Parkway split to the point where Westheimer Parkway crosses Buffalo Bayou. George Bush Park is operated by Harris County although the US Army Corps of Engineers has jurisdiction since it is within the reservoir[5].

Archeology of Barker Reservoir

During the past fifty years, there has been a rise in the interest in the understanding of who and what occurred in the Houston area prior to the modern era. The encouragement and imperatives of various state and federal antiquities legislation has enabled researchers to find evidence of prehistoric peoples and cultures. Although it was relatively late in coming to the Houston area, archeological research in west Houston has benefited from the protection afforded by the creation of Barker Reservoir and its companion Addicks Reservoir under the jurisdiction of the US Army Corps of Engineers. In particular, the widening and channelization improvements of Buffalo Bayou in the mid-1980's led to archeological surveys of Barker Reservoir.

By 1986, thirty-eight percent of the 11,607 acres in the Barker Reservoir study area had been surveyed. Archeological investigations were made on thirty-one prehistoric sites. These prehistoric sites were clustered in two groups. One group was a cluster of floodplain mounds that were found within an eight acre area near Buffalo Bayou. A second group consists of twenty-four sites in a 75 acre area near the Harris-Fort Bend County line in the western portion of Barker Reservoir.

The data from the sites in the vicinity of the Cinco Ranch suggest that the occupations were by relatively small groups of people who may have moved in an annual seasonal route. There was no evidence of a permanent occupation of the sites. The people who occupied the sites date from about 1000 BC to 300 BC, a period known as the Late Archaic/Early Ceramic. They appear to have been very mobile foragers who exploited an extensive area, ranging as far as the lower Brazos River valley where chert was procured. Fragments of vessels were found that appear to be jars or bowls used in food preparation, cooking or storage. However, no evidence of the manufacture of ceramics was found in Barker Reservoir sites.

In addition to the prehistoric sites, twenty-one historic sites within Barker Reservoir were identified and investigated[6].

Historic Aboriginal Inhabitants -- the Akokisa

The vast expanse of Barker Reservoir, though surrounded on all sides by a great, modern city, allows us to peer back in time to an era when the landscape was only beginning to be touched by civilization. Although there are paved roads, buildings and mowed sports fields in the reservoir, a short walk off the road takes you to a different place and time. The prairies, river woodlands and East Texas pine forests stand here in the reservoir much as they did in the 1700's.

Texas, of course, was populated by indigenous peoples prior to the arrival of Europeans. During historic times, the coastal area is known to have been inhabited by the Akokisa, Karankawa, Bidai, Atakapa and Patiri tribes. Of these groups, the Akokisa were the most likely inhabitants prior to Anglo-American settlement and they are also the most likely to have occupied the Barker and Addicks Reservoir areas. The Han and Coaque Indians encountered by Alvar Nunez Cabeza de Vaca in the 1530's were mostly probably Akokisa[7].

The Akokisa did not live in permanent settlements, but rather, they migrated between the coastal areas and the inland sites on a seasonal basis. In the winter, large groups of people congregated in villages and semi-permanent camps. During the late spring, they dispersed to the littoral areas along the bays and the Gulf to take advantage of seasonal aquatic resources. The summer was spent wandering in search of food.

As one might expect, the Akokisa bands set up camp near the mouths and confluences of streams and rivers. They practiced some limited agriculture, for example, raising maize; however, the bulk of their diet was gathered from the land. Birds' eggs, fish, wild fruit and game, including deer, bear and bison, could be found on the coastal prairie and woodlands in quantities sufficient to support the population. Some of the Late Ceramic sites in the Addicks area show evidence of the use of efficient hunting tools, such as the bow and arrow and fish weirs. Yet, the search for natural food was very much a determining factor in the daily lives of the Akokisa.

The timeless existence of the native peoples of the Gulf coast began to change in the early 1700's. The colonization activities of the great nations of Europe were becoming evident in the region. The Spanish had claimed the area of Texas in the 16th century, but they neglected the land far to the east because of its distance from Mexico City. However, when French explorers began to cross the Sabine River to trade with the native peoples, the Spanish sought to establish a presence in the area[8].

A Spanish outpost, El Orcoquisac, and the Nuestra Senora de la Luz Mission were built in 1756 near the mouth of the Trinity River, at a site near the present day Wallisville, for the Akokisa and the Bidai tribes. The Spanish Governor of Texas, Jacinto de Barrios, placed the garrison on the site of a French trading post in a move to oppose French presence and to curtail their trade with the Bidai and Orcoquiza (the Spanish rendering of the Akokisa name). Indeed, Barrios enriched himself through fur trade with the natives and contraband trade with the French at Natchitoches. For fifteen years, the Spanish tried to establish sovereignty over the region, but the foibles of bureaucracy and the difficulties of maintaining such a far-flung outpost resulted in the withdrawal of the Spanish missionaries and soldiers from the area in 1772[9].

Things would never be the same for the native peoples, however. All indications are that, even in the best of times, the Akokisa population was fairly sparse. In the Spanish period, around 1700, the population of the upper coast reached a peak at approximately 1200 individuals. By 1820, their numbers had declined to about 300. Finally, succumbing to the inevitability of history, the Akokisa joined their relatives, the Atakapas, in southwest Louisiana in 1830's. It was widely reported by the new settlers from the United States that the land around the new town of Houston was largely uninhabited[10].

Hike and Bike Trails

From a parking area about one mile north of Westheimer Parkway, the old Barker Clodine Road, now closed to automobiles, offers a paved route through the heart of the reservoir for walking, hiking or bicycling. The Barker Clodine Trail crosses Buffalo Bayou on the old road bridge to provide access to the north side of the bayou. Although there is a bike and pedestrian gate at the north end of the trail near the LH7 Ranch, there is very little parking. High water in the reservoir may also flood the trail at times.

Between the Barker Clodine Trail and the reservoir levee, there are a number of hiking trails that cross the interior of the reservoir. These trails are not heavily used and can be difficult to follow if the vegetation is high. This is especially true of the Cow Trail, an informal dirt trail that follows the south side of Buffalo Bayou. Beginning near the bridge over Buffalo Bayou, the Cow Trail connects the Barker Clodine trail with the spillway at Highway 6. As this little-traveled trail cuts through the heart of the reservoir, it provides a unique opportunity to see wildlife, including deer, bea-

Photo credit: Louis F. Aulbach

An extensive network of hike and bike trails provide rugged adventure within Barker Reservoir.

ver, turtles and snakes. Be alert. The Cow Trail, unfortunately, is often muddy or under water because it is so close to the bayou.

Close to the old Beeler Road junction with Barker Clodine Road are two hiking trails that go east from the road. An unnamed trail goes perpendicular to the road into the center of the reservoir and ends near a north-south pipeline easement. A second trail leaves the Barker Clodine Road a short distance north of the unnamed trail. It tracks diagonally to the northeast until it connects with the east-west segment of the Noble Road Trail. From there it is a straight path to the levee. The trail passes to the north of Barker Lake and connects with the levee road and the parking area at the end of Briar Forest Drive.

The Bayou View Trail is a short trail in the interior of the reservoir that heads north off the Noble Road Trail and ends at Buffalo Bayou.

A gravel and rock road, closed to automobile traffic, on top of the Barker Reservoir levee forms a hike and bike trail that connects with the Barker Clodine trail and the trails in Terry Hershey Park. A parking area, located at the spillway for Barker Reservoir, is the junction of hike and bike trails in Terry Hershey Park, going east, and the Cow Trail in the reservoir, going west to the Barker Clodine trail[11].

At the end of Briar Forest Drive there is a parking area from which you can access the trails and lakes in Barker Reservoir. Another good place to park is on the north side of Buffalo Bayou at the spillway. In addition, the Corps of Engineers Office is located on Highway 6 at the spillway on the south side of the bayou. They have informational brochures about the reservoir, the hike and bike trails, and the regulations for use of the reservoir. You can also get a good map of the area from them. The public is welcome.

Habermacher Family

In addition to the prehistoric sites, at least twenty-one historic sites within Barker Reservoir have been identified and investigated. Many of these historic sites relate to the settlement of the area by the Habermacher family. The story of this family exemplifies the pattern of German immigration into Texas in the 1800's.

Thomas and Marie Habermacher arrived in Texas in 1832 with their sons Casper, Joseph, Lawrence, John and Stephen, and their daughter Catherine. On the census records of 1850, the Habermachers indicated that they came from France, but, according to Prince Carl Solms-Braunfels, the head of the German immigration society that gave us the German communities of New Braunfels and Fredericksburg, they were actually Alsatians of German heritage. Prince Solms-Braunfels notes in his journal of 1844-1845, too, that Marie Habermacher had been born in Turin, Italy[12].

The Habermachers settled in Harrisburg initially. Mrs. Dilue Rose Harris recalled in her memoirs that Mr. Habermacher and his son Stephen stopped at the Harris plantation in Stafford's Point in May, 1834, on their way to work on William Stafford's cotton gin on Oyster Creek[13].

By 1844, when Prince Solms visited them, Thomas Habermacher had lived on 107 acres of the William Hardin League from at least 1841. About the same time, Joseph Habermacher is known to have owned 300 acres in the Joel Wheaton survey as well as 100 acres in the Jesse Sitton survey, farther to the west, where the Habermacher Settlement site is.

It appears that the elder Habermacher settled on land to the east of the present Barker Reservoir in the William Hardin survey, probably in the area now crossed by Dairy Ashford Road. Each of his sons then acquired farm land of their own in the vicinity of, but to the west of their father's farm, probably in the Joel Wheaton survey. Joseph Habermacher also acquired land west of the Joel Wheaton survey in the Jesse Sitton survey that became the family homestead known as the Habermacher Settlement[14].

Sometime in the early 1840's, Thomas Habermacher built his farm near the San Felipe Road. Although Miles Bennet makes no mention of Habermacher's farm on his journey on the San Felipe Road in early 1839, by 1844, Habermacher had established his farm as welcome rest stop on the road between the Wheaton farm where the road crossed Buffalo Bayou and the settlement at Piney Point. The San Felipe Road continued south of the bayou from the Wheaton farm to Thomas Habermacher's place before turning to the east to Houston. In 1846, Alwin Soergel wrote that he came upon an inn owned by the German Habermacher in the "middle of nowhere[15]."

The area did not remain remote and uninhabited for long. Not only did the Habermacher family live in the area, but other immigrants, especially from Germany, began to come into the area. By 1850, the Habermacher sons had established themselves as farmers in the area. Each of them had families of their own and, according to the Harris County Census of 1850, each family had accumulated a modest amount wealth.

Stephen Habermacher, the eldest son of Thomas and Marie Habermacher, had married Anne Sophia Coates on December 28, 1846. In 1850, he was 36 yrs old and his wife was 22 years old. They had no children, but as a farmer, he had property valued at $250.

Casper Habermacher was also a farmer. He had married Eliza Jane Cates on April 18, 1844, and, by 1850, they had two daughters, Mary Anne , age 4, and Susan A, age 2. At age 31, Casper and his twenty-five year old wife had property valued at $1,000.

Lawrence Habermacher and Amanda Wheaton were married November 19, 1846. By 1850, when Laurence was 28 years old and Amanda was 22 yrs old, they had two daughters, Catherine E, age

3, and Martha Anne, age 1. They worked a farm and had property valued at $500.

John Habermacher was a 25 year old farmer in 1850, and he was married to Artumasia McFarland who was 19 years old. They had no children, but they did have property valued at $300[16].

According to the 1870 census, Stephen Habermacher was a farmer and Lawrence Habermacher was a teamster. They paid taxes on mules, wagons and cattle. Casper had moved to Austin County, married a wealthy widow and prospered in the cattle business[17]. Joseph Habermacher, at age 58, was a farmer with a young wife Ann, 26 years old, and two small children, Stephen, age 1, and Joseph, age 6-1/2 months. Nineteen year old William Habermacher was a stock driver who lived with the Wilson family with his fifteen year old wife Ophelia.

By the early 1870's, John C. Habermacher had a store in the village of Quinan on Wharton-Richmond Road, near Hungerford. He had the local post office in his store[18].

August T. Marks, a twenty-three year old immigrant from Prussia in 1870, owned 1,600 acres and a stagecoach inn on the banks of Buffalo Bayou. Marks sold the land and inn to W. J. Habermacher, Sr. in 1871. Habermacher moved his family into the inn which had been operated by a Mrs. Silliman prior to Civil War and probably was the inn owned by Elizabeth Wheaton during the 1840's. The inn thereafter became known as the Habermacher House[19].

Joseph Habermacher continued to live on his farm during the 1870's. His farm, now known as the Habermacher Settlement, is located near the intersection of Old Beeler Road and Barker Clodine Road in Barker Reservoir. The homestead, encompassing an area of 25 x 25 meters, contained the early home of Joseph Habermacher and his family. The early settler's home was one or two rooms and small in size. The small dwelling was abandoned as the family moved closer to the intersection of Old Beeler Road and Barker-Clodine Road where the rail station was established and the community of Habermacher was developing. The Texas Western Narrow Gauge Railway rail stop was built along Old Beeler Road about 1877. The settlement may have had as many as five buildings including the homesteads, a church or community building, the train depot, and a school.

The Habermacher post office, mentioned earlier, opened on December 6, 1880 with Joseph Habermacher as the postmaster. However, by this time, the settlement was in decline. Joseph Habermacher was in his late 60's and the railway was failing. The post office was discontinued on May 17, 1881. Joseph Habermacher sold his land to Isaac Stafford who later sold it to Ben Fort Smith in the 1890's[20].

The Habermacher community appears on the 1896 map of Harris County, and Habermacher Station remained on the county maps until 1908. Only through the creation of the Barker Reservoir in 1945 was the Habermacher Settlement preserved for a glimpse of local history. Otherwise, it may easily have become paved over and developed into highways, malls and neighborhoods like those that lie outside the levee.

Texas Western Narrow Gauge Railway

Few streets in the city of Houston are as straight and long as Westheimer Road from the Galleria to Highway 6. The reason for this is that Westheimer Road, as it extended west from the city, was built on the road bed of the pioneer narrow gauge railway in Texas.

The Texas Western Narrow Gauge Railway was chartered January 18, 1875 for the purpose of shipping cotton loaded at Pattison and the Brazos bottomlands to the markets of Houston. More grandiose plans called for the Texas Western Narrow Gauge Railway to be the first railroad to reach the rich silver bearing region on the Rio Grande by 1876. The rail line was opened the 42 miles to Pattison on April 23, 1877, making shipments of cotton from the Brazos valley to Houston[21].

Although the promoters may have had grandiose plans for the railway, records show that its assets included one wooden shop, two engines, nineteen old flat cars, ten new flat cars, one old box car, four new box cars, one caboose and two old coaches and that income for the first fiscal year amounted to $14,861!

From its depot at the corner of St. Emanuel Street and Commerce Avenue, the Texas Western Narrow Gauge Railway made its way to the edge of town. From there, the line went due west to a point beyond the Habermacher Station in what is now Barker Reservoir. At that point, the line turned northwest at an angle of about 30 degrees and headed directly to the town of Pattison near the Brazos River.

Texas Western Narrow Gauge Railway was extended across the Brazos River to Sealy in 1881, giving it a total of fifty-two miles of track, but the railroad was unable to participate in through traffic because of the narrow gauge.

Due to poor economic conditions, the railroad was forced into receivership. It was purchased by Col. Elijah Smith of Portland, Oregon for $200,000, and reorganized in 1880 as the Texas Western Railway Company. Scheduled stops were made at Habermacher Station until 1890, and the rail service continued until 1899 when it ceased operations[22]. A marker was erected commemorating the Texas Narrow Gauge in Pattison by the state and Waller County Historical Survey Committee and is the only physical reminder of what was once a vital economic link in the State's railway system[23].

LH7 Ranch

As Buffalo Bayou enters Barker Reservoir, it begins a turn to the north. The course of the bayou makes a broad arch across the reservoir before flowing back to the southeast as it crosses Highway 6. As it makes this sweeping bow, the bayou brings us to the place where the Texas Longhorn cattle breed was saved from extinction. The northern half of Barker Reservoir was carved from the famous LH7 Ranch. A small remnant of this giant of the Texas cattle industry remains just beyond the boundary of the reservoir on Barker Clodine Road.

The story of the LH7 Ranch is one of the great stories of Texas -- German immigrants on the forbidding prairie, wild longhorn cattle on the vast open range, the great cattle drives of the 1880's, rodeos and trail rides, and ultimately, urban development.

Godhif Marks and his wife Sophia left Prussia for Galveston, Texas in 1847. Sophia was pregnant at the time and during the passage, she gave birth to a son. They named him August Texas Marks - his first name was the month of his birth and his middle name denoting the prospect of hope in their chosen new home. August Texas Marks, born August 15, 1847, en route to Texas[24].

Photo credit: Louis F. Aulbach

Buildings from the LH7 Ranch have been located on a small tract of land situated off Barker Clodine Road.

Marks and his family arrived in Galveston when one of the infamous epidemics of the coastal areas was raging. Like many Germans at this time, he took his family to the interior of Texas, and he settled in western Harris County near the German community that had grown up on Bear Creek, present day Addicks. The Marks' raised crops and rounded up wild Longhorn cattle that roamed the vast open ranges.

By 1850, Sophia, at age 33, has remarried, although the circumstances of the situation are not clearly known. Christian Streipe, a 40 year old farmer, has taken Sophia and August into his family. From the 1860 census, however, we see that Sophia is the head of the household that consists of her four children only, including the teenager August. They had land valued at $790.

After the Civil War, August Texas Marks was a young man in his 20's. On Christmas Eve, 1870, August married Anna Marie Elizabeth Schultz, the 18 year old daughter of a neighboring German family. By 1871, the young Marks owned 260 acres at Addicks. Building on his experience with longhorns on the family farm, he became a cowboy who participated in the trail rides to the rail heads of the Midwest.

Marks and wife Elizabeth had five children by 1881. Emil Henry Marks was born in Addicks on October 26, 1881. Tragically, Elizabeth died in childbirth in 1887 at age 35, leaving August to care for the family. However, when one daughter was quarantined in a pest house for smallpox, August broke the quarantine and brought his daughter home. The daughter recovered, but August contracted smallpox and died in January, 1891[25].

Emil Henry Marks was 6 years old when his mother passed away and he lost his father just three years later. After his father's death, the nine-year-old Emil was raised by an aunt and uncle on a cattle ranch on the Brazos River. Emil went to work in his uncle's store and saloon[26].

Eventually, Emil inherited a small part of the family homestead. He had just 63 acres so he let his longhorns run on the open range. Emil married the 20 year old Maud Smith in 1907 and with this small ranch and a few longhorns, Emil and Maud Marks established the LH7 Ranch[27].

The LH7 brand had been registered in 1898. Emil claimed that the letters had no special significance, although there were seven members of their family.

In 1917, Marks sold his land near Addicks and purchased a section of virgin prairie at Barker. In December, 1917, Marks moved the ranch from east of Addicks to 640 acres near Barker. In the spring of 1918, Marks and his neighbors gathered at the Barker site for the spring branding of the new calves. They held riding and roping contests. And, this gathering ultimately grew into the annual ranch rodeo that continued for 30 years[28].

Although the LH7 Ranch cross bred Brahman cattle from India with Longhorns, the LH7 Ranch had one of nation's largest herds of authentic longhorn cattle with 500 head of pure Texas longhorns. The ranch had 6,670 head of crossbred cattle on 36,000 acres between Highway 90 and Hockley. By the 1930's, the LH7 Ranch had become one of the largest cattle operations on the Gulf Coast.

The Depression, however, had a devastating effect on the ranch. In 1936, the partnership with W. A. Paddock was dissolved. Marks was left only with his longhorn herd and 1,006 acres of land.

Photo credit: Louis F. Aulbach

Built after the floods of 1929 and 1935, the gates of Barker Reservoir keep flood waters from downtown Houston.

In 1945, U. S. Army Corps of Engineers claimed 450 acres of the LH7 Ranch for Barker Reservoir. The rodeo grounds were part of the land that was to become part of the reservoir, and the rodeos were abandoned.

For 30 years, 1907 to 1936, thousands of urban visitors came to the LH7 Ranch Rodeo to see Marks' herd of pure bred Texas Longhorns. The rodeos had ceased, but in January, 1952, Marks and three others rode in the first Salt Grass Trail Ride from Brenham to the Houston Livestock Show and Rodeo. Today, several trail rides are an integral part of the annual event commemorating Houston's cattle heritage.

Emil Marks rode and worked cattle into well into his 80's. He died on September 15, 1969, a few weeks before his 88th birthday. Emil and Maud's youngest daughter Maudeen inherited what was left of the LH7, and, even today, she continues to run pure bred Texas Longhorns[29].

North of Buffalo Bayou and east of the Barker Clodine Trail in Barker Reservoir, on former pastures of the the LH7 Ranch, is the Local Training Area of the 5th Army Reserve, U. S. Army Corps of Engineers[30].

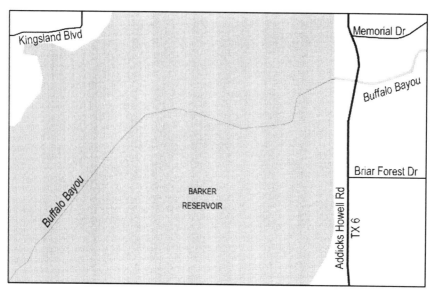

Map by Rachel A. Garcia

Buffalo Bayou exits Barker Reservoir near the community of Addicks where it crosses Highway 6 south of Memorial Drive (above). From there, the bayou passes through the western sections of Terry Hershey Park (below).

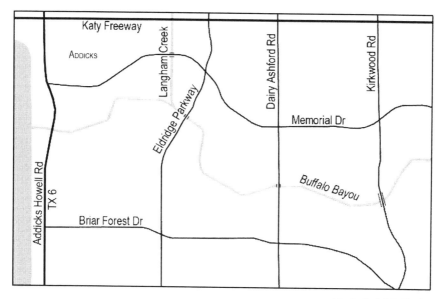

Map by Rachel A. Garcia

Chapter 3
Addicks

From the top of the levee where Buffalo Bayou passes through the floodgates, the view across the reservoir resembles the nature of this land before the European settlement began in the 1820's. The woodlands provide a zone of comfort for the bayou. The grassy prairies, especially south of the bayou, are dotted with a few small lakes among the tall grass. In the dry season, the bayou is a slim channel emerging from the woods before approaching the steel and concrete towers of the gates. In wet weather, a shallow lake pools up behind the levee. The trees stick out of the muddy brown water and the prairie grasses stand like pin pricks where they break the water's surface.

Turn around, and you look down at the spillway as the water pours out through its concrete mouth. Bayou water is channeled down the concrete-sided streambed for about 150 yards before it passes under the bridge at Highway 6. State Highway 6, also known by its former name, Addicks-Howell Road, parallels the eastern face of Barker Reservoir. The six-lane traffic artery seems endlessly busy, shuttling cars and trucks from northwest Harris County through Interstate 10 on the north to Sugar Land and Fort Bend County on the south. Once a two-lane country road between the rural communities of Addicks and Howellville, a small village along the Union Pacific rail line that parallels the Alief Clodine Road, Highway 6 is the major north-south thoroughfare for the western suburbs of Houston.

Looking about 1-1/4 mile to the north, the few buildings and homes that remain of the community of Addicks can barely be seen where the old Addicks Howell Road dead ends into the Katy Freeway access road. Most of the remnants of the town have been absorbed into the frontage businesses and the residential development of recent times. Yet, the people who came here in the mid-

1800's played an important part role in the story of Houston. With the support of the farming communities that were strung like beads to the west of town along the north side of Buffalo Bayou, Houston would become one of the most prosperous agricultural centers of Texas.

About 1850, German immigrants began to homestead along Bear Creek, Langham Creek and South Mayde Creek. The community was known by different names over the years, including Letitia, Bear Hill and Bear Creek. It took the name of Addicks in 1884 in honor of the town's first postmaster Henry Addicks[1].

Eventually, a railroad stop was established for the community near the Missouri, Kansas and Texas line in 1891, and Addicks became the commercial center for local farmers and ranchers.

The creation of the Addicks Reservoir brought changes to the Addicks community. In 1947, forty homes were destroyed or moved to the community's present location on the south side of the railroad tracks and it became a suburb of the City of Houston.

Highway 6

From Highway 6, Buffalo Bayou truly becomes an urban recreational waterway. Although the city limits of Houston follow the far western boundary of the Barker Reservoir, the bayou is too primitive and inaccessible within the reservoir for extensive recreational use. Regulations governing the reservoir also prohibit the use of watercraft, such as canoes or kayaks, within the reservoir.

Buffalo Bayou can be canoed or kayaked from Highway 6. The hiking and biking trail of Terry Hershey Park has its western access point at Highway 6, as well. The parking lot on the west side of the road, north bank of the bayou, is a good place to park. There is usually plenty of space. The hiking and biking trail is on the south side of the bayou, adjacent to the US Army Corps of Engineers Office. The wide, concrete trail winds down the south bank of the bayou and under the bridge. It follows the south side of Buffalo Bayou east toward Eldridge Road, about one and a half miles.

The put in access for canoes or kayaks is somewhat difficult on the west side of Highway 6. The slope of the concreted bank of the spillway channel is not too steep, however, it can become slippery if it has been wet. With some caution, it may be possible to carry your boats to the water from the parking lot to the bayou under the bridge. The concrete rip-rap at the eastern edge of the Highway 6 bridge is extremely dangerous to canoes. Rocks, jagged concrete and exposed reinforcement bars lie just at the surface where the bayou exits from under the bridge into the downstream channel.

An alternate put in on the south bank, downstream of the bridge, is also possible. There is no parking on this side of the road. However, it may be possible to use the driveway for access to the easement, which is usually chained closed, as a place to unload your boats. The parking lot of the business on the south bank is another unloading possibility. Unload and park in the lot across the street. It is a fairly long way to carry your boat and gear down to the bayou. The steep bank presents another challenge, but once in the water, you can leave the pavement and cars behind.

San Felipe Road

Before heading down the bayou, either in your boat or on the trail, pause for a moment at the Highway 6 bridge to recall that this is the site of one of the most historic crossings of the bayou. The traditional route of the San Felipe Road crossed Buffalo Bayou here.

Stephen F. Austin designated the community of San Felipe, on the western bank of the Brazos River, as the seat of government for his colony in 1822. A number of colonists, and prospective colonists, had already moved into Texas by that time. Several of them had settled along the San Jacinto River which had ocean access to the Gulf of Mexico.

John R. Harris settled on Buffalo Bayou, upstream of the bayou's mouth on the San Jacinto, in 1824, and he began shipping goods between New Orleans and Texas. The San Felipe Road was the main route between the seat of Austin's Colony and Harris's town of Harrisburg on Buffalo Bayou. The goods needed by the colonists were transported to the inland destinations of the Brazos Valley from the Gulf Coast ports such as New Orleans[2].

By the mid-1830's, the village of San Felipe, situated 50 miles due west of present day Houston on the west bank of the Brazos River, had become a hub from which eight or more roads projected.

The San Felipe Road was probably the most important of these roads for commerce. It followed a direct route eastward through the present Fifth Street in Katy. From this point, the road turned south and crossed Buffalo Bayou in this location near the modern road crossing. The road curved south of the bayou to pass beyond the forested area known then, as now, as Piney Point. From there, it was a relatively direct line, taking the same route as the present day West Dallas Avenue, to the junction of Buffalo Bayou and Brays Bayou where Harrisburg was situated.

Santa Anna followed the route in his march to San Jacinto in 1836. In an attempt to subdue the rebellious Texans, he burned San Felipe de Austin and then did the same to Harrisburg, before moving on downstream to the fields owned by Peggy McCormick on the San Jacinto River.

We know that the specific route of the road crossed at the Highway 6 point from the earliest times. Arthur McCormick, Peggy's husband, drowned as he attempted to make the crossing of a severely swollen Buffalo Bayou in this location. McCormick had just received title to his land at San Jacinto in August, 1824 when he perished[3].

As early as 1839, the Wheaton family had established a farm where the road crossed the bayou at today's Highway 6. Mrs. Elizabeth Wheaton ran an inn and stagecoach stop that was renowned for its hospitality. We cannot say exactly when the Wheaton farm was established, but the journal of Miles Bennet indicates that he stopped there in February, 1839. Joel Wheaton was granted a first class headright of one labor in 1840, but it appears that he had settled in the area prior to that. Since Joel Wheaton received a first class headright, we know that he was living in Texas on the day that independence from Mexico was declared, March 2, 1836[4].

Miles Bennet refers to the inn as "Mrs. Wheaton's" in 1839. Elizabeth Wheaton may have managed the inn, while her husband farmed, yet Joel Wheaton is not mentioned after the granting of the headright. The German diarist, Prince Carl of Solms-Braunfels, calls the place "Mrs. Wheaton's" in his journal in 1845. Ferdinand Roemer, writing in 1847, noted that the farm belonging to Mrs. Wheaton was larger and more "pretentious" than the neighboring farms. In the census of 1850, Elizabeth Wheaton is identified as a 45-year-old head of the household with property valued at $2500[5].

Although it is not clear whether the Wheaton farm was on the north or the south side of the bayou, we might infer from the itinerary of Miles Bennet that the inn was on the south side. Bennet describes the winter trip in 1839 to deliver military goods to San Antonio. He delayed at the Wheaton farm because of flooding and bad weather. Ultimately, Bennet detoured by going southwest through Richmond. Had the farm been on the north bank, he would have then proceeded along the high ground through the community of Cane Island (the modern town of Katy).

The fate of the stagecoach inn on the bayou becomes unclear after 1850. A Mrs. M. Silliman reportedly ran the inn prior to the Civil War. Afterwards, the property was owned by August T. Marks. In 1871, he sold the inn and the property to W. J. Habermacher, Sr. The Habermachers moved into the inn and it thereafter was known locally as the Habermacher House. The bayou crossing became known as the Habermacher Crossing[6].

Whether there was a topographic feature that is not visible today, or some other reason, this point for the crossing of Buffalo Bayou was as much used by the early Texas settlers as it is by modern Houstonians. Even the aboriginal tribes had a special feeling for this spot. The Habermacher Mound was located about 700 hundred yards downstream from the outlet works of Barker Dam on the south bank of the bayou. It was a relatively large midden that had been well known, and well scavenged, for many years. During the construction of Barker Dam, the stream channel was straightened and deepened, and Habermacher Mound was leveled by construction of the new channel. It is believed that the old house that had been an inn was razed at this time as well[7].

Subdivisions

From Highway 6, Buffalo Bayou takes a course through over thirty neighborhood subdivisions before coming to Memorial Park. The heavily wooded area on the north bank became prime residential property after World War II. In the half century since then, middle and upper income residential developments have been built along the bayou, following the winding route of Memorial Drive. Residential developments also have sprung up in the prairie along the south side of the bayou. Canoeing, biking or hiking along the bayou in this area provides a unique glimpse at Houston's contemporary and varied architectural styles. Although Terry Hershey Park permits access to the bayou between Highway 6 and the West Belt, the banks of Buffalo Bayou from West Belt to Shepherd Drive are largely private property. Access to and egress from the bayou is largely restricted in these areas because of the private ownership of the land. Be respectful of private property and mindful that trespass may be unlawful.

Fleetwood

From the canoe or kayak put in at Highway 6, the Fleetwood Subdivision extends along the north side of the bayou for about 3/4 of a mile as the channelized stream makes a left curving arch. Fleetwood is one of the older communities in the Memorial area, with homes built between 1972 and 1988. As is often the case in the older neighborhoods, the homes are nestled among landscaped yards that have larger trees than many of the newer communities in the area.

Vincent Kickerillo developed Fleetwood and built homes of light colored brick in French, Tudor and traditional designs. The median size of the 457 homes in the neighborhood is 3,288 square feet. The median year of construction for the homes in Fleetwood is 1977[8].

Briarhills

An office complex sits on the southeast corner of Highway 6 and Buffalo Bayou. Within a quarter of a mile, the Briarhills Subdivision begins along the south bank, and it continues for the next half mile or so.

The Briarhills Subdivision was developed in three phases. In each phase, there are distinctly different homes styles. During the late 1970's, contemporary houses and patio homes were built. Beginning in the early 1980's, the neighborhood saw the construction of closely spaced "soft contemporary" and traditional patio homes. The final phase of construction during the early 1990's introduced two-story brick traditional homes to the neighborhood.

The total number of homes in Briarhills is 665. Median year of home construction is 1980. The size of the homes varies widely, as might be expected from the pattern of development, ranging from 1,800 square feet in size to 3,400 square feet. Median size of homes in the neighborhood is 2,381 square feet.

Briarhills has excellent recreational facilities for its residents, including a five acre park that includes a clubhouse, a pool, tennis courts and basketball courts[9].

Memorial Thicket

As the bayou makes a sharp right turn and begins to head due east, the Memorial Thicket Subdivision begins on the north side of the bayou. Actually, it is the eastern section of the subdivision that is south of Memorial Drive and adjacent to the north side of Buffalo Bayou. Another section is across Memorial Drive and it extends to Addicks-Howell Road.

Memorial Thicket was developed by former Houston Mayor Bob Lanier in the 1970's, prior to his term in office from 1992 to 1998, as a gated community. The median size of the 150 homes in Memorial Thicket is 3,634 square feet. The median year of construction of the homes is 1982[10].

Terry Hershey Park

About one mile downstream from Highway 6, you come to the junction of Buffalo Bayou and South Mayde Creek. The land along both sides of these streams is part of Terry Hershey Park, a county park named in honor of Buffalo Bayou preservation activist Terry Hershey.

Terese Tarlton Hershey has been active in conservation matters for over forty years. A 1943 graduate of the University of Texas, Hershey served on the Texas Parks and Wildlife Commission and is a founding member of The Park People, a Houston-area alliance that works to preserve parks and open spaces[11].

The Terry Hershey Park headquarters is located on the north side of Memorial Drive just west of Eldridge Road. The park encompasses of the flood control easement along South Mayde Creek and Buffalo Bayou, and the parks extends along both sides of South Mayde Creek to its junction with Buffalo Bayou. The park provides recreational access to Buffalo Bayou from Highway 6 eastward to beyond Wilcrest Drive.

Asphalt hike-and-bike trails follow South Mayde Creek on both sides to its junction with Buffalo Bayou. On the west side of South Mayde Creek, a pedestrian bridge crosses the bayou and connects with the paved trail on the south side of Buffalo Bayou that goes right to Highway 6 and left to Eldridge Road. Along the north side of Buffalo Bayou, the Terry Hershey Park hike-and-bike trail, initially proposed by Harris County landscape architect Mike Cunningham in 1987, extends another 6-1/2 miles from Eldridge Road to beyond Wilcrest Drive. A future extension of the trail will go all the way to Beltway 8[12].

There is a canoe and kayak access point for Buffalo Bayou on South Mayde Creek about 50 yards upstream of its junction with Buffalo Bayou. This access is merely a series of steps placed in the grass-covered bank of South Mayde Creek. The steps descend down the rather steep bank for about fifteen feet to the normal water level in the creek. Other than the steps, there is little else to assist in putting in at this point.

There is adequate parking on Memorial Mews, a street that parallels South Mayde Creek's eastern bank. Although at times, the parking may be limited due to the popularity of the park's other recreational facilities, there is usually sufficient parking near the turnaround at the end of the road. The canoe access is adjacent to the turnaround.

The first bridge after the put in at Terry Hershey Park is at Eldridge Road, a quarter of a mile downstream. There are rocks in the channel near the bridge that can be hazardous, especially in low water. Immediately past the bridge, Turkey Creek enters from the north. Turkey Creek Rapids is at the mouth of the creek and it forms a swift current in the right channel. Below Turkey Creek, there is an area cluttered with chunks of concrete rip-rap. Be alert.

In May, 2002, in relatively low water, a trip from Terry Hershey Park to the Woodway Drive bridge, a distance of about 20 miles, took approximately 8-1/2 hours to complete. There were five or six logjams, two of which required getting out of the boats to portage.

Ant Hills

Much of the popularity of Terry Hershey Park derives from the paved trail that offers excellent opportunities for walking, hiking, jogging, roller skating and bicycling. The paved trail follows the north side of the bayou from Eldridge Road. Along the south side of the bayou from Eldridge Road to beyond Wilcrest Drive is a network of dirt trails, known as the Ant Hills, that can challenge the skills of the average mountain biker.

Enter the Ant Hills from the south side of the bayou at Eldridge Road. Go under the bridge and pick up the trails that go east through the trees and gullies along the south bank. This is a single track trail that runs up and down the banks of the bayou, providing some short climbs and downhills. Otherwise, the trail is generally flat. There are upper trails and lower trails, and the upper trails tend to be more difficult. Just beyond Wilcrest is an area called the Bowl where it is possible to do jumps.

Although it is only four miles from Eldridge Road to Wilcrest Drive, the Ant Hills can provide a circuit of over 8 miles of mountain bike trails with a beginner rating by the Mountain Bike Association[13].

Eldridge Road

Eldridge Road, or Eldridge Parkway, as it is called as it runs north from Buffalo Bayou into Addicks Reservoir and on to northern Harris County, has become a major artery for north-south traffic in western Harris County. It is an extension of a Sugar Land road named for William T. Eldridge. Eldridge was first manager of Imperial Sugar Company in Sugar Land. He built the company town around the sugar factory, providing 435 homes for the workers, stores and the farms in Sugar Land before his death in August, 1932[14].

Snuggled between Terry Hershey Park and Eldridge Road, fronting the north side of Buffalo Bayou for a quarter mile, is the western section of the Thornwood Subdivision. The eastern section of the neighborhood is east of Turkey Creek and north of Memorial Drive. Many of the 388 French chateau, Tudor, Spanish and traditional style homes in the neighborhood are situated among the mature pines, oaks and magnolias of the area[15].

Nottingham Forest's western section is situated along one mile of the north side of Buffalo Bayou on eleven acres east of Eldridge Road. The subdivision was developed by Vincent Kickerillo in the 1960's with home styles of English, colonial, Spanish and the typical "squarish house" dressed with shutters. A larger section of Nottingham Forest is on the east side of Dairy Ashford Road. The median size of the 932 homes in Nottingham Forest is 2,790 square feet. The median year of construction is 1967[16].

Directly across the bayou from Nottingham Forest is the Stonehenge Subdivision. Stonehenge begins about three quarters of a mile from Eldridge Road and fronts the south bank of the bayou for a short one quarter mile.

Adjacent to Nottingham Forest on the north side is the Westchester Subdivision which continues along the bayou for one half mile to Dairy Ashford Road. The 366 homes in Westchester average 2,806 square feet in size and they were built in the late 1960's. Located near greenbelts and trails on Buffalo Bayou, the Southern Colonial, English Tudor and a few Spanish style homes of Westchester have pleasant wooded yards filled with elm, pecan, oak and pine trees[17].

Dairy Ashford Road

Suburban development accelerated after World War II along the major highways in Houston. For nearly thirty years, the city's western boundary ended near today's Post Oak Road, and it was extended that far only because of the annexation of Memorial Park in 1926. However, the substantial growth of residential development between 1950 and 1966 took the city limits as far west as Dairy Ashford Road[18]. Between Dairy Ashford Road and the West Belt,

Buffalo Bayou continues its easterly course through the popular Memorial neighborhoods.

Terry Hershey Park also extends as far as the West Belt, and it provides a broad park zone from the edge of the water to the back fences of the homes on the boundary of the neighborhood. This is especially true on the north side of the bayou where flood control retention ponds offer open green space in periods of normal flow.

Access to the bayou at the Dairy Ashford bridge is not good. There is no provision for parking or for the loading of boats near this crossing. Any attempt to put in or take out here would be difficult at best.

There is a stream flow gauge on the bayou on the south bank at the bridge on Dairy Ashford Road over the rectified channel. It was placed here in 1945 when the bayou was channelized, and it is known as the Buffalo Bayou at Addicks gauge. Readings from this gauge can be found on the USGS Stream Flow web site (http://waterdata.usgs.gov/tx/nwis/current/?type=flow).

Immediately after the Dairy Ashford bridge, the current picks up speed and forms the Dairy Ashford Rapid, a mild Class I riffle in low water. In higher water, the rapid washes out.

Dairy Ashford Road is one of the older roads in this part of Harris County. Originally, it was the link between two communities in the western part of the county, Dairy in the south and Ashford in the north.

Dairy, and also called Dairy Station, was a community on the Southern Pacific Railroad near Brays Bayou. The area was first settled in 1861 when Reynolds Reynolds (yes, that is his name according to the Handbook of Texas) claimed 1,250 acres of land at the headwaters of Brays Bayou. In 1894, the county surveyors named the community Dairy, however, during the process of the application for a post office, the name was changed to Alief in honor of the first postmistress, Alief Ozella Magee[19].

Ashford was a community in northwestern Harris County that was also known as Thompson Switch. It was located on the Houston and Texas Central Railway near the present intersection of US 290 and Highway 6. In 1910, J. T. Thompson planned a town site which he named Satsuma for the Satsuma orange groves he had planted. The town never developed much beyond a shipping point on the railroad, but the road between the two railroad communities, Dairy and Ashford, has become a well known part of suburban Houston[20].

Prehistoric sites in west Houston are not very numerous. Most of the known sites were identified and excavated in conjunction with the development of Addicks and Barker Reservoirs. With the exception of the Habermacher Mound site near Highway 6, the only other prehistoric archeological sites between the reservoirs and the Turning Basin are near Dairy Ashford Road.

These sites were identified by the survey done by the Houston Museum of Natural Science in 1947, prior to the initial channelization of Buffalo Bayou in conjunction with the creation of the two reservoirs. The first site is on the south side of Buffalo Bayou approximately 200 feet east of the old Dairy Ashford Road. A second site is located on the north side of Buffalo Bayou about 2000 feet east of the Dairy Ashford Road.

Although the information about these sites is limited, they were probably midden sites from which few artifacts were recovered. The construction of the rectified channel has severely disturbed both of the sites[21].

Ashford South

As you proceed beyond the Dairy Ashford bridge, the bayou is bordered on both sides by the Ashford South Subdivision. It is the only subdivision within the City of Houston that spans Buffalo Bayou.

The northern section fronts the bayou for about a quarter of a mile, while the larger part of the subdivision extends along the south bank for about a half mile. Ashford South is a neighborhood of about 395 modest homes built in the mid-1960's to mid-1970's. The size of the homes ranges from 1600 to 2400 square feet[22]. At the eastern edge of the neighborhood is its sewage disposal plant on the south bank.

Nottingham Forest

The eastern section of the Nottingham Forest Subdivision begins a quarter of a mile east of Dairy Ashford Road on the north side of Buffalo Bayou, immediately adjacent to Ashford South's north side section. The neighborhood holds the bank of the bayou for about one half mile before the River Forest subdivision which occupies the remaining quarter mile of bayou before you get to Kirkwood Road[23].

Country Village

Although not directly on the banks of the bayou, the Country Village Subdivision is set back from the south bank in deference to a large gully and section of the old stream bed. Situated in the wedge shaped tract near the intersection of Kirkwood and Briar Forest Drive, Country Village has homes built in the 1970's. One section of Country Village consists of contemporary-style patio homes of 1700 to 2200 square feet[24].

As late as 1992, the civic groups of this area opposed the extension of Kirkwood Road from Memorial Drive to South Kirkwood at Buffalo Bayou[25]. Today, the bridge at Kirkwood Road provides access to the hike and bike trails in Terry Hershey Park on the north side greenbelt. A parking area on the south side of the bayou is a convenient place to leave your vehicle. Unfortunately, the access to the bayou for canoeing or kayaking at Kirkwood Road is poor. No developed boat launch is in place although it may be possible to carry your boat down the high bank and through the trees to the bayou from the far eastern side of the parking area where a gully enters the bayou.

Cenacle Retreat House

The desirability of the forest habitat for urban living gives the Memorial area an appeal that contrast dramatically with the tract houses built on the coastal prairie found south of Buffalo Bayou. The River Forest Subdivision sits on the western edge of the pine forest that dips down from East Texas to the Houston area. The bayou stands as a razor, cutting the landscape between piney woods and prairie.

Tucked into a corner of tranquil River Forest is the Cenacle Retreat House, a Roman Catholic retreat house that opened in 1967.

Set on eight heavily wooded acres along Buffalo Bayou at Kirkwood Road, the center, owned by the Cenacle Sisters, provides programs that emphasize spiritual renewal[26].

The property is cut by steep ravines formed by an oxbow channel of Buffalo Bayou and the sisters utilize the terrain for gardening and landscaping. Loretta Coussirat of the Cenacle Retreat House oversees the landscaping of the reflective gardens and she teaches how personal spiritual renewal can be understood in the terms of the way recycling plays a role in these woodland gardens[27].

Like paddling deep among the overhanging willows of the bayou corridor, the Cenacle Retreat House offers a place to contemplate something other than the concrete and noise of the big city.

Lakeside Country Club

Across the bayou from the Cenacle Retreat House is a somewhat different approach to relaxation in the urban environment. On the south bank of Buffalo Bayou, just east of the Kirkwood Road bridge, the Lakeside Country Club has over one mile of bayou frontage, extending all the way to Wilcrest Drive.

Lakeside Country Club is a private, 18-hole golf club located at 100 Wilcrest Drive. Designed by architect Ron Prichard, Lakeside Country Club opened in 1952 as the last exclusive, private country club developed in the city of Houston[28]. In those early days, you had to drive out Westheimer Road from town to Hayes Road and then turn north to the country club. Today, Wilcrest Drive crosses the bayou, and the area is generally thought of as "close in." The development of the surrounding neighborhoods has seen the facility change from a true country club to one of the most popular clubs in suburban Houston.

Typical of this surrounding development is Lakeside Place. Situated on the south side of Lakeside Country Club, at the intersection of Wilcrest Drive and Briar Forest Drive, Lakeside Place is a neighborhood of traditional and contemporary homes built in the 1970's and 1980's that range in price from the $120,000's to $315,000 according the 1998 data.

Yet, in spite of the effects of suburban growth, Lakeside Country Club strives to fit well into the natural ecology of the bayou and it is the only Houston golf course to be certified as an Audubon Cooperative Sanctuary. Memorial Park Golf Course and River Oaks Country Club, the two other golf courses along Buffalo Bayou in Houston are enrolled in the program and working toward certification[29].

Yorkchester

A large gully enters the bayou from the north side immediately downstream of the Cenacle Retreat House. The sewage disposal facility for the River Forest subdivision is located on the west side of this gully about one quarter mile from the bayou.

The Yorkchester Subdivision is a small neighborhood on the east side of River Forest with about one quarter mile of frontage in the north-curving arch of Buffalo Bayou beyond Kirkwood Road. Patchester Road on the east side separates the subdivision from the neighboring subdivisions of Wilchester and Wilchester West[30].

Wilchester

The remaining three quarters of a mile of the north bank of the bayou before you get to Wilcrest Drive are part of the Wilchester and Wilchester West Subdivisions. Wilchester and Wilchester West contain 1,124 custom homes built between 1960 and 1968. The typical designs are Tudor, Colonial and two-story New Orleans style homes. These homes, which average 2,820 square feet, are set among the native oaks and pines that remain from the forest where the subdivision was developed. The wooded lots average 9,605 square feet in size.

The homes of Wilchester differ from those of Wilchester West in that Wilchester West have gaslight lamps in front[31].

Wilcrest Road

Wilcrest Road crosses Buffalo Bayou east of Wilchester Subdivision, on the north, and Lakeside Country Club on the south. Canoe and kayak put in facilities on Buffalo Bayou have been added on the north bank east of the bridge. These facilities consist of steps embedded in the steep grassy bank. Unfortunately, there is no designated parking or loading place on Wilcrest Drive, so you will have to use the county access driveway. Use caution because the traffic on Wilcrest can be heavy at times. You will have to park your vehicle in the Gaywood or Memorial Glen neighborhoods beyond the Terry Hershey Park green space.

Just past Wilcrest Road is a small waterfall extending completely across the channel. In low water, be aware not to get stuck on the rocks.

Gaywood

The Wilcrest Drive bridge marks the beginning of the final segment of Terry Hershey Park. Since the park is largely a result of the flood control channelization of the bayou, this one and a quarter mile segment also is the last of the straightened and rectified channel of Buffalo Bayou until Shepherd Drive. The uniform width and the smooth curves and bends of the bayou will give way to a wilder and more natural waterway as it flows east of West Belt.

On the north side, the Gaywood Subdivision reaches the bayou frontage for about a quarter mile past Wilcrest Drive. The Gaywood homes were built between 1955 and 1963. The median year of construction is 1960. The neighborhood consists of 119 homes, each on a lot of about 1/3 acre. The soaring pines and the absence of sidewalks, curbs and gutters along the streets creates a sense of spaciousness to the yards of the homes which are a mix of ranch, traditional and contemporary styles. The median size of the homes in Gaywood is 2,402 square feet[32].

Gaywood is one of three sister neighborhoods in the wedge created by the junction of Buffalo Bayou and Rummel Creek which enters from the northwest at a 45 degree angle. One quarter mile past Wilcrest, adjacent to Gaywood, is the Memorial Glen Subdivision. Memorial Glen occupies the north bank for one mile before the West Belt. Considered a 'close in' neighborhood, Memorial Glen enjoys a good reputation for its natural setting with yards that are abundant with trees. Most of the 2,200 to 3,500 square foot homes of the subdivision were built in the early 1960's[33].

The third neighborhood of this group is the Rustling Pines Subdivision. This neighborhood is just off Memorial Drive and it is contiguous to Gaywood and Memorial Glen. It is also adjacent to the Edith L. Moore Nature Center and Rummel Creek. Most of the 155 homes of Rustling Pines were built between 1961 and 1965[34].

The hike and bike trail of Terry Hershey Park extends beyond Wilcrest Drive to the Sam Houston Tollway as the Quail Trail continues along the north bank of the bayou. Horseshoe Bend is a scenic oxbow that was created during the channelization of the bayou. A concrete dam provides access across the oxbow to a set of stairs that go to the local neighborhood park. Brentwood Park is located at the junction of Rummel Creek and Buffalo Bayou adjacent to the Memorial Glen subdivision. The sewage disposal facility for the neighborhoods occupies the tip of land at the junction of the creek and the bayou.

Lakeside Forest

The south side of Buffalo Bayou between Wilcrest Drive and the West Belt encompasses two neighborhoods, Lakeside Forest and Walnut Bend.

For about three quarters of a mile from the bridge at Wilcrest, the Lakeside Forest Subdivision lies among and beyond the oxbows and gullies on the south bank, perhaps accounting for the "lake" in its name for there is no lake in the subdivision. A more likely explanation, though, is that the neighborhood gets its name from its proximity to Lakeside Country Club which is across the street.

Large and multi-acre lots with hundreds of trees are typical in this neighborhood of Georgian, contemporary, Mediterranean, French and Tudor style homes. Lakeside Forest provides privacy and a sense of isolation although the neighborhood is within the City of Houston. The subdivision of 291 homes that average 3,056 square feet in size is laid out with horseshoe-shaped streets and cul de sacs. The median year of construction of the homes is 1972.

Immediately south of Lakeside Forest is its companion subdivision, Lakeside Estates, a neighborhood of slightly smaller homes built a few years earlier. The home styles of 270 homes in the Lakeside Estates range from English traditional, Tudor, and colonial styles to Spanish and New Orleans designs. The median year of construction for these homes, which average 2,473 square foot, is 1971[35].

Walnut Bend

The Walnut Bend Subdivision, next to both Lakeside Forest and Lakeside Estates, is a neighborhood with 900 homes built in traditional, Mediterranean, Spanish and contemporary styles. The median year of construction for the homes in Walnut Bend is 1967. They average 2,264 square feet in size.

The quarter mile of bayou frontage of Walnut Bend is separated from the West Belt by a quarter mile of undeveloped property that is cut by a deep gully[36].

Rummel Creek

Rummel Creek headwaters are near the intersection of Interstate 10 and the Sam Houston Parkway, a short distance north of I-10 and west of the Beltway. It flows into Buffalo Bayou at the West Belt bridge. The name of the creek comes from one of the early settlers to the area, Wilhelm Rummel.

Wilhelm Rummel was one of the many German immigrants to Texas in the late 1840's and early 1850's who settled west of Houston along the north side of Buffalo Bayou. As early as 1830, Karl Kolbe had settled in the area. He maintained contact with his friends and family in Germany, and Wilhelm Rummel's trip to Texas was inspired by Kolbe's presence here[37].

In 1847, August Bauer immigrated to Texas and wrote his family of the wonderful opportunities available here. As a result of August Bauer's letter about Texas, his father Carl Siegismund Bauer sold the Bauer-Rummel mill and his home in Saxony and he used the money to bring his family to Texas in 1848. Although Carl Bauer was 56 years old, the chance to live in freedom was enough to cause him to leave Germany. Wilhelm Rummel, who was Bauer's partner in the mill, but was more the age of his son August, decided to come, too[38].

On October 10, 1848, the Rummel and Bauer families sailed from Bremen on the ship Neptune. There were seventeen members of the two families that arrived in Galveston after a difficult voyage of nine weeks. The two German families drove their wagons west of Houston to a place about nine miles out where five other German families were camped on a wooded creek. We know this creek as Spring Branch. On this spot, the grateful travelers joined with the others in a thanksgiving service that is recognized as the founding of the worship community that became St. Peter's Church.

Wilhelm Rummel settled on the west side of Spring Branch in a beautiful grove of oak trees and giant pines. Although he is listed as a farmer in the census of 1850, Rummel's knowledge and experience with sawmills were put to use in the erection of a log cabin church for the community in 1854 on a fourth of an acre that he and his wife donated for the church.

When the community decided to build a modern frame church, they chose Wilhelm Rummel to head the project. Wilhelm and son Carl, both whom worked at the new McGuffey sawmill in the Spring Branch area, selected the timbers and the lumber as each piece came from the mill. The new church was dedicated in 1864. The old frame St. Peter's Church can still be seen on the site near the point where Long Point Road crosses Spring Branch, east of Campbell Road[39].

The timberlands along the north side of Buffalo Bayou were an important resource for those who settled in the area west of Houston. The city was a major economic center for the state and the growth of commerce and population in Houston during the 1870's and 1880's spurred the demand for basic building materials. Logging and sawmills were common in the area because of the abundance of quality timber in the pine forest.

Edith L. Moore Nature Sanctuary

By the early 20th century, however, the timber industry west of Houston waned. Richer resources lay in other areas and the railroads could transport lumber from farther distances.

In 1926 and 1927, Jesse and Edith Moore purchased two tracts of remote and heavily timbered land west of the present day West

Belt. The Moores established a small gasoline-powered sawmill and built a dairy barn. In 1931, they began to build their home along Rummel Creek using the loblolly pines on the site. An analysis of the growth rings indicates the logs were 50 years old. By the time the Moores settled in the area, it had become reforested with second growth trees.

The Moores made their livelihood from dairy farming and logging. And, although the Moores divorced in 1959, Edith continued to live in the log cabin they had built until her death in 1975. She willed her log house and 17.5 acres to the Houston Audubon Society as a nature preserve[40].

The Edith L. Moore Nature Sanctuary, 440 Wilchester, was established by the Houston Audubon Society to preserve this remnant of the native riparian forest that once stretched west of Houston along Buffalo Bayou. In accordance with the donor's wishes, it is maintained as a bird sanctuary. Although it is only a fraction of the Moore's original 180 acres, this pocket wilderness hosts an annual migration of 200 species of birds on the central eastern flyway. Among the common sightings are twenty species of warblers, red-bellied woodpeckers, brown threshers, cardinals, chickadees and tufted-titmouses. The peak birding times are April to mid-May.

From the Moore cabin, you cross the thirty foot wooden bridge over Rummel Creek to a far wilder side of the property. The sanctuary harbors squirrels, rabbits, armadillos, possums, raccoons, lizards, turtles, giant bullfrogs and water snakes among the native forest consisting of hickory, elm, loblolly pine and a variety of oak trees. Other native species in the preserve include a variety of shrubs, such as the cherry laurel, redbud, blackberry and yaupon. And, don't forget, poison ivy is there, too.

The Edith L. Moore cabin was restored in 1988, and, in 1997, the cabin was declared a State Historical Site by the Texas State Historical Society. It currently serves as the headquarters of the Houston Audubon Society[41].

Sam Houston Parkway

Sam Houston Parkway crosses Buffalo Bayou several yards past Rummel Creek. This roadway is known by various names, including

Sam Houston Tollway, Beltway 8 and West Belt Drive. You may find any of those names on the map you are using. We will refer to the road as West Belt Drive.

Concrete rip-rap in the water at the West Belt bridge blocks much of the bayou and makes a clean run through the rapid difficult at normal water levels. Immediately after the bridge, a pipe crosses the bayou close to the normal water level and may be a potential hazard. Portage is possible on the south bank.

The gauge on Buffalo Bayou at West Belt Drive is on the downstream side of the bridge about 100 feet downstream from Rummel Creek. The current flow for the bayou at this gauge can be found on the internet (http://tx.waterdata.usgs.gov/nwis/uv/ ?site_no=08073600&PARAmeter_cd=00065,00060). Unfortunately, there is no access to the bayou from the West Belt right of way at this time.

Memorial Bend

The completion of the Sam Houston Tollway from Interstate 10 to US 59 may have been a wonderful thing for cross town commuters, but in some cases, there are less than desirable results for others. This was certainly the case for residents of the Memorial Bend Subdivision which was bisected by the construction of the toll road.

Memorial Bend, a neighborhood on the north side of Buffalo Bayou, is bordered on the west by Rummel Creek and on the east by Memorial Drive, significantly, at a "bend" in Memorial Drive. The median size of the 355 homes is 2,300 square feet, and the median year of construction of the homes in Memorial Bend is 1957. You can imagine the consternation of the residents when, during 1988, the thick pines that lined the median of West Belt Drive were cleared to make way for the Sam Houston Tollway[42].

Briargrove Park

Buffalo Bayou, downstream of the West Belt bridge, follows its natural course. The channelization of the bayou that resulted from the creation of Barker and Addicks Reservoirs ends at West Belt Drive. A twisting, winding stream carves its way for about 20 miles from West Belt to Shepherd Drive. In contrast to the public land of Terry Hershey Park, both side of the bayou are private property to the water's edge.

Briargrove Park, a heavily wooded subdivision south of Buffalo Bayou and east of West Belt Drive, extends for almost two miles along the south bank. Some of the more elaborate homes in this neighborhood of well kept homes and manicured lawns overlook the bayou. Canoers and kayakers should respect the property rights of the land owners in this section as well as along all other areas of the bayou.

The homes of Briargrove Park are mostly soft contemporary styles with brick front and high ceilings. Deed restrictions that limit each home to 1-1/2 stories has helped to maintain a consistent look throughout the neighborhood. Most of the 1,341 homes in Briargrove Park were built in the mid-1960's and they average 2,466 square feet in size[43].

Rivercrest

Between Briargrove Park and Gessner Road, the Rivercrest Subdivision occupies the south bank for about a half mile. An exclusive, well to do neighborhood, Rivercrest has several homes that have sold in the millions[44].

Buckner Haven

The north bank of the bayou from West Belt to Gessner Road has several isolated residential streets. Three quarters of a mile from West Belt is a tract that appears as the Texas Baptist Haven on a 1975 map of the area. It appears as the Buckner Haven Subdivision on a 1999 city map[45].

Bunker Hill Village

Although the city limits do not extend to the water's edge of the bayou, Bunker Hill Village lies a short distance beyond the banks of the bayou at Gessner Road. As one of the six Memorial Villages, the area was settled in the 1800's by German farmers who established sawmills to cut the local timber.

By 1936, the community consisted of scattered dwellings near one of the sawmills. In the period after World War II, there was a movement to incorporate the communities in the Spring Branch area. The failure of the communities to agree on a single plan of incorporation caused a number of the communities to incorporate individually[46].

Bunker Hill Village was incorporated in 1954, yet it was still essentially a rural community with shell roads, septic tanks and water wells. Zoning ordinances were established with restrictions to prohibit businesses and it was decreed that no house can be built on a lot smaller than 20,000 square feet[47].

The quest to become a prestige suburban community was enhanced when the noted architect Frank Lloyd Wright designed a house for William L. Thaxton in Bunker Hill Village in 1954. The Thaxton house was a one story, concrete-walled house built in triangles on a 60-degree L-plan. The house itself was set far back on the property which is at the end of a cul de sac. It is one of only four buildings in Texas designed by Frank Lloyd Wright and the only one in the Houston area[48].

As an incorporated suburban community adjacent to Hedwig Village and Piney Point Village, Bunker Hill Village has 1,262 homes that average 3,596 square feet in size. The median year of construction is 1965, however, many of the original flat roof contemporaries and ranch style houses have been restored or torn down.

The name of the village has a distant connection with one of the earliest Anglo settlers in the area, Isaac Bunker. Isaac Bunker was a partner of John D. Taylor who received a grant of land from Stephen F. Austin in August, 1824. Taylor sold his land to William Scott later that year and Bunker's land, in the upper corner of the Taylor league was surveyed as the Isaac Bunker Survey.

Whispering Oaks

A half mile downstream from Buckner Haven, and a mile and a half from the West Belt, is the Whispering Oaks Subdivision. Whispering Oaks lies mostly north of Gessner Road and it is in both

Bunker Hill Village and the City of Houston. A few homes of the 229 homes in the neighborhood border on Buffalo Bayou and on Stoney Creek, a small tributary. The homes are substantial, well-built styles including 1 and 1-1/2 story English designs and contemporaries. The median size of the homes is 2,847 square feet and the median year of construction is 1960[49].

Gessner Road

Gessner Road crosses the bayou at the end of the Whispering Oaks Subdivision. There is no access to the bayou on either side of the bridge.

Stoney Creek enters Buffalo Bayou immediately below the bridge from the north. One of the largest storm sewers on the bayou is also below the Gessner Road bridge. Extreme caution should be exercised in this area during periods of run off from heavy rains.

The Woodlake Preserve extends from Gessner Road along the south bank of Buffalo Bayou for a mile to the bridge of Briarforest Drive.

Sandalwood

East of Stoney Creek is the Sandalwood Subdivision that fronts the bayou for three quarters of a mile. Sandalwood was developed from the 300 acre estate of oilman Jim Rush by developers Martin Nadelman and Howard Singer who divided the estate into lots in 1956.

The red brick colonial home that Rush built in 1930 was unique. Some of the walls were one foot thick and the beams taken from the keel of a sailboat.

Although it is not obvious to the casual passerby on Memorial Drive, Sandalwood is a lakeside community. There are 175 homes located among three lakes that flow into Buffalo Bayou. Walking trails circle around the lakes in an area that is thick with pine trees[50].

Briarforest Drive

A ledge of limestone creates a small rapid just before you get to the Briarforest Drive bridge. The channel to the far left is usually the best route.

Camp Hudson

Many Houston men who were young during the 1950's and 1960's may recall their participation in boy scout camp outs at Camp Hudson on Buffalo Bayou. Although it appears on an old Houston street map of the 1950's, subsequent street maps from the 1970's and 1980's do not show the camp. Instead, Briarforest Drive cuts diagonally through the property from Memorial Drive on the north side of the bayou to the Briarforest Drive extension on the south side.

According to information provided by Mark Andrus, an avid paddler and one of the boy scouts who remembers camping there in his youth, Camp Hudson was given to the Sam Houston Area Council of the Boy Scouts in 1925 by E. A. Hudson, who owned the Hudson Furniture Company located at 711 Travis Street. Hudson was president of the council for ten years, and he was elected President Emeritus in 1932.

The camp property comprised about 100 acres in the heavily wooded area along the banks of Buffalo Bayou. By 1957, the boy scout retreat, located at the end of an old gravel road, had been developed with a training center and other scouting facilities.

By the 1970's, the suburbs had encroached on the Memorial area. The camp no longer seemed remote and in the country. Civilization and housing built up around the site. In 1973, the boy scouts sold the property that was Camp Hudson[51].

As a reminder of its past, the name of Camp Hudson remains in the names of the residential developments along Briarforest Drive in the area of the former camp. Two of these are Hudson Forest and Hudson Courts.

Map by Rachel A. Garcia

After leaving Terry Hershey Park near Beltway 8 (above), Buffalo Bayou follows an unchannelized course through Piney Point and the Memorial Villages before entering the forested suburbs of west Houston between Voss Road and Chimney Rock Road (below).

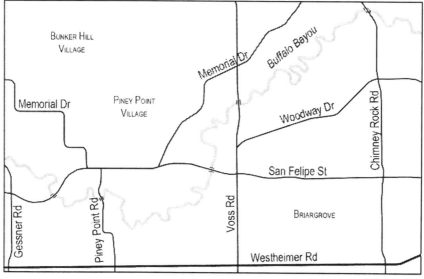

Map by Rachel A. Garcia

Chapter 4
Piney Point

Across from the former Camp Hudson property is Piney Point Gully, a major drainage that enters Buffalo Bayou from the south. On the west bank of Piney Point Gully, near Westheimer Road, is the site of the Rosewood Medical Center. Rosewood was a two hundred bed hospital built in 1963. The hospital was closed in 2000 and it was demolished to make room for residential and retail development along the Westheimer Road corridor[1].

The east bank of Piney Point Gully is the western extent of Piney Point Village. For approximately one mile, Piney Point Village stretches across Buffalo Bayou. On the north bank, Piney Point Village begins at the edge of the Camp Hudson property. A small portion of the village extends to the south side of the bayou just as the bayou drops in a broad arch that began after the West Belt. Buffalo Bayou reaches the "point" in this bend within a mile past Piney Point Gully, reaching its southern most extent just north of the intersection of Woodway Drive and Lazy Hollow Drive. Past Piney Point, Buffalo Bayou and the tree growth recede to the north.

Although it may not be as evident today, the dense pine forests along the north bank of the bayou were a prominent protrusion into the coastal prairie to the south. Travelers from Harrisburg recognized this geographical landform on the route known as the San Felipe Road, and the landmark was given the name, Pine Point, that remains in a variant spelling until this day. At Piney Point, Buffalo Bayou reaches it farthest southerly extent, coming to within a quarter mile of the latitude delineated in the 1870's by the roadbed of the Texas Western Narrow Gauge Railway and in modern times by Westheimer Road.

Within a mile downstream of the Briarforest Drive bridge is the South Piney Point Road bridge. South Piney Point Road connects Memorial Drive on the north with Fondren Road on the south. There is a U. S. Geological Survey gauging station on the south bank on the upstream side of the bridge at South Piney Point Road. Officially, it is known as USGS 08073700 Buffalo Bayou at Piney Point, TX[2].

After the South Piney Point bridge, there is a long outcrop and scattered boulders along the right bank that may present a hazard to boaters.

Piney Point and the Canfield Family

From the early days of Texas colonization, the Piney Point community was a well known stop for travelers on the San Felipe Road. It was the first stop on the way out of Houston. After the victory at San Jacinto, Piney Point was well documented in the writings and journals of travelers during the time of the Texas Republic.

Miles Bennet, driving three ox wagons with supplies for the Texas Army in San Antonio, listed it in his journal as one of his encampments on the San Felipe Road from Houston in February, 1839: "To Piney Point 9 miles on Buffalo Bayou[3]."

Prince Solms-Braunfels, in his book describing his travels in Texas during 1844 and 1845, makes note that there is no water between Houston and Piney Point. The Pine Point Spring had a reputation as a good source of drinking water for those traveling the San Felipe Road[4].

Ferdinand Roemer, a 27 year old German with a recent Ph.D. in paleontology, noted that the San Felipe Road along the coastal prairie out of Houston became an endless swamp due to rain. In November, 1845, he met a group of farmers transporting corn from the Colorado River area to Houston. They were camped on a rise near the forest. From them, he learned that this was Piney Point[5].

Alwin Soergel rode on horseback along the San Felipe Road toward Piney Point in February, 1846. From Houston, it was a distance of nine miles over a fairly poor road, and, in the rain, the prairie became a swamp and the road was nearly impossible to follow. Soergel and his companions saw a light of a distant farm house and the owner showed them a hospitality that impressed them. They had come to Piney Point[6].

German traveler C. von Sommer rode from Houston in 1846 along the San Felipe Road, arriving at the Piney Point Farm owned by a Mr. George, at that time. They were offered room and board for $2.50 a night in a house that they noted to be similar to most of the others in the area, a two bedroom house with kitchen and a porch[7].

Travelers knew they were approaching Piney Point when the pine trees along the bayou dipped south into the open prairie, hence the name of the piney point. Well known for its accommodations and hospitality, the way station at Piney Point was an important part of the road system extending from the ports of Harrisburg and Houston to the interior of the young republic.

When the railroads were built to the Brazos River valley, the commercial importance of the San Felipe Road declined. Piney Point, however, retained some significance when it became a stop on the Texas Western Narrow Gauge Railway in 1877.

Actually, the route along the south side of Buffalo Bayou dates from the earliest days of the colonial period of the 1820's. A large group of settlers from Austin's colony established farms in the vicinity of the San Jacinto River and along Buffalo Bayou. The road from the settlements of Harrisburg, Lynchburg and others south of the bayou was the most direct route to Austin's headquarters at San Felipe. One of the earliest documented travelers of the road was Arthur McCormick, the famous Peggy McCormick's husband, who was following this route in 1824 on his return to his farm at San Jacinto when he drowned near the Wheaton Farm while crossing Buffalo Bayou.

During 1842 and 1843, surveyors for Harris County mapped the road from Houston to Piney Point and from Piney Point to the county line. The county designated the route, which became known as the San Felipe - Harrisburg Road, as a public road in February, 1844. Buckman Canfield was appointed as the overseer of the San Felipe Road from Houston to Piney Point and Stephen Habermacher was overseer from Piney Point to county line. The importance of this road to local commerce is seen in the public maintenance established for its upkeep[8].

The community of Piney Point dates from the early 1820's when John D. Taylor, who came to Texas in 1822 with several others and initially settled north of the San Jacinto River, applied for a grant as one of Austin's Old Three Hundred and received title to a league of land along Buffalo Bayou on August 10, 1824. He built a house east of a ravine, now known as Piney Point Gully, on a tract of land that is now located in the Windermere subdivision[9].

For reasons unknown to us, Taylor sold his land to William Scott later in 1824 and moved to Harrisburg where, in the census of March, 1826, he was listed as a farmer and stock raiser. His household included his wife Maria, his daughter and 2 servants. He died at Harrisburg about 1829[10].

We are not sure what was happening at Piney Point during the next few years for there is no mention of it in the historical record, but the mid-1830's brought the Texas Revolution and a re-orientation of priorities. Since Santa Anna led his army from San Felipe to Harrisburg along this route, it is possible that the Mexican army stopped at Piney Point, but we do not know. However, the victory of the Texians in 1836 and the establishment of the City of Houston as the capitol of Texas revived traffic along the road. Opportunities abounded in the new republic and many men sought their fortune in Texas.

Buckman Canfield arrived in Texas from New York in February, 1833 with his wife Harriet and their infant son William B. Canfield. Not much is known about Canfield's activities for the next few years, except that a daughter Hannah Canfield was born to them in 1834. Canfield served admirably during the Texas Revolution and, as a result, earned a headright.

By late 1837, Canfield seems to have developed a plan. He purchased two slaves in Houston and, in 1838, he purchased 300 acres with an old house near the Pine Point Spring. The land was acquired from the owners of the John Taylor survey and it was part of Taylor's reserve not sold to Stephen F. Austin. Canfield proceeded to build his homestead on a portion of the land that lay on a slight rise in elevation from the prairie. The modern location of Canfield's farm is near Piney Point Road and Vargo's Restaurant at 2401 Fondren Road[12].

By 1839, Buckman Canfield had established himself as a hog raiser, cattle rancher and small crop farmer at Piney Point. He also had a reputation as a hunter and a fisherman. Son John D. Canfield was born in 1841, and the Canfield's seemed to be prospering.

After moving to Piney Point, Buckman Canfield began to buy the properties surrounding his own. In June, 1838, he bought a lot from the estate of Stephen F. Austin, who had died on December 12, 1836, that was just to the east of his property. Canfield claimed two tracts of land to the south of Piney Point in 1841, one as his 320 acre headright and the other as a 177 acre military claim. He bought the remaining 548 acres of the Taylor league from William P. Harris on December 8, 1842. To complete the consolidation of his holdings about Piney Point, in 1844, Canfield purchased the 360 acres lying between his two tracts from fellow Texas veteran Edward P. Whitehead[12].

In a little over ten years, Buckman Canfield was well on the road to prosperity and he had accumulated a significant amount of land for his farm at Piney Point, which now totaled 1,893 acres, as well as additional land for speculation. He owned 2,583 acres on the Brazos River south of Houston and another tract of 4,428 acres on Mill Creek in Montgomery County.

Sadly, on June 6, 1844, Buckman Canfield met an unfortunate fate. His body was found in Buffalo Bayou a short distance below his dwelling. He had been shot in the face and neck with number 14 buck shot while sitting near the edge of the Buffalo Bayou.

The crime scene investigation determined that the murderer had discharged the fatal shot from a high point on the opposite bank, about forty feet higher than where the victim, Canfield, was sitting[13].

A Harris County grand jury indicted three black slaves for murder of Buckman Canfield. Indictments against two of them were later dropped. One of those, Hester, a female household slave of the Canfield's, was spared prosecution and, under the perverse logic of the slavery system, was later sold for the benefit of the Canfield family. Castro, a slave of R. C. Campbell, a local attorney, was convicted of Canfield's murder in November, 1844 and sentenced to hang by a jury of twelve local farmers[14].

The motive for Canfield's murder was thought to be robbery since Castro, the convicted slave, had $582 on him when he was captured. The money was returned to the Canfield family. The execution of the convicted man was carried out by having him sit in a wagon under a tree limb. The loose end of a noose was tied around his neck and the wagon was driven off[15].

The situation may have been particularly difficult for Harriet Canfield. She was on her own on the frontier with two young sons, William, age 12, and John D., age 3, and a daughter, Hannah, age 10. Since Buckman Canfield died without a will, his wife Harriet was appointed as the executor of his estate. The appraised value of the estate, filed in 1845 was over $12,000[16].

Within the year, the 35 year old Harriet Canfield remarried and she became Mrs. James J. Todd on January 22, 1845. Todd, however, in a sad turn of events, died before the birth of their daughter Mary Elizabeth Todd in 1846. Subsequently, Harriet Canfield Todd married Benjamin Moore George on April 5, 1846. A son Edmund W. George was born in 1848, but Benjamin George died some time before 1850[17].

The decade of the 1840's was a tumultuous time on the frontier for the Harriet Canfield Todd George household. But, they did not fail to prosper, however, during these hard times. By 1850, the forty year old Harriet George was widowed three times, yet, according to the 1850 census data, she herself had property valued at $2,000, a substantial amount for that time, and she was living at Piney Point with her five children, three slaves, four ranch hands and a German cabinet maker named William Bathke. Harriet would not inherit her share of her late husband Buckman Canfield's estate until 1854 when she would receive the Piney Point property and a one half interest in Canfield's Brazos River land and Montgomery County land.

The Canfield children proved to be as industrious has their parents for the most part. William Canfield, Harriet's 18 year old son, owned property and a sawmill while still living with the family at Piney Point in 1850. When Buckman Canfield's estate was settled in 1854, William Canfield received 2,000 acres of the Mill Creek property in Montgomery County and a 984 acre tract elsewhere[18].

Hannah Canfield, at age 20, married William A. Morse in 1854 and later that year, she received a one half interest in Canfield's Brazos River property. They had a son Charles Canfield Morse and a daughter Ella Morse. In 1867, Hannah married J. T. Hurtt after the death of her husband William. Hannah married A. P. Sulliman in 1874. She and daughter Ella died in 1890[19].

John D. Canfield, thirteen years old and Buckman Canfield's youngest son, inherited 2,952 acres of property in Milam County from his father's estate in 1854.

There is no doubt that life in rural Texas during the mid-1800's was challenging. Most early Texans learned to survive and prosper as best they could, overcoming adversity as a matter of course. Edmund W. George, the son of Harriet and Benjamin George, born in 1848, died in childhood, some time after 1850. William Canfield and John D. Canfield became young Confederate soldiers. Both died during the siege of Vicksburg in the summer of 1863[20].

In many ways, though, the Canfield story resonates with the themes that typify the early settlement of Texas. A young family comes seeking the opportunities for a better life in Texas during the pre-revolutionary period. They acquire land and settle in the difficult environment of Texas. The husband hopes to exploit the abundant natural resources of the land. He establishes a sawmill in the pine forests near the growing town of Houston. The ready market for cut timber in Houston is the basis for his prosperity, but tragic events result in his death and the family faces an uncertain future. In the case of the Canfields and many other frontier families, the wife loses one or more husbands within a short period of time while raising several young children on the frontier. Through perseverance and hard work the family survives and succeeds.

Harriet Canfield continued to live at Piney Point after the death of each of her husbands until her death in 1893. At the time of her death at age 83, Harriet Canfield George had assets of $11,650, including 1,000 acres at Piney Point and a house valued at $1,550.

Charles Canfield Morse, son of Hannah and grandson of Buckman and Harriet Canfield, took his place as the landowner at Piney Point in 1893[21].

Piney Point Village

The community of Piney Point became a station on the Texas Western Railway in 1885 as the railroad followed the same straight line path of modern Westheimer Road. The station was approximately at the current intersection of Westheimer Road and Fondren Road[22].

Located along Buffalo Bayou about 10 miles west of downtown, Piney Point was part of a settlement of German farmers who came to the Spring Branch area during the second half of the 1800's. The heavily forested land north of the bayou still had several sawmills as late as 1936[23].

The 2.2 square mile village that lies in a roughly rectangular tract extending from Buffalo Bayou on the south to Beinhorn Road and Hedwig Village on the north was incorporated in 1954. Governed by its own mayor and city council, the 3,380 residents of Piney Point Village have engineered a post-World War II transition from a rural farming and logging community to an exclusive residential suburb of Houston.

By ordinance, lots in Piney Point Village cannot be subdivided smaller than 40,000 square feet. The 1,075 homes in the village were built, on average, around 1972 and the median value of a home is $780,000. Not surprisingly, Piney Point Village was designated "the richest town in Texas" according to *Worth* magazine's ranking of the 250 richest towns in America in 2002[24].

Briarbend

About one half mile past the South Piney Point Road bridge, the Houston city limits is encountered along the south bank of the bayou. Piney Point Village continues along the north bank for another three miles of the bayou which is the village boundary.

Within a mile and a half downstream of the South Piney Point Road bridge is the Briarbend subdivision. The homes in Briarbend are limited to 1-1/2 stories. They are primarily one story ranch styles that were built in the 1950's. The size of the 137 homes ranges from 1,900 to 2,400 square feet[25].

Adjacent to Briarbend is the Charnwood subdivision. Nestled between Briargrove and the Memorial Villages, homes in the Charnwood subdivision were built in the 1950's and 1960's. Styles in Charnwood include ranch, traditional, Tudors and brick contemporary homes. It has the added advantage of being close to Kinkaid and Duchesne schools[26].

The neighborhood park, Briarbend Park, is located off the isolated extension of Woodway Drive in the subdivision. Parking is available along the street although it is somewhat limited. Access to the bayou has been developed with trails to the water and a bulkhead along the waterline at the Bob Arthur Canoe Launch. The park is one of the best access points to Buffalo Bayou in this upper section of the bayou, and it is within a half mile of San Felipe Road, the traditional starting point of the Buffalo Bayou Regatta.

Kinkaid School

Across the bayou from Briarbend Park and a little upstream are the grounds of the Kinkaid School. Founded in 1906 by Margaret Hunter Kinkaid, Kinkaid School moved to this forty acre, wooded site in Piney Point Village in 1957[27].

Located on the 3.9 acres along Buffalo Bayou is an outdoor nature classroom for Kinkaid students known as Kinkaid's Backyard. Dedicated in 1993, the land that once had been a landfill unfolds on two levels, extending back from the football field scoreboard to Buffalo Bayou.

The upper level of Kinkaid's Backyard is a controlled, yet carefree habitat of flowering plants and vines, and a teaching deck. The lower level is an untended wetland with a vernal pool in an area that periodically floods. Bat houses on the upper level are inhabited by Mexican freetail bats. At times, Kinkaid has a floating classroom as the students are able to explore the bayou by canoe.

Environmental science classes at Kinkaid's Backyard conduct monthly tests of Buffalo Bayou's water quality index. They have determined that most of the pollutants in the bayou come from runoff from streets, yards and businesses in the watershed. At times, bacterial levels in Buffalo Bayou rise due to the sewage treatment plant upstream of the Kinkaid School[28].

Just beyond the Kinkaid School is the Biarbend Park Rapid which extends for about 100 feet before coming to the bulkhead of the Park.

Memorial Villages Water Authority

From the bulkheaded shoreline in Briarbend Park, the once notorious wastewater treatment plant of the Memorial Villages Water Authority can be seen on the opposite bank. The bubbling flow of effluent from the plant enters the bayou from a pipe near the north bank. Boaters should be alert to this possible hazard in the water. Air freshener is also recommended.

In 1985, this wastewater treatment plant was on the Texas Water Commission's Worst of Texas list. The plant was dumping more than 1 million gallons of raw sewage per day into Buffalo Bayou on rainy days. In fact, it had been dumping raw sewage into Buffalo Bayou since 1974[29].

Although the Memorial Villages Water Authority had been cited for dumping raw sewage into Buffalo Bayou since 1978, it only came into compliance with state standards in 1988 with the construction of a new treatment plant[30].

The new treatment plant was again a cause for concern in June, 1993. Surging storm waters caused erosion above a bend in the bayou near Farnham Park Drive, just above San Felipe Drive, that ate away a high bluff and sent stately old trees into the bayou. Forty feet of bank collapsed forming a cliff-like drop off that endangered the 36 inch sanitary sewer line below the road to the wastewater treatment plant. Fortunately, repairs were made and a crisis for the 11,000 homes that use the treatment plant was averted[31].

San Felipe Street

Within three quarters of a mile below Briarbend Park is the San Felipe Street bridge. On the south side is an office complex of several buildings. The Buffalo Bayou Regatta begins here and much of the set up for the launch of boats takes place in the parking lot and easement on the downstream side of the bridge.

The Buffalo Bayou Regatta began in 1970 as an event to raise funds for local canoe racers who desired to attend the national championships of the United States Canoe Association. Originally called the Buffalo Bayou Canoe Race, it soon picked up its more evocative name, the Reeking Regatta, because of the dismal water quality of Buffalo Bayou[32].

In those early days of the event, the bacteria and contamination levels in the bayou were 100 times the standard for boating and 1,000 times the accepted standard for swimming. The Regatta organizers hoped to draw attention to the harm that pollution has done to Buffalo Bayou and the ongoing attempts to improve it.

Since 1987, the Buffalo Bayou Regatta has been sponsored by the Buffalo Bayou Partnership[33], an organization dedicated to improving the bayou. In recognition of the efforts of many people to bring the quality of the water in Buffalo Bayou to acceptable standards, the name of the Reeking Regatta was changed, after the 1990 race, to the Buffalo Bayou Regatta. By 2002, the regatta was part of a larger event, The Bayou Beckons 2002, a festival of events celebrating Buffalo Bayou[34].

The course for the Buffalo Bayou Regatta begins at the San Felipe Street bridge and ends at Sesquicentennial Park, a distance of fifteen miles. The race course is both unique and difficult. Racers must contend with both shallow and deep water sections, tight corners, portages and many obstacles.

Billed as the premier canoe race in Texas, the Buffalo Bayou Regatta offers more trophies than other races and it has the longest sprint races in Texas. With hundreds of entrants, the regatta is easily the largest canoe race in Texas.

Hunter's Creek Village

Beyond the office complex at San Felipe Street, on the south bank, is the small tip of Hunter's Creek Village that extends across the bayou. The eastern boundary of this segment is Voss Road. The larger portion of the village is on the north side and is adjacent to Piney Point Village. This boundary line begins about one mile downstream of the bridge. Hunter's Creek Village continues along the north bank for three miles.

German farmers settled in this vicinity and established sawmills to cut local timber during the second half of the nineteenth century. As late as 1936 the town site consisted of a sawmill and several dwellings. The community was incorporated in 1954 as Hunter's Creek Village[35].

In a manner similar to the other Memorial Villages, Hunter's Creek Village residents sought to transform their rural farming community after World War II into an upscale suburb of Houston. By city ordinance the lot size must be at least one half acre. Of the 1,430 homes in the village, the median year of construction was 1963. As befits the large lots, the homes have a median size of 3,606 square feet.

The two story homes situated among the pines, oaks and cherry laurels have proven to be a desirable community for the 4,598 residents. With a per capita income of $70,577, according to the 1990 census, Hunter's Creek Village was one of the ten wealthiest suburban communities in the nation[36].

Houston Country Club

About one half mile downstream of the Voss Road bridge, the Bering Ditch enters from the south. The Houston Country Club, on the south bank, begins at the Bering Ditch and extends for approximately two and a half miles along the south side of Buffalo Bayou.

The Houston Country Club, Houston's first country club, dates to an organizational meeting at the home of Colonel S. F. B. Morse on October 28, 1901. In March, 1904, several businessmen acquired 56 acres on San Felipe Road and built a $5,000 clubhouse. The Houston Golf Club, the forerunner of the Houston Country Club, had 110 charter members and its facilities were located on a tract of land directly across Buffalo Bayou from Glenwood Cemetery[37].

As Houston's oldest continuously running country club, the Houston Country Club has moved twice prior to relocating to its present west Houston site. In 1908, the popularity of golf prompted the club to acquire 156 acres at the intersection of Harrisburg Boulevard and the present day South Wayside Drive for a clubhouse and golf course. That site is now the Gus Wortham Park Golf Course[38]. In 1957, the Houston Country Club opened its facilities at 1 Potomac Drive.

The golf course situated along the banks of Buffalo Bayou was designed by Robert Trent Jones, Sr. In 1987, Ben Crenshaw, Masters Champion, and his partner Bill Coore completed an extensive renovation of the old course. Houston Country Club is a private facility for members only[39].

At the far end of the Houston Country Club property, the bayou makes a tight right turn around a high point of land known as the Farther Point. A channel cuts off to the left under the Farther Point Drive Bridge, and, if the level of the bayou is high enough, boaters can select either route. The Farther Point Rapids are created here by naturally-occurring outcrops of sandstone and clay

Tanglewood

Within a quarter mile downstream of Farther Point is the Chimney Rock Road Bridge, followed immediately by the entrance of Spring Branch Creek on the north side of the bayou. The Indian Trails residential development is on the south bank of the bayou in the small tract of land between the Houston Country Club property and Chimney Rock Road.

The larger and more extensive neighborhood of the Tanglewood Subdivision lies south of the Houston Country Club and Indian Trails, but beyond Chimney Rock Road, it extends along Buffalo Bayou as far as Sage Road.

The Tanglewood Subdivision opened in the summer of 1949 as a residential neighborhood developed by William Giddings Farrington. At that time, the houses were built far to the west of downtown off a narrow shell lane called San Felipe Road. The property had previously been part of about 2,000 acres owned by the Bering brothers, August, Conrad and Charles. The Berings had used the land to plant crops to support their households[40].

Most of the homes were the wide "rambling ranch" designs that were popular in the 1950's. Developer Farrington named the subdivision after "Tanglewood Tales" by Nathaniel Hawthorne. Since his term of office ended in 1993, former President George H. Bush has made his home in Tanglewood[41].

Chimney Rock Road

The Chimney Rock Road bridge over Buffalo Bayou was built in 1988. Although the extension of Chimney Rock across the bayou had been a controversial project since the early 1950's and objected to by neighborhood groups, the City of Houston voted to commence the road work in 1987.

The extension and widening of Chimney Rock to Wirt Road was intended to create a thoroughfare connecting I-10 and the Southwest Freeway to alleviate the lack of north-south access in west Houston. A more expensive alternative of extending Chimney Rock to Antoine Road was rejected.

Ultimately, however, the route to Wirt Road proved to be more costly than planned. In 1988, the Duchesne Academy, owned by the Catholic Diocese of Galveston-Houston, filed suit against the City claiming the fine arts building was ruined by its proximity to the new road and had to be rebuilt on the other side of the street. The settlement added about $3 million more to the cost of the project[42].

Duchesne Academy

Located north of Buffalo Bayou on the northwest corner of the intersection of Chimney Rock Road and Memorial Drive, the Duchesne Academy is a part of the Network of Sacred Heart Schools offering college preparatory courses with a curriculum rooted in Catholic doctrine. The Network of Sacred Heart Schools consists of twenty-one schools across the United States operated by the Society of the Sacred Heart, an organization founded by Saint Madeleine Sophie Barat nearly 200 years ago.

Established in 1960, the Duchesne Academy program includes Lower, Middle and Upper Schools. The physical facilities include two main classroom buildings, a fine arts building and theater, a gymnasium, tennis courts, sports fields and a 300 seat chapel. The chapel, which was dedicated in 1979, has a prominent steeple that is visible from the nearby streets[43].

Spring Branch

The homes on the east side of Chimney Rock Road, north of the bayou, overlook the deep gully of Spring Branch Creek. This major tributary of Buffalo Bayou rises in the heart of that part of Houston known as Spring Branch. Some of the earliest settlers to the area which would become known as "Houston" settled in Spring Branch. It is one of the most historically important areas along Buffalo Bayou.

The Spring Branch Creek, as the name implies, is feed by springs, and Spring Lake on the Proetzels Branch is indicative of the source of fresh water that attracted the first settlers to the area. The creek angles away at forty-five degrees to the northwest from its junction with Buffalo Bayou near Chimney Rock Road to a point near Long Point Road. Although it is not a community defined by specific political boundaries, Spring Branch is thought of as the area bounded by Silber Road on the east, Gessner Road on the west, Buffalo Bayou on the south and Kempwood Road on the north. What began as a small, rural farming community now encompasses the six affluent residential neighborhoods of the Memorial Villages as well as the adjacent working class neighborhoods within the City of Houston.

Among the earliest individuals to settle in the area was Karl Kolbe, a German immigrant, who built his log cabin on the banks of Spring Branch where it joins Buffalo Bayou. Who was Karl Kolbe and why he came to Texas is a mystery. Little is known of his personal life, whether he was married and had a family, how old he was and when he died. Although some suggest an arrival date of about 1830, it has not been documented earlier than 1845. We do know that he came to Texas several years before the much-studied German immigrations during the Texas Republic and afterwards[44].

An attempt to attract colonists to Texas from Germany was considered by Stephen F. Austin about 1830, yet he made no formal program to bring Germans to his colony. In contrast, the Galveston Bay and Texas Land Company formed by Joseph Vehlein of Mexico City, David G. Burnet and Lorenzo de Zavala set out to bring one hundred German or European families to Texas in 1830. Kolbe may have been influenced by the activities that preceded these formal immigration plans[45].

Like many of those early settlers who entered Texas on their own during the period of colonization, Kolbe simply chose a place he liked and built his home. He selected a forested region that was fifteen miles from the nearest town, Harrisburg. His site was remote and isolated from the main roads of the area. The road to San Felipe crossed the prairie south of the Buffalo Bayou and the Washington Road was off to the northeast. Yet, although Kolbe pioneered an isolated farm, he seems to have remained in touch with his friends in the German province of Saxony over the next eighteen years.

One of those with whom Kolbe corresponded was Carl Siegismund Bauer. When the Revolution of 1847-1849 broke out in Europe, Bauer sent his son August to Texas to avoid the fighting. August lived in Texas during 1847 and he wrote a glowing description of Texas to his father. On the basis of August Bauer's letter about Texas, Carl Siegismund Bauer sold the Bauer-Rummel mill and home in Saxony. With the proceeds from the sale, Bauer prepared to move his family to Texas. He also persuaded his partner Wilhelm Rummel to bring his family[46].

By the late 1840's, Houston had become the destination for many families from Germany, often because of the reports of the opportunities that the new republic held for immigrants.   Five German families now lived in the community on the Spring Branch Creek, about nine miles due west of Houston. The families of Karl Kolbe, Daniel Ahrenbeck, Jacob Schroeder, Louis Hillendahl and Henry Hillendahl were the core of the community of farmers and dairymen that would flourish over the next half century. In 1848, the nucleus of the Spring Branch community attained a critical mass with the arrival of the two additional families from Saxony[47].

On October 10, 1848, the ship Neptune sailed from Europe and arrived in Galveston nine weeks later after a difficult voyage. The families of Wilhelm and Caroline Rummel and Siegismund and Chistiana Bauer, totaling seventeen immigrants, arrived in Texas after narrowly averting shipwreck in the Gulf off Galveston. Kolbe, Ahrenbeck and Schroeder met the immigrants in Houston and they convinced the new families to settle in Spring Branch[48].

The Rummel and Bauer families drove their wagons west of town to the place where five other German families were camped alongside the wooded creek. They settled near a beautiful grove of oak trees and giant pines that lay across the creek and northeast of the camp. In the evening of that same day, the newcomers from Saxony led the community in a thanksgiving service that began the formal worship community that became "St. Petri Gemeinde," St. Peter's Evangelical Lutheran Church[49].

St. Peter's Church has been called the "heart of Spring Branch." Although the German immigrants did not come to Texas primarily to gain religious freedom, the desire to worship freely and in their own way was a significant factor in the organization of the community[50]. In a pattern of nineteenth century settlement that is also found in the northern parts of Harris County, these Evangelical Germans formed a close knit and highly religious farming community in the hinterland of the larger, and more cosmopolitan, city of Houston.

August Bauer, son of Carl Bauer, had purchased a book of sermons before leaving Annaberg, Saxony in 1847. When the families gathered in Texas in 1848, the young August Bauer was appointed as the religious leader of the community[51].

With the beginning of the year in 1849, the farmers began to clear the surrounding forest land for farms and to cut trees for a log cabin church. Unfortunately, the fallen timbers proved too tempting, and some enterprising loggers for the railroad apparently stole the stockpile of logs that had been set aside. Undeterred, new logs were cut for St. Peter's Church and, this time, they were taken to the home of Wilhelm Rummel who with his wife had donated a 1/4 acre tract of land upon which the log cabin church finally was built in 1854, five years after the first worship service[52].

The Rev. John Hardtle became the first pastor of St. Peter's Church, arriving in August, 1856. He went to work immediately and the first baptism was recorded August 3, 1856 as that of Louis Wilhelm Schaeltroop. Under his direction, the parish began to develop into the prominent institution of the community. Hardtle established the first school in Spring Branch at St. Peter's Church. August and Emilie Bauer donated four acres of land for the school's playground, and Rev. Hardtle dedicated the first cemetery for the community on land that was adjacent to the northwest boundary of the school's playground[53].

The cemetery at St. Peter's Church holds graves of many Spring Branch pioneers. The first burial was on December 21, 1856. Three years later, the yellow fever epidemic of 1859 took the lives of several parishioners, including the pastor, Rev. B. M. Hailfinger, whose lone headstone marks the mass grave of the thirty-six victims. Rev. Hailfinger had just arrived as the resident minister in 1859. He opened the school on September 9 and he died 19 days later. He is the only minister interred in St. Peter's Church Cemetery[54].

In 1864, St. Peter's Church was damaged by fire and the community decided to build a modern frame church to replace the ten year old log cabin structure. At the time, the timber business was prospering in the heavily wooded Spring Branch area. The Bauer family, who owned one of the three local sawmills, donated the land for the church. Lumber was acquired by Wilhelm Rummel and his son Carl who worked at the McGuffey sawmill[55].

Wilhelm Rummel and his son carefully selected the timbers and lumber as each piece came from the mill. They specifically chose beams of 12 inch heart pine to be used for the sills and the framework. And, in 1864, the new church, a stone structure with hand pegged attic beams, was dedicated[56].

Nearly a century later, in 1961, a new, brick St. Peter's Church was built adjoining the old church. The old St. Peter's Church, built in 1864, was moved a short distance to the west to make room for the new church, and in 1968, the small frame chapel was restored, making it one of the oldest churches in continuous use in Harris County. In the old church are many reminders of the past. The interior retains the original church pews and the raised preaching pulpit. An 1839 edition of Martin Luther's German Bible is on display. The original organ from St. Peter's Church, however, has been donated to St. John's Church in Sam Houston Park and is on display there[57].

St. Peter's Church, located at 9022 Long Point Road, stands today as an enduring example of the determination of the early settlers of the Houston area. Yet, while buildings and organizations may represent the progress made to develop a city, the story of the people give life to the history of the area.

The first immigrants to settle in Spring Branch around 1848 were farmers and timber men. While the timber was exploited during the initial decades of the settlement of the area, farming became the primary industry for the next one hundred years. Three of the families who came to the area in 1848 provide examples of the transformations that have taken place.

Carl Siegismund Bauer was 56 years old when he arrived in Texas. Born in 1792 in Wiesa, Saxony, Bauer was an experienced stone mason who also owned a sawmill in partnership with a younger man, Wilhelm Rummel. He brought his family and, with Rummel, he established a sawmill operation in the woods of Spring Branch.

Yet, sometimes unforeseen events change one perspective on things. Bauer's wife died within ten months of their coming to Texas. By 1851, he had decided to move on to Round Top. Carl Bauer turned over his property in Spring Branch to his son August and moved to Round Top with the rest of his family. He lived there until his death on January 27, 1873 at age 80. August Bauer continued to operate in the lumber business in Spring Branch and then, later, in northern Harris County. Bauer Street, extending along the north side of Spring Branch Creek between Hammerly Drive and Emnora Street, is a reminder of his legacy to Houston[58].

Wilhelm Rummel, Carl Bauer's partner, was 36 years old when he brought his wife, Carolina, and their four children to Texas. According to the 1850 census, Rummel was a farmer and had assets of only $100. Although we know that he also supplemented his income by working in the local sawmill, Rummel earned additional money, as late as 1857, by hauling goods between the plantations of the Brazos River bottoms and the city of Houston. One of his clients, John Greer, gave him a bell that had been used to call slaves in from the fields for St. Peter's Church in Spring Branch[59].

Little more is known of the Rummel family in the area, but name of Rummel Creek, a tributary of Buffalo Bayou near West Belt, is a lasting reminder of the pioneer family.

When the ship Neptune brought the Bauer and Rummel families to Texas in 1848, the greeting party from Spring Branch included the Hillendahl brothers. In their mid-thirties, Louis Hillendahl, age thirty-five in 1848, and Heinrich, one year younger, also had recently immigrated from the Hanover region of Germany with their families.

Louis Hillendahl and his wife Dorothea had four children and property valued at $200 at the time of the 1850 census. Heinrich and his wife Elizabeth had three children. Both he and Heinrich began to establish their farms in the early 1850's[60].

Heinrich acquired his first eighty acres in 1851 for $2.00 an acre, and eventually the Hillendahl farm extended from Long Point Road to Westview Drive and from Pech Road to 150 feet west of Monarch Oaks Drive. The Hillendahl's raised a variety of vegetables, including beets, onions, cabbage, collards, turnips, tomatoes, beans and peas, that were transported to Houston's market square each day. Their operation was typical of the many truck farms that served the needs of the city. At its greatest extent, the Hillendahl farm included two barns, a workshop, a smokehouse, hog pens, chicken coops, a storm cellar and an old hand dug well[61].

Life in rural Texas was not without its difficulties. Elizabeth, Heinrich's wife, died in 1854. Heinrich buried her in a plot in the northwest corner of the farm, and that piece of land became the family cemetery for three generations. Heinrich's second wife Maria was buried there in 1907, and the cemetery also contains the graves of four of Heinrich's children and several members of his son Arnold's family[62].

By the early 1960's, the urban development in Spring Branch had made farming less attractive. Arnold Hillendahl, Jr. sold most of farm in 1962 and a large part became the Monarch Oaks Subdivision with 150 homes. Today, the small family plot of nineteen graves is in a parking lot of a former K-Mart store and a Firestone auto service store at 8355 Long Point Road, at the corner with Pech Road. The Hillendahl cemetery has city, county and state registrations to remain a cemetery and it will never be moved. A trust fund provides for the maintenance for the pebble stoned graveyard that is surrounded by a 4-foot hurricane fence and lies largely unnoticed among the stores along the busy street[63].

For over a century, the extended Hillendahl family owned property in Spring Branch. A store at what is now Campbell Road and Long Point Road served as a station for horseback mail carriers in the 1850's, and it was called Hillendahl Station after the pioneer family. When the Missouri, Kansas and Texas Railroad was built, the community became known as Hillendahl, and it continued to be called by that name until 1930 when Spring Branch became more popular[64].

When efforts to form a corporation known as Spring Branch failed in the mid-1950's, a group of affluent communities known as the Memorial Villages were formed from the town of Hillendahl and surrounding area. Spring Valley is the incorporated residential community on site of Spring Branch.

St. Mary's Seminary

Immediately past Spring Branch Creek, on the north side of the bayou, is the property of St. Mary's Seminary of the Catholic Diocese of Galveston-Houston. The seminary was moved from La Porte in 1954 by Bishop Wendelin J. Nold. It is located at 9845 Memorial Drive, near the intersection of Antoine Drive and Memorial Drive.

St. Mary's Seminary's Romanesque-style facilities include an administration building, a chapel, a dining hall, a convent, two residence halls, a classroom and recreation building. A library and indoor gymnasium-auditorium were dedicated in 1966[65]. The buildings were designed by Maurice Sullivan, a partner of Birdsall Briscoe[66].

Sherwood Forest

At the far eastern edge of the St. Mary's Seminary property, Little John Creek enters the bayou. This is also the beginning of the Sherwood Forest Subdivision, a neighborhood that continues along the north bank of Buffalo Bayou for about one mile. The names of streets in Sherwood Forest are derived from the legend "Tales of Robin Hood."

Woods Bayou flows into the bayou from the north about one mile beyond Spring Branch Creek in an area that's thickly wooded. There are several springs along this section of the bayou. Woods Bayou has a concrete dam that has created a small, scenic lake. The dam appears on a 1952 map of the area and must have been built prior to that[67]. A small rapid creates a riffle near the dam.

A short distance downstream, there is the ghost of an old bridge across Buffalo Bayou. This is probably the old Post Oak Road bridge across Buffalo Bayou. A 1916 map shows the route of Post Oak Road passing west of the modern Woodway Drive bridge[68].

As you pass the relatively straight stretch of bayou before the Woodway Drive bridge, the site of the old Swiss Chalet Restaurant is on the opposite side of the street on the south side of the bayou. A mid-rise condominium of seven stories was constructed on the site of famous eatery that operated from the 1950's to the late 1990's. The new condominium, built in 2004, includes twenty units and is named "The Venti" which is Italian for twenty[69].

Woodway Drive

By 1961, Woodway Drive had become a major thoroughfare connecting with Memorial Drive in Memorial Park and providing access to the suburbs of west Houston that are on the south side of Buffalo Bayou.

There is reasonably good access at Woodway Drive and the Loop 610 feeder for canoes and kayaks. On the south side of Woodway Drive and on the north bank of Buffalo Bayou, there is a gravel parking area on land that is part of a thirty-five acre sliver of Memorial Park on the western side of Loop 610. Parking is plentiful. In the fall of 2002, as a result of the construction on the Woodway Drive bridge, a graded roadway replaced the trail that led down to the bayou through the heavy brush. It remains to be seen whether a paved access road to the bayou will be built at this point. The recently released master plan for Memorial Park anticipates the further development of this access point for commercial and private float trips down Buffalo Bayou through Memorial Park.

The parking area originally served the Memorial Park Archery Range that was located on this section of Memorial Park. After arrows were found in the lawn of the exclusive hotel across the bayou from the range in the late 1980's, the archery range was closed[70].

In May, 2002, in relatively low water, a trip from Terry Hershey Park to the Woodway Drive bridge took 8-1/2 hours. There were five or six log jams, two of which required getting out of the boats to portage[71].

Riverway

For a half mile past the Woodway Drive bridge, the Riverway business complex is on the south side of the bayou. Encompassing approximately twenty-five acres, Riverway contains a major hotel and several high rise office buildings.

Seymour Sacks lived on the tract of land near Memorial Park at Woodway Drive and Buffalo Bayou. When he sold several parcels to developers in the late 1970's and early 1980's to the Riverway developers, he retained his single family dwelling. In 2001, Seymour Sacks' 1.5 acre home site was purchased by developer Jerry Crawford who demolished the old Sacks house. Crawford is planning a residential condominium tower for the site[72].

On the western end of Memorial Park, several small brooks and ravines were dammed up and terraced in the 1940's, forming a lake. This lake, located around the first bend past the Woodway Drive bridge, was filled in to permit the construction of the hotel in the Riverway complex.

A twelve inch pipeline crosses the bayou near the end of the Riverway property. The structure is high above the water level and neither the pipeline nor the supports present a hazard to boaters.

West Loop

About three quarters of a mile below Woodway Drive, the bayou flows under the West Loop.

The first section of the West Loop, between Memorial Drive and the Southwest Freeway, was opened in 1963[73]. Since then, the West Loop has become one of the most heavily traveled and continuously-congested highways in the state. Although congestion is extremely high, efforts to expand the freeway have been defeated because any expansion would require the loss of highly-prized Memorial Park land. In 2002, a small concession was made to improve traffic flow along the West Loop. A swap of 1/4 acre of Memorial Park for 4/5 acre of land owned by Texas Department of Transportation provided for the frontage road on the west side of the West Loop[74].

Houston Arboretum

As the bayou passes under the multiple bridges that make up the West Loop, there is an office and residential building complex on the south bank. The north bank, for the next 3/4 mile, is the thickly wooded oasis of urban "wilderness" that is the Houston Arboretum.

The Houston Arboretum and Nature Center, 4501 Woodway Drive, preserves one hundred fifty-five acres of woodland, ponds and prairie[75]. Over five miles of trails are maintained to enable you to explore this remnant of the forest environment that existed at the time of the founding of the city. Although the forest is not virgin growth, it has been protected since the 1920's when the Hogg family transferred the property to the city.

Robert A. Vines, a noted botanist and author of the definitive work on trees in Texas, first proposed the creation of an arboretum within Memorial Park. Houston's City Council approved the concept in 1951 and set aside two hundred sixty-five acres (later reduced to one hundred fifty-five acres by highway right of ways) for the arboretum and botanical garden[76]. Vines subsequently served as the Director of the Arboretum. During his tenure, Vines found that Memorial Park has seventy-five native species of plants. This is half the total native species found in East Texas[77].

During the 1980's, the Houston Chapter of the Native Plant Society of Texas has assisted the Arboretum in developing five acres of prairie in the Arboretum. The Houston Arboretum's pond, located near the prairie, is home to twenty species of dragonflies and damselflies including the Golden-winged Skimmer, the Slaty Skimmer and the Banded Pennant.

Birds that nest in the Houston Arboretum include the Wood Duck, the Red-shouldered Hawk, the Barred Owl, the Great Horned Owl and the Pileated Woodpecker. During the winter, the American Robin, the Hermit Thrush, the Gray Catbird, the Cedar Waxwing, kinglets, the Brown Creeper and the American Woodcock can be seen in the Arboretum[78]. Bird watchers can easily position them-selves in prime birding habitat on the Charlotte Collins Couch Birding Walkway. This 150 foot elevated trail to a deck overlooking Buffalo Bayou was dedicated on November 11, 2000. The heavy brush and undergrowth make it difficult, if not impossible, to see the Walkway from the bayou[79].

Railroad Trestle in Memorial Park

Slightly less than a mile from the West Loop, a railroad trestle crosses Buffalo Bayou and marks the end of the Arboretum. On the south side, the railroad tracks also serve to separate the office complex from the Tall Timbers Subdivision. The trestle is a some-what unusual, but substantial, steel pipe structure on concrete ped-estals.

As early as 1922, the Galveston, Harrisburg and San Antonio Railroad crossed the bayou in the area of the modern Memorial Park on a track known as the Eureka Cutoff. Going south from the Eureka Junction, located near the modern intersection of White Oak Bayou and T. C. Jester Boulevard, the rail joins the former Southern Pacific Sunset line from Harrisburg to Richmond at the West Junction near South Main Street[80].

Since the merger of the Union Pacific Railroad and the Southern Pacific Railroad in 1997, the line crossing the Southern Pacific Railroad bridge has become the main rail route from downtown to the west[81].

The "railroad rapids" occurs soon after the bridge. Riffles cre-ated by the solid rock and clay bottom and the occasional large rocks form one of the most serious rapids on the bayou.

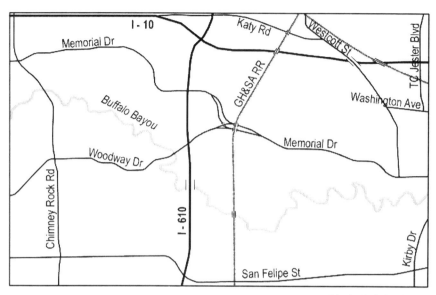

Map by Rachel A. Garcia

From Chimney Rock Road, Buffalo Bayou crosses under Woodway Drive and the West Loop. For the next few miles, the bayou provides a wild and scenic experience as it flows through Memorial Park on the north and River Oaks on the south.

Chapter 5
Memorial Park

The area that we know today as Memorial Park received its first mention in recorded history when Jane Long, "the Mother of Texas", wrote in her diary about the "pinery" in which they were camped. Long was traveling to San Antonio in September, 1822 to seek a pension from Governor José Félix Trespalacios, an associate of her husband James Long who was killed earlier in the year. The group camped for two days in the woods and the men hunted for food on the outlying prairie[1].

By the mid-1820's, settlers who were attracted to Texas by the promotional efforts of Stephen F. Austin began to find their way into the country. In addition to those who sought land in the heart of Austin's Colony along the Brazos River, others found places on the San Jacinto River and its tributary Buffalo Bayou. In 1824, grants of land were issued to Nathaniel Lynch near the mouth of the San Jacinto River, to the Vince brothers along the lower end of Buffalo Bayou, to John R. Harris near the junction of Brays Bayou, and as far west as John D. Taylor who settled in the area we know of as Spring Branch[2].

Allen C. Reynolds arrived in the area in 1826. In 1831, Reynolds received a grant of a league of land, approximately 4,428 acres, on the south side of Buffalo Bayou in the Memorial Park area where he operated a sawmill and a grist mill on the bayou[3].

John Reinermann, his wife and sons Heinrich (Henry) and John, Jr., settled along the north side of Buffalo Bayou near Memorial Park. Having sailed from Oldenburg, Germany in 1834, the Reinermann's were on board the schooner Sabine from New Orleans when it wrecked near Galveston Island on December 22, 1834. The von Roeder and Kleberg families were also on that ill-fated voyage. While they eventually moved on to the German settlements in the interior near Cat Springs and, ultimately, into the history of Texas and the King Ranch, the Reinermann's chose to stay on Buffalo Bayou[4].

Unfortunately, within the year, John Reinermann died. Although the Reinermann's had built a log cabin, planted orchards and cultivated a few small fields, the elder's death in 1835 brought hardships to the pioneer family. John Reinermann was laid to rest in the family cemetery on the farm in what is now the Cottage Grove Subdivision[5].

The Reinermann family was determined to remain in the area. Henry Reinermann married Louisa Margerethe Schermann on December 19, 1840, although the census records of 1850 indicate that Henry and Louisa had two children by then, Louisa, born in 1838, and Frederick, born in 1838. After Henry's untimely death in 1844, his widow Louisa married Joseph Sandman on April 27, 1845. They had a son Joseph Sandman, Jr., in 1846[6].

In an effort to secure title to their land, John Reinermann's widow applied for a land grant from the State of Texas on the grounds that he qualified for the grant since he was an immigrant to the area before the Texas Revolution. A league and a labor of land were granted by the State of Texas to the heirs of John Reinermann on April 28, 1847. The 4,428 acres of the grant lie on the north side of Buffalo Bayou, west of and adjoining the John Austin two-league grant on which the City of Houston was established in 1836[7].

By the late 1840's, Louisa was no longer married to Joseph Sandman, and she had married Christian Ledovic Bethje with whom she had a daughter, Bertha, in 1850. Christian Bethje, 28 years old, listed himself as a farmer in the 1850 census and his household included his 34 year old wife Louisa and their combined family of four children. They had property valued at $5,250 which indicated that they were prospering. By the 1860's, their farm in the Memorial Park area had its own sawmill, several cultivated fields, three hundred head of cattle and various farm animals[8].

In 1869, members of the Reinermann family bought a house on fifteen acres and moved to the Brunner Addition located along the Washington Road (near today's Shepherd Drive). Some of the heirs continued to live on the original property, but by 1883, the original homestead was abandoned. The heirs sold off tracts from the north and west part of the original Reinermann grant to various timber operators. Later, they sold the remainder to land speculators, although they retained a tract as late as 1915 which became the eastern part of Camp Logan. The Reinermann home, which was located a few blocks northwest of the modern intersection of Washington Avenue and Shepherd Drive, was demolished in the 1920's[9].

An archeological survey of Memorial Park and the Camp Logan facility in 1989 found no evidence of historic occupation in Memorial Park prior to 1917. The Reinermann homestead is believed to have been near what is now 5302 Darling Street in Cottage Grove[10].

Although the physical evidence of this pioneer family seems to have passed away, these early settlers of Houston remain with us in simple, but subtle way that you might notice the next time you drive in the area around Memorial Park. John Reinermann's name is perpetuated by Reinerman (sic) Street which runs south from White Oak Bayou to Buffalo Bayou, five streets west of Shepherd Drive. Joseph Sandman's name is perpetuated by Sandman Street, a north-south street two blocks east of Reinerman Street. Christian L. Bethje's name is perpetuated by Bethje Street, a short street one block east of Sandman Street, near where Durham Street curves back to join Shepherd Drive. Durham Street was constructed over Bethje Street in the Brunner Addition as the southbound, one way companion to the northbound Shepherd Drive.

Throughout the nineteenth century, the area of Memorial Park lay well beyond the City of Houston. On the Wood Map of 1869, it was west of all platted additions of the city. Similarly, on the August Koch Bird's Eye Map of 1873 and the Bird's Eye Map of 1891, the wooded area of Memorial Park was not a part of Houston[11].

By 1917, the Hogg family had assembled a block of land that included the current Memorial Park. With the coming of World War I, the United States leased the land owned by the Hogg family for Camp Logan. Camp Logan was established as an emergency training center for troops during the war.

After World War I, Mike and Will Hogg reacquired control of the land that was Camp Logan. Through the efforts Catherine Emmott and Ilona Benda, the City of Houston purchased the land that had been Camp Logan for a park as a memorial to the servicemen of the World War[12]. Will and Mike Hogg, Henry Stude, and the Reinerman Land Company contributed land to the project, and the

1,503 acres of wooded land on the site of Camp Logan were annexed by Houston in December, 1926 as Memorial Park[13].

Even before the area was established as Memorial Park, it was a recreational area for the growing and prosperous city. In 1921, the fourteen year old Army Emmott and his friend John Henry Cabiness frequently paddled Buffalo Bayou from Post Oak Road to Shepherd Drive in a canoe that Emmott built. Long weekends were spent exploring the bayou and catching large numbers of frogs which they sold to the Brazos Hotel in downtown Houston[14].

Riding stables were established during the 1930's on the western side of Memorial Park along Post Oak Road. One of the few remaining private stables in the area are owned by the Bayou Club. With a reputation as one Houston's most exclusive clubs, the Bayou Club, established in 1939, has its clubhouse and stables on the northwestern edge of Memorial Park at 8550 Memorial Drive. The Houston Polo Club plays on the field near the Club[15].

By the early 1940's, picnic grounds in Memorial Park had been located along Buffalo Bayou. In many of the clearings, the bayou was considered suitable for swimming or wading. Today, however, due to pollution and bacteria levels, water contact is not recommended.

Yet, today, Memorial Park has become the focal point of much of the city's recreational activity and the park is recognized as the crown jewel of Houston's park system. The Memorial Park Conservancy estimates that more than 10,000 visitors a day take advantage of the amenities that the park offers[16].

Joggers happen to make up the bulk of the daily visitors to Memorial Park, but the other facilities are also well used. The Arboretum is a special preserve for understanding the natural environment. Sports enthusiasts can take advantage of the golf course, the tennis courts, the polo field and fields for soccer, softball and baseball. A trail system accommodates joggers, cyclists and mountain bikers, hikers and horseback riders, while a swimming pool and a fitness center is also available. New boat launches for canoeing and kayaking Buffalo Bayou are planned for the Woodway Drive bridge and the area along the east side of the railroad right of way. These boat launches will augment a proposed string of boat launch points in Memorial Park, at Shepherd Drive, at Waugh Drive, in downtown, at El Mercado, at North York Park, at Lockwood Drive and at Hidalgo Park[17].

With such a diverse group of users, Memorial Park is not without controversy. The Ho Chi Mihn Trail, a six mile, single track, expert-level trail for mountain biking is frequently closed after rain due to concerns over the destruction of the forest terrain. Ho Chi Mihn Trail is a favorite of the mountain bikers since it can be dangerous and strenuous due to hard ground, loose sand, exposed roots and deep creeks for fast up and down rides which are dangerous for beginners. Unfortunately, these same qualities have led to the trail's popularity and overuse, although Memorial Park also has about nine miles of single track trails and fire roads that are essentially flat bike trails for all skill levels[18].

From today's perspective amid the growth of Houston to the fourth largest city in the United States and demands on the prime property that is Memorial Park, we must admire the foresight that the Hogg family had in providing the land for Memorial Park with the strict covenant that the land only be used as a park[19].

As early as 1936, the Houston Independent School District board had petitioned the city to transfer acreage in Memorial Park to the new University of Houston. The board had anticipated that Work Projects Administration funds would be available for building the first unit of the university. Eventually, the university acquired about 110 acres of land from the Settegast and the Taub estates, and the new campus on St. Bernard Street (which was later named Cullen Boulevard) opened in 1939[20].

Similar efforts to partition the park for the purposes of an airport, a National Guard armory and to drill for oil have been thwarted. The recent swap of land on the west side of the West Loop, in 2002, however, seemed to re-open the old wounds from the loss of land in the Arboretum to the construction of the West Loop. A quarter acre of park land, which had been donated to the park by Harry C. Wiess and his wife in 1942, was traded for four fifths of an acre owned by the Texas Department of Transportation for a frontage road on the west side of the West Loop. Although, in this case, the park was a beneficiary of the transaction, all the parties in the matter were concerned that integrity of Memorial Park was preserved[21].

Memorial Park Golf Course

The Memorial Park Golf Course is one of the most popular facilities in Memorial Park. So popular, in fact, that all 144 tee times are usually booked within 45 minutes each day[22].

The golf course actually pre-dates the establishment of the park. After World War I, the base hospital of Camp Logan was converted to a charity hospital that was operated by the American Red Cross. A 9-hole, sand green course was built near the hospital in 1923 for use by convalescent soldiers. When the Jefferson Davis Hospital on Elder Street opened in 1924, the former base hospital was closed and the golf course was opened to the public[23].

With the creation of Memorial Park in 1926, the golf course became part of the Houston Parks Department. In 1935, the Parks Department began construction on a first class, 18-hole golf course to replace to older course. Designed by architect John Bredemus, the course, which he referred to as his "greatest golf course ever," opened in July, 1936[24].

After nearly sixty years of use, the golf course was showing its age. In 1994, a campaign to restore the golf course to its original grandeur was begun. It was hoped that it would be possible to preserve the historical quality while, at the same, provide for the proper maintenance of the course in the future. The newly-renovated 600 acre course opened in 1995 with a lighted driving range, putting and chipping greens, a new clubhouse and a golf museum created from the original clubhouse structure[25].

With the renovations, a number of environmental improvements were made to the Memorial Park Golf Course. The golf course has enrolled in the Audubon Cooperative Sanctuary program in which the Audubon International certifies that the golf course meets certain environmental goals regarding wildlife and habitat management, pesticide use, water conservation and water quality management. Some of the specific improvements include the development of five acres of native wildflowers and grasses, the reduction in the amount of managed turf, and introduction of lower-maintenance grass varieties. In order to reduce the need for fertilizer, there are also plans to divert water from Buffalo Bayou, which is rich in nutrients, for irrigation[26].

The River Oaks Country Club, the golf course across the bayou, is also enrolled in the Audubon Cooperative Sanctuary program, while the Lakeside Country Club, upstream at Wilcrest Drive, is the only Houston golf course to be certified as an Audubon Cooperative Sanctuary[27].

Camp Logan

In the first week of April, 1917, the Unites States Congress passed a resolution declaring that the country was in a state of war with Germany. Although the war had been going on in Europe since August, 1914, the United States was unprepared to engage in the conflict. The need to rapidly mobilize a military force for service in Europe prompted the federal government to establish training facilities throughout the country. Because the land which is now Memorial Park had previously been a National Guard facility, and possibly because much of the land was owned by the well-connected Hogg family, the United States leased a tract of land just beyond the western city limits from the Hogg family to build an emergency training center. This training facility was named Camp Logan in honor of Major General John A. Logan, a prominent Union officer in the Civil War.

Within four months after the declaration of war, the American Construction Company of Houston had been hired as the primary contractor for Camp Logan. The $2 million construction project began on July 20, 1917 and within four days, 2,500 men were on the job working 7 days a week.

The first phase of construction called for the completion of 1,000 buildings within a month. To meet the deadline, construction materials for Camp Logan were shipped by rail to Eureka Junction on the Southern Pacific Railroad. Eureka Junction, a rail yard on White Oak Bayou near the place where T. C. Jester Boulevard now crosses the bayou, permitted the construction materials to be shipped to a location in close proximity to the construction site.

By August 15, the first phase had been completed. The speed of construction set a record for World War I camps, and within three months, more than 30,000 men were living and training at Camp Logan[28].

Camp Logan was a tent camp with a troop capacity of 44,899 men. The tents were placed on raised wooden platforms and located along graded streets near mess halls and latrines. Most of the tents had four foot wooden walls. The streets in Camp Logan were unpaved or surfaced with oyster shell or cinders.

In addition, there were 1,329 buildings in the camp and all of the buildings were of wooden frame construction. Most of the buildings were set on wooden blocks. Some buildings, however, were placed on concrete footings while the bathhouses had concrete slabs with plumbing, drains and sewers[29].

The general layout of Camp Logan was a rhomboid shaped wedge, or four sided figure, with the short end along a line from the intersection of Crestwood Street and Memorial Drive to the intersection of Washington Avenue and Westcott Street. The camp perimeter then followed the path of Washington Avenue northwest to the Southern Pacific Railroad tracks. The perimeter turned southwest along the railroad tracks to the Memorial Drive, and finally, back east along Memorial Drive to Crestwood Street

The Base Hospital was in the southeastern corner of Camp Logan, near the Crestwood - Memorial Drive intersection. Camp Headquarters and the administration building was located on the south side of the present day intersection of the Arnot Street and Haskell Street. Various training units were situated along the Washington Avenue line, including engineering, supply, sanitary and ammunition training units. Three artillery brigades filled the remaining space as far as the railroad tracks. Four infantry brigades were situated along the railroad tracks as far as the Memorial Drive area. Six infantry brigades were located along the Memorial Drive line back to the area of the hospital. The central area of the camp, now occupied by the golf course, was an open area.

In addition to the 3,002 acres of developed encampment, another 6,558 acres were undeveloped and available for training drills, marches and schools for chemical warfare, bayonet practice, and hand grenade use. Drill fields were between one and two miles northwest of the camp proper while two other drill fields were on the south side of Buffalo Bayou. The Remount Depot was located just west of the main camp, and a rifle range was built about seven

Postcard courtesy of the Robbie Morin Collection

Camp Logan was organized as a tent camp supplemented with wooden buildings in regimental units of about two thousand men each.

miles to the west on Hillendahl Road. An artillery range was another three miles farther out[30].

A complete trench system was dug west of the main camp at Camp Logan, but the trenches were abandoned after heavy rains flooded the area. In general, the problem of poor surface drainage was not adequately handled by the open ditches along the roads. Standing water provided breeding grounds for mosquitoes and there was a serious outbreak of dengue fever in the camp in March, 1918[31].

For its part, the City of Houston was obligated to certain commitments in order to obtain the award of the training facility. Washington Avenue, the main road from downtown to Camp Logan, was improved. Other roads also were built to make the camp more accessible. Water for Camp Logan was also to be provided by the city. The Layne and Bowler Company, the contractor hired by Houston, drilled a 600 foot deep water well south of Washington Avenue that produced over 1 million gallons of water per day. Water from this well, as well as from several other wells drilled near the camp, was piped into a 200 foot square earthen reservoir located in the southeast quadrant of the intersection of Washington Avenue and the modern Westcott Street[32].

The federal government also wanted the City of Houston to provide assurances that there were no vice districts within five miles of the proposed training camp. In a show of good faith, within the two or three months that the proposal was being considered, the city closed down a notorious red light district on the east side of downtown[33].

Entertainment and recreation for the troops was an important aspect of life in camp. The YWCA had a Hostess House on base and the YMCA's four clubs were located within the brigade encampments for soldiers during their time off duty. A library was established and operated by the American Library Association. The 108th Engineers, whose duties included the training and use of horses, often held impromptu rodeos to display their horsemanship in addition to entertaining the troops[34].

Relations between the Army at Camp Logan and the civilian community were generally good although the racial incident involving the 24th Infantry soldiers during the first month of the operation of the camp did not get things off to a good start.

The primary purpose for Camp Logan was to train the 33rd Infantry Division of the Illinois National Guard and other units for duty in France during World War I. Most of the troops serving at Camp Logan were white. During the construction of the facilities and the deployment of the first troops to the camp in July and August of 1917, however, the 3rd Battalion, 24th Infantry, a unit of black soldiers from Illinois, arrived on July 28 and was stationed at Camp Logan as construction guards. While the U. S. Army itself was segregated into white and black units, a situation that persisted until after World War II, the assignment of a black unit from a northern state to a city in the segregated south proved to be a prescription for disaster[35].

As construction guards, the soldiers of the 24th Infantry lived in a camp about one mile east of Camp Logan, on a tract of land near the northwest corner of the intersection of Washington Avenue and Reinerman Street in the Brunner Addition. Reacting to rumors about an incident involving the arrest of a black soldier by Houston police officers in the Fourth Ward at noon on Thursday, August 23, 1917,

Sgt. Vida Henry led about one hundred fifty armed black soldiers on a riotous march to downtown at eight that evening[36].

The mob left their quarters near Reinerman Street and marched the four blocks down Washington Avenue to Brunner Avenue, now Shepherd Drive, repeatedly discharging their weapons into the neighborhood before turning south and going to the end of Brunner Avenue. Upon reaching the end of Brunner Avenue the black soldiers took the road through the wooded area along Buffalo Bayou to Shepherd's Dam where they crossed the structure to Shepherd's Dam Road, now South Shepherd Drive, on their way to the San Felipe Road. Since their destination seems to have been the Fourth Ward, they turned down San Felipe Road, now West Dallas Avenue, and headed for Houston.

The riot took the lives of twenty people and eleven others were seriously injured. Shortly after 10 pm, Sgt. Henry told the men to return to camp under the cover of darkness. Henry then killed himself with a gunshot to the head.

Order was brought to the city with a curfew imposed by the mayor on the morning of August 24th. On Saturday, August 25th, the black soldiers of the 3rd Battalion were placed aboard a train and sent to Columbus, New Mexico. Military tribunals convicted one hundred ten of the soldiers who participated in the riot. Nineteen were hanged and sixty-three were sentenced to life in federal prison[37].

The first thirty days of Camp Logan proved to be a traumatic and tragic experience for Houston. But, once things settled down, the events at Camp Logan became fairly routine. The 33rd Infantry left to serve in France in June, 1918. They fought in the Amiens and Verdun sectors and participated in the St. Mihiel and Meusse-Argonne offensives. Returning to the United States in May, 1919, the division was demobilized June 6, 1919 at Camp Grant, Illinois[38].

On November 10, 1918, the armistice was signed that brought an end to the conflict in Europe. Camp Logan, having served as a training center for nearly twenty months, was deactivated. On March 20, 1919, the facility was turned over to the U. S. Public Health Service and the building which had been used by the American Red Cross was converted into Houston's first charity hospital[39].

Shortly after the Hogg Family regained possession of the Camp Logan land, most of the remaining structures were removed. Yet, even today, the outline of the systems of roads and drainage ditches is visible in Memorial Park. More significant, though, is the enduring imprint of the Camp Logan experience on the character of Houston.

River Oaks Country Club

About a half mile beyond the railroad bridge, the backyards of the homes in the Tall Timbers Subdivision can be seen on the south side of the bayou. Homes along Willowick Road and Pinehill Drive sit high on the the steep bank and several have landscapes and terraces extending to the bayou. At the end of the long, hairpin turn that curves around the point where Pinehill Drive is located, the River Oaks Country Club begins. Situated directly across from the picnic loop in Memorial Park, about 1-1/2 miles below the railroad bridge, the greens and fairways of the golf course are visible from the bayou.

The River Oaks Country Club Estates was developed in the 1920's as a residential neighborhood with golf course[40]. Although the golf course community is a popular idea today, in the 1920's, it was a new concept.

The William L. Clayton Summer House was the first house built in the newly opened River Oaks Country Club Estates. The house, at 3376 Inwood Drive, is set on a wooded site overlooking the River Oaks Country Club and its principal facade faces the country club, not the street[41].

Attorney Hugh Potter recognized the potential of this plan and he obtained an option to purchase two hundred acres surrounding the River Oaks Country Club in 1923. With his friends Michael and Will Hogg, Potter developed River Oaks as a residential garden suburb along Buffalo Bayou[42].

The River Oaks Country Club, at 1600 River Oaks Boulevard, opened in 1923. Designed by Donald Ross and Rees Jones, it is one of the most exclusive clubs in the area, if not the country. With its stately fairways, lush greens, and the Old World ambience of the clubhouse, the River Oaks Country Club has been called the best version of the Augusta National anywhere in southeast Texas[43].

River Oaks Country Club is enrolled in the Audubon Cooperative Sanctuary program. A large water pump for the River Oaks Country Club stands on a steel beam construction that consists of a platform that can be raised or lowered by means of a large electric pulley to correspond to the water level of the bayou. By pumping water from the bayou, the golf course can reduce its dependence on fertilizers and ground water[44].

The River Oaks Country Club occupies the south bank of the bayou for about one and one half miles. A ravine at the point of a bend in the course of the bayou separates the golf course from the property of Ima Hogg's Bayou Bend. The suspension bridge for Bayou Bend can be seen straight ahead as the stream turns back to the northeast. The sumptuous and often elegant homes of the River Oaks Subdivision line the south side of the bayou for the next one and one half miles to the Shepherd Drive bridge.

River Oaks

The first known resident of the area that we know as River Oaks was Allen C. Reynolds. Reynolds, who was born in Connecticut in 1786, grew up in New York and served in the War of 1812 as a captain in the United States 27th Infantry. After the war, Reynolds apparently visited Louisiana for his name appears in Jean Laffite's diary. In 1826, at age 40, Reynolds sailed for Texas, and for a while, he ran a mercantile establishment in Galveston with his partner William T. Austin[45].

Reynolds first acquired property in Brazoria County while he applied for a land grant of one league in what is now Harris County as early as 1826. He moved his wife and four children to Texas in 1830, and in 1831, Reynolds was granted a league of land by Stephen F. Austin that encompassed 4,428 acres extending south of Buffalo Bayou to the present day Bellaire Boulevard. The tract ranged from about Shepherd Drive on the east to the Southern Pacific Railroad tracks near Weslayan Street on the west.

Reynolds built a residence north of the present Weslayan Street and Highway 59 intersection, and from 1831 to 1835, he operated a sawmill and grist mill on Buffalo Bayou. He reportedly transported the lumber he cut down the bayou in his boat, taking it to Harrisburg since the town of Houston was yet to be conceived. In 1835, he sold all his property to James Spillman and moved away[46].

Reynolds bought the William and Peter Kerr land grant in Washington County in 1835, and he built his home on Hidalgo Bluff, a few miles upstream of Hidalgo Falls on the Brazos River.

Allen Reynolds died, at age 51, in Washington County on March 14, 1837 and is buried on Hidalgo Bluff. He had no idea that the land he owned would become a part of the City of Houston or that it would include River Oaks, Greenway Plaza and the City of West University Place. Yet, with an estate of $100,000, Reynolds seems to have done all right for himself[47].

Mitchell Louis Westheimer was a young German immigrant to Texas in the late 1850's. Born in Baden, Germany in 1831, Westheimer purchased at auction a parcel of 640 acres from within the A. C. Reynolds Survey that extended from present day Westheimer Road to Bellaire Boulevard. His farm became known as the Westheimer Plantation[48].

A miller by trade, Westheimer became successful in a variety of business ventures. In addition to a flour mill, he was a hay merchant, and he helped to build the first streetcar rails in Houston. The Westheimer Plantation had a large, plantation-style house, stables and a racetrack. In 1866, Westheimer established a free school for his employees' children and the neighboring children.

In 1895, Mitchell Westheimer donated a portion of land from his plantation to Harris County for a short cut road through Sealy to Columbus. This road, still called Westheimer Road, runs for thirty miles from Houston to Fulshear and it is longest major street in Texas. He died in 1906.

In the mid-1920's, to complement the country club at the north end of River Oaks Boulevard, Lamar High School was built at the south end of the street on the site of Westheimer's plantation and the school he had established[49].

In 1920, Thomas H. Ball, Kenneth Womack and William S. Farish bought 180 acres of wooded land west of town for a private golf club in which members could buy lots for homes. The venture was called River Oaks Country Club Estates.

The River Oaks Country Club Estates was platted as sixteen lots of about 2 acres each across the south edge of River Oaks Country Club. To provide access to the new development, the road to the country club from Westheimer Road was paved and it was named Ball Boulevard. Later, the name was changed to River Oaks Boulevard[50].

Tom Ball, born in 1859 in Huntsville, was a local Huntsville politician who espoused prohibition and was elected to the U. S. Congress in 1896. He helped secure the first federal aid for the development of the Houston Ship Channel in 1899 and resigned from Congress in 1903 to practice law in Houston. So well respected was Ball that, in 1907, the community of Peck was renamed Tomball in his honor. In his early sixties at the conception of the River Oaks Country Club Estates, the subsequent development of the subdivision fell to younger and more energetic men like Will Hogg. Tom Ball died in Houston on May 7, 1944[51].

In 1922, Will Hogg sponsored the River Oaks Corporation for development of a restricted River Oaks Addition. Houston attorney Hugh Potter obtained an option to purchase 200 acres surrounding the River Oaks Country Club in 1923. By May, 1924, Will Hogg had put together a block of land for a residential garden suburb of 1,100 acres along Buffalo Bayou that absorbed the original layout of the River Oaks Country Club Estates. Will Hogg, his brother Mike Hogg and Hugh Potter became the developers of River Oaks[52].

With a vision of a grand subdivision that would allow the citizens of Houston to escape the noise, dirt and congestion of the city, the developers began to convert the farmland and woodlands lying three miles west of downtown into a "distinguished experiment in fine living[53]."

River Oaks was a master planned community designed by landscape architects Hare and Hare of Kansas City. The design included home sites, a fifteen acre campus for the River Oaks Elementary School, two shopping centers, esplanades, underground utilities, rigid building codes, deed restrictions and a centralized community control to assure exclusivity. The development became a model of community planning[54].

While many of these features were touted as new concepts in residential development, the "park" design, with curving drives through tall, native trees, had actually been introduced thirty years earlier in the Magnolia Park neighborhood on the east side of Houston[55].

Although the developers attempted to introduce innovative social ideas to urban planning and development, the concept that may have been ahead of its time was, unfortunately, still tied to the conventions of the past. The gentleman's agreement that excluded blacks, Jews and minorities from home ownership in River Oaks persisted well into modern times[56].

The first house built in River Oaks was the William L. Clayton Summer House at 3376 Inwood Drive. Designed by architect Birdsall Briscoe, the great grandson of John R. Harris, founder of Harrisburg, in 1923, the Clayton House was set on a wooded site overlooking the River Oaks Country Club. The house is a Colonial Revival style based on George Washington's home at Mount Vernon[57].

William Lockhart Clayton, cofounder of the cotton brokerage firm Anderson Clayton and Company, intended the house to be his summer retreat since it was several miles outside the city. In fact, Inwood Drive was not paved until 1925[58].

River Oaks proved to be popular from the beginning. Cleveland Harding Sewall, a successful wholesale grocer, built his home on six acres in the heart of River Oaks in 1925. His house, at 3452 Inwood Drive, was designed by architect Ralph Adams Cram and is an excellent example of the Spanish Colonial Revival style[59].

Cleveland Sewall died in 1942, and his widow, who died in 1973 at age 84, willed the property to Rice University. The house was left to deteriorate pending the sale of the property. As is often the case, the wrecking ball is the fate of many significant structures in Houston. The Harris County Appraisal District records for 2002 indicate that the lot on which the house stood is vacant[60].

Will Hogg and his partners greatly expanded the concept envisioned for the River Oaks Country Club Estates by platting several sections in the River Oaks Addition. An eighty acre section was set aside as the Homewoods subdivision. It consists of about sixteen lots on the east side of the River Oaks Country Club, along both sides of Lazy Lane. The largest lot was reserved for the Hogg family and it became Bayou Bend[61].

River Oaks was an independent community for three years until it was annexed by the City Houston in 1926[62]. Although conceived as a subdivision of summer homes, the planned community actually became popular for primary residences. The mobility offered by the automobile made outlying suburban living possible. Houstonians seemed to readily adopt this way of life, and the open coastal prairie to the south of Buffalo Bayou was available to accept this pattern of growth.

By the end of 1937, Houston had annexed the Briarwood Addition, a newly opened western section of River Oaks. In the late 1940's, Frank Sharp developed the Royden Oaks Subdivision adjacent to River Oaks, near the intersection of Willowick Street and San Felipe Road. The growth of Houston to the west of town continued decade after decade. By the 1990's, River Oaks, once the far western suburb, had become the geographic center of the city[63].

Crestwood Acres

For three and one half miles from the bridge at the West Loop, the north bank of Buffalo Bayou is a wild and natural growth of tall pines, towering sycamores and dense underbrush in Memorial Park. Shortly after a sharp right bend of the bayou, a ravine enters from the north side, and on the left side of the gully, the cleared brush and manicured landscaping indicates that the boundary of Memorial Park has been crossed.

The tract of land stretching from the eastern edge of Memorial Park to Westcott Street and lying between Memorial Drive and Buffalo Bayou is a secluded enclave of upper income residences and condominiums. In recent years, a considerable amount of redevelopment has taken place in this area. Older homes have been torn down and gated communities and condos have risen in their place.

Crestwood Street runs south along the park boundary at Memorial Drive. The street then makes several curves into the heart of bayou's north bank where it dead ends. The Crestwood Acres Subdivision lies on each side of Crestwood Street. Recent developments have carved a handful of smaller subdivisions and condos from the older neighborhood. Much of the new development has not been without controversy.

In 1992, Paragon Homes was granted approval to build nineteen homes in the Crestwood Acres Subdivision despite protests from other residents. Over thirty families in the subdivision expressed concern over drainage, erosion and traffic problems in the neighborhood, fearing that additional construction and development would only exacerbate the problem. The residents pointed out that in 1985, a ten unit condominium facility was sixty feet from the banks of the bayou, yet, by 1992, erosion had placed the site within twenty to thirty feet of the water[64].

The City, however, rejected the claims of the residents and issued a permit to Jerry Deutser, owner of Paragon Homes. Deutser planned to build nineteen garden homes in Crestwood Acres that sell in the $300K to $350K range[65].

By 2003, six subdivisions occupied the Crestwood tract beginning at Memorial Drive and ending at the cul-de-sac in the Sanctuary Subdivision. On the corner of Memorial Drive is section one of Arlington Terrace. Other parcels of the original Crestwood Acres have also been separated off to create the Park at Crestwood, the Crestwood on the Park Condo and Crestwood Court subdivisions.

Arlington Court

The most dramatic redevelopment of the residential neighborhood has been the Arlington Court Subdivision. Located along Memorial Drive, Arlington Court is a gated residential development of the Morgan and Company, a firm headed by Houston businessman Niel Morgan. Morgan bought out and removed the older homes at this location in the 1990's and has developed the two section subdivision of slightly over fifteen acres into eighty lots[66].

Glen Cove

After a half mile on a southerly course, the bayou turns back to the north around the tip of the Sanctuary Subdivision at the end of Crestwood Street. The acreage adjacent to the bayou is the Hogg Bird Sanctuary, a park of the City of Houston. The tract north of the bird sanctuary is the lower end of the Glen Cove Subdivision.

There are 173 modest, one story homes in the Glen Cove neighborhood, most of which were constructed in the 1940's. The large lots of Glen Cove, the deed restrictions and the proximity to Memorial Park have made the neighborhood attractive for redevelopment. The new homes have been primarily low density housing and single family dwellings.

A similar pattern of redevelopment is occurring in the Camp Logan Subdivision which is across Arnot Street and north of the Glen Cove Subdivision. The 279 bungalows and cottages of the Camp Logan Subdivision were built in the 1930's and 1940's. These homes, which average about 1500 square feet in size, are rapidly being replaced by town homes ranging from 2,500 to 3,500 square feet.

While most of the Glen Cove Subdivision is north of Memorial Drive, there are about sixteen homes on Glen Cove Street, a short, dogleg lane south of Memorial Drive on a high terrace above the bayou[67].

Memorial Cove Lofts

Memorial Cove Lofts, located at 6007 Memorial Drive, one block west of the Westcott Street and Memorial Drive intersection, is a new twenty unit condominium that was created out of the Glen Cove Subdivision. Each unit is a two story unit with a mix of warehouse loft features, including exposed concrete floors and ceilings, high windows and exposed mechanicals, and modern kitchen and bathroom features. The floor plans for the Memorial Cove Lofts range from 1,680 to 3,219 square feet with prices in December, 2002 from $375,000 to $699,000[68].

Bayou Bend

Buffalo Bayou makes a small "S" turn bend as it flows past Glen Cove. As the bayou turns to a northeasterly course, the suspension bridge of Bayou Bend can be seen in the middle distance of a quarter mile straight away. The pedestrian bridge provides access to the Bayou Bend Gardens and Museum from the parking area on the north side of the bayou. The Hogg Bird

Sanctuary, 100 Westcott Street, is on the north side of the bayou and occupies the small stretch of land along the bayou terrace adjacent to the parking lot.

Across the gully from the River Oaks Country Club Golf Course, the Bayou Bend property occupies the point of land in a north-curving bend in the bayou. Situated between two deep ravines, Bayou Bend is located at 2940 Lazy Lane in the Homewoods section of River Oaks. The public access for Bayou Bend is across the bayou at 1 Westcott Street. The property was the estate of Ima Hogg and it now houses the Bayou Bend Collection of the Houston Museum of Fine Arts[69].

Few families have played as prominent a role in the make up of Houston in the twentieth century as the Hogg family. From River Oaks to Memorial Park to the Houston Symphony to the Museum of Fine Arts, the Hogg family remains a continuing legacy in the city. The Hogg family, however, came to Houston only after a half century in East Texas and Austin.

Joseph Lewis Hogg and his wife Lucanda McMath Hogg came to Texas in 1839 from Alabama and settled on a farm two miles northeast of Rusk in Cherokee County. Joseph Hogg was active in politics and he helped to write the Texas Constitution. He fought in the Mexican War of 1845 and during the Civil War, he served as a brigadier general for the South[70].

Joseph and Lucanda had two sons, James Stephen Hogg and Thomas Elisha Hogg. James was born on the farm near Rusk on March 24, 1851. After his father's death, James Hogg looked to his older brother Thomas as father figure. As a young man, James was strongly influenced by the writings and poetry of his brother. After a successful career in local politics, James Hogg became the first native-born governor of Texas, serving from 1891 to 1895[71].

About 1874, Hogg married Sarah Ann Stinson and their first child, William, was born in 1875. Daughter Ima was born in 1882, son Michael was born in 1885, and son Thomas was born in 1887[72].

After the death of his wife of tuberculosis in 1895, Hogg returned to private law practice in order to support his young family. He subsequently amassed a sizable fortune through shrewd investments in real estate and oil lands. James Hogg purchased the Varner Plantation near West Columbia in 1901. Certain that it would have oil, he stipulated in his will that the property not be sold until fifteen years after his death[73].

James Hogg died on March 3, 1906 at age fifty-five at the home of his partner Frank Jones in Houston, and he is buried in Austin. His oldest son, Will Hogg, at age thirty-one, moved to Houston in 1906 to manage his father's interests on his death[74].

William Clifford Hogg was born on January 31, 1875 and attended public schools in Austin before entering Southwestern University at Georgetown. Ultimately, he received a law degree from the University of Texas in 1897. Will Hogg practiced law in San Antonio before joining his father's firm in Austin and was working in St. Louis at the time of his father's death[75].

Will Hogg was an assistant to Joseph S. Cullinan of the Texas Company (which later became Texaco) until 1913 when Hogg, Cullinan and James Autry formed Farmers Petroleum Company. In 1918, twelve years after his father's death oil was discovered on the Varner Plantation, providing the Hogg family with a source of wealth that would propel them into prominence[76].

During World War I, Will Hogg served in Washington at $1 per year in the special intelligence service. When he returned to Houston after the war, Hogg managed the family properties and investments. He also served as the chairman of City Planning Commission of Houston. At this time, Will Hogg was the driving force that produced the development of River Oaks and city's acquisition of Memorial Park[77].

Ima Hogg was the second of the Hogg children. She was born on July 10, 1882 in Mineola in Wood County. Ima was named by her father after a character in an epic poem written by his brother Thomas Elisha Hogg whom he admired greatly. The name is short for Imogene, yet it was an incongruous moniker that her father failed to recognize. Her grandfather rushed to Mineola when he heard the news of her birth to protest the name, but Ima had already been christened. Fortunately, Ima Hogg accepted her name with grace and humor throughout her life[78].

Showing a gift for the piano and music from the age of three, Ima Hogg entered the University of Texas in 1899 and went to New York to study music in 1901. From 1907 to 1909, she studied music in Berlin and Vienna. She moved to Houston in 1909 and taught piano. In 1913, she helped to organize the Houston Symphony Orchestra[79].

In late 1918, Ima Hogg became ill with depression and, while in her late thirties, she spent two years in Philadelphia under care of a specialist in mental and nervous disorders. She returned to Houston in 1923[80].

The development of River Oaks during the early 1920's seemed to come at just the right time. Bayou Bend was designed and built between 1926 and 1928 for Ima Hogg and her two brothers Will and Michael Hogg. Architect John F. Staub, with his associate Birdsall P. Briscoe, built the two story, twenty-four room house at Bayou Bend. The fourteen acre estate also had a two story garage and service building adjacent to the house[81].

At last, situated in her new home and, perhaps, sympathetic to the plight of other less fortunate because of her own experiences, Ima Hogg led efforts in 1929 to charter the Houston Child Guidance Clinic. This public service agency was established to provide therapy and counseling for disturbed children and their families[82].

Will Hogg died on September 12, 1930 at age 55 while on vacation in Europe with his sister Ima Hogg. The funeral services were held at their home at Bayou Bend, and he was buried in Oakwood Cemetery in Austin[83].

Will Hogg left the bulk of his estate to the University of Texas, and the Hogg family remained committed to the cause of mental health. With an initial endowment from the estate of Will Hogg, the Hogg Foundation for Mental Health was established at the university in Austin in 1940 through the efforts of Ima, Michael and Thomas Hogg and their families[84].

As the remaining Hogg siblings disposed of the estate of their brother Will, the thought of how to establish a public legacy seems to have been on their mind. Ima devoted her resources to the restoration of the family homestead in Cherokee County. The property, located two miles northeast of Rusk, was deeded to city of Rusk in 1941 by Ima Hogg, Thomas E. Hogg and Mike Hogg. Rusk then turned the property over to Texas Parks Board and the birthplace of James Hogg became Jim Hogg State Historical Park[85].

In 1943, after the death of Mike Hogg, Ima Hogg donated the extensive collection of works of Frederic Remington owned by Will and Mike Hogg to the Houston Museum of Fine Arts. The Hogg collection consists of forty-one works representing a comprehensive survey of Remington's career. It includes the painting entitled "Fight for the Water Hole" which has become an icon of American art[86].

After the marriage of Mike Hogg in 1929 and the death of Will Hogg, Ima Hogg lived at Bayou Bend alone until her death. Bayou Bend is very much a creation of Ima Hogg and, in many aspects, is a vivid reflection of her character and personality. Ima Hogg's love of architecture and furnishings seem to have been inspired by her childhood experiences in the Governor's Mansion during her father's two terms as governor from 1891 to 1895.

In 1920, Ima Hogg sat for a portrait in Wayman Adams' studio in New York. Admiring a simple armchair in the studio, she was surprised to learn it was made in colonial America. She obtained a similar Queen Anne chair for herself and Ima Hogg's collecting career had begun[87].

By the 1950's, Ima Hogg's collection of American antiques had become nationally recognized. Motivated by a sense of public service that had been instilled in her family for generations, Ima Hogg donated Bayou Bend to the Houston Museum of Fine Arts in 1957. She continued to live in her home until 1965 as she oversaw the transformation of her home into a museum[88].

The Bayou Bend Collection of American decorative arts and paintings is comprised of works produced from the 1660's to the 1860's that are displayed in twenty-four different settings in the main house. The Bayou Bend Collection, one of the finest such collections in the United States, was opened to the public on March 5, 1966[89].

Ima Hogg died on August 19, 1975, at age 93, due to complications from injuries suffered in an automobile accident while traveling in London. Miss Ima, as she was affectionately known, is buried in the Oakwood Cemetery in Austin in the Hogg family plot[90].

Bayou Bend Gardens

The construction of Bayou Bend began in 1927. Looking at the thicket and brush that covered the 12.8 acre lot, Ima Hogg conceived of a plan for a series of gardens set along the bayou woodlands. Recalling the lessons of her studies that included landscape architecture and garden design, Miss Hogg adapted the tenets of the discipline to her home as well as to the Houston climate. Her gardens became a spectacular mixture of native and imported plants, with the most predominate plants being azaleas and camelias[91].

Over the course of nearly fifty years, the gardens of Bayou Bend evolved from the initial formal "outdoor rooms" designed in conjunction with the house to a complex series of informal garden spaces that often were inspired by the limitations of the terrain or the vicissitudes of nature. Through each one, Ima Hogg was there, designing, planting and inspiring[92].

There are ten gardens at Bayou Bend, if you count the Woodland Trails as a "natural" garden. Two of the gardens were created at the time of the construction of the house between 1927 and 1928. These original gardens are the East Garden and the Clio Garden[93].

As you approach the house from the driveway to Lazy Lane, the East Garden is an extension of the east facade of the house. Separated from the house by a covered walkway, it was designed to be an "outdoor room[94]."

The azaleas, provided to Miss Hogg by John F. Grants, and the camellias of the East Garden are among the first introduced in Houston. Especially prominent are the Duchesse de Caze pink camellias which are an old and rare variety that was brought from Avery Island, Louisiana. The East Garden was redesigned in the period between 1932 and 1936 by Ruth London[95].

The second of the original gardens is the Clio Garden. Located off the northwest corner of the house adjacent to the new public entrance to Bayou Bend, the garden consists of geometrically patterned flower beds that were laid out by Ima Hogg in 1928.

The Clio Garden was modified in 1939 with the addition of the statue of Clio, the Muse of History, who represents the Past. The statue of Clio was made by the Antonio Frilli Studios in Florence, Italy in 1939, and it is based on a work in the Vatican Museum in Rome[96].

The White Garden, designed in 1934-1936 by Ima Hogg and her gardeners, is located east of the entry drive near Lazy Lane. In contrast to the regular circular and rectangular patterns of the East Garden and the Clio Garden, the White Garden lies deep in the woods and draws its character from the ravines on eastern edge of the property.

The White Garden was a favorite place for Alvin Wheeler who was the gardener at Bayou Bend for thirty years. In 1971, Ima Hogg dedicated the White Garden to Wheeler's memory and a plaque, two bronze deer and a bench were placed in the garden. The garden was restored in 1996 by Jon Emerson and Associates[97].

After the completion of the White Garden, Ima Hogg conceived of a new garden on the back lawn of Bayou Bend that returned to her earlier concepts to integrate the house and the garden with an outdoor room. A new feature to this garden would be a centerpiece statue. The Diana Garden was designed in 1936-1939 by C. C. "Pat" Fleming and Albert Sheppard in collaboration with Ima Hogg to frame a replica of the Diana of Versailles. In 1937, Miss Hogg purchased the statue Diana from the Antonio Frilli Studios in Florence, Italy[98].

The statue of Diana was the first of three that Ima Hogg purchased in each of the years from 1937 to 1939. A statue of Euterpe was purchased in 1938 and it became the basis for a new garden on the northeast side of the back lawn. A statue of Clio was purchased in 1939 and was placed in the Clio Garden. Each stature was sculpted from white Carrara marble.

The figures from classical Greek mythology represent the themes about which Ima Hogg felt strongly, the Past, the Present and the Future. Clio, the muse of history, represents the Past. Diana, goddess of the hunt, represents the Present. Euterpe, muse of poetry and music, represents eternity and the Future[99].

The terrace along the rear of the house takes its name from the Diana Garden. The Diana Terrace offers excellent views of the Diana Garden that lies at the far end of the back lawn of the estate. Will Hogg purchased the pink flagstones of the Diana Terrace from the City of Houston. Sidewalks of downtown were being "upgraded" to concrete in 1927 and 1928, and Hogg made the best of the opportunity to re-use the stones. The walkway on the west side of the terrace that leads to the Winedale Cottage and the Clio Garden consists of antique pink brick salvaged from a demolished building. The manufacturer's mark on several of the Lucas bricks from the local Lucas Brickyard are clearly visible in the brickwork[100].

The brick walkway leads to the Winedale Cottage. This small house was built with the typical German interiors found in the settlements in central Texas in the 1860's. Ima Hogg was inspired to add the cottage after she restored the historic Stagecoach Inn in Winedale community of Fayette County. In 1963, Miss Hogg purchased the simple farmstead of 190 acres. By 1967, the Inn had been restored and seven historical buildings had been relocated to the property which was given to the University of Texas as the Winedale Historical Center, an outdoor museum and study center dedicated to Texas history[101].

A pathway leads past the Clio Garden and around the back of the Diana Garden. The Euterpe Garden is set along the trail on the northeastern corner of the back lawn. The statue of Euterpe is specifically situated between two large trees that have stood on the lot since before the house was built, a loblolly pine and an American sycamore. The Antonio Frilli Studios in Florence, Italy made the statute in 1938. Sculpted in Carrara marble, it was modeled after a work in the Vatican Museum in Rome.

The original design of the Euterpe Garden was created during 1938-1939 by Pat Fleming and Albert Sheppard in coordination with Ima Hogg. Nature did its share of modifications when Hurricane Carla hit the Gulf Coast in 1961. A number of the trees in the Euterpe Garden were destroyed. Hurricane Alicia, in 1983, also downed many trees in the garden, but the statue endured both storms without damage[102].

To the east of the circular drive in the front of the house, the Butterfly Garden is set deep in the trees near the edge of the ravine along that side of the property. Created in the years 1941 and 1942, the Butterfly Garden was the last garden of Ima Hogg's active gardening period. The lighthearted design, created in conjunction with Pat Fleming and Albert Sheppard, seemed to be an appropriate finale to Miss Ima's fifteen years spent landscaping the grounds. At age sixty, Ima Hogg felt that she had finished the landscape design of Bayou Bend[103].

In addition to the forest devastation in the Euterpe Garden, the natural forces of Hurricane Carla offered Ima Hogg, in her 79th year, another opportunity for garden design. When the 1961 storm downed several trees in the woodlands on the northeast corner of the

East Garden to form a small clearing, Miss Ima created the Carla Garden and named it in honor of the storm. It was at this same time, in 1961, that Miss Ima requested the River Oaks Garden Club to assume the permanent supervision of the gardens of Bayou Bend[104].

The Carla Garden was designed in 1970 by Janet Wagner and Harriet Osborn. Further modifications to the garden were made, in 1983, when a large tree in the Carla Garden was destroyed by Hurricane Alicia[105].

In another episode of unplanned landscape design, a leak from a nearby fountain inspired the Waterfall Garden. Located immediately to the east of the East Garden, this small garden is built around a cascade of water in the tributary gully that feeds the large ravine on the east boundary of the estate.

The final garden at Bayou Bend lies along the west side of the circular drive at the front of the house. The Topiary Garden was given to Miss Hogg by the River Oaks Garden Club for the United States Bicentennial in 1976. Beginning in 1975, Ima Hogg collaborated with A. Gregory Catlow in the design of Topiary Garden, choosing topiary figures of a turkey, a squirrel, a rabbit and a deer to represent typical Texas wildlife. She selected an eagle to stand for the United States. The animals are arranged in a circular, brick-paved garden around a central star of clipped dwarf yaupon that represents the Lone Star State. Ima Hogg died in August, 1975 before the garden was completed, yet it is as much her own creation as is the whole of Bayou Bend[106].

The Woodland Trails at Bayou Bend, though not gardens in the strict sense, lead you through the woods of the bayou floodplain at the far north end of the estate. Winding beyond the Clio Garden on the west side, around the back of the Diana Garden and then out into the forest north of the Euterpe Garden, the trails offer a glimpse of the second growth forest of native pines, elms and oaks with an understory of flowering dogwood and redwood.

Bayou Bend was featured in the first Azalea Trail that was held in the spring of 1934. At this event, Ima Hogg introduced camellias to Houston and helped to make the azalea the popular plant that it now is. The gardens have changed little over the years and they continue to reflect Ima Hogg's vision as the highlight of the annual Azalea Trail[107].

Bayou Bend Towers

As you pass under the suspension bridge crossing to Bayou Bend to Ima Hogg's Bayou Bend, the towering white building on the left bank dominates the skyline above the trees along the bayou. Bayou Bend Towers, at 101 Westcott Street, is a 22 story, luxury high-rise condominium constructed by the Campeau Corporation of Toronto in 1983. The building itself appears as three rectangular blocks joined together with each successive block one story taller than the other[108].

Ahead, at the bend, is the parking garage of about five stories adjacent to the Bayou Bend Towers.

Birdsall Street

Birdsall Street begins on the north bank of Buffalo Bayou, two blocks east of Westcott Street, and it goes north for about twelve blocks before terminating at the I-10 feeder road. The name of the street probably derives from architect Birdsall Briscoe, a friend of the Hogg family who previously owned the land through which the street passes. Yet, the name beckons us to recall two prominent families linked not only to the early days of Houston, but to the very beginnings of the settlement of Texas.

Birdsall Parmenas Briscoe was born in Harrisburg, on June 10, 1876, to Andrew and Annie Briscoe. He was the grandson of Andrew Briscoe, the first chief justice of Harris County and the great-grandson of John R. Harris, founder of Harrisburg, whose wife Jane was a Birdsall.

Birdsall Briscoe learned architecture during apprenticeships with Houston architects C. Lewis Wilson and, later, Lewis Sterling Green. He began private practice in 1912 at age 36. From 1919 until his retirement in 1955, Birdsall Briscoe shared an office with noted architect Maurice J. Sullivan[109].

Briscoe had a reputation as an exceptional designer and he is best known for the elegantly composed and detailed houses he built in several Houston neighborhoods. His association with the Hogg family began in 1920 when he remodeled the Patton-Varner House near West Columbia for Ima and Will Hogg. During the period from

1920 to 1940, Briscoe worked mostly in the Houston neighborhoods of Courtlandt Place, Shadyside, Broadacres and River Oaks. His finest works, between 1926 and 1940, exhibit an array of historical architectural styles[110].

Birdsall Briscoe built the first house in River Oaks, a summer home for the William L. Clayton family. The Colonial Revival style home is a small-scale, finely detailed, 20th century adaptation of the style represented by George Washington's home at Mount Vernon[111]. In 1924, he designed a pink stucco surfaced house in the Country Club Estates of River Oaks which became known as the Redbird House because of the redbirds that were incorporated into the grillwork of the French doors at the front entrance. He also assisted John F. Staub in the design of the Hogg family home at Bayou Bend. Birdsall Briscoe died in Houston on September 18, 1971 at age 95 and is buried at Oak Hill Cemetery in Goliad[112].

Rainbow Lodge

Once the bend has been made and the bayou turns back to the southeast, the banks along the north side have been cleared of underbrush so that a single story structure higher on the bank can be seen through the trees.

The Rainbow Lodge, at 1 Birdsall Street, was a restaurant with a hunting and fishing decor that offered outdoor elegance in the midst of the natural beauty of Buffalo Bayou.

The structure that was Rainbow Lodge was built as a private residence in 1935. The house was transformed into a restaurant in 1976 when the main dining room was added to the ground floor. The master bedroom became an elegant dining room with a balcony overlooking the east gardens which include two landscaped acres and a waterfall. The original home now serves as the main entrance and the bar area for the restaurant that seats 140 persons for dinner.

Proprietor Donnette Hansen installed the Tied-Fly Bar at the Rainbow Lodge in 1993. The spectacular twenty foot semicircular bar was created by Vermont artist Bill Herrick with a top carved to resemble a busy trout stream. Rainbow Lodge's menu includes wild game dishes with venison, quail, elk, wild boar, buffalo, duck, salmon, trout and lobster, and some not so wild chicken, beef and pork[113].

In mid-2006, the Rainbow Lodge moved to a historic cabin located on Ella Boulevard at White Oak Bayou. The original site on Buffalo Bayou became Brenner's Steakhouse on the Bayou, owned by the Landry's Corporation[114].

In earlier times, around 1890, long before the development along Memorial Drive and even before the roadway itself, St. Mark's Methodist Church, an African-American church of Houston located at 1615 Patterson Street, baptized its members in Buffalo Bayou near present site of the Brenner's Steakhouse[115].

Memorial Terrace

The bayou continues in a southeasterly course past the Rainbow Lodge for about a quarter of a mile. Development along the north bank includes residences and condominiums such as the Two Elk Glade and the Asbury Estates. On the south bank lie two large, private home sites in the River Oaks Homewoods Section.

As the bayou curves back to the northeast, the land east of Asbury Street has been subject to recent commercial development. The Memorial Terrace Joint Venture owned eight acres of wooded land along Memorial Drive of which they sold 2.3 acres to Huntington Properties, Inc., a Houston based shopping center developer, for a 30,000 square foot retail center[116].

A popular restaurant at 5525 Memorial Drive, the One's A Meal Restaurant owned by Sotirios Xenakis and his daughter Demetra Xenakis, was demolished in 2002 to make way for the new shopping center[117].

Rienzi

On the opposite bank, high upon the stately lawn, is Rienzi, a European decorative arts wing of the Houston Museum of Fine Arts. Rienzi is the 4.4 acre estate and former home of Harris Masterson III and his wife Carroll Sterling Masterson. Located at 1406 Kirby Drive, the home site is bounded on two sides by wooded ravines on the banks of Buffalo Bayou[118].

After Masterson bought the lot from Ima Hogg in 1952, intending to build a home following his marriage the year before, he and architect John F. Staub walked the Rienzi property and spotted a magnificent 250 year old magnolia tree near the back of the lot that became the focal point for the location of the house[119].

Reinzi, built in 1953, is a one story, Palladian style contemporary villa of nearly 12,000 square feet. The design of the house features a symmetrical facade, a balustrade and a parapet, all of which overlook a reflecting pool and more than 4 acres of gardens. The house was expanded in 1972 to include a grand ballroom and a gallery[120].

The reflecting pool originally was a swimming pool, however, when a new city ordinance required that swimming pools be fenced in, Masterson felt that a fence would spoil the beauty of the landscape. The pool was rebuilt as a shallow refection pool[121].

The Rienzi gardens, designed in the mid-1950's by Texas landscape architect Ralph Ellis Gunn, are filled with grand Southern varieties, including evergreen and deciduous magnolias, camellias and bulbs, although the azalea is the prominent flower. The wooded landscape, like its neighbor and Azalea Trail companion Bayou Bend, is a blend of formal and informal gardens. The undeveloped ravines near the bayou are lined with native plants such as loblolly pine, ash and magnolia[122].

Rienzi is named for the maternal grandfather of Harris Masterson, Rienzi Melville Johnson. Johnson, born in 1849, served in the Confederate Army during the Civil War although he was only a young teenager. Later, he became the editor in chief and publisher of the Houston Post. He subsequently served in the Texas state Senate as well as the United States Senate. Rienzi Johnson died in 1926[123].

Masterson began to acquire British painting and decorative arts while in England during World War II. During their travels, the Mastersons added to their collections which include paintings from the 17th, 18th and early 19th centuries, 18th century English furniture, objects by Faberge, and an outstanding collection of almost 800 pieces of 18th century Worcester porcelain[124].

Carrol Masterson died in 1994 and Harris Masterson lived at Rienzi until his death in 1997. The estate was donated to the Houston Museum of Fine Arts and it opened to the public in May, 1999[125].

Detering Street

At the end of the bayou straight away, the Left Bank development can be seen above the trees. The Left Bank, completed in 2000, is a 293 unit, Class A apartment complex built by Winther Investment, Inc. and it is located on Memorial Drive near its intersection with Detering Street[126].

Detering Street is named for Carl A. Detering, a local businessman and developer, who was instrumental in the construction of Memorial Drive during the mid-1950's[127].

Born on July 20, 1904, Detering lived above his father's grocery east of the intersection of Studemont Street and Washington Avenue. He established the Detering Company at that location in 1926. Still family owned and operated, the Detering Company continues to offers a unique product mix of brick, millwork and windows at its original location at 3028 Washington Avenue[128].

In 1960, Carl Detering bought the historic Liendo Plantation in Waller County and began to restore it. The Liendo Plantation was the home of Leonard W. Groce who, leaving school in Georgia, joined his father in Texas in 1822. His father, Jared Groce, was convinced to bring his household to Texas by Stephen F. Austin in late 1821. Arriving from Alabama in January 1822 with fifty wagons of belongings and ninety slaves, Jared Groce was granted ten leagues of land because of the extensive property he brought with him. He was the wealthiest settler in the Austin colony, and his son Leonard was brought in to manage the operations of the plantation[129].

The cotton from this plantation was shipped through the port of Harrisburg prior to the Texas revolution and was a major source of wealth for the colony. Cotton, later, became the source of wealth for many of the prominent citizens of the city of Houston, and these "cotton factors" (cotton brokers) dominated the agricultural industry of Texas well into the twentieth century.

After the estate of Jared Groce was divided among his children following his death in 1839, Leonard Groce began to establish his own plantation. In 1841, Groce bought 3,000 acres for his Southern style plantation from Justo Liendo who had received a land grant from the Mexican government[130].

Groce built the two story, fourteen room house of the Liendo Plantation, named in honor of the original owner of the property, in 1853, using longleaf yellow pine imported from Georgia. The chimneys and foundation of the house were made of bricks from Brazos River clay[131].

Liendo was a typical Southern plantation with over three hundred slaves. It was a self-contained community and sufficient in all its needs. Conveniently located on the road between Houston and Austin, Groce entertained many of the prominent citizens and travelers of the period at Liendo[132].

The Groce family provided material support for the armies of Texas from the time of the Texas Revolution, the Mexican War and the Civil War. Liendo Plantation became Camp Groce during the Civil War, and it was converted into a prisoner of war camp to house the Union infantry troops captured at battle of Galveston. After the fall of Galveston, a Civil War prisoner of war camp commanded by General George A. Custer was built at the gates of the Liendo Plantation[134].

The hospitality shown to Custer during his time at the Liendo Plantation from September to December of 1865 is thought to be the reason that the home survived the post-war period without significant damage. After the Civil War, however, Liendo suffered from the changes in the economic base and the harsh economics of Reconstruction. The plantation could no longer be profitable. Leonard Groce died in 1873, and his son, Leonard Groce, Jr., sold the Liendo Plantation and its 1,100 acres to Edmund D. Montgomery and his wife Elisabet Ney[135].

Franzisca Bernadina Wilhelmina Elisabet Ney was born on January 26, 1833 in Muenster, Westphalia, Germany. She studied sculpture in Germany and married Scottish physician and scientist Edmund D. Montgomery in Madiera in 1863. They immigrated to Georgia in 1871 and they came to Texas in 1872. While Dr. Montgomery pursued his scientific interests, Elisabet raised their children and managed the Liendo Plantation for the next twenty years[136].

Elisabet Ney resumed her sculpting career in 1892 and opened a studio in Austin. Over the next fifteen years, she became famous for her portrait busts of prominent Texans, especially her statues of Stephen F. Austin and Sam Houston. Ney died in Austin on June 29, 1907[136].

In poor health after having suffered a stroke, Dr. Montgomery deeded the Liendo Plantation to Theodor Low in 1909 who then sold it to W. P. Gaines. Gaines sold it to George W. Harris in 1910, although Dr. Montgomery, having retained the right to use a portion of the main house, stayed at Liendo until his death in 1911. Montgomery was buried next to his wife in a grove of live oaks on the grounds of Liendo Plantation[137].

Mrs. Laura B. Harris, the widow of George W. Harris, sold the Liendo Plantation to Miss Willene Compton in 1943. It was purchased by Phylis and Carl Detering in 1960, and for the next ten years, the Deterings faithfully restored Liendo and acquired period furnishings from Europe and the deep South for the house[138].

Carl Detering and his son Will raised red Brahman cattle for a living on the 1,000 acre homestead until the elder Detering died on May 8, 2001 at age 96. Carl Detering is buried at Liendo Plantation, and Will Detering continues to own and operate Liendo today[139].

Located northeast of the town of Prairie View, between Waller and Hempstead, at 38653 Wyatt Chapel Road, the Liendo Plantation is a Texas historic landmark and is listed on the national register of historic places[140].

Rice Military Addition

As you approach Detering Street and the back of the Left Bank complex, there is a prominent storm sewer outlet on the north bank. The bayou turns to the right and takes a course that is nearly due easterly. The large drainage easement on the Reserve at Aloe Subdivision offers a buffer to the development on the north side of the bayou. The two to three acre home sites of the River Oaks, Section 1, as well as the smaller lots of Section 12, along the south bank show evidence of construction and development extending down to the water's edge.

Within a quarter of a mile, the bayou makes a ninety degree turn to the left and flows due north. It is in this northward course that Buffalo Bayou follows the route of the western boundary of the original two leagues of the John Austin Survey. The easement along the left bank gives way to the buildings and the parking areas of the Bayou on the Bend Apartments.

The Bayou on the Bend Apartments, in the 5200 block of Memorial Drive, was a thirty-one unit complex on a four acre tract that was developed by J. Frederick Welling and his sister Mary Jane Carvel in 1959. A single family dwelling occupied the site and it was removed prior to the construction of the apartments. Located adjacent to the bayou, the complex has been flooded by the rising waters of Buffalo Bayou several times over the years. The damage done by Tropical Storm Allison in 2001 was severe, and the complex lay vacant for several months.

In July, 2003, Commerce Equities, a firm owned by developer Matt Dilick, purchased a fifty percent interest in the land on which the Bayou on the Bend complex sat. The old apartments were demolished and a 242 unit mid-rise apartment project, completed in 2004, replaced them[141].

The quarter mile straight away ends as Buffalo Bayou turns sharply to the right and parallels Memorial Drive for nearly a half mile on its way to Shepherd Drive. The erosion at the bend is rapidly eating away at the shoulder of Memorial Drive, and soon, the Harris County Flood Control District, the owner of the easement, will have to take action to prevent further loss of bank to the bayou.

As the bayou parallels Memorial Drive at this point, its north bank is part of the Rice Military Addition, a subdivision immediately west of the Brunner Addition. The initial tract of land for the Rice Military Subdivision, bounded by Westcott Street, Asbury Street, Buffalo Bayou and the Houston and Texas Central Railway tracks, was sold by J. S. and W. M. Rice to the Bankers Trust Company on August 29, 1910, giving the "Rice" name to the subdivision. The boundaries of the original plat of the subdivision in the 1920's extend from Westcott Street on the west to Bethje Street and the Depelchin Children's Center on the east. From north to south, Rice Military extends from Washington Avenue to Buffalo Bayou[142].

Rice Military's lack of deed restrictions has led to a varied array of single family homes, condominiums, two and three story town-homes and exotic locales such as the Wabash Antiques and Feed Store at 5701 Washington Avenue and the famous Beer Can House at 222 Malone Street[143].

John and Mary Milkovisch transformed their house in the Rice Military Addition into a fanciful work of art by covering the exterior with flattened aluminum beer cans. Cans and pull tabs dangle in the wind from the roof. The zany landscaping of the Beer Can House includes an artificial lemon tree made of metal wire and plastic lemons. Other trees are made of artificial fruit and vegetables[144].

After her husband's death in 1988, Mary Milkovisch, born on December 16, 1916, promoted the Beer Can House to folk art experts and she appeared on national television. Mary, who retired from her job at the cosmetics counter at the Foley's store downtown in 1978, died on March 18, 2002, at age 86. In November, 2001, the Orange Show Foundation purchased the Beer Can House about for $200,000 in order to preserve it[145].

A vacant lot now stands on a site of some historic interest. Harold Wilcox operated the Aeroplane Repair Company at 5318 Washington Avenue from 1919 to 1925. The aircraft plant assembled Curtiss JN-4's that were then shipped to Ellington Field on trailers[146].

In a final note to remind us of the "military" heritage of the subdivision, an original building from Camp Logan was at 5801 Washington Avenue at Birdsall Street on the southwest corner. The low, one story wood frame building may have been a storage facility for the Army, but it had been a night club and other small businesses in recent times, and it is now a victim of the redevelopment along Washington Avenue.

The transformation of the small bungalows and shotgun houses in the Rice Military Addition to multi-story town homes began in the 1990's and continues today. In 2002, there were 1,300 homes in the Rice Military Addition of which the median size was 1,903 square feet. Lots average 2,584 square feet. The median year of construction of 1995 reflects the recent redevelopment of the area. There is no telling how much longer the historic character of the neighborhood will remain or whether it will be remembered[147].

Clements Spaceway

The park space north of Memorial Drive between the dead end of Reinerman Street and the Shepherd Drive intersection is the Clements Spaceway. Previously known as Spencer Middleton Clements Park, the Clements Spaceway, at 5100 Memorial Drive, provides a limited amount of parking. The spaceway is about 150 yards west of Shepherd Drive[148].

Spencer Clements, a Houston hotel executive, founded the Homeplace Inns of America in 1986 as a chain of small quality motels located in small Texas towns. How or whether this Spencer Clements is related to the Clements Spaceway is just one of the unsolved mysteries of Buffalo Bayou[149].

DePelchin Children's Center

From the Clements Spaceway, the new building of the De-Pelchin Children's Center stands prominently on the tract of land on the northwest corner of Shepherd Drive and Memorial Drive. The DePelchin Children's Center, located at 100 Sandman Street, is a non-sectarian, community-supported institution caring for dependent children of Harris County[150].

The organization which today bears her name was established in April, 1892 by Mrs. Kezia Payne DePelchin. Kezia Payne was born on July 23, 1828 in the Madeira Islands, and spent her early life in England. Her mother died in the mid-1830's, and she arrived with her father in Galveston in 1837. Kezia Payne's father married her governess, Hannah Bainton, in 1839, but a yellow fever epidemic took her father's life, although Kezia survived the illness. Nearly destitute, the thirteen year old Kezia and her stepmother arrived in Houston in 1841.

Kezia's stepmother taught her to play the piano and, during the 1840's, Kezia Payne worked as a music teacher. Since she had acquired an immunity to yellow fever after having survived it in childhood, she did charity work among the poor and nursed the victims of the yellow fever epidemics in Houston. During the 1850's, Kezia Payne continued to teach and she operated a number of different schools[151].

On August 23, 1862, at age 34, Payne married itinerant Belgian musician Adolphe DePelchin at Christ Church where she was the organist. DePelchin was a widower with a young child whom Kezia had grown very fond of. Yet, the marriage was brief. DePelchin was financially reckless and the couple soon separated, yet, his name would endure and be associated with philanthropy in Houston into the twenty first century[152].

During the Civil War, Kezia Payne DePelchin served in the nursing corps in Houston. And, afterwards, returned to teaching. The 1866 City Directory, lists Kezia DePelchin as a music teacher located on Milam Street between McKinney Avenue and Lamar Avenue. DePelchin worked at the German-English school in 1875, and, when Houston's public school opened in 1877, she taught in the Fourth Ward[153].

Kezia DePelchin continued to nurse the victims of the yellow fever epidemics in cities throughout the South, and she was appointed head nurse of the City Charity Hospital. In 1888, at age 60, she became the first matron of Bayland Orphans' Home for Boys[154].

When the Bayland Home was moved from its site on Galveston Bay to a thirty-six acre site in the Woodland Heights area of Houston in 1900, DePelchin was able to call on her old friends for assistance. She asked Mrs. T. W. House to help her provide a place for three orphaned babies since the Bayland Home only accepted children from 6 to 12 years old. On May 2, 1892, DePelchin christened the "Faith Home" at 2410 Washington Avenue[155].

Later that year, Kezia DePelchin contracted a fever and became ill with chest congestion. She died on January 13, 1893 at the age of sixty-four. DePelchin was buried at public expense since she had given all of her personal funds for charitable causes[156].

Houston's community leaders immediately launched an effort to ensure that her work would continue. Within a week of her death, the DePelchin Faith Home was organized by one hundred Houston women in her honor as a non-sectarian, community-supported institution for dependent children. The DePelchin Faith Home was chartered on January 20, 1893[157].

DePelchin Faith Home moved to a larger building at the corner of Chenevert Street and Pierce Avenue in 1903. By 1909, there were forty-seven children under care in the facility[158].

Recognizing the importance of the Faith Home to the community, a group of influential Houstonians, including Jesse Jones, the publisher of the Houston Chronicle, built a larger facility for the DePelchin Faith Home. With seventy-five children to care for, the orphanage moved to a bigger home at 2710 Albany Street in 1913. The historic DePelchin orphanage, a three story Mediterranean style stucco building with many rounded arch windows, housed disadvantaged children from 1913 to 1938 when a new DePelchin Faith Home was built off Memorial Drive. As a part of the revitalization of the Midtown area, the old facility was renovated in 2000 as fifteen residential flats known as the Villa Serena[159].

Ben Taub, the director of DePelchin Faith Home, began buying property on Shepherd Drive in 1931. With the aid of the Works Progress Administration, the construction of nine new buildings for the DePelchin Faith Home began in 1937. The twelve acre site included five cottages, an administration building, a hospital and a dining hall when the facility, at 100 Sandman Street, opened on September 15, 1938. A sixth cottage was added in 1939[160].

In 1939, the DePelchin Faith Home became the first Houston institution to serve the needs of dependent black children[161]. The name of was changed to the DePelchin Children's Center in 1983. And, in 1992, the Houston Child Guidance Center, at 3214 Austin Street, and the DePelchin Children's Center merged[162]. A new and larger building for the DePelchin Children's Center was completed in 2002.

Shepherd Drive

The bridge at Shepherd Drive is visible from the bayou several hundred yards upstream since the bayou set its course nearly due east, toward downtown. The bridge marks the location of a man-made feature on the bayou, originally situated far to the west of the city, that was well known as early as the mid-1890's. A dam was built at a point immediately upstream of the present bridge.

The dam on Buffalo Bayou was the idea of David P. Shepherd. Shepherd, who otherwise is largely forgotten in the history of Houston, gave his name to the dam on the bayou and, subsequently to the road leading to the dam from the San Felipe Road and the bridge of iron and wood that was built just above the dam about 1895.

Characterized as a "get-rich-quick" type of personality, D. P. Shepherd, like many other young Houstonians in the second half of the nineteenth century, had grand ideas for commerce and enterprise. He was a cousin of banker B. A. Shepherd and the uncle of the future Governor Pat M. Neff. Born in Virginia in 1838, David Philip Shepherd came to Houston and, by 1866, was the superintendent at the Southwest Telegraph Company. He and his wife Olivia lived on Main Street between Rusk Avenue and Walker Avenue[163].

In 1892, D. P. Shepherd began construction of a water mill on Buffalo Bayou. By March, 1894, the construction of a dam was under way. Made of cedar logs and brick bats from Fred Rice's brick yard in Brunner, Shepherd's Dam created a ten to twelve foot head of water that backed up for about three miles. The impounded water became a resort for skiffs, fishing and bathing, and a bath house was built on the bank to allow city visitors to change clothes[164].

Shepherd had acquired ten acres on the north side of the bayou as a rectangular tract that was centered on what is now Shepherd Drive. A two acre tract was also owned by Shepherd on the south side of the bayou, immediately east of the modern bridge. His plan was to build a sawmill and a flour mill at this location. This design was merely one part of a larger scheme of dams, mill races and navigation locks up and down the bayou[165].

Shepherd actually organized a company to carry out his ventures, the Shepherd Water Power Company. In addition to the dam at the present day Shepherd Drive, he planned to build one other dam on the bayou at Sabine Street. His vision for Buffalo Bayou was to create a system of dams and mill races to power flour and grist mills as well as factories using the power of water in a manner similar to what had been successfully accomplished in New Bedford, Massachusetts[166].

One critical element in his plan was a scheme to divert water from the Brazos River into Buffalo Bayou in order to build up the water supply and to provide a consistent flow. Since such a diver-

Postcard courtesy of the Hildegard Cox Collection

The lake formed behind Shepherd's Dam was a popular recreation spot at the turn of the twentieth century. The bridge across the bayou at the dam was an important roadway connecting neighborhoods on each side of he bayou.

sion plan required the approval of the state, the rejection by the legislature of his proposal brought his company to financial ruin[167].

Every few years, a rise in Buffalo Bayou would wash out part of Shepherd's Dam and Shepherd would have to spend more money to repair the dam. He used up his savings, mortgaged his land, borrowed money, then finally quit. The last wash out of the dam was about 1910 or 1912. Financial problems wrecked the plan, and the dam became known as Shepherd's Folly. The failed project was the subject of local ridicule. The 1913 J. M. Kelsen Map of Houston cleverly labeled the road to the dam as "Shepherd's Damn Road[168]."

Although floods washed away his dam, a remnant of the structure could still be seen from the Shepherd Drive bridge as late as 1938. The name of the street and the bridge crossing near the site of his dam remains the sole legacy of David Shepherd and his grandiose scheme[169].

Yet, before we dismiss D. P. Shepherd's dreams as a far-fetched delusion, we should recall that by 1927, the Brazos Valley Irrigation Company had obtained a permit to take 99,000 acre feet of water annually from the Brazos River to irrigate the rice crops north of

Sugar Land[170]. This system then merged with the Briscoe Irrigation Company which had developed a network of canals to provide Brazos River water for irrigation and industrial uses to Fort Bend, Brazoria and Galveston Counties. In the 1930's, the entire system was sold to the American Rice Growers Association. The Briscoe Canal, which draws water from the Brazos below Sugar Land, and the American Canal, which taps the water from Oyster Creek in Sugar Land, became part of the American Canal Company of Texas. The company was acquired by the Brazos River Authority in 1967, and the canals continue to be major components in the management of the Brazos watershed in this area[171].

You can canoe past the large pumping station on the Brazos River for the Briscoe Canal opposite the town of Thompsons, a few miles below Sugar Land, and the pumping facility for the South Texas Water Company Canal a couple miles farther downstream, near the community of Juliff.

Near Fulshear, the Brazos River is less than ten miles from the upper reaches of Buffalo Bayou. It makes you realize that Shepherd's idea was, perhaps, only a little ahead of its time.

Shepherd Drive itself, as the first major north-south thoroughfare on the west side of town, tells the story of Houston's population growth, suburban residential expansion and the desire for west side, cross-town transit that has been replayed time and again over the past several decades, often with a certain amount of associated controversy.

Nineteenth century residential patterns seemed to follow a concentric circle around the downtown area. Prominent businessmen lived on the southern periphery of downtown, gradually moving south out Main Street toward Brays Bayou. Neighborhoods like Courtlandt Place, Southmore, Shadyside, Montrose and Hyde Park were the places to live in the times prior to World War I. Working class families filled the neighborhoods north of the bayou, creating the Fifth Ward, Sixth Ward, Brunner and Houston Heights neighborhoods by 1920.

The opening and development of River Oaks in 1926 seemed to finally signal that the growth of Houston would be to the west and southwest. In the post-World War II era, Houston's new suburbs developed in the slice of the area between the modern I-10 toward

Katy and the modern Southwest Freeway to Sugar Land and Richmond.

The controversies caused by the development of thoroughfares connecting the north and the south suburbs could fill a book of its own. Post Oak Road became the West Loop, and it is still a source of contention as the Harris County Toll Road Authority proposes a toll road through, or under, Memorial Park along the Southern Pacific rail corridor.

Chimney Rock Road was finally opened across Buffalo Bayou in the 1980's. The West Belt divided quiet neighborhoods. Kirkwood Road went in over the protests of the locals. Fondren Road still retains its two lane, winding country road character, protected from "improvement" only because of the folks in Piney Point Village. Highway 6 is a six lane, undivided "superhighway" drawing an asphalt line from Jersey Village to Sugar Land.

And, finally, think of the Grand Parkway linking Richmond and Katy through Cinco Ranch today, and you can recognize the pattern that began with Shepherd Drive a century earlier. Perhaps it is just the natural part of urban growth that takes places that once were "way out in the country" and transforms them into part of the city.

By the beginning of the twentieth century, residential development in Houston had spread north over Buffalo Bayou to the Fifth and Sixth Wards and southwest down Main Street and the Montrose area. In addition, outlying suburban communities sprung up away from the downtown area, namely, the Houston Heights to the northwest and Brunner to the west. But, for the most part, much of the surrounding land was farm land. The 1913 Kelson map shows the Shepherd Dam Road extending south from the bayou as far as Richmond Road where it ends in open fields. A smaller road connects across the dam on Buffalo Bayou to Brunner Avenue in Brunner Community which ends at White Oak Bayou[172].

By 1928, Shepherd Drive, as seen on the 1928 Fantham & Fantham map, extends to the south as far as Rice Boulevard where West University Place has grown around the campus of Rice Institute. Similarly, Brunner and the Houston Heights have been annexed by Houston and Shepherd Drive connects to Brunner Avenue which, in turn, connects with Lowell Avenue in the Houston Heights Annex subdivision north of White Oak Bayou[173].

On the 1942 Ashburn Map of Houston, Shepherd Drive extends from Rice Boulevard on the south to West 12th Street in Houston Heights Annex on the north, absorbing both Brunner Avenue and Lowell Avenue[174]. The transition from its origin as a country lane to a major highway is complete by the 1950's. The 1952 Humble Oil Map of Houston shows Shepherd Drive as a fully developed thoroughfare from Aldine Bender Road on the north to Rice University on the south. The segment from its junction with Washington Avenue to Aldine Bender Road is an alternate route for US 75[175].

As with Shepherd Drive, major streets in the city are often named for prominent citizens, or for others who made major contributions to the development of the City. Bagby Street is named for Thomas Bagby, an early Houston businessman. Holcombe Boulevard honors Oscar Holcombe, mayor of Houston for many years. Allen Parkway is named for the Allen brothers who founded the city.

Kirby Drive joins Allen Parkway at the Shepherd Drive bridge and is named for John Henry Kirby, the father of industrial Texas. Kirby, who owned the two largest lumber companies in Texas, was also the president of the Houston Baseball Association in 1895. He built his magnificent mansion in 1928 at 2006 Smith Street, and it can still be seen off the southwest edge of the Pierce Elevated in downtown. Yet, as fame and fortune are so often fleeting, John Kirby filed for bankruptcy in 1933[176].

With this idea of a naming convention for streets, it might suggest from today's perspective that Shepherd Drive is named for a well known Houstonian, someone more prominent than David P. Shepherd. In fact, more than once, it has mistakenly been reported that Shepherd Drive is named in honor of Benjamin A. Shepherd, one of the most influential and successful businessmen in Houston during the nineteenth century. Without a doubt, B. A. Shepherd certainly deserves some measure of civic recognition.

Benjamin Armistead Shepherd, born in Fluvanna County, Virginia on May 14, 1814, began work as a clerk in a country general store. In 1833, at age 19, he moved to Nashville in order to work in an established mercantile firm in that city. It was there that he made the acquaintance of Sam Houston who was relocating to Texas, and the two men became life-long friends[177].

As Sam Houston was finding his destiny in Texas, Shepherd was learning his trade. In 1837, he moved to New Orleans, where he worked as the chief bookkeeper and credit advisor in a large wholesale commission house. The fortunes and opportunities of the new republic of Texas attracted Shepherd and he moved to Galveston in 1839. By 1844, Shepherd had settled in Houston where he formed a partnership with A. J. Burke in the mercantile trade under the name of Burke and Shepherd[178].

Although Benjamin Shepherd chartered the Commercial and Agricultural Bank, the first bank in Texas, in 1847, he devoted most of his time during this phase of his career to the mercantile business and other ventures. In one such venture, Nathaniel K. Kellum sold his house, thirteen acres of land on Buffalo Bayou and a brick kiln to Shepherd in 1850. Shepherd then sold the house, which is now known as the Kellum-Noble House in Sam Houston Park, to Abram Noble in January of 1851[179].

By 1850, Shepherd was well established in Houston as a thirty-six year old businessman and a family man with his wife Mary, a twenty-seven year old native of Tennessee, and their five children. He listed real property assets as $30,000 in the census records which made him one of the more prosperous citizens of the community[180].

In 1855, B. A. Shepherd sold his interest in the mercantile business and became exclusively a private banker. The skills that he acquired while managing the credit operations as a merchant prepared him for financial dealings at a higher level. As a private investment banker, Shepherd became involved in a number of business ventures in a city that was the commercial hub of the state[181].

By 1860, Shepherd had quadrupled his real estate holdings to about $125,000 and his personal property was valued at $150,000[182]. At age forty-six, Benjamin Shepherd was one of the wealthiest men in town. His business interests were consistent with the industries that were generating Houston's prosperity including the Houston Direct Navigation Company and the Houston and Texas Central Railway. He organized a company to grade and construct a plank road on the Washington Road[183].

When the Civil War began, Shepherd retired from banking due to the uncertainty of financial matters in the Confederacy, and although he started no new businesses during the Civil War, he continued in various businesses in which he had been involved[184].

His City Cotton Mills, located on the site of the later Cleveland Compress near the modern Jensen Drive, produced a rough-goods material, called Osnabergs, that was used for slaves' clothing, cotton-picking sacks, wagon covers and tarpaulins for the Confederate army. Not immune to setbacks, the City Cotton Mills were destroyed in a fire and Shepherd suffered the total loss of the company since insurance was not available during the war[185].

As a director of the Eureka Manufacturing Company, Shepherd had more success. After the war, Eureka Manufacturing operated a sawmill, a grist mill and a woolen mill adjacent to tracks of Houston & Texas Central Railroad four miles from town (an industrial site still in use on the south bank of White Oak Bayou at T. C. Jester Boulevard)[186].

The post-Civil War period brought a return to stability in business and B. A. Shepherd reopened his private bank. In 1867, he acquired a controlling interest in the First National Bank owned by Thomas M. Bagby. The two banks merged and Shepherd became the bank's president. Informally, the bank continued to be known as "Shepherd's Bank" which he managed for twenty-five years[187].

The partnership with Thomas Bagby extended beyond the banking business. Their business interests brought gas street lamps to the City and they introduced the first mule-drawn trolleys to Houston. In 1874, Shepherd served as the vice president of the Board of Trade and Cotton Exchange[188].

The Shepherd residence was in the Fourth Ward on Lamar Avenue between Milam Street and Travis Street. With his wife Mary, they raised five children while two others died in childhood. By 1870, son Joseph was a retail grocer and dry goods owner. Neither of Benjamin Shepherd's sons took an active role in the banking business[189].

Shepherd sought to retire from the active life of Houston business and, in 1875, he moved to San Jacinto County where he founded the town of Shepherd. The town was near a former Coushatta village and it was on the proposed route of the Houston, East and West Texas Railway. Yet, he was never far away from a promising investment. In 1883, he built the Shepherd Building, an imposing Victorian structure, at 219 Main Street[190].

Benjamin A. Shepherd established a trust fund the proceeds of which were to be distributed to Houston's needy in 1889. He had amassed a fortune over the years, but cared little for public acclaim and never sought public office. He died on Christmas Eve, 1891. His grave in Glenwood Cemetery is marked with a small obelisk[191].

Sallie Shepherd Perkins established the Shepherd School of Music at Rice University in the memory of her grandfather, Benjamin A. Shepherd, who inspired her with his love of music. In 1950, Perkins signed an agreement with Rice University to staff a small music department. After her death in 1968, Rice received the bulk of the bequest for the complete music school[192].

And, although the name of Shepherd Drive is not truly his, there was a street named in his honor. Shepherd Street, on the east side of downtown off Canal Street, named for B. A. Shepherd, was subsequently renamed Delano Street[193].

Shepherd Drive Bridge

If the water level is up, you can float the few hundred yards above the Shepherd Drive bridge with ease. On your right, you pass the back yards of the homes along Teil Way. This wooded lane was named for Lucille Potter, the wife of River Oaks founding partner Hugh Potter, whose nickname was Teil[194].

It is in this section of the bayou that the tidal influence on Buffalo Bayou begins. Fresh water flowing downstream meets the brackish water that has backed up from Galveston Bay. The U. S. Geological Survey gauge, located on the south bank and on the downstream side of the bridge, measures the ebb and flow of the daily tide.

Although daily readings of the level of the bayou at the Shepherd gauge began in 1936, peak flows were measured as early as 1929 when a high reading of 19,000 cfs, or 43.5 feet, was recorded on May 31, 1929. The maximum gauge height recorded on Buffalo Bayou was 49.0 feet on December 9, 1935. The bayou was running a very swift 40,000 cfs! Those who remember Tropical Storm

Allison on June 9, 2001 can compare its reading of 36.58 feet, or 14,000 cfs, with the earlier record levels[195].

Buffalo Bayou, although prone to sporadic flash floods, actually has a rather low mean flow. Measurements during the period of unregulated flow, prior to the construction of Barker Dam in 1945, indicate an average discharge of 272 cfs. After the creation of Barker Dam, the average of 26 years of regulated flow was only 274 cfs.

The lowest levels of flow at Shepherd Drive were recorded on May 24, 1939 and on November 5, 1950 when the bayou trickled along at 1.3 cfs[196]. The low levels of flow occurred before the urban development in west Houston. The wastewater effluent releases that accompany suburban growth now provide a minimum level of flow much higher than the historic lows. Encouraging, isn't it?

The swimming hole that was formed by the remnants of Shepherd's Dam made the north bank of the bayou a popular picnicing area well into the 1920's. Residents of the Brunner neighborhood along Washington Avenue would come down the road from Brunner Avenue to the dam site. The trolley made a turn around in the intersection of Brunner and Washington Avenues, and it made the excursion to the bayou picnic area a popular destination on weekends. That is gone now. The tree and shrub growth is so thick that joggers along Memorial Drive can hardly see the canoers on the bayou.

On the south bank of the bayou, the Kirby Drive intersection at Shepherd Drive houses one of the gateway entrances to the River Oaks Subdivision. These monumental gates were designed and installed by John F. Staub in 1927. Similar gateways exist at the other roadway entrances to River Oaks, and the one on West Gray opens to the River Oaks Shopping Center, the first neighborhood shopping center in Houston[197].

This section, downstream of Shepherd Drive, is a transition zone for Buffalo Bayou. From Piney Point Road to Shepherd Drive, Buffalo Bayou most closely resembles the bayou as it may have looked to the first Europeans. Below Shepherd Drive, there are few sandbars. The property along the bank is publically-owned, the stream bed has been channelized, and the banks show the evidence of the "scraping" that occurred in the 1950's.

In 1949, the U. S. Army Corps of Engineers began a project to strip the bayou from Shepherd Drive to downtown of trees, channelized the bayou, clear and re-grade the banks[198]. The proposed improvements were intended to improve the drainage and flooding in downtown. The construction of the six lane Memorial Drive, which opened on the north bank of Buffalo Bayou from Shepherd Drive to downtown on January 10, 1956, joined with the six lanes of Buffalo Drive, now Allen Parkway, to give unprecedented access to the city center by automobile. In the process, Buffalo Bayou from Shepherd Drive to Sabine Street was cleared of trees and stripped of vegetation by 1958[199].

Fortunately, the concreting of the banks of Buffalo Bayou did not happen. In a fortuitous combination of civic protest from a nascent group of local conservationists and the delay of funding for the project, Buffalo Bayou was spared the fate that befell Brays Bayou and White Oak Bayou.

When the water level is low, there is a small riffle downstream of the bridge at Shepherd Drive. A long bar of fine, white sand historically formed below the Shepherd Drive bridge. Well documented as late as 1938, a smaller sandbar stills forms along the north bank in the place where school boys from St. Thomas High School skipped off to swim in the mid-1940's. While shouting to the less adventurous among them who watched from a perch on the old ornamental concrete bridge railing of Shepherd Drive where a plaque reminded them that the structure was officially designated Shepherd's Dam Bridge[200].

The old bridge has been replaced and the plaque is long gone, along with the memory of Shepherd's Dam. Few swimmers are seen here these days. Water contact is not encouraged since the bacteria count at Shepherd Drive, in December, 1994, was higher than the federal levels as acceptable for swimming. Fecal coliform concentrations in Buffalo Bayou exceeded state standards in over 75% of the samplings during the period from 1998 to 2000. Paddlers, though, still use the sandbar and its eddy as a take out point for canoe trips on the bayou[201].

Houston Tuberculosis Hospital

If you pull in at the sandbar below Shepherd Drive, look up and over the south bank, beyond the huge opening for the new storm sewer, to the trees on the tract of land bounded by West Dallas Avenue, Shepherd Drive and Allen Parkway. This is the former site of the Houston Tuberculosis Hospital.

Infectious diseases played a more significant role in every day life in the early twentieth century than today. In 1900, tuberculosis was the chief cause of death in the United States. Efforts of the local community to combat "the white plague," as tuberculosis was known, began in 1911 when Dr. Elva A. Wright organized the Houston Anti-Tuberculosis League at a meeting at the Rusk Settlement House in the Frost Town neighborhood[202].

The City acquired two tracts of land in the spring of 1913 for the Houston Tuberculosis Hospital. John F. Markham sold a parcel of 21.25 acres to the City on March 29, 1913, and two weeks later, on April 11, an additional 13.27 acres of land were acquired from J. M. Frost. John Miles Frost II, was the son of John Miles Frost, a prominent Houston businessman, and the grandson of Samuel Miles Frost, the developer of the Frost Town subdivision in 1838. As, perhaps, an interesting insight into the character of John M. Frost, he sold the property with the restrictions that the property not be used for immoral purposes or for the sale of alcoholic beverages. He further stipulated that it not be used for a cemetery. Those restrictions are in force even today[203].

The Houston Tuberculosis Hospital was built on the 34.6 acres west of the city limits on West Dallas Avenue. In June, 1924, the City and Mrs. Allie Kinsloe Autry signed an agreement for the construction and maintenance of a school for tubercular children on the site. Mrs. Autry provided the funds for the construction and the equipment for the buildings of the Autry Memorial School and the City would operate and maintain them. The Autry School, built in 1925 on the Houston Tuberculosis Hospital property, was located near the northeast corner of Shepherd Drive and West Dallas Avenue, at 4210 West Dallas Avenue[204].

Allie Kinsloe Autry was the wife of James Lockhart Autry II, an associate of Will C. Hogg and J. S. Cullinan, who served as a director of the Texas Company, later Texaco, until 1913. Autry's grandfather, Micajah Autry, came to Texas to fight in the Texas revolution and perished defending the Alamo. Mrs. Autry's generous donation may have been prompted by the death of her young son James Lockhart Autry III in 1922[205].

Although the right of way for Buffalo Drive, now Allen Parkway, built to provide access to the newly developed River Oaks Subdivision, removed about ten acres from the hospital site, the twenty-five acre complex was sufficient for its purpose. The Houston Tuberculosis Hospital included a number of individual ward units with 124 beds. The Autry Memorial Hospital School Building had an additional capacity of fifty beds[206].

The Houston Tuberculosis Hospital was the only hospital in the city dedicated to tuberculosis patients. By 1924, the hospital complex lay at the north end of Gross Street which bisected the tract. Although the buildings were near Buffalo Drive, access was from West Dallas Avenue on Gross Street. The first building along Gross Street was the Nurses House, situated about half way down the road and on the west side of Gross Street. Farther on, there was a ward building on each side of Gross Street. A third ward building, which also houses the office, is immediately north of the ward on the east side of the street. A ward for black patients was separate from the other ward buildings, reflecting the social customs of the time. The black ward was in the northwest corner of the tract near the intersection of Shepherd Drive and Buffalo Drive. The laundry building was at the far north end of Gross Street[207].

An expansion of the Houston Tuberculosis Hospital was opened in 1930. A large, centrally located Administration Building was built on the west side of the street on land between the former Nurses Home, which became the superintendent's dwelling, and west side ward (designated as No. 2 at this time). Offices and a kitchen were located on the 1st floor and a nurses home was on the 2nd floor[208].

A laboratory was constructed on the east side of the street across from the Administration Building. The southmost ward on the east side became Ward No. 4, while the northmost one was Ward No. 1. The ward on the west side of Gross Street was Ward No. 2. A new laundry building was built to the east of the street between

wards No. 1 and No. 2, and the former laundry became a maintenance crew dwelling.

Significant additions were made to the western side of the
complex as well. Two new wards were built in the vicinity of the
original ward for black patients. The Presbyterian Ward was built
to the west of the Administration Building and south of the black
ward. A new ward for black female patients, designated Female
Colored Ward No. 3, was built north of the Presbyterian Ward,
and the original black ward became the Male Colored Ward No.
3. A new Nurses Home was built north of this ward[209].

Reflecting the continuing need for the care and treatment of
tuberculosis, a new hospital was proposed for the new Medical
Center that would allow the Tuberculosis Hospital to take advantage of the student, intern and nursing groups being trained at the
Baylor Medical School[210].

The Houston Tuberculosis Hospital remained in service until
1948 when treatment by medication made isolation unnecessary.
The disease, however, did not disappear and it persists as a threat
to health in the community. Tuberculosis cases in Houston and
Harris County declined to a twenty-six year low, in 1999, of 456
new cases. In thirty years of recording the number of cases,
beginning about 1970, the lowest number of new cases of tuberculosis recorded was 441 cases in 1975. The highest number was
786 in 1995, reflecting the sporadic resurgence of the disease that
warrants constant vigilance[211].

One of the more interesting episodes related to the Houston
Tuberculosis Hospital happened in 1944. An airplane flown by an
Army pilot crashed and exploded on the grounds. The pilot was
stationed at Ellington Field, and, although he survived the crash,
the explosion and fire caused damage to the buildings of the
hospital[212].

Ellington Field dates to World War I when it housed the
largest aviation training facility in the nation. Deactivated after the
war, Ellington Field was razed by fire in 1927[213]. With the outbreak of World War II, Ellington Field was rebuilt, in 1941, as an
Army Air Force Base. In the wake of the end of World War II,
Ellington Field survived as the only post-WWII navigator training

school. Later, the base was the training facility for pilots for the Korean War[214].

During the 1970's, President George W. Bush was a reserve pilot in the 147th Fighter Wing at Ellington Field. An F-102, similar to the one that the President flew, with Bush's name near the cockpit, is on display at the base. Ellington Field continues to be the home to the 147th Fighter Wing of the Texas Air National Guard and several smaller units of the Texas Army National Guard[215].

In tribute to the fiscal diligence of the City fathers, a claim for $60 was approved for payment to the City by the Army Air Forces at Ellington Field to compensate for the damage to city property on the hospital site caused by the crash of that airplane[216].

Today, the site that once was Houston Tuberculosis Hospital is a part of the Center Serving Persons with Mental Retardation complex. The Center Serving Persons with Mental Retardation, located at 3550 West Dallas Avenue, is a private, non-profit United Way agency serving the needs of individuals with developmental disabilities[217].

Established in 1950, the organization has evolved through a series of names, including the Houston Center for the Mentally Retarded and the Center for the Retarded. However, its commitment to the service of this special segment of the community has been unwavering.

An outstanding example of the work done by the Center is the Cullen Caners. The Cullen Caners, a workshop to repair cane chairs, is operated by the Center Serving Persons with Mental Retardation. Opening for business in 1979, the Caners provide cane repair service to the public and they have revived the disappearing art of caning. There are eleven caners employed at the workshop who can repair cane, rush and wicker furniture.

The average cane chair repair job costs about $100. In 2002, the Caners repaired 762 items and provided $54,000 in income for the Center[218].

St. Thomas High School

From the sandbar below Shepherd Drive, your view up the grassy slope of the north bank is capped with the white limestone fascade of St. Thomas High School. Sitting high and prominent, as if upon a hill, the stately building nestled among a grove of trees projects a sense of excellence and dignity.

Officially named St. Thomas College, St. Thomas High School is a college preparatory school for boys which has operated under the direction of the Basilian Fathers since its founding in 1900. Its reputation for academic excellence is well deserved. Ninety-five percent of its graduates attend college[219].

The Congregation of the Priests of St. Basil was founded in France about 1799 and the priests of the community devoted themselves to education. They became a formal religious community in 1822 with St. Basil, 330 AD to 379 AD, bishop of Caesarea, as their patron. The order expanded to Canada in 1850, and in 1899, the priests of the Congregation came to Texas to establish a college preparatory school near Waco. The following year, a similar school was founded in Houston by Rev. Nicholas Roche and two other Basilians. Although the rural Waco school was not as successful as the venture in Houston, and it was abandoned in 1915 due to low enrollment, St. Thomas High School flourished[220].

The school began in an old two story frame building at the corner of Franklin Avenue and Caroline Street. Adjacent to St. Vincent Church, the building had been erected by the Franciscan Fathers as a monastery in 1861. Shortly afterwards, the structure was damaged during the famous 1900 hurricane, and the school was moved to the Mason Building at corner of Capitol Avenue and Main Street. The old building was subsequently moved to the Sacred Heart Church on Pierce Avenue when the property was sold and it was used as a parochial residence for a decade[221].

In 1903, Fr. Roche purchased a block of land bounded by Austin Street, LaBranch Street, Hadley Avenue and McIlhenny Avenue for the construction of a permanent facility for St. Thomas High School, Houston's first college preparatory school for boys. St. Thomas High School occupied the building at Hadley Avenue and Austin Street from 1906 to 1940[222].

In 1929, a thirty-two acre tract of land for the future expansion of St Thomas High School was purchased at what is now the northeast corner of the intersection of Shepherd Drive and Memorial Drive[223].

Maurice Sullivan, the partner of Birdsall Briscoe, designed a building constructed of reinforced steel and concrete faced with Cordova shell stone. The front walls of the imposing structure slant obliquely from the ends to form an apex at the rounded entrance pavilion where four massive columns rise to support a semicircular parapet. In 1940, Rev. T. P. O'Rourke moved St. Thomas High School to its current home on the sixteen acre campus on the north bank of Buffalo Bayou[224].

Brunner

Before we get too far downstream from the Shepherd Drive bridge, it is worth pausing to note that the north side extension of Shepherd Drive was originally named Brunner Avenue. It was the main street of the town of Brunner, a residential community centered on the intersection of its two main streets, Brunner Avenue and Washington Avenue.

The Brunner family immigrated to Texas from Germany in the early 1850's. We can surmise this because the Brunners do not appear in the 1850 census and both Anton, born in 1845, and his younger brother John, who was born in 1850, are listed on the 1870 census as having been born in Bavaria[225].

By 1850, there were many settlers in Harris County who had arrived from Germany. A large number of them moved to the forested land and the prairies that lay west of Houston and north of Buffalo Bayou. It was there that they established farms, often near friends from the old country or relatives who had made a similar journey to the new land of Texas.

Within a year of their arrival in Texas, both of the parents of the Brunner children passed away. The young Brunner children moved to a relative's farm where Anton Brunner lived and worked for five years. In his late teens, Anton moved to Houston to learn a trade as a shoemaker[226].

Houston was notorious for its wide, unpaved streets that became muddy quagmires during the frequent rainy periods. Early photos of men in the downtown area with their pant legs tucked into high top boots are a reminder of the necessity of quality footwear at that time.

Moisture and mud are the enemy of leather and the local climate kept boot makers in high demand.

Anton Brunner seems to have excelled at his trade since at the age of twenty-one, in the 1866 City Directory, he is listed as a boot maker with a shop on Congress Avenue, between Main Street and Travis Street[227].

By 1870, Anton Brunner, a skilled shoemaker, was living in the Third Ward with his wife, Bertha, and he had brought his twenty year old brother John into the trade. Within two years, his business of repairing shoes and making factory made shoes was successfully established[228].

Anton Brunner's marriage to Bertha Bethje was especially fortuitous for the young businessman. Bertha Bethje, born in 1850, was the daughter of Christian and Louisa Bethje. Bertha's mother Louisa Schermann had married Henry Reinermann, son of John Reinermann, who had come to Texas on the ill-fated voyage of the schooner Sabine. Shipwrecked off Galveston Island, the Reinermann's, as well as the others in their party from Germany, including the von Roeder and Kleberg families, were delayed in their plans to settle in Austin County. The Reinermanns ultimately decided to stay in Harris County and John Reinermann received a grant of land on the north bank of Buffalo Bayou that included the area that is now the site of Memorial Park in Houston[229].

After her husband's death in 1844, Louisa Reinermann married Joseph Sandman on April 27, 1845. By 1850, Joseph Sandman had apparently died, and Louisa was married to Christian Ledovic Bethje. The Bethje's lived on the Reinermann family farm in the Memorial Park area which in 1860's had is own sawmill, cultivated fields, 300 head of cattle and various farm animals[230].

Yet, the prosperity of the growing town of Houston had its effect on the outlying rural populations. Then, just as is often the case even today, the lure of the city and its high paying jobs drew workers off the farms. In 1866, C. L. Bethje began to work for the Houston and Texas Central Railway. Bethje's City Directory listing as living in the "northern suburb" may also indicate that he had moved to lodgings in what would become the Sixth Ward, close to the H&TC shops[231].

In 1869, some members of the Reinermann family bought a house and 15 acres in the area that would become the Brunner Addition. Although some of the Reinermann heirs continued to live on the original property and some lived in the new house west of town, in 1870, C. L. Bethje, his daughter Eliza, and Anton's brother John were all living with Anton and Betha Brunner in their house in Houston's Third Ward. By 1883, the original Reinermann property was abandoned[232].

As the Brunner business prospered, Anton began to invest in real estate. In 1888, he filed a plat of the land three miles west of Houston where the Reinermann house stood. This tract of land between Buffalo Bayou, on the south, and the Houston and Texas Central Railway tracks, on the north, was divided into a rectangular grid of 137 blocks centered on Washington Road, extending from Patterson Street on the east to Reinerman Street (now spelled with one "n") on the west. It was called the A. Brunner Addition[233].

The lots in the Brunner Addition were very aggressively marketed and they were sold for between $150 and $300 each. The community of Brunner prospered quickly, obtaining its own post office as early as 1888, and getting shuttle transportation to Glenwood Cemetery, the end of Houston's electric street car line, in 1892. By 1895, there was a direct line from downtown to Brunner Avenue[234].

The Brunner community provides one of the earliest examples of how affordable public transportation can promote suburban development. Brunner had a population of two hundred persons by 1894, and, within two years, it had five hundred residents and a host of community establishments, including a German school, a public school, a Baptist college, a Baptist Church, a Lutheran Church and a saloon[235].

Similar developments combining suburban living and public transportation into downtown Houston followed with Magnolia Park and the Houston Heights. However, the city embarked on a different course in the mid-1920's when the Hogg family created the River Oaks development and based its success on the use of the private automobile to commute to downtown along multi-lane, limited access roadways, such as the scenic thoroughfare, Buffalo Drive (built in 1927 at Will Hogg's urging and later renamed Allen

Parkway). Nearly ninety years later, Houston is still attempting to come to grips with the public transportation issue.

In ways that the citizens of Houston still enjoy the wooded suburban life of west Houston, Houstonians at the turn of the nineteenth century relished the country-style recreation and ambience found in Brunner. The streetcar could be taken in the early evening or on Sundays to the end of the line where there was a turnaround near the modern intersection of Washington Avenue and Durham Street. From this stop, it was a short walk down Brunner Avenue to the wooded banks of Buffalo Bayou. Picnics were popular pasttimes, and scenic, and sometimes romantic, views of the bayou could be had from the wooden bridge at Shepherd's Dam[236].

As an independent town, Brunner's existence was short lived. With a growing population, the community received its first postmaster, George W. Chaney, on May 2, 1894. A rise in local importance was noted when the Vollmer community post office, its neighbor to the north, was closed, on September 15, 1898, and mail was sent to Brunner[237].

The McAshan and City Mission Methodist Church, now the Shepherd Drive Methodist Church, located at 600 Shepherd Drive at Blossom Street, was organized in 1899 in Brunner. The congregation met in McClure's Assembly Hall until the sanctuary was built in 1901[238].

The first development for oil in the Houston area came in 1903 when oil was discovered in a forty foot water well on the property of George Parker in Brunner[239].

The prospects for this small, but vibrant community appeared to be strong. Yet, the expansion and importance of the larger city of Houston was not to be denied. On January 31, 1905, the post office in Brunner was closed, and its mail was sent to the Houston Post Office. In 1915, the town of Brunner and its four hundred eighty-two residents, the majority of whom voted their approval, were annexed into the city of Houston[240].

Brunner was very much a victim of its own success. The suburban residential community offered an affordable rural living environment far from the dirt and clamor of the downtown, yet, it was accessible to the city for the average worker because of the streetcar system. In a short time, others had the same idea that inspired Anton Brunner.

In 1895, Conrad Schwarz subdivided his farm land just east of the Brunner Addition. Schwarz called his subdivision the Magnolia Grove Addition and he developed it as a German working class neighborhood with simple one story Victorian style homes[241].

Just west of the Brunner Addition was Smokeyville. Smokeyville, sometimes called Smokeytown, was a small freeman's town located along Washington Road in the Reinermann tract. It had 2 churches and a school. Identified on local maps as late as 1922, Smokeyville became surrounded by neighborhoods of working class European immigrants[242].

After World War I, development along Washington Road increased. The construction of Camp Logan at the far end of Washington Road had improved the roadways to that part of town, and, during the 1920's, the Rice Military Addition and Camp Logan Addition were platted just west of the Brunner Addition. Ultimately, all of the neighborhoods fell victim to the process of urban homogenization, and the area that encompasses the Brunner Addition, the Magnolia Grove Addition, the Rice Military Addition and the Camp Logan Addition became known as the West End[243].

Time, and sometimes the process that we often refer to as progress, has a way of obliterating the past. The story of Brunner, the man and the town, is a story of what makes Houston the place of opportunity. An orphaned immigrant works hard, learns a trade, establishes a business and becomes a successful businessman. He develops a tract of land which he names in his family's honor and watches it become a successful and prosperous community. Yet, in the end, his town is swallowed up by the relentless growth of the larger metropolis. His namesake avenue is renamed for someone else, not even remotely related to him. And, the name of his town and subdivision is wiped out within half a century to be known only to those who ply the arcane stories of the long forgotten past.

The Reinermann home which was located a few blocks northwest of the modern intersection of Washington Avenue and Shepherd Drive was demolished in the 1920's. Brunner Avenue was renamed Shepherd Drive in the 1930's. It is, then, not a little ironic that, although the name of Brunner has been wiped off the books, both of the town and the street, the names of his in-laws and extended family are perpetuated in the streets that Anton Brunner established for his town: Reinerman Street, Sandman Street and Bethje Street.

The Houston Riot of August 23, 1917

The working class community of Brunner was a quiet suburb of the expanding city of Houston. Yet, the peace and tranquility along the banks of Buffalo Bayou was shattered by a racial riot of historic proportions on the night of August 23, 1917. The violence that occurred that Thursday night is sometimes referred to as the Camp Logan Riot. Other sources call the events the Houston Riot of 1917, and that is probably a better appellation since the actions of the mutinous soldiers assigned to Camp Logan took place away from the actual premises of the military base.

The construction work at Camp Logan had begun on July 25, 1917 on orders of the War Department to meet the growing need for trained men to fight in World War I[244]. Camp Logan was a huge encampment to be built on 3,002 acres of what is now Memorial Park. The camp was to include 1,329 buildings and it had a troop capacity of 44,899 men. To guard the construction site while it was being prepared for the mostly white troops that would eventually train there, the Army ordered six hundred forty-five black soldiers from the Third Battalion of the Twenty-fourth United States Infantry regiment from Columbus, New Mexico, to Houston. The soldiers were bivouacked away from the permanent Camp Logan site in an area immediately west of Reinerman Street and north of Washington Avenue, adjacent to the Brunner neighborhood[245].

From the minute they arrived in Houston, the African-American soldiers of the Third Battalion faced racial discrimination. Many of the men had been raised in the south and were familiar with segregation but they expected to be treated differently as Army servicemen. Local residents, including members of the police department, public officials and even streetcar conductors viewed the presence of the black soldiers as a threat to the racial harmony that existed in Houston at that time.

On August 23, 1917, around noon, police arrested a black soldier for interfering with the arrest of a black woman in the Fourth Ward. A black military policeman, Corporal Charles Baltimore who was attached to the Third battalion inquired about the soldier's arrest. There was an argument and a Houston policeman hit Baltimore over the head. Baltimore and the other black enlisted men with him ran, with shots from the white policemen's guns ringing over their heads. They captured Baltimore nearby and took him to police headquarters where he was soon released.

However, before Baltimore could return to camp, a rumor started that he had been shot and killed whereupon a group of black soldiers decided to march to the police station. Almost simultaneously, a rumor started that a white mob was approaching the camp. At that news, black soldiers rushed into supply tents, grabbed rifles and began firing wildly in the direction of the supposed mob. The armed soldiers marched down Washington Avenue, crossing to the south side of Buffalo Bayou on Shepherd's Dam Road (now Shepherd Drive) turned up San Felipe Road and headed for town.

The acts of violence took place in two locations along Buffalo Bayou. The first was the suburban residential community of Brunner, located on the north side of Buffalo Bayou and centered at the intersection of Washington Avenue and the modern Shepherd Drive. The second scene of rioting took place on the south side of Buffalo Bayou along San Felipe Road, now known as West Dallas Avenue, in a residential area of the Fourth Ward known as the San Felipe District.

There was a third scene of violence in the episodes of this night that is not strictly part of the riot, but is rather more of an epilogue. Sergeant Vida Henry, the leader of the mutinous troops, stood alone near the tracks of the GH&SA Railway along the eastern edge of the Fourth Ward, probably close to the modern intersection of South Main Street and Wheeler Street. At about 2:05 am on Friday, August 24, Henry took his own life with a single shot from his revolver.

The events of that August day began when reports circulated in the camp on Reinerman Street that Corporal Charles W. Baltimore, an off duty military policeman from the Third Battalion, had been roughly treated by a Houston policeman and arrested. Later, rumors that Baltimore had been killed provoked intense feelings of anger and frustration among the troops. The unrest among the soldiers continued to build during the early evening, and when Sergeant Vida Henry of I Company reported the situation to Major Kneeland S. Snow, the commandant, Snow ordered Henry to collect the rifles and ammunition from the men. About 8:00 pm, shortly after sunset, as Henry was gathering the rifles and ammunition, a soldier screamed that a mob was coming toward the camp. Private Frank Johnson yelled for the troops to get their guns. A shot was fired and bedlam broke out as the soldiers raided the supply tent for their weapons, and shots were fired wildly into the residential neighborhood. Ironically, Sergeant Henry emerged as the leader of the mob of over one hundred soldiers who spilled out of the bivouac area and into the Brunner community intent on marching to the Fourth Ward jail to release their imprisoned comrade.

The mob of soldiers marched one block east on Louis Street, now Center Street, to Roy Street, where they peppered the home of Peter Morrison at 1119 Roy Street with rifle fire. Fortunately, there were no injuries to the Peter Morrison family, but when the soldiers turned south on Roy Street, across Washington Avenue, to Lillian Street, two young men at 4910 Lillian Street were not so lucky. Frederick Winkler, age nineteen, a machinist, was shot and killed on his front porch as he turned on the porch light. William J. Drucks, twenty-six, was shot in the right arm, but he ultimately recovered and lived until 1975.

Although the main body of the mutinous soldiers headed down Roy Street, it is clear from the other reports of casualties that a fairly large body of soldiers fanned out across several blocks and numerous streets, shooting at random targets and demonstrating their well-honed marksmanship skills at any opportunity that presented itself.

E. A. Thompson was among the first to be killed by the rioters, presumably near Washington Avenue. Adam R. Carstens, a forty-eight year old house painter with a large family, was shot and killed near Parker Street and Center Street. M. D. Everton, a member of Company H, 5th Texas Infantry, was found dead near Carstens. He had been shot in the liver and in the right shoulder, and he had been bayoneted in the abdomen.

Washington Avenue was the main street of Brunner, a working class residential community that had only been annexed by Houston in 1915. The local residents would certainly be out on the streets in the dusk of a scorchingly hot summer's day socializing and completing the errands of the day. Manuel Garredo, who lived at 4900 Washington Pond Avenue, was shot and killed. Senelton "Senator" Satton, a barber, was shot through both thighs and bayoneted through the heart and neck. Sammie Foreman, a member of Company F, 5th Texas Infantry, was shot in the leg, but did not suffer a serious injury. More seriously injured were W. A. Thompson, who was shot in the hip, and Alma Reichert, who was shot in the stomach. George W. Butcher, 41, who worked as an ice man and who lived with his wife and seven children on Kiam Street in the Cottage Grove Addition[246], just north of Brunner, was shot in the left chest and right side, but he recovered from his wounds.

The mob of soldiers headed south to converge at the narrow bridge across Buffalo Bayou at Shepherd's Dam at the end of Brunner Avenue. For those who were unaware of what was taking place in their neighborhood that evening, the consequences were dire. Charles W. Wright, a barber, came out of his home on Wood Street, now Floyd Street, near Brunner Avenue to investigate all the commotion. He was shot in the stomach and killed. Jitney driver E. M. Jones, 53, drove his last fare of the day and was found dead on a shell road near Brunner. He had been shot several times and his right arm had been severed by a saber. Earl Fendley, age 16, who had been with a group of friends on Washington Avenue earlier that evening, was found in the road near Shepherd's Dam, shot through the heart and bayoneted.

The soldiers converged on the narrow bridge at Shepherd's Dam and then made their way up the dirt road through the riparian forest along the banks of the bayou to the San Felipe Road. The San Felipe Road ran due east, directly into the heart of the Fourth Ward. It would place them near enough to their intended location, the jail on the banks of Buffalo Bayou at the corner of Bagby Street and Capitol Avenue. This route also offered an unobstructed path to the city. Although they encountered the small, black community of Green Pond adjacent to the College Memorial Park Cemetery established by Jack Yates, and across from Yates' Houston College, there were only a cluster of houses in the Stanley Subdivision near the Magnolia Cemetery (near modern Montrose Boulevard). The road passed through scattered rural farms and fields until it reached the western edge of the San Felipe District near present day Taft Street.

After marching for an hour or so, the soldiers stopped to rest in the 1600 block of San Felipe Road, near Gillette Street, about three miles from where they had begun their journey. The mob numbered slightly less than one hundred men now, since some of the rioters had wearied of the quest and had drifted back to camp. It was still a well armed and formidable force.

As they resumed their march to town, the mob encountered a captain and a lieutenant from Camp Logan. Although the soldiers almost shot the officers, they decided instead to allow them to pass, perhaps indicating that the mob was focusing its hostility, not on its own military comrades, but on the Houston police.

Within 10 minutes, the mob was at the call box on San Felipe Road at Wilson Street. Mounted officers Ross Patten and W. H. Long were at the call box and Long was making a call. A dozen soldiers fired on the police, killing Patten's horse and wounding him. Patten and Long took cover in an adjacent house. Patten would die from his injuries two weeks later.

At just that time, a vehicle driven by businessman Charles W. Hahl approached the scene. Police officers Rufus Daniels, W. C. Wilson, Horace Moody and C. E. Carter had commandeered the car for a ride to the action. The car stopped when they heard shots fired on Patten and Long. Sergeant Henry ordered his men to take cover in the City Cemetery on the south side of the street. Daniels then proceeded to charge the troops in the cemetery with only his hand gun, and he was instantly killed. Carter, Wilson and Moody took cover in a nearby garage. Moody was shot in the leg and severely injured. Moody later died while doctors were amputating his leg.

The firing ceased, and the soldiers brutalized the dead body of Rufus Daniels, battering his face and bayoneting his body. The mob, then, continued toward downtown.

Four blocks later, at Heiner Street, the troops encountered a seven passenger touring car driven by James E. Lyon. This car had two civilian passengers and police officers John E. Richardson and Ira Raney, who had hitched a ride to get to the area of the action.

The mob disarmed those in the touring car and held them in the road with their hands up. When Richardson inadvertently let his hands down a soldier struck him over the head with butt of his rifle. At that point, Raney and the civilian passenger Eli Smith took off running in opposite directions. The fifty-six year old Smith was an easy target for expert riflemen[247]. Smith was later found in the ditch at Heiner Street. He had also been bayoneted in the hip and the left arm pit, a thrust that penetrated his heart. Officer Raney's dash placed him in the illumination of the car's lights where he was shot. Raney's body was beaten and bayoneted like that of Officer Daniels.

Lyon jumped as a soldier took aim at him with his rifle and he was only hit in the arm. Lyon ran for two blocks where a police officer found him and took him to a hospital. Lyon survived with only minor wounds in the leg and arm.

Asa Bland, the other civilian passenger in the touring car, was shot over the left eye, but received only a slight graze wound. He was knocked unconscious by a soldier and lay motionless in the middle of the San Felipe Road. Officer Richardson feigned death nearby.

Soon, a second car arrived at the Heiner Street intersection. This vehicle carried Captain Joseph Mattes from Camp Logan, three enlisted soldiers and Officer Edwin Meineke. Mattes stood up in the car as if to address the mutineers, but about forty of the rioting soldiers took aim at the approaching car and fired on those in it. Both Mattes and Meineke, as well as one of the enlisted men, were killed immediately. The driver of this second car ducked under the steering wheel and crashed the car, but he saved his life. The other enlisted soldier was covered by the fallen body of Mattes, and he escaped injury.

The rapid sequence of violent and bloody events seemed to call for a natural hiatus. The Houston police, choosing to avoid a confrontation with the superior strength of the mob of professional soldiers, monitored the situation from a perimeter of two blocks or more. Although the exact time and location of the incidents are unclear, two other men sustained injuries in the melee. Police detective T. A. Binford received a minor wound to the knee, and wholesale grocery salesman William H. Burkett who lived in the

Fourth Ward received a gun shot to his left side and was hit with shotgun pellets, but he survived these serious injuries[248].

It had been a little over two hours of violent rioting and, after the soldiers mistakenly killed their own Captain Mattes, thinking he was a city policeman, they argued over the next course of action.

The deflated mob retreated a few blocks to the south and gathered near the railroad tracks on the eastern edge of the Fourth Ward. Although Sergeant Henry urged the mob to attack the jail, many of the soldiers had lost interest in the venture and they drifted away and back to camp. Others wanted to hide in the woods or stay with friends in the area. Finally, after two hours of discussion, Henry concluded that the soldiers no longer wanted to continue, so he sent them away and told the men to return to camp.

Henry had asked some of his comrades to kill him, but they all refused. Alone and in despair, about 2:05 am, Henry took his own life. The next morning, his body was found by some young boys near the railroad tracks.

On August 24, 1917, Governor James E. Ferguson declared martial law in Houston and he placed Brigadier General John A. Hulen, commander of the Texas National Guard, in charge of the city. That day, three hundred fifty Coast Guardsmen arrived from Galveston and six hundred two infantrymen arrived from San Antonio to enforce a curfew that was imposed on the city. All recruits in the Houston area waiting for transfer to units were restricted to City Auditorium. By 9:30 am on Saturday, August 25, 1917, all of the troops of the 3rd Battalion were placed on Southern Pacific trains and sent to San Antonio and New Mexico to await trial. The civil authority was restored to the city on Monday, August 27, 1917.

In the riot of August 23, 1917, eleven innocent citizens lost their lives, five police officers were killed in the line of duty, and thirty citizens suffered severe wounds. Four of the rioters died. Two of the mutinous soldiers were accidentally killed by their own men, one soldier was shot by a citizen and died later in a hospital, and Sergeant Vida Henry died by his own hand.

Punishment for the black soldiers was swift and harsh. Between November 1, 1917 and March 26, 1918, three separate courts martial were convened at Fort Sam Houston in San Antonio, and they indicted one hundred eighteen men of Company I, 24th Infantry, 3rd

Battalion. Seven of the soldiers who rioted testified against the others in exchange for clemency. One hundred ten of the mutinous soldiers were found guilty of at least one charge, nineteen of them were hanged, and sixty-three of them received life sentences. Two officers of Camp Logan faced courts martial, but were released. No civilian citizens of Houston were brought to trial.

It was a sad and tragic day in Houston history. Ironically, the outbreak occurred on the evening that the local Chamber of Commerce had prepared a watermelon feast and picnic for the African-American soldiers. Racial incidents occurred at virtually all camps in the south where African-American troops were stationed in World War I, but the incident at Camp Logan was by far the worst. Except for the racial incident involving the soldiers from the Third Battalion 24th Infantry, relations between the Army at Camp Logan and Houston's civilian community were good and remained so for the duration of the camp's existence.

Several sources discuss the reasons, the motivations and the causes for the riot, but I have chosen here to present simply the chronology of the events and the identities of the persons involved on that dangerous night in town in the summer of 1917. Please take the time to read the other sources on this episode in order to form your own opinion on the other aspects of the events.

Map by Rachel A. Garcia

After leaving the Memorial Park area, Buffalo Bayou is a part of the city parkland from Shepherd Drive to Sabine Street known as Buffalo Bayou Park. Tightly nestled between Memorial Drive, on the north, and Allen Parkway, on the south, the bayou and its environment is a vast manicured green space of recreational opportunities and hike and bike trails.

Chapter 6
Buffalo Bayou Park

Buffalo Bayou Park is a green space extending from Shepherd Drive to the Sabine Street Bridge. Hiking trails, bike trails and pedestrian bridges provide access to the rolling hills and wooded bayou banks that are encased by the roadways of Allen Parkway and Memorial Drive. The paths of the park offer excellent views of the historic sights of the old "west end" of Houston.

St. Thomas High School Stadium

To the east of the Priests' Residence at St. Thomas High School is the Football Stadium. This athletic facility for football, track and other sports is aligned north to south and it is tightly fitted into the school property. When the school was built in 1942, the extent of the property ranged from Shepherd Drive on the west to Patterson Street on the east. Memorial Drive was a small country lane running along the north bank of the bayou as far east as Waugh Drive.

In the early 1970's, in response to financial needs for improvements to the school facilities, such as the need to air condition the classrooms, St. Thomas High School sold the land where the old football stadium stood to developers.

The Bayou Park Village Apartments were built on the land between St. Thomas and Cleveland Park. These apartments can be seen along Memorial Drive[1].

Cleveland Park

Cleveland Park is located at 200 Jackson Hill Street, and it is adjacent to east side of the Bayou Park Village Apartments. Although the baseball field appears to be the whole of the park, Cleveland Park land encompasses the large part of the north bank of

Buffalo Bayou from Shepherd Drive to Waugh Drive. Cleveland Park is named in honor of William D. Cleveland, Sr. who began a wholesale grocery company after the Civil War and, by the turn of the 20th century, had become very successful in the business which was continued by his son for another generation[2].

In 1906, A. J. Vick owned the land on north side of Buffalo Bayou, west of the Butler Brick Works near the GH&SA Railway spur. By 1917, the land on the north bank of the bayou from Shepherd Drive (or Brunner Avenue as the road on the north side was called) to Waugh Drive (known as Irving Avenue on the north side) was divided into several large tracts owned by numerous individuals.

A 44.5 acre tract on the north bank at Waugh Drive was a city park called Vick's Park. A two acre tract owned by T. S. Vick was immediately north of Vick's Park was part of the Vick's Park Addition. The homes in the Vick's Park Subdivision, which averaged about 1,105 square feet, were built in the mid-1920's on lots that averaged about 5,430 square feet. In 2003, only two single family homes in the Vick's Park Addition were still standing[3].

An oxbow lake formed by a large, northerly bend in Buffalo Bayou, was known as Vick's Lake. In the early years of the twentieth century, the Vick's Lake area was a popular spot for picnicing and canoeing[4].

By 1925, the land along the bayou had been acquired by the City and was consolidated as Cleveland Park. As late as 1951, maps of the park show the Cleveland Park Lake, located in Cleveland Park, on the north side of Buffalo Bayou, east of Waugh Drive and south of Willia Street. The site of the lake, since drained and filled, is now Spotts Park[5].

Jackson Hill

On the "curving" corner of Jackson Hill Street at Eugene Avenue, the Houston public school system built the William D. Cleveland, Sr. Elementary School in 1927 on property that was adjacent to Cleveland Park. The Cleveland Elementary School, located at 320 Jackson Hill Street, was named for William Davis Cleveland,

Sr. and the school served the community for fifty years until it was closed in 1977.

In 2000, the Finger Companies purchased the four acre site for $5.1 million. Construction of the Jackson Hill Luxury Apartments, an apartment complex with 316 units, began in October, 2002. The developer Marvy Finger completed ten apartment buildings and parking garage of the Jackson Hill Luxury Apartments in 2003 on a tract of land that overlooks the scenic green space of Buffalo Bayou Park[6].

Buffalo Drive, a Suburban Parkway

The south bank of Buffalo Bayou, below Shepherd Drive, was actually developed before the north bank. Buffalo Bayou Park was designed about 1921 by the city planning commission to reach from Shepherd's Dam to Market Square, but lack of funding meant that little development took place at that time[7].

Concerns about traffic problems in the mid-1920's led to a 2.25 mile parkway corridor that was designed to integrate traffic engineering with urban design and civic landscaping by architects Hare and Hare. Buffalo Bayou Park and Buffalo Drive, now Allen Parkway, were constructed in 1925-1926 along the south side of Buffalo Bayou to create a linear park spanning westward from the Civic Center in downtown Houston to the garden suburb of River Oaks[8].

The Freedmenstown-Reservation neighborhood gained unwelcome prominence after the construction of Buffalo Bayou Park and, in 1944, the San Felipe Courts complex was constructed on a highly visible, thirty-seven acre site at foot of the Buffalo Bayou Park development to advertise a progressive example of slum clearance housing for low income families[9]. But, before the park land received this notoriety, the rural area along the San Felipe Road was home to two historic cemeteries and an academic institution for African-American students in Houston.

Houston College

The years following the War Between the States were difficult times in Houston. The social changes brought about by the emancipation of the slaves presented challenges to the citizens of Houston for which no one was prepared. Few institutions or organizations of social welfare existed to adequately care for the large numbers of former slaves who migrated into the city in the late 1860's.

Fortunately, there were a few strong leaders who emerged from among the African-American community. One of these was John Henry (Jack) Yates. The 30-year-old Jack Yates helped to organize the Antioch Baptist Church, and he became its first pastor in 1868[10].

As the first generation of freed men and women adjusted to their new way of life, it became apparent to many of them that education was the key to success. In 1885, Jack Yates and other leading blacks established the Houston Baptist Academy. The school opened in rented facilities in the Third Ward, in a residence called the Cooper Place which was located at the corner of Bell Avenue and San Jacinto Street, a block south of the current South Texas College of Law[11].

Within a decade, the success of the school prompted Reverend Yates to reorganize the Houston Baptist Academy as the Houston College, and, in 1894, he relocated the institution to a wooded, three acre tract of land beyond the western limits of Houston on the San Felipe Road. In spite of the name, the Houston College offered only courses in primary, secondary and industrial education. Yet, the school offered a special opportunity to the black children of the community who sought an alternative to the Colored High School of the public school system[12].

Even after the death of Jack Yates in 1897, the Houston College operated for another generation before its closure in 1921. Located in the modern 3200 block of West Dallas Avenue, the Houston College was on the north side of West Dallas Avenue between Dunlavy Street and Terrell Street. The buildings of the institution included a domestic science building, a laundry, a boys dormitory and a girls dormitory. An additional dormitory was located on the south side of West Dallas Avenue[13].

The spirit of educational opportunity that characterized the Houston College persisted even after the school closed. In 1927, the Houston Colored Junior College was established. In 1934, it was renamed the Houston College for Negroes, and by 1947, the institution had become the Texas State University of Negroes. Finally, in

1951, true to the legacy of Jack Yates, the college became Texas Southern University[14].

Today, as you paddle along Buffalo Bayou past the Shepherd Drive bridge, nothing of the former Houston College is visible. The tract of land, which is designated as the Houston Baptist Academy Addition, was previously occupied by the 1960's vintage Allen House Apartments on the south side of Allen Parkway. The land is currently under preparation for redevelopment as the Regent Square complex[15]. A small sliver of the original tract on the north side of Allen Parkway is the Adath Yeshurun Cemetery which was acquired by the Congregation Adath Yeshurun in 1895[16].

College Park Cemetery

After Jack Yates moved his Houston Baptist Academy to a site west of the city limits, he established the College Park Cemetery across the street, on the south side of the San Felipe Road, about 1896. College Memorial Park, as the sign over the gate says, got its name because it was across the road from Yates's Houston College.

College Park Cemetery, 3605 West Dallas Avenue, is one of the city's oldest cemeteries, and among the approximately 6,000 burials in the 5.45 acre cemetery are former slaves from east and central Texas and from Louisiana as well as their descendants who lived in the Fourth Ward's Freedmenstown neighborhood. Burials began in the late 1890's and continued until the 1970's, although most of the burials date from the 1930's[17].

In general, the persons buried at College Park were ordinary citizens. A number of small, plain stone markers, some of which are handmade of cement, reflect the eloquent, though simple, respects paid by the families of Freedmenstown. But, a few historical figures do rest at the cemetery. Among these are the Rev. John Henry "Jack" Yates, founder and pastor of Bethel Baptist Church, and his son Rutherford B. H. Yates, the first African-American to establish a printing press in Houston. When Jack Yates died in 1897, he was originally buried at Olivewood Cemetery, but his body was later moved to College Park. John Sessums, Jr., the first African-American member of the Houston Light Guard, is also buried in the cemetery. A Texas Historical Marker marks the site of his grave[18].

By the 1920's, the community of Green Pond had grown up near the college and the cemetery. Within one block to the west, on Gross Street, were the African-American churches of the Free Gospel Church and the Nazarene Baptist Church in addition to the community's Green Pond School[19].

The cemetery fell into disrepair in the 1980's and there were episodes in which portions of the cemetery were either sold or up for sale. In 1997, members of the Bethel Baptist Church began a program to cleaning up College Park Cemetery when they found that the cemetery was in such poor condition during a search for the grave of the church's founder Jack Yates. Since that time, various groups have volunteered their efforts to maintain the cemetery. College Memorial Park received the recognition of a Texas Historical Marker on August 1, 2003[20].

John Sessums, Jr.

John Sessums, Jr. was buried in College Park Cemetery after his death on July 7, 1928. His final rites at the grave site were attended by about 2,000 people from both the African-American community and the white citizens of the City. For such a display of respect, especially at that time in the country's history, John Sessums must have been a remarkable individual. As noted on his tombstone, Sessums was the only drummer that the Houston Light Guard, one of the City's local militia units during the nineteenth century, ever had. He was also the only African-American member of the Light Guard during that time. As the members of the Light Guard who attended his funeral recognized, they could not have been as successful as they were without him[21].

The story of John Sessums, though, can be seen in a larger context than just his role with the Light Guard. His career parallels the history of local militias in Texas and the United States during the post-Civil War era. His participation in both the white militia unit of the Light Guard and various black militias units exemplifies the adjustments that the society had to make after the Civil War. Unfortunately, by 1900, Southern society, including Texas, had turned to laws requiring segregation and the disenfranchisement of blacks, and the spirit of tolerance, frequently seen in the late nineteenth century, was lost until after the Civil Rights movement of the 1960's[22].

During Reconstruction, African-Americans had been recruited into black militia units, often to protect Republicans from white Democratic violence. Most of the black militia units were disbanded after the Texas Democrats regained political power in the mid-1870's. However, in 1878, Captain A. M. Gregory, a young African-American officer in the black militia, suggested to the Texas Adjutant General John B. Jones that a black regiment be formed. Given the go ahead, Captain Gregory began recruiting new companies for the black regiment in late 1878. The influential Richard Allen of Houston, a former African-American state legislator, was appointed as the regimental quartermaster[23].

As early as January, 1880, John Sessums was the captain of a black militia in Houston. His Davis Rifles, a unit of the Texas Volunteer Guard, consisted of sixteen men and they participated in events in May of that year. Although the details of Sessums' recruitment into the militia are not known, his association with Richard Allen may have been a factor. The young Sessums, who was about thirty in 1880, was the son of John Sessums, Sr., a local minister and a member of the board of directors of the Emancipation Association of which Richard Allen was the chairman[24].

John Sessums earned a reputation for intelligence and military discipline, and under his leadership, the Davis Rifles entered and won drill competitions across the region. Formally known as Company L, 1st Colored Regiment/Battalion, Davis Rifles (Houston), the militia unit commanded by Captain John Sessums won the first prize of $250 at the drill contest in New Orleans on October 9, 1882. That was just one of many victorious competitions for the Davis Rifles over the decade of the 1880's that inspired pride in both white and black citizens of Houston. In their dashing uniforms of light blue pants, dark blue coats in the cut frock style, white helmets and white waist belts, the Davis Rifles made quite a presence. In the summer of 1887, the Davis Rifles were sponsored at a national competition in Washington, D. C. by a group of white citizens who were eager to have the black militia unit of Houston recognized nationally[25].

During this same time, John Sessums was also a member of the Houston Light Guard. Although it is not certain how or when he joined the Light Guard, it is believed that he was a member as early as the late 1870's. The Houston Light Guard was organized in 1873, and in February, 1874, the unit appeared for the first time at "the great carnival of King Comus," the Mardi Gras of New Orleans. By 1875, the unit was participating in contests with other units across the state, and they won their first prize at the drill meet in Austin in 1876[26].

The Light Guard fared well over the next few years, winning many competitions, but also failing at some of them. In 1881, Thomas Scurry was promoted to Captain. Scurry was determined to make the Houston Light Guard the best military company in the country, if not the world. It may have been at this time, that John Sessums was asked to join the Light Guard. Sessums was already known for his Davis Rifles, and Scurry may have wanted to bring the special skills that Sessums possessed to the Light Guard. Sessums was definitely a well known member of the Light Guard by June, 1886[27].

The transformation of the Houston Light Guard under Captain Scurry was certainly dramatic. From 1884 until 1888, the Light Guard perfected their drill skills to such a level of precision that the unit won nearly every contest that it entered. During Captain Scurry's tenure as commander, from 1881 to 1889, the Houston Light Guard gained a reputation for drill excellence and won several prizes totaling $17,000. After the drill competition in Austin in 1888, the unit was barred from competition in further contests. At the Interstate Drill at Galveston, in June, 1889, the Houston Light Guard was not allowed to compete, but the unit was awarded a special prize of $500 for an exhibition drill[28].

Members of the Light Guard knew the contribution that John Sessums made to the success of the unit. Precision drill requires the accurate timing and choreography that can be enhanced by the rhythmic cadence of a well played drum. When the Houston Light Guard held their first company meeting in their new armory on January 22, 1892, toasts were offered to the captains that had guided the unit so successfully, including Thomas Scurry, James A. Baker and George L. Price. The contributions of John Sessums were acknowledged as one final toast was offered "lastly to John Sessums, the mascot and drummer." In later years, W. A. Childress, President of the Houston Light Guard Veteran's Association, said that "John was a lifesaver at times when everything on the trip would not go its merriest. Besides furnishing drum music to wake up, march by, and retire by, he was a constant source of entertainment." They lived by his perpetual drum beats, and for that reason, John Sessums was bestowed the title of "Perpetual Drummer" for the Houston Light Guard in 1910[29].

In May, 1890, John Sessums formed a Zouave company. A Zouave company was a cadet militia group for youths from the ages of ten to fourteen who performed precision drills while dressed in uniforms derived from the infantry regiments in the French Army recruited from the Zouaoua (or Zwawa), a Berber tribe from the Jurjura Mountains. Units in both the Union and Confederate armies in the Civil War were patterned after the French Zouaves. The unique movements in the Zouave drill were performed by cadets under Captain John Sessums with "agitation, motion and perspiration" that were highlighted by the conspicuous uniforms of red Zouave trousers, blue jackets and a regulation, fez style, red Zouave cap[30].

Throughout the decade of the 1890's, John Sessums dedicated himself to these African-American youth groups. The names of the groups changed from time to time, depending upon who the sponsor was, but for the twenty to forty black youths of Houston who participated in the Zouaves at any one time, the travel to distant cities to perform exacting drills was a treat not common to black children of that era.

From the initial cadets of the Buckley Zouaves of 1890, to the Packard Zouaves sponsored by businessman Si Packard, to the Captain James Lawlor Zouaves who traveled to the 1895 Southern Cotton Exposition in Atlanta, and finally to the Anderson Zouaves who performed at the Dallas State Fair in 1898, John Sessums tried to provide the youth of his world the same opportunities that had been given to him[31].

After the retirement of the Houston Light Guard from drill competition in 1889, John Sessums continued his work with the Davis Rifles, a black militia company. On January 7, 1890, John

Photo credit: Louis F. Aulbach

Captain John Sessums, Jr. is buried in College Park Cemetery on West Dallas Avenue. The image of a snare drum is etched on his tombstone. A Texas Historical Marker recognizes his remarkable contributions to Houston's history.

Sessums was reelected as Captain the Davis Rifles, a position he had held since the unit's beginning. But, in September, 1890, John Sessums formed a new company called the Scurry Rifles. Interest in the militias, however, began to wane in mid-1890's. The last encampment of black militia units took place in September, 1893 with only three companies and a company of juvenile Zouaves from Houston[32].

The State Adjutant General Woodford H. Mabry tried to revive interest in the black militia units in 1896 when he ordered "colored battalion of infantry" to their annual encampment at the Afro-American Fair in Houston in late August, 1896. Governor Charles Allen Culberson commissioned John Sessums as first lieutenant of the Sheridan Guards on August 10, 1896, and Sessums took command of the Cocke Rifles, which was Section B of the Sheridan Guards. Needless to say, the Cocke Rifles under John Sessums took the high score of event drill competition[33].

As the United States and Spain edged toward war over Cuba, both black and white militias prepared for possible active duty. Captain John Sessums ordered the Cocke Rifles to drill practice twice a week on Monday and Friday nights during the winter of 1897 in order to be in top shape to go to Cuba if war were to break out. Yet, when the call came to Texas, no black militia units were accepted in the four regiments that the state formed. The only African-Americans from Texas to serve in the Spanish-American War were among two companies recruited into the federal army[33].

After the war, the U. S. Congress passed the Militia Act of 1903, also known as the Dick Act, which reorganized the state militias and formulated the concept of the National Guard. The black militias in Texas were permanently disbanded, and organizations to which persons like John Sessums had belonged ceased to exist. For African-Americans, it was just another disenfranchisement that would take several decades to remedy[34].

John Sessums joined the Houston Light Guard Veteran's Association in 1902 when it was formed, and he proudly remained active in the organization until his death. The Houston Light Guard Veteran's Association purchased a tombstone for Sessums that is embossed with the emblem of a drum. The epitaph says it all: "Only drummer of Houston Light Guard. Faithful unto death[36]."

Adath Yeshurun Cemetery

The Adath Yeshurun Cemetery, also known as Beth Yeshurun I, dates from 1895. A group of new Eastern European immigrants, who were opposed to the reforms advocated by the local Jewish community, broke away from Congregation Beth Israel in 1887 and formed the Orthodox Congregation of Adath Yeshurun in 1889[37].

The new brick synagogue and frame buildings of the Adath Yeshurun Congregation were built in the Second Ward on the land that became Union Station in 1910. About 1895, the Adath Yeshurun Cemetery was established on the Houston Baptist Academy Subdivision, Lots 1 and 8 in each of Blocks 1, 2 and 3[38].

After the merger of the Conservative Congregation Beth El and the Orthodox Congregation Adath Yeshurun in 1945 to form the Conservative Congregation Beth Yeshurun, the cemetery became known as Beth Yeshurun I. It is located at 3500 Allen Parkway, on the north side of Allen Parkway, between Terrell Street and Dunlavy Street[39].

Rochow Street - A History of Development

Beyond the Adath Yeshurun Cemetery, Buffalo Bayou curves slightly to the left. The imposing new residential tower on the corner of Allen Parkway and Rochow Street with its bonnet-like structure crowning the roof line rises high above the upper contour of the south bank. At thirty stories, it would be hard to miss even if it did not have a distinctive architectural design.

This prominent corner on Allen Parkway, however, is no stranger to architectural prominence. For nearly seventy-five years, the site was occupied by the elegant Spanish-Mediterranean style buildings of the Gulf Publishing Company.

Yet, as difficult as it may be to imagine today in this traffic-congested quadrant of Houston, as late as 1917, the tract was undeveloped farm land. Spurred by the development of the River Oaks Country Club Estates, the River Oaks Subdivision of Will Hogg, Hogg's promotion of the construction of Buffalo Drive as a major thoroughfare, and the development of a crafts and manufacturing district adjacent to the roadway, local developers in the mid-1920's began to subdivide tracts along West Dallas Avenue for new residential neighborhoods.

One such developer was the Rochow family who platted the Rochow Subdivision into five tracts from West Dallas Avenue to Allen Parkway with Rochow Street along the eastern boundary.

The Rochow's were a third-generation, construction trades family who came to Houston about 1920 after a half century in the Midwest. Their story began when the thirty year old Carl Rochow, his wife Christina, age thirty-two, daughter Augusta, age six, and sons Charles, age five, and the infant Robert immigrated from Germany in 1865. It is possible that he may have come from the village of Rochow, in modern Lithuania (pronounced "Rah'- kov"), but that is not conclusive. Ultimately, they settled in southeastern Illinois in the town of Saline Mines where Carl worked as a coal miner until at least the early 1870's. His son Otto was born there in 1867[40].

By 1900, Carl Rochow, at sixty-five years old, had established himself as a contractor in Indianapolis, Indiana. He and his wife Christina lived across the street from his son Robert and his family with whom he participated in the contractor's trade. Robert Rochow, by this time at age thirty-six, had begun his own family. He and his wife Bertha, who had immigrated from Germany in 1885 at age thirteen, had two sons Carl and Max, ages four and three, and an infant daughter Augusta[41].

Over the next decade, Robert Rochow continued in the general contracting business and, by 1910, had migrated some 80 miles west to Danville, Illinois. His father, Carl, now seventy-five years of age, had moved in with Robert and his family[42].

After the passing of the elder of the family, the Rochows sought other opportunities. They arrived in Houston around 1920 and initiated the development of the Rochow Subdivision with the construction of single family homes. The subdivision was drawn from West Dallas Avenue to Buffalo Drive (which later became Allen Parkway). The eastern boundary was a street named for themselves, Rochow Street, and the western edge of the subdivision lay east of Dunlavy Street. The subdivision was divided into five tracts, each separated by a one block street, Vick Avenue, D'Amico Avenue, Leonidas Avenue and Byrne Avenue (which now is called West Lamar Avenue). By 1924, there were five homes completed in Block 5, facing West Dallas Avenue. Four other homes were still under construction on the Byrne Avenue side of the block. Blocks 1 to 4 were, as yet, undeveloped[43].

The Rochow clan, headed by the patriarch Robert, positioned itself for the development of the subdivision. The three families lived along the north side of West Dallas Avenue, with Robert and son Carl living next door to each other in the 3400 block, while younger son Max and his family lived in the 3200 block near their contractor's yard, office and related buildings on the northwest corner at Rosine Street. Robert was the building contractor. Carl was a contractor and carpenter, while Max rounded out the trades as a plaster mason[44].

Commercial development on the site began in 1926 when Ray L. Dudley, founder of the Gulf Publishing Company, selected the 2.6 acre site on Block 1 at the northern end of the subdivision for construction of a Spanish-Mediterranean style building. With a red tile roof, a stucco exterior, and heavy ornamentation carved from cast concrete, the structure, designed by Wyatt Hedrick of Hedrick

& Gottlieb in 1927 and completed in 1928, was a prominent feature on Allen Parkway for the next seventy-five years[45].

While additional commercial construction was added to Block 2, such as the Parke Engraving Company Building in 1936 and various auxiliary buildings for the Gulf Publishing Company, the residential development continued as well. By 1943, the Rochow Subdivision was fully developed with approximately 46 single family homes on lots in Blocks 3, 4 and 5[46].

The waning years of the twentieth century brought changes to the Rochow Subdivision. The redevelopment of the areas within the Loop had gained momentum by this time, and the neighborhoods along West Dallas Avenue were no exception. By 2002, there remained only twenty-four single family homes in the subdivision. These were located on Block 5, near West Dallas Avenue, and more than half of these homes had been built since 1998. Block 3, bounded by Damico Avenue and Leonidas Avenue, is a multi-family residential property owned by the ERP Operating LTD Partnership of Chicago. Block 4, bounded by West Lamar Avenue and Leonidas Avenue, is vacant commercial property owned by the ERP Operating LTD Partnership[47].

On May 16, 2001, the white stucco walls and delicate ornamentation of the Gulf Publishing Company building were torn down to make way for a luxury apartment complex. Today, Allen Parkway Place, located at 3333 Allen Parkway, offers 250 units for lease on the thirty floors of the residential development owned by Simmons Vedder and Company and designed by the architectural firm of the Steinberg Collaborative[48].

Max P. Rochow, Jr. was born on August 12, 1923 as his father, Max, Sr., and others of the Rochow family began work on their subdivision. By the time that he had served in World War II as a 1st Lieutenant in the U. S. Army, Max saw the Rochow Subdivision flourish with commercial and residential development. Max, Jr., who passed away on August 29, 1983, found a permanent place in Houston and is buried in the Houston National Cemetery. He did not have to suffer the changes that have transformed the Rochow Subdivision[49].

Star Engraving Building

In addition to the Gulf Publishing Company building, the Star Engraving Company building was one of three printing plants constructed during the 1920's and 1930's that comprised a Spanish village craft district along Buffalo Drive (now, Allen Parkway)[50].

Star Engraving Company was incorporated in 1911 and it was well known for the manufacture and sale of high school class rings. The company was acquired by Roy J. Beard in 1922, and it announced the construction of its new building on the southwest corner of Buffalo Drive and Rosine Street in April, 1930[51].

Star Engraving Company building is a one and two story loft type business office building and manufacturing plant that is made of reinforced concrete in a Spanish Mediterranean style. The structure is significant for its cast in place concrete construction and steel sash windows which provide for an economical, durable and fireproof construction with generous provisions for day lighting and passive ventilation. Designed by Houston architect Rezin D. Steele, this structure is his most intact commercial building. Steele, who practiced in Houston from 1893 until his death in 1936, also designed the Sidney Lanier Junior High School (1925)[52].

The City of Houston, under the direction of Mayor Robert C. Lanier, purchased the Star Engraving Company Building, at 3201 Allen Parkway, in order to preserve it and use it as a cultural center. The building was added to the National Register of Historic Places in 1995[53].

The Buffalo Motel Ushers In the Automobile Age

Houston began to embrace the automobile as its primary means of personal transportation as early as the late 1920's. The Depression and World War II delayed things a bit, but after the war, the local economy surged, the City's population exploded, the City expanded the local highway system and the automobile became an integral part of Houston's lifestyle.

Will Hogg spearheaded the move to suburban living with the development of River Oaks. Residents of the suburb commuted to downtown along Buffalo Drive, the City's first major parkway. The four lane roadway, which is now Allen Parkway, paralleled Buffalo Bayou's south bank from downtown to Shepherd Drive. Getting to work in your personal car was a breeze.

By 1951, a sign of things to come could be seen in the Buffalo Town House Hotel Tourist Court on the southeast corner of Waugh Drive and Buffalo Drive. The Buffalo Motel, as it was later called, was an automobile traveler's complex that consisted of a filling station directly on the corner, a restaurant along Waugh Drive to the west and the motel lobby and dwellings along Buffalo Drive to the east. Additional townhouse residential units comprised six buildings at the rear of the property[54].

This configuration of lodgings, a restaurant and a service station on a prominent corner of a main thoroughfare is familiar to us today. Holiday Inn, La Quinta, Motel 6 and many other hoteliers have joined with the likes of Denny's, the Waffle House and every brand of gas station to set up along our highways and freeways. It is a scene that is common now, but in the 1950's, it was *avant garde*.

In the early 1960's, Gus Wortham's American General Insurance Company acquired the Buffalo Motel, and construction began on the first of the five buildings of the American General Center in 1963. The office complex now occupies a prominent location among the revitalized neighborhoods and new developments along Allen Parkway. And, the automobile is still the Houston commuter's transportation of choice[55].

The Waugh Drive Bat Colony

There is a noticeably pungent odor along the Buffalo Bayou at Waugh Drive. The acrid smell of ammonia is especially strong on the jogging path under the bridge. It is there that you will find Houston's foremost colony of bats.

Since at least 2003, and possibly earlier, a colony of Mexican Free Tail bats has taken up residence in the Waugh Drive Bridge. The original, long span bridge was built between 1922 and 1924 to replace an earlier low water crossing. It was named for Private Tom T. Waugh who died in World War I. His father, T. L. Waugh was city's street and bridge commissioner. The current bridge is a modern structure with a box beam design using large concrete slabs with beams separated by expansion joints. The expansion joints are 3/4 to 4 inches wide and 16 inches deep, and those cracks provide an ideal nesting place for the bats. The bridge, which spans the length of the bayou gorge, provides ample room for the 250,000 to 300,000 bats who make up the colony[56].

Although this colony is much smaller than the 1.5 million bats of the colony in Austin, the Houston Waugh Drive bats are unique in that they apparently do not migrate. Mexican Free Tail bats (*Tadarida brasiliensis*) usually arrive in March and return to Mexico in November. The Waugh Drive colony is here all year around[57].

The best time of year to see the bats is in July and August. The bugs in Houston are at their best in late summer, and the bats have had their "pups" so both mothers and babies are foraging for mosquitoes and insects along the bayou. Shortly before dusk, the activity of the colony begins under the bridge. For the next hour or so, bats can be seen swarming under the bridge. However, unlike the dramatic exits of other colonies, such as those in Austin or at Carlsbad Caverns, the Waugh Drive colony does not exit in a black cloud against the dimly lit sky. Rather, these bats head right down the bayou toward downtown, catching food on the wing that inhabits the trees and brush on the banks of the bayou[58].

The best place to see the bats is at the Waugh Bat Colony Observation Deck on the south bank of Buffalo Bayou at Waugh Drive and Allen Parkway. The deck, donated by the Lyondell Chemical Company and dedicated in May, 2006, provides a convenient spot from which to await the bat activity each evening[59].

A Monument to Gus Wortham

The south bank of Buffalo Bayou from Montrose Boulevard to Waugh Drive is a profound, but subtle, tribute to one of Houston's most significant benefactors, Gus Wortham.

The most visible, and public, recognition of Wortham is the Gus S. Wortham Memorial Fountain which is located on bayou park land near Waugh Drive. The Wortham Fountain was designed by William Cannady and construction was completed in 1978. The spray and mist created by the nozzles at the end of the copper tubes that radiate from the center of the fountain provide the fountain with its common name, the Dandelion Fountain[60].

Even more impressive is the tract of land which is bounded by Allen Parkway on the north, West Dallas Avenue on the south, Montrose Boulevard on the east and Waugh Drive to the west. Most of this tract is owned by the American General Corporation, the gigantic insurance conglomerate that was founded by Gus Wortham in 1926[61].

This site was mostly rural pasture land throughout the nineteenth century and the first two decades of the 20th century. By 1924, however, there was some development on the tract. The A. T. Lucas Brick Company occupied a large block next to the Magnolia Cemetery and the complex included three dry kilns, a dirt shed, an office, a reservoir, a general storage building and a caretakers dwelling. The only other improvements on the tract were a handful of scattered dwellings or farms on Link Road (now Peveto Street)[62].

In the economic prosperity of the post World War II period, businesses and residences began to appear along Waugh Drive. The Buffalo Town House Hotel Tourist Courts at Allen Parkway, the Ineeda Laundry on Peveto Street, and the Carnation Milk Company on Waugh Drive at D'Amico Street were the commercial developments. A few residential dwellings also were built along Waugh Drive and West Dallas Avenue[63].

In the 1960's, the American General Corporation began to acquire the land for its own business development. Over the next twenty years, the forty-four acre American General Center took shape. The center eventually came to consist of five high rise office buildings, three parking garages and a health spa. The complex's flagship high rise, the America Tower, was constructed in 1982 and contains 956,380 square feet of improved space. A 2007 market appraisal of the American General Center placed its value at a cool $200,421,755.00[64].

Gus Sessions Wortham was born in Mexia to John Lee and Fannie Sessions Wortham on February 18, 1891. He began his career in insurance in 1912 when he went to work for the Texas Fire Rating Board in Austin. In 1915, Gus and his father moved to Houston and founded the John L. Wortham and Son insurance agency. In 1926, Gus Wortham and Houston businessmen Jesse H.

Jones, James A. Elkins and John W. Link organized the American General Insurance Company, with Wortham was president and John W. Link as chairman of the board. It was one of the first multi-line insurance companies, writing both fire and casualty insurance and that proved to be a key to the company's success that has persisted through the Depression, World War II and the post war period to the present day[65].

After years of successful acquisitions, the American General Insurance Company became a general business holding company in 1980. Twenty-one years later, in 2001, the American General Corporation was acquired by the American International Group. The American International Group became a component of the Dow Jones Industrial Average on April 8, 2004. The AIG logo was added to the exterior facade of the Wortham Tower in the spring of 2007 to join the ever-waving American flag atop the building[66].

Gus Wortham married Elizabeth Lyndall Finley on October 4, 1926, and they had two daughters. Throughout his life, he was devoted to his family, the Houston Symphony Orchestra, the Grand Opera and the general well being of the city. During the 1950's and 1960's, Wortham was a member of the "8-F Crowd" - a group of business leaders who met for lunch in Suite 8-F of the Lamar Hotel to chart Houston's civic affairs. He served two consecutive terms as the president of the Houston Chamber of Commerce[67].

In the 1970's, Wortham helped to rescue a neglected cemetery that lay adjacent to his American General Center. It was said that he hand picked his final resting place in Magnolia Cemetery because it gave him a view of his American General headquarters building[68].

Henrietta Steiner buried her family members John P. W. Steiner and Arthur Steiner on a tract of land on the north side of the San Felipe Road near the western edge of Houston in 1884. Shortly thereafter, the First German Methodist Church of Houston (now known as the Bering Memorial Methodist Church) established this tract as the Magnolia Cemetery for its members. In 1892, the Magnolia Cemetery Company amended its charter to permit membership privileges to persons who were not members of the church[69].

The Magnolia Cemetery was originally a ten acre tract extending from the San Felipe Road (now West Dallas Avenue) to Buffalo Bayou. In 1929, the trustees of the Magnolia Cemetery deeded about two and a half acres of unused cemetery land to the City of Houston to provide the right of way for Buffalo Drive and to pay the cemetery's part for paving the roadway[70].

By 1970, the Magnolia Cemetery had fallen into a state of disrepair. The trustees of the Magnolia Cemetery sold an unused section of land on the north end to Gus Wortham's American General Insurance Company in 1974. That parcel later was converted into park space for visitor and local citizens. In 1970, an acre on the cemetery's south end was sold to establish a perpetual care endowment. This tract on West Dallas Avenue is still owned by AIG American General Life Insurance and is vacant commercial land[71].

Today, the Magnolia Cemetery, 809 Montrose Boulevard, consists of six acres in a peaceful, park-like environment and contains about 4,000 burials. After his death on September 1, 1976, Gus S. Wortham was buried in a mausoleum in the cemetery. When his wife Elizabeth Wortham died July 12, 1980, she joined him in eternal rest in the picturesque tomb[72].

Vick's Lake -- A Popular Park on Buffalo Bayou

A little to the east of Waugh Drive, Buffalo Bayou flowed north into a small lake, called Vick's Lake because of the land holdings of the Vick family along the north bank. A century ago, Houston residents escaped the hectic pace and the heat of summer in the city by spending a relaxing day in the park, much as we do today. Picnicking among the shady trees along Buffalo Bayou was popular. So was canoeing the bayou and paddling on Vick's Lake. The bayou swimming hole in Vick's Park was considered to be one of the city's best. Vick's Park was on the north bank of Buffalo Bayou between the modern Studemont Street and Waugh Drive. It was named for the family that had owned the land.

Three young men of the Vick family in their early twenties left Tennessee about 1880 and came to Texas. By 1900, the three had married, started families of their own and established themselves in the communities that were developing northwest of Houston along the Washington Road. The Vick brothers and their families lived in close proximity to each other near the modern intersection of Washington Avenue and Waugh Drive. Tobe S. Vick raised cattle on his farm lying between Washington Road and the bayou. Andrew Vick, the oldest brother at age forty-five, was joined by the youngest brother, B. S. Vick, as owners of rental property[73].

The industrial site that developed near Chaney Junction, the intersection of the Houston and Texas Central Railway with the Galveston, Harrisburg and San Antonio Railway spur, offered opportunities for employment for several hundred men. Both the Fidelity Cotton Oil Company and the Butler Brick Works were major employers. Many of the factory workers and their families lived in the scattering of neighborhoods along Washington Road.

The Vicks lived in this neighborhood and rented houses to these workers who held jobs as oil mill laborers, house carpenters, day laborers, dairy men, farmers, wood cutters and coal burners. The largely working class neighborhood was surprisingly integrated for the time. According to the 1900 census records, the homes around the Vick families were occupied by twenty black families and twenty-one white families who were evenly distributed in the block patterns of the census[74].

In addition to Tobe Vick's farm, Andrew Vick owned a large tract of land west of the Butler Brick Works on the GH&SA spur which included most of what would become Vick's Park. In a situation that may have been outstanding foresight or it may have been merely fortuitous, the Vicks rode the crest of the boom in housing and residential development that accompanied the growth of Houston in the two decades that spanned the turn of the century[75].

The increase in the population of the Sixth Ward after the Civil War spilled over to the Brunner community in the late 1880's which was platted west of town on the Washington Road. Encouraged by the success of Brunner, which by 1895 had 500 inhabitants, and by the establishment of trolley service on Washington Road in 1891, land owners and farmers turned their land holdings into small residential subdivisions that dotted the outskirts of Houston along the major roadway out of town. Strung like beads on a string, the Moodyman, Butler, Brown, Riverside Park, Vick's Park, Hartman, Leverkuhn, Renard Frisco, Magnolia, and the Magnolia Grove Additions extended along Washington Road from the GH&SA cutoff to the Brunner Addition[76].

The Vicks Park Addition, tightly sandwiched between the Hartman Addition to the west and the Riverside Park Addition to the east, consisted of two rows of lots located along Vida Street. Named for Andrew Vick's daughter Vida, Vida Street was the main avenue of the small subdivision. It ran south from Washington Road to the edge of the high bluff overlooking the valley of Buffalo Bayou where, in 1910, the 48 year old Tobe Vick lived on his two acre farm at 47 Vida Street with his wife Zadella and their two young children. Tobe still considered himself a cattle stockman[77].

Perhaps inspired by the success of his real estate ventures, Andrew Vick moved on to San Antonio to explore the opportunities there. By 1910, Andrew and his son Ivan, living with their extended families at 325 West French Place in San Antonio, describe themselves as real estate speculators[78].

The forty-four acres of land on the north bank of Buffalo Bayou between the modern Studemont Street and Waugh Drive became Vick's Park by 1917, a city park. Later, the park would be incorporated in the property along the bayou to the west as a part of Cleveland Park. The channelization of Buffalo Bayou in the mid-1950's removed the northward curving bend in the bayou at Waugh Drive. The oxbow that was Vick's Lake was filled and contoured during the construction of Memorial Drive and the Waugh Drive cloverleaf. Today, the former park site is the City of Houston's Spotts Park[79].

The Vick's Park Addition has been carved up by the widening and extension of Heights Boulevard on the south side of Washington Avenue, as well as by the extension of Yale Street south to connect with Waugh Drive along the route of the former Vida Street. Today, only two homes of the addition, built about 1926, remain. Lying between commercial tracts on the north and an office building to the south, these remnants of the Vick's Park Addition are soon to be lost to the rapid pace of development occurring along the Washington Avenue corridor. Tobe S. Vick's former homestead is an office building and parking garage at 55 Waugh Drive, owned by the Parkway Investments Partners[80].

By 1920, the Vick brothers no longer appeared in the records of Houston. Their park has been transformed under another name. Their subdivision will soon be renewed into something else. In the fading light of history, Vick Avenue, located across the bayou one block south of Allen Parkway at Rochow Street, will linger as the sole reminder of the Vick family legacy in Houston's "western" suburbs.

GH&SA Railway Spur

In 1880, the Galveston Harrisburg and San Antonio Railway built a connecting track that joined its main line, south of town, with a rail yard on the north side of Buffalo Bayou in downtown Houston. This "entrance" into the city greatly enhanced the railroad's potential for rail service while also connecting it with the other large rail line of the city, the Houston and Texas Central[81].

In March of the same year, Thomas R. Chaney, founder of the Howard Oil Mill Company, began the construction of a factory to be located adjacent to the intersection of these two great railroad lines. Over the next three decades, this rail junction, called Chaney Junction, was to become the focal point of an industrial district for the local economy's first major oil boom, the cottonseed oil boom[82].

Cotton was produced commercially in Texas from the days of the Austin Colony, and within a decade after the Civil War, Texas had became the leading cotton producing state in the United States. Cotton was "ginned" to separate the fibers from the seeds, and large quantities of baled cotton were shipped through the ports of Houston and Galveston. However, with each pound of cotton ginned, two pounds of cotton seeds were left over. For the most part, the seeds were disposed of as a waste product. Advances in technology during the 1870's, however, made the milling of cotton seeds commercially viable, and by 1882, there were fourteen cottonseed oil mills in Texas, producing a total of five million barrels of oil per year. The processing of cotton seed was one of the earliest large-scale industries in Texas[83].

To complement the mill operations at Chaney Junction, the Inman Compress Company of Georgia decided to build a compress on the tract of land adjoining the Howard Oil Mill. George W. Harris, president of the Inman Compress in Georgia, arrived in Houston in the summer of 1882 to oversee the construction of the compress. The Inman Compress of Houston was organized on

August 9, 1883 and was operational for the fall cotton crop. Cotton compresses used screwjacks, and later haydraulic presses, to reduce the bales of cotton that came from the cotton gins to roughly half their size so that the bulky bales could be packed for shipment by sea[84].

Shortly after midnight on August 28, 1886, the Howard Oil Mill caught fire and was completely destroyed. The flames lit the night sky and could be seen clearly from the city. Fire hoses had been attached to the hydrants, but when the valves were turned, the hydrants failed to provide water to fight the fire. The whole facility and five box cars of cotton belonging to the Houston and Texas Central Railway were consumed by the fire. The only items saved were two oil tanks of 4,500 barrels and 3,500 barrels of oil, respectively. The loss was estimated at $250,000. The Howard Oil Mill Company was determined to rebuild the mill. The cottonseed oil business was extremely competitive at this time, and the interim offered an opportunity to one of Howard's chief competitors[85].

On March 5, 1887, the Southern Cotton Oil Company was organized in Philadelphia with Henry C. Butcher as president. A few days later, the officials of the Southern Cotton Oil Company were in Houston to locate a site for one of eight new oil mills for the company. The company planned to build mills for producing cottonseed "crude" across the South, and the Houston facility was one of the first. In early April, Butcher and P. Oliver, his General Manager, negotiated agreements with the H&TC Railway to secure tracks for the proposed new oil mill. On May 7, 1887, the Southern Cotton Oil Company acquired about forty-four acres land for the new mill in the Hollingsworth Survey, on Lots 5, 6 and 7 for $4,783. The mill was located along the east side of the GH&SA Railway spur, south of Washington Avenue. By October, 1887, the mill had received six new presses to bring its production to full capacity, and it was in operation day and night[86].

Not to be outdone, the Howard Oil Mill Company was hurriedly rebuilding its mill. In August, 1887, a stand pipe to deliver 700,000 gallons of water in case of a fire was set on the premises[87]. They were not going to get caught short the next time!

The economic influence of the cotton industry on the local community was fully evident as Houston began the 1890's. In

January, 1892, the newspaper reported the National Cotton Oil Company, the new name for the Howard Oil Mill Company, employed 200 to 225 men with a payroll of $2,000 to $2,500 per week. The Southern Cotton Oil Company employed 250 men with a weekly payroll of $3,000. The cotton compresses in Houston, of which the Inman Compress was one of three, collectively employed about 400 persons with a weekly payroll of over $3,000[88].

The production volumes were equally as significant. The value of goods produced by the local economy was enormous. The output of the National Cotton Oil Company mill in 1892 was 12,000 tons of oil cake and cotton seed meal, 1.25 million gallons of crude oil and 2000 bales of lint. The Southern Cotton Oil Company mill produced 12,600 gallons of oil, 31 tons of oil cake and 25 bales of lint. The mill of the National Cotton Oil Company was significantly larger than its neighboring competitor, and the National mill was the largest cotton oil mill in Texas at the time. Taken together, the mills of Houston consumed more cotton seed and produced more oil, cotton seed meal and cake than anywhere else in the world. At the turn of the century, cottonseed processing was second only to the lumber industry in Texas in value of the product, and Texas was the leading processor of cottonseed in the US[89].

The success of the cotton industry in the late nineteenth century and early twentieth century was due to the improvements in processing the plant that expanded the commercial uses for the cotton and cotton seeds. Ginning technology to separate the cotton fibers from the cotton seeds was perfected in the early 1800's, but the seeds were discarded because there was no commercial process to make the seed products usable. After the Civil War, however, techniques for milling the cotton seeds were developed so that the seed products could be used. After cotton was ginned to remove the seeds, the mills reduced the seeds to four by products: linters, hulls, meal and cottonseed oil[90].

Cotton linters were processed for textiles. Cottonseed hulls provided roughage in cattle feed, and the ashes of the hulls were used as fertilizer and to produce lye for soap. Cottonseed meal was used as a high protein supplement for livestock feed. The most valuable product from the milling process, however, was the oil or "crude." The crude oil was used to make commodities such as soap and candles because it was inedible and unsuitable for cooking purposes. A major breakthrough in the process for refining cotton-seed oil brought changes to the industry. In 1899, David Wesson developed the process for making cottonseed oil edible, and that year he installed the process at the Southern Cotton Oil Company plant at Savannah, Georgia. Refined oil quickly found uses in cooking oil, margarine and mayonnaise. As one contemporary writer reported: "Cottonseed was garbage in 1860, fertilizer in 1870, cattle feed in 1880 and 'table food and many things else in 1890[91]'."

In 1909, the Proctor and Gamble Company acquired the rights to the hydrogenation patent for cottonseed oil and produced the first all vegetable shortening in 1911. Originally named "kipso," the product became popular when it was renamed Crisco, an abbreviation of "crystallized cottonseed oil." Crisco was promoted as a vegetable oil with more purity and healthfulness than lard from slaughterhouses and meat packing companies which were perceived in a bad light at that time. Proctor and Gamble also bought large quantities of cottonseed oil to produce Ivory Soap. The Southern Cotton Oil Company so successfully marketed Wesson Oil that the company was renamed the Wesson Oil and Snowdrift Company in 1925. Many of the cottonseed oil products that contributed to Houston's turn of the century prosperity remain familiar household names today, even though the connection with cotton has been largely overlooked[92].

The success of the cotton business attracted other businesses to the Chaney Junction industrial development. By 1896, Michael Butler's Brick Works was established west side of the Galveston Harrisburg and San Antonio railroad tracks, near Buffalo Bayou. The facility for making bricks included four kilns, several drying sheds and a steam and hot air drying house. By 1907, the Butler Brick Yard had expanded to seven kilns[93].

The Dickson Car Wheel Company relocated its foundry from the site on Steam Mill Street in the Fifth Ward to a site on the west side of the tracks just north of the Butler Brick Works. In these expanded facilities, the company was producing 400 railroad car wheels per day in 1913[94].

Directly across the railroad tracks from the Butler Bricks Works, the Bayou City Rice Mills built a four story rice mill that was flanked by a single story rough rice warehouse and a one story clean rice warehouse. Incorporated in January, 1902, the mill was receiving train car loads of rice at the mill by 1903[95].

The Fidelity Cotton Oil and Fertilizer Company was granted a permit to do business in Texas on July 22, 1905. It acquired the former Southern Cotton Oil Company mill along the GH&SA tracks south of Washington Avenue, and continued the operation of the mill in 1907 with essentially the same plant and facilities that were on the site in 1896[96].

The Industrial Cotton Oil Company, formerly the National Cotton Oil Company, operated its mill and its refinery which was expanded by 1907 to provide for the improved refining processes that new technologies brought to the cottonseed industry[97].

The Inman Compress, by 1907, had moved its compress facility to the east side of town near the International and Great Northern Railroad yards at Harrisburg Road and Velasco Street. The former Inman Compress site at Chaney Junction lay vacant. The development of processes to compress cotton at the gin into high density bales by the 1890's eliminated the need for some cotton compresses[98].

In 1918, the GH&SA Railway completed a new entrance into Houston between Chaney Junction and West Junction. The original 1880 entry between Chaney Junction and Stella was partly abandoned, leaving only a siding that ran south from the junction near Center Street, across Buffalo Bayou to West Dallas Avenue. Although this change did not seriously diminish the prospects for the industrial district, the mixture of business in the area did change. Reflecting the over capacity in the cottonseed oil business and the subsequent consolidation of mills and plants, the American Cotton Oil Company mill, formerly the Industrial Cotton Oil Mill and the National Cotton Oil Mill, was no longer in operation by 1924. The refinery, located just north of the mill, was also deactivated by this time. The Butler Brick Works, located near the bayou, also closed and vacated the site by this time. Otherwise, the industries along the GH&SA siding south of Washington Avenue to Buffalo Bayou prospered in the aftermath of World War I[99].

The three main businesses operating in the industrial district in 1924 were the Fidelity Cotton Oil & Fertilizer Company, Dickson Car Wheel Company and the Standard Rice Company. A diversification of the business mix reflected a change in the foundations of Houston's economic base from cotton to rail transportation and other agricultural products, such as rice. The consolidation of the cotton-seed oil industry continued during the Depression, especially in response to the introduction of solvent extraction that permitted larger capacity and more efficient mill operations. The cotton indus-try declined further after 1940 with the advent of synthetic fabrics. Eventually, the Fidelity Cotton Oil mill closed and the site was redeveloped by Henke and Pillot, Inc. in 1946[100].

In Houston's post-World War II economy, the industrial zone at Chaney Junction, especially along the railroad spur from Washing-ton Avenue to Buffalo Bayou, showed a variety of business that comprised Houston's modern economy. The cotton mills and refin-eries were gone. The Dickson Car Wheel Company was acquired by the Pullman Car Company and the foundry was taken over by another railway equipment manufacturer, the American Brake Shoe and Foundry Company. The rice mills continued to be operated by the American Rice Growers Cooperative Association. The whole-sale grocery operations of Henke and Pillot highlighted the new concept of suburban supermarkets. And, the Ed Sacks and Company plant for waste paper was opened on the tract of land previously used by the Butler Brick Works[101].

Eventually, though, these industries gave way to the changing development patterns of Houston. Henke and Pillot was sold to the Kroger Corporation of Cincinnati in 1956 and the warehouses were moved to other locations. The American Rice storage silos, which had been vacant for several years, were destroyed by a five alarm fire on January 14, 1988. The rice silos were one of the last reminders of Houston's agricultural heritage within the inner Loop area. The silos were imploded in 1996, and since 2004, the property has been transformed into the 100 acre Memorial Heights residential development[102].

In 2004, Ameriton Properties, a subsidiary of developer Arch-stone-Smith, purchased the 2.75 acre Sacks Paper Company site on the north side of Buffalo Bayou along Memorial Drive at Stude-mont. Construction of a high rise residential tower on the site began early 2008. With the completion of that structure, the transformation of Houston's early industrial zone into a residential development will be complete. Even the railroad spur that laid the foundation for the area has disappeared from view. The only remnants of the historic past are the concrete footings for the railroad trestle that lie in the sandy bottom of Buffalo Bayou and the notched bulkhead that supported the rail right of way along Memorial Drive[103].

Sears, Roebuck and Company

By the end of the 1920's, Houston, as an American city, was showing signs of the changes in society that were occurring across the United States. Some of these broad patterns can be seen in the development along Buffalo Bayou and the commercial development adjacent to the GH&SA Railway spur.

If River Oaks ushered in the suburban residential way of life that was connected to the business center by modern roadways, like Buffalo Drive, and a dependence on the private automobile, then the suburban retail department store concept began with the opening of the Sears, Roebuck and Company store on Buffalo Drive (now named Allen Parkway).

By 1920, the population of the United States living in cities outnumbered the rural population. At the turn of the twentieth century, the situation had been the reverse. Robert E. Wood, president of Sears, Roebuck and Company saw this change and recognized the effect on retail merchandising. He opened an experimental retail store in Chicago in early 1927, and by the end of the year, he had twenty-seven retail outlets to complement the mail order catalog operations. By 1929, Sears had three hundred nineteen retail stores and by the country's entry into World War II in 1941, there were more than six hundred Sears stores nationwide[104].

Houston's Sears, Roebuck and Company store was built in 1929 on a three acre site at the present day intersection of Allen Parkway and Montrose Boulevard. It was the first suburban department store in Houston. With its main entrance facing Lincoln Street (now Montrose Boulevard), truck loading docks on the north side facing Buffalo Drive and the rail docks along the east side, the Sears store seemed to be the most advanced commercial venture in the region. Designed by the firm of Nimmons, Carr and Wright, the brick art deco structure was an architectural example of the type of high quality development along Buffalo Drive as it emerged as the major corridor between downtown and River Oaks. The new $1,000,000 retail department store opened for business on the corner of Buffalo Drive and Lincoln Street in August, 1929[105].

Situated in a prominent position on the south bank of Buffalo Bayou, located adjacent to the railroad spur from Chaney Junction, and convenient to residential neighborhoods that stretched in a broad arch across the southwest side of the city from South Main Street to River Oaks, the Sears, Roebuck store seemed to ideally positioned for success. Yet, after only a decade, the store was relocated to South Main Street, near its current day intersection with US 59. The unpredictable nature of the bayou had shown its hand. On December 9, 1935, Buffalo Bayou rose in flood to its historic high level, reaching an estimated flow of 40,000 cfs. The first floor of the Sears store flooded, and substantial losses were incurred. The subsequent "flood" sale, in which damaged goods were displayed and sold on the second floor of the building, was an event to remember and was well patronized by bargain-seeking shoppers[106].

By 1942, the Olympia Arena was operating on the site of the old Sears store. Then, in 1943, the building was the temporary, first home of the Baylor College of Medicine. Baylor College of Medicine moved from Dallas to Houston before the Texas Medical Center could construct the building it had promised, so students at Baylor attended classes during the first four years, until 1947, in the old Sears warehouse[107].

Arthur G. Robinson purchased the former Sears store in the 1950's for a storage business. His public storage operation was the first of its kind in Houston and a prelude to the mini storage facilities that are so common today. Robinson and his family operated the Robinson Public Warehouse for over forty years. The building was often unnoticed since a large "RPW" written on the east-facing wall of the tower section of the structure was its only identifying sign[108].

By 2001, the RPW building was for sale and it stood there inconspicuously collecting the ugly marks of graffiti on the wall near the loading dock. Ameriton Properties, a subsidiary of Archstone-Smith, had plans to acquire the Robinson Public Warehouse at 2323 Allen Parkway in 2004. Ameriton was going to build a residential development called the Village at Allen Parkway on the three acre RPW tract and the 8.3 acres owned by Reliant Energy, behind the RPW warehouse. Instead, the Aga Khan Foundation purchased the 11.3 acre tract in 2006 in order to build an Ismaili Center on the site[109].

The Aga Khan Foundation is a non-denominational, international development agency established in 1967 by His Highness the Aga Khan. The foundation is chartered under Swiss law with independent affiliates in fifteen countries. It promotes solutions to social problems and is a vehicle for philanthropy in the Ismaili Muslim community. Ismaili Muslims are the second largest Shia community in the world with fifteen million followers. About 15,000 Ismaili Muslims live in the Houston area[110].

The Ismaili Center envisioned for the Allen Parkway site will include a prayer hall, classrooms, offices and a social hall. This facility will complement the Ismaili Jamatkhana and Center at Houston which opened in Sugar Land on June 23, 2002. The former Sears building was demolished in 2008 and the tract was cleared and landscaped in preparation for the future construction[111].

Rosemont Bridge

On March 26, 2011, a new pedestrian bridge over Buffalo Bayou, called the Rosemont Bridge, was opened near the Montrose-Studewood bridge. The Rosemont Bridge has a seven hundred eighty linear foot span of concrete and steel over the bayou in a bifurcated walkway that permits access to both the hike and bike trail on the north side of Memorial Drive as well as hike and bike trail along the north bank that lies south of Memorial Drive. A single path provides access to the south bank of Buffalo Bayou and the trails there. In a nod to the historic location of the new bridge, the upper walkway connects into the bulkhead of the former right of way of the Galveston, Harrisburg and San Antonio Railway. Funding for the bridge project came from the Memorial Heights Tax Increment Reinvestment Zone Number 5[112].

The Allen Parkway side of the Rosemont Bridge exits into a segment of the Buffalo Bayou Park called "Harmony Walk" where the City has acquired an art work, entitled "Tolerance," from the internationally renowned artist Jaume Plensa. Plensa's Tolerance, a

Photo credit: Louis F. Aulbach

Tolerance, the sculpture by Spanish artist Jaume Plensa, consists of seven stainless steel human figures, as seen at the left. The figures are in a small park adjacent to the Rosemont Bridge on Allen Parkway.

sculpture of seven stainless steel human figures, was a gift to the City by private donors in conjunction with the Houston Arts Alliance and the Greater Houston Community Foundation.

The figures in the sculpture represent the seven continents. Each figure is formed specifically to sit on a unique boulder hand-selected by Plensa from his native Spain. Each figure is ten feet high and is made of his signature stainless steel alphabetic mesh. The alphabet mesh represents a mix of languages including Latin, Hebrew, Arabic, Chinese, Japanese, Korean, Greek, Hindi and Cyrillic. At night, each figure is lighted from within. The sculpture, as a whole, celebrates Houston's openness, diversity and international character.

The Tolerance project came about through the efforts of Mica Mosbacher and Dr. Mahmoud Eboo who represented His Highness the Aga Khan who personally contributed to the realization of the project. The Plensa art work graces the banks of Buffalo Bayou in front of the proposed Ismaili Center on Allen Parkway[113].

Allen Park Inn

The land on the east side of the GH&SA railroad tracks, located in the 2100 block of Allen Parkway, lay relatively undeveloped through the first half of the twentieth century. In 1951, the Black-

Brollier, Inc., Concrete Pipe and Products Manufacturing Plant No. 2 was located on the site. A small Ramada hotel was built there in 1960, and in 1974, the hotel was acquired by Rebecca and Robert Harris. Under the Harris ownership, the hotel became the Allen Park Inn, and the facility was expanded to include 249 rooms with the addition of new buildings.

The Allen Park Inn was never a thriving business. With vacancy rates of 65 to 70 percent, the inn with a staff of 100 employees survived for many years as a business hotel with several corporate clients. Rising waters from Tropical Storm Allison in 2001 affected the hotel lobby, its restaurant and its ballroom. The flood damage was so extensive that the Allen Park Inn closed for good in late 2001[114].

ZOM Texas, Inc. acquired the 7.3 acre site of the former Allen Park Inn and, in the second quarter of 2006, the Bel Air Apartments, at 2121 Allen Parkway, opened. Inspired by the grand resort hotels of the early 1900's, the Mediterranean-style complex, designed by Looney Ricks Kiss of Memphis, is built around seven landscaped courtyards. The Bel Air is a 4-1/2 story apartment complex with units that range from 720 to 1700 square feet in size. The apartments sit atop 1-1/2 levels of parking. Since the site is located in the flood plain of Buffalo Bayou, the Bel Air was designed so that 25% of the garage would accommodate the flood waters from the bayou[115].

Temple Terrace

The land immediately east of the Bel Air complex was developed as a residential community in the mid-1930's as the Temple Terrace Subdivision. Earlier than that, though, the area has a history that dates to the earliest days of the town of Houston.

About 1838, John S. Stanley built a race track, stables, several houses and slave quarters on land that lay west of the Houston Ranch and northwest of Mirabeau B. Lamar's Oak Grove estate. The race track was on sixty-nine acres along Buffalo Bayou, about 1-1/2 miles west of town, and within sixty feet of the San Felipe Road. Horse racing was a popular sport in the early days of the Republic, and many of the prominent citizens of Houston participated in the Houston Post Oak Jockey Club which frequently met at Stanley's race track. The officers of the jockey club included Robert Barr, the first postmaster general of Texas, Lardner C. Stanley, G. W. Adams and Henry Kessler. The club was organized on September 23, 1839 in a meeting at Kessler's Arcade in Houston. Races at the track were held during the late 1830's to the early 1840's[116].

Today, Temple Terrace is a small neighborhood of middle class, brick homes west of Taft Street. In 2008, many of the homes were in moderately good condition with values of less than $100,000, however, the land values put the total value of lots in the $200,000 - $300,000 range[117].

Redevelopment of tracts within the subdivision has brought new homes to the area. The construction of eleven town homes in the Townes of Buffalo Bayou Subdivision, located on Allen Parkway at Stanford Street began in 1996. The Townes of Buffalo Bayou project was a joint venture of the Work Organization of developer Shannon Work and Carlos Vruderer of Guatemala, the landowner. Home values of the Townes of Buffalo Bayou average about $350,000 in 2008[118].

Other portions of the Temple Terrace Subdivision have been converted to commercial development. The tract of land on the east side of Stanford Street at Allen Parkway became the home of KHOU-TV in 1960. The television station known as Channel 11 started in Galveston as KGUL-TV on March 23, 1953. The station moved to Houston in 1958. In June, 1959, KGUL became KHOU, and the station changed its city of license to Houston with the FCC license showing both Houston and Galveston as service areas. On April 20, 1960, the KHOU relocated its offices and studios to its present location at 1945 Allen Parkway. From the late 1950's to 1984, the CBS affiliate was owned by Corinthian Broadcasting of Indianapolis. In 1984, the station was sold to the Belo Corporation[119].

Although the studios occupy a prominent and visible site on the south bank of Buffalo Bayou, the prestige of such a location was tarnished somewhat during Tropical Storm Allison in 2001. The studios of KHOU were flooded as the bayou overflowed its banks, and the television station went off the air for about an hour and a half. Builders and developers in Houston have often underestimated or ignored the forces of nature found in Buffalo Bayou. The Sears building, having survived the 1929 flood of 43.5 feet, was inundated six years later when the flood of 1935 reached 49.0 feet. Twenty-five years later, the KHOU facility was built on a site in the flood plain that would be breached by the 36.6 feet flood waters of TS Allison, only the third highest level on record[120].

The headquarters of the Service Corporation International was built on former home lots of the Temple Terrace Subdivision, east of KHOU, in 1975. SCI, founded in 1962 by Robert L. Waltrip, is the largest funeral and cemetery services company in North America. This corporate giant has its roots in a family business that began in 1925 with the establishment of the Heights Funeral Home by Mrs. S. P. Waltrip and her son Robert E. Waltrip. After the death of his father in 1951, Robert L. Waltrip took over the business and grew it into the industry leader. In 2008, the company operated over 1,340 funeral homes and about three hundred sixty-five cemeteries in the United States, Puerto Rico, Canada and Germany. The corporate initials on the high rise office building are visible from many vantage points along the bayou green space west of the central business district[121].

Sam Houston's Ranch... in Houston!

It is very difficult to see Taft Street from the water level of Buffalo Bayou. The bayou begins a sharp left turn at this point, and, over the years, the current has created a steep cut bank on the right side. To prevent Allen Parkway from falling into the bayou, a concrete bulkhead, about twenty feet high, both supports the roadway and keeps the bayou's natural erosion power at bay.

If you were to climb to the top of the bank and stand on the sidewalk at the foot of Taft Street, you could peer into the distance to the south and see West Dallas Avenue on the elevated horizon. With a little imagination, you can see back to the time of the first years of the Republic and, in your mind, envision a small log cabin, bounded on the east by a timber post fence, that was recognizable as belonging on Sam Houston's Ranch.

During the formative months of the new Republic and its new capital at Houston, several persons sought to stake out new land holdings in the vicinity of the town. In early 1837, Sam Houston acquired thirty acres west of town on the San Felipe Road. He built a log cabin there and established a farm that became known as the "Houston Ranch[122]."

Other prominent farmers, veterans of the Texas army and members of the new government also settled on tracts of land on the edge of Houston. John Woodruff, a farmer from Brazoria, built a home on fifty acres on the east side of Houston's Ranch on a tract that later became the Castanie Subdivision. To the west of Sam Houston's Ranch was Mirabeau B. Lamar's homestead of one hundred fifty acres which he called Oak Grove[123].

After President Lamar engineered the relocation of the capital of Texas to Austin in 1839, the land on the outskirts of Houston became less valuable or practical for government officials to own. In late 1843, Sam Houston sold parts of his farm to Lewis Levy for about $75 per acre as land prices around Houston had fallen nearly twenty-five percent after the loss of the capital of the Republic[124].

In 1845, George Baker purchased part of the Houston Ranch from Levy, and in a series of purchases in subsequent years, Baker acquired the remainder of the ranch tract and several adjacent tracts to become one of the major land owners along this section of the San Felipe Road. As Baker consolidated his holdings, the delineation of specific tracts such as the Houston Ranch was blurred. In the case of the Houston Ranch, for example, the western boundaries of the thirty acre farm became no longer visible on survey maps as it was incorporated into larger tracts of land owned by Baker[125].

However, through a quirk of fate, the eastern boundary of the Houston Ranch has remained identifiable on survey maps, even today.

At the time that Sam Houston acquired his ranch, he chose it in the vacant lands south of the John Austin Survey. Since the San Felipe Road generally followed the east-west line of the southern boundary of the John Austin Survey, the deed describing the Houston Ranch began at the San Felipe Road and described a rectangular tract of thirty acres lying perpendicular to the road. This alignment of the tract placed the Houston Ranch at 10 degrees southeast (later surveyed as 12 degrees southeast) since the road dipped slightly to the southwest[126].

In the late 1840's, the San Felipe Road was straightened to run due west along the John Austin south boundary line. This realignment placed the road a short distance north of the Houston Ranch, as seen on survey maps after 1847 and even today. The realignment also left the eastern boundary of the Houston Ranch as an intrusion into the adjoining tract which is Lot 40 of the Obedience Smith Survey A-696. Although the boundary lines of other tracts in the area were normalized to the straightened San Felipe Road, the intrusion of the Houston Ranch never was. It is this 2-1/2 acre intrusion that can be identified and which allows us to definitively place the location of the Sam Houston Ranch[127].

By following the legal description of the Houston Ranch from the earliest deed records, we can trace the boundary lines over the streets of a modern Houston street map with it generally lying south and west of the intersection of West Dallas Avenue and Taft Street.

According to descendants of George Baker, a photo taken in 1916 shows a cabin which is believed to have been the original cabin on Sam Houston's Ranch. A timber post fence to the east of the cabin is probably the eastern boundary of the property. If that is the case, then, the cabin was in the vicinity of the modern Taft Street[128].

Although a lot of attention has been given to Sam Houston's log cabin "Presidential" residence in Houston, little notice has been made of Sam Houston's country retreat southwest of town. Now, at least, we know where it was.

Buffalo Bayou Park

The construction of Buffalo Drive (Allen Parkway) in 1925 divided the Spring Garden tract and the adjoining Vauxhall Gardens tract belonging to Garrett Hardcastle in half. This land on the south bank of the bayou was cleared of its riparian growth in the early 1950's when Allen Parkway was expanded and re-graded. The resulting green space was acquired by the City for park land in 1981. The subsequent development of this broad park land, totaling 124 acres generally confined between Allen Parkway and Memorial Drive and extending from Shepherd Drive to Sabine Street, has become the popular Buffalo Bayou Park[129].

The portion of the park on the north side of Allen Parkway, near Gillette Street, includes a large point of land created by a broad loop of the bayou. When Memorial Drive was opened from Shepherd Drive to downtown on January 10, 1956, the tip of this point of land was separated from the rest to form a somewhat isolated, tree-lined park along the south bank of Buffalo Bayou that lies north of Memorial Drive and opposite the Glenwood Cemetery. The Houston Police Officers Memorial occupies this site[130].

The broad green space that lies between Allen Parkway and Memorial Drive and extends from near Taft Street to Sabine Street is a park land that contains some of Houston's finest public art in addition to the City's extraordinary recreational spaces. The simple, but peaceful environs of Jane's Garden are located near Taft Street. Internationally acclaimed British sculptor Henry Moore's "Large Spindle Piece" rests defiantly on the small knoll near the end of Gillette Street. Farther to the east are the playgrounds of Eleanor Tinsley Park, a park within a park that also includes the Shady Grove sculpture.

On the other side of the bayou, the Buffalo Bayou Park is home to the enigmatic sculpture entitled "Passage Inacheve" which sits in a meadow-like opening along the hiking trail just west of the foot bridge over the Tapley Tributary. Lastly, to the east near the Sabine Street bridge, shrills and thrills of youngsters of many ages can be heard at the Lee and Joe Jamail Skatepark.

Police Officers' Memorial

Although highly visible from both Allen Parkway and Memorial Drive, the Houston Police Officers' Memorial is difficult to get to by car and almost inaccessible on foot. Its isolation is appropriate and thought provoking. The pink granite monument in Buffalo Bayou Park opposite Glenwood Cemetery pays a final and lasting tribute to those police officers of the City who died in the line of duty.

Shaped in the fashion of a Greek Cross, the Memorial consists of five stepped, forty foot square pyramids in a ziggurat design. The central pyramid rises 12.5 feet above ground, while four inverted pyramids sink to a depth of twelve feet. A bubbling reflection pool at the apex is surrounded by four polished Texas pink granite slabs inscribed with the names of the officers who have fallen while in service to the citizens of the community. In 1992, that granite slab was engraved with the names of eighty-six police officers.

The Police Officers' Memorial, located at 2400 Memorial Drive, was designed by Jesus Bautista Moroles, a native Texan who was born in Corpus Christi in 1950 and raised in Dallas. The monument, which was seven years in planning and cost $1.2 million, was dedicated on November 19, 1992. From the vantage of a small shelter to the west of the Memorial, an officer keeps vigil on the site day and night. The first honor guard was the Chief of Police Sam Nuchia.

Sculptor Jesus Moroles was contracted in 2004 to make restorations to the Police Officers' Memorial where pieces of stone had fallen off the entrance, holes had formed as the ground shrunk away from the granite, and mineral deposits corroded the fountain at the top. Today, the Memorial stands as a proud tribute to these public servants amidst the salute of the national, state and City flags[131].

Jane's Garden

Jane's Garden is a pocket park across Memorial Drive from the Police Officers Memorial in a small rise amid mature oak trees. It was created about 2002 by friends and family of Jane Howe Gregory a master gardener and nature enthusiast. Paths, benches and engraved moss rocks make the small park an enchanting and inviting place to stop and contemplate[132].

Henry Moore Sculpture

A major exhibit of monumental works by pre-eminent British sculptor Henry Moore was recently held at the famous Royal Botanical Gardens at Kew in London. Twenty-eight of Moore's outdoor sculptures were gathered from across England and sited in Kew Gardens from September, 2007 to March, 2008, making it the first exhibition of its kind in London. It was also one of the most well-attended events ever held at Kew Gardens[133].

But, did you know that we have one of Henry Moore's sculptures right here in Houston?

"Large Spindle Piece" was created by Moore in 1969 and was originally part of Moore's Spindle series which was placed in London's Hyde Park to honor the sculptor. In 1979, the tall bronze sculpture was purchased by the Knox Foundation and given to the City of Houston[134].

Originally, the sculpture was to stand in Tranquility Park. However, when Moore came to Houston, he deemed the proposed site there unsuitable, saying it was too complicated, too confined and that the architecture surrounding it would interfere with the lines of the piece. Instead, he selected a prominent knoll along Buffalo Bayou, between Allen Parkway and Memorial Drive, where the sculpture stands today[135].

Moore's Spindle series evolved from a visit he made to the Vatican in 1925. He was fascinated by Michelangelo's depiction of God creating man with the touching index fingers in the Sistine Chapel fresco. Describing his "Large Spindle Piece," Moore said, "Sculpturally, it's two points just about to meet. This work is on the same theme, only the two fingers are going out, not in[136]."

The "Large Spindle Piece" is a twelve foot tall cast bronze abstract sculpture mounted on a circular cast concrete base that is painted matte brown. Although this is a significant work of art, there is no plaque or sign near it that identifies the sculpture or the artist. Upon close inspection, the artist's signature and designation of the sculpture's number in the series ("4/6") can be seen near the base. A foundry mark of Hermann Noack of Berlin also appears on the lower edge, facing the Houston skyline. Unfortunately, as is the case with so many stunning pieces of art around the world, this sculpture has been marred by graffiti, a small amount of which is shown in the photo.

Henry Moore was born in 1898 in Yorkshire, England and died on August 31, 1986, at the age of 88, at his home in Hertfordshire. As is befitting such an important British sculptor, his body is interred in the Artist's Corner at St Paul's Cathedral in London. He had an interesting career in the arts, including a period during World War II when he was commissioned as a war artist, notably producing powerful drawings of Londoners sleeping in the London Underground while sheltering from the blitz. These drawings boosted Moore's international reputation, particularly in America[137].

Photo credit: Linda Gorski

Henry Moore's "Large Spindle Piece" brings the elegance of world class art to Houston.

However, Moore is best known for his abstract monumental bronze and carved marble sculptures which can be seen in many outdoor spaces around the world as public works of art. Occasionally, Moore created his large scale works using fiberglass, as in the "Large Reclining Figure" on display at Kew. The lightweight nature of fiberglass was especially suited to the production and transportation of a few of his larger works[138].

Although Moore's works are exhibited in major cities around the world, Moore's iconic spindle on Buffalo Bayou is Houston's best kept art secret.

Eleanor Tinsley Park

East of the Henry Moore sculpture, the bayou pulls close to Allen Parkway. On a high ridge above the bayou, the City established a small "park within a park" named in honor of former City Council member Eleanor Tinsley.

Eleanor Burleson Tinsley, born on October 31, 1926 in Dallas, was a graduate of Baylor University. After moving to Houston with her husband in 1953, Tinsley was elected to the school board of the

Houston Independent School District in 1969 and served on the board until 1973. In 1979, Eleanor Tinsley was elected as Houston's first woman at-large Council member. During her tenure on Council, she vigorously promoted park development and the City's authority to control local signage and billboards. Tinsley served on City Council for sixteen years until term limitations caused her retirement in 1995[139].

The Eleanor Tinsley Park sits on high ground that was a portion of the Hardcastle Subdivision of 1866 which became the Freedmenstown neighborhood shortly after the Civil War. The construction of Allen Parkway left the end of the old subdivision on the north side of the roadway and it was included in the park land along the bayou. The low lying areas on the east side of the park contain a boat dock, playgrounds and volleyball courts today, however, these ravines and slopes had been developed as the Vauxhall Gardens by Garrett S. Hardcastle between 1855 and 1857. Vauxhall Gardens was a popular recreation spot where German festivals were held in the latter part of the nineteenth century. Over a century later, this location continues to be a venue for the City's finest festivals[140].

On the western end of Eleanor Tinsley Park, there is small plaza among the trees which contains a unique sculpture by local artist Tim Bailey. The corten steel and copperized steel sculpture called "Shady Grove" was installed at Eleanor Tinsley Park in 2001. The City of Houston initially proposed a park dedicated to organizations devoted to victim's rights in 1997, and this plaza and its municipal art were dedicated "in honor of all victims of crime" during National Crime Victim's Rights Week in April, 2002[141].

Passage Inacheve

Buffalo Bayou Park on the north side of the bayou, across from Eleanor Tinsley Park, also is a well used green space. As the hiking trail on the north bank emerges from under Memorial Drive, it enters an isolated grassy area that is bounded on the east by the tree line of the Tapley Tributary. In this open space along the trail is a work of municipal art entitled "Passage Inacheve" which means "incomplete pass" in French.

Passage Inacheve is a galvanized steel and concrete art work by Linnea Glatt which includes photographic images by Francis Merritt Thompson. Glatt is a Dallas artist who was born in 1949 in Bismarck, ND. The piece was acquired by the City in 1990[142].

Tapley Tributary

The north bank of Buffalo Bayou near Sawyer Street is separated, and somewhat isolated, from the Sixth Ward neighborhood by Memorial Drive. As a result, this part of Buffalo Bayou Park is a pleasant green space that receives much less use than the companion park land on the south bank of the bayou. The hiking trail coming from the Waugh Drive area passes under Memorial Drive and emerges in the grassy meadow where the unique art structure entitled "Passage Inacheve" stands. Heading east from the "Passage Inacheve," the hiking trail crosses a rustic footbridge over a small stream that has been named in honor of Charles Tapley[143].

In the late 1970's, Charles Tapley, a local landscape architect, designed an innovative site along the north bank of Buffalo Bayou west of Sabine Street that included a tributary with riparian plantings and seating areas with attractive granite steps. However, after a quarter of a century of neglect, Tapley's initiative was in dire need of revitalization. In 2004, the Buffalo Bayou Partnership sponsored a project to restore Tapley's site to its original vision[144].

Tapley's design included several resting places along the hiking trail and on the upper slopes of the bayou's bank that entice the visitor to sit and view the beauty of the bayou. The simple, yet elegant, granite benches are placed within view of the bayou and the tributary. High on the slope near the new Lee and Joe Jamail Skatepark is the largest of Tapley's seating stones. The triangular granite benches form a shady circle amidst the small cluster of trees. This set of granite stones is the largest seating area of the tributary site. Other stones that provide rest stops for an individual or couple are located at places near the creek and along the trail.

Within the tributary, Tapley created rapids and cascades to tumble the water as it flows from the wetland pond to its confluence with the bayou. Directly below the bridge over the stream, a set of granite blocks creates a small rapid where the water bubbles over the blocks and channels while flowing under the canopy of cypress trees. A few yards later, the stream flows over the circular cascade of large granite stones that open into a block-lined pool. Along the course of the tributary, there are individual granite seating stones in the form of square blocks.

The goal of the restoration of the Tapley Tributary was to demonstrate the benefits of wetland habitat within the urban environment. Undesirable and invasive plants were removed from the drainage, and wetland plants, such as cattails and lilies, that improve water quality were planted in the tributary. Since the Tapley Tributary is the storm water outfall from White Street and the Sixth Ward neighborhood, the wetland plants which have root structures that can remove minerals, heavy metals and toxins from the water, help to improve the urban runoff that flows into Buffalo Bayou. River birch and cypress trees were added to the 150 yard long stream to help stabilize the banks and provide an attractive bayou woodland. The enhancements and management practices used in the restoration of Tapley Tributary will be applied to other sites along the bayou[145].

And in case you think Charles Tapley's resume is limited to Buffalo Bayou, you'd be wrong. Tapley actually opened his architectural practice in 1960 and has designed parks, churches and other buildings around the country. In addition to his master plan for Buffalo Bayou which called for natural wide banks instead of a "concrete slip and slide" draining to the Houston Ship Channel, Tapley also designed Tranquility Park in downtown Houston. He designed the color scheme for the repainting of the University of Houston-Downtown's main building. Tapley also helped found the Lynn R. Lowrey Arboretum at Rice University and is currently on the architecture faculty at the University of Houston[146].

Take time to stop in the Tapley Tributary park space. The natural beauty and peacefulness of this bayou tributary with the backdrop of our great city is a rare treat and a grand tribute to Charles Tapley's vision.

Washington and Glenwood Cemeteries

Beyond Studewood Street and past the Memorial Heights homes, the wooded north bank of Buffalo Bayou extends for a little over one half mile toward downtown. The trees and brush that occupy the slopes above the roadway of Memorial Drive conceal the tombstones of Washington Cemetery and, a little farther down where the bayou turns left under the road, Glenwood Cemetery. These cemeteries are the final resting place of many of Houston's foremost businessmen, civic leaders and ordinary citizens.

The Washington Cemetery, located at 2911 Washington Avenue, was established in 1887 when a group of local German businessmen formed the Deutsche Gesellschaft, an association to establish a cemetery for German citizens of Houston. Known officially as the German Society Cemetery, the cemetery was located beyond the city limits of the time on a twenty-seven acre tract of land the Deutsche Gesellschaft purchased from the heirs of John Lawrence and Thomas Hart on February 8, 1887. The first burials took place on March 20, 1887 when J. Turner and Annie Fraser were interred[147].

One section of Washington Cemetery, consisting of forty-two grave sites, was set aside for the burials of Confederate veterans of the Civil War. Another section, designated as the Stranger's Rest, contains about 2,000 burials. Little information is known about those who are buried in the Stranger's Rest. Perhaps they were drifters, paupers or persons who died accidentally and had no other place to be buried. Each burial is a single grave space identified only by a brick-size marker with an engraved number[148].

The cemetery's early years strongly reflected its connection with Houston's German community. The cemetery records were maintained in German until 1901, and many German families are represented among the graves. It was commonly referred to as the "Old German Cemetery." But, as a result of the anti-German sentiment that arose in Houston and the nation during World War I, the German Society Cemetery was renamed Washington Cemetery in 1918[149].

One of most intriguing persons buried in Washington Cemetery is Emma Seelye, the only woman to become a member of the Grand Army of the Republic, a Union Veterans organization. Of course, to be a member of the GAR, Mrs. Seelye had to have served in the Union Army during the Civil War. That's where the story gets interesting[150].

Mrs. Seelye was born Sarah Emma Evelyn Edmundson in New Brunswick, Canada in 1841. In 1858, at age 17, she ran away from home to avoid an unwanted marriage. She masqueraded as a man while she worked as a publisher's agent in the Midwest. Then, on May 25, 1861, Sarah Edmundson enlisted as a man in Company F, 2nd Michigan Volunteer Infantry Regiment under alias Franklin Thompson of Flint, Michigan. Sarah, as Franklin Thompson, served two years in the Union army as a male nurse, as the brigade post-master and as an agent on special assignments for the secret service. Not surprisingly, in her service as a spy, she penetrated the Confederate lines "disguised" as a woman. Sarah Edmundson's secret military career came to an end when she became ill with malaria in 1863. Fearing that medical treatment would result in her discovery, she deserted her regiment and lived in Ohio as a female[151].

In 1864, Sarah Edmundson wrote the story of her exploits as a Union spy and a master of disguise in a book entitled: "Nurse and Spy in the Union Army" by S. Emma E. Edmonds. The book sold over 175,000 copies. The proceeds of her book were donated to charity for soldiers at the war front[152].

After the war, Sarah Emma Edmundson married Linus Seelye, and they had three children. She and her husband moved to La Porte to be with her stepdaughter and family in 1893. They built a home on Main Street in La Porte[153].

On April 22, 1897, Sarah Seelye became only woman member of Grand Army of the Republic when she joined the McClellan Post, GAR in Houston. She suffered a relapse of malaria and died in LaPorte on September 5, 1898 at age 57. The remains of Sarah Seelye were transferred to the GAR plot in the German Cemetery in Houston in 1901. Her grave is indicated by a simple metal marker. In the 1990's, Sarah Emma Edmundson Seelye was inducted into the US Army Military Intelligence Hall of Fame at Fort Huachuca, Arizona[154].

At the time of its creation, Washington Cemetery consisted of 27 acres. In the mid-1950's, the City of Houston took 5.7 acres of Washington Cemetery for the construction of Memorial Drive. Fortunately, since the south end of the cemetery had never been developed, no burials had to be removed. The current size of the cemetery property is 48.37 acres. Glenwood Cemetery bought the

Washington Cemetery in 1999 and the two cemeteries are maintained jointly[155].

Glenwood Cemetery

Glenwood Cemetery lies immediately to the east and adjacent to Washington Cemetery on land that was settled shortly after the founding of Houston by the prominent attorney and legislator Archibald Wynns. Wynns was born in Paris, Tennessee on December 25, 1807 and while living in Tennessee, he was admitted to the bar in that state as well as Illinois. He married Martha Elizabeth Edmunds while still in Tennessee, and they came to Texas in 1837. By January, 1839, Archibald Wynns had bought a large, narrow tract on the north bank of Buffalo Bayou from S. P. Hollingsworth where he established a plantation[156].

Archibald Wynns was one of the rising stars of Texas. Upon his arrival in Houston, he opened a law office on Congress Avenue with William Lawrence. The two of them formed one of the leading law firms of the new republic. In addition, both Wynns and Lawrence were elected to the Congress of the Republic of Texas. Archibald Wynns was first elected to the House of Representatives in 1838, and in 1841 and 1842, he represented Harris County in the House in the 6th Congress of the Republic. William Lawrence was elected to the House of Representatives of the 3rd and 4th Congress of Texas, 1838-1840, as a representative from Harrisburg. In 1842, Lawrence was elected as a senator from Harris, Galveston and Liberty Counties for the 7th, 8th and 9th Congresses. Wynns also served as the alderman from the Fourth Ward in 1840[157].

The combination of public service and the legal practice proved successful for Wynns. His declared real assets of $10,000 in the 1850 census placed him, at forty-two years old, among the wealthiest residents of Harris County. The Wynns family was prospering in Texas as well. A year after coming to Texas, their first son George was born. He was followed by daughters Julia, Florida, then sons Thomas and Charles, and lastly, daughter Ella in 1857[158].

Archibald Wynns' untimely death at age fifty-one on August 21, 1859, while in Jackson, Louisiana, cut short his promising career. Fortunately, his estate which was valued at $7,000 in real assets and

$7,500 of personal assets in 1860, greatly benefited the family. Martha and the Wynns children continued to live in Houston in their home on the corner of Rusk Avenue and La Branch Street. Daughter Florida Wynns McLelland Bishop, when she died, was buried in Glenwood Cemetery about fifty yards from where she was born[159].

After the death of Archibald Wynns, his plantation was the site of a brick quarry operated by William H. King. King was a successful master brick layer who served as the mayor of Houston in 1859 and who, by 1860 at forty-six year old, had accumulated real assets of $26,000 and personal assets of $12,000. He and Elias Thorpe, a brick maker, operated the W. H. King Brick Yard located at the west end of State Street, and the business was in operation as late as 1869. However, it appears that King had died by 1870 since only his wife and family are recorded in the 1870 census. The brick yard was purchased by investors for development as Glenwood Cemetery[160].

In anticipation of the establishment of the cemetery, a group of business leaders purchased about twenty acres in Lot 7 of the Hollingsworth Survey in January, 1870. On November 5, 1870, Alfred J. Whitaker placed an ad in the local newspaper to promote the proposed charter for the Houston Cemetery Company. Whitaker was the spokesman for the effort to provide Houston with a rural cemetery park, and he later was appointed as the superintendent of the improvement project for the new cemetery[161].

Alfred Whitaker was a twenty-seven year old, trained botanist who came to Houston from England in 1859. He was already a fairly wealthy man, as indicated by assets of $30,000 declared in the 1860 census, and he established a successful nursery and seed business as he made Houston his new home. By 1870, Whitaker and his Texas-born wife Courtney had settled with their four young children into a large and stylish home in the western suburbs. Three household servants assisted the Whitakers, and a nurseryman and three gardeners were employed in Whitaker's landscaping business. He was the obvious choice to oversee the development of the new park-like cemetery[162].

On May 12, 1871, the Texas Legislature incorporated the Houston Cemetery Company for Alfred Whitaker and "such other persons as may associate with him" and authorized the company to acquire land for cemetery purposes. This legislation introduced new concepts of regulation and responsibilities for cemeteries in Texas although the ideas had previously been included in rural cemeteries such as Green-Wood in Brooklyn and Laurel Hill in Philadelphia. The Houston Cemetery Company was required to survey the grounds of the cemetery and plot the lots, drives and walkways, a map of which was to be filed with the county registrar of deeds. Additionally, and perhaps more significantly, the company was to maintain a permanent fund for the maintenance and improvement of the cemetery. This was a major departure from the way cemeteries had been dealt with in the past[163].

Work on the new cemetery began with the clearing of lots and roadways on roughly sixty acres that were thickly grown with short leaf pine, sweet gum, wild peach, cottonwood, oak and an occasional magnolia and "picturesquely broken with frequent ravines and numerous rustic ridges." By late October, 1871, the cemetery had been laid off into fifteen sections, each named with a letter and encircled by a graded avenue. The road into the cemetery passed through thirty foot wide entry and descended a deep ravine with precipitous banks over which a bridge was being constructed. The cemetery itself was enclosed with a picket fence five to six feet high. Several names were under consideration for the cemetery. Alfred Whitaker proposed the place be called Montepose, but the name Glenwood was selected at the meeting of the stockholders and directors in February, 1872[164].

Enthusiasm for the new cemetery was expressed throughout the community. The Masonic Grand Lodge held a dedication for Glenwood Cemetery on Friday, June 14, 1872 that commenced with a large procession through the city to the grounds. The first burial in Glenwood was then held on June 19, 1872. Since the City of Houston condemned St. Vincent's Cemetery as a burial ground, local Catholics secured a section of Glenwood Cemetery for their use. Later in 1872, the remains of a number of burials in the Episcopal Cemetery were unearthed and reinterred in Glenwood[165].

Under Whitaker's guidance, Glenwood was designed in the style of a Victorian-era cemetery park to resemble beautiful gardens with winding paths and elaborate stone sculptures. On Sunday, January 18, 1874, Glenwood attracted a large crowd of ladies and gentlemen who showed up to view the flowers and the rural scenery and to walk among the thought provoking monuments. Especially prominent was the recently erected Sessums Monument, a resplendent marble sculpture depicting a broken oak clad with encircling vines. The City's mule-drawn street car service, which began running to Glenwood Cemetery along Washington Road in 1874, popularized the regular weekend outings to the cemetery which would continue for years[166].

The popularity of the cemetery park exceeded the expectations and the development plans of the cemetery company. In August, 1875, there were suggestions that Glenwood Cemetery could be "transformed from a plot of vine grown woods, rough declivities and deep ravines" into a beautiful cemetery if the company would spend some money to build bridges, lay out the avenues and make the place attractive. By July, 1878, many improvements had been made and the cemetery was reported to be in a "most flourishing condition" and open to accept visitors[167].

Houston families made the visit to Glenwood a regular feature of special commemorative days during the year. However during 1883 and 1884, the upgrade of the street car line to a street railway made it difficult to get to the cemetery. The street railway line to Glenwood Cemetery was completed on October 10, 1884 after two years of construction, and the public responded overwhelmingly. On Saturday, November 1 and Sunday, November 2, 1884, over 3,000 men, women and children visited Glenwood Cemetery and brought flowers to the graves which had been cleaned and trimmed by the cemetery's workmen[168].

Throughout the decade of the 1880's, the well kept grounds of Glenwood attracted hundreds of people on pleasant weekends and even more visitors on special days such as Easter, All Saints Day and Memorial Day. The grounds were noted for being scrupulously clean, and the finely cultivated shrubbery and flowers were neatly trimmed and well maintained by the cemetery management. A new bridge over the ravine near the entrance to Glenwood Cemetery was built in September, 1885 to replace the old bridge. The celebrations of Memorial Day, known as Decoration Day by Union and Confederate veterans groups, filled the cemetery with reverential graveside ceremonies and beautiful floral displays by the ladies' groups. So large were the crowds at Glenwood that on June 10, 1891, the City

Council approved the construction of a double track for the street railway along Washington Avenue to handle the visitors[169].

Yet, on Decoration Day, May 31, 1895, the celebration was not observed to the same extent as it had been previously. Fewer old soldiers turned out for the event although flowers were placed at Glenwood Cemetery by ladies' groups. Although fewer veterans of the Civil War survived thirty years after the conflict, the decline in participation at the cemetery events indicated that there were other issues. A group of lot owners in Glenwood Cemetery met on February 21, 1896 to discuss the management of the cemetery. They selected W. D. Cleveland as the chairman of the committee to meet with Thomas Tinsley, president of the Houston Cemetery Company, to address issues of proper care of the cemetery grounds. The lot owners felt that the plants were not watered, the lots were not kept up, and the bridge across gully was dangerous and in need of replacement. There seemed to be a general neglect of the cemetery by its management[170].

Tinsley, a New York financier who had gained a controlling interest in the cemetery company, rejected the claims of the owners' committee and stated that he would make no changes in the management of the cemetery. The lots owners filed suit in the District Court of Judge Sam H. Brashear on March 27, 1896 and requested that a receiver be appointed to oversee the operation of Glenwood. Judge Brashear decided in favor of the lot owners and, on April 24, 1896, he appointed William Christian as the receiver for the Glenwood Cemetery property[171].

On May 22, 1896, Court of Appeals of the First District upheld the appointment of a receiver in the Glenwood Cemetery lot owners suit against Tinsley. The opinion in the case was one of the first of its kind to recognize the principle that corporations accept a public trust and have obligations to its shareholders. In September, 1896, William Christian, receiver for the Glenwood Cemetery property, was authorized by the court to proceed with improvements to the bridge and to address other maintenance items on the property[172].

Glenwood Cemetery was returned to its floral beauty and finely cultivated appearance. On Memorial Day, May 31, 1897, approximately 5,000 people witnessed the impressive ceremonies that were performed by the Union and Confederate veterans associations at

Glenwood. The tradition of observing National Decoration Day and other special commemorative events continued at the cemetery into the twentieth century.

The Houston Cemetery Company was reorganized as the Glenwood Cemetery Association on July 24, 1904, and in 1969, the Glenwood Cemetery Association was succeeded by Glenwood Cemetery, Inc., Texas non-profit corporation. Glenwood Cemetery bought the adjoining Washington Cemetery in 1999, and the combined cemeteries occupy a total of over 118 acres. Seventeen acres are available for future development[173].

The Glenwood Cemetery Historic Preservation Foundation was established in 1999 to preserve the historic heritage of the grounds and the monuments. While most of the earlier cemeteries of Houston were woefully negligent in the grave location and maintenance of the burials of prominent Houstonians, Glenwood Cemetery is a permanent record of many of the civic leaders, noted businessman and ordinary citizens who have made Houston a prosperous city of the nineteenth, twentieth and twenty-first centuries[174].

Glenwood Cemetery is also the location of the Houston Firefighters' Memorial. Volunteer firefighters bought a lot in Glenwood Cemetery for members of the department in May, 1888. On May 27, 1889, the selection committee for the Firemen's Monument for Glenwood Cemetery chose a design for the monument. It was to be a 25 to 30 foot marble and granite monument with a life size statue of a fireman. The granite shaft came from Aberdeen, Scotland, and the statue was carved from marble in Carrara, Italy. The oldest living volunteer firefighter at the time, Robert Brewster, reportedly modeled for the 5 foot, 2 inch tall statue. The Firemen's Monument was unveiled at the cemetery on May 1, 1890[175].

The monument on the firefighters lot in Glenwood Cemetery was moved to the front of Fire Station No. 1 at 410 Bagby Street (now, Landry's Aquarium) in 1976. In 1992, the monument was returned to its original location in Glenwood Cemetery. The Houston Firefighters' Memorial is the site of an annual memorial service for firefighters who have died in the line of duty[176].

Within the fenced boundary of Glenwood lies a small, but separate cemetery belonging to the Trinity Lutheran Church. In June, 1880, land for the cemetery was purchased on the east side of

Glenwood Cemetery. On March 11, 1881, the Trustees of the German Evangelical Lutheran Church requested permission from City Council to establish a cemetery adjoining Glenwood Cemetery. The entrance to the triangular shaped cemetery of 4,426 square feet is on Sawyer Street, near the east end of State Street, however, the gate is locked, except for funerals. Burials in the cemetery are reserved for church members. Trinity Lutheran Cemetery may be accessed through Glenwood where it is separated only by shrubbery[177].

Federal Reserve Bank

On the south bank of Buffalo Bayou, between Taft Street and Gillette Street, the stylish, new Federal Reserve Bank building stands brilliantly on the horizon. The oversized dimensions of the structure make the building seem comfortable in its surroundings when it is viewed from a distance. When seen up close, the Federal Reserve is an imposing fortress exuding the strength of our financial system. Less obvious is the rich history of the site upon which it stands.

The story of this tract of land, situated about one and one half miles west of downtown, begins shortly after the establishment of the town of Houston and involves one of the less well-known heroes of the Texas Revolution. Phineas Jenks Mahan, who was born in Bucks County, Pennsylvania on January 22, 1814, came to Texas in 1832 at age eighteen. He enlisted in Texas army on November 3, 1835 in the company of Captain Thomas K. Pearson. After the Siege of Bexar, Pearson's company was dispatched to Goliad. While Mahan's squad was guarding the horses, they were surprised by soldiers of Mexican General Urrea's army early in the morning of February 27, 1836. Mahan was captured and imprisoned at Matamoros. He was released on January 29, 1837, and eventually made his way to Houston. On August 1, 1838, the Houston Town Company conveyed the 55 acres of Lot 6 of the Hollingsworth Survey to Elisha Floyd and Sidney Collins who then sold it to Phineas J. Mahan on September 22, 1838 for $3,000. That fall, Mahan established his homestead near the center of Lot 6, locating his home and his business north of the San Felipe Road (present day West Dallas Avenue) and west of Spring Gully[178].

Phineas Mahan referred to himself as a practical gardener who was involved in "market gardening" and the cultivation of bees. From his farm, which he named Spring Garden, he sold fruit trees, shade trees, ornamental trees, grapevines and gardening tools. As early as 1841, he was also selling starter seeds at William Dankwerth's Store on Market Square. His operations had varied success initially and he almost lost his farm on at least one occasion, but, in later years, Mahan was more successful[179].

Phineas Jenks Mahan published the recollections of his experiences in the Texas revolution in a volume entitled "Reminiscences of the War for Texas Independence" in 1872. On May 3, 1875, Mahan died at the age of 61 years and was buried in the family burial ground, probably located on the Spring Garden property. His wife Emeline Hood Mahan filed his will for probate on September 23, 1876. All of his property, including Spring Garden, was left to his wife Emma, who was to provide for their three children, Emma, Franklin and Alexander. Emma Mahan and son Alexander J. H. Mahan moved to town to share a dwelling at Congress Avenue and LaBranch Street with Mrs. Samantha E. Compton, a widow. On October 1, 1880, Emma Mahan sold the 46-1/4 acres of Lot 6, Block 2 that had not previously been sold to Abraham Groesbeeck for $10,500. After the property was sold, Phineas J. Mahan's remains were removed from Spring Garden and reinterred in Glenwood Cemetery, Section C, Lot 143 on March 1, 1881. Emma Mahan died about 1891[180].

By the time that Abraham Groesbeeck purchased the Spring Garden, he had been a successful entrepreneur and influential businessman in Houston for over thirty years. Groesbeeck was born in Albany, NY about 1821. He came to Texas in 1838 with his cousin John D. Groesbeeck, a surveyor who platted the town of Galveston in that year. After living in New Orleans, where he married about 1847, Groesbeeck, wife Anna and his son Leonard moved to Houston about 1850[181].

In the mid-1850's, Abraham Groesbeeck joined with William M. Rice and others who, as merchants and entrepreneurs, prospered with the growing city. In 1859, these businessmen incorporated the Houston Cotton Compress Company, and during the Civil War, they made substantial fortunes with their blockade running operations. In

1868, Groesbeeck and others organized the Houston Ship Channel Company. He served as president of this venture designed to straighten, clear and deepen the Buffalo Bayou channel to Houston. Groesbeeck also had a long association with the Houston and Texas Central Railway, serving as the company president and as a director from about 1860 until the railroad was sold to Charles Morgan in 1877. When the Houston and Texas Central Railway extended its tracks to Limestone County in 1870, it established a community which was named Groesbeck in honor of Abraham Groesbeeck. The town was incorporated in 1871 and, a few years later, became the county seat[182].

The Spring Garden property was acquired for the Houston Brick Works, one of Groesbeeck's new business ventures in the early 1880's. By September, 1881, he was advertising the quality products provided by the Houston Brick Works. About the same time, Groesbeeck bought the old Capitol Hotel on the northwest corner of Texas Avenue and Main Street. He demolished the two story frame structure that served as the Capitol of the Republic from 1837 to 1839, and then replaced it with a five story brick hotel which he also named the Capitol Hotel[183].

But this time, Groesbeeck's business ventures were less successful than in the past. He lost the Capitol Hotel and other properties due to delinquent taxes. His former business associate William Marsh Rice acquired both the Capitol Hotel and Groesbeeck's interests in the Houston Brick Works in 1885. Abraham Groesbeeck died in Houston on January 23, 1886, at age 65[184].

Frederick Allyn Rice, William Marsh Rice's younger brother, took over as president of the Houston Brick Works Company. By April, 1887, the company was manufacturing 40,000 to 50,000 pressed clay bricks per day in facilities on the north bank of Buffalo Bayou at Sabine Street and on the Spring Garden property. Competition in the local brick market was intense, and the Spring Garden operations of the Houston Brick Works were transferred to a tract in the Brunner Addition on Lot 2 of the John Reinerman Survey in 1891. Nevertheless, on June 29, 1897, the City of Houston raised the assessment of the Spring Garden tract from $13,800 to $19,425. By 1898, price cutting by the Butler Brick Works had caused significant losses for the Houston Brick Works. In the midst of this difficult business climate, William Marsh Rice was murdered in New York on September 23, 1900, and his business holdings were managed by his estate until claims against his will could be settled[185].

At this time, the newly organized Houston Golf Club was looking for a place to establish its facilities. In March, 1904, William Marsh Rice, Jr., a charter member of the Houston Golf Club, executed a lease on the Houston Brick Works Spring Garden property to the golf club for $1 per year. On these 46.25 acres located on the San Felipe Road, west of town, they built a clubhouse and a nine hole golf course[186].

The Houston Brick Works Company ceased to exist in 1907. The assets of the company, including the Spring Garden property, were transferred to Rice Institute (renamed Rice University in 1960) on December 19, 1907. Shortly thereafter, P. B. Timpson, treasurer of the Houston Country Club, was notified that the club's lease on the Spring Garden property would terminate at the end of October, 1909, so the Houston Country Club relocated to a site on Harrisburg Boulevard in 1908. As a result, the Spring Garden land lay vacant from then until 1916[187].

The City of Houston acquired the Spring Garden property from the Rice Institute in November, 1916 in exchange for some lots in downtown Houston and taxes due. The city built a garbage incinerator at the north end Golf Links Place near the head of Spring Gully. The site was used by the city as a dumping ground and garbage trench. A few city maintenance buildings were located on the west side of Spring Gully[188].

In the late 1920's, an eleven acre tract west of Spring Gully was set aside for a new hospital that would be accessed from the new Buffalo Drive (renamed Allen Parkway in 1961), the roadway that was built in 1925 along the south bank of Buffalo Bayou. On February 3, 1931, Alfred C. Finn and Joseph Finger were selected by the City to design the new city-county hospital which was designated as the "Outpatient and Ward Building, City and County Hospital[189]."

The designs for the new twelve story, skyscraper-style hospital were submitted on October 24, 1931, but construction was delayed because of the lack of funding for the project. Finally, funds were made available through the Public Works Administration, a federal agency created in 1933 to fund public works projects. The construction of the new Jefferson Davis City County Hospital was approved by the City Council in November, 1934, and Albert Finn was awarded the contract in September, 1935. Ben Taub, Chairman of the Jefferson Davis Hospital, presided over the ground breaking ceremonies for the hospital on March 23, 1936[190].

The cornerstone for the new $2 million hospital was laid on July 19, 1936 by Mayor Oscar F. Holcombe and County Judge W. H. Ward. The main building of the Art Deco structure was built in form of a cross with the central section consisting of twelve stories flanked by wings of eleven stories each. Texas limestone was used as a trim feature to lighten the buff brick face of the building. A two and three story Out Patient Wing was set off to the east side of the main building[191].

The rest of the tract contained the support facilities for the hospital complex. South of the main building and situated along Gillette Street, there was a seven story Nurses Home. The Power Plant and Laundry Building was built in the southwest corner of the tract, and adjacent to it was a one story "Colored Nurses Home." Construction on Jeff Davis Hospital complex was completed on October 28, 1937. However, a two story Convalescent Ward was added to the west side of the main building in 1949[192].

As a part of the improvements to the site to provide vehicular access to the nurses residence and the power plant, Gillette Street was widened and extended from West Dallas Avenue (formerly the San Felipe Road) to Buffalo Drive. The Spring Gully was filled in and a storm sewer was installed to handle the natural drainage of the land. The only indication of this historic drainage is a small outlet on the grassy slope near Buffalo Bayou. Trees and brush have grown up around this remnant of the former gully so it can be located if you look for it below the north end of Gillette Street.

The Jefferson Davis Hospital opened in 1938. The new five hundred bed facility was listed by the American Medical Association as the largest general hospital in Texas in 1941. Yet, it was already overcrowded and lacking enough beds. The city and county were just beginning to understand the extent of the medical needs of the community. Overcrowding led to a serious outbreak of staphylococcus infections in the maternity ward at the hospital during 1957 and 1958, and that led to a temporary loss of accreditation in 1961. Nevertheless, Jeff Davis Hospital had a remarkable record of service. It opened the nation's first trauma center, and the City's first tuberculosis clinic was established in the complex. During the 1970's, Jeff Davis had the distinction of being the first charity hospital in the United States to deliver 10,000 babies in a year[193].

Nonetheless, the hospital was considered to be obsolete by the late 1970's and it closed in 1989 after fifty years in operation. Houston apartment developer Marvy Finger bought the old Jeff Davis Hospital site from the Harris County Hospital District in January, 1999, and paid about $3 million to have the structure razed. Experts from the D. H. Griffin Company strategically detonated charges that set off fifteen sharp blasts followed by a ripple of smaller explosions. Within seconds, the historic Jefferson Davis Hospital was reduced to a pile of concrete rubble by a series of rapid fire explosions on Saturday morning, May 15, 1999[194].

The redevelopment of the Jeff Davis Hospital tract was delayed because the site had been contaminated by gasoline leaking from petroleum storage tanks on adjacent city-owned property. In 1998, the City of Houston Brownfields Redevelopment Program initiated a lengthy remediation program for the Jeff Davis tract. Subsequently, in 2000, Marvy Finger sold the property to the Federal Reserve Bank for about $20 million. The Federal Reserve Bank acquired the land to build a replacement for the downtown building it had occupied since 1958. The ground breaking ceremony for the new Federal Reserve Bank took place on October 16, 2002. By 2003, over 10,000 gallons of gasoline had been removed from the groundwater on the Jeff Davis Hospital site, but the cleanup was far from finished. To meet the Federal Reserve's construction schedule, an expedited program using a horizontal well extraction system began in October, 2003 in order to complete the cleanup for the opening of the new building which was planned for 2005[195].

The new Federal Reserve Bank at 1801 Allen Parkway opened in mid-May, 2005. Designed by seventy-one year old architect Michael Graves, the structure's long and narrow length and porch-style entry, reminiscent of a shotgun house, reflects the character of the nearby Freedmenstown neighborhood. The main building is made of red bricks interspersed with a blue tile pattern, and green glazed tiles cover the roof in a Southwestern style. The use of columns and a cathedral-like front door present an imposing structure, but the roof terraces and windows on the third and fourth floors tend to soften the visual effect. Graves wanted the building to be "a monumental, yet an approachable focal point for all of Houston[196]."

Since the bank is the Houston branch of the Federal Reserve Bank of Dallas, the sign over the main entrance included the word "Dallas," however, within a few days, a new sign was put in place. It reads simply: "Federal Reserve Bank Branch[197]."

The main entry way to the Federal Reserve Building is watched over by "The Guardian." A twelve foot tall bronze sculpture, "The Guardian" depicts an eagle with its wings spread and perched on a pyramid base -- a portrayal inspired by the two images on the back of a U. S. one dollar bill. The 4,000 pound sculpture rests on an eighteen foot column, and the eagle's wing span is twenty feet. Sculptor Ken Ullberg, a Swedish immigrant who works out of Corpus Christi, created "The Guardian" and it was cast by Art Castings of Colorado in Loveland, Colorado. The new 280,000 square foot, $95 million Federal Reserve Building held its official opening to the public on October 27, 2005[198].

City Hospital and Potter's Field at Spring Gully

Spring Gully was a natural topographic feature that separated Mahan's Spring Garden from land owned by Garrett Hardcastle. In 1858, the City of Houston purchased twelve acres adjacent to the Spring Garden property, along the west line of Lot 5 of the Hollingsworth Survey, for a city hospital. The city hospital was located some distance from the center of town since the hospital served poor and indigent citizens who had contracted the infectious diseases that often struck Houston during the nineteenth century. The city hospital was a place to quarantine, as well as treat, the victims of yellow fever, cholera or smallpox during the seemingly annual epidemics. These illnesses were thought of as a pestilence, and the hospital was commonly called a "pest" house. The yellow fever epidemic of 1878 was particularly devastating and there was a serious lack of space in the City cemeteries. In 1879, the City Health Officer recommended that a new City Cemetery and Potter's Field be opened on a portion of the tract of land where the pest house was located[199].

During the winter of 1890-1891 Houston experienced a small-pox epidemic. The seriousness of the crisis prompted the State Health Officer, on Jan 3, 1891, to place Houston on quarantine for the containment of smallpox. Dr. James M. Boyles, City Health Officer, protested that decision since he felt that the City had the disease under control. Houston's quarantine operations were centered at the City hospital site and a number of structures were hastily built for that purpose. Outside of the pest house, there existed only four cases of smallpox, and those cases were successfully isolated[200].

However, by the time the epidemic had abated, the magnitude of the City's effort was evident in Dr. Boyles' report to City Council on April 14, 1891. Dr. Boyles reported that a total of $17,009 had been spent to combat the smallpox epidemic. Of that sum, $4,008 was spent to build hospital wards, to purchase tents and to provide them with equipment. Two hundred eighty-seven patients were treated at the hospital and sixty-two persons were treated in their homes during the epidemic. Expenses for clothing provided to patients whose apparel was removed and burned came to $3,037.67. Their bedding and the hospital buildings were also burned as a precautionary measure[201].

What was not reported were the number of deaths during the epidemic and the account of the burials in the graveyard at the pest house. The City seems never to have had a systematic record of burials in the City cemeteries, and during the time that the pest house and the Potter's Field were in use, no account of the numbers or names of the persons buried were maintained. The City Cemetery and Potter's Field was declared to be full in 1904 and was closed. However, the City Hospital remained in use, and burials may have continued until about 1910[202].

The City continued to use the City Hospital tract for the treatment of infectious diseases. A new, one story hospital, called the City Detention Camp, was constructed beyond the north end of Timpson Street along the new Buffalo Drive. However, by 1927, it was recommended that the pest house on Buffalo Drive be abandoned in favor of the Jefferson Davis Hospital on Elder Street[203].

In 1939, the City began the construction of the San Felipe Courts, a low income housing project encompassing thirty-seven acres of the Hardcastle Subdivision, Freedmenstown and the City Hospital-Potter's Field tract. From May, 1941 to June, 1942, the remains of nine hundred twenty-eight persons were exhumed from the cemetery and moved to Brookside Memorial Park. By 1943, the first three hundred units of the San Felipe Courts were occupied, and by the end of 1944, there were over four thousand residents living in the housing complex that would become known as Allen Parkway Village in 1964[204].

In 1996, the remains of 3 or 4 bodies were disturbed during utility excavations prior to the redevelopment of the dilapidated Allen Parkway Village. These unmarked graves were uncovered under the playground and the buildings along Gillette Street. Further investigations found a total of four hundred thirty burials remained at the old cemetery site. The remains were reinterred in a cemetery tract established at the southwest corner of Allen Parkway and Heiner Street which is maintained by the City of Houston Housing Authority[205].

Archeological investigations have determined that no intact human burials were found on the Jeff Davis Hospital site which is across Gillette Street. However, a thorough investigation of the undeveloped old cemetery land remains to be completed. Until then, the playground that occupies the tract across from the Federal Reserve Bank is closed.

Freedmenstown - A Neighborhood on the Bayou

With the end of the Civil War and the emancipation of the slaves on June 19, 1865, the City of Houston faced a crisis. How would it adjust to a peacetime economy, and how would its newly freed residents adjust to a way of life they had never known? One of the most pressing issues for those who suddenly became freed from the protection and care of their former masters was where would they live.

Help came from sympathetic businessmen and influential citizens of Houston. In particular, Garrett S. Hardcastle set aside a tract of land that he owned as a residential development for these newly free persons. The Hardcastle Subdivision soon became known as Freedmenstown[206].

Hardcastle came to Houston in 1836 from the eastern shore of Maryland. He was a devoted Methodist and when the Shearn Methodist Church was organized in 1841, he was made a steward of the church, a position he held until his death in 1884. From the mid-1850's, Hardcastle began to acquire land along the north side of the San Felipe Road (present day West Dallas Avenue). On July 14, 1855, he purchased land from William R. Baker that lay between his own land on the west and the land of Clement R. Hobson on the east. Hardcastle acquired the twenty acres that Hobson owned on May 6, 1857, and he moved into Hobson's former home on the property[207].

As the Assessor and Collector of taxes for Harris County, Garrett Hardcastle and other Methodists paid the taxes for freed slaves and helped them keep their properties. By 1866, twenty-two dwellings in the subdivision were occupied by freed slaves. In time, besides Freedmenstown, four adjoining additions in western part of the Fourth Ward became largely black-owned residential neighborhoods: W. R. Baker Addition, the Castanie Addition, the Senechal Addition and the Hopson Addition. The highest percent black ownership was in Freedmenstown[208].

In 1874, the local newspaper reflected a somewhat less than generous view of the residents of Freedmenstown. It noted that the area had to be patrolled by the police in order to preserve order and curb the vandalism. The neighborhood was second only to Vinegar Hill in notoriety, and the children ran naked while the place reeked of "idleness and crime." Nevertheless, residents such as Richard Allen, the first African-American state legislator from Houston, pursued the ideals of good schools and voting rights for blacks in spite of the rising specter of "Jim Crow" laws that would come into place by the end of the nineteenth century[209].

Although the black community in the adjacent subdivisions seemed to thrive and prosper, the Hardcastle Subdivision/Freedmenstown declined. In 1908, City officials created the fifteen block "Reservation" in the Freedmenstown district in an attempt to plan and reserve a geographic district for all of the prostitutes of the City. The Reservation was formally abolished as an entity of the City in 1915[210].

Freedmenstown continued to lose its identity in the pre-World War II period. As one of the nation's first urban renewal projects, the San Felipe Courts (later Allen Parkway Village) were constructed in 1939-1940 on the Hardcastle Subdivision, Freedmenstown and part of the New City Cemetery of 1879 as housing for white working class families[211].

The final indignity for the original Freedmenstown came in 1984 when the National Register of Historic Places designation of the Freedmen's Town Historic District in the Fourth Ward went to the black community that was south of West Dallas Avenue and between Genesee Street, West Gray Avenue and Arthur Street[212].

Jim Mozola Memorial Disc Golf Course

The Jim Mozola Memorial Disc Golf Course is a nine hole disc golf course along the north bank of Buffalo Bayou between the Tapley Tributary and Sabine Street. Disc golf, an offshoot of the Frisbee craze, is similar to regular golf, but uses golf discs and players aim for a Disc Pole Hole. The first disc golf course was established in 1975 at Oak Grove Park in Pasadena, California, and today, there are over 2,500 Disc Golf Courses in the U.S. and 390 sanctioned professional tournaments.

The Jim Mozola Memorial Disc Golf Course was established in 1997, and it was redesigned in March, 2008. The course is rated as a very difficult course with water in play on most holes and some baskets on steep hillsides[213].

Lee and Joe Jamail Skatepark

The other recreational facility on the north bank in Buffalo Bayou Park caters to athletic prowess of the young generation. The Lee and Joe Jamail Skatepark is a world class, state-of-the-art skate boarding facility. The 30,000 square foot, all concrete skate park, with facilities for 100 continuous skateboard riders of all skill levels, opened on June 1, 2008[214].

In 2005, The Houston Parks and Recreation Department partnered with Public Use Skateparks for Houston (PUSH) to create a skateboarding facility in the downtown area. The Parks and Recreation Department allotted the land on the sloping banks of the bayou below the former fifteen million gallon water reservoir of the City Water Department on the corner of Memorial Drive and Sabine Street for the new park[215].

Initially, the skate park was to be the Central Houston Skate Park, but on June 4, 2007, prominent trial lawyer Joseph Jamail donated $1.5 million to the Houston Parks Board for the skatepark with the provision that it be named the Lee and Joe Jamail Skatepark, in honor of his wife who died in January, 2007[216].

The Sabine Street Bridge, A Long Forgotten Beauty

With the recent opening of the Sabine-to-Bagby Promenade, the neglected reaches of Buffalo Bayou on the edge of the central business district received a beautification that has been long overdue. An especially pleasing result has been the highlighting of the Sabine Street bridge at the western terminus of the Promenade.

As early as 1891, there was a bridge across the bayou at Sabine Street that connected the Sixth Ward with the Fourth Ward. This initial crossing appears to have been more of a foot bridge than a main thoroughfare since its location seemed to indicate a crossing at the end of Heiner Street on the south which simply extended across the bayou to an area near the end of Sabine Street on the north. However, the subsequent development of both the Sixth Ward and the south bank of Buffalo Bayou along Heiner Street led to the construction of a primary roadway spanning the bayou in 1924[217].

In the early 1920's the City Council passed a bond issue for the improvement the city's streets and bayou crossings. Included in this program were new bridges at Shepherd's Dam, Heights Boulevard and Sabine Street[218].

The Sabine Street bridge, completed in 1924, was designed by W. W. Washburn, the City bridge engineer, and his work was strongly influenced by the City Beautiful movement which is evident in the design of the bridge and the use of neoclassical ornamentation and railing. The bridge is 240 feet long with two lanes of traffic on forty foot roadways which are flanked on each side by wide cantilevered sidewalks. It spans the bayou on six reinforced concrete girder and floorbeam units which are erected over four-column bents and abutments. Its special design, its railing and the artistic use of ornamentation make the Sabine Street bridge architecturally significant. In addition, it is the sole surviving concrete bridge constructed under the 1920's civic improvement program[219].

Improvements were made to the Sabine Street bridge in 1987 to restore the bridge to its original splendor after decades of neglect. At that time, minor changes were made to the roadway which was narrowed in order to expand the size of the sidewalk on the west side of the bridge. In the renovations of 2006, the bridge is portrayed as a gateway to recreation on Buffalo Bayou. Stairways at each corner of the bridge provide access to the foot paths near the bayou through arched portals capped with stylized stainless steel canoes. With the inclusion of the bridge in the Promenade, this historic structure can assume a place of prominence as one of the hidden jewels of Houston[220].

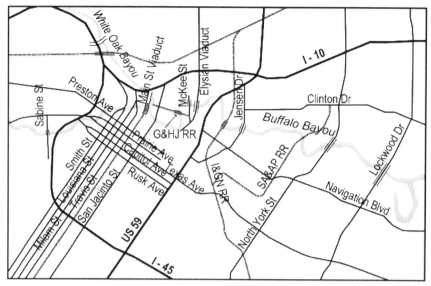

Map by Rachel A. Garcia

From the Sabine Street bridge, Buffalo Bayou enters the western edge of the historic downtown district of Houston. The recently developed Sabine-to-Bagby Promenade joins the adjacent Sesqui-centennial Park to provide pedestrian access along both sides of the bayou from Sabine Street to Smith Street.

Chapter 7
The Sabine Promenade

The Hopson Addition

As you head downstream toward the Sabine Street bridge, you will notice a tributary entering the bayou on the south bank near the street where Allen Parkway Village ends. This is the outlet of the Crosby Street storm sewer. This sewer drains rain water and runoff from a large part of the Fourth Ward and the Montrose area. The significantly large outlet tunnel attests to that capacity.

In periods of low water in the bayou, the stone plaza that has been constructed at the base of the outlet provides a pleasant arena to watch the birds and turtles that inhabit that tree lined tributary. A staircase descends from the sidewalk on Allen Parkway to platforms on the lower level. The circular arrangement of the granite slabs dam the outflow to create a pool while allowing the overflow to drain down the short tributary to its confluence with Buffalo Bayou some two hundred feet away.

Crosby Street is also the western boundary of the Hopson Addition, a subdivision established in 1860 by Mrs. Sarah Ann Hopson[1]. The subdivision was one of five along the San Felipe Road, now West Dallas Avenue, that became the neighborhood where many African-Americans settled after emancipation in 1865. In the early days of Houston, and prior to the Civil War, this part of town had a much different history than that of the post war period of which we are most familiar.

The most notable early settler in the area was John Woodruff. Woodruff had been a farmer and stock raiser in Brazoria County prior to 1836. John Woodruff served in the Texas Army in the fall of 1835, and with the approach of Santa Anna's army in April, 1836, the Woodruff family abandoned their farm and fled east in the Runaway Scrape, hiding in the timberlands near Clear Creek at the time of the battle at San Jacinto. In December, 1836, Woodruff moved his family to the new town of Houston, settling on land southwest of the town. Woodruff established his farm on fifty acres of land that today extends along the south side of West Dallas Avenue from near Clay Street on the east to Genesee Street on the west[2].

John Woodruff opened his home on the San Felipe Road as a boarding house, and among his boarders were some of the most influential members of the government of the Republic, including General Edward Burleson, Anson Jones, William Harris Wharton, and William Fairfax Gray, Clerk of the Senate. Woodruff's good connections served him well as he won contracts with the Republic to supply beef and other meats under contract for the Military Hospital in Houston and other governmental units. By 1838, his slaughterhouse and cattle operations were highly successful. However, when the capital of the Republic was moved to Austin in 1840, Woodruff transferred his stock raising operations to the new capital as well[3].

Woodruff sold his fifty acre farm to Robert C. Campbell in 1840. Campbell sold the fifty acres to Justin Castanie on July 3, 1846. Castanie platted this tract as the Castanie Subdivision on April 12, 1848, and the area had a scattering of residential structures prior to the Civil War[4].

Other entrepreneurs recognized the livestock potential in the prairies south of the bayou. In the early 1840's, Clement R. Hopson began acquiring property on the north side of the San Felipe Road near the former Woodruff tract. Hopson and his partner John J. Cain established a "tallow factory" or slaughterhouse on the banks of Buffalo Bayou by 1846. In 1850, however, Hopson moved his operations to the new town of Corpus Christi. In a partnership with Corpus Christi founder Henry Kinney, Hopson operated a beef packing company in what is now downtown Corpus Christi during the 1850's. This led to the sale of a portion of his land on the San Felipe Road to Garrett Hardcastle in May 6, 1857. In 1860, Mrs. Sarah Ann Hopson subdivided the Hopson tract on the south bank of Buffalo Bayou into the Hopson Addition. These residential developments set the stage for the post-Civil War growth of the

African-American community in this part of the Fourth Ward and the rise of Freedmenstown in Garrett Hardcastle's subdivision[5].

During the late nineteenth and early twentieth centuries, the businesses of local African-Americans concentrated in the area to the east of Hopson's Addition. This commercial district formed in the vicinity of the Antioch Baptist Church, one of the spiritual centers of the community. By 1926, the Houston Negro Chamber of Commerce was housed in the Pilgrim Temple Building at 222 West Dallas Avenue at Bagby Street. Designed by noted architect Alfred Finn, this building was the focal point of the black business community for over forty years[6].

Plans for Houston's freeway systems were formulated in early 1954, and by August of that year, the right of way for Interstate 45, built on the west side of the downtown district, had been cleared of residential and light commercial structures. The portion of the Fourth Ward neighborhood bounded by Smith Street and Dallas Avenue was separated from the rest of the neighborhood along West Dallas Avenue. Many of the Fourth Ward's most important buildings were eliminated and the geographical integrity of the community destroyed. When this section of the freeway opened on December 12, 1955, the Antioch Baptist Church, built in 1879 at 313 Robin Street, was cut off from its community and placed in the commercial district that was developed as Allen Center. The community in the western part of the Fourth Ward declined rapidly and the redevelopment that began in the 1990's is transforming the area into a different type of neighborhood[7].

Heiner Street, named for Houston architect Eugene Heiner, became the access road on the west side of Interstate 45. The parcel bounded Heiner Street on the east and Crosby Street on the west, and lying between West Dallas Avenue and Allen Parkway, is the only recognizable property of the Hopson Addition still extant. Today, this tract is dedicated, in a special way, to many anonymous residents of Freedmenstown and the San Felipe District.

During renovation of Allen Parkway Village in 1996, a number of unmarked graves were uncovered under the playground and buildings along Gillette Street. These graves were in addition to ones disturbed during the original excavations on the site. From 1879 until about 1908, the city operated a hospital (a "pest house" for victims of pestilence and disease) and a cemetery in this area which served the freed slaves and indigent whites residing in Freedmenstown and the surrounding area. In 1941-1942, during the construction of the San Felipe Courts (which is now called Allen Parkway Village), the remains of 928 persons who had been buried in the pauper's cemetery were removed to Brookside Memorial Park. Obviously, a significant number of burials in the former city cemetery were missed. To date, an additional 430 graves have been uncovered during redevelopment of Allen Parkway Village. The playground at the corner of Gillette Street and Allen Parkway is closed until further investigations can be done[8].

The remains from the recently discovered graves were reinterred in the land along Heiner Street which the city condemned for $10 and which the City of Houston Housing Authority maintains. The fenced area adjacent to the Housing Authority building contains the numbered, but anonymous, graves of those who have been given a final resting place on this historic spot[9].

The Interstate 45 bridge over Buffalo Bayou was renovated in 2000. To highlight the presence of Buffalo Bayou, four "bayou beacons" were installed on the bridge to mark the site of the bayou. The thirty foot ornamental steel light towers are designed by local architect Rey de la Reza and sculptor Paul Kittelson. These markers may help us to recognize the bayou waters below the freeway, but also the effects on the community that the freeway has had and the stories of the people who lived in this part of Houston[10].

West End Ball Park

Baseball was played in Houston as early as 1861 when the Houston Base Ball Club was formed. The Houston Stonewalls triumphed over the Galveston Robert E. Lees on April 21, 1868 at the San Jacinto Battleground in the first game reported in the local newspaper. For two decade after that, amateur base ball clubs flourished in Texas towns, following a trend that led to the formation of professional base ball clubs in the East by 1871[11].

In 1888, the local sport went "professional" and adopted the name "baseball" as Houston was a founding member of the Texas League with its team the Houston Red Stockings[12].

For the next decade, the Houston team enjoyed some competitive success, winning pennants in 1889, 1892 and 1896. However, the team and the league was less successful financially, and the league folded on July 5, 1899[13].

Professional baseball returned to Houston in 1903 as the new South Texas League was formed. The revitalized team also began play about this time in their new ball park, called the Ball Park. Located in the Fourth Ward about seven blocks south of Buffalo Bayou from the Sabine Street bridge, the Ball Park was situated on land that previously was the farm and home of Houston mayor John D. Andrews, who served from 1841-1842. After his death, the tract lay undeveloped for many years while the Fourth Ward developed around it. The Ball Park, at the corner of Andrews Street and Heiner Street, was situated on the southern edge of the San Felipe District, the foremost black community of the city, but it was also near the grandiose homes of prominent citizens along the streets extending south of town. Today, the site is under Interstate 45 and the Reliant Energy substation near Jefferson Avenue[14].

Houston rejoined the Texas League in 1907, and two years later, the club took the name Buffaloes, or Buffs, which remained with them for the next fifty-three years. The team continued to have winning seasons and they won pennants in 1905, 1909, 1910, 1912 and 1913[15].

The local support for the baseball team was sufficient enough that in 1923 the St. Louis Cardinals purchased the controlling interest of the club. The legendary Branch Rickey made the Houston Buffs one of the premier clubs in his famous farm system[16].

On April 11, 1928, the Houston Buffs played the first game in their new 11,000 seat stadium on Calhoun Road which the Commissioner of Baseball Kenesaw Mountain Landis, who attended opening day, called "The finest minor league baseball park in America." Today, the site is occupied by the Fingers Furniture Company store[17].

In 1962, Houston joined Major League Baseball's National League. The Houston Colt .45's opened in a temporary stadium on South Main Street prior to emerging for the 1965 season in the Astrodome as the Houston Astros. Since 2000, the Houston Astros have played at Minute Maid Park (formerly, Enron Field), initially dubbed the Ball Park at Union Station, on Texas Avenue at Crawford Street[18].

Go Astros!

Sam Houston Park

The view for boaters on the bayou as they approach Interstate 45 is that of a maze of bridges. There are separate bridges for the north bound and south bound lanes of the freeways. Sliding off of these main lanes is an intricate array of entrance and exit ramps, each forming its own bridge over the bayou. All in all, there are eight distinct bridge structures associated with the I-45 freeway at this point. In order, going downstream, they are: 1) the West Dallas Avenue exit ramp, 2) the I-45 south main lanes, 3) the Allen Parkway exit ramp, 4) the I-45 North main lanes, 5) the Memorial Drive exit ramp, 6) the I-45 North entrance ramp from Allen Parkway, 7) the McKinney Avenue exit ramp, and 8) the Walker Avenue entrance ramp.

Each of these bridges is supported by large concrete pillars, many of which are located within the stream bed of Buffalo Bayou. At normal water levels, these mid-channel obstacles do not present any major difficulty to boaters. However, when the rate of flow increases to levels above 1,000 cfs or more, the pillars become dangerous obstacles for canoers, kayakers and other boaters to negotiate. Caution should be carefully observed when weaving through the strong currents and billows that form around the bridge supports.

The nest of concrete associated with I-45 also obscures the view of the historic Sam Houston Park which lies on the south bank of the bayou where the bayou begins its gentle turn to the northeast. With a glance over the right bank immediately before the McKinney Avenue ramp, the tops of a number of the houses and buildings of the park can be seen from the bayou.

Sam Houston Park has the distinction of being the first public park land acquired by the City of Houston. In June, 1899, Mayor Samuel Brashear purchased land for a city park that included the old Samuel Young brickyard on the north side of Buffalo Bayou and the Noble and Byers property on the south side. Although the tracts had played a significant role in Houston for over fifty years, the properties had fallen into disrepair by the time of the purchase. The Noble family home, which had been built by Nathaniel Kelly Kellum in 1847, was the main structure on the property, and it was salvaged for use as the headquarters for the park[19].

As early as 1837, the banks along this area of Buffalo Bayou were identified as a source of clay for making bricks. It was about this time that a man named Hathaway had a brick yard near the foot of McKinney Avenue. The demand for building materials in the early days of Houston inspired others to try to exploit the natural resources in the area, and by 1842, Nathaniel Kellum was advertising high quality bricks for sale from his brick yard near the foot of Lamar Avenue[20].

Kellum, who was born in Virginia about 1818, arrived in Houston in early 1839. He began to purchase lots in town in May, 1839, but eventually, the twenty-one year old Kellum set up a kiln and brick yard operation on the southwest edge of town. Nathaniel Kellum married Elmyra Cotton on January 23, 1842, and he set out to establish himself in the community. In July, 1842, the local newspaper reported that Kellum's bricks were of a quality similar to those bricks which were imported from the United States. With the success of his brick business, Kellum then sought to acquire ownership of the land for his enterprise[21].

In a series of transactions in 1844 and 1845, Kellum put together the tract of about thirteen acres where he had established his operations and, later, built his home. Kellum purchased 2.1 acres for $200 from James J. Holman on February 9, 1844, adjoining the property that he was already using as his brick yard. On May 16, 1844, he purchased eight acres where he had his brickyard for $500 from Thomas M. Bagby. This tract had previously belonged to William N. Mock and was resided on by R. P. Stewart, but Augustus C. Allen had forced the property into foreclosure in 1839, and it was sold to Bagby in a sheriff's sale in 1843. Lastly, on November 22, 1845, Nathaniel Kellum bought eight town lots adjoining his property on the east from Francis R. Lubbock for $150. These lots comprised a tract known as the Hospital Lot where Ashbel Smith had established the General Military Hospital for the Republic of Texas in 1837.

The hospital ceased to exist in 1841 after the capital was moved to Austin and the army was disbanded[22].

In 1847, Nathaniel Kellum began construction of a stately white brick house in the style of a Louisiana plantation from bricks fired in the kiln at his brickyard. The two story, Southern colonial brick structure displays an Old Louisiana French influence in its double verandas that are supported by narrow, square brick pillars[23].

Nevertheless, despite these accomplishments, Kellum began to liquidate his land holdings in Houston in 1849. On October 13, 1849, Kellum granted his power of attorney to Benjamin A. Shepherd to sell his former residence and brickyard, comprising about fourteen acres, a two story building, out houses and other improvements. On January 29, 1851, Shepherd sold the Nathaniel Kellum brickyard property to Abram W. Noble for $2000 with a promissory note due on April 1, 1852[24].

Kellum may have been motivated to find a better place to raise his growing family, especially following the births of his sons Robert in 1844, Nathaniel in 1846 and Ruthven in 1849. By November, 1850, the Kellum family had settled in Grimes County about ten miles northwest of the town of Anderson. The land that Kellum acquired included a sulphur spring that had been identified as early as 1836 as the Navasota Sulphur Springs. Jacob DeCordova's map of 1849 identified spring site as White Sulphur Springs, but the J. H. Young map of Texas in 1850 referred to the place as Kellum's Sulphur Springs[25].

By the mid-1850's, Kellum had built a resort and health spa around his mineral springs. The complex included a two story, fifty room hotel, eighteen cottages, a bathhouse and several reservoirs. Spring water was pumped into the hotel. Accommodations could be had for 400 to 500 persons with board, lodging and bathing priced at $1 per day. The hotel was the social center of the resort with musicians on the staff and, every Tuesday evening, parties and dances were held in the second floor parlor[26].

During the mid-nineteenth century, Texans sought recreation and the healing influences on mineral waters at springs in the countryside. Thousands of visitors enjoyed the small resorts and health spas like Kellum Springs and Piedmont Springs, located about ten miles to the southwest of Kellum Springs. Like Kellum

Springs, Piedmont Springs developed extensive facilities. A four story hotel with a hundred rooms was built there about 1860, and the resort became even more popular than Kellum's, with entertainment that included billiards, poker and horse racing[27].

A small community grew up around Kellum's resort, and, on October 11, 1859, Kellum was appointed the postmaster of Kellum's Springs, Texas. The success of Kellum's venture in his resort was evident by 1860 when he declared that he owned real estate valued at $20,000 and held personal assets of $25,000. Nevertheless, the difficulties of the Civil War led to a decline in business at the resort. In newspaper ads in August, 1862, Kellum assured the public that Kellum Springs was indeed open for business. In deference to the hardships of the war, however, Kellum wrote that dance parties at Kellum Springs were suspended for the duration of the conflict[28].

The economic downturn in the aftermath of the Civil War led to a significant decline in business at resorts like Piedmont Springs and Kellum Springs. Nathaniel Kellum died prior to 1870 and the valuation of the property dropped to about $3,000. Nevertheless, on August 29, 1877, the Navasota Tablet reported that groups of ladies and gentlemen from Navasota, Anderson and the surrounding countryside made weekly visits to both Kellum Springs and Piedmont Springs and they enjoyed the resorts. On July 29, 1879, Grimes County Sentinel reported that Grimes County had some of finest springs and summer resorts in Texas, including Kellum Springs and "the celebrated Piedmont springs." Eventually, though, after the death of Kellum's wife, the upkeep of Kellum's hotel deteriorated to a large extent and the building was condemned[29].

Yet, the Kellum Springs area served as a community gathering place well into the 1890's. On July 13, 1894, Dr. J. J. Burroughs, the populist candidate for Congress, and Congressman Tom Ball met in a debate at Kellum Springs. Two years later, in the next election campaign, the Honorable Tom Ball, the Democratic candidate for the First Congressional District, and Joe Eagle, the populist, held a debate at Kellum's Springs on August 27, 1896. The newspaper reported that both the debate and the associated barbecue were a success. Nevertheless, Kellum Springs, as well as the other mineral water spas and resorts in Texas, closed and were largely forgotten in the twentieth century[30].

After Kellum's departure from Houston, the Kellum house and brick yard property became the home of the family of Abram Noble. Abram Washington Noble, born in Lawrence County, Mississippi on February 28, 1815, brought his wife Louisa and their young daughter to Nacogdoches County, Texas in 1840, following his older brothers Edward who came to Texas in 1837 and Stephen who came in 1838. Louisa Noble died in 1849 and Abram Noble settled his family, which by then included five children, in Houston in 1849, but it is unclear whether the move to Houston occurred before or after the death of his wife. In April, 1849, Abram Noble married Zerviah Metcalf Robinson Kelly, a widow from Connecticut with a daughter, Catherine, who was born in 1834. In early 1851, the large extended family moved into the Kellum house. Shortly thereafter, on February 10, 1851, Zerviah Noble opened a school in her home for children under twelve years old. She was assisted by her seventeen year old daughter Miss C. A. Kelly, and several of her stepchildren were students[31].

Zerviah Noble lived and taught school in the Kellum-Noble House until the 1890's. She operated it as a private school at first, then as one of Houston's first public schools. When the City's public school system was established in 1877, her school became the Fourth Ward Public School[32].

Abram Noble took over Kellum's brick yard business about 1851. By 1860, he employed one brick maker and four laborers at his brick yard, and he was moderately successful in the venture. During the Civil War, Noble served as a captain in the Confederate army. Zerviah and Abram W. Noble divorced in 1865, and Abram moved to Kaufman County in that same year. Zerviah Noble retained the Kellum-Noble house and continued her career as a teacher and principal there almost until her death in 1894[33].

In June, 1899, Mayor Samuel Brashear purchased the land, which included the Noble property, that became the city's first public park. In 1902, Mayor O. T. Holt formed the Parks Department to maintain the City Park. When it opened, the City Park was decorated with flowers and plants, and it was made appealingly bucolic with wooden footbridges, an old mill and a picturesque pond. A small zoo featured native Texas wildlife including squirrels, rabbits, prairie dogs and alligators. By 1913, the park had been named in honor of Sam Houston[34].

As other parks were developed in the city, the use of Sam Houston Park declined. The zoo was relocated to a new thirty-four acre site in Hermann Park on January 11, 1925. By the early 1950's, Sam Houston Park and its main facility, the Kellum-Noble house, were in danger of being demolished. Fortunately, a group of concerned citizens recognized the value of the historic brick home and its park land. The Harris County Heritage Society was formed in 1954 to save the house and the park, and the downtown city park has become the focal point for the preservation of historic Houston structures. The Kellum-Noble House is the oldest surviving brick structure in Houston, and it sits on its original location[35].

The original purchase of land for the city park in 1899 included not only the Kellum tract, but also the land on the opposite bank that had been the Samuel Young Brick Yard. Buffalo Bayou had cut through the overlying Acadia clay loam and possibly into the Ochlockonee clay strata, exposing a seam of clay that was suitable for the manufacture of bricks. The clay deposits of the south bank at this location were exploited as early as 1837, and brick making from the deposits on the north bank of the bayou are documented as early as 1860. During the mid-1800's, the two brick works operated on the north side of the bayou opposite Kellum's operation. These two businesses were the Stanley Brick Yard and the Samuel Young Brick Yard[36].

Lardner C. Stanley was in Houston as early as 1837 and he operated a sixty-three acre vegetable farm just west of town on the north side of Buffalo Bayou. By 1850, the fifty-two year old Stanley still listed his occupation as a farmer, however, in 1860, he was a brick maker. His operation employed William Johnson, as a brick maker, and Ruthven Needham as a machinist. The Stanley Brick Works continued in operation through 1870, perhaps until Stanely's death in that decade[37].

In the late 1860's, Samuel W. Young, a newcomer to Texas from Pennsylvania in his early twenties, began to acquire land from Henry Evans on the north bank of the bayou west of Stanley's operations. In 1869, Young bought a 2.1 acre track south of J. W. Johnson's brick yard and he established a brick making operation of his own. Young's brick business grew to be the largest in this area, and although the brick yard was heavily damaged by fire in October, 1875, Young continued to operate his business through the 1880's. In January, 1891, Young's Brick Yard was sold for $500 to R. G. Thacker to satisfy a judgment against Samuel Young[38].

By the mid-1890's, the brick yards had depleted the clay resources of the site and they left a large ravine lying east of Young Avenue (the modern Riesner Street) and south of Washington Avenue, extending as far as the City Water Works facility. A large oval depression and ravine remained to the west of Young Avenue in what is now the Municipal Courts parking lot[39]. The six acres at the lower end of Houston Avenue were a part of City Park acquisition in 1899, and the land remained attached to the park for the next several decades. As a part of the right of way for the construction of Interstate Highway 45 in the 1950's, the former Young's Brick Yard is now under the elevated portion of the freeway, and it is used for parking and other similar purposes by the City.

Two Forgotten Cemeteries of Downtown Houston

As you paddle downstream on Buffalo Bayou past the Sabine Street bridge, you emerge from under the noisy main lanes and access ramps of I-45 to a pleasant view of the downtown Civic Center. The recent landscaping of the Sabine Street Promenade provides an elegant green space that opens to the City Hall Annex, a modern civic building that is flanked on the south by Sam Houston Park and on the north by the new William P. Hobby Center for the Performing Arts. The access ramp extensions of Walker Avenue and McKinney Avenue separate the City Hall Annex from the entities on each side. Today, little evidence remains on this site of the two cemeteries that were the resting place of prominent Houston residents of the early Republic of Texas.

In the 1840's, the Masonic Cemetery was established by Holland Lodge No. 1 on 3/4 acres on the banks of Buffalo Bayou in the far southwest part of town off Bagby Street at Lamar Avenue. George H. Bringhurst was a Mason who served as the secretary and the treasurer of Holland Lodge No. 1 for more than thirty years. Bringhurst was the City surveyor for ten years during the 1840's and he owned property on Bagby Street. Quite possibly, through his efforts that the land for the Masonic Cemetery was acquired. Nevertheless, James West, the land owner to the northeast of Nathaniel Kellum, donated two acres of his land for the Masonic Cemetery in 1843. Since the Masonic Cemetery and the adjacent Episcopal Cemetery have traditionally been linked, the Episcopal Cemetery may have been established at this time as well. Together, the two cemeteries consisted of about two acres of land in a long and narrow strip extending from a one lot "set back" from Bagby Street to the bayou[40].

Those buried at Episcopal Cemetery included Stephen Richardson, one of Stephen F. Austin's Old Three Hundred settlers. The twenty-eight year old Richardson was shipwrecked near the mouth of the Brazos on December 22, 1822. He went on to San Felipe de Austin and established a business with Thomas Davis. In January, 1838, Richardson moved to Harrisburg where he operated a steam sawmill until about 1848. He moved to Houston in early 1849 and he died in Houston on July 6, 1860 at age sixty-six[41].

Moseley Baker, a veteran of San Jacinto and a legislator in the Republic, died on November 4, 1848 of yellow fever in Houston. He was buried initially in the City Cemetery on Elder Street, but was later moved to the Episcopal Cemetery. The remains of Baker and his wife were moved to the State Cemetery in Austin in 1929[42].

Also buried at the Episcopal Cemetery are the children of Mrs. Priscilla Hadley Key, a descendant of Francis Scott Key who wrote the Star Spangled Banner, our national anthem. These children were also the grandchildren of Obedience Smith[43].

The most notable burial in the Masonic Cemetery was that of Anson Jones, the last president of the Republic of Texas, who died on January 9, 1858. Jones' remains were subsequently moved to Glenwood Cemetery[44].

The City Council prohibited interments in the Episcopal Cemetery and the Masonic Cemetery in 1879. At that time, some of the bodies in the Episcopal Cemetery and the Masonic Cemetery were unearthed and reinterred in Glenwood Cemetery. There is some indication that, in spite of the ban, the last burial in the Masonic Cemetery was in 1900. Without a doubt, though, both cemeteries were neglected and fell into disarray. Many of the headstones lay broken and scattered. The two acre tract surrounded by a five foot metal fence was unkempt and overgrown with weeds. With the construction of the new City Hall on Bagby Street and the civic center development on the west side of downtown, more graves were removed from the Episcopal Cemetery and reinterred in Brookside Cemetery in 1938[45].

In 1959, the expansion of the Civic Center with the construction of the City Hall Annex on the west side of Bagby Street and the expansion of Sam Houston Park required the removal of the two cemeteries. An additional eighty bodies were moved from the site to Glenwood Cemetery[46].

Today, there is no visible sign of the two old cemeteries. The exit ramp from I-45 to McKinney Avenue covers part of the cemetery tract while the exhibits of Sam Houston Park have replaced the remainder. The Three Coyotes of the Neuhaus Fountain, a 1992 work by California sculptor Gwynn Murrill, lie over much of the former Masonic Cemetery. The Neuhaus Fountain, dedicated on September 17, 1992, is named in honor of Hugo Victor Neuhaus, Sr. and his wife Kate Rice Neuhaus. The cagey bronze scavengers seem to be appropriate protectors of the ghosts of early Houston[47].

City Hall Annex

The McKinney Avenue entrance ramp to I-45 separates Sam Houston Park from the civic center complex. An open space on the south bank of Buffalo Bayou is criss-crossed by the Walker Avenue entrance ramp and the access road to Allen Parkway. However, the pedestrian walkway of the Sabine Street Promenade provides one with an excellent view of the downtown skyscrapers. Looking due east at this point, the four story, white building in the foreground of downtown is the City Hall Annex.

The tract of land where the City Hall Annex sits today was owned by James West in 1851. By 1866, the tract had been divided into lots. George H. Bringhurst owned a lot with a house on the west side of Bagby Street between Walker Avenue and McKinney Avenue. Andrew Opperman, a laborer, lived on the southwest corner of Bagby Street and Walker Avenue, next to the Bringhurst property. By the 1890's, the City Hall Annex tract, Block 151, had been extensively developed. A grocery store was established on the corner of Bagby Street and Walker Avenue by Italian immigrant Michael DeGeorge, and there were small one story dwellings located along Bagby Street. Numerous single story dwellings, rented by African-Americans, filled the bayou side of the tract[48].

Michele (Michael) DeGeorge, born in September, 1849, had immigrated in 1882 and came to Houston where he established the grocery store. With the success of the store, DeGeorge, who had brought his wife and young daughter Rosalie to Texas in 1884, built a ten room home at 918 Bagby about 1895 for his growing family which then included daughter Lena and sons Jasper and Bernardo[49].

The large DeGcorge home was a prominent landmark of the Fourth Ward neighborhood for over fifty years. Its expansive, two story porch overlooking the corner of McKinney Avenue and Babgy Street was capped by an inspiring, third floor turret. The landscaped yard was neatly enclosed by a handsome fence.

In 1898, DeGeorge began the commercial real estate business which would be the family profession for over 100 years. DeGeorge developed two hotels with architect Joseph Finger. The DeGeorge Hotel, at the corner of Preston Avenue and LaBranch Street, was built in 1913 and is now called the DeGeorge at Union Station. The Auditorium Hotel, on Texas Avenue at Louisiana Street, was built in 1926 (it is now the Lancaster Hotel)[50].

Residential development in Block 151 reached a peak in the first decade of the twentieth century. Along Bagby Street, there was a store on the north corner and three single story dwellings in addition to the two story DeGeorge house. Twenty-six single story dwellings were located on the tract behind the front row of lots in 1907, and there was one tenement building. Michael DeGeorge, a 60 year old real estate "capitalist" in 1910, continued to live with his family in his fine home at 918 Bagby Street, and fellow Italian immigrant Joseph Guseman and his family lived a few doors down at 906 Bagby Street[51].

In the mid-1920's, the construction of Buffalo Drive and its connection with Walker Avenue caused some of the houses on the lower section of Block 151 to be removed. Only fourteen single story dwellings remained on the back portion of the tract in 1924. Michael DeGeorge died in 1927, but members of the family continued to live in the house on Bagby Street. Rosalie DeGeorge lived with her sister Lena and brother-in-law Tanny C. Guseman in the big house which proved suitable for their three children. In 1930, the house was still valued at $20,000. But, after the completion of the new City Hall across the street in 1939, the family moved from the house[52].

By the 1950's, much of Block 151 was cleared to serve as parking for the new Sam Houston Coliseum which had been built across Walker Avenue. The DeGeorge house stood vacant on the corner of the tract and six single story dwellings and three two story dwellings remained on the back of the lot. The DeGeorge property along Bagby Street was covered with "shanty houses." In preparation for the development of the civic center and the construction of ramps for the new Interstate 45 freeway, the DeGeorge house was demolished and the rest of Block 151 was cleared. The City Hall Annex was built on the site in 1967[53].

The Hobby Center

Immediately ahead is the pedestrian bridge of the Sabine to Bagby Promenade. Designed by the SWA Group, the 189 foot long steel-trussed, arched bridge has a ten foot wide wooden walking path and is supported by two sets of steel columns, one on each side of the bayou. The bridge connects the hike and bike paths on each side of the bayou along the Promenade, it offers an excellent viewpoint for the entry to the Hobby Center for Performing Arts. And, of course, the most prominent feature at this point on the bayou is the seven story, red brick parking garage for the Hobby Center[54].

The Hobby Center and its grand garage occupy an irregular city block bounded on the east by Bagby Street, on the north by Rusk Avenue, on the south by Walker Avenue and on the west by Buffalo Bayou. The larger than standard block is the result of the meander the bayou near Rusk Avenue and by a historic topographical feature, a deep ravine that extended from the block that is now Tranquility Park to the right of way along Rusk Avenue and then to the bayou. The contour of the land along what would become the modern Rusk Avenue created what appeared to be a hill above the ravine. It was in this area in 1866 that the original site of the Antioch Missionary

Baptist Church was relocated. About 1875, Jack Yates moved his church from the Brush Arbor on "Baptist Hill" in the Hathaway neighborhood to its current site on Robin Street[55].

After the Civil War, the western edge of the city had a dozen or so dwellings along this section of the bayou. Many of the residents were African-Americans who rented the houses on the streets off Laura Street (renamed Rusk Avenue in 1892). By 1890, these few homes were run down and in poor condition. The growth of the city at the turn of the 20th century resulted in the increase in the number of houses on the block to thirty-six single story dwellings in addition to five scattered dwellings near the bayou. The development of the block was stable in the 1920's and there were thirty-one homes on the tract in 1924[56].

In anticipation of the new civic center to be built on the west side of town, Fire Station No. 2 was built on the corner of Rusk Avenue and Bagby Street in 1926. That same year, the first new civic building was constructed and it was the new public library, now known as the Julia Ideson Library. The fire station served both the library and the county jail that was across the street. In 1927, developer Will Hogg, who had been acquiring land on the west side of town, offered the land to the city for the new civic center[57].

On January 15, 1928, the remarkable Jesse H. Jones convinced the Democratic Party to hold their nominating convention in Houston. Jones offered the City Auditorium as a venue that could handle the event, but he said that if it were not large enough, "the city of Houston will build a temporary structure that will comfortably seat all." The City Auditorium did not meet the requirements of the convention committee, and in the spring of 1928, construction crews began an expedited effort to build an immense wooden structure that was hastily cobbled together for the 1928 Democratic National Convention[58].

In June, 1928, the Democratic National Convention met in Sam Houston Hall, a pine edifice erected on the block bounded by Walker Avenue, Bagby Street, Rusk Avenue and Buffalo Bayou. Franklin Delano Roosevelt gave the keynote address as the party nominated Alfred E. Smith for President. Needless to say, Republican Herbert Hoover won the election in November[59].

The Depression of 1929 interrupted the further development of the new west side civic center. However, by the late 1930's, federal funds became available for local civic projects and the temporary Sam Houston Hall was replaced by the Sam Houston Coliseum. At the same time that the Coliseum was going up, the Music Hall, adjacent to the Coliseum, was constructed with an entrance on Bagby Street. Designed by Alfred Charles Finn, the Coliseum opened in October, 1937 and the Music Hall was completed in March, 1938[60].

Oddly enough, as construction of the Sam Houston Coliseum neared completion, someone noted that the plans did not include any space for the animals of the Houston Fat Stock Show and Rodeo, a major tenant of the hall. An annex that could double as parking space was quickly added. The two story Stock Exposition Building and Garage with a Cattle Shed was ready when the Houston Fat Stock Show and Livestock Exposition opened in 1939[61].

The last event held in the Sam Houston Coliseum was an Amway show in December, 1993. The Sam Houston Coliseum and Music Hall were demolished in 1999 to make room for the Hobby Center for the Performing Arts[62].

The Hobby Center of the Performing Arts opened on Friday, May 10, 2002. Named for the family of former Lieutenant Governor William Pettus "Bill" Hobby, Jr., the Hobby Center contains two theaters, Sarofim Hall, a 2,650 seat theater for musicals, and Zilkha Hall, a 500 seat theater for local theater and dance groups. The Arista restaurant on the second floor, above the lobby, takes advantage of Robert A. M. Stern's design using glass and vaulted ceilings, making the lobby a "window on the city[63]."

Out front, on the corner of Bagby Street and Walker Avenue, is an untitled sculpture in cast bronze. Designed by British sculptor Tony Cragg, the abstract sculpture is a towering 80 feet high and weighs 5,300 pounds. It had to be shipped by boat from Rotterdam[64].

In addition to the main building, a $10.5 million, seven story garage, which holds 800 cars, sits on the back part of the tract near Buffalo Bayou. A covered walkway from the garage to the main entrance forms an arcade between the complex and the administration building which "is like a big arrow saying the bayou is there," according to the architect. In any event, from the bayou, you do get a wonderful view of the long side of the parking garage[65].

Although the fine new garage for the Hobby Center dominates the south bank of the bayou, a remnant of the historic past lies near the water line of the bayou. Two sets of concrete pillars, one on each side of the bayou, stand apart from the modern, recently-constructed facilities and pathways. These pillars were the supports for a covered walkway into the Sam Houston Coliseum Garage from the parking lots on the north bank of the bayou. During the active days of the Coliseum, patrons of the events would park in the city lots across the bayou and they could walk comfortably into the hall over the covered walkway. Now, the pillars do nothing except provide us with a reminder of the former popular hall.

Bayou Place

Downstream, at the far end of the Hobby Center Garage, are the twin bridges of Rusk Avenue and Capitol Avenue. When a new reinforced concrete bridge was completed at Capitol Avenue in early 1915, it was the longest flat bridge in Houston. The bridge provided access for the growing west side of town to the downtown area, anticipating the move of the civic center to Bagby Street two decades later[66].

The combined thoroughfare of Capitol Avenue and Rusk Avenue separates the Hobby Center from Bayou Place across the street. The west bound lanes form the Capitol Avenue bridge and the east bound lanes are the Rusk Avenue bridge. The two bridges were created in the late 1950's as Memorial Drive was built as a limited access thoroughfare into the downtown district. The inbound lanes of Memorial Drive connect to Texas Avenue while the outbound traffic enters Memorial Drive from Prairie Avenue. Capitol Avenue and Rusk Avenue are the feeder lanes, or access lanes, for Memorial Drive.

The roadway itself is formed by the convergence of Capitol Avenue and Rusk Avenue as they merge on the west side of Bagby Street. The triangular traffic island created by this convergence has been developed as the Sweeney Triangle, a small park with ornamental trees, landscaping and park benches. The Sweeney Clock, a fifteen foot high timepiece that stood at the J. J. Sweeney and Company, 419 Main Street, on the northeast corner of Main Street and Prairie Avenue from 1908 to 1928, was installed at this location in 1971. From this little park, the historic site that is now Bayou Place - Phase II can be viewed with its recently renovated front entrance at 315 Capitol Avenue[67].

In the nineteenth century, the course of Buffalo Bayou through this area created a point of land that extended out from the blocks of town like a finger toward the west. The bayou flowed in a north-westerly bend before turning sharply to the east and going in a straight path to near Smith Street and Prairie Avenue. The peninsula-like characteristics of the terrain were enhanced by the ravine that ran through Block 87 and followed along the street right of way of Rusk Avenue west of Bagby Street until the gully curved abruptly to the north and entered the bayou. This tract, somewhat isolated by the topography around it, was the homestead of John H. Stephen Stanley, an early Houston resident[68].

J. H. S. Stanley, born in England about 1800, immigrated with his family to Texas in the early 1840's. In the 1850 census, he listed his occupation as a bookkeeper, but by 1855, Stanley was the local Houston agent for Thomas Affleck's Central Nurseries in Brenham. To accommodate his family, which included his wife Elizabeth, and their four teenage children, Stanley built a large home on the western edge of downtown at the foot of Capitol Avenue at Bagby Street. On this two acre tract which backed up to Buffalo Bayou, he also planted a grove of ornamental trees around his home to display the kinds of trees and shrubs that were available from the Affleck nursery. A live oak that was in Stanley's garden still stands on the site today. This oak has been estimated to be about 400 years old, and Stanley certainly appreciated its beauty and developed his gardens around it[69].

By 1860, J. H. S. Stanley called himself a photographic artist and, in 1866, he had a shop on Main Street between Preston Avenue and Prairie Avenue. His large extended family which included his son Alfred and his daughter Elizabeth and her children lived in the compound that was known as "the Stanley place." Alfred J. Stanley, known as "Fred," was employed as the bookkeeper and confidential clerk for T. W. House, a local merchant and a fellow immigrant from England[70].

Fred Stanley's association with the prominent businessman T. W. House proved be be extremely beneficial. In 1870, Fred Stanley, who had assumed the role as the head of the family by this time, had accumulated real assets valued at $100,000 and personal assets of $11,000. His father still lived with him at the home on Capitol Avenue, as did daughter Elizabeth Vasmer and her children[71].

In 1874, Fred Stanley was elected as the Alderman from the Fourth Ward. He served on the Finance Committee and his efforts and expertise were instrumental in the City's program to resolve the issue of the City debt. Stanley retired from the Board of Aldermen in January, 1876 due to recurring health problems. Fred Stanley died at his home on September 12, 1877 from "carbuncle" (possibly indicating that he suffered from diabetes, kidney or liver disease)[72].

Elizabeth H. Vasmer and her grown children with their families continued to live at the Stanley place through 1880. But, in 1882, the Stanley heirs, which included Elizabeth Vasmer and her sister Ada Link, the wife of Joseph B. Link, a minister, sold the two acre family homestead to the Freedmen's Aid Society of the Methodist Episcopal Church for $7500[73].

When the county began to look for a site on which to build a new county jail, the old Stanley place was a unanimous choice by the County Commissioners. To them, the site was well suited for the proposed new jail and courthouse since the place was isolated to a great extent by its location on the western edge of downtown and secluded by the topographic features of the area which included the gully along the south and Buffalo Bayou on the north. Situated on such a site, the jail and criminal courts would not disturb the adjacent neighborhood[74].

The Commissioners Court authorized the purchase of the Stanley place from the current owner, J. S. Dunlavy, for $15,000, and instructed the county judge to proceed with the bid process. The judge advertised for bids on June 16, 1895 with the opening of the bids scheduled for July 16, 1895. Local architect Eugene T. Heiner completed the plans for the new county jail and courthouse on September 13, 1895. And although there were questions, and hearings, about the quality of the construction work done on the building, the new jail opened in October, 1896[75].

The jail building designed by Heiner was typical of the style for such structures of that time. It was one of thirteen jails that he designed during the twenty years following his first jail project for Galveston County in 1878. The building was a three story pressed brick structure with concrete trimmings throughout, except for the front entrance and portico which was faced with solid granite. The general plan call for the court rooms and offices to be in the front part of the building with main entrance facing Capitol Avenue. The jail portion was to the rear, with the entrance to the jail to the left side of the building and with the sheriff's residence on the right[76].

Court offices occupied the first floor of the front section and a large, 50 foot by 60 foot court room was on the second floor. Spectators could watch the court proceedings from a large balcony above the court room on the third floor. The jail occupied three stories and included forty-four steel cages. The locks for the cells operated on a single, common lever and the cells could be locked or unlocked independently, as well. Jail cells for female prisoners and juveniles were located in the rear wing[77].

Within a decade, the new jail proved to be inadequate to handle the needs of this growing county. The remedy, however, was not immediately forthcoming. In the prosperity of the post World War I period, though, the old courthouse was razed in 1926 and a new criminal courts and county jail was constructed in its place. Designed by Wyatt C. Hedrick, Inc. of Fort Worth, the Harris County Criminal Courts and Jail Building, located at 624 Bagby Street, was completed in the autumn of 1927. Built in the Greek classic style, the ten story structure included a basement, a mezzanine and eight floors. Granite steps led to the main doorway of the building that faced Bagby Street. An immense spreading live oak, a *Quercus fusiformis*, that had been a notable feature of the old Stanley place, retained its distinguished presence at the front entrance of the courthouse and jail[78].

In the early 1960's, the courthouse and jail building was demolished to make room for Albert Thomas Convention Center. The center was named in honor of Albert Thomas who served as the Congressman from Harris County from 1936 to 1966. Thomas had graduated from Rice Institute (now, Rice University) in 1920, and he was the first Rice alumnus to serve in the U. S. Congress. Work on the convention center began in 1966. In order to preserve the site's large live oak tree, thought to be the oldest tree in Harris County, a basement wall was left in place to protect the tree's root system[79].

The Albert Thomas Convention Center never achieved the kind of success that had been hoped for it. By the 1990's, the City made plans to redevelop the property, and in 1991, David Cordish of Baltimore was awarded a sixty year lease on the center. On December 31, 1997, the convention center was re-opened as Bayou Place, an entertainment complex of restaurants, theaters and music venues. The renovation of the west hall of the center has added about 200,000 square feet of office space at Bayou Place. The Planet, a leading provider of information technology solutions, opened its new, state of the art world headquarters at 315 Capitol Avenue on December 12, 2007[80].

Gracing the entry way to the offices in the Bayou Place - Phase II development is the grand old live oak. By this time, the large oak tree had become legendary and the City has erected a plaque nearby calling it the Old Hanging Oak[81].

The Hanging Oak and Hangman's Grove

This story began four or five years ago when Linda Gorski and I were walking along the banks of Buffalo Bayou in the downtown area trying to identify the sites that might hold good stories for this book on Houston along Buffalo Bayou. We came upon the large oak tree in front of what was then the Albert Thomas Convention Center, and we noted that the sign by the tree said it was the Old Hanging Oak. We made a note to find out more about the story of the tree. Then, a couple of years ago, we ran into Stephen Hardin at a local event and he told us that he had just published a book on the 1838 executions of two convicted murderers in a location that was later called Hangman's Grove. That's when we began to link the stories together. With a little help from the late Jim Glass, things began to fall into place. What follows is what we found out.

In 1836, Houston emerged as a town from the wilderness on the frontier of Texas. Today, you would scarcely see anything that resembles a wilderness in Houston, but the traces of the past are still there and they are intertwined into our local history.

Buffalo Bayou, unlike most rivers in Texas, runs east-west instead of north-south. It is the dividing line between the East Texas Piney Woods to the north and the Coastal Prairie to the south. The banks along the bayou were covered with a riparian woodland and the nearby prairie was dotted with small thickets of oak and other native trees. Our story involves three of these tree clusters.

As you might know, large trees, especially very large oak trees, are held in high esteem in many parts of the country. Some trees even have their own societies that rank their magnificent trees by size, age, girth, etc. We came upon Houston's own "special" live oak tree while exploring the banks of Buffalo Bayou. Houston's largest live oak tree sits in front of The Planet, an internet hosting company located in the newly renovated section of Bayou Place, formerly the Albert Thomas Convention Center.

This tree, which is located on the corner of Capitol Avenue and Bagby Street, appears to my untrained eye to be a Texas Live Oak, Quercus fusiformis. A marker that has been placed in front of this tree by the City of Houston estimates the age of this live oak to be about 400 years.

As a side note, we did try to verify the age of the tree that the marker says might be 400 years old. Determining the age of a tree is not as easy as it may seem. Several sources say that the only accurate way to determine the age of a tree is to count the growth rings. To do that, you have to cut it down (!) or use a boring tool. Since we had access to neither of those options, we tried the other technique which is to measure the circumference of the trunk of the tree.

One morning in August, we drove over to the tree with a measuring tape and a pencil. Two mounted patrol officers gave us a long, hard look, but they refrained from asking us what we were doing. We strung the tape measure around the tree trunk, twice in fact, to find that the tree is 175 inches around. Then, we plugged that number into the step by step calculations offered by four different web sites for a sure fire answer. We got four widely different results, ranging from 136 years to over 300 years. None actually approached the 400 year number, though. So, the true age of our oak tree will have to wait for a more scientific analysis. What we do know, is: that tree is old.

The marker also has given the tree the name of The Old Hanging Oak. It is a name which we feel is unfortunate for this tree, and it is a name that is historically inaccurate in many ways. In particular, the marker repeats the undocumented legend that, during the period of the Republic of Texas, eleven criminals were executed by hanging from this tree.

It is almost a part of the myth of the American West that every town on the frontier had a "hanging tree" on the square or somewhere in the locality. In Texas, several towns boast of "hanging trees," including Clarksville on whose tree, in 1837, a murderer named Page and two others were hung, and Goliad, where, in 1857, trials were held and men were hanged from the local oak for the murder of Mexican freighters. Comanche, Seguin, Cold Spring and Hallettsville also boast of their hanging trees, just to name a few[82].

In a perverse sense of pride, these legendary trees are pointed to in the local histories. Whether these trees actually performed the roles assigned to them is a matter for local historians to document or debunk. Legends, however, are difficult to deflate, and their advocates do not give up the tantalizing story easily, no matter how outlandish it may be.

Generally, the naming of a hanging tree refers to a single event in the distant past. So significant was this event that it remains in the memory of the town and the local population long after the event. It may have a basis in fact, but the legend takes on a life of its own. So, then, does Houston have an event in its past that would give rise to the legend of the hanging tree? In fact, it does.

On Wednesday, March 28, 1838, convicted murderers John Christopher Columbus Quick and David James Jones were executed. The gallows were located, according to the local newspaper that day, "in a beautiful islet of timber, situated in the prairie about a mile south of the city." As described by the first hand account of John Herndon, a young lawyer who arrived in Houston from Kentucky in January, 1838, the hangings were a gruesome affair that out of curiosity drew almost everyone in the young city to the place that would later be called "Hangman's Grove[83]."

"Wednesday, March 28. A delightful day, worthy of other deeds. One hundred forty men ordered out to guard the criminals to the gallows. A concourse of from 2000 to 3000 persons on the ground and among the whole lot not a single sympathetic tear was dropped. Quick addressed the crowd in a stern, composed and hardened manner, entirely unmoved up to the moment of swinging off the cart. Jones seemed frightened altho' as hardened in crime as Quick. They swung off at 2 o'clock p.m. and were cut down in thirty-five minutes, not having made the slightest struggle... Cavanaugh and self went out to the graves and cut off the heads of Quick and Jones and brought them in for dissection..."

"Thursday, March 29. ...Commenced dissecting and examining the heads. Phrenologically, Jones had a very bad head, all moral power very deficient... Quick had a much better head. His moral powers pretty well developed and intellectual tolerably well..."

"Friday, March 30. ...Finished the dissection of Quick's and Jones heads. Preserved the brains of Jones..."

"Saturday, March 31. ...Buried the remains of Quick's and Jones heads...[84]"

For the young town, the executions made a big impression. Nearly every person in town witnessed the event and it was remembered by the citizens of Houston for decades. The place of execution soon became known as Hangman's Grove. But, since the early 20th century, the exact location of Hangman's Grove has been a matter of debate among modern historians. The debate continues even today.

Historian Stephen L. Hardin wrote the story of the 1838 Quick and Jones hangings in his popular book entitled *Texian Macabre*. In exquisite detail, Hardin tells the story of how the prosecution of these criminals changed the sense of lawlessness that had captivated the capital of the Republic in its first years of existence. The executions set a new tone of civility for Houston[85].

As a historian, Hardin relied on the notes of Andrew Muir, a historian of Houston from a generation earlier, when he identified the location of the execution site as "in the vicinity of Main and Webster." Both men were quite vague in saying where the place was. This can be seen on the map included in Hardin's book[86].

By 1839, a year after the events described above, the name Hangman's Grove appears in an advertisement in the Telegraph and Texas Register as well as in the deed records of Harris County. The February 13, 1839 edition of the Telegraph contains an advertisement by the company of Heddenberg and Vedder which mentions their tract of land which includes part of "hangman's grove." In fact, the ad is a warning notice to the public forbidding the cutting and removal of timber from the tract. About a month later, on March 26, 1839, the John W. N. A. Smith Survey report describes Hangman's Grove as extending along the James Wells Survey west boundary line for .65 miles[87].

Hangman's Grove was mentioned in another newspaper ad on June 19, 1839 by the Hedenberg and Vedder mercantile firm for fifteen acres within one mile of the city. Similarly, on March 2, 1841, Mary O'Brien sold fifteen and one half acres near Hangman's Grove to Emma Blake. The land was located in the Girard tract about a half mile from Houston. The Girard tract was in the James Wells Survey. On January 1, 1840, James Wells and his wife sold thirty-one and one half acres from his headright to Auguste Girard, Charles J. Hedenberg and Philip V. Vedder, a triangular piece of land in the extreme southern part of the Wells survey. Following the details of the Smith Survey report, Andrew Muir identified this Hangman's Grove, about 1950, as near City of Houston Block 245, bounded by Lamar Avenue, Dallas Avenue, Chartres Street and St. Emanuel Street[88].

The question is: which place is the real Hangman's Grove? Main at Webster or Block 245? We can assess each possible site by asking if the place is the site of a documented event. And, did the site remain in the popular memory because of that event?

For Block 245, we have found no documentation or reports of a significant event of a hanging or an execution in the grove near this block. In addition, according to the survey report, the grove extends for over a half mile. Much larger than the "islet" description for the location of the Quick and Jones executions. The survey report also notes that the grove of timber begins a half mile from the city. Subsequent deed records and other accounts make no mention of this "Hangman's Grove" after 1841.

The evidence for Muir's Main at Webster location as the actual site of the Quick and Jones executions is somewhat better. This location is referred to as Hangman's Grove in a number of newspaper stories throughout the nineteenth century. The Galveston Daily News of January 28, 1874 reported on cases of small pox, one of whom was a black man who had been sick for sometime and lived "at Hangman's Grove, in the west of the city." On August 12, 1876, the Galveston Daily News reported that a dueling incident between two African-Americans took place "in the pine woods known as Hangman's Grove, near State Fair Park." The fairgrounds were located near Webster Street and west of Main Street. Frank Barnes, who lived "in the vicinity of Hangman's Grove, in the western part of the city" was the victim of a robbery, according to Galveston Daily News of June 17, 1877. Each of these newspaper accounts points to the general knowledge that the Hangman's Grove was a thicket of trees in the area that is southwest of downtown Houston[89].

An article in the Galveston Daily News of August 5, 1893, offers even more information regarding Hangman's Grove. The story reported that there were only three other hangings that took place at the City's Hangman's Grove, one, in 1854, was a Mr. Hyde, in 1867, was a Mr. Johnson, and another Mr. Johnson about 1869. After that, hangings took place in the jail yard of the county jail in downtown. These included the executions of Henry Quarles in 1878, John Cone in 1881, Burt Mitchell in 1885, William Caldwell in 1889, and Henry McGee in 1891. Walter E. Shaw was convicted of murder and hanged at the City Jail on August 5, 1893[90].

Well into the late nineteenth century, the cluster of trees that was called Hangman's Grove was a well known locale to the people of Houston. Most likely, this was because the grove was still there and had changed little since 1838. It was a landmark on the prairie southwest of town. The clincher in terms of the exact location of Hangman's Grove, however, comes in 1887. The Galveston Daily News of August 23, 1887, reported that Peter Gabel owned the twenty acre grove of trees in south part of the Fourth Ward that was known as old Hangman's Grove. Gabel fenced off the tract and thus blocked several unsurveyed streets including Calhoun Street, Gray Street and Pierce Street, Baker Street, Hopson Street and Crosby Street, Anson Street, Bagby Street and Brazos Street[91].

The Gabel tract which contained Hangman's Grove had been purchased by Gabel's wife's first husband John Stein from Obedience Smith in 1843. The deed records clearly define the bounds of the land where the grove was, as late as 1887. Lastly, the Bird's Eye map of Houston, printed in 1891, clearly shows Hangman's Grove. It provides a final bit of evidence that the grove of trees that acquired the name of Hangman's Grove after the executions of 1838 was still a prominent feature of town over fifty years later. The subsequent suburban development of the land had the effect of removing the grove as a local landmark. As a result, few, if any, references can be found to Hangman's Grove after 1900. Even Dr. S. O. Young, writing in 1913, places the location of Hangman's Grove "just on the southeast corner of the old cemetery out of the San Felipe Road." That is the right direction, but not quite the right place. By the time of the study of Houston's history in the 1940's, the location of the grove had been forgotten[92].

So, then, what about the Old Hanging Oak?

John H. S. Stanley built his homestead in the isolated tract on the west side of town in the 1840's. Stanley was the local representative of Thomas Affleck, a nurseryman in Brenham. He planted a grove of ornamental trees around the Stanley home. The Stanley family lived on the property until the 1880's when it was sold and later acquired by the County in 1895 for a courthouse and jail. The four story courthouse and jail was built on the Stanley land and the large live oak tree which graced the property was left in place to stand at the front entrance to the building. When this courthouse was demolished in 1926 for the construction of a new, eight story courthouse and jail complex, the live oak again survived and became a landmark in its own right at the front of the courthouse.

When asked if any hangings had taken place from the oak, T. A. Binford, who served as the sheriff of Harris County from 1918 to 1937, said that the criminals were hanged from the rafters of the jail, but beneath the tree, the relatives and mourners gathered and waited. In 1942, the live oak at the courthouse was simply referred to as "an immense spreading oak." By 1984, noted reporter and newsman Ray Miller called it "the Courthouse Oak, also known as the Hanging Oak." When the City was upgrading the Civic Center complex in the early 1990's, the marker placed at the tree called it "The Old Hanging Oak[93]."

No hangings or executions took place at this fine live oak tree. It was called the Courthouse Oak in the past. Wouldn't this be a better name for our beloved old tree today?

The City Water Works

The bayou is congested as you paddle under the Rusk Avenue (inbound to downtown) bridge and the Capitol Avenue (outbound) bridge. The pilings for these bridge constrict the routes, especially in higher water. Above, too, are the elevated lanes of Interstate 45, and the concrete supports for that roadway also contribute to the maze in the waterway.

You can negotiate the currents and the bridge pilings as the bayou rounds the west end of Bayou Place. If you look up to the north bank, the roof line of the former City Water Works building is visible above the trees and shrubbery of Landry's Aquarium entertainment complex. Immediately to the east of the large Water Works building, the conical roof of an earlier pump house is barely visible. Landry's incorporated these historic structures into their facility instead of demolishing them, and they should be commended. The larger structure now contains the shark tank which fits nicely into the story of Houston's early experiences with the water system.

The planning for a great city as envisioned by the Allen brothers did not include the installation of what we consider to be basic infrastructure. They made no plans to provide drinking for the residents who flocked to the new town. Early enterprises, such as the attempt in 1838 to sell the water from Beauchamp Springs, failed. William Lawrence and A. F. Woodward held a meeting to organize the Houston Water Works Company on December 15, 1838 with the intention of piping water from Beauchamp Springs, located on White Oak Bayou near where Houston Avenue crosses that bayou today, to the city. The company was never operational, although Thomas D. Beauchamp had been selling water from the springs in thirty gallon barrels to Houston's thirsty citizens since June, 1838. The price was $0.75 per barrel[94].

For nearly forty years, Houston residents relied on rain water captured in cisterns or bayou water for their water needs. That was indeed a poor situation, so finally, in 1878, a franchise was awarded to a New York group which formed the Houston Water Works Company. The franchise agreement authorized and required this new water works company to operate a water system to supply water "for extinguishing fires and other purposes." Fire suppression was the primary goal of the new municipal water system since the hazard from fires was of great concern to the businessmen of the town. Providing fresh and clean drinking water was a secondary consideration at this time. By September, 1878, the Houston Water Works Company had built a dam on Buffalo Bayou above Capitol Avenue. The company established a plant on Buffalo Bayou at Artesian Street, laid water pipes and began pumping water from the bayou into the city system[95].

The service provided by the water company, however, was largely unsatisfactory to the local residents. In 1884, T. H. Scanlan and Associates of Chicago purchased the Houston Water Works Company and promised to expand the water system in order to improve services to public buildings, stores and residences. The new operators installed a new boiler, steam powered turbine pumps and a brick reservoir. The upgraded water system's new capacity was eight million gallons a day[96].

Complaints about the water system continued, however, especially when the system failed on occasion to provide enough water pressure to fight fires. Nevertheless, the city's water system took a turn for the better in 1887. In that year, Henry Thompson drilled an artesian well to 180 feet at Franklin Avenue and La Branch Street that flowed 1,400 gallons per hour. Beneath the city lay the nation's third largest underground reservoir of water. By 1891, Houston had fourteen artesian wells. The Water Works complex expanded to three buildings which housed Worthington Duplex Pumps with suction pipes to the bayou. Well water was provided to residents, but during emergencies, the company pumped water from Buffalo Bayou into the system and mixed it with ground water to provide enough pressure to fight fires[97].

On October 6, 1906, during the administration of Mayor Baldwin Rice, the City bought the Houston Water Works Company for

$901,700, and shortly thereafter completed sixty-six new artesian wells to improve the quality of the water system. Within a year, the additions and improvements to the water works complex significantly enhanced the municipal water system. The main building contained two large pumping systems, a five million gallon per day Worthington pump and an eight million gallon per day Worthington pump. The smaller round building with the conical roof included two other Worthington pumps with a combined capacity of three million gallons per day. A round the clock crew of five to seven employees maintained the water system continuously[98].

The Central Pumping Station, the large building still visible today, was built in 1926-1927 and contained a steam-driven flywheel that powered pumps drawing water from artesian wells. In May, 1929, the Central Water Works plant was flooded by twenty feet of bayou water and the pumps went out of commission. Again, in December, 1935, the bayou rose eight feet higher than in 1929 and the system ceased operating, yet, the plant remained the city's primary pumping station until the Lake Houston reservoir was completed and began service in 1954. This pump station continued in operation until 1980 when the new pump station facility on the west side of Sabine Street at Buffalo Bayou was built[99].

Texas Avenue

After passing the old Water Works, Buffalo Bayou flows due east for a short distance. The walls of Bayou Place on the south bank form a palisade, of sorts, while the north bank is overshadowed by the elevated roadway of Texas Avenue. If you peer beneath the canopy of the road, you can get a glimpse of the ferris wheel at the Aquarium. This is the largest ferris in downtown Houston. The fact that it is the only ferris wheel in downtown Houston does not diminish its significance. It anchors the entertainment area of Landry's showcase restaurant complex provides dramatic aerial views of the central business district.

In the earliest days of Houston, the bayou was the edge of town and the place where Texas Avenue now crosses the bayou was the site of Stockbridge's ford. The water in the bayou was about four feet deep at that point and the white sand bottom was hard enough to allow draymen and teamsters to drive their oxen carts across the bayou. It was a good place for watering their animals as well. With a firm bottom, shallow water and fine sand, the site also became known as Stockbridge's swimming hole and it was especially suited for beginner swimmers[100].

At this time, the bayou's course did not make the ninety degree turn to the left as it does today. It continued ahead to near Smith Street before turning back through the city block and making a radical "S" turn before turning east again beyond Preston Avenue. A gully began near Milam Street and ran between Texas Avenue and Prairie Avenue to the bayou. Where the gully crossed Smith Street, there was a large spring which had minnows and a large overhanging oak tree. The spring was probably the reason that, in April, 1837, when three hundred Comanche warriors arrived in Houston to discuss a treaty with the new government of the Republic of Texas, they set up camp in this area. During the spring of 1837 and the spring of 1838, leaders of the major native American tribes in Texas, the Comanches, the Lipan Apaches, the Cherokees and the Tonkawas, came to Houston to meet with President Sam Houston and the members of the Texas Congress. The issues relating to the Indian situation, however, were not resolved. In the election of 1838, Mirabeau B. Lamar campaigned on the policy of the eradication and removal of Indians from Texas. After his election, Lamar enforced that policy. The troubles with the native tribes on the Texas frontier persisted until the 1880's[101].

Landry's Downtown Aquarium

Calvin Stockbridge owned the land on the north bank (the west side in this section of the bayou where it runs more northerly) where Landry's Downtown Aquarium is located today. He purchased the sixteen acres on April 7, 1838, and in June, he built a toll bridge across the bayou near what is now Preston Avenue. This caused a controversy with Bernard Caraher who sued to prevent its use. Caraher operated a ferry near there with a license that he acquired from William K. Wilson which had been granted on May 17, 1838[102].

The Stockbridge bridge over Preston Avenue was deemed "unsafe" by county inspectors and it washed away in 1839. The city had built a free bridge over Buffalo Bayou at Preston Avenue in November, 1838, and it, too, washed away in 1839. Elam Stockbridge, son of Calvin Stockbridge, oversaw the construction of a second bridge at Preston Avenue, but in 1841, it also washed away[103].

The importance of a transportation link to the farms and plantations of the Brazos River was not lost on the City officials. In December, 1843, construction of a new bridge at Preston Avenue began. This bridge was more substantial than the previous structures. It was one hundred feet long, sixteen feet wide, and set on twenty-five foot high piers of four posts each and spaced fifty feet apart. This bridge was the longest and most substantial in Texas at the time, and it became known as the Long Bridge[104].

The five major trails leading to and from Houston had intersecting cross-trails that allowed wagons and oxen teams to reach the Washington Road and enter the city over the Preston Avenue bridge. The Long Bridge at Preston Avenue was used by more than four hundred wagons a day during the 1840's. The steady procession of freighters were bringing cotton to the city and shipping goods out to the interior of the state. Nearly eighty percent of the commerce of Texas crossed the bridge[105].

The bayou, however, was difficult to tame and and continued to pose problems. The flood of 1853 washed out the Long Bridge built in 1843, and it had to be rebuilt. By 1885, there was a 160 foot long iron bridge at Preston Avenue, and in 1914, a concrete bridge was built[106].

During the 1840's, Elam Stockbridge operated the town's first grist mill that relied on three oxen on a treadmill for power. He married Melinda G. Bachelder on July 4, 1843, and by 1850, the thrity-five year old Stockbridge was a successful merchant with a young family of two sons and a daughter. In his occupation as a trader, Stockbridge was very successful during the next decade. His real assets in 1860 were valued at $50,000 and he had personal assets of $45,000. His personal life, however, fared less well. Their young daughter Adaline died in 1850. Their infant daughter Ella died in March, 1858. And, Elam's wife Melinda passed away on

December 18, 1858 at age thirty-seven. Each of these family members are buried in the City Cemetery which is known today as Founders Memorial Park. In addition, his oldest son Judge developed mental problems[107].

Beset with these personal problems and on the onset of the Civil War, Elam Stockbridge moved to the City of Brenham where he could care for his son Judge who had been declared insane. Fortunately, his wealth did not suffer too badly during the war, and by 1870, Stockbridge was a farmer in Brenham with land holdings valued at $20,000 and personal assets of $35,000. After Elam's death sometime before 1880, his son Luther took custody of Judge who lived with him and his family in Brenham where Luther worked as a printer[108].

While the Stockbridge fortunes were in decline, the prospects for New Yorker Benjamin Charles Simpson were on the rise. The twenty year old machinist arrived in Houston in 1859. With the coming of the Civil War, he enlisted in the Fifth Texas Infantry and rose to the rank of third sergeant of Company A before being wounded at Second Manassas and, later, captured at Gettysburg on July 2, 1863. He escaped to Canada from Fort Delaware and returned to Houston in February, 1865 as a crew member of a blockade runner[109].

After the war, Simpson formed a partnership with Charles Wiggins and G. A. Branard to manufacture and sell agricultural implements. The foundry for Simpson, Branard and Company was established on the former Stockbridge property near the Long Bridge at Preston Avenue. Wiggins, a master machinist was the superintendent at the foundry. The company advertisements, in 1866, suggest that they had a wide range of agricultural products for sale. By 1870, the company was reorganized as the Phoenix Iron Works, with Simpson and Wiggins as founders. As evidence of the high quality of the products manufactured, the Phoenix Iron Works was awarded a medallion "For the best stationary engine made anywhere 1871" at the Texas State Fair in Houston[110].

For the next two decades, the Phoenix Iron Works produced fine iron products at the site on Preston Avenue. But, after the death of B. C. Simpson, on May 16, 1888, the company declined, and by 1896, it had completely closed down. For a few years, the Henke and Pillot company used the site for a cotton yard. In the 1920's, it was the Preston Wagon Yard, but for the next four decades or so it was an undeveloped tract of land. After the Farmer's Market moved into its new building on the opposite bank of the bayou in 1929, the grassy area on the north bank of Buffalo Bayou between Sabine and Preston Streets was the location of Houston's first fruit market. The area became known as Watermelon Flats and it functioned as an adjunct to the market until the Farmer's Market itself shut down in the 1950's. In 1987, the grassy area became the site of the Watermelon Flats Show, an open air art show. Watermelon Flats was established as the site of the Buffalo Bayou Artpark in 1992[111].

In the 1960's, the City of Houston established the headquarters of the Fire Department in a four story building on the former site of the Phoenix Iron Works. The building opened on February 1, 1968, with Fire Station No. 1 occupying the first two floors and the offices of the department on the upper floors. The Fire Department headquarters moved to larger facilities on Dart Street in 1985, and Fire Station No. 1 closed in 2001[112].

The Houston City Council approved a forty year lease on the former Fire Station No. 1 property with the Landry's corporation for a dining and entertainment venue. Landry's Downtown Aquarium opened in early 2003 with an array of restaurants, a Ferris wheel and a train to a shark exhibit in the old City Water Works building. The facility is a popular place in the revival of downtown entertainment for all age groups[113].

Wortham Theater Center

The Farmers Market in Houston dates to the earliest days of the city. The first plat of the town of Houston included a block bounded by Travis Street, Milam Street, Preston Avenue and Congress Avenue that was set aside by the Allen brothers for a public market. By the first decades of the twentieth century, the growth of Houston strained the capacity of the market house to serve the needs of the population.

The market at Market Square was so congested that farmers and housewives petitioned the city for more suitable accommodations. In the mid-1920's, a site on Preston Avenue was selected as centrally located, convenient, with good sanitation and capable of future expansion. A larger and more modern facility was planned for a new location on Buffalo Bayou[114].

The new Farmer's Market was a part of the project to channelize Buffalo Bayou from approximately Texas Avenue to Smith Street. The work of clearing and straightening the bayou and grading its banks for bulkheads and retaining walls began in 1927. The large "S" turn in the bayou extended from Texas Avenue through City blocks 60, 40 and 38 while passing under the Preston Avenue bridge before turning back to the east at Smith Street. The channelization project would make the course of the bayou run straight from Texas Avenue, under the Preston Avenue bridge, and then turn toward Smith Street, resulting in the reclamation of land in the blocks bounded by Preston Avenue, Smith Street, Texas Avenue and the bayou. On this eight acre tract, the city built the new Farmer's Market. The Farmer's Market was opened to the public on March 21, 1929[115].

The Farmer's Market, located at 500 Preston Avenue, was built to provide adequate quarters for the direct grower-to-consumer sale of Texas-grown produce. Local truck farmers grew a wide variety of vegetables, including snap beans, onions, cucumbers, squash, potatoes, beets, carrots, spinach, lettuce, peppers, tomatoes, egg-plant, turnips, radishes and cabbage, which they sold to the public at the downtown market. In the 1930's, it was commonplace for ten to fifteen thousand people to shop at the Farmer's Market each day[116].

The structure was a reinforced concrete building with a floor area of 114,583 square feet in a series of one story sections built in modern industrial, open air design. Eight roofed areas extending for a length of 300 feet on the top floor contained three acres of floor space for 318 stalls for vendors. The lower level contained parking spaces for 1,200 vehicles. Rest rooms, offices and a restaurant occupied the northeast side of the building[117].

After World War II, the growth of the city spurred the opening of markets in the suburbs and a decline of the downtown city market ensued. The Henke and Pillot Company was one of the grocers leading the way to spread suburban supermarkets throughout the city. Henke and Pillot had a long association with services to the farmers and the market during the last quarter of the nineteenth and the early twentieth century, but by mid-century, the grocery chain was in the forefront of the market forces that led to the closure of the downtown market house. In 1956, the company was acquired by the Kroger Corporation of Cincinnati and in the early 1960's, the Henke and Pillot stores were re-branded as Kroger. With its widely distributed supermarket locations, Kroger has dominated the Houston grocery market for over fifty years. The Farmer's Market was razed in 1958 to permit automobile access into the downtown district with the extension of Memorial Drive to Texas Avenue and Prairie Avenue[118].

The site of the market was used as a surface parking lot for two decades until the City Council, in 1980, made the two blocks bounded by Texas Avenue, Smith Street, Preston Avenue and Buffalo Bayou available for a lyric center. The Wortham Theater Center, located at 550 Prairie Avenue, officially opened on May 9, 1987. The building was designed by Eugene Aubry of Morris Aubry Architects and it was named in honor of Gus S. Wortham whose foundation gave $40 million of the $66 million needed to build the facility. The center includes two theaters named in honor of Alice and George Brown and Roy and Lillie Cullen as the Brown Foundation donated $6 million to the cost of the center while the Cullen Foundation contributed $7.5 million[119].

The Brown Theater, a large venue with 2,423 seats and a 17,000 square foot stage, is home to major performances of the Houston Ballet and the Houston Grand Opera. The smaller Cullen Theater, with 1,100 seats, is ideal for solo artists, chamber music, small touring shows and recitals. The interior stairway of the Wortham Center is decorated with eight shimmering, multi-colored steel columns which resemble twelve to twenty-eight foot tall sheaves of grain tied together in an offering. This magnificent design was made by Albert Paley, a former jewelry maker[120].

The construction of the Wortham Theater Center was accompanied by the establishment of park along Buffalo Bayou adjacent to the theaters in commemoration of Houston's and Texas' 150th birthday in 1986. Designated as Sesquicentennial Park, the park was planned for two phases of development. Phase I of Sesquicentennial Park, completed in August, 1989, consisted of a 2.2 acre park that included a grand entrance, a fountain, a multilevel waterfall and stairways from street level around Wortham Center to the Carruth Promenade along the banks of Buffalo Bayou below. Named for Allen H. "Buddy" Carruth, long time chairman of Wortham Foundation, the promenade was connected with the Sabine to Bagby Promenade in 2006 to provide an extensive pedestrian walkway system along Buffalo Bayou west of Allen's Landing[121].

Phase II, completed in May, 1998, added 8.2 acres of park land to the project that extends from Texas Avenue to Smith Street along both sides of Buffalo Bayou. The foremost feature of Phase II, erected between the Wortham Theater Center and the Promenade, is Mel Chin's Seven Wonders of the Community. The seven pillars of this sculpture reach seventy feet high. Each illuminated pillar consists of 150 stainless steel reproductions of drawings created by Houston children who were born in 1986 and the steel displays are set on thirty foot masonry bases[122].

To create the Seven Wonders of the Community, Mel Chin, a local artist who was born in Houston's Kashmere Gardens neighborhood in 1951, reviewed the artwork of 1,050 children and then incorporated a laser cutting of each drawing into 3 foot by 4 foot stainless steel panels. The drawings were grouped on the pillars to depict seven distinctive aspects of life in Houston: agriculture, transportation, manufacturing, energy, philanthropy, medicine and technology[123].

The Phase II development of Sesquicentennial Park also included the creation of The Commons in the block bounded by Preston Avenue, Smith Street and a curve of Buffalo Bayou. Various art works and landscaping areas were added to the park space on both sides of the bayou and its walkways, including The Big Bubble, The Grotto, The Upper Garden and The Lower Garden. The Bush Monument was added to the north bank in 2004, and the Baker Monument was dedicated in 2010[124].

The Big Bubble is a whimsical creation of artist Dean Ruck that lies in the channel of the bayou upstream of the Preston Avenue bridge. When the large red button, located in the northeast alcove of the bridge, is pressed, a burst of air from the bayou floor sends an enormous bubble of water to the surface -- with startling effects on the unsuspecting passersby[125]!

The area of the park on the east bank of the bayou and north of Preston Avenue is The Common, a 1.25 acre semi-circular lawn that slopes gently to the bayou and is the staging area for outdoor events. A balustrade railing borders the northern edge of The Common and artist Dean Ruck assembled a collection of porcelain-enamel photographs, which are mounted along the balustrades, that trace the history of Houston's waterfront[126].

In late 2009, the City Council approved a plan to establish a monument to former U. S. Secretary of State James A. Baker III in The Common. Renowned artist Chas Fagan of Charlotte, North Carolina was commissioned to sculpt a statue of Baker. A set of plaques commemorates not only the accomplishments of James A. Baker III, but highlights the role of four generations of the Baker family in the story of Houston. The Common was renamed Baker Common in honor of the family, and the formal dedication of the Baker Monument was October 26, 2010[127].

The story of the land that has become the Baker Common goes back to the first decades of Houston when Edward W. Taylor, the older brother of Horace Dickinson Taylor, bought City of Houston Block 37 in a tax foreclosure sale on July 25, 1849. The nine Taylor children, natives of Massachusetts, were orphaned in 1831 when their parents died in typhus fever epidemic. Two of the Taylor sons moved to Charleston, South Carolina while Edward Taylor came to Texas in 1837 to establish a mercantile business in Independence. Horace Taylor, who was born in 1821, went to stay with his Charleston brothers in 1836 and 1837, and then he joined his brother Edward in Texas in 1838[128].

Horace Taylor served in the Texas army during the Mier Expedition from October 17, 1842 to January 17, 1843. After a brief visit to his brothers in Charleston beginning in the summer of 1845, Horace Taylor returned to Texas in January, 1848. Eventually, Horace settled in Houston where he and his brother Edward opened a cotton commission business in a rented warehouse at Travis Street and Commerce Avenue. Horace lived frugally in bachelor quarters in their downtown warehouse on the bayou, while Edward built a home and garden for his family on three plus acres in Block 37 and 38, located "on the edge of town[129]."

About 1850, Edward Taylor joined the successful firm of William Marsh Rice and E. B. Nichols. He then sold the home he had just built and his part of the cotton commission business to his brother Horace. Horace Taylor, who had married Emily Baker on December 1, 1952, moved into his brother's vacant home on Block 37 where they eventually raised eight children on the homestead[129].

The Taylor home was situated on Preston Avenue in the center of Block 37, just on the edge of the top of the bayou's bank which angled diagonally across the block from Smith Street near the end of Congress Avenue. It gave the appearance of sitting on a high and imposing hill. The main part was constructed with a hip roof and it had a long porch that extended across front and down Smith Street side. The house was enlarged six times with additions to the rear of the house so that it eventually included ten rooms. Picket fences surrounded the whole place and extending all the way down to the bayou. The home was set among the trees of the heavily wooded tract that included native varieties of sycamore, prickly ash, bois d'arc, sweetgum, holly, box elder and mustang grapes. Some of the magnolias growing there were nearly one hundred feet tall[130].

In addition to his business interests, Taylor served as alderman for the First Ward. After the Civil War, he became the mayor of Houston. In a one year term in 1866. Horace Taylor played a vital role in this pivotal time for the city. He was determined to revitalize the city and the civic infrastructure after the years of neglect during the war. To show the way, Taylor refused to accept his $3,000 salary as mayor. He set out a program that improved the streets with a layer of new shell and he had street signs posted with names on the street corners for the first time. A culvert was installed in the large gully at Caroline Street and Congress Avenue to improve transportation to the east side of town[131].

Horace Taylor died on November 9, 1890, at age sixty-nine. In 1892, the Taylor family built a one story wood frame store building on Preston Avenue between the home and the bridge. The original Taylor home was demolished about 1906 and the site became a cotton yard. The commercialization of the tract continued and by 1924, the two blocks were occupied by structures of the Taylor Lumber Company and various other businesses, including a plumber's supplies store located on the corner of Preston Avenue and Smith Street[132].

In 1928, the City obtained most of Block 38 from the Taylor family through eminent domain in order to complete the channelization of Buffalo Bayou. In the 1930's, structures on Block 37 contained businesses related to the new Farmer's Market that was built on the opposite side of Preston Avenue. These businesses included wholesale produce stores in the building along the north side of Preston Avenue and a hotel on the second floor of the building. The City acquired the tract in 1964 and it was used as a parking lot for nearly three decades[133].

In 1990, in preparation for the development of the site for Sesquicentennial Park, archeological investigations of the Taylor homestead were conducted by Moore Archeological Consulting. The fascinating details of Taylor's urban farmstead, officially recorded as Texas archeological site 41HR695, provide us with a revealing glimpse of everyday life in Houston during the nineteenth century[134].

A pedestrian foot bridge, built on the Preston Avenue bridge as a part of Sesquicentennial Park, permits access to parts of the park on the west side of Buffalo Bayou. The west side of the park consists of features along the street level and features along the hike and bike trail at the edge of the bayou. These features include the Upper Garden, the Lower Garden, the Grotto and the George H. W. Bush Monument.

The Upper Garden, on the north side of the Preston Avenue bridge, offers a panoramic view of the park and the downtown skyline. The wooded garden is on a hill that rises eight feet above adjacent streets and it sits above an old, existing twenty-five foot concrete retaining wall that was part of the channelization of the bayou in 1928. The Grotto lies below the balcony of the Upper Garden. It was an existing storm sewer that has been enhanced with scenic concrete rockwork and landscaping to create a pool of water with a spillway in dense foliage[135].

The Lower Garden lies below the concrete retaining wall and is connected to the Upper Garden by a circular stairway and an ADA accessible ramp. Lower Garden, south of the Preston Avenue bridge, is filled with native plants and it is built to withstand flooding. In fact, all of Sesquicentennial Park is in the one hundred year floodplain so silt deposits caused by the frequent flooding of the bayou are controlled by the use of fire hoses to wash the surfaces[136].

In 2004, a portion of the Upper Garden at the intersection of Bagby Street and Franklin Avenue was set aside for a monument honoring long time Houston resident George H. W. Bush. The George Bush Monument, formally dedicated on Thursday, December 2, 2004, includes an eight foot bronze statue of Bush which is surrounded by four bas-relief panels depicting highlights of his life. Two bronze eagles flank the entry to the memorial. Chas Fagan created the statue and twin eagles while Houston sculptor Wei-li "Willy" Wang created the bas-relief panels which are mounted on pink granite boulders[137].

Bush, a pioneer in the offshore drilling business, moved to Houston in 1959. His political career began in 1966 when he was elected to the U. S. Congress from Houston. His first legislative action was to prevent the Army Corps of Engineers from making Buffalo Bayou a concrete canal. Oil man George Mitchell and environmentalist Terry Hershey founded the Bayou Preservation Association in 1966, and they approached the newly elected Congressman to intervene in the Corps of Engineers' plan to straighten and pave Buffalo Bayou from Shepherd Drive to downtown. The success of Bush's efforts can be seen in the luxurious green space that now exists in that place[138].

Bush's political career peaked when he served as the 41st President of the United States from 1989 to 1993. One of the bas relief panels depicts Bush presiding over the end of the Cold War, shaking hands with Mikhail Gorbachev and seeing the fall of the Berlin Wall[139].

The Bush Monument is a quiet and contemplative space on the edge of Houston's busy downtown. The view of the skyline from its elevated vantage point is spectacular. Yet, ironically, the statue of the man who saved the bayou from becoming a concrete drainage ditch stands above the only section of Buffalo Bayou that has been channelized with concrete retaining walls.

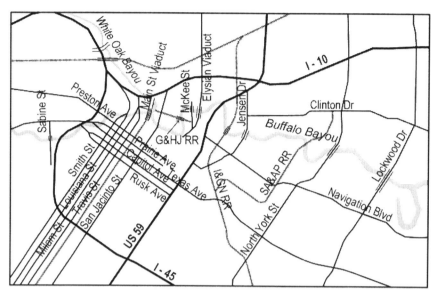

Map by Rachel A. Garcia

Between the Preston Avenue bridge and the Main Street Viaduct, the course of Buffalo Bayou lies within the west side of the historic downtown district. From the earliest days of the founding of Houston, the residents of the city and their business activities took place along this section of the bayou.

Chapter 8
The Historic Downtown

Grand Central Station

As you turn the corner at Sesquicentennial Park and head east on the bayou, leaving the Bush statue behind you, the massive retaining wall constructed during the 1928 channelization project becomes obvious. Although the retaining wall is little noticed from the street level, it is quite imposing from the water level. The covering of vines helps to disguise the wall, but a large, painted gauge that measures the level of the bayou stands out on the concrete wall. The yellow gauge measures a height of forty feet to the railing along the sidewalk of Franklin Avenue.

Franklin Avenue had been built across the bayou in 1931 as part of the channelization improvements and the construction of an elaborate, new railroad depot that fronted on the new Franklin Avenue Extension. Evidence of the extension of the street can be seen in the elevated roadway that is supported by the tall, concrete pillars lining the bayou as far as the Smith Street bridge[1].

In earlier times, the north bank sloped up to the Washington Road where the Houston and Texas Central Railway had its passenger depot. The railroad brought farm products from the Brazos Valley onto Houston, and the Washington Road was used by teams of oxen carts and mule wagons as farmers delivered their goods to the city. The banks of the bayou along Washington Avenue served as a gathering place for these out of town visitors, and an informal fair was held on the north bank of Buffalo Bayou in the years after the Civil War. In 1870, John T. Brady organized the "state fair" of the Agricultural, Mechanical and Blood Stock Association of Texas, and it was a popular success[2].

The location of the state fair was on the north bank of Buffalo Bayou south of Washington Avenue. Today, the topography of the area has been changed by the channelization of the bayou. Washington Avenue has been re-routed and connected with Franklin Avenue. The original fair grounds would now be situated on the lanes of Franklin Avenue and the parking lot of the U. S. Post Office. The popularity of the fair prompted the fair association to look for a more suitable location and, in 1871, it bought 1,400 acres on the south side of town, in the modern Midtown area south of the Pierce Elevated, and moved the fair to that large tract of land which they called the Fairgrounds[3].

The typical prize categories at the fair of 1872 included handicrafts of tanned sheep skins, leatherwork for saddles, moss mattresses, gentleman's pantaloons, coat and vest, as well as factory products such as jeans, osnabergs, cottonades, cotton knitting yarns, cotton tweed and sewing silk. Although several of the first place awards went to entries from around the state, many blue ribbons were awarded to local artisans and Houston area factories such as the Eureka Mills and the Houston City Mills[4].

In 1874, the state fair was apparently quite a large event. The City was buzzing with excitement as a large number of Indians came to the fair and camped near McGowen Street and Travis Street. The Indian wars were still active on the Texas frontier at this time, and the Battle of the Little Big Horn was still two years hence. Fortunately, it seems that their presence at the fair was mostly uneventful[5].

The state fair continued in Houston through 1878, but it was discontinued after that when interest in the event waned because of the economic depression of the late 1870's and a resurgence of yellow fever in 1879. A group of businessmen in Dallas organized the event in 1886, and Dallas has been the site of the State Fair ever since[6].

Near the railroad terminal tracks, the switching yards and the parkways near the depot was Henke's Wagon Yard, a campsite established in the mid-1870's as an adjunct to Henry Henke's New Orleans Store at 807 Congress Avenue. Farmers and haulers who brought goods to Houston gathered in Henke's wagon yard near Washington Avenue. Henry Henke provided a place for them to camp and exchange their produce for goods and supplies that they needed back on the farm[7].

Not far from Henke's campground, on a triangular strip of land bounded by Preston Avenue, Washington Avenue and Buffalo Bayou, about four blocks west of the Houston and Texas Central Railway depot, was Vinegar Hill, a notorious slum where drinking, gambling and brawls were common, and cocaine addicts frequented its dives[8].

After 1865, a cluster of houses and buildings in the wedge shaped tract of land formed by the intersection of Washington Avenue and Preston Avenue and bounded on the east by Buffalo Bayou was occupied by a large number of poor African-Americans. The banks of the bayou at this point, where it made a hairpin turn around the end of Horace Taylor's homestead in City Blocks 37 and 38, rose to noticeable elevation on the high bank. The tract closest to the bayou, platted as Block 45B NSBB, extended from Washington Avenue to Preston Avenue and was divided into two sections by a small thoroughfare called Tin Can Alley. For over forty years, this community (if that term can be applied) and its residents had one of the worst reputations for crime and vice in the city. The community was called Vinegar Hill[9].

Vinegar Hill got its name from either of two sources. Some say that the place was so called because of the infestation of vinegaroon scorpions in the area. Another account indicates that the name came from the acrid smell of the fumes of a nearby vinegar factory which was located adjacent to the Macatee cotton sheds two blocks to the east[10].

Although most petty criminals become nameless after a few years of local notoriety, the story of one notorious person from Vinegar Hill is still legend today, over 140 years later. For over a decade, from the late 1860's until her death in 1880, Caroline Riley was the "Queen of Vinegar Hill," the foremost scoundrel of the district. According to newspaper accounts, Riley came to Houston and settled at Vinegar Hill about 1867. The earliest documented evidence of her presence is found in a crime report in Flake's Bulletin, a Galveston newspaper reporting on Houston events, on July 30, 1868 when she was the victim of abuse by one of the other residents named Ben Brown[11].

But, Caroline Riley was not usually the victim of crime. She was in and out of the municipal courts and the city jail many times during the 1870's, and she was associated with drunkenness, violence, gambling, the sale of cocaine and prostitution during her career. Riley was arraigned several times on the charge of maintaining a "disorderly house," an all-inclusive term used to describe such places as a house of prostitution, an illegal gambling casino, or a site where drugs are constantly bought or sold. All of the above seemed to apply to Caroline Riley's house[12].

On August 4, 1869, Caroline Riley, even then already considered a local nuisance, was sentenced to three years in the penitentiary for knowingly receiving stolen money from a black youth. Yet, for some reason, possibly through her political connections, she was back in town and her disorderly house was back in operation within one year[13].

Vinegar Hill consisted of twenty or thirty tenement houses and shacks which housed about fifty black women and a similar number of small children. It was "a settlement of one and two room box-shaped, dilapidated structures" scattered over the area in no systematic pattern with no fences, dividing lines, or walk ways except narrow foot paths. Within this "congregation of shanties and men-coops," the worst men and women, both black and white, engaged in "debaucheries and orgies[14]."

A saloon on the corner of 9th Street and Washington Avenue was the primary business in Vinegar Hill. It was a low class drinking establishment filled with "castaway wretches of both sexes and all colors" with "worn, haggard, suspicious, whisky-beaten countenances." A short distance from the saloon was the home of Caroline Riley, "the palace inhabited by the Queen of Vinegar Hill." Revelries were commonplace on six of the seven nights of the week. Patsy Bennett, a member of Riley's crew, played ragtime so loudly on the piano that the music disturbed all the residents of the surrounding neighborhood. It was on Saturday nights, though, the riots of debauchery, in which "every base deed known to criminology" was found, were at their peak[15].

Caroline Riley, herself, was an intelligent, but cunning and treacherous woman. She was a large, heavy set, dark complexioned woman of about 300 pounds who had only one eye, but who had no problem handling the rowdy patrons of her establishment. A newspaper reporter who visited Riley's house in March, 1874, said she bore the face of "years of dissipation, sin and crime." In a room that was dimly illuminated by a kerosene lamp, the place of such debased behavior was decorated with religious pictures on the walls. Among these pictures was a portrait of the Messiah and a picture depicting the Apostle Peter being saved by the Lord on the Sea of Galilee. Ironic decorations for this type of establishment, indeed[16].

The newspaper expose of March, 1874 may have prompted the local residents' outrage over the activities taking place in Vinegar Hill, or it may have simply given voice to the complaints from residents of the other neighborhoods. Whatever the case, the local law enforcement agency acted to close down the vice operations. City Marshal Thompson began to clean up the crime in Vinegar Hill. On April 23, 1874, Caroline Riley was tried in Judge Sam Dodge's Criminal Court "for keeping a disorderly house," found guilty and fined $150 plus court costs[17].

The crackdown forced Riley into retirement, and for a time, the notorious activities in Vinegar Hill may have ceased. The Queen of Vinegar Hill was not a credit to her ethnic community, and it was reported that she had paid more fines in municipal court than all other African-Americans in Houston combined. Yet, even though her operations in Vinegar Hill had been broken up, she still had run ins with the law. On July 25, 1877, Caroline Riley and Frances Williams, were arraigned in Recorder's Court and fined $1 "for uproarious conduct" on Louisiana Street. In April, 1880, Riley was arrested and was in the City jail when on April 12, she died suddenly while in the custody of City Marshal Morriss. The City buried the indigent Queen of Vinegar Hill in the City Cemetery without fanfare[18].

Even without Caroline Riley, Vinegar Hill continued to be a public nuisance and a vice district. Prostitution was known in the area that benefited from its proximity to the railroad terminal and the traveling public. Thieves and criminals frequented the area and "the syrens and divinities of the place" entertained their clients. Things had gotten so bad that in March, 1879, the citizens of the nearby neighborhood petitioned City Council to take some action. Council deferred on the matter, however, saying a total clean up was not possible[19].

In frustration over the lack of action against what was a public nuisance, a group of fifteen or twenty young men, including three or four African-Americans from the Fourth Ward, descended on Vinegar Hill on June 6, 1879, and set out to destroy the entire place. Homes were broken into, furniture and bedding destroyed, windows broken out, doors knocked in, and buildings were set on fire. Fortunately, the fires were put out before much damage was done, but the perpetrators did not fare so well. For their vigilante actions, each of them faced charges of arson, burglary, assault and malicious mischief[20].

In spite of the attempts by the more upstanding citizenry and local law enforcement officials to remove the blight of Vinegar Hill, improvements to the area came only when real estate developments encroached on the neighborhood. The growth of passenger service to Houston on the railroads led to the construction of hotels and businesses along Washington Avenue in the Vinegar Hill area. Eventually, the slum was revitalized as the property was converted into small businesses and hotels serving the railroad customers.

The Houston and Texas Central Railway built its rail yard along Railroad Street, north of Washington Avenue, and a small depot was built on Railroad Street at 4th Street. Passenger business on the railroad did not justify an elaborate terminal at this time although, on one occasion, the railroad depot drew a big crowd. In late October, 1886, the Texas Central Depot became the center of local interest when the fierce Apache chief Geronimo was on display at the depot while a prisoner of war of the US Army and en route from Fort Sam Houston in San Antonio to confinement in Florida with thirty-two Apache braves, their women and children[21].

With the growth of the railroads in Houston and the acquisition of the Houston and Texas Central Railway by the Southern Pacific Railroad in 1883, a modern, three story brick Grand Central Station was constructed in 1887 for $80,000 to replace the earlier depot. The grand depot was located on the north side of Washington Avenue and it extended for the length of the entire block between 7th Street and 8th Street[22].

Railroads were an important transportation link between Houston and the rest of the country. Passenger traffic on the railroads increased significantly. By the 1890's, hotels were built in the vicinity of the depot to accommodate the traveling businessmen and the general public. The Grand Central Hotel was across from the depot on the southeast corner of Washington Avenue and 7th Street. The hotel Dining Hall offered ten course dinners costing fifty cents in 1899. The Lawlor Hotel was located across the street from the Grand Central Hotel, on the southwest corner of Washington Avenue and 7th Street and it was near the top of the bank of Buffalo Bayou. By 1906, the extensive Brazos Hotel was built between Buffalo Bayou and Washington Avenue, across from Grand Central Station on the lots that had formerly been the occupied by the Grand Central Hotel and the Lawlor Hotel. The array of four story structures stretched for over a block and was a popularly priced hotel that catered to the traveling salesmen who arrived in Houston by passenger train. The Macatee Hotel was one block east of Grand Central Station, and the Grand Central Hotel was relocated one block to the west of its former location[23].

In the early 1920's, the Tennison Hotel, a "railroad station hotel" serving business travelers arriving by train, was built to the west of the station on the site where the Grand Central Hotel had moved. The Tennison opened in 1922 as a "popularly priced" hotel with rooms costing $2 per night. The Tennison, one of a handful of Houston hotels designed by architect Joseph Finger, was commissioned by Henry Booker Tennison. Henry Tennison and his brother James operated a sheet metal manufacturing company in Mount Pleasant, Texas with warehouses in Houston and Dallas[24].

By the time that the Tennison Hotel was built, the Vinegar Hill neighborhood had changed from a dingy cluster of run down houses into a large block of businesses, stores, a garage, a bakery and this fine hotel. The commercialization of the large City block continued through the post-World War II period, but its fortunes waned as the railroads gave way to the automobile for person transportation. After the demolition of Grand Central Station in the early 1960's, the Tennison Hotel declined rapidly and it finally closed in 1972. The building was vacant until it was acquired by Ray Ferguson who began to transform the old hotel into upscale apartments and office space in 2000. Financial difficulties have plagued the project, which was renamed One Bayou Park, and it went into foreclosure in 2003. Today, the crudely remodeled hulk of Finger's Tennison Hotel stands alone, except for the nondescript concrete bunker that housed the City Fire Alarm Building, on Vinegar Hill. The remainder of "the Hill" is covered by the right away and ramps for the elevated I-45 that passes overhead[25].

The early twentieth century was the heyday for railroads in Houston. The terminal that was built in 1887 showed the importance of train traffic to the city's economy, and as its influence grew, the station reflected the prominence and prestige of the rails. Grand Central Station itself was remodeled twice, once in 1906 and, again, in 1914. By 1924, the Grand Central Depot consisted of a passenger depot in the center of the main building with railroad offices on the second and third floors. Other offices were located on the east wing, and the baggage room and mail offices were on the west wing. Two 600 foot long train sheds extended over the tracks on the north side of the depot to protect the passengers from the elements[26].

Plans were made for a new passenger depot in 1929. Construction began in May, 1933, and the new Grand Central Station opened on September 1, 1934. The project was a joint venture between the Southern Pacific Railroad and the City of Houston. The total cost of $4,347,000 for the facility and tracks as well as improvements to the city streets and the bayou was divided equally between the city and the railroad company[27].

The modernistic station was designed by Wyatt C. Hedrick of Houston. The exterior of the building was Texas Cordova cream-colored limestone set on a base of Texas pink granite. The main waiting room was a large, two story chamber with a floor of marble and terrazzo and walls with a marble wainscoting topped with a cream-colored marble. Wood trimmings were of black walnut. Decorative panels at each end of the main room consisted of murals by John McQuarrie of San Francisco, one depicting Stephen F. Austin and Baron de Bastrop in 1823 and the other of Sam Houston entering the town in 1837. The main waiting room was flanked by offices and a restaurant on the west wing. Racial segregation was the undeniable tradition of the day, and a smaller "colored waiting room" was located in the east wing of the depot. Railroad offices, a lunch room and the baggage room also occupied the east wing[28].

Grand Central Station was razed in 1961. It was replaced by the new U. S. Post Office which still occupies the site on the north bank of the bayou[29].

The Boyle Hotel -- A Site Overlooking the Bayou

The bridge ahead is the Smith Street bridge which was built in 1925. From this point on until you reach the wharf area at the foot of Main Street, there are several bridges across Buffalo Bayou, one for every street that comes to the bayou. A second bridge merging into Smith Street comes right after the first. This is the exit ramp from I-10 that feeds into downtown. In the space between Smith Street and Louisiana Street along the new Congress Avenue elevated street bed, the south bank of the bayou is an unkempt mess of roadway substructure, trees, brush and trash. But, there are stories here, too.

One of the more intriguing mysteries of early Houston is the location of Water Street. As a roadway, it appears on the earliest plats of the town, including the Borden plat of Houston of January 18, 1837. Although most discussion of the phantom Water Street involves the area around the wharf or the foot of Main Street, the 1837 plat shows that the street extends from Austin Street (originally Homer Street) west as far as Smith Street. Water Street appears to be the unplatted right of way between the blocks and lots of the town plat and the water's edge of Buffalo Bayou[30].

In the wharf area, Water Street may have been the roadway used to move goods and cargo between the warehouses along Commerce Avenue and the boats docked at the wharf. Beyond the wharf area, there seems to have been little use for the Water Street right of way, especially as the city came to learn of the fluctuation of the bayou's water level. Development along what was designated as Water Street was subject to frequent flooding. One exception to that idea occurred in the unplatted right of way between Louisiana Street and Smith Street at Congress Avenue.

The Borden plat of Houston of January 18, 1837 shows three gullies entering Buffalo Bayou from Louisiana Street to Smith Street. This topography probably indicates a low bank in this area that was unsuitable for general development. Yet, by 1869, there was one small structure on one lot near the northwest corner of Louisiana Street and Congress Avenue. By 1885, the site contains two frame dwellings[31].

More significant development of the tract occurred by 1890 when a large two story building was constructed on the "top of the bank" along the bayou at the site. This building housed the "Colored Variety Theater," four small stores along Louisiana Street including a barber shop and a restaurant, and a larger saloon and billiards hall facing Congress Avenue. Two other small structures were on the west side of theater building. The variety theater was an entertainment center for shows, like vaudeville, that included dances, music, songs and skits. As the laws of segregation came into being late in the nineteenth century, the blacks found business and entertainment activities among themselves. The variety theater at this site catered to the African American residents of Houston, and their music, common throughout much of the South, evolved into the style that later became ragtime[32].

Associated businesses occupied store fronts along Congress Avenue and Louisiana Street. The saloon and billiard parlor served a clientele in much the same way that such places do today. The establishments held similar dangers for their customers. For example, On December 18, 1892, A. Allen, the son of black legislator Richard Allen was accidentally shot at 11 am in the bar room of the "negro dance house and variety theater" at the end of Louisiana Street. His wounds were serious, but not fatal. Guns, bars and billiards were a dangerous mixture even then. And, at 11 o'clock in the morning! Contemporary news accounts referred to the place as the "honka tonk" and it seems it may not be much different from venues of a similar description today[33].

This variety theater was short lived. Within another two years, the building succumbed to one of the major hazards of the city, fire. On the evening of February 21, 1894, the frame building of thirty-one rooms caught fire in the upper part of the second story and burned. A daring, and somewhat humorous rescue was made of a woman, known as Daisie, who had been ill and had remained in her room that evening. She escaped the fire from the second floor by jumping upon an awning and sliding down a post to the ground, escaping the flames without a stitch of clothing on. A more tragic event was the death of Lulu Taylor, a San Antonio woman who was one of singers in the variety show. She ran back upstairs to save her trunk with valuables and money in her room. Her charred remains were found there[34].

The owner of the building, Frank Dunn, suffered the loss of the structure valued at $5,000 and the furnishings of $2,000, all of which were uninsured. The African American proprietor of the theater, R. L. Andrews, had a similar uninsured loss of $2,000 for the fixtures. The property, however, did not remain vacant for long. Situated near the downtown business district and adjacent to Grand Central Station, it was a good location for the hotel built by the Boyle family on the site later in 1894[35].

The two story Hotel Boyle had fifty-three rooms situated on the bank of Buffalo Bayou. The office of the hotel was located on the corner at 220 Louisiana Street, while the dining room was at 218 Louisiana Street and two stores were at 216 and 214 Louisiana Street. The hotel kitchen was located in the back along the bayou in a one story addition. The construction site on the banks of the bayou was precarious, at best, and in 1896, the city engineer reported to City Council that the sewer at the foot of Congress Avenue was in bad shape and the erosion was endangering the foundation of the Hotel Boyle[36].

W. T. Boyle came to Houston from Dallas in 1894 with his wife and his three grown sons, and the three men were the proprietors of the Hotel Boyle. After the unexpected death of son Charles in 1896, W. T. Boyle and his son J. T. Boyle continued to operate the hotel. They were successful enough in this venture that they were able to acquire the former Hutchins House, a prestigious old hotel that had fallen into some disrepair. On March 1, 1897, the Boyle family sold their interest in the Hotel Boyle and took over the management of the Hutchins House. Unfortunately for the Boyle family, the Hutchins House was destroyed by a pre-dawn fire on October 19, 1901[37].

The Hotel Boyle continued to operate under the proprietorship of F. D. Burke. But, that hotel had its problems, too. Fire, caused by an explosion of gasoline, broke out in the hotel in 1908. Mrs. Burke, the wife of the proprietor, leapt fifty feet from the hotel roof to escape the flames that engulfed the building. Mrs. Burke landed amid logs, stumps and timber behind the building. The fall knocked her unconscious and she sustained internal injuries. The hotel was repaired and continued in business for another twenty years[38].

The final episode for the Boyle Hotel came in 1928. By this time the hotel was owned by the city and managed by R. W. Green. Three city offices were located in the lobby. About 3:15 am on December 11, 1928, the Boyle Hotel caught fire. Manager Green awakened the thirty to thirty-five guests, and some of them escaped by jumping out back windows into Buffalo Bayou. Sadly, three men died in the fire. The two story, brick Hotel Boyle was destroyed[39].

This site on the banks of Buffalo Bayou was never intended for development by the Allen brothers. Subsequent construction on the site ended in failure and tragedy. No new structures were built there after the 1928 fire. The channelization of the bayou during this same time made the tract of land unsuitable for use. The site today is home only to trees, riparian vegetation and stray trash. No sign of its prior history can be seen. Yet, it should be remembered.

Louisiana Street Spring

When the Allen brothers established the Houston Town Company in 1836, they paid a lot of attention to the promotion and sale of town lots, but they thought little of services for the new residents, such as a municipal water supply. As a result, the residents of Houston were on their own to find drinking water and water for use in their homes.

For the first fifty years, residents of Houston relied on cisterns to capture and store rain water for personal use. Bayou water and some shallow wells were used to supplement the supplies of water when necessary. Although some cisterns were above ground structures, many homes and businesses had subterranean cisterns. Excavations at the Horace Taylor home site in Sesquicentennial Park uncovered a sixteen foot deep, bottle-shaped brick cistern that was a water supply for his large farmstead. Recent excavations in the Frost Town area have unearthed smaller, but more common, residential cisterns[40].

Even when the City Waterworks opened in 1879, the city water system pumped water directly from Buffalo Bayou, and bayou water was as unappetizing then as it is now. In 1887, two artesian wells were drilled and brought on line to supply the public water system[41]. The discovery that Houston was built over a vast reservoir of ground water permitted the city to grow apace for another half century or so until the Lake Houston and Lake Livingston surface water systems were constructed.

Today, evidence of the reservoir of fresh water in the ground beneath the City can be seen along Buffalo Bayou, if you know where to look.

An early Houston writer had remarked that there was a spring at the head of a gully that began near the southeast corner of Preston Avenue and Louisiana Street. A large puddle usually collected on Louisiana Street. While the street is now paved and the spring is buried, you can still see the free flow of spring water pouring forth from the large drain under the Louisiana Street bridge[42].

Monument Circle

By the first decade of the twentieth century, railroads were one of the principal industries in the economy of Houston. Business transportation and personal travel into the city largely came on the railroads, and most of that traffic arrived and departed from the Southern Pacific's Grand Central Station on Washington Avenue. Much like today's airports, the train station was the hub from which visitors arrived in the city. From the station, they took taxicabs, public transportation or walked across Buffalo Bayou into the downtown district to the hotels and business they wished to visit. The limited access across the bayou on the bridge at Louisiana Street prompted the city to conceive of an elaborate bridge across Buffalo Bayou in order to welcome visitors to the city and to provide easy access to the business district.

Mayor Horace Baldwin Rice announced on August 30, 1912 that a reinforced concrete covering over Buffalo Bayou would be built between Louisiana Street and Franklin Avenue. The existing Franklin Avenue and Louisiana Street bridges would be replaced with a girder type triangular structure that occupied the space of the two bridges, and in the center would be a statue of General Sam Houston[43].

The bayou covering would be two hundred feet at its widest point and was to have a monument to keep the traffic divided and regulated. The proposed covering over Buffalo Bayou would connect with the Houston Ice and Brewing Company covering on the north side of Franklin Avenue, and it was intended to hide the unsightly view of the bayou from strangers coming to town from the passenger station who might get the wrong impression of the City's "real waterway[44]."

The new triangular bridge at Franklin Avenue and Louisiana Street was dedicated on February 6, 1915. The reinforced concrete bridge had an area of 44,120 square feet and it cost $130,000. Built at grade level and "ornamented with a handsome balustrade and standing lights," it was hailed as "one of the handsomest bridges in Houston" and the "most beautiful bridge spanning the bayou[45]."

On January 18, 1915, the City began a campaign to raise $50,000 to erect a monument of Sam Houston in the space set aside for it. Not every person, though, liked the original idea. Mayor Ben Campbell, who succeeded Rice, favored an equestrian statue. The controversy over the center piece of the bridge persisted. As late as 1921, the traffic circle consisted of a fifty foot diameter bed of four hundred English daisies planted with a large Phoenix Canariensis palm in the center[46].

Yet, the expanding economy of Houston in the post-WWI years brought more people to the city, and the traffic congestion near Grand Central Station continued to be a problem. On November 28, 1922, plans for a "monster bridge" over Buffalo Bayou from Smith Street to Franklin Avenue were announced at City Council. This enormous bridge would cover one city block from Grand Central Station to the downtown district and it would relieve the traffic congestion on this side of town. The bridge was to be so expansive that the space would even provide a place for a fire station or a curb market for farmers on the bridge[47].

George P. Macatee of the Macatee Interests, owner of the land on the north bank, offered to donate the land for the project to cover over the bayou ravine from Smith Street to Franklin Avenue, providing that the City buy or remove the Boyle Hotel on the south bank and not improve the assets of a private landowner[48].

The large covered bridge was to be built in conjunction with a Buffalo Bayou bridge with a sixty foot roadway and sidewalks that would connect Congress Avenue and Smith Street to the north bank at 6th Street. Financing for the larger project, however, proved to be difficult to obtain, but nevertheless, the bridge at Smith Street was constructed. The new bridge at Smith Street was built by Charles K. Horton for a cost of $180,000 and it opened on August 7, 1925[49].

The City did eventually acquire the Boyle Hotel, but it was destroyed by a fire in 1928. Additional factors, however, came into play. On May 31, 1929, Buffalo Bayou flooded to such an extent that the pavement was washed out from several downtown bridges, including the bridges at Milam Street, Smith Street, Preston Avenue and Franklin Avenue. The effects of this event may have altered the plans for the large bridge project. In any case, a more limited project was undertaken along the north bank of the bank in this location. The Franklin Avenue extension was constructed as an elevated roadway on the north bank in 1931. This road is clearly evident from the bayou today, even though it is relatively unnoticed by motorists using the streets on their way into downtown Houston[50].

All thoughts of an extensive covered concrete platform over Buffalo Bayou were dismissed after the flood of Buffalo Bayou that occurred on December 8, 1935. With water rising to levels about seven feet higher than the flood of 1929, the Capitol Avenue bridge was submerged, the new Farmer's Market was flooded and damage to the Houston Ice and Brewing Company platform and buildings, a different approach to development of the bayou was needed[51].

The bayou between Smith Street and Franklin Avenue has seen little improvements in modern times except for the landscaping on the north bank and the hike and bike trail near the normal water level. The south bank is overgrown with brush and filled with construction debris. A positive sign for the future is the new home for the Houston Ballet on Congress Avenue.

The property at the corner of Smith Street and Preston Avenue, on the diagonal from the Wortham Theater Center and just south of where an exit from I-10 enters downtown, contains a 115,000 square foot, six-story mid-rise that has become the Houston Ballet Center for Dance. The Ballet's new home opened in the Spring of 2011. The $53 million structure is connected to the Wortham Theater Center by an aerial walkway angled across the intersection of Smith Street and Preston Avenue[52].

The replacement of the elevated section of Congress Avenue also offers hope that the hike and bike trail along the south bank will be completed from Sesquicentennial Park to Travis Street.

Where the Franklin Monument Circle once welcomed untold numbers of businessmen and visitors to downtown Houston, a new gateway to the city welcomes vehicular traffic exiting from Interstate 10. In 1999, a concrete and bronze art work by Team Hou Architects, entitled The Downtown Houston Gateway, was erected in the location of the previous entry way, and proudly calls out "Welcome to Downtown Houston[53]."

Franklin Avenue and the Donnellan Crypt

You would not ordinarily think of the banks of Buffalo Bayou in downtown Houston as an ideal burial spot, but in the nineteenth century, the south bank near Franklin Avenue entombed the remains of a number of members of the family of prominent early Houstonian Timothy Donnellan.

Timothy Donnellan, one of Houston's earliest settlers, arrived about 1839 from New Orleans with Emily De Ende and their young son Henry. Most likely, Timothy was several years older than Emily, who was about eighteen years old when their son Henry was born in Louisiana in 1838. According to the Handbook of Texas, Emily was the daughter of the French General de Adendy of New Orleans[54], however, her name is written De Ende in all other documents. Donnellan was a violinist[55] who immigrated from Ireland, and he quickly established himself in the Houston community. By 1840, Donnellan had obtained a patented title to one hundred acres in Harris County, and he owned ten town lots in Houston[56]. During 1842 and 1843, he served as an alderman from the First Ward[57].

Although Donnellan established himself in Houston, he had left some unpaid debts in New Orleans. About five years after his arrival in Houston, the firm of Curtis and Buddendorff of New Orleans filed notice in the Galveston newspaper that Timothy Donnellan had failed to pay a debt of $141.04. The debt had been turned over to P.

Edmunds for collection, but it is unknown whether the debt was ultimately repaid[58].

Timothy Donnellan and Emily De Ende formalized their marriage on May 11, 1841 in Harris County[59]. Their second son, Benjamin Franklin Donnellan, was born on April 15, 1841 and christened at St. Vincent de Paul Catholic Church in Houston on July 20, 1841, with his aunt, Harriette De Ende, as godmother[60]. About 1844, a daughter Emily[61] was born to the Donnellans. A third son, Thurston John Donnellan, was born in Houston on July 6, 1845, and christened at St. Vincent de Paul on November 21, 1846[62].

When Tim Donnellan died in 1849, he was buried in a large, red brick vault[63] built in the south bank of Buffalo Bayou at the west end of Franklin Avenue. The 1850 census places the residence of Emily Donnellan between William Hutchins of the Hutchins House Hotel and Paul Bremond, a successful merchant, both of whom lived on the west side of town along Franklin Avenue[64]. The Donnellan family probably lived nearby, and perhaps the banks of the bayou where the crypt is located was a favorite place of the elder Donnellan.

Nevertheless, in 1850, Emily Donnellan was a thirty-year-old widow with three young children, Henry, age twelve, Emily, age eight, and Thurston, age five. The young son Benjamin Franklin apparently died some time before 1850. Although Emily was left moderately prosperous with real estate of $5,000 at the death of her husband, the need to provide for her young family must have presented a significant challenge. At this time, then, two of Emily's relatives, Harriet and Franklin De Ende -- probably her sister, age twenty-four, and her brother, age twenty-three -- came to live in the Donnellan household[65].

In the early 1850's, Emily Donnellan met Francis Dwyer, a tin and copper workshop owner from New York[66]. Dwyer was a successful tinner who owned his own shop on Main Street, between Franklin Avenue and Commerce Avenue[67]. Emily Donnellan and Francis Dwyer, a man about twelve years her senior, subsequently were married on December 24, 1856[68], and a daughter Mary was born to them about 1858[69].

When the census was taken on September 30, 1860, the Dwyer household consisted of Emily De Ende, thirty-eight, Francis Dwyer, fifty, and their combined children. Henry Donnellan, twenty-two, was working as a tinner, possibly an apprentice in his stepfather's shop. The other children were Emily Donnellan, fifteen, Thurston Donnellan, fourteen, and Mary Frances Dwyer[70]. A son, Frank Beauregard Dwyer, born August 21, 1861, rounded out the Donnellan-Dwyer household[71]. The Dwyer home was in Block 4, North Side Buffalo Bayou[72], directly across the bayou from the Donnellan crypt at the end of Franklin Avenue. The 1866 Houston City Directory referred to the location of the Dwyer residence as "near the H&TC Railroad Depot[73]."

A tinner was a skilled craftsman who made and repaired items made of tin. In the mid-nineteenth century, many utilitarian kitchen products were fabricated by craftsmen of this cottage industry. Items such as cake stamps, milk pails, basins, cake and pie pans, cups, and coffee pots were the kitchenware most in demand, but decorative goods, such as chandeliers[74], were also made by the best artisans of the trade. Francis "Frank" Dwyer, who reported real estate of $8,000 and personal estate of $5,000 in the census of 1860, was one of the best of his trade in Houston.

In early 1860, the Galveston News noted that Frank Dwyer was one of the best "mechanics" in the area. The paper also reported that he maintained a good stock of stoves and tinware on hand in his store[75]. Dwyer's advertisements touted his supply of stoves, hardware, tinware, woodware, nails, and castings. His services included the installation of house pipe, gutters, and roofing, and Dwyer guaranteed his work[76].

Dwyer's reputation was such that when the meeting to organize the Mechanics Association in Houston was held at Levy's Hall in July, 1865, Frank Dwyer and his stepson Henry Donnellan were selected for the committee that was formed to draft the constitution and by-laws of the organization[77].

During the War Between the States, Henry and Thurston Donnellan both served in Company B, Second Texas Infantry. Henry's extensive Compiled Service Record shows that he enlisted on August 7, 1861 as a Private, and was promoted to Sergeant at the end of 1862. The unit was present at Shiloh, Corinth, and Vicksburg. When Vicksburg was surrendered in July 1863, Henry received four months back pay at $17 per month and was paroled. He is described as age twenty-three, born in New Orleans, height 5' 6", with black eyes, dark hair, and dark complexion, civilian occupation of Tinner. The regiment was reorganized in 1864 and stationed at Galveston. For the last several months of the war, Henry was detailed to the Ordnance Department in Houston, utilizing his skills as a tinner[78].

Being younger, Thurston apparently did not enter the Army until late in the war. Though he has no formal service record, his wife received a Confederate pension after his death. In the pension file, several witnesses stated that he served as a drummer, but did not travel east of the Mississippi River, due to his age[79]. When the United Confederate Veterans held their national reunion in Houston in 1895, there were sixty members of the 2nd Texas Infantry present. Those assembled marched from the Cotton Exchange to the reunion headquarters accompanied by the fife and drums used the night before the battle of Shiloh, the musicians being Herman Holtkamp, fifer, Thurston Donnellan, kettle drum, and William Hartung, bass drum[80].

With two stepsons in the army, Frank Dwyer was sympathetic to the needs of the soldiers. In response to a plea for assistance to the beleaguered Texas troops, Dwyer made a donation of twelve dozen tin cups to the men of Forney's Division in May, 1865[81]. In the wake of the imminent defeat of the Confederacy, the Division had withdrawn to Hempstead during March and April, and disbanded there in late May, 1865[82].

In the mid-1860s, as Houston's economy began to recover from the effects of the Civil War, Henry Deschaumes established a store selling tinware on Preston Avenue between Main Street and Travis Street[83]. Deschaumes, an immigrant from France, had operated a tin shop in Bastrop from the mid-1850s through, at least, 1860. Although it may have seemed that Deschaumes was in direct competition with Dwyer, there appears to have been enough business for both companies, and a rivalry did not exist between them. In 1866, Henry Donnellan had moved from his stepfather's business to work as a tinner with Deschaumes and Company[84], yet he continued to live with the family. In his place, Dwyer had hired A. C. Richer[85], a 27-year-old immigrant from France, as a tinner in his shop. Prior to coming to Houston, Richer was a tinner in Jefferson, Marion County, Texas, where he lived (and also probably worked) with other young craftsmen from Europe at the home of John Fisher, a German-born shoe and boot maker[86].

The winter of 1866-1867 proved to be especially tragic for the Donnellan family. In late 1866 or early 1867, Frank Dwyer died. On January 24, 1867, Henry D. Donnellan was appointed the administrator pro tempore of the estate of Frank Dwyer, and he posted a bond of $1,500[87]. Henry Donnellan was the logical heir to inherit the business of his stepfather. Henry had apprenticed with him and worked in the shop prior to joining Deschaumes. So, Henry, at age twenty-nine, immediately took over the company and formed a partnership with A. C. Richer. The Donnellan and Richer Company[88], however, was destined to be short lived.

On Sunday morning, February 10, 1867, Henry Donnellan and A. C. Richer, partners in the tin business that was located "below the Kennedy Building," returned to their home on Buffalo Bayou for dinner. While waiting for dinner, the two men attempted to defuse a shell taken from a large pile of ordnance that was exposed in the shallows of Buffalo Bayou. The ordnance had been dumped into the bayou after the surrender of the Confederacy in 1865[89]. John Kennedy had leased his two-story brick building on Travis Street, just north of Congress Avenue, to the Confederacy for use as an ordnance depot[90]. At the end of the war, looting of the depot was occurring and Kennedy had the remaining ordnance removed from the building and dumped into Buffalo Bayou from the Milam Street bridge, then known as "the iron bridge[91]."

Henry Donnellan was working on the detonator cap to defuse the shell, but the bomb exploded. Both arms and both legs were torn off Richer and his limbs were hanging by shreds. Donnellan's left arm and elbow were badly mutilated. He had a wound in the abdomen, a severe laceration of the left leg and several fingers were torn off his hand. The two men were promptly attended to by Dr. W. P. Riddell, who resided nearby on Prairie Avenue between Smith Street and Louisiana Street, and Dr. Stewart, but to no avail. Both young men were fatally wounded[92]. The remains of Henry Donnellan were interred in the family vault on Buffalo Bayou.

On February 26, 1867, I. C. Lord, the executor for Donnellan and Richer, advertised in the Houston Daily Telegraph for the settlement of any indebtedness to the firm of the two men who had been killed[93]. A week later, on March 3, 1867, I. C. Lord and B. F. De Ende, the attorney for the family, posted a notice calling for the settlement of indebtedness to the estate of the firm of Donnellan and Richer. They also requested that any claims against the company be presented[94]. On April 18, 1867, B. F. De Ende was appointed administrator pro tempore of the estate of Henry D. Donnellan, and he was empowered to bring suit to recover possession of the land near Houston for the estate[95].

Although he was not living with them in 1860, B. F. "Franklin" De Ende, Henry Donnellan's uncle, returned to the Dwyer household by 1866. At that time, De Ende was working as a clerk at the County Courthouse[96], and by 1867, he was an attorney. On May 1, 1867, B. F. De Ende was appointed the administrator of the estate of Henry D. Donnellan and was ordered to file an inventory of the property belonging to the estate, which he did later that month[97].

In late 1867, Emily Donnellan died[98], and she was buried in the family vault along with her husband Timothy and her son Henry. On March 19, 1868, Thurston J. Donnellan, the twenty-three-year-old son of Emily and Timothy Donnellan and the oldest adult male of the family, petitioned the court for the guardianship of his half-sister Mary Dwyer, age ten, and his half-brother Frank Dwyer, age six, who were without living parents[99]. On April 4, 1868, Thurston Donnellan was appointed the guardian of Mary Dwyer and Frank Dwyer and ordered to file an inventory of the property of the minors, which was appraised by B. F. De Ende, H. H. Dooley and W. A. Daly[100].

After several tumultuous years, the Donnellan family began to see some stability as they entered the decade of the 1870s. When the census was taken on August 2, 1870, Emily Donnellan, age twenty-six, was heading up the household that included her half-sister Mary, age twelve, and half-brother Frank, age seven. It also appears that their aunt Harriet De Ende McArthur (spelled McCarthy in 1870) and another relative from Louisiana (possibly her son) Alexander, age fifteen, had come back to live with the family at this time[101]. Although Thurston Donnellan was the legal guardian of the minor Dwyer children, it appears that he left them in the care of his older sister.

In June 1880, Emily Donnellan's household, still located on the property at the "head of Washington Street by the Bayou," included Mary Dwyer Treadway, her husband Theo Treadway, age twenty-seven, a native of Illinois, their son Frank, age four, and their daughter Lillian, age two. Aunt Harriet McArthur also lived with them[102].

Thurston John "Thuse" Donnellan began painting at age eighteen and he studied art in Chicago and New Orleans[103]. As early as 1860, Donnellan was painting scenery for plays at the Perkins Theater[104]. In the early 1870's, Thuse Donnellan performed in concerts locally. A noted benefit performance on Thursday, April 7, 1870, at the Perkins included a rendition of the popular tune "Shoo Fly" performed with the "cow bells[105]." Other successful concerts included one on June 14, 1872, that was attended by "the elite of the city" and reported as an outstanding performance[106].

Needless to say, popular entertainment and musical concerts today are somewhat different than those of the 1870's. However, it is interesting to note that the popular song performed by Donnellan, "Shoo Fly" remains today as a popular children's song. Just check it out on Google. The lyrics are provided below, and if you would like to hear this "Top 40" tune from early Houston, several versions are available on the internet (http://www.divtune.com/).

Shoo Fly (public domain)

Shoo fly, don't bother me,
Shoo fly, don't bother me,
Shoo fly, don't bother me,
For I belong to somebody!

I feel, I feel, I feel like a morning star
I feel, I feel, I feel like a morning star

Shoo fly, don't bother me,
Shoo fly, don't bother me,
Shoo fly, don't bother me,
For I belong to somebody!

Thuse Donnellan, an accomplished artist, sculptor, and musician, is best known for his portraits of General Sam Houston[107].

Three of these portraits of Sam Houston are in the city of Houston. One is at City Hall and others are in the Houston Public Library and at Rice University[108]. Donnellan married Jessamine Hawthorne, a native of Baltimore, Maryland, on December 31, 1873[109]. Jessamine taught dancing in Houston[110].

The grave vault of the Donnellan family seems to have been prominent and visible throughout the last decades of the nineteenth century, and the tragic story of the family was a familiar part of the local history. On Wednesday, November 21, 1877, the Galveston News reported that the Houston police had found an old bomb shell under the Iron Bridge at Milam Street from the Civil War that was similar to the one that had killed Henry Donnellan[111]. A decade later, on Decoration Day, April 6, 1888, the Galveston Daily News reported that "the graves of Henry Donellan [sic] and Ritchie [Richer], situated near the site of the old Houston and Texas Central Depot, were also profusely decorated[112]." The honors placed on the graves of Henry Donnellan and A. C. Richer indicate that they both were Confederate veterans. It is unclear whether the two were both entombed in the vault or in separate graves although the implication of this article is that they were buried together. No other record has been found to indicate the whereabouts of Richer's burial.

The industrial development along the north side of Buffalo Bayou and along Washington Avenue in the latter part of the nineteenth century had an adverse effect on the Donnellan home and property. The Hamilton Ice Works was constructed on the north side of Washington Avenue across the street from the Donnellan home some time prior to 1885[113]. The Houston Ice Company acquired those facilities and, by October of 1890, had expanded the ice plant significantly. The Simpson, Hartwell and Stopple Foundry was built adjacent to the ice plant about this same time[114]. By 1896, the Houston Ice and Brewing Company had completed a major expansion of their facilities in both Block 15 and Block 4, where the Donnellan home was located. By this time, the home had been demolished and replaced by other structures[115]. The census records of 1900 indicate that Emily Donnellan was living at 305 Lamar Avenue with her twenty-four-year-old nephew Frank Treadway and his half-sister Emily Anderson[116], age sixteen, who was born in July, 1883 to Mary Treadway Anderson and her husband, William Maurice Anderson[117].

By 1885, a wooden bridge had been built across the bayou to connect Franklin Avenue with 5th Street on the other side[118]. The wooden bridge was replaced with an iron bridge by 1907 as traffic to the businesses across the bayou increased[119]. Franklin Avenue became an important thoroughfare to the northwest side of town and, as a result of the continued encroachment on the integrity of the vault, all of the remains in the Donnellan Grave Vault were removed on December 3, 1901 by Wall and Stabe Undertakers and re-interred at Glenwood Cemetery[120]. An article in the Houston Chronicle on April 26, 1906, which listed over three hundred Confederate veterans buried in Houston cemeteries, included Henry Donnellan in the "Donnellan place" at the foot of Franklin Street bridge[121]. Although the article failed to recognize that the remains had been moved to Glenwood Cemetery in 1901, it does show that the Donnellan crypt was still visible on the banks of the bayou. However, the construction of an enormous platform over the bayou prior to 1924 buried the vault beneath the roadbed and bridge supports that extended from Louisiana Street to Franklin Avenue and beyond for about one hundred feet[122].

Thurston John Donnellan died in Houston on April 2, 1908 at age sixty-eight[123]. He was buried in Glenwood Cemetery where the remains of Timothy and Emily Donnellan, his parents, and Henry Donnellan, his brother, had been buried in 1901. On Sunday morning, June 18, 1911, Miss Emily Donnellan, daughter of Timothy and Emily Donnellan, died in Houston. Her funeral was held on Monday at the home of her nephew F. D. Treadway on Louisiana Street, with interment in Glenwood Cemetery. She was survived by her sister Mary F. Anderson, her brother F. D. Dwyer, her nephew F. D. Treadway and her nieces Mrs. Lillian M. (Treadway) Lillienthal of Houston and Mrs. Randolph Dickson of Galveston[124]. The Donnellan family members are buried in unmarked graves[125].

Jessamine Donnellan, widow of Thuse Donnellan, died on Friday, August 13, 1937, at age seventy-nine, in a Houston hospital[126]. Thuse Donnellan's younger half-brother Frank Dwyer also died in 1937 and was buried in Washington Cemetery[127].

The Donnellan crypt is a large vault made of red brick with a small wooden door in the lower right corner. A fine degree of workmanship is seen in the arched header to the doorway, which is boarded up with timbers. Located in the bank of Buffalo Bayou under the Franklin Avenue bridge at Louisiana Street, the vault has survived a number of phases of construction along the bayou, including the channelization of the bayou in the mid-1920's. Remnants of former bridge pilings stand under the modern bridge and a concrete ramp extends from the water line to the base of the vault to prevent erosion from undermining the vault's integrity.

Despite years of progress, construction, and development in the downtown area, the Donnellan Grave Vault endures as an impressive, but little known, monument to an early Houston family.

Houston Ice and Brewing Company's Magnolia Brewery

Immediately after passing under the Franklin Avenue bridge, we can see the remnants of one of the largest and most famous breweries of Houston. Several structures on the south bank of the bayou have survived from the late nineteenth and early twentieth century when the Houston Ice and Brewing Company operated the Magnolia Brewery at this location, and by 1903, nearly 200,000 barrels of fine quality beer were produced annually for thirsty Houstonians.

The Houston Ice and Brewing Association was incorporated in 1887, with Hugh Hamilton as the president of the company, Bertrand Adoue as the vice-president and Hyman Prince as the secretary and treasurer. The story, however, begins much earlier and it revolves around the company's founder Hugh Hamilton and his expertise in the ice manufacturing business which was critical to the commercialization of breweries and the growth of the beer industry[128].

Beer, historically, was a warm beverage. In the United States, the first lager beers were produced in the early 1840's. Jonathan Wagner is credited with making the first lager beer in North America in Philadelphia in 1842. As spring ales, they were brewed in the winter and allowed to ferment in the cold air of winter. Lager beer is brewed in cool conditions with a slow acting yeast, then stored ("lagered") in cool conditions to clear the beer of particles and flavors. Brewing usually was a family operation and was done on a small scale. These were craft brewers[129].

For industrial production, brew masters had to move away from the craft brewing techniques. The brew masters had to exercise a high degree of control over the temperature of the beer so they could brew the beer all during the year, not just in the cooler months. Many brewers used natural ice in their operations. Ice was cut in the winter from frozen streams and lakes in the north and stored in sawdust insulated containers until it was needed. However, the year round production of lager beer required a level of ice production that could not be maintained through ice harvesting alone[130].

In 1859, Ferdinand Carre patented in France an absorption process for making artificial ice, as they called it. The Carre process got a boost in Texas during the Civil War when the supply of natural ice from the north was cut off. Daniel Livingston Holden installed a Carre machine in San Antonio during the war and improved his Carre machine to produce clear ice while using distilled water. In 1873, David Boyle established the first ammonia compression plant for making artificial ice in Jefferson, Texas. These early attempts at refrigeration systems involved a labor intensive method with a series of 10 x 14 foot plates immersed in water with an ammonia refrigerant. An alternate method was the can ice system which required distilled water to prevent bubbles, but it was simple and less labor intensive. It made ice in three hundred pound cans. The use of ammonia, though, in the production of artificial ice was troublesome and dangerous[131].

At the Centennial Exhibition in Philadelphia in August, 1876, there was a major breakthrough in the technology of making artificial ice. Raoul Pictet, an inventor from Geneva, Switzerland, exhibited his new ice making machine. Pictet's machine differed from the more common liquifaction process using ammonia. His ice machine employed a vaporization and expansion process using the less expensive and less hazardous fluid of anhydrous sulphurous acid. The Pictet ice machine itself was quite compact, consisting of a 6-1/2 foot long cylindrical, tubular copper boiler with a diameter of 14 inches that was submerged in a steel vat. The Pictet process, with an eight horsepower engine, could manufacture 550 pounds of artificial ice in an hour. With that kind of productivity, the demand for the manufacture of artificial ice and cold air for refrigerating rooms and for breweries skyrocketed. Refrigeration began to be commercialized and breweries became the largest users of the new refrigeration technology. By the end of the decade, the modern era of beer brewing had begun in the United States with the support of the industrial advances in commercial refrigeration, automatic bottling machines, pasteurization and railroad distribution. There were over 2,500 breweries in the United States by the late 1870's, producing about ten million barrels of beer per year (at thirty-one gallons per barrel)[132].

The story of breweries in Houston began about 1849 with German immigrant Peter Gabel who opened a brewery on Preston Avenue at Caroline Street. Shortly thereafter, Henry Schulte, who had partnered briefly with Gabel, opened his own brewery near Frost Town and then moved to the banks of Buffalo Bayou at San Jacinto Street and Commerce Avenue. The Floeck family operated a brewery on their tract near Jackson Street. Each of these breweries were family owned craft breweries and probably produced modest quantities of beer in season. They operated on a small scale up to and through the Civil War, and into the 1870's as well.

By 1877, there were three breweries in Houston. Frederick Hahn had a brewery at the corner of Crockett Street and Beach Street where he also resided (on the banks of White Oak Bayou, four blocks east of Houston Avenue). Gerhard Schulte had taken over the operation of his brother's brewery about 1866 at the same location on San Jacinto Street. John Wagner and Charles Hermann were proprietors of Gabel's brewery on Preston Avenue[133].

At this same time, the other component necessary for commercial brewing was beginning to appear in Houston. Elisha Hall and R. R. Everett established the Houston Ice Manufacturing Company. The ice house, or manufacturing facility, was located on the north side of Buffalo Bayou, near the City Water Works. Their retail office was on the south side of Prairie Avenue between Main Street and Fannin Street[134].

Within two years, there was a significant expansion of the ice business in Houston. Elisha Hall brought C. C. Wiggin and B. C. Simpson into the Houston Ice Company and expanded the manufacturing of artificial ice at their plant located near Wiggin and Simpson's Phoenix Iron Works where the expertise for making the boilers and vessels necessary for the ice production process was available[135].

In addition to the Houston Ice Company, Leigh Hutchins and Company operated the Pictet Ice Company, bringing the advanced ice making technology invented by Raoul Pictet to Houston in 1879. The Pictet plant was located on the south side of Washington Avenue between 5th and 6th Streets. Hyman Prince established an ice company as well, although he was probably a dealer rather than a manufacturer of ice. Prince's office was on the south side of Preston Avenue between Main Street and Fannin Street[136].

The increased availability of ice and refrigeration had its effect on the breweries of Houston, too. John Wagner and Charles Hermann continued to operate the Peter Gabel Brewery on Preston Avenue as they had in the past. They were "bottlers of beer for family use" and proprietors of Gabel's saloon in the craft brewing tradition that had been common for the previous three decades. But, the beer business was changing[137].

Houston's other brewery, owned by Gerhard Schulte and located on Commerce Avenue, enhanced its offerings of locally brewed beer with beer from the W. J. Lemp Company of St. Louis, Missouri. Rail cars refrigerated with an abundant supply of manufactured ice permitted larger breweries in the Midwest to ship their beer to places far beyond their own town. Regional beer distribution networks followed the railroad connections into major cities of Texas and the South where it was believed that the climate was too warm to produce quality lager beer. Seizing this opportunity, in 1879, Gerhard Schulte became the Houston agent for William J. Lemp's St. Louis lager beer[138].

Other regional brewers came to the Houston market, too. At this same time, the Eberhard Anheuser Company Brewing Association of St. Louis was represented in Houston by Henry Suess. Advertising itself as the "Largest brewery in the West. Bottling capacity 100,000 bottles per day," the Anheuser Company's secretary Adolphus Busch formed his first venture to provide beer to Houstonians. Busch and his companies would be associated with brewing in Houston from 1879 through the current day[139].

It was in this environment that Hugh Hamilton, the man who would be the most significant personality in the brewing of beer in Houston, came to town.

Hugh Hamilton was born in County Tyrone, Ireland, in July, 1852. Raised in Glasgow, Scotland, Hamilton came to the United States at age seventeen and began working at the Cramps Shipbuilding Yards in Philadelphia. It was there that he learned the boilermaker's trade. Hamilton went to San Antonio, Texas initially, but in 1878, he made his way to Houston on foot, walking from San Antonio. The twenty-six year old Irishman found lodging at the Green Tree House which was operated by Mrs. Julia W. Cleary. The boarding house's location on Preston Avenue near the Phoenix Iron Works may have been planned or fortuitous, but it would be significant in both his personal life and his business career[140].

Immediately upon settling in his new town, Hamilton bought the ice factory owned by Wiggin and Simpson, one of the first such factories in Texas, and rebuilt the plant to make it more efficient. His skills as a boilermaker and pipe fitter allowed him to modernize and improve upon the ice making process so that this plant could produce five tons of ice per day. Hamilton sold his ice for ten cents a pound, and the potential seemed unlimited[141].

In 1880, Hugh Hamilton and Company, proprietors of the Crystal Ice Manufacturing Company, proudly advertised that they made "artificial ice, as clear, solid and lasting as any natural ice." Hamilton had formed his company with his friend Michael M. Mooney of San Antonio and Emile Hoencke, a local merchant who had a groceries and provisions store on the corner of Dallas Avenue and Smith Street. The office and plant was located near the City Water Works on the north side of Buffalo Bayou, and retail operations were handled from their office at 247 Preston Avenue. An ice house for the company was located at the corner of the Houston and Texas Central Railway and 2nd Street[142].

About this same time, Hugh Hamilton fell in love with the daughter of the proprietress of the Green Tree House. Mary Wickham married Hugh Hamilton at Annunciation Church in Houston on November 21, 1881. The family grew and prospered along with the ice business. Daughter Julia was born in October, 1882, followed by another daughter Mary in June, 1884 and son Hugh, Jr. in August, 1885. Daughter Agnes came along in June, 1887, but Hamilton's wife Mary suffered a hemorrhage following the birth of Agnes, and Mary Wickham Hamilton died on August 13, 1888. After Mary's death, Hugh Hamilton married Lily Imhoff. Tragic events, though, followed and that marriage ended when Lily died in childbirth on October 16, 1896. Both mother Lily and infant daughter were buried in Glenwood Cemetery[143].

During the decade of the 1880's, competition intensified in both the ice manufacturing business and the beer business in Houston. The local breweries expanded their business as suppliers of beers from the large regional breweries, and de-emphasized their own local brewing. The W. J. Lemp Western Brewery of St. Louis built an establishment on the former Gerhard Schulte property at the corner of San Jacinto Street and Commerce Avenue. The Joseph Schlitz Company of Milwaukee distributed beer from their agent's office 46 Franklin Avenue. And, later in the decade, the Lone Star Brewing Company of San Antonio established an office on the northeast corner of Travis Street and Preston Avenue and tried to break into the Houston market[144].

An advertisement by the W. J. Lemp Western Brewery in 1884 showed why these local operations would not succeed in the changing beer business. Lemp's ad promoted their St. Louis keg and bottled beer and proudly announced that they had "a full supply of beer and lake ice." Lake ice as a means of keeping beer cool was on the way out. The future was in manufactured ice, and no one knew this better than Adolphus Busch as he dreamed of a national beer business from his St. Louis brewing operations[145].

Adolphus Busch established the American Brewing Association in Houston as the agent for the Anheuser-Busch Brewing Association's Budweiser Bottled Beer by 1882. Busch, in St. Louis, was the president of the American Brewing Association, but Isidor Japhet, a local wholesale liquor dealer and merchant, was vice president. They built an ice factory and cold storage facility at the corner of 2nd Street and Railroad Street, and boasted that they had "the largest ice plant in the south" and they sold Dixie Pale and Hackerbrau bottled beer and American Standard keg beer. If you think that a cold beer on a hot afternoon today is refreshing, can you imagine what a "cold" beer in Houston in the 1880's was like? The future was cold beer, with an emphasis on cold[146].

The demand for ice was not lost on Hugh Hamilton. Hamilton expanded his ice manufacturing operations throughout the 1880's and was a principal in Houston's two commercial ice production companies, his Crystal Ice Manufacturing Company and the Central Ice Manufacturing Company, a dealership operated by Hyman Prince, but the plant was managed by Hugh Hamilton. Both of these ice companies were located on the north bank of Buffalo Bayou along Washington Avenue between 4th Street and 6th Street. Hamilton also began to manufacture and sell his ice making machines. By 1886, the Crystal Ice Factory was the manufacturer of "Hamilton's Celebrated Ice Machines" that were made to order for any size, could be shipped anywhere in Texas and were the best and cheapest machines in use[147].

In 1889, Hugh Hamilton decided to compete directly with Busch's American Brewing Association in the cold beer market. Hamilton became the agent for the Christian Moerlein Brewing Association of Cincinnati. The Christian Moerlein Brewery was the most prominent brewery in Cincinnati and it sold beer throughout the US and even internationally. Its beer was considered to be one of the superior products on the market and, with beer vaults located adjacent to the Crystal Ice Factory at the corner of Washington Avenue and 4th Street, Hamilton was in direct competition with the American Brewing Association of Adolphus Busch a few blocks away. Hamilton advertised that he could provide "the finest beer on the market" from supplies that were replenished daily. Not surprisingly, many people agreed with that. Moerlein beer was thought to be the best on the market at the time, and the brewery's distribution system was one of the most extensive of its day. The brewery continued to operate after the death of its founder Christian Moerlein in 1897, but closed in 1920 with the enactment of Prohibition and did not re-open after the law's repeal[148].

The next move by Hugh Hamilton was even more audacious. In 1892, he joined with his old friend Hyman Prince, with the Galveston investment firm of Adoue and Lobit, and with William M. Rice to build a large brewery plant on the site where his ice plant was located. Formally established in February, 1893, this venture was the Houston Ice and Brewing Association, and its brewery was called the Magnolia Brewery[149].

Well known local architect Eugene Heiner designed and built the Houston Ice and Brewing Association's new main building on the northwest corner of Washington Avenue and 4th Street. The elaborate and ornate five story brick structure was completed in 1893, and it housed two large ice machines that had a total capacity of 100 tons of ice per day. Water for both the ice and beer operations was obtained from three artesian wells, 800 feet, 300 feet and 150 feet in depth, giving the brewery the capability of producing 60,000 barrels of beer annually[150].

The Houston Ice and Brewing Company employed the German born Fritz Kalb as their brew master, and Hugh Hamilton excelled in making the refrigeration which enabled his brewers to make a uniform product all year round. The Magnolia Brewery began producing a general brand called Magnolia and a selection of bottled beer brands, including Extra Pale, Richelieu, Standard and its most popular, Southern Select. On February 25, 1894, the Houston Ice and Brewing Company proudly announced that they had proven that the climate of Texas and Houston, in particular, could be adapted for the brewing of beer. By 1895, they were brewing more than 35,000 barrels a year[151].

Business for the Houston Ice and Brewing Company was good. In the years around the turn of the twentieth century, the company was producing about 250 tons of ice each day and and reaching its capacity of 200,000 barrels of beer annually. In one extraordinary venture, the company was running two power boats to Key West, Florida to ship its beer to Cuba. This success allowed the company to improve its facilities. By 1907, the Houston Ice and Brewing plant and associated buildings, located on the north side of Buffalo Bayou along Washington Avenue, included the main building and an extensive brewing complex consisting of cold storage rooms, freezing tanks, ice storage, a wash room and beer cooling and storage cellars. The Magnolia Brewery facilities on the south side of Washington Avenue included the bottling works, the office and stables surrounding a brick-paved courtyard[152].

A few years later, in 1912, the Houston Ice and Brewing Company expanded across the bayou to Franklin Avenue into a three story building redesigned by the firm of H. C. Cooke and Company and built on the foundations of a late nineteenth century structure. Magnolia Building, constructed partially over Buffalo Bayou, was connected with buildings on the north bank by a concrete platform over the bayou. The adjacent two story structure on the corner of Franklin Avenue and Milam Street served as the company's executive offices and tap room and also housed the Magnolia Cafe. The Houston Ice and Brewing Company, at its greatest extent, in 1915, consisted of ten buildings on twenty acres extending across both sides of Buffalo Bayou. It was an imposing presence in downtown Houston[153].

Belgian born Frantz H. Brogniez was the brew master for the Houston Ice and Brewing Company at the time the new Magnolia Building was built. Brogniez was already famous in the industry for his quality beers, but his work at the Magnolia Brewery was extraordinary. Under Brogniez, the Magnolia Brewery's Southern Select beer won the Grand Prize at the International Congress of Brewers in 1913. The general public concurred with the judges' assessment in the best way possible. The Houston Ice and Brewing Company became the largest brewing company south of Milwaukee[154].

As the Magnolia Brewery was growing in prominence in the second decade of the twentieth century, it was also faced with intense competition in the beer market. Price wars over beer were common, and many of the small craft breweries did not survive. There was a lot of consolidation in the industry. Local brewers grew at the expense of the craft breweries and of the large regional brewers with extensive distribution networks. The number of breweries in the United States declined to about 1,400 in 1914. Attempts to gain a competitive edge led some brewers in Texas to espouse questionable practices and, in 1915, several breweries in Texas were accused of violations of Texas anti-trust statutes and of making contributions of corporate funds to political campaigns[155].

In addition to this difficult economic environment, brewers faced the rising influence of the temperance movement in the United States. The temperance lobby became quite politically astute at this time and displayed an influence in Washington that jeopardized the beer industry. The onset of the hostilities of the world war permitted the prohibition lobby to ride a "wave of virulent xenophobia that came with World War I" aimed at German immigrants and other groups who regarded alcohol consumption as a part of their cultural traditions. On April 4, 1917, the day Congress declared war on Germany, Texas Senator Morris Sheppard introduced the prohibition amendment in the U. S. Senate. By the end of 1917, the proposed constitutional amendment was approved by Congress. The Texas legislature ratified the federal amendment in 1918, and by 1919, the 18th Amendment to the U. S. Constitution, commonly known as Prohibition, was ratified by the necessary number of states[155a].

In anticipation that the 18th Amendment would go into effect (which it did on January 17, 1920), Hugh Hamilton began to diversify away from the brewing business. In summer of 1918, the Houston Ice and Brewing Company installed $600,000 of new machinery to convert the brewery into a business that manufactured food products. The Magnolia Dairy Products Company, as this new venture was called, produced a variety of dairy products, including Honey Boy Ice Cream, buttermilk, cottage cheese, Magnolia Brand Butter and condensed milk. The logo of a magnolia blossom in a lone star, carried over from the familiar brewery logo, was imprinted on the company's packaging. By January, 1920, the 69 year old Hugh Hamilton, once the foremost brewer in Houston and, perhaps, Texas, declared himself to be a manufacturer of dairy products[156].

In mid-summer of 1922, Hugh Hamilton traveled to Milwaukee for medical treatment, and on Friday night, August 4, 1922, he died there. His body was returned to Houston and Hugh Hamilton was laid to rest in the family plot in Washington Cemetery alongside his first wife Mary and their son Hugh, Jr. who died in an automobile accident in 1911[157].

James H. Studdert, the secretary of the Houston Ice and Brewing Company and a long time associate of Hugh Hamilton, took over the management of Magnolia Dairy Products Company, and by 1924, had renamed it the Lone Star Creamery. Studdert operated the creamery well into the 1930's, but he relocated it elsewhere. In March, 1925, the building formerly occupied by the Magnolia Creamery was converted into a "first class popular priced hotel." The new owner, E. F. Williams, christened the new establishment as the Magnolia Hotel. The hotel, fitted with the most modern steam heating system, accommodated two hundred fifty guests, and each room was supplied with hot and cold water[158].

In the same year, architect Alfred Finn designed alterations to the part of the Magnolia Brewing complex at 110 Milam Street for the Dixon Packing Company, as the former Houston Ice and Brewing Company structures were put to other commercial uses[159].

The redeployment of the former Houston Ice and Brewing Company complex of buildings along the bayou was short lived. The rising waters of the Buffalo Bayou flood of May 31, 1929 damaged a portion of the complex and the concrete platform over the bayou. Then, the flood of December, 1935 did even greater damage to the buildings. Significant parts of the the Magnolia Hotel and the Dixon Packing Company were undermined by the swift current of Buffalo Bayou and portions of the buildings crumbled into the bayou[160].

The Houston Ice and Brewing Company, which closed during Prohibition, had its sprawling industrial plant devastated by the floods of 1929 and 1935. Although the 21st Amendment which repealed Prohibition was ratified in December, 1933, many regional and craft breweries in the United States were unable to re-open for business. Only about one hundred sixty breweries were able to be revived after Prohibition, and the Magnolia Brewery was not one of them. The Houston Ice and Brewing Company closed for good in 1950[161].

In 1967, historical preservationist and architect Bart Truxillo acquired the old Magnolia Brewery building at 715 Franklin Avenue. Truxillo renovated what was left standing of the neo-classical structure, and during the early 1970's, it was the site of the Bismarck Restaurant, a fashionable downtown eatery managed by famed Houston restaurateur Manfred Jachmich. For the last several years, the second floor Magnolia Ballroom has been a popular place for meetings, parties, high school proms and other special events[162].

Today, from your boat on the bayou, you can still see the reinforced concrete foundation posts and support beams of the former Magnolia Building. The remains of the concrete infrastructure that supported the part of the building that extended about thirty feet into the channel of Buffalo Bayou lie under the modern bridge at Franklin Avenue. The Pink Monkey nightclub, which occupies the basement of the Magnolia Ballroom building, uses the deck on the old foundation as a patio which is decorated with hanging baskets and potted plants[163].

Passing downstream, imagine the concrete platform that covered the bayou and extended as far downstream as the last ragged-edged structure on the south bank. These are other parts of the Magnolia Brewery complex. The Dixon Meat Packing Company was the last tenant of the 7,000 square foot, four story building at 110 Milam Street that dates from 1906. Although vacant for more than thirty years, this building was redeveloped in 1996 with the ToC nightclub on the first floor and residential lofts on the upper floors[164].

The small fragment of the Houston Ice and Brewing Company embodied in the few structures in the corner of Milam Street and Franklin Avenue is an excellent reminder of the City's most historic brewery operation, but it scarcely reflects the full extent of the sprawling complex that consisted of ten buildings on twenty acres along the bayou. Nothing remains of the ice factory and main brewery on the north side of the bayou.

Milam Street Bridge

The hike and bike trail emerges from beneath the Franklin Avenue bridge on the north side of Buffalo Bayou. As the trail winds along the bank, the landscaped slope forms a small park which is accessible when the water level of the Bayou is within its normal range. Ahead, we see the trail go under the Milam Street bridge. This bridge is fairly modern. It was built in 1947, but this crossing of Buffalo Bayou dates to the time before the founding of the City of Houston[165].

As Stephen F. Austin worked to establish his colony in Texas in the 1820's, he encouraged the immigration of men of economic means such as Jared Groce. Groce transplanted his plantation from Alabama to the Brazos Valley near modern day Hempstead, and within a few years, Groce was producing quantities of cotton that could be exported from Texas. In the mid-1820's, Groce transported one hundred bales of cotton to the junction of White Oak and Buffalo Bayou. Near what is now the Milam Street bridge, Groce and his crew forded the bayou. His wagons bumped along a trail hacked through underbrush and giant trees across the future site of

Houston to Harrisburg where he loaded the cotton on John R. Harris's steam-powered barges for the trip to Galveston[166].

The importance of this "road" was not lost on the Allen brothers. In 1837, the town of Houston contracted with David Harrison to build a bridge across the bayou at this point. Augustus C. Allen donated the timbers and heavy planks for the bridge which was 300 feet long and was constructed at a cost of $1,500. The low wooden bridge at the foot of Milam Street was completed in October, 1838, and it was Houston's the first bridge over Buffalo Bayou. A bridge over the other important crossing of Buffalo Bayou at Preston Avenue was completed shortly afterwards in November, 1838[167].

The young town of Houston had to learn about the hydrology of Buffalo Bayou from the very beginning. A few months after its construction, the Milam Street bridge was damaged by a flood in February, 1839, and it had to be repaired by David Harrison. In the 1840's, a second bridge made of wood and concrete was built at the foot of Milam Street to accommodate the increase in commercial traffic into the city. That bridge was destroyed by the floods of October and November, 1843. Finally, about 1850, the bridge was replaced with a "little iron bridge" that served for a long time thereafter. The bridge is nicely depicted on the 1873 Houston Bird's Eye Map[168].

At the end of the Civil War, an incident took place at the Milam Street bridge that would have repercussions for the city for the next one hundred forty (or more) years. The story begins with John Kennedy, an Irish immigrant who came to Houston in 1842 and opened a bakery. The young Kennedy was quite industrious and soon expanded his business enterprises and land holdings in Houston. In the late 1840's, he took over the trading post operations after the Torrey brothers abandoned their Houston business and he opened the Kennedy Trading Post in the narrow two-story brick building at 813 Congress Avenue across from Market Square. Kennedy was an early parishioner of St. Vincent de Paul Church, Houston's first Catholic church, and he and his wife Matilda contributed to the building fund for the church building and donated a lot for the cemetery[169].

By 1860, John Kennedy had erected a flour mill at Congress Avenue and the Dry Gully, the large drainage that ran down what would be Caroline Street, that produced twenty-four barrels of flour a day. He also built the Kennedy Building, a three story structure located at 220 Travis Street and Congress Avenue. It was this building that Kennedy leased to the Confederacy in 1862 for use by the ordnance department as an arsenal[170].

After the surrender of the Confederacy in 1865, soldiers who were returning to their homes in Texas raided the Kennedy building, taking items that they might need to re-establish themselves on their farms in the countryside. The government stores in Houston were appropriated by soldiers and families of soldiers while ordinance stores "were either carried off or destroyed, and guns, shot and shells were thrown into Buffalo Bayou." After his place had been looted, Kennedy disposed of the remaining ordinance by taking it to the Iron Bridge at Milam Street and dumping the munitions and into bayou[171].

The disposal of the ordinance from the arsenal was part of a broader effort to deprive the approaching Union forces of the equipment and supplies of the Confederacy. During the war, blockade runners and ammunition barges had operated between Houston and Galveston. Ordnance and supplies came to Houston by the shipload, and in June, 1865, there were three of these vessels at the dock in Houston. These barges, "loaded with rifles and cannon balls were driven up stream as far as possible and sunk." The low water bridge at Milam Street was as far upstream as the barges could be moved, and there they were scuttled[172].

Although significant amounts of material and munitions had been disposed of in the bayou, no organized effort was made to remove the ordnance from the bayou. Houston seemed content to let the bombs and guns lie in the mud of the stream bottom. Nevertheless, the citizens were reminded of this episode periodically, especially during periods when the tide was very low.

On Sunday morning, February 10, 1867, Henry Donnellan and A. C. Richer, partners in the tin business returned to their home on the north side of Buffalo Bayou via the Milam Street bridge for dinner. While waiting for dinner, the two men were examining a shell that had been exposed in the shallows of the bayou. The shell exploded and both men were fatally wounded. The tragic event stunned the whole town and it remained in the local memory for years thereafter, such as on Wednesday, November 21, 1877, when the police found an old bombshell under the Iron Bridge at Milam Street that was "similar to the one that killed Henry Donnellan[173]."

For the next thirty years, the disposed munitions attracted little interest. However, in late January, 1906, a low tide exposed the remains of the Civil War disposal effort. One of the old barges, although mired in the mud, had been visible above the surface for many years. Now, the shallows of the bayou were exposed and the City authorized the Houston Yacht and Power Boat Club to clear the bayou above Main Street in order to construct a "harbor for pleasure craft and launches." On January 30, 1906, "a blast was placed under the ancient wreck of an old ammunition boat" and the explosion attracted a large crowd to the scene. A hundred or more men and boys gathered along the banks of Buffalo Bayou below the Milam Street bridge and began digging and scraping the bottom of the bayou with sticks and other implements looking for cannonballs, bombshells and other dangerous Civil War relics[174].

In the forty years since the munitions were disposed of, this was the largest number of relics recovered from the site. Many of the bombshells were still quite dangerous. The gunpowder was found to be dry and very explosive, even after having been submerged for so long. The memory of those who had died in the past while handling these relics of the war was carefully noted as a precaution to those who were collecting the souvenirs. The items recovered included Civil War era rifles and cartridges that were shipped to Texas from France, cannonballs, and some money and a diamond ring. Mayor Baldwin Rice and two City Commissioners inspected the excavation and were pleased that the "three old hulks have been removed" from the waterway[175].

The iron bridge at Milam Street was replaced with a concrete bridge by 1924, and no more was heard about the buried Civil War artifacts and cannonballs in the mud of Buffalo Bayou. That is, until 1947, when a new concrete bridge was built to replace the earlier one. During the construction of this bridge, which was designed by J. G. McKenzie and built by the C. E. Lytle Company, 351 cannonballs were uncovered and taken to Fort Sam Houston for disposal[176].

This information caught the attention of real estate developer, history buff and treasure hunter Carroll A. Lewis, Jr. In February,

1968, Lewis and the Southwestern Historical Exploration Society, a group of like minded persons who shared Lewis's interest in history and quest for hidden treasure, probed the area below the Milam Street bridge. The soundings that they took indicated that objects seemed to be buried in about five feet of mud, close to the bridge[177].

In the early summer of 1968, Lewis organized an excavation of Buffalo Bayou near the Milam Street bridge in hopes of locating and recovering artifacts from the sunken ships or barges. His efforts to find these Civil War relics relied on the eye witness accounts of three Houston residents who participated in the 1906 excavations at Milam Street. Each of them had vivid memories of the event that took place over sixty years earlier, even though each was only a young boy at the time[178].

John Gresham claimed that he and his grandfather, John S. Taylor, boarded the sunken boat at Milam Street during the low tide which was accentuated by a north wind that had blown the bayou water out and exposed the ruins. Gresham and his grandfather boarded the old Confederate ship which his grandfather recognized as the Confederate blockade runner Augusta. Taylor had served as the cannoneer of the ship while a member of Hood's Texas Brigade. The schooner Augusta had made a trip to New Orleans, Mobile and back. While docked near the Milam Street bridge, the 65 feet long and 20 feet wide schooner was sunk about thirty feet downstream from the bridge with its bow pointed out toward the middle of the bayou. Gresham recalled that the forward cabin of the ship was extant and the muzzle of an iron cannon was sticking out. The deck of the boat was gone, but the ribs were still visible. Among the ruins, they picked up about forty cannonballs which later were taken to Fort Sam Houston and exploded by the Army[179].

W. L. Cleveland remembered the old boat that could be seen in the middle of the bayou near the Milam Street bridge when the water was low. He recalled the time that it was blown up after some divers had recovered several boxes of rifles from the boat[180].

Felix Joe Richard was there when a north wind caused a low tide in Buffalo Bayou and a boat was exposed. The boat was about sixty feet long and twenty-five feet wide. There was another boat across the bayou, but it appeared to be buried more deeply in the mud. Richard went onto the boat and found boxes of shells, boxes that could have had rifles in them, cannon balls and a cannon that was bolted down to the main deck[181].

On July 20, 1968 at 8:00 am, the Southwestern Historical Exploration Society set a thirty ton drag line on the Milam Street bridge to dig the bayou mud. Believing that the sunken boat was near the middle or closer to the south bank, they dredged that area first. Six and a half hours later, at 2:30 pm, a 3" Parrott type cannonball was found at a site ten feet from the bridge in center of bayou. Subsequent digging recovered an impressive array of ordnance and military equipment, including three Parrott cannon projectiles of CSA manufacture, two 3" Blakely cannon projectiles of British manufacture, a 12 lb Borman fused cannon ball, a Williams wiper Minie ball and a 10" Brass Naval ordinance cannon fuse dated 1861. Other military items included three Blakely brass nipple fuses, pistol balls of 28, 31, 36 and 44 caliber, rifle balls of 50, 58, 69 caliber, an Enfield bayonet, a musket wrench, grape shot, and an octagonal, 36 caliber rifle barrel with its front sight attached. Additional items included a belaying pin, square nails, spikes, chest locks and keys and other items that would have been the typical cargo of a Confederate supply ship[182].

Carroll Lewis, who supervised the Southwestern Historical Exploration Society recovery of the Civil War relics, said that his organization would not do any additional excavations, but he felt that many more artifacts were left in the bayou to be recovered. This recovery operation was financed by the Houston Antique Gun Collectors Association for display at their annual meeting on August 4, 1968 and they had satisfied that commitment. He did say, however, that the artifacts would be on display at the Houston Museum of Natural Science[183].

The display of the Civil War relics from the Milam Street bridge took place at the Museum of Natural Science in 1974. After the exhibit, the whereabouts of the recovered artifacts is unknown and the items were most likely retained in the personal collections of the treasure hunters.

During March of 2010, a combination of a strong low tide and a gusty north wind created low water conditions in Buffalo Bayou that were similar to those of 1906. This time, however, even though the old pilings and bulkhead of the bayou were exposed and the muddy bottom of the bayou visible to a large extent, no Civil War artifacts were seen lying on the stream bed. If they are there, they are mired deeply in the sediments of the bayou.

Dickson-Siewerssen Building

Throughout the 19th century, the low water bridge at Milam Street marked the extent of upstream navigability of Buffalo Bayou and the Houston Ship Channel. Commercial boats could not pass under the bridge. Milam Street also formed the western extent of city's wharf district along Commerce Avenue. Although the block of Commerce Avenue between Travis Street and Milam Street was a few blocks away from the primary commercial center of the city, this block was the home for business and commercial endeavors from, at least, the end of the Civil War.

Today, from the bayou, one can easily see the two story Dickson-Siewerssen Building encompassing the entire 800 block of Commerce Avenue. Situated on the south side of the street, the elegant turn of the century structure has been updated into a modern office complex while retaining its original brick facade. This historic building, nevertheless, is one of the least known architectural remnants of Houston's downtown business district[184].

As early as 1869, the Wood map shows that there were four buildings along the south side of Commerce Avenue in SSBB Block 16. The Houston Bird's Eye Map of 1873 depicts these structures as two story buildings. The Houston Bird's Eye Map of 1891 shows a slightly different configuration of the buildings, some of which are shown as three stories in height. By 1907, a major reconstruction of these lots produced the buildings essentially as they exists today[185].

With the growth of the ranch and cattle business after the Civil War, the trade in hides and wool expanded in Texas and Houston. Although it was not a major commercial factor in Houston's emerging post war economy as was cotton, there was a persistent presence of hide and wool dealers in Houston throughout the nineteenth and early twentieth centuries. As early as 1877, William D. Alexander, of Alexander and Company, and David Rosenthal were dealers in hides, pelts and wool in Houston, and their offices were located "on the west side of Commerce Avenue between Milam Street and Travis Street[186]."

The hides and wool business at this time was one in which dealers and business owners changed frequently. The place of business, however, was fairly stable and over the decades of the 1870's and 1880's, a succession of dealers worked out of the storefront on Commerce Avenue. In 1879, Thomas M. Anderson was the dealer in hides, wool and cotton with an office there, although he resided in Palestine, Texas. A year later, in 1880, Theodore H. Zanderson, a San Antonio resident, operated his hides business from that same location while boarding at the Hutchins House hotel, a block away, when he was in town[187].

The nature of the hides and wool business required that a dealer travel into the ranching country as well as take care of the shipping and transport part of the trade in the commercial center like Houston. As a result, the owners often hired clerks to run the office while they were soliciting business from ranchers in the hinterlands. An industrious young man could work his way up the ladder from clerk to partner to principal owner. And, just such an example was the case in Houston in the store on Commerce Avenue.

Charles Siewerssen, a twenty-seven year old from Louisiana, and his younger brother Emile, arrived in Texas in late 1877 and they settled in Houston. Charles Siewerssen hired on as a clerk with the Henry Henke company, and Emile Siewerssen got a job as a clerk with the Thomas M. Anderson Company, working at the store on Commerce Avenue. As the hides and wool business changed hands and was taken over by Theodore H. Zanderson, Emile Siewerssen stayed with the company, and by 1880, Emile had been promoted to agent for the company, while his brother Charles began working at the T. H. Zanderson company as a clerk[188].

Emile Siewerssen learned the hides and wool business well, and by 1884, he was a principal of Zanderson, Hartwell and Company along with George Hartwell, another local businessman. Zanderson handled his side of the business from San Antonio. The Houston office was still at the location at the corner of Commerce Avenue and Milam Street which by this time had been assigned the street number of 2 Commerce Avenue[189].

The business evolved once again in 1884, and Emile Siewerssen and George H. Hartwell became partners in the firm which they called Hartwell, Siewerssen and Company. Charles Siewerssen expanded his role and became a traveling hide buyer. The offices and warehouse for the hides and wool company remained in the same building which was one of six businesses operating in that block of Commerce Avenue. The hide and wool dealers shared the block with a diverse group of enterprises, including an agricultural implements warehouse, a lime, cement and drain pipe company, the Periera and Randolph Company which sold mixed paints and oil, Vinson's Warehouse and M. C. Welborn, a Commission Merchant[190].

Toward the end of the 1880's, Emile Siewerssen acquired control of the hide and wool company and renamed it E. Siewerssen and Company. His brother Charles moved to an inside job and became the company's bookkeeper. The Siewerssens brought the family together in the business just as the family stayed stayed together in town. By 1880, Charles had moved into a house with his brother Emile, and sister Lillie joined her brothers in Houston by 1886 when they moved into a house on the northeast corner of Walker Avenue and Chartres Street[191].

In late 1889, the Siewerssen company began to rely less on sending a representative out into the countryside and more on advertising to make contact with their customers. On October 1, 1889, the E. Siewerssen Company advertised in the the newspaper's Houston Business Directory. They had a prominent ad in each year's Houston city directory and they advertised regularly in the daily newspaper. The company acquired the retail space next door at 4 Commerce Avenue and expanded its products in 1891 to include "Liverpool salt, hay, corn, oats, bran, etc.," but that enterprise was short lived, and the business soon returned to its main lines of hides and wool. The store space at 4 Commerce Avenue was apparently better suited to their operations and, in 1896, the company offices were at 806 Commerce Avenue, two doors from the corner, after the new street numbering system was put in place in Houston[192].

After the renovation of the buildings along the 800 block of Commerce Avenue about 1905, the Siewerssen hide and wool company shared the commercial row with a blacksmith and carriage shop next door on the corner. The blacksmith occupied the store that

Siewerssen did previously. On the east side of Siewerssen was a large store which occupied numbers 808 through 814 Commerce Avenue. This merchant of wholesale dry goods, notions, gents furnishings was the original store and warehouse for the Hogan-Allnoch Dry Goods firm. The Hogan and Allnoch company of Victoria sold out to the Graves Dry Goods Company in 1906, and they moved to Houston to enter the wholesale dry goods business here. Hogan-Allnoch later moved their store to 520 Preston Avenue before constructing their final location on the corner of Texas Avenue and Austin Street in 1922[193].

Emile Siewerssen and his siblings continued to operate their business on Commerce Avenue through the first quarter of the twentieth century even though the hides business diminished significantly and the wool trade moved elsewhere. The family moved to a new house after 1900 and the two unmarried brothers, Emile and Charles shared the home with their unmarried sister Lillie and their widowed sister Ida Magee. Emile and Charles died some time before 1930, and the hides business closed about mid-1930. Lillie Siewerssen passed away in 1932[194].

By 1950, the stores along the 800 block of Commerce Avenue had become businesses in Houston's "Produce Row" that extended for several blocks along Commerce Avenue. The block was home to a wholesale meats and sausage manufacturing company, a wholesale poultry supplier, a poultry and wholesale produce company, a cold storage warehouse, a wholesale bananas distributor and a wholesale produce store. Yet, the economics of the downtown markets had changed by the 1970's and the buildings along Commerce Avenue had declined in value and were often vacant[195].

In 1970, the law firm of Kronzer, Abraham and Watkins purchased two buildings spanning the 800 block of Commerce Avenue. Ralph Anderson of Wilson, Crane, Anderson and Reynolds was hired as the architect for the renovation of the structure now known as the Dickson and Siewerssen buildings. The renovations included gutting the buildings back to the basic wood structure and opening the second floor to the roof. Only the original brick masonry, the heavily timbered second floor and the oak ceiling rafters were retained, while skylights were added to provide light for the foyer area that opens to the roof above. The structure that had

housed four separate establishments in two buildings was reconfig-
ured as modern office space in one building. In recognition of its
innovative restoration, the project, in June, 1972, received an award
at the 9th Annual Environmental Improvements Awards Competition of the Houston Municipal Art Commission and the Houston
Chapter of AIA. The law firm of Hill, Brown, Kronzer and Abraham
moved into its new office space in January, 1975. Today, the 27,302
square foot Dickson and Siewerssen building, with a spectacular
view of Buffalo Bayou from its front door, is owned by the Frank T.
Abraham Trust and occupied by the law firm of Abraham, Watkins,
Nichols, Sorrels, Agosto and Friend[196].

Houston Flour Mills

The Travis Street bridge follows immediately ahead. Built in the
early 1970's, the Travis Street bridge is the feeder road from downtown to the northbound lanes of Interstate 45. The roadway cuts
across NSBB, Block 6 which was the site of commercial ventures
for a hundred years.

During the 1870's and 1880's, the Houston Flour Mills operated
in a five story building situated in the northwest corner of the block,
adjacent to the Houston and Texas Central Railway tracks. The plant
used a stone mill with double roller mill that was powered by a
George Corliss 175 horsepower engine enabling a production capacity of two hundred twenty-five barrels of flour and three hundred
barrels of meal per day. The Houston Flour Mills was managed by
David P. Shepherd from the early 1870's until the mill closed in the
mid-1880's. After the death of L. J. Latham, the owner of the mill,
the company's property was put up for sale by the estate in July,
1886, and the mill closed shortly thereafter[197].

Although David Shepherd was associated with the Houston
Flour Mills for several years, he is best known for his attempt to
build a mill complex on Buffalo Bayou upstream of town, near the
community of Brunner. In the 1890's, Shepherd constructed a dam
on the bayou that became known as Shepherd's Dam. The road
across the dam was Shepherd's Dam Road that today is Shepherd
Drive, a major thoroughfare on the west side of Houston.

By 1907, the flour mill site was used as a factory by the Texas Bag and Fiber Company. To the east of the plant, the Henry Henke company built a large, two story grocery and feed warehouse. The Henke and Pillot Company later expanded their warehouse as a part of their wholesale grocery business[198].

In 1913, the old mill was replaced by a large, three story reinforced concrete warehouse that was occupied by the Southwest General Electric Company. By 1950, the Black Brothers Furniture Company had acquired both facilities on Block 6 and was using them as furniture warehouses[199].

The two warehouses were removed from the site in the early 1960's. The foundations remained, and most of those were removed a decade later with the construction of the I-45 feeder. The land in the block was incorporated into the Johnny Goyen Park along with the landscaping of the bayou hike and bike trail in 1999. Yet, today, portions of the concrete foundation of the former Henke and Pillot warehouse are still visible near the railroad tracks and the University of Downtown Academic Building[200].

American Brewing Association

The University of Downtown Academic Building is a stylish recent addition to the campus of the City's downtown university. Adjacent to the main university building, the former M and M Building, the Academic Building houses classrooms, food facilities, the Wilhelmina Cullen Robertson Auditorium, the Technology Teaching and Learning Center and a parking garage for campus visitors. The South Deck, an expansive patio off the Academic Building, extends over the railroad tracks and offers a dramatic view of downtown Houston. All of which contrasts with the more industrial nature of the businesses that previously occupied the block on which the building sits[201].

The development of refrigeration and the making of artificial ice changed the way beer was made and sold in the United States. Refrigerated rail cars allowed breweries in the Midwest to ship their beer products to distant cities, including places like Houston. As a result, the local breweries could no complete with the high volume, all year round production of beer makers in St. Louis, Cincinnati and Milwaukee.

By the late 1870's, the Eberhard Anheuser Company Brewing Association of St. Louis advertised itself as the "largest brewery in the West. Bottling capacity 100,000 bottles per day." They had an agent in Houston in 1879, but the energetic young secretary of the company had grander plans. When Adolphus Busch took over the company, he established the American Brewing Association in partnership with local Houston businessmen, and Isadore Japhet, a Houston liquor merchant, became vice president of the association[202].

By 1882, the American Brewing Association had built "the largest ice plant in the south" on NSBB Block 12, located between 2nd Street and 3rd Street on Railroad Street. They were the agent for the Anheuser-Busch Brewing Association Budweiser bottled beer, but also supplied Dixie Pale and Hackerbrau bottled beer in addition to American Standard keg beer. The beer was shipped by refrigerated railroad cars from the brewery in St. Louis and stored in the icehouse in Houston[203].

Improvements in commercial refrigeration led Adolphus Busch to introduce the large scale brewing of Anheuser-Busch beer to Houston where the warm climate had previously prevented such enterprises. The American Brewing Association constructed their brewing facility in a six story building which covered the entire block on Railroad Street. The gala grand opening of the brewery was held in February, 1894 with 10,000 people in attendance to celebrate a cold beer[204].

The brewery employed some innovative ways to keep the beer cold. The walls of the beer cellars, the brew house, the cold storage rooms and the ice storage rooms were lined with cork for insulation. A tunnel from the building went twenty feet down before turning and going the thirty to forty feet to the bayou. Two pipes along the base of the tunnel delivered bayou water for cooling the beer as water in pipes circled the brewing vats to draw off the heat[205].

The American Brewing Association faced strong competition from the Houston Ice and Brewing Company upstream and across the bayou at Franklin Avenue, but it proved to be a successful enterprise that operated in Houston until 1918 when the effects of the temperance movement caused breweries to close and Prohibition was on its way to becoming the law of the land.

The icehouse and refrigeration facilities were bought by the American Ice and Storage Company which operated on the site until a fire in 1948 closed it down. The South Texas Junior College, the predecessor to the UH-Downtown, acquired the former icehouse in 1967 for parking. In January, 1996, during the ground breaking for the new academic building, the foundation of the icehouse once owned by the American Brewing Association was uncovered[206].

M and M Building

The building immediately to the east of the UH-Downtown Academic Building is, naturally, the main building of the University of Houston-Downtown. This splendid, ten story red brick structure sits on the high bank of Buffalo Bayou at its junction with White Oak Bayou. The university's building began life as the Merchants and Manufacturers Building, and before that, the historic Samuel L. Allen Cotton Warehouse was located on the site.

Sam Allen was one of the brothers of the founders of Houston, Augustus Chapman Allen and John Kirby Allen, and his place of business on the block overlooking the City wharves reminded the citizens of Houston of the presence of the Allen family in the commercial interests of the town, a presence that stood throughout the nineteenth century.

The story of how Augustus C. and John K. Allen came to Texas and established the town of Houston is well known. It has been retold many times and is the basis for every history of Houston. What is less known is the story of how the whole Allen family was transplanted into this frontier town and how they invested everything they had in the future of Houston. And, remarkably, all six Allen brothers became prominent figures in the economic and social life of Houston and Texas.

Although an advertisement in the newspaper of August 30, 1836 touted the establishment of the new town of Houston, efforts to clear the pine grove and drain the prairie ponds at the site of the 62 blocks platted in November of 1836 by Gail Borden as the new town did not begin until after the First Congress of the Republic had designated the new town of Houston as the capital of the Republic in December, 1836. By January 1, 1837, a few log cabins and several tents were evidence of the vast construction underway. The Allen brothers had promised to build a capital in time for the Congress to reconvene on April 1, only a few months away. Nevertheless, in early 1837, amid these rudimentary beginnings, the father, mother, a sister and four brothers of A. C. and J. K. Allen arrived from Canaseraga, a village in Allegany County, New York about sixty-five miles south of Rochester, to make their home in Houston[207].

Augustus C. and John K. Allen had been in Texas since 1832. Their parents, Rowland and Sally Allen, at ages fifty-five and forty-nine years respectively, left the place where they had lived for decades to join the enterprise of their eldest son and his younger sibling. Along with them came their other four sons, Samuel, George, Henry and Harvey. Ranging in age from twenty-eight years old to seventeen years old, these young men were well suited to the opportunities that the new town offered. The Allen's daughter and sibling to the city's founders also came to Houston in 1837, but little can be found in the historical accounts about her, even her name. In the census records of 1850, however, there is a Julia Allen, age twenty-three, who lives in the household of Henry Allen and his family. If this person is the last Allen sibling, then she came to Houston at about age ten, but not much is known about her. Her story may only be known to the family and descendants of the founding family[208].

It was not long after the Allen family moved to Houston that the untimely death of John Kirby Allen happened. He died of congestive fever on August 15, 1838 and was buried in the City Cemetery, now known as Founders Memorial Park. Since he died intestate, there was a question about how to handle his interests in the Houston Town Company. In an attempt to expedite the matter, the brothers waived their rights to share of John Kirby's his estate in favor of their parents. That agreement only delayed the day of reckoning. Sally Allen, their mother, died on September 20, 1841. Rowland Allen, their father, passed away less than two years later on June 6, 1843[209].

After the deaths of their parents, the four Allen brothers decided that they each wanted their share of John Kirby's estate, and they began negotiations with Augustus, the oldest brother, in 1843, to determine how to assign the various interests from the estate. Charlotte Allen, Augustus' wife, took a keen interest in the negotiations since it was her inheritance that funded a large part of the early enterprises of Augustus and John K. Allen. As the discussions dragged on, Charlotte became dissatisfied with the methods used in the settlement of the Allen brothers' business, so much so that she and Augustus became estranged during the process[210].

In addition to the separation from his wife, Augustus Allen's health was deteriorating. As a result, he decided to leave Houston. By 1850, Allen had signed over to his wife the bulk of his enterprises in Houston and had left for Mexico to pursue new opportunities. In 1852, he was appointed as the United States Consul for the port of Tehuantepee, Mexico, southeast of Vera Cruz. Augustus Chapman Allen died in 1864 on a visit to Washington, D. C., and he was buried in Greenwood Cemetery, Brooklyn, NY[211].

After thirteen years, the City of Houston had lost both of its founders, but the four brothers and the wife of one of the founders had established themselves as major participants in the city's business and social communities.

Samuel L. Allen was a cotton commission merchant, and for a time, he worked in partnership with Thomas M. Bagby. Their cotton yard, offices and warehouses covered more than a block on the west bank of White Oak Bayou at its junction with Buffalo Bayou. Eventually, Sam Allen operated the business as a sole proprietor at that location through the remainder of the nineteenth century[212].

Henry R. Allen was active in numerous business enterprises. He helped establish the Houston Chamber of Commerce in 1840 and promoted the development of the Houston Ship Channel. As a small businessman, Henry Allen opened a daguerreotype studio on the east side of Main Street near the wharf and continued to operate the business from June 11, 1845 until about February 15, 1847. Afterwards, he pursued other business enterprises[213].

Harvey H. Allen succeeded Andrew Briscoe as the Chief Justice of Harris County. That is the same position that is now called the County Judge of Harris County. It was, and is, one of the most influential political positions in the area[214].

Only one brother chose a more bucolic life. George Allen and his wife Harriet established a farm in the Houston area and raised their family there. One of their sons, Samuel Warner Allen, would, however, follow in the tradition of his uncles and become a prominent local businessman later in the century. After George Allen's untimely death on June 5, 1854, his namesake Samuel L. Allen took his young nephew to work with him as a clerk at his cotton warehouse[215].

Although the interests of John K. Allen had been distributed among the four brothers who remained in Houston, none of the brothers became extremely wealthy from the inheritance. From the declarations in the 1850 census, Samuel L. Allen had assets of $5,000, Henry R. Allen had assets of $5,000, Harvey H. Allen had assets of $2,000, and George Allen had assets of $500. They were by no means poor, but, to put each brother's wealth in perspective, in 1850, there were forty-four persons in Harris County with assets of more than $5,000, and of those, fifteen persons had assets of $20,000 or more[216].

Over the next decade, Sam Allen's business enterprises prospered significantly and he declared real assets of $75,000 and personal assets of $5,000 in the 1860 census. Henry Allen's business did well, too, and he had real estate worth $20,000 and personal assets of $500. Similarly, Harvey Allen had real assets of $15,000 and personal assets of $5,000[217].

The Civil War and its immediate aftermath had dramatic economic consequences for the Allen brothers, just as it did for almost everyone in Houston. Sam Allen's commission business survived, but, as indicated by the 1870 census, his net worth had declined to real assets of $21,000 and personal assets of $700. Henry Allen retained only real assets of $3,000. Harvey Allen did not survive the duration of the war. He died unexpectedly at age forty-three on April 22, 1863 in Houston[218].

Although Charlotte Allen was not enumerated in either the 1850 census or the 1860 census, she did declare real assets of $25,500 and personal assets of $1,650 in the 1870 census. No doubt, her net worth declined in a similar fashion as those of her brothers-in-law[219].

During the 1870's, the Allen family tried to recover from the effects of the war and Reconstruction, as did every person in Houston. Although in his sixties, Sam Allen continued to work as a commission agent and his business cotton warehouses on Buffalo Bayou operated as in the past. The growth of railroad transportation was advantageous to Sam Allen, and he promoted his business as having a warehouse fronting on the Houston and Texas Central Railway. From his office on the corner of 1st Street and Railroad Street, Sam Allen watched as cotton became "king" in Texas, and most of that cotton was shipped through Houston. And, from his home a few blocks away, on the corner of Allen Street and Walnut Street on the North Side of Buffalo Bayou, between the GH&H Railroad and Texas Transportation Company depots, Samuel L. Allen was never far away from the railroads that made his enterprise successful[220].

Henry R. Allen was elected to the 12th Texas Legislature in 1870, but disagreements with members of his own party led to the end of his political career in 1871. The bright spot for the Allen family was the emergence of Samuel Warner Allen. After the war, Samuel W. Allen returned to work as a clerk in his uncle's cotton commission business. Then, after three years of work with his uncle, Samuel W. Allen opened a lumber yard in 1868 and went on to acquire interests in sawmills in East Texas. In 1879, Allen had mills in Egypt in Montgomery County and Hartley in Liberty County, both conveniently located on the I&GN Railroad line. By 1882, Samuel W. Allen, as a lumber manufacturer and wholesale dealer, operated one mill at Hartley Station in Montgomery County with a capacity of 400,000 board feet per month, two mills at Africa in Liberty County with a capacity of 600,000 board feet per month, one mill at Matthew's Switch in Liberty County with a capacity of 300,000 feet per month, and one mill at Corrigan Station in Polk County with a capacity of 500,000 board feet per month[221].

By the 1880's, the three elder Allen's settled into their roles as well-respected, "early settlers" of Houston. Henry Allen and his wife Margaret lived in retirement at the home of their daughter and son-in-law Dr. M. Perl and their family. Mrs. A. C. Allen, as she still referred to herself in the 1880's, was a boarder at the H. H. Milby family boarding house on Main Street. Samuel L. Allen, in his 70's, began to wind down his business by 1882, and he leased portions of his warehouse complex to the Houston Press Company and the

William D. Cleveland grocery company. By the end of 1890, the prominent S. L. Allen Warehouses on north bank of Buffalo Bayou were vacant, except for a small area leased by W. D. Cleveland[222].

In the last decade of the century, the generation of Allen's who played such an important role in the founding of Houston passed from the scene. Henry R. Allen passed away some time prior to January 3, 1895. Charlotte M. Baldwin Allen died at age 90 on August 3, 1895, and she was buried in Glenwood Cemetery. Two months later, Samuel L. Allen died at age 87 on October 12, 1895, and he was also buried in Glenwood Cemetery[223].

The economic fortunes of Samuel Warner Allen deteriorated by 1900. The Sam Allen Lumber Company went bankrupt and lawsuits dragged on until October, 1901, when assets of the company were turned over to the trustee of the bankrupt firm. The story that the Allen descendants tell is that Samuel W. Allen forced the family business into bankruptcy in order to cash in his interests at ten cents on the dollar and liquidate his losses. The fifty-seven year old Allen then left town and moved to Washington state[224].

At the turn of the twentieth century, the Samuel L. Allen Warehouses on NSBB Block 9 consisted of a small two story warehouse on the northeast corner of 2nd Street and Railroad Street and a 1-1/2 story warehouse which extended along Railroad Street from 2nd Street to 1st Street. An additional one story cotton and cattle shed occupied the north side of the block along Girard Street[225].

In the first decades of the twentieth century, Houston's economic growth put the locally available warehouse space in demand. Situated in close proximity to the transportation network of rail, ship channel and highways, the Sam Allen warehouses were occupied during this time by a variety of companies, including the James Bute Company (home decor, wall paper and paint), the William L. Heffron Company (roofing materials, lime and cement), the American Brewing Association (beer), and the American Ice and Storage Company (ice and cold storage)[226].

By the mid-1920's, developers realized the importance of the location of the Allen warehouses. In 1928, the old, historic Sam L. Allen warehouse and associated structures on Block 9 were razed and construction was begun on the Merchants and Manufacturers Building. The Merchants and Manufacturers Building, given a prestige address at One Main Street, was designed by the firm of Giesecke and Harris, and it exemplifies the beautiful and elaborate Art Deco decoration of the period[227].

The ten story M and M Building, completed in 1930, occupied the entirety of Block 9. Its main entrance was built to open on to the Main Street Viaduct, which opened in 1913, at street level which, for the viaduct, was three floors above ground level. A concrete platform at the third level covered the loading docks of the railroad tracks on the south side of the building at ground level. A loading dock from Buffalo Bayou provided access to shipping and barge traffic from the waterway to the Houston Ship Channel. A tunnel from the bayou dock permitted goods to be transferred to the loading areas at ground level. A garage and automobile parking was located on the second floor, while wholesale and retail arcade stores were located on the third floor. Offices and storage facilities occupied the remaining seven floors[228].

Made of stone and bricks, the M and M Building was originally intended as a manufacturer's haven with a site, on the Bayou between railroad tracks and roadways, accessible by auto, train and water. It gained some notoriety for having 40,000 window panes. Yet, the building opened just as the Depression was devastating the local economy. Over the years, the building changed owners, as well as tenants, without producing much financial success[229].

In 1968, South Texas Junior College bought the building for its academic programs. A few years later, in 1974, the University of Houston acquired the assets of the South Texas Junior College and opened the UH-Downtown as a four year college. By the late 1970's, the Texas Legislature approved the UH-Downtown as a freestanding university in the University of Houston System[230].

In 1980, the Merchants and Manufacturers Building, one of the city's finest examples of Art Deco architecture was added to the National Register of Historic Places. Constructed of Bayou Brick, a popular brick made from sands quarried along the Buffalo Bayou, the building was resplendent in a soft red hue. Over the decades, the structure faded in glory. It was painted a muddy yellow in 1965 and, then again in 1979, but it still looked like a dilapidated warehouse[231].

In conjunction with a series of beautification projects along Buffalo Bayou in downtown, James Ketelson, the CEO of Tenneco, Inc. solicited over $400,000 in contributions from downtown businesses, including his own company, for the exterior renovation of the UH-Downtown's main building. In 1985, architect Charles Tapley designed a new, multi-colored paint job to make the school more attractive, while paying tribute to the building's heritage. The soft red hue of the new color scheme reflected the original brick color of the building. A flesh tone and a light tan color were used to highlight the minor columns and stonework along the sides of the structure. The building's Art Deco relief designs were highlighted with turquoise. "Where brick existed, brick colors were used; where stonework was, stone colors were used[232]."

Today, over a quarter of a century later, the former Merchants and Manufacturers Building is still one of the finest looking buildings in downtown Houston.

Johnny Goyen Park

From the third level platform of the UH Downtown Main Building, it is easy to descend to the grassy banks of Buffalo Bayou using the UH Downtown Stair Tower. Three flights of open stairs offer expansive views of downtown as you reach the green space that joins with the hike and bike trails along Buffalo Bayou. This space was dedicated as Johnny Goyen Park in 1988, in honor of City Council member Johnny Goyen. Goyen is the longest serving Council Member in Houston's history. First elected in 1957, he served continuously until 1981[233].

Desel Boettcher Warehouse

Looking south from the vantage point on Johnny Goyen Park, you can see the Spaghetti Warehouse, a popular restaurant on the corner of Travis Street and Commerce Avenue, directly in front of you. The Spaghetti Warehouse occupies the former Desel-Boettcher Building. The Desel-Boettcher Company was a wholesale produce company that was formed in 1904 when F. A. Boettcher went into partnership with C. M. Desel. Desel had begun in the produce business in 1901 and Boettcher arrived in Houston in 1903. With the success of their business, they became the first tenants of the building at 901 Commerce Avenue when it opened in 1912. The two story brick building was owned by B. A. Riesner and measured approximately 78 feet by 100 feet. A basement level was also incorporated in the design that had offices on the first floor, second floor storeroom for non-refrigerated stock and produce and cold storage in basement. An elevator provided for the transfer of their produce between floors[234].

The Desel-Boettcher Company had its headquarters in Houston and branches in Victoria, Corpus Christi and Brownsville. F. A. Boettcher died in Houston on August 8, 1934 at the age of 71, and the company began selling off its branch operations in 1940[235].

The Desel-Boettcher warehouse was bought by the Spaghetti Warehouse in 1974 as a second location for the Dallas-based restaurant chain. The Spaghetti Warehouse was founded in 1972 by Robert Hawk, a vice-president at Pier 1 Imports. Hawk built his first restaurant in a former pillow factory in Dallas's warehouse district. The menu offered the authentic Italian recipes of chef Victor Petta, Jr., who also invented the restaurant's patented system of spaghetti preparation[236].

Hawk then sought to expand the company through the acquisition of warehouses and factories in the inner city where real estate was inexpensive and development in the historic areas brought tax breaks or tax credits for renovating the buildings[237].

Spaghetti Warehouse, Inc. was acquired in 1998 by Consolidated Restaurant Companies, a holding company of the private equity firm of Cracken, Harkey and Company. In June 2007, Consolidated Restaurants sold the chain to the Los Angeles-based investment firm Frandelli, Inc., which is a subsidiary of the Korean conglomerate SK Group[238].

Frandeli Group was established in late 2005 by a venture capital firm to acquire, invest, develop, and operate restaurant companies. From 2006 to 2008, Frandeli expanded rapidly, acquiring three separate companies that operated Papa John's as franchisees and the Spaghetti Warehouse chain. Doug Pak, co-founder of the Frandeli Group, serves as CEO and President while Azam Malik, the President of Spaghetti Warehouse Restaurants, Inc., oversees the restaurant's operations. Currently, the Spaghetti Warehouse operates twenty locations in nine states[239].

The Spaghetti Warehouse occupies a historic location on Houston's Produce Row. But, even before that name came into use in the first decades of the twentieth century, the site on Block 2 was part of the Commerce Square envisioned by the Allen brothers at the founding of the city. Unfortunately, business owners discovered fairly early on that the blocks that made up the wharf area were subject to flooding by the rising waters of the bayou. Nevertheless, that did not prevent businesses from attempting to establish operations there. The most ambitious attempt was the city's first electric generating station[240].

Houston Electric Light and Power Company

Gas lights were introduced in Houston shortly after the Civil War and were in widespread use in businesses and homes by 1880. The inventions by Thomas A. Edison in the late 1870's with the new source of energy of electricity were about to change the lives of Americans and Houstonians in particular. Edison's improvements to the incandescent light bulb and his development of an electric power distribution system led to the installation of the country's first incandescent light and power station for private consumers in New York City in 1882[241].

In the late spring of the same year, Emmanuel Raphael obtained a franchise to build a plant utilizing Edison's concept of generating electrical current by means of a central dynamo, then distributing it in small quantities to thousands of homes and commercial buildings. Raphael received a charter for the Houston Electric Light and Power Company on May 20, 1882, and the company constructed its plant on Buffalo Bayou at the foot of Main Street near Commerce Avenue, approximately on the site of the parking lot behind the Spaghetti Warehouse. The plant, completed in December, 1882, was a two story brick generating station with a 125 horsepower Lawrence generator, two tubular boilers constructed locally at the foundry of Alexander McGowen, and a one hundred foot smokestack[244].

The difficulties of introducing a new technology to society and making it an economical and profitable business are monumental.

The Houston Electric Light and Power Company had technical problems resulting in chronic low load conditions and financial problems caused by an inadequate rate structure. The company went into receivership in March, 1886 and was acquired by its rival, the Houston Gas Light Company, in 1887[243].

Other investors, however, saw the potential for electrical power and chartered the Citizens' Electric Light and Power Company on July 29, 1889 and built a power plant on Buffalo Bayou at McKee Street. Rather than compete for the electrical power market in Houston, the Houston Gas Light Company sold its interest in the Houston Electric Light and Power Company to Citizens' Electric in January, 1891. The plant on Commerce Avenue closed, and that was probably a good thing since the location of that plant was, and is, subject to frequent flooding[244].

Within the past twenty years, named storms such as Tropical Storm Allison in 2001 and Hurricane Ike in 2008 have sent the bayou waters over most of Block 2. Yet, even sudden, and unanticipated, rain events, frequently inundate the area, such as when the bayou rose into the Spaghetti Warehouse during the first week of March, 1992 or when heavy afternoon downpours on Friday, July 2, 2010 caused the bayou to flood out of its banks downtown near the Spaghetti Warehouse[245].

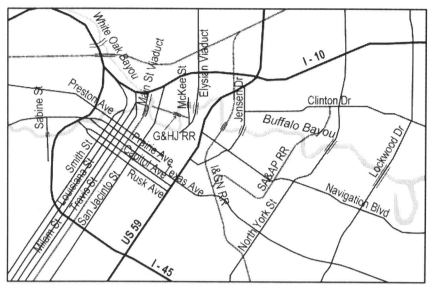

Map by Rachel A. Garcia

The Allen brothers established the town of Houston at the junction of Buffalo Bayou and White Oak Bayou where they established the city wharves and initiated the great commercial center that grew up around the original "Port of Houston." Centered at the foot of Main Street, the historic downtown district was the heart of business activity throughout the nineteenth century and early twentieth century.

Chapter 9
Allen's Landing

Main Street Viaduct

For the first seventy-five years of Houston's existence, the two city block area of the city wharves at the foot of Main Street was the focal point of the commercial interests of the city. Shipping vessels crowded into the dock area and lined up along both sides of Buffalo Bayou, awaiting an opportunity to offload their shipments and take on new cargo for other ports. The broad, sloping bank from Commerce Avenue to the bayou was the scene of the steady activity required to load and unload boats, and small one story buildings housed the offices of those supervising the wharf while long, single story sheds provided for temporary storage of the goods in transit.

By 1900, however, changes at the wharf were underway. Ocean going vessels had grown larger in size and required deeper water in Houston's ship channel. Dredging of the ship channel as far as Main Street had reached a practical limit by the end of the nineteenth century and the larger ships docked at the wharves near Harrisburg while only sloops, tugboats, barges and smaller vessels still came up the bayou to the downtown docks. At these docks, the wide avenue of Main Street opened fully to the wharf area and the three and four story buildings of the city that lay at and beyond Commerce Avenue were the skyline of Houston. Even the dome of the new 1910 County Courthouse could be seen rising in the distance.

In 1912, the scene at the foot of Main Street started to change. The U. S. Army Corps of Engineers was dredging a deep channel for the Houston Ship Channel that would be christened in 1914 as the new Port of Houston at what is now the modern Turning Basin, just upstream of Harrisburg. As early as 1908, the increase of vehicular transportation into and out of the downtown area prompted the City Council to authorize the construction of an enormous bridge to the north side of Buffalo Bayou, and the construction of the Main Street Viaduct in 1912 began to change the face of the City at Main Street. The Main Street Viaduct, and its companion at San Jacinto Street, were to be constructed as monumental spans over Buffalo Bayou. These civic improvements, being both functional enhancements to the infrastructure of the City while striving to be visually pleasing, represented an early influence of the City Beautiful movement in Houston[1].

In October, 1912, after months of delay, contractors began to pour the concrete for the south abutment pier of the arch in preparation for the completion of the main span over the bayou. The north abutment was constructed of solid concrete upon a base of seven hundred pilings, each twenty-five feet long, that were driven into the banks of the red clay hill before reinforced concrete was poured into the coffer dam[2].

When completed, the Main Street Viaduct formed a bridge that was sixty feet wide and 1,600 feet long with a reinforced concrete arch of 170 feet in diameter spanning Buffalo Bayou and thirty continuous concrete slab and girder spans extending to the north while crossing the tracks of the Southern Pacific Railroad, the Missouri, Kansas and Texas Railroad and White Oak Bayou. The single open-spandrel arch, a solid arch ring resting on massive abutments constructed using a Kahn reinforcement system, was designed to provide adequate clearance for boat traffic on the bayou[3].

Designed by F. L. Dormant, the City engineer, and built by the William P. Carmichael Company of St. Louis at a cost of $312,000, the Main Street Viaduct's single concrete arch incorporated the latest technology for reinforced concrete with the "Kahn system." The Kahn system of reinforced concrete was initially used for large factory buildings, but by 1909, the design was promoted for use in the construction of bridges. The reinforcing bar of this system was a diamond shaped rod which had horizontal extensions, like "wings," which were broken away and bent up or down to counter the shearing forces in concrete beams, adding twenty to thirty percent more strength to the beam. The bridge was touted as the longest reinforced concrete bridge in Texas, notable for the length of its main span, the longest of its type in Texas[4].

The Main Street Viaduct included an exceptionally wide deck to accommodate both vehicular traffic and the tracks of the Interurban line which ran down the middle. On August 26, 1912, the Houston Electric Company was granted a permit to operate street cars lines over the viaduct while abandoning the route on San Jacinto Street. The new permit for lines on the viaduct was extended until October 23, 1933[5].

On San Jacinto Day, April 21, 1913, the Main Street Viaduct was dedicated as part of a day of special celebrations which included the inauguration of the new City administration, the anniversary of the Battle of San Jacinto and a huge parade through the streets of downtown. Festivities began at four o'clock in the afternoon as the Honorable Ben Campbell took the oath of office from the outgoing mayor H. Baldwin Rice[6].

Upon completion of the Main Street Viaduct, the old steel and wooden bridges at San Jacinto Street, Capitol Avenue, Franklin Avenue, Preston Avenue, and Hill Street (now, Jensen Drive) were scheduled for replacement with concrete ones. In mid-June, 1913, the demolition of the old San Jacinto Street commenced and preparations for that new reinforced concrete bridge began[7].

The Viaduct connected Main Street to First Street on the north side of Buffalo Bayou and then continued on to the Montgomery Road. Automobile traffic increased through the next several decades and the bridge has served the transportation needs of downtown Houston for over ninety years.

In 1980, the Girard Street approach ramp to the Main Street Viaduct was reconstructed and defective deck slabs were replaced. At the same time, the sidewalks and sections of the original railing were also replaced, replicating the original design. On the first day of 2004, the Houston Metro Rail line was inaugurated after an absence of sixty-four years and the light rail line began service from the University of Houston Downtown campus station on the Viaduct at One Main Street to locations to the south as far as Reliant Stadium. Today, nearly one hundred years later, the Main Street Viaduct still stands as a resplendent monument at the foot of Main Street and it remains a vital thoroughfare into downtown[8].

City Wharves

As one passes under the tall arch of the Main Street Viaduct, the site of the founding of the City of Houston comes into full view. It was here on the south bank of Buffalo Bayou that the twenty-one year old Francis R. Lubbock, who in 1861 became the governor of Texas, and a few of his friends rowed a small yawl taken from the steamer Laura in its voyage upstream from Harrisburg and found the first indications of the construction of the new town of Houston on January 1, 1837:

"We ...by close observation discovered a road or street laid off from the water's edge. Upon landing we found stakes and footprints, indicating that we were in the town tract. ...A few tents were located not far away; one large one was used as a saloon. Several small houses were in the course of erection. Logs were being hauled in from the forest for a hotel to be erected. ...A small number of workmen were preparing to build cabins, business houses, and this hotel[9]."

After the Battle of San Jacinto on April 21, 1836, John Kirby Allen and his older brother Augustus Chapman Allen were determined to establish a commercial center for the new Republic of Texas. Although they had been looking at the possibility of acquiring the town site of Harrisburg from the Harris estate, the revolution complicated the negotiations and made the prospect of an acquisition nearly impossible. Augustus Allen began searching for a more suitable location for their new town, "having spent days making surveys and soundings in a skiff, and recording every sounding showing shoal water or deep, and proving that ample depths of water prevailed for all purposes of navigation[10]."

The Allen brothers were looking for three features in a location along the bayou to establish their town. Since there were no roads (as we think of them) or railroads in Texas in 1836, the best means of transportation was by waterway. John R. Harris had shown that vessels could travel from New Orleans and other ports up Galveston Bay to the San Jacinto River and Buffalo Bayou as far as his town of Harrisburg. Buffalo Bayou was influenced by tidal flow and had sufficient water at nearly all times for vessels to sail to Harrisburg. Augustus Allen felt that the head of tide for Buffalo Bayou lay even farther upstream than Harrisburg and he tested the bayou to determine the extent of the tidal flow. To his satisfaction, Buffalo Bayou was tidal as far as its junction with White Oak Bayou. In addition, the bayou maintained a sufficient depth for ships up to that point as well. The junction with White Oak Bayou provided the last piece of the puzzle. The junction of the two streams formed a turning basin that would allow the large ships coming upstream to the new town to turn around to return to the Gulf.

The primary difficulty for navigation up Buffalo Bayou was having sufficient water depth in the channel so that ships did not run aground en route. Although Galveston Bay seemed to offer an attractive entry point to the interior of Texas in the early days of colonization, the concerns over the ability a vessels to enter the river basins of the upper bay were well known. In early 1822, three schooners from New Orleans sailed up Galveston Bay for destinations on the San Jacinto River. The Revenge, a schooner, went aground briefly on Red Fish Bar, an oyster reef stretched across the bay from what is now San Leon to Smith Point. This event served as a warning to ships with a draft of over five feet. Later, in 1834, the steamboat Cayuga, a ninety-six foot long side wheeler with a draft of about five feet, crossed Red Fish Bar with delicate precision. However, that successful voyage showed that large steamers could negotiate the channel into Buffalo Bayou and with that the steamboat era commenced[11].

In late 1836, the surveyors laid out the plat of the town of Houston and the streets were staked out in such a manner to conform to the banks of Buffalo Bayou and to assure "maximum wharfage and commercial opportunities." A. C. and J. K. Allen hired the eighty-five foot long steamboat "Laura" to make its way up Buffalo Bayou, in water no deeper than six feet, to land at the new town of Houston to prove it could be done. The Laura arrived at the town of Houston on January 22, 1837, the first steamboat to make the trip. The two City blocks, numbered SSBB Blocks 2 and 3, north of Commerce Avenue and between Travis Street and Fannin Street were set aside as Commerce Square[12].

From the very beginning, businesses were shipping directly from warehouses on Commerce Avenue. Small river steamboats began operating regularly scheduled trips between Houston and

Galveston. These shallow draft steamboats could make the journey in about ten hours, a true advantage in travel since there were no roads going inland. These shallow draft steam packets transferred goods and passengers to Galveston[13].

Under the direction of newly elected mayor Charles Bigelow, the construction of a wharf to extend five hundred feet from Main Street to Fannin Street along the water was begun in 1840. The City wharves were to be six feet above the low water line, twenty feet wide, and most likely, bulkheaded. On January 29, 1842, the City established the Port of Houston, and in 1843, the Texas Congress granted it the right to remove obstructions and improve the bayou. Charles Gerlach was appointed as the wharf master. And, from this point on, the City was engaged in constant struggle to maintain access to the port for vessels entering Galveston Bay[14].

The shipment of cotton, especially from the cotton growing lands of the Brazos Valley, was important to many merchants. In 1846, two Galveston cotton merchants contracted a Trinity River boat builder to construct a steamer able to carry a load of 1,000 bales of cotton. This state of the art vessel reflected the standards necessary for ships operating in the Houston Ship Channel at this time. It was a one hundred ten foot steamboat with a draft of only four and one half feet[15].

During the 1850's, the Houston Navigation Company was organized by local merchants and steamboat captains to promote the shipping business of Houston. Under the guidance of its commodore Captain John H. Sterrett, the company's small fleet of steamboats regularly made the trip from Houston to Galveston in about eight hours. Yet, these businessmen faced a recurring problem with the channel. Buffalo Bayou had silted in so badly that only shallow draft boats could reach the city wharves. So, in 1857, the merchants in Houston joined with the City to pay for the deepening and straightening of Buffalo Bayou above Harrisburg. Not much work on the bayou was done at this time, however, and then, the War Between the States intervened[16].

After the Civil War, the business interests of Houston endeavored to get the local economy back in order. Houston merchants, boat owners and ship captains revived the Houston Direct Navigation Company to operate steamboats and barges between Houston and Bolivar Roads, by-passing the port at Galveston and its associated wharf fees. At the same time, the Bayou Ship Channel Company was formed to improve the bayou to a depth of twelve feet for the largest ships to reach Houston. This company had many of the same directors as the Houston Direct Navigation Company, and through their efforts, the U. S. Corps of Engineers recommended, in 1870, that a channel of one hundred feet wide and six feet deep be dredged. No funds, however, were appropriated for these improvements to the ship channel, and nothing was accomplished. Nevertheless, business activity at the foot of Main Street at this time was illustrated in a popular drawing of the stern wheel packet steamer St. Clair loading cotton at the City wharf[17].

As is often the case, it takes a strong leader and visionary personality to accomplish great things. Shipping magnate Charles Morgan bought the Bayou Ship Channel Company in 1874, and within two years Morgan had dredged the channel to the town of Clinton. Morgan dredged a nine foot deep channel through Morgan's Point and up Buffalo Bayou to his railroad terminal located on the north side of Buffalo Bayou opposite Harrisburg. In April, 1876, the schooner-rigged side-wheeler Clinton docked in Houston as the first ship to sail the new ship channel. It offloaded seven hundred fifty tons of freight and left with two hundred fifty head of cattle[18].

Things were looking up for progress on the ship channel when, in 1877, Congress authorized a channel twelve feet deep and one hundred feet wide. However, actual work on the improvements was slow in coming. Eventually, the U. S. government purchased Morgan's improvements to the ship channel and accepted the primary responsibility for the channel in 1890. In 1896, Congress authorized the deepening of the Houston Ship Channel, but only to Harrisburg, not to Houston. The plan called for the dredging of the ship channel to a depth of twenty-five feet with a terminus at Long Reach. Yet, by 1909, the channel had only been dredged to eighteen and one half feet[19].

The efforts to improve the ship channel picked up speed thanks to the influence of Houston Representative Tom Ball. Work commenced in 1912 and was completed about two years later. The Houston Ship Channel formally opened on November 10, 1914 after it had been dredged to twenty-five feet from Bolivar Roads to the

Photo credit: Louis F. Aulbach

The features of Houston's commercial success were the City wharves, the rail-roads and the turning basin formed at the junction with White Oak Bayou.

Turning Basin. Unfortunately for the City Wharves, the possibility of ships coming all the way to downtown was long forgotten. Activity at the wharf at the foot of Main Street declined significantly after 1913[20].

In 2005, the U. S. Army Corps of Engineers completed a project to deepen the Houston Ship Channel to forty-five feet (from forty feet) and widen the bottom to five hundred thirty feet. The finest of ocean going vessels still navigate the channel to Houston, but only as far as the Port of Houston at the Turning Basin[21].

By the mid-1960's, the old City wharves were in need of revital-ization and the City acquired 1.76 acres of land at 1001 Commerce Avenue for a development of a city park at the former docks. Construction began in 1966 and a circular promenade was built over a portion of the reconstructed concrete wharf that was designed to replicate the original port. Pedestrian walkways from Commerce Avenue made for easy access to the overlook on the bayou. On its dedication in May, 1967, the park was named "Allen's Landing Memorial Park" although historically the landing had previously only been known as "the landing," "the wharf," "the municipal wharf," "the foot of Main Street" and other such names. Charlie Lansden of the Chamber of Commerce said, however, that when they worked to make the site a city park, they just made up the name[22].

Thirty years later, the park was badly in need of repair. On October 27, 2000, the ground breaking for the redevelopment of the Main Street Wharf at Allen's Landing was held. The goal of this project was to return the area to its original appearance. The restoration of the decaying bulkhead and the construction of a concrete wharf replicated the port that flourished in the nineteenth and early twentieth centuries. Today, the park with its walkway atop the wharf, an entry plaza at Main Street and Commerce Avenue, the terraced grass lawn, public art, historical signs, benches and lights make this park the centerpiece for our renewed appreciation for the site of the founding of the City of Houston[23].

Houston's Carnival

Not all of the activity near the foot of Main Street was toil and work. There were times when the City was light hearted and frivolous, as in the story of the arrival of the "King."

The regal flotilla pulled up to the wharf at the foot of Main Street. After the royal entourage exited to the landing amid the fanfare of the occasion, King Nottoc stepped off the elegant vessel and strode up the path to Commerce Avenue as the throngs of admirers cheered wildly and thousands of Houstonians clogged the downtown streets. The celebration of the No-Tsu-Oh carnival had begun. Often, King Nottoc arrived without revealing his identity. As in 1909, at the coronation of the queen of the carnival, Captain James A. Baker revealed himself to be the king when he placed the crown on the head of the queen, Miss Lillie Neuhaus. Such exuberant festivities were similar in each of the annual celebrations of No-Tsu-Oh from its beginnings in 1899 to the final carnival in 1915[24].

The No-Tsu-Oh festival (Houston spelled backwards) was a week long civic celebration of the importance of cotton to local economy. The Mardi Gras-style festival was presided over by King

Nottoc (cotton spelled backwards) who usually was a prominent businessman chosen for the event. A local debutante was selected as the queen and her coronation at the grand ball was the highlight of the six days of parades and festivities.

The origins of the No-Tsu-Oh festival derive from an earlier event established in the mid-1880's by the local produce growers and wholesalers. This festival, called the Fruit, Flower and Vegetable Festival, was short lived. However, the concept had a certain appeal and the No-Tsu-Oh Association was organized to bring the No-Tsu-Oh Carnival to Houston in December, 1899. Later festivals were held in November[25].

A prominent event during the early No-Tsu-Oh festivals was the football game between the University of Texas and the Agricultural and Mechanical College of Texas. The rivalry of this game exists today as the annual contest between UT and Texas A&M[26].

The popularity of No-Tsu-Oh began to wane prior to the 1915 festival, and the carnival atmosphere of the festival seems to have degenerated to the level of "tin-horn parades and garrulous horseplay" as noted on the Houston Chronicle editorial page of November 18, 1915. The Chronicle begged: "Let it be our last 'Carnival[27].'"

With the arrival of World War I, the No-Tsu-Oh festival ceased and faded into history.

H&TC Railway bridge over White Oak Bayou

The view from the City Wharves, or Allen's Landing, to the north looks directly into the mouth of White Oak Bayou. A railroad trestle crosses White Oak Bayou only a few yards from its junction with Buffalo Bayou. This railroad line belongs to the Southern Pacific Railroad today, but its location here dates back to the beginnings of the railroad industry in Houston.

Railroads in Houston have their origin in a charter for the Galveston and Red River Railway was issued March 11, 1848 to Ebenezer Allen of Galveston. It was five years later before ground was broken for the Galveston and Red River Railway and twenty-five miles of track were laid by the end of 1853. The railroad was renamed the Houston and Texas Central Railway in 1856, and soon the tracks reached the cotton growing regions near Cypress, Hockley and Hempstead. Cotton could be delivered directly from the farms to the warehouses at the port of Houston for shipment to the world[28].

A group of Galveston businessmen chartered a short railroad line, named the Galveston and Houston Junction Railroad, in 1861 to join the Galveston, Houston and Henderson Railroad with the Houston & Texas Central Railway. The Civil War delayed the improvements to the line, but after the war, the tracks were laid through the Frost Town subdivision and Aaron B. Brown, a local bridge builder, was hired to construct the bridges across White Oak Bayou and Buffalo Bayou to connect the two rail lines[29].

The Houston and Texas Central Railway reached Red River City in 1873, connecting with the Missouri, Kansas and Texas Railroad to form first all-rail route from Texas to St. Louis and the East. The rail line became a vital link for the shipment of cotton and other goods to the port and then out of Houston to the markets of the world. Charles Morgan, the shipping magnate who had established his terminal at Clinton, purchased the Houston and Texas Central Railway in 1877 in an attempt to gain a competitive advantage in the transportation of goods. The Southern Pacific Railroad was also intent on the expansion of its enterprise and, in 1883, it acquired Morgan's interests in the Houston and Texas Central Railway. The rail line is still operated by Southern Pacific today and the company's trains cross this prominent trestle over White Oak Bayou every day[30].

The Legacy of the Texas Steam Mill Company

We are all familiar with the fact that on August 30, 1836, John K. Allen and his brother Augustus C. Allen advertised the new town of Houston to be established on the south bank of Buffalo Bayou near its junction with White Oak bayou. Many persons of the time spoke of the Allen brothers as land speculators, or even worse, but few persons would have used another term for the pair, namely, visionaries. One excellent example of their visionary qualities can be found in the story of the Texas Steam Mill Company.

Some time in the earliest stages of the creation of the town of Houston, in late 1836 or very early 1837, the Allen's, or perhaps more likely, Augustus Allen, convinced the distinguished mathematician and scientist Elijah Hinsdale Burritt to build a sophisticated industrial enterprise in Houston.

Elijah Burritt was born in New Britain, Connecticut on April 20, 1794. He was trained as a blacksmith and, then, he graduated from Williamstown College in Massachusetts. He published his first book "Logarithmick Arithmetick" in 1818. The book contained a new and correct table of logarithms of the natural numbers from 1 to 10,000, extended to seven places[31].

Burritt married Ann W. Watson of Milledgeville, Georgia on October 28, 1819, and there he edited a weekly paper for several years. After an incident in 1829 involving an abolitionist pamphlet which caused him to flee the state, Burritt returned to New Britain where he was the principal of a private school. It was during this period that Burritt published his most significant works[32].

His "Universal Multipliers" was published in August, 1830. The book was used for computing simple and compound interest, and it also included tables of annuities. Burritt sold the copyright to this book in November, 1830 for $10,000[33].

An astronomy textbook, "The Geography of the Heavens," which was published in 1833, and the accompanying volume of celestial maps entitled "Atlas, Designed to Illustrate the Geography of the Heavens" was printed in 1835. The "Atlas of the Heavens" was a set of six hand-colored engravings of sixteen inch by fourteen inch celestial charts of constellations with figures derived from Greek and Roman mythology. Even today, these engravings are highly prized. A set sells for about $4500[34].

Yet, in spite of this apparent success, Burritt, at age forty-three, decided to embark on a challenging new adventure. He was "going to Texas." The letter written to his wife Ann in the early morning of his departure from New Haven reveals the strong emotions that he felt:

"The commencement of this Texas Expedition has been full of toil and sacrifice. It has pressed upon my spirits, not to say upon my frame, with the weight of many mountains. My energies, mental and feeling sound, have grappled with the great duties and consignments involved in it, for the last month or two, with so ever present consequences that I am dealing with the elements of my own destiny

and those of my family. There is nothing of sport or of pastime in it, to me[35]."

Within one year of the announcement of the establishment of the town of Houston, Burritt had recruited a colony of skilled craftsmen and artisans to join him with their families in the new Republic of Texas. On August 30, 1837, Burritt and his associates left New Britain, Connecticut for Houston, transporting equipment and machinery along the interior waterways of the Ohio and Mississippi Rivers through New Orleans to Galveston on September 29 and, then, to Houston on October 3[36].

The Texas Steam Mill Company was incorporated by an act of the Congress of the Republic of Texas on December 16, 1837 and it was established to "operate by steam power or otherwise in Texas a saw mill, a grist mill, a planing mill, a lathe and shingle mill" and any other manufacturing or mechanical business they wish to pursue[37].

Burritt himself outlined the terms of the agreement with the Allen brothers:

"The owners of the city lots in Houston and vicinity have donated all the timber upon a 1,000 acres immediately opposite the city (as here represented) with a fee simple of 2 acres for our buildings and garden together with the privilege of cultivating as much other ground in the neighbourhood as we please[38]."

The location of this steam saw mill tract was on the east bank of White Oak Bayou, immediately north of its junction with Buffalo Bayou. The site is prominently displayed on the Girard map of Houston of 1839[39].

The Burritt party arrived in Galveston aboard the brig Elbe on September 29, 1837, one month to the day from their departure from New Britain[40].

A brig is a vessel with two square-rigged masts. Brigs were especially popular in the eighteenth and early nineteenth centuries. They were fast and maneuverable and were used as both naval war ships and merchant ships. The vessels fell out of use with the arrival of the steam ship because they required a relatively large crew for their small size and were difficult to sail into the wind[41].

While Burritt waited for a boat to take him to Houston, he and his friends found the conditions at Galveston to be quite extraordinary:

"There are several thousand persons hanging about the place, said accommodations only for about 500. The daily arrival of Emigrants from the States averages from 50 to 100 -- all hungry -- all worn out with the fatigues of their journey. There is nothing to be had here to eat, except fresh meat and bread. One of our fellow passengers had about a ½ a bushel of potatoes left from his stores, which he sold for $3. -- and another gentleman has just informed me that he paid $10 a bushel yesterday! Sweet potatoes bring $3 and $4 a bushel. Common bar soap is $1.00 per pound, milk $1.00 a gallon, eggs $1.00 - $1.50 a dozen. Flour was 30 cents a barrel the day before our arrival, but so much was brought in by our vessel that the price fell to 15 cents. I bought a barrel of sugar yesterday at 15 cents and a barrel of pork for $28. Rice is 12 ½ cents. Molasses $1.12 cents a gallon. Lamp oil is $2.50. Spinner Candles $1.00 a pound. Thick Cowhide boots $10.00. Shoes (men's) and clothing in proportion. If Mr. Ward could come over here immediately with the articles I have named, say even but $1000 worth, he could not fail to realize $3,000 clear profits. The best single article which could be brought is Irish potatoes. They are just as certain to fetch $2 a bushel here as they are 20 cents there![42]*"*

Elijah Burritt and other key personnel took a boat to Houston on October 3rd to look over their site and handle other business. His observations provide a unique assessment of the town as well as a glimpse of the frontier nature of the town:

"Houston is 15 miles above Harrisburg and is just this distance too far up the bay for the seat of Government, so far as navigation is concerned, the head of which is properly at Harrisburg. Steam Boats ascend beyond that with difficulty. The grounds at Houston are however, decidedly, preferable. They rise about 40 feet above the water and they maintain an unbroken level for many miles. I think the ground opposite Houston is handsomer than Houston itself, and would have been chosen for the site of the city had it been prairie instead of a dense forest."

"Brother William Cornwall Smith (our engineer) and two hired men went with me to spy out the country. We staid [sic] in Houston

2 days. Selected a location for our buildings, and the 2nd night slept under a rude shelter constructed with our own hands in the wild Forests of Texas, and there ate our first meal by the light of the fire which cooked it. An Indian brought along a fine deer for the hind quarter of which I paid him 50 cents[43]."

Burritt returned to Galveston on October 9 to find that the Racer's Storm had destroyed all but one of the thirteen vessels in the harbor at Galveston. The Racer's Storm was a major hurricane that was first observed near Jamaica by the British vessel HMS Racer, and subsequently, the storm has taken its name. Their ship, the Elbe, was beached high on land and a total loss. The boat, nevertheless, was pressed into service first as a hotel, then converted into a multi-cell jail for the county and city of Galveston which it functioned as for six years[44].

Fortunately, all members of the colony were safe and "all our property escaped unimpaired." The women of the party, though abandoned by the Elbe's Captain's Mate and half the crew during the Racer's Storm, endured the wreckage of the storm with the falling masts and spars "cool and collected" and without panic. Elijah Burritt and his party left Galveston for Houston with their goods on October 12, 1837[45].

The Racer's Storm was the least of the difficulties for the members of the Texas Steam Mill Company. Six members of the party contracted yellow fever in Houston and died. Nathan Hosmer Andrews, Burritt's cousin and a skilled carriage maker, died in Houston of fever on Oct 27, 1837. Jabez Cornwall, a director of the company and Burritt's brother-in-law, died on November 9, 1837. Elijah Burritt himself died of yellow fever on January 4, 1838. Even after Elijah Burritt's death, the Texas Steam Mill Company took about six months to get started and recorded its land on June 23, 1838. Nevertheless, after the death of so many members of the company, the project was abandoned and the survivors returned to Connecticut[46].

Although the Texas Steam Mill Company venture ended in complete failure, that does not deny the "vision" of the Allen brothers in this enterprise. No steam saw mill, or other mills, were ever built on the tract awarded to the company. In 1902, the city built its first sewage treatment facility on the site. The full extent of the extraordinary nature of this business venture can only be found in a review of the estate of Elijah Burritt.

Elijah H. Burritt died intestate about January 4, 1838 in Harris County. His sister Mrs. Emily Taylor (nee Emily Burritt) was the sole heir and blood relation in the county. She inherited his estate of approximately sixty books and several fine scientific instruments which were sold at auction to Robert A. Irion, the secretary of state of the Republic of Texas, on April 15, 1838 for the rather meager sum of $467 for the lot[47].

The key to Burritt's intentions for the Texas Steam Mill Company lay in his books. In addition to books on religion, philosophy, mathematics, astronomical navigation, geography and political science, there was an inordinate number of technical publications on the construction and development of railroads. For instance:

Mitchell's Compendium of the Internal Improvements of the United States: Comprising General Notices of All the Most Important Canals and Rail-roads, Throughout the Several States and Territories of the Union, Together with a Brief Notice of Works of Internal Improvement in Canada and Nova Scotia.
By Samuel Augustus Mitchell, Mitchell, Samuel Augustus, 1792-1868
Published by Mitchell & Hinman, 1835

Lectures on the Steam-engine: In which Its Construction and Operation are Familiarly Explained: with a Sketch of Its Invention and Progressive Improvement: and an Account of the Present State of the Liverpool Railway, and the Performances on It, and of Steam Carriages on Turnpike Roads.
By Dionysius Lardner
Published by J. Taylor, 1832

Treatise on Rail-roads and Internal Communications: Compiled from the Best and Latest Authorities, with Original Suggestions and Remarks.
By Thomas Earle
Published by J. Grigg, 1830

A Practical Treatise on Rail-roads, and Interior Communication in General: With Original Experiments, and Tables of the Comparative Value of Canals and Rail-roads ...
By Nicholas Wood
Published by Knight and Lacey, 1825

Report on steam carriages. By Parliament, Great Britain. Parliament. House of Commons. Select Committee on Steam Carriages, Great Britain Parliament. House of Commons, Benjamin Chew Howard, Great Britain, United States. Congress (22nd, 1st session: 1831-1832). House, United States. Congress. House. Committee on Internal Improvements, United States. Congress House, United States, Congress.
Published by Duff Green, Printer, 1832

An historical and practical treatise upon elemental locomotion, by means of steam carriages on common roads: showing ... the rise, progress, and description of steam carriages; the roads upon which they may be made to travel ...
By Alexander Gordon
Published by Printed for B. Steuart, and W. Blackwood, Edinburgh, 1832

A treatise on practical surveying,: which is demonstrated from its first principles. Wherein every thing that is useful and curious in that art, is fully considered and explained.
By Robert Gibson, John D. Craig, Jun Fielding Lucas, Joseph Cushing, J. Robinson, John W. Suggett, Mathematical tables: difference of latitude and departure ...
Published by Published by F. Lucas, Jun. and Joseph Cushing. J. Robinson, printer., 1818

A system of geometry and trigonometry: together with a treatise on surveying: teaching various ways of taking the survey of a field : also to protract the same and find the area: likewise, rectangular surveying, or, an accurate method of calculating the area of any field arithmetically without ... By Abel Flint
Published by Cooke & Hale, 1818

From these titles[48] in Burritt's collection, it seems reasonable to conclude that Burritt intended to do more than simply build a steam saw mill. The articles of incorporation mention the company's plan operate a saw mill, a grist mill, a planing mill, a lathe and shingle mill, but, also, any other manufacturing or mechanical business they wish to pursue. Augustus Allen was a man of grand ideas. Allen knew the potential that a railroad could bring to his commercial center and he placed the manufacturing center in a prominent location in town.

Although the Burritt venture failed, Augustus Allen continued to pursue his vision for a railroad. Allen was a director of the Houston and Brazos Rail Road which was chartered on January 26, 1839. However, lacking the technical expertise of Burritt and his craftsmen, the Houston and Brazos Rail Road was unable to construct a viable rail system. It's charter was revoked. It was not until 1853 that Texas' first railroad, the Buffalo Bayou, Brazos and Colorado Railway, began operations. By 1912, Houston was a major regional rail center that boasted of a network of seventeen railroads -- the embodiment of Allen's vision[49].

Willow Street Pump Station

The front page of the Houston Chronicle on December 19, 2007 blared: "Bayous are flush with fecal bacteria[50]!"

Although the city has made significant progress in wastewater treatment since the 1980's, Buffalo Bayou still does not meet state standards for contact recreation activities such as swimming or wading because, at times, the levels of bacteria from human and animal waste are elevated beyond what is acceptable[51].

Houston has had to deal with the pollution of Buffalo Bayou many times in its history. In 1895, in response to a demand from the US Army Corps of Engineers to clean up the scum-covered Houston Ship Channel, the City Council approved a $300,000 bond issue to construct the city's first wastewater treatment plant, the Willow Street Pump Station[52].

The Willow Street Pump Station, completed in 1902, is located on White Oak Bayou, a short distance above the confluence with Buffalo Bayou. The Romanesque Revival style building can be seen on the east bank, opposite the University of Houston-Downtown campus at One Main Street. The name of the facility derives from its address on Willow Street which was renamed North San Jacinto Street some time after 1907 (probably after the construction of the San Jacinto Street bridge in 1914)[53].

By 1907, the City Street Cleaning Department was added to the site, and in 1915, the crematory facility was constructed adjacent to the sewage pumping station. During the early twentieth century, wagons pulled by horse and mules hauled merchandise in the city. The trolley system also used mules to pull the cars. If, and when, these animals died on the job, the city street cleaning crews handled the removal of the carcasses and their disposal at the Willow Street facility[54].

The Willow Street Pump Station was built on the south half of the tract initially set aside in 1837 by A. C. Allen for a steam saw mill. The president and several others members of the Texas Steam Mill Company fell victim to shipwreck in the Racer's Storm of October and to yellow fever in late 1837 on their journey to Houston. The company collapsed and the steam saw mill envisioned by Allen never materialized. The site lay vacant until the 1880's when the Houston Press Company Compress was constructed on the site. Ziegler's Warehouse and Gin occupied the site in 1890, but the structure was dilapidated and falling down by 1896[55].

The Willow Street Pump Station was an essential component of the city's sewage disposal system as the North Side Sewage Treatment Plant, located on Buffalo Bayou east of town at Japhet Street, was constructed in 1917. Subsequent wastewater treatment facilities have been built on the bayou at 69th Street and at Lockwood Drive in order to keep up with the growth in the population of Houston throughout the twentieth century[56].

The Willow Street facility eventually was decommissioned, fell into disuse and lay in ruins until 2003 when the University of Houston leased the property from the City of Houston and renovated the buildings into a community conference and exhibition center. The beautifully restored facility was listed on the National Register of Historic Places in 2004[57].

Championship Park

Championship Park, at the confluence of White Oak and Buffalo Bayous, across from Allen's Landing, is a park-like space created on a flood control facility. Access to the park is located on Wood Street, just off North Main Street near the U of H-Downtown. It was named in honor of the Houston Rockets basketball team who won the franchise's only two NBA Championships in back-to-back seasons in 1994 and 1995[58].

International Coffee Company

The only structure remaining on the blocks that comprised the City Wharves at Allen's Landing Park is a three story building painted in a subdued green hue. This building, that once was the site of the International Coffee Company, is in deplorable condition with boarded up doors and windows on the lower floors and blown out windows on the third floor. Yet, despite these conditions, the building is a visible reminder of the prosperity and commercial activity at the Port of Houston during the nineteenth and early twentieth century that characterized the economic growth of Houston and the surrounding region.

The International Coffee Company was owned by the W. D. Cleveland and Sons Wholesale Grocery Company and the structure is the only remaining feature of the extensive business enterprises of William D. Cleveland. A grocer, merchant and cotton factor, Cleveland's business career, which encompassed over fifty years, was centered around SSBB Block 3, the tract of land between Main Street and Fannin Street and north of Commerce Avenue to the bayou. His warehouse and offices were the last in the line of businesses that operated from the wharf area which was the focal point of the City's shipping industry from the earliest days of 1837[59].

In the twenty-five years from the founding of Houston until the beginning of the Civil War, a number of merchants operated businesses shipping and receiving goods at the Port of Houston. Several companies consigned shipments on steamers to and from Galveston, among these are names that are familiar even today: John Dickinson, Rice and Nichols, Bremond and Van Alstyne, H. D. Taylor, B.

A. Shepherd, John Kennedy, L. J. Latham, Groesbeeck and Company, and Allen and Bagby. Few of these entrepreneurs were as successful as William Marsh Rice[60].

William Marsh Rice came Houston in October, 1838, at age 22, after the Panic of 1837 sent the United States into a deep recession. He ran the bar of the Milam Hotel and was issued a headright to 320 acres of farm land. On June 28, 1840, the City issued him a first class license for a mercantile business, and Rice began a business which supplied goods from the eastern states of the U. S. to settlers in Texas. Rice eventually formed a partnership with Ebenezer B. Nichols who also arrived in Texas about 1838. Although both men were about the same age, Ebenezer Nichols was the senior partner of the firm of Nichols and Rice. The firm began dealing in dry goods, groceries, hardware and crockery for both wholesale and retail sales, but the company eventually developed into a large import and export business. The W. M. Rice Warehouse on Commerce Avenue, on the west side of Main Street, served inland settlers with goods from New Orleans and New York[61].

Nichols moved to Galveston in 1850 and established a firm of cotton factors and commission merchants. Cotton planters relied on cotton factors, who were also called commission merchants, to sell their crops for them. Cotton factors often purchased goods for their clients and handled the shipment of these goods to the client. This relationship with planters could be extremely profitable[62].

Rice, who remained in Houston, took over the firm and renamed it William Rice and Company in 1856. Although Nichols was successful in his Galveston ventures, William Marsh Rice went on to become one of the wealthiest men in Texas by the time of the Civil War with a net worth of about $750,000. Rice was only one of many examples of an ambitious and talented young man finding his opportunity in the City of Houston while rising from junior partner to the head of a successful commercial enterprise[63].

Even with the success of these early Houston businessmen, the opportunities for others did not diminish. In the late 1840's, another young entrepreneur came on the scene named Alexander Sessums. The Sessums family came to Houston about 1838. Blunt Newsome Sessums, his wife Mary Ann, daughter Messiniah Elizabeth and young Alexander left Lauderdale County, Alabama in late 1837 with their eight slaves and relocated to Houston. In 1840, the Sessums family was established in town with a home on Franklin Avenue. By 1850, the twenty year old Alexander Sessums was working as a clerk at the company of John Dickinson and learning the trade that would be his career[64].

John Dickinson was born in Scotland in 1820. He made his way to Houston by the early 1840's and formed a business partnership with a Mr. M. Cavanaugh. Cavanaugh was a merchant who imported goods, wares and merchandise through Galveston as early as January, 1843, and Dickinson worked his way up in the company to become a partner. However, on October 1, 1847, Dickinson and Cavanaugh dissolved their partnership, and Dickinson continued the business himself. Dickinson imported a general assortment of goods from New York and Boston for his establishment. The items that he offered for sale included prints, satinetts, jeans, fashionable hats and caps, brown and white domestics, flannels, tickings, kerseys, linseys, saddlery, boots, shoes, clothing, hardware, wooden ware, castings, shot and lead, fish, pickles, liquors and wines[65].

Alexander Sessums soon became a partner with John Dickinson in the dry goods business, but John Dickinson had ambitions to move up to the more lucrative cotton trade. On July 1, 1856, the partnership of Alexander Sessums and John Dickinson in the mercantile firm of John Dickinson and Company was dissolved so that Dickinson could pursue a cotton factorage, general commission and exchange business in Houston. Sessums acquired his interest in the mercantile business[66].

In addition to his business, John Dickinson was also active in city politics at this time, serving on City Council and chairing the City's Finance Committee. His involvement in the City's ownership of the Houston Tap Railroad led to Dickinson's election as a director and the secretary of the Houston and Brazoria Tap Road Company when it was organized in Houston on January 20, 1857[67].

The decade preceding the Civil War brought enormous prosperity to Houston and to the businessmen who were able to capitalize on the commercial activity. By late 1860, a number of Houston merchants had become very wealthy. John Dickinson and his neighbors in the Quality Hill section of Houston, William J. Hutchins and William Marsh Rice, were among the top in this elite group. John

Dickinson reported real assets of $150,000 and personal assets of $215,000. William J. Hutchins, a forty-six year old merchant from New York, had real estate valued at $300,000 and personal assets of $400,000. And, the forty year old William Marsh Rice surpassed them all with real assets of $250,000 and personal assets of $500,000[68].

The Civil War posed difficult challenges for the businessmen of Houston, and even after the war, some struggled to recover the success of the pre-war period. Rice was able to conserve much of his business by moving to Matamoros, Mexico during the conflict, and after the war, he moved to New Jersey. William Hutchins lost over half the value of his enterprises and, in 1870, declared assets of only $217,750. John Dickinson fared more poorly than his counterparts. Dickinson had real estate valued only at $25,000 and personal assets of $3,000[69].

John Dickinson and Company, Cotton and Wool Factors, continued to operate from their offices located on Main Street between Franklin Avenue and Commerce Avenue, but the business was declining. Dickinson retired by 1870, and he was forced to seek protection from his creditors. He filed a bankruptcy petition in federal court on June 27, 1871[70].

On August 9, 1871, while on a trip to Saratoga, New York, John Dickinson died. His remains were returned to Houston on December 16, 1871, and he was buried in Glenwood Cemetery after funeral services at the Episcopal Church[71].

After Alexander Sessums acquired the interests of John Dickinson in the mercantile business in July, 1856, he pursued the same course of business that he had seen others do so successfully. As he had seen before and had done himself, Sessums hired a young clerk to help him with the business. This new employee was William Davis Cleveland[72].

William D. Cleveland was born near Pleasant Hill in Dallas County, Alabama on September 1, 1839. He came to Texas at an early age with his parents Ezra and Sarah Cleveland who settled in Austin County between Brenham and Bellville. Ezra Cleveland served as the district clerk of Austin County in the 1850's, and William, as the third of seven children in the Cleveland family, was anxious to get on his own when he moved to Houston in 1858[73].

The relationship between Sessums and Cleveland appears to have been both a good business partnership and a strong personal friendship. Alexander Sessums married Mary Runnels on May 4, 1854, and their first child was born on July 7, 1858. It does not seem to be merely a coincidence that they named their son Davis -- the middle name of William Davis Cleveland[74].

At the time that War Between the States broke out, Alexander Sessums had a successful company, but it was scarcely as profitable as the merchant and brokerage companies of Rice, Hutchins, Dickinson and others. Sessums, in 1860, had real assets of $21,000 and personal assets of $20,000, a small fraction of the net worth of his former partner and mentor and others in that group of businessmen. As the war began, Sessums attempted to maintain his business operations and he used his skills to aid the war effort. His most trusted employee, William D. Cleveland, however, joined Terry's Rangers, enlisting, at age 22, in Company B, 10th Texas Infantry on October 23, 1861. As 2Lt. William D. Cleveland, he served with distinction during four years of the war, until he was captured at Franklin, Tennessee on November 30, 1864[75].

After the war, Sessums welcomed his friend back to the firm, and Cleveland returned to employment with Alexander Sessums in his mercantile business located on the southeast corner of Main Street and Franklin Avenue. By 1866, Sessums was investing in the future of Houston along with the leading businessmen of the time. He became one of the stockholders, along with other prominent men including B. A. Shepherd, W. M. Rice, T. M. Bagby, W. J. Hutchins, J. T. Brady and A. McGowen, in the new Houston City Mills. And, on August 26, 1867, Sessums was elected as president of the National Bank of Texas in Galveston[76].

Sessums expanded his business operations to Galveston in the late 1860's while leaving the Houston operations to William Cleveland. By July, 1870, Sessums had moved to Galveston where his work as a commission merchant would grow. As the economic recovery in Texas began to flourish in the 1870's, Sessums decided to concentrate exclusively on the commission business. In a transaction that was finalized in March, 1872, he sold his interest in his Galveston-based wholesale grocery business to Lawther, Block and Company of Galveston. In Houston, William D. Cleveland acquired control of the local firm and renamed it "Wm. D. Cleveland, Wholesale Grocer and Commission Merchant." It was still located in Sessums' former building at 37 Main Street, on the corner of Main Street and Franklin Avenue[77].

In the winter of 1873, Alexander Sessums devoted himself to his company's commission business. In late January, although he was suffering from a severe cold, he went into work in the morning of January 31. His partner and brother-in-law Dr. Josiah Camillis Massie found him at the office in critical condition. He returned home, but the congestion and hemorrhaging ultimately caused his death. Alexander Sessums, at age forty-three, died on Friday night, January 31, 1873 at midnight after a short and painful illness. Funeral services for Alexander Sessums were held on Sunday, February 2, 1873 at the Baptist Church in Galveston. He was then buried in Glenwood Cemetery in Houston[78].

In February, 1873, Mary Sessums, his wife, was appointed the administratrix of the estate of Alexander Sessums, and she advertised for any claims against the estate to be presented. The claims were overwhelming and the firm of A. Sessums and Company was bankrupt. The office furniture and other remaining assets of A. Sessums and Company were auctioned off on May 29, 1873[79].

In spite of the enormous difficulties imposed on the family by the sudden and unexpected passing of her husband, Mary Sessums handled the estate and looked after the interests of their son Davis. Davis Sessums, at sixteen years old, was an exceptionally intelligent young man, and through the efforts of his mother, their family and friends, he enrolled in the University of the South at Sewanee, Tennessee in 1874. In four years, Davis graduated from the university with honors, and after briefly attending the law school at the University of Virginia, he returned to Sewanee to take the position of headmaster at Sewanee High School. At the same time, he entered the theological department at the university which prepares students for the Episcopal ministry[80].

In August, 1882, Davis Sessums was ordained to the priesthood of the Episcopal Church. He served as rector at Grace Church in Galveston among others before going to Christ Church, New Orleans in 1888. On April 15, 1891, Rev. Davis Sessums, rector of Christ Church in New Orleans was elected as coadjutor bishop in the

Episcopal Diocese of Louisiana. Rev. Davis Sessums had married Alice Castleman Galleher, the daughter of Right Rev. J. N. Galleher, STD, Bishop of the Episcopal Diocese of Lousiana, on December 18, 1890, and Sessums then succeeded Bishop Galleher after the bishop's death[81].

The friendship between the William D. Cleveland and Alexander Sessums was well known, but the influence of this bond extended to the Sessums family for years afterwards. When the Right Reverend Davis Sessums and his wife Alice had their first son in 1903, they named him Alexander Cleveland Sessums. Their second son, born in 1906, was named Davis, Jr[82].

The economy of Houston was slow to recover from the effects of the Civil War and Reconstruction that followed. The recessionary period of the 1870's left the City with poor finances and a huge debt. Business leaders banded together to bring the City out of this depressed state, and W. D. Cleveland assumed a leadership role in the community. Although he had lost his former partner, friend and mentor, Cleveland was himself an astute businessman and inspiring civic leader and, at age thirty-three, stepped into the role that he seemed destined for. During the 1870's, William D. Cleveland served without pay on the City Council during the time when the City was struggling financially and he often paid for city improvements with his own funds. He was a founding member of the Board of Trade and Cotton Exchange when it was organized on May 15, 1874, and he served as its president three times, from 1875-1876, 1884-1891 and 1902-1904[83].

During the 1870's, William Cleveland expanded his interests into both the mercantile trade and the cotton factor business. By 1877, Houston was recognized as the best produce and grocery market in Texas and the W. D. Cleveland company was a leading enterprise in that marketplace. While handling flour, grain, bacon and the general range of groceries, Cleveland also made a specialty of Texas sugars and syrups. His interests in the cotton trade increased so much that the W. D. Cleveland Wholesale Grocers, Cotton Factor and Commission Merchant company's operations moved into additional office space at 9, 11, 13 and 15 Franklin Avenue, on the southeast corner of Travis Street and Franklin Avenue. At this same time, Cleveland ventured into the another aspect of the cotton business and he was elected as the vice-president of the Buffalo Warehouse and Cotton Compress Company which was located on the north side of Buffalo Bayou, east of the modern day McKee Street. Within two years, he was the president of the compress company[84].

In March, 1880, the W. D. Cleveland Company purchased 600,000 bricks for the construction of a new four story building to be located on the northeast corner of Main Street and Commerce Avenue, the same site where Doswell and Adams established Houston's first large general mercantile store in 1837. The new building was completed in the fall and the advertisements for the new store promoted its extensive stock of staples, fancy and family groceries, whiskey, cigars and tobacco[85].

Business was good, and by the summer of 1885, the Cleveland company leased additional warehouse space for the grocery operations in the former Sam Allen warehouse across the bayou at 2nd Street and Railroad Street. Realizing that he could no longer effectively manage the business alone, Cleveland brought long time employee Caesar M. Lombardi into the company as a partner. Lombardi had been with the W. D. Cleveland Company since 1871 and was knowledgeable of all aspects of the business. With this new partner on board, the name of the company was changed to W. D. Cleveland and Company[86].

The commission business, in particular, was doing very well. The local newspaper reported that late in 1880, William D. Cleveland sold 3,071 bales of cotton to A. H. Lea for $150,000, and this was thought to be "the largest single cotton transaction ever made in Texas." The Buffalo Compress company was reorganized into the Union Compress and Warehouse Company, and on May 7, 1888, William D. Cleveland was elected as a director of the company. Cleveland also invested in the up and coming cottonseed oil business along with other local business notables, including T. W. House, E. A. Sewall, T. H. Scanlan, T. J. Boyles, J. S. Price and James A. Baker, as the Merchants and Planters Oil Company was incorporated on April 11, 1889 with capital stock of $125,000[87].

In the spring of 1893, the Cleveland enterprises suffered a major setback. On April 7, 1893, the wholesale house of W. D. Cleveland and Company caught fire. Fanned by a high east wind, the flames were uncontrollable and the building on the corner of Main Street and Commerce Avenue burned to the ground. The fire was thought to have started on the second floor and spread throughout the building. About $125,000 worth of stock was lost in addition to the $10,000 building, which was fully insured. That same day, William Cleveland pledged to resume business immediately. They would begin clearing the debris as soon as possible so that they could start the construction a new building. In the interim, Cleveland said that the business would lease the old electric light plant, located across the street in SSBB Block 2, and continue operations from there[88].

Within a year, the new building for W. D. Cleveland and Company was completed. It was a three story structure, with a basement floor, located at 1013-1019 Commerce Avenue, on the northwest corner of Commerce Avenue and Fannin Street. Perhaps as an extra precaution against fire, the building was constructed of "cement and shells and is virtually an adobe building." It was an example of pre-reinforced concrete construction with oyster shell as reinforcement instead of rebar, and it was given the nickname of "the Concrete House[89]."

In the spring of 1894, W. D. Cleveland and Company began to manufacture their own baking powder and roasted coffee under the Apex Brand. Advertisements for the products cited the company's ability to control the production process in order to insure the freshness and purity of the items. The manufacture of yeast powder and the roasting of coffee were done in a two story building constructed to the northwest of the company's main offices, on the sloping bank between the main building and the bayou[90].

In 1898, after twenty-seven years with the company, partner Caesar Lombardi decided to leave W. D. Cleveland and Company. Lombardi had immigrated to the United States with his family in 1858. His father was a bar keeper in New Orleans and Caesar, age twenty-four, was working as a clerk in a men's store when he came to Houston about 1871 and joined the W. D. Cleveland Company as a clerk. Lombardi was a partner in the firm for the last thirteen years with the company. It was during these years that the company expanded both its wholesale grocery business and its involvement is many aspects of the cotton trade[91].

Caesar Lombardi sent his son Maurice to Yale University and decided to pursue other opportunities in Portland, Oregon. Eventually, Caesar and his wife Caroline moved on to Berkeley, California to be with Maurice and his family. Maurice was employed there as an engineer with an oil company, and Caesar was the president of the local newspaper[92].

After Lombardi's departure in 1898, William D. Cleveland brought his two sons, William D. Cleveland, Jr. and Alexander Sessums Cleveland, into the company. His son Alexander had been born the year after the death of his close friend and business associate Alexander Sessums, and Cleveland named his young son in his honor. The company now became W. D. Cleveland and Sons[93].

At the end of the nineteenth century, W. D. Cleveland and Sons was the largest wholesale grocery company in Texas. The company also had extensive holdings in the cotton compress and warehouse business with the development of the Cleveland Compress and Warehouse Company on the east side of Hill Street (now, Jensen Drive) at Buffalo Bayou. Nevertheless, financial difficulties plagued the company that had grown and endured since 1866. The firm had assets of $441,000 while facing liabilities of $758,000, and on August 10, 1899, the company filed a voluntary petition of bankruptcy in federal court[94].

The sixty year old William Cleveland faced this challenge in the same manner as he had each one in the past. On the strength of his reputation, the creditors of W. D. Cleveland and Sons agreed to a settlement on September 15, 1899 that would allow the company to resume business operations. In the first decades of the twentieth century, Cleveland revitalized his wholesale grocery business and developed its operations around the facilities at the foot of Main Street (Allen's Landing) that shaped the site as we know it today[95].

W. D. Cleveland bought the International Coffee Company of Galveston in 1907. He then built a building behind his main building to serve as the headquarters for his coffee roasting and distribution business. The construction of the three story building for the International Coffee Company required that a long concrete retaining wall be built south of the wharf so that the new structure would lie at the same elevation as the existing company building at 1019 Commerce Avenue. Although W. D. Cleveland and Sons had been roasting coffee in a small building near the same location since 1894, that two story structure was replaced by the larger International Coffee Company where coffee imported from Central America could be manufactured under the Sunset Coffee label and distributed throughout the southwest from the transportation hub of Houston. Within two years, the International Coffee Company was advertising its Sunset Coffee brand throughout Texas with the pitch that their product was roasted and packed in Houston in "air-tight sealed tins, dust proof, germ-proof, and impervious to moisture." It sold for the price of thirty-five cents a pound or three pounds for a dollar[96].

The year 1912 was a pivotal year for the Cleveland enterprises. On February 21, 1912, a great fire swept across the Fifth Ward, and in the process, burned over forty city blocks including the plant, sheds and the adjoining railroad yards of the Cleveland Compress Company and the 32,000 bales of cotton in its warehouse. The loss to the Cleveland company was estimated at $1.9 million. Later that year, however, the worst happened. William Davis Cleveland died of heart trouble at his home at 806 San Jacinto Street on Sunday evening at 5:15 pm on December 24, 1912. He was seventy-three and was buried at Glenwood Cemetery following his funeral on December 25[97].

The sons, who had been involved in the company for nearly fifteen years, vowed to continue the business. William D. Cleveland, Jr. and A. S. Cleveland headed up the wholesale grocery and cotton factor business of William D. Cleveland and Sons for almost two decades thereafter, but ultimately, the company ran its course as the Great Depression set in. In March, 1930, the great enterprise of one of Houston's pioneer family firms closed for good[98].

For a person of such prominence in the business and civic affairs of Houston, there are very few reminders of William D. Cleveland in the city today. Cleveland Park, a city park acquired in 1910, is located on the north bank of Buffalo Bayou on the east side of Jackson Hill Street. The original tract extended from the east side of Waugh Drive to an area west of Jackson Hill Street, but with the redevelopment of the Waugh Drive-Heights Boulevard interchange, Spotts Park was created out of the eastern part of Cleveland Park. In 1927, the William D. Cleveland Elementary School was built at 320

Jackson Hill Street on a parcel of land just north of Cleveland Park. The school was closed by the Houston Independent School District in 1977 after fifty years of service. The property was sold and the Jackson Hill Luxury Apartments were built on the site in 2003 by the Finger Companies.

After the close of the W. D. Cleveland and Sons business, the two buildings on Commerce Avenue that were the center of the Cleveland business operations for so many years were leased for secondary warehouse uses during the next four decades. The main building which fronted on Commerce Avenue had various businesses using it at times for cold storage vaults, wholesale grocery, wholesale meats and sausage manufacturing. The International Coffee Company building saw use as coin machine storage on the first floor and wholesale grocery storage on the second and third floors[99].

The revival of the old downtown in the mid-1960's as an entertainment district brought a new life to the Cleveland buildings. The most famous, and certainly most renown, establishment at this time was the Love Street Light Circus and Feel Good Machine, a nightclub with psychedelic lighting and music. The inspiration of local artist David Adickes, the music venue with innovative displays of color patterns was an outgrowth of the experiences that Adickes had at San Francisco's "Summer of Love" in the late spring of 1967. He was fascinated by the use of overhead projectors and colored oils to produce spectacular productions of artistic color. On his return to Houston, the forty year old Adickes put together about $25,000 and opened his club on June 3, 1967[100].

The third floor of the building, where earlier in the century gas roasters had produced Sunset Coffee, became Houston's premier psychedelic nightclub. An emerging artist, Billy Gibbons, prior to forming ZZTop, performed here in a band called Moving Sidewalks. An entire wall of the club was covered with Adickes' iconic poster of Love Street, a four Day-Glo colored silk screen with the image of Theda Barra. Without tables or chairs, the audience reclined against foam-covered "benches," lying on the floor while watching the dazzling images on the ceiling and walls and listening to the sounds of rock music[101].

After about eighteen months, David Adickes had seen enough of his experimentation with colors and patterns and the nightclub business. He had made about $25,000 from the venture and, realizing that he had recovered his investment, he sold the nightclub to one of his partners for practically nothing. The Love Street Light Circus and Feel Good Machine continued on for another year and a half before it finally closed after its last show on June 6, 1970[102].

Although the Love Street Light Circus and Feel Good Machine of David Adickes was only a temporary contribution to Houston's art scene, Adickes began a prolific series of sculptures in the early 1980's that have become outstanding examples of outdoor art in Houston, the surrounding region and the United States. In 1982, David Adickes was commissioned to design a sculpture for a downtown building. The "Virtuoso," a thirty-six foot tall concrete sculpture of a cello player with a music sound system that plays twenty-four hours a day, is located at the Lyric Center office building on the corner of Smith Street and Prairie Avenue, two blocks south of Buffalo Bayou. David Adickes created "The Winds of Change," an eight foot bronze statue of George H. W. Bush in 1989. The statue is found in Terminal C at Bush Intercontinental Airport, Houston. The monumental "Tribute to American Statesmanship" is and assemblage of busts of Stephen F. Austin, Sam Houston, Abraham Lincoln and George Washington. The sculpture, which Adickes created in 2008 and which he whimsically calls "Mount Rush Hour," is on the corner of Elder Street and Bingham Street and visible from I-10 eastbound and I-45 southbound lanes near downtown[103].

Other works by David Adickes include his 1994 creation called "A Tribute to Courage" which is a sixty-seven foot tall statue of Sam Houston set on a ten foot granite base in Hunstville, Texas. In 2006, Adickes erected a sixty foot tall statute of Stephen F. Austin in Brazoria County. Inspired by Mount Rushmore, Adickes has created three sets of twenty foot tall busts of all forty-three presidents of United States. One set is in "Presidents Park," an outdoor educational museum in Lead, South Dakota about forty miles from Mount Rushmore, a second set is in a park near Williamsburg, Virginia, and a third set of presidential busts sits at his studio lot in Houston waiting for a place to call home[104].

By 1973, the W. D. Cleveland Warehouse on Commerce Avenue was demolished. The International Coffee Building was boarded up, vacant and allowed to deteriorate. Tropical Storm Allison of 2001 flooded the building with bayou water that reached within two feet of the first floor ceiling. The structure seemed destined for the wrecking ball until the Buffalo Bayou Partnership acquired the building in 2001[105].

A temporary rehabilitation of the The International Coffee Company building was performed by French students working under French artist Georges Rousse for the FotoFest 2002 exhibit. Long term plans for a $3 million renovation of the building came in 2003 when the project was awarded to Lake/Flato Architects of San Antonio. The plans include the use of the second floor for office space for the Buffalo Bayou Partnership and the third floor as office space or an event venue. A restaurant or cafe with a banquet room could also become part of plan. The first floor, due to its propensity for flooding from the rising waters of Buffalo Bayou, would become a canoe, kayak and bike rental concession[106].

The renovation of the International Coffee Company Building, which is sometimes referred to as the Sunset Coffee Building, and the surrounding grounds will enhance the public's access and awareness of the place where Houston had its beginnings. Over one hundred seventy years of commercial and historic activity have taken place at the City Wharves on Buffalo Bayou, now the public green space of Allen's Landing Park. The renovation of the one remaining structure of the historic period will point us to the future. The incorporation of a portion of the west wall of the former W. D. Cleveland Building, a rare surviving example of pre-reinforced concrete construction with oyster shell as reinforcement instead of rebar, into the landscape of grounds will remind us of the past.

Star Bottling Works

From the docks at Allen's Landing Park, we set out downstream in the former course of the Houston Ship Channel. The bayou ahead is noticeably wider than it was back upstream, above the entrance into the historic turning basin. The bayou flows in a straight channel between parallel banks about one hundred feet apart for as far as one can see. A quarter of a mile ahead, the bayou turns sharply to the left.

At the end of the wharf, the Fannin Street bridge crosses in front of us. Built in the late 1970's, the Fannin Street bridge is best described as a functional, modern street bridge. It angles off the street grid of the downtown district to meet a similarly angling San Jacinto Street bridge to form a triangle on the north side of the bayou where both streets merge into North San Jacinto Street. Although the Fannin Street bridge improves the traffic flow in downtown, the bridge itself obscures our view of the scenic and historic San Jacinto Street bridge, a petite companion to the Main Street Viaduct. You will see people at all times of the day walking across the Fannin Street bridge to the large, red brick building that anchors the north side of the bayou. It is the Harris County San Jacinto Street Jail[107].

While the City wharves were the center of activity at the port, the tracts of land at the end of Fannin Street were less busy. In early times, a small gully ran to the bayou from Fannin Street and a small iron bridge on Commerce Avenue permitted traffic to cross the drainage. Because of the way the street grid was laid out, the bayou flows close to the City blocks on the south bank. In fact, these blocks, SSBB Block 4 and Block 5, are only partial City blocks, having a depth of only one City lot[108].

The earliest reported structure in Block 4 was the De Chene Hotel. In 1840, the hotel, located on Fannin Street at Buffalo Bayou, provided accommodations to visitors to Houston that was enhanced by the hotel's front gallery where gents "tipped their chairs back against the wall, spat tobacco juice over the railing and watched the bayou boats heading for the Main Street landing[109]."

For the most part, though, the block on the banks of the bayou between Fannin Street and San Jacinto Street was undeveloped until 1884 when the Star Bottling Works was built on the northeast corner of Commerce Avenue and San Jacinto Street. The soft drink industry that we know today, with the familiar names of Coca-Cola, Pepsi and Dr Pepper, had its origins in the post Civil War nineteenth century. The story of the Star Bottling Works is Houston's contribution to the story of soft drinks[110].

Beverages that we call soft drinks have been around for centuries, and they are associated with the medicinal benefits perceived to come from the naturally carbonated mineral waters found in natural springs. In 1767, English chemist Joseph Priestley developed a way of infusing water with carbon dioxide to make carbonated water or, as it is sometimes called, soda water. By the mid-nineteenth century, pharmacists in America began to add herbs and chemicals to flavor artificial mineral water in order to improve the taste of the drink[111].

It was about this time that ginger ale, a drink created in Ireland about 1851, was brought to America. Ginger ale, derived from ginger beer, proved to be very popular and it was thought to be the most popular soft drink in the United States from 1860 to 1930. Another popular drink was root beer, a carbonated beverage flavored with sarsaparilla and sassafras that first went into mass production in 1876[112].

In 1880, the Star Bottling Works opened at 99 Congress Avenue at the corner with Fannin Street. The proprietor, Robert Cotter, was a forty-three year old druggist who had immigrated to Texas from England in the late 1860's. Cotter was associated with Matthias D. Conklin, another Houston druggist who worked for the R. F. George and Company. In 1870, Robert Cotter took over the George pharmacy at 76 Main Street and established the R. Cotter and Company, wholesale druggists. By 1879, Cotter and his partner Conklin were selling a variety of medicinal treatments of their own manufacture such as IXL Chill Cure, IXL Sarsaparilla and IXL Liver Pills in addition to other products including Triumph Mexican Chewing Gum and Pure Extract Jamaica Ginger. With the bottling company, Cotter branched out into beverages such as soda, sarsaparilla and ginger ale[113].

Local merchant and grocer W. D. Cleveland took an interest in the fledgling beverage company and, in 1882, he became the president of Star Bottling Works. Robert Cotter was the vice-president and general manager of the manufacturing operations that produced soda, sarsaparilla, ginger ale and other beverages. However, within a couple of years, Houston contractor August Baumbach acquired the Star Bottling Works and moved its operations to a new building located on the northwest corner of Commerce Avenue and San Jacinto Street. On June 8, 1884, the Star Bottling Works announced that it was in full operation and ready to fill orders for soda water, sarsaparilla, Belfast ginger ale, essences of peppermint and ginger, Vichy, Selzter and syrups of all flavors[114].

August Baumbach was born in Hamburg, Germany in April, 1853, and he immigrated to United States in 1871. He arrived in Houston about 1878 and began to work in his trade as a brick mason. By the time that he acquired the Star Bottling Works, he had become a general contractor overseeing the construction of brick buildings in Houston and around the state. His two major projects in 1886 were the Chambers County Courthouse in Wallisville, a brick and stone Renaissance Revival style structure, and the Falls County Courthouse in Marlin. In 1889, Baumbach completed the construction of a fine brick assembly hall at the Texas Agricultural and Mechanical College. He also handled local projects such as the addition to the truck house of the Fire Department on the corner of Prairie Avenue and San Jacinto Street in 1894[115].

The mid-1880's were a pivotal time in the emerging carbonated water beverage business. In 1885, pharmacist Charles Alderton invented Dr Pepper in Waco, Texas. A year later, Dr. John S. Pemberton invented Coca-Cola in Atlanta, Georgia. The competition in the soft drink market was intense as local bottlers sought to bring new beverages to the public. In the enthusiasm of this market, the Star Bottling Works of Houston tried, perhaps, a little too hard because it was slapped with a lawsuit by the Moxie Nerve Food Company of Maine. The bill of injunction, filed on February 2, 1887 in U. S. Circuit Court by Moxie Nerve Food Company against August Baumbach and the Star Bottling Works, alleged that Star Bottling was fraudulently manufacturing a liquor similar to their product. Moxie claimed that Baumbach used a similar bottle, similar packing, a similar label and similar ingredients in a drink called "Standard Nerve Food" which infringed upon their trademarked beverage. In a landmark case, on July 12, 1887, August Baumbach and Star Bottling were injoined to stop the trademark infringement against the Moxie Nerve Food Company[116].

Despite this setback, August Baumbach continued to operate his bottling company along with his general contracting business, managing both enterprises from his office in the Star Bottling Works plant on Commerce Avenue. In 1889, though, he turned over the management of the bottling company to August Bonner[117].

August Bonner was Italian immigrant who came to Houston about 1878. Bonner worked as a bar tender until he was able to open his own establishment, the First and Last Chance Saloon, on Milam Street at the south end of the Iron Bridge, in 1880. He began his employment with Star Bottling about 1886, and worked his way up to management of the company by 1889. Baumbach and Bonner became partners in Star Bottling in 1890. Eventually, in 1892, August Bonner became the sole proprietor of the Star Bottling Works as the company expanded its business as a manufacturer of soda, sarsaparilla (in the Old West this was called "sasparilla"), ginger ale, mineral waters and other beverages[118].

August Bonner continued to operate the Star Bottling Works at the same location, designated as 1117-1119 Commerce Avenue in the new street numbering system of 1892, until his death on August 20, 1896. The fifty-two year old Bonner took a fatal dose of morphine and died at his boarding house about 11 pm[119].

Henry H. Kuhlman purchased the Star Bottling Works from the estate of August Bonner in early 1897. Kuhlman moved the plant across the street in 1900 to the building at 1216-1220 Commerce Avenue. After the sale of the company to G. Geaccone about 1902, the Star Bottling Works was relocated to 20 NE Crawford Avenue at the corner of Magnolia Street in 1903. Geaccone moved the plant to 1102 Wood Street at corner of Vine Street in 1908 and sold the company to Italian immigrant Joseph R. Navarro in 1910. Navarro and his partner M. Lamana expanded the product line to include Mignon Limon splits and Jersey Creme, a soda fountain syrup from the Jersey Creme Company of Fort Worth[120].

In 1915, the Star Bottling Works, which advertised itself as "the oldest manufacturers of soda water in Houston," relocated to their new facility at 1010 N. San Jacinto Street. Joe Navarro operated the company at this location until his tragic death on June 24, 1932 when an assailant, armed with a sawed-off shot gun, burst from the darkness near the Navarro home on Holly Street and fired into Navarro's left side while he, his wife and daughter sat on the front porch. The murder was thought to be the result of a personal quarrel and not a gangster killing. His son Roxie Navarro, who worked as the bookkeeper for the company, took over the Star Bottling Company. After the death of his father J. R. Navarro, Roxie J. Navarro became the proprietor and manager of Star Bottling Works until it closed in 1962[121].

The lot on the northwest corner of Commerce Avenue and San Jacinto Street was cleared by 1907. All of the lots in SSBB Block 4 were mostly empty, except for a couple of small structures, until the construction boom of the mid-1920's when the Texas Packing Company facility was built in 1924 on the corner at San Jacinto Street. This two story building at the Commerce Avenue street level housed the cold storage rooms for the packing operations. The rear of the building includes a total of five levels as the structure extends down to the water level of Buffalo Bayou. In 1931, an addition was made to the Texas Packing Company building that doubled the size of the structure to what we see today. Although it is a one story structure at the street level, the rear of the building extends four levels to the bayou. The high water events that occur when the bayou floods make the lower levels of this building unsuitable for any commercial use. The debris that is often seen stuck to the walls of the building attest to that[122].

San Jacinto Street bridge

San Jacinto Street is a main artery for traffic leaving the downtown area. It has been an important connection to the north side of Buffalo Bayou since 1883 when the first bridge was constructed at this location. As a vital link to the Fifth Ward, the bridge provided access to the City for the workers who lived north of the bayou. The need for a bridge was so critical to the residents of the Fifth Ward that twice they threatened the City Council with secession from the City if more attention was not paid to their needs, including a bridge[123].

When the Houston City Mills was destroyed by fire in August, 1875, it was argued that the mills could have been saved if a bridge had existed to permit fire fighters from the Fifth Ward get to the scene of the fire. After a second petition for secession in the early 1880's, the City Council made a few concessions to the Fifth Ward residents and, in January, 1883, an order was placed for the construction of a Swedish-designed, iron drawbridge across Buffalo Bayou at the foot of San Jacinto Street. Since it was necessary for the bridge to allow clearance to ships coming upstream to the City wharves, it had to be a movable bridge. In this case, it was a three hundred fifty foot long pivot bridge, revolving on a pedestal on the north side of the bayou[124].

During the second decade of the twentieth century, Houston, under the leadership of Mayor H. Baldwin Rice, initiated a program of civic improvements that were inspired by the principles of the City Beautiful movement. A new bridge at San Jacinto Street was commissioned to form a link between the business section in the heart of Houston and the Fifth Ward manufacturing and jobbing districts[125].

The demolition of the old San Jacinto Street bridge began on June 17, 1913 to make way for the new bridge to match a similarly designed bridge at Main Street. Like the nearby Main Street bridge, the San Jacinto Street bridge uses the same spanning technology of a long, solid barrel arch ring to span the main channel of the bayou. The reinforced concrete design enables much greater vertical lift than other construction techniques and the bridge could be built with enough clearance for navigating Buffalo Bayou without a movable span. The arch of the bridge rises twenty-eight feet, nine inches from the average water level which had a depth of ten feet[126].

The central, and most striking feature of the San Jacinto Street bridge is a one hundred ten foot open-spandrel concrete arch and buttress type abutments. The bridge abutments are flanked on either side by reinforced girder spans and retaining wall approaches. Designed by E. E. Sands, the city engineer of Houston, and built by the William P. Carmichael Company of St. Louis at a cost of $155,000, the San Jacinto Street bridge is one of only a very few of open-spandrel concrete arch bridges in Texas[127].

The construction of the bridge at the San Jacinto Street site also presented some difficult engineering challenges. Since there was no natural rock foundation at this location, the bridge's arch foundation was placed on four hundred fifty-five precast concrete twenty foot long piles which were driven twenty-three feet below the water level. In order to connect to Willow Street on the north side of the bayou, the bridge was built on a fifteen degrees left forward skew. Stretching for a length of three hundred twenty-five feet, the San Jacinto Street bridge is seventy feet wide, including a fifty foot concrete roadway with ten foot wide cantilevered concrete sidewalks on each side. The arch ring contains eight hundred sixteen cubic yards of concrete while the total amount of concrete for the entire bridge is about 5,500 cubic yards incorporating about two hundred tons of reinforcing bars[128].

Improvements in 1997 included the replacement of the original deck and sidewalks while the railing was replaced with a modern open balustrade. The result, nevertheless, is a beautifully styled bridge. Although obscured by the Fannin Street bridge and blocked from view by the Harris County buildings on both sides of Buffalo Bayou to the east, the San Jacinto Street bridge is just one of the many hidden gems of the Bayou City. One that can be best seen from the bayou itself[129].

Schulte Brewery

Immediately downstream of the San Jacinto Street bridge, two multi-story buildings stand at the bayou's edge along the south bank. The first one, right on the corner of San Jacinto Street and Commerce Avenue, is a six story, red brick structure on Commerce Avenue, but the rear of the building rises nine stories from the level of the bayou. Similarly, the second building, also a red brick structure, is three stories on Commerce Avenue, but it rises five stories from Buffalo Bayou. Both buildings were constructed in the early part of the twentieth century as commercial warehouses. The two buildings together occupy the entire city block known as SSBB Block 5. Block 5 is one of the truncated blocks containing only one row of lots along Commerce Avenue. Today, both are part of the Sheriff's Office prisoner processing operations. In the nineteenth century, this city block was the site of one of the city's first breweries and, later, one of the city's early beer distributors.

When you talk of commercial beer brewing in Houston, and for that matter, in Texas, too, you have to begin with Peter Gabel. His brewery, established in 1849, was the first brewery in Texas, predating the famous Kreische Brewery in La Grange by a decade[130].

Peter Gabel was born in Herxheim am Berg, Rhein Pfalz, Germany on November 4, 1813 to Peter and Madeline Gabel. His father died when he was two, and his mother died when he was six. Peter Gabel was taken in by relatives and taught the trade of a cooper (a barrel maker) and a brewer. Hoping to improve his fortunes, at age twenty-seven, Gabel immigrated to Lewiston, Pennsylvania in 1840, and then, to St. Louis before arriving in Houston in November, 1844[131].

Peter Gabel's first job in Houston was cutting wood in Germantown, a platted subdivision north of White Oak Bayou that was a heavily wooded pine forest and a ready supply of lumber for construction. In 1845, Peter Gabel went into partnership with Jacob Werlin in a soap factory located on Market Square. The soap business soon failed, and Gabel went back to the trade that he knew best, working as a cooper or barrel maker for McKinney and Williams of Galveston who operated a tallow making business called "Tallow Town." Tallow Town was located downstream of Frost Town, on the Samuel May Williams League that was situated east of Houston, on the south side of Buffalo Bayou. Apparently, Gabel was quite skilled at making barrels and that led to work for Martin M. Shepherd making wooden cisterns, and later, he made barrels and hogsheads for the sugar plantations on the Brazos River. Yet, still unsatisfied with his situation, Peter Gabel was caught up in the gold fever of 1849 and made preparations to leave for California. He returned to Houston to put his affairs in order, but then, met a woman who also was an immigrant from Germany and he fell in love[132].

Maria Gebhardt Stein had come to the United States with her parents and eventually lived in New Orleans. Her first marriage to a man named Thiel produced two sons, and after Thiel's death, she married John Stein. John and Maria Stein moved to Houston where Stein died, and during the probate of John Stein's estate, she met Peter Gabel. Mrs. Maria Stein and Peter Gabel were issued a marriage license on June 18, 1849 and were married shortly thereafter. Marriage motivated Peter Gabel to settle down, and after his marriage, he built a brewery on one of the downtown lots he had purchased a few years earlier. The first brewery in Houston was opened in 1849 on Preston Avenue, near the courthouse square[133].

Beer was not a common drink for Houstonians who were not of German heritage. They were not used to the "peculiar beverage" made by Peter Gabel. They were more familiar with whisky toddies and mint julips than with the "frothy, new-fangled German fluid." It may also be the case that Gabel was not all that good a brewer, as well. In the 1850 census, he still listed his occupation as a cooper. Fortunately, he met the twenty-three year old Heinrich (Henry) Schulte, a recent immigrant from Prussia, and they formed a partnership in 1850. Henry Schulte was a brewer by trade and he probably headed up the beer making at the brewery, at least until 1854, when he left to form his own brewery[134].

In 1857, Peter Gabel doubled the size of his brewery, constructing a two story frame building on the north side of Preston Avenue between Caroline Street and San Jacinto Street with a cellar beneath that was about twenty feet deep. In addition to the brewing operations, Gabel opened a distillery to produce whiskey. During the Civil War, he focused on the distillery and closed the brewery. Corn whiskey sold for $1500 a gallon in Confederate currency. Later, after the war, he imported wines from Europe which he distributed to dealers around the state. The wine operations included large vaults in his building filled with wine in casks and with bottles stacked from floor to ceiling. Dealing primarily in Rhine wines, Peter Gabel was known for having the finest wine cellar in the Southwest[135].

After the Civil War, Gabel also was active in real estate investments. By 1870, he had real estate holdings in Houston and Harris County of between $75,000 and $80,000. Eventually, he turned the brewery over to John Wagner and Charles Hermann. By 1879, Wagner and Hermann were operating the P. Gabel Brewery and advertising the company as "bottlers of beer for family use." Beer and ale were sold in half and quarter barrels as well. When Gabel started the brewery in the 1850's, he sold only two barrels of beer per week at $9 per barrel, but, by the 1870's, the brewery was selling eighty to one hundred barrels a week[136].

For much of the nineteenth century, Peter Gabel was a prominent Houston citizen. He was a founding member of the Houston Turn Verein and an active participant in the Volksfest Association and its festivals. Affectionately referred to as "Uncle Peter," Peter Gabel died at his home at 312 San Jacinto Street at 4:30 pm on January 7, 1896, after a brief illness. He came to Houston without much to his name, but through hard work and perseverance, he found his place in the community. He left an estate estimated to be between $172,000 and $250,000. The old wooden malt house of his brewery which was known as Gabel's Wine Cellar, where he kept finest white Rhine wines in the deep cellar which only saw candle light, was demolished on July 3, 1897[137].

When Henry Schulte left the partnership with Peter Gabel, he established a brewery of his own. On December 12, 1854, Schulte sold to Peter Gabel his interest in the ten acre tract known as the William F. Hodge property that Schulte and Gabel had purchased from Levi Butler on June 1, 1853. With the $450 that he received from this sale, Schulte bought the adjacent tract of land to the south and established a brewery on that site in a partnership with F. P. Hoffman. The partnership with Hoffman, however, was dissolved a year later in 1855. Henry Schulte then purchased the property on Buffalo Bayou between San Jacinto Street and Caroline Street where he erected three substantial brick and frame buildings for his brewery[138].

By the end of the Civil War, the Henry Schulte and Company was well established at the corner of San Jacinto Street and Commerce Avenue. But, Henry had other ambitions. Perhaps because the beer market was such a narrowly focused opportunity, or perhaps for some other reason, Henry Schulte turned his interests to the grocery business and gave the brewery to his brother Gerhard Schulte. Gerhard, about eleven years younger than his brother, was born in Westphalia, Germany and was trained as a brewer. He and his wife Anna immigrated to Houston during the 1850's and lived on the site of the brewery with their children. By 1868, Gerhard was in charge of the brewery operations after Henry had relocated to Galveston. Under Gerhard's leadership, the Schulte and Company Brewery became one of the city's suppliers of lager beer, ale and "porter," a dark-colored style of beer similar to stout (as in Guinness Stout, a popular beverage today)[139].

In November, 1866, Henry Schulte joined the George Schneider and Company grocery business in Galveston. By March, 1868, Henry Schulte and Louis LeGierse had become partners with George Schneider in George Schneider and Company, wholesale grocers and "dealers in western produce" located in the Kuhn's Building on the Strand in Galveston. Henry Schulte retired from George Schneider and Company in 1870 to establish a firm with Louis LeGierse, a company that was a wholesale grocer and a dealer in western produce, liquors, wines, cigars and tobacco. He later retired from LeGierse and Company in 1873[140].

In the spring of 1877, Henry Schulte retired from business in Texas all together. His well respected integrity and fine business qualifications had made him quite successful. In a decision that was rare, but not unique, Henry Schulte left Texas and resettled in his native Germany with his wife and six children. Then, on November 4, 1877, Henry Schulte, at age fifty, died suddenly and unexpectedly in Frankfurt, Germany[141].

The local beers produced by the breweries of Gabel and Schulte were pioneering efforts in the story of making beer in Houston, but after a quarter of a century, the taste for beer in Houston underwent a change. Beer drinkers began to fancy the new, "imported" brands from St. Louis and Cincinnati. The Schulte Brewery began to shift away from local brewing to being the agent for a nationally distributed beer. By 1879, Gerhard Schulte was the local agent for the William J. Lemps Company of St. Louis and he was selling their St. Louis Lager beer from the Schulte Brewery[142].

As the 1880's began, Gerhard Schulte also diversified his businesses. His large brewery and home on Block 5 had served as a residence for several of the workers at the brewery for many years, but in 1882, he opened his home as a public boarding house. As the proprietor of the Schulte House, Schulte advertised that they "have the most comfortable and airy rooms to be found in the City." The Schulte House was located at 89 Commerce Avenue, with the main two story structure set back near the bayou and close to Caroline Street. An arbor extending completely across the front of the boarding house offered expansive views of the downtown skyline[143].

At this time, the competition in the beer market increased significantly as major breweries from the Midwest shipped their products to Houston by rail in refrigerated cars. By 1884, the Anheuser-Busch Brewing Association of St. Louis and Joseph Schlitz of Milwaukee had established distributors in the City to compete with the William J. Lemp Company. William J. Lemp and Company built its Ice and Beer Depot on the northeast corner of San Jacinto Street and Commerce Avenue in 1885 on the lots adjacent to Schulte's brewery. Gerhard Schulte, though, curtailed his own activity in the beer business and focused on his boarding house. August Moser became the agent for W. J. Lemp's Western Brewery and operated the establishment on Commerce Avenue. The incorporation of the Houston Ice and Brewing Company in 1887 brought a new type of large scale brewery to Houston, as well[144].

Gerhard Schulte and his wife Anna operated the Schulte House for the next fifteen years or so until Gerhard passed away about 1899. Anna Schulte then continued to run the boarding house through the summer of 1901. In August, 1901, however, Mrs. Anna Schulte, desiring to retire at age sixty-five, offered the Schulte House at 1211-1213 Commerce Avenue for lease. The Schulte House had twenty-four rooms with lavatories both upstairs and downstairs, and the boarding house was available for a one to three year lease for $75 per month. Mrs. Olga Remmer was the proprietor of the Schulte House in 1908 as the old establishment came to its last days when the development of new commercial warehouses along Commerce Avenue began[145].

Schuhmacher Warehouse

The beginning of the twentieth century was a time of economic growth and prosperity for Houston. The establishment of a deep water port at the Turning Basin was only one of a number of factors that increased the commercial activity in the City. This activity was seen in the construction of a number of new commercial warehouses along Commerce Avenue, and one of these warehouses belonged to the Schuhmacher Company, a new venture in Houston formed by successful businessmen from La Grange, Texas.

John Schuhmacher, at six weeks old, arrived with his parents in Galveston, Texas on November 30, 1846 aboard the sailing vessel James Edward. His parents, Henry and Elizabeth Schuhmacher, immigrated from their home in Coblenz, Germany, and after about a year in Galveston, made their way to La Grange. In 1862, when John Schuhmacher was sixteen years old, he enlisted in the Confederate Army and served at Galveston. After the war, he went to New York where he worked for a time at a vinegar factory before returning to La Grange[146].

About 1868, John Schuhmacher formed a partnership with Frederick Carl "Fritz" Streithoff and they opened a grocery business in

La Grange. Hildegard Cox, a daughter of Fritz Streithoff, recalled that her father kept a dollar from the first sale of their company. John Schuhmacher also retained a 1796 silver dollar as a keepsake from that earliest transaction of the firm. Streithoff did not remain in the partnership for long, and in 1868, he left for other business pursuits and, eventually, owned a saloon on the town square a couple of doors down from Schuhmacher's bank. Streithoff served as the mayor of La Grange and the Fire Chief in subsequent years. This episode, however, was the origin of the Schuhmacher Company that would be managed and controlled by heirs of John Schuhmacher until 1960 when the company was sold to the Fleming Company[147].

With the success of his grocery and general merchantile business, John Schuhmacher also opened a bank. His son Henry Charles Schuhmacher was running the wholesale grocery operations by 1900, and after John Schuhmacher's death in 1907, Henry led the expansion of the Schuhmacher Company into other cities in southeast Texas. The Schuhmacher Company was incorporated in 1903 with capital stock of $250,000. Henry C. Schuhmacher was the president while members of the extended family filled the other executive roles. Charles Perlitz was vice president and Max R. Robson was the company's secretary and treasurer[148].

The Schuhmacher Grocer Company, as they initially called it, opened in Houston in 1908 and the wholesale business's first location was 519-525 Preston Avenue. By 1910, the Schuhmacher Company had moved into their new three story warehouse at 1209 Commerce Avenue, formerly the site of the Schulte House and Brewery. As a recent entrant into the Houston market, the company faced a challenging environment with the other wholesale grocers of the City, including Carson, Sewall and Company, William D. Cleveland and Sons, Henke and Pillot, the Holm-Schmidt Company and Theodore Keller. Nevertheless, by 1913, the Schuhmacher Company had stores in LaGrange, Eagle Lake and Victoria, as well as Houston[149].

Henry Schuhmacher successfully guided the company through the prosperous times of the 1920's and the difficult times of the Depression. On January 1, 1940, the Schuhmacher Company branched out into the retail grocery business and it acquired a controlling interest in the Minimax Stores. Henry Schuhmacher died on September 28, 1940, but his sons John W. and Henry C., Jr., who had worked with their father in the company, took over the family business. Minimax had three grocery stores in Houston in 1935, and under the leadership of John Schuhmacher, the Schuhmacher Company became one of the largest independent retail grocery organizations in Texas with eleven Minimax Super Markets in Harris County by 1948. The slogan promising "minimum prices and maximum quality" seemed to appeal to Houston grocery shoppers[150].

In 1960, the Fleming Companies, Inc. acquired the Schuhmacher Company of Houston. Eventually, the large warehousing operations were relocated to larger facilities on the west side of town. The Schuhmacher Warehouse and the General Warehouse Company's adjacent six story building at 1201 Commerce Avenue became vacant. Both structures, the Schuhmacher Warehouse built in 1910 and the General Warehouse Company building constructed in 1927, were acquired by Harris County and renovated for use by the Sheriff's Department. Today, the two buildings that occupy the whole of SSBB Block 5, comprise the Sheriff's Prisoner Intake Facility[151].

Sheriff's Department Jails

As one paddles downstream under the San Jacinto Street bridge, a modern skywalk or pedestrian bridge can be seen connecting the prisoner processing center on the right bank of the bayou with the stylish, modern building on the left bank. The walkway is without windows and is totally enclosed. It is not meant for sightseeing, but instead, allows the Sheriff's Department to transfer prisoners between the jails on the north side of the bayou to the processing center and the courts on the south side of Buffalo Bayou.

Harris County maintains three jails in this area on the north side of Buffalo Bayou that has been called the "detention zone" by county officials, while other buildings in the vicinity house offices of the Sheriff's Department. The exterior facade of each jail that is visible from the bayou is pleasing and appealing to the eye. Although they have the appearance of exclusive condominiums overlooking the City's famous waterway, most of the windows are false fronts and do not open or allow sunlight in to the cell blocks of the jail.

Situated where White Oak Bayou joins Buffalo Bayou, the Harris County Jail building at 701 N. San Jacinto Street is a striking, nine story red brick high rise with a prominent position facing Allen's Landing and the downtown skyline. Near the front of this building was the site of the ferry operated by W. K. Wilson from about 1837 to 1839. The construction of a bridge across White Oak Bayou at Vine Street about 1839 allowed residents and travelers from the north side to enter the town center via the low water bridge at Milam Street, and the ferry was no longer needed[152].

During most of the nineteenth century, the block on which the jail sits, NSBB Block 51, was relatively undeveloped. Over the years, a few scattered structures occupied the site, but it was usually little used or vacant. Block 51 was owned by James T. D. Wilson after the Civil War and was the site of the Wilson Coal and Wood Yard around 1896, possibly serving the Hartwell Iron Works across the street at that time. The first major development of the site came during the prosperous years after World War I when, in 1927, the Houston Terminal Warehouse and Cold Storage Company built a five story building with a basement on Block 51. Harris County acquired the warehouse building in 1989 and renovated it into a nine story high rise jail facility on the 2.8 acre site[153].

The bayou frontage lots along the north bank of Buffalo Bayou have historically been used by the Direct Navigation Company, the predecessor to the Port of Houston Authority, to support the shipping trade at the City Wharves. From the time that the railroad tracks were laid across White Oak Bayou in the late 1850's, rail sidings and warehouse sheds were in use on the north side lots. During the days of "King Cotton," the cotton sheds and cotton platforms of the Direct Navigation Company assisted the brokers and commission agents in the shipment of millions of bales of cotton out of the Port of Houston. Remnants of these platforms and docks can still be seen near the water line although the development above the bank has taken a much different direction in recent times[154].

The industrialization of the north side of Buffalo Bayou accelerated in the first decade of the twentieth century. The Peden Iron and Steel Company was established in 1890 and incorporated in 1902 by

Edward Andrew Peden and his father David Dantzler Peden. In 1905, the Peden Company built its extensive warehouse at 700 N. San Jacinto Street and, in 1929, it constructed an office building for its operations across the street at 1100 Baker Street. This elegant Art Deco structure was acquired by Harris County in 1992. The four story structure with a basement, known as the Peden Building, houses the offices of the detectives of the Harris County Sheriff's Office[155].

In November, 2002, the 1200 Baker Street Jail was opened. Located immediately east of the Peden Building, the new jail replaced the old Central Jail on Franklin Avenue which had been built in 1982. The new county jail was built with 4,200 beds for prisoners, but by 2007, that was too few accommodations. Although the 1200 Baker Street Jail is a five story facility stretching across one and one half city blocks, plans are underway to add another jail and processing center with a capacity of an additional 2,500 beds. This new jail will be built on NSBB Block 45, east of the 1200 Baker Street jail, on the tract currently used for a parking lot[156].

As the bayou makes a sharp turn to the left beyond the jail parking lot, the razor wire and chain link fence high on the left bank tells you that you have come to the third jail facility on the north side of the bayou. The building backs up to the bayou, but its address is 1307 Baker Street. This is the County's minimum security jail which can house 1,052 inmates in a dormitory style setting. The 4.75 acre site has been used by the Sheriff's Department since 1998 and it shares the facility the Joe Kegans State Jail[157].

The Kegans unit of the state jail system, whose entrance is 707 Top Street, was established in October, 1997, and it has a capacity of 667 prisoners. The Joe Kegans State Jail has a transitional program to assist state jail felons in the process of reintegration into society by teaching them skills to gain and hold meaningful employment[158].

Caroline Street Gully

Beyond the Sheriff's Prisoner Intake building is the closed right of way for the foot of Caroline Street. It and the whole of the block between Caroline Street and Austin Street are currently used as a parking lot. At the end of Austin Street, there is usually water pouring from either or both of the storm drains that empty into Buffalo Bayou. The unimposing concrete panel of civil engineering art at the foot of Austin Street, which is the outlet for both the Austin Street and Caroline Street storm sewers, scarcely reveals the importance of the Caroline Street drainage to the town of Houston. The simple, yet engaging, circle and square storm sewer outlet is all that remains of the large ravine that extended up Caroline Street.

A number of ravines cut through the Houston town site in 1837. Most prominent among these was the large gully at the lower end of Caroline Street. The size of the ravine decreased significantly south of Congress Avenue, and it continued to gradually narrow until it disappeared between Prairie Avenue and Texas Avenue. As the gully flowed toward the bayou, it curved to the east near Commerce Avenue and cut through SSBB Block 6 (of the Houston town plat) to a depth of about forty feet before dropping into Buffalo Bayou near the end of Austin Street[159].

According to James L. Glass, a noted local historian and map maker who studied the history of Houston from 1836 to 1839, the Caroline Street gully may have played a pivotal role in the layout of the town of Houston. On the sixty-two block rectangular plat of the town, the east-west streets of Houston were laid out at angle of North 55 degrees West while the north-south streets were at an angle of South 35 degrees West.

Supposedly, the streets were offset from a true north-south alignment in order to conform to the curvature of Buffalo Bayou and to assure "maximum wharfage and commercial opportunities." However, the Caroline Street gully was a significant topographic feature of the land where the Allen brothers wanted to locate their town. By aligning the plat of the streets to the gully, the Allen's were able to maximize the number of available town lots for sale. Any other alignment meant that several blocks would have been cut diagonally by the gully and many lots would have been unsellable[160].

The Dry Gully, as it was sometimes called, varied from twenty to forty feet deep and was a significant barrier separating the business district from the residential neighborhood of Quality Hill to the east. As a result, bridges were built across the gully at Franklin

Avenue and at Congress Avenue. An 1852 painting by Thomas Flintoff shows St. Vincent Church situated near the corner of Franklin Avenue, just west of the wooden bridge across the Caroline Street gully. John Kennedy, who also owned property on Market Square, operated a grist mill that was located at Congress Avenue and the Caroline Street Gully[161].

After the Civil War, mayor Horace Taylor set out to revitalize the City after a period of neglect due to war. Among the civic projects, which included adding new shell to the streets and the posting of street signs with names on street corners, was the installation of a culvert in the gully at Caroline Street and Congress Avenue. Thus began a process that, by the end of the century, would result in the closing and filling of the Dry Gully. By 1873, the drainage south of Commerce Avenue had been filled in, and only the ravine, winding through Block 6, remained. Block 6 was undeveloped as late as the early 1900's, but by 1924, a major sewer outlet had been constructed at the end of Austin Street and Block 6 was partially covered with the tracks of the International and Great Northern Railroad[162].

Today, Caroline Street shows no evidence of the deep ravine that was its lower end. Block 6 lies vacant and is used as a parking lot. From the street level, no trace of the gully can be seen, and the history of this topographic feature is securely buried beneath tons of fill dirt, asphalt and concrete.

St. Vincent de Paul Catholic Church

In the 1850's, after only about fifteen years of existence, the City of Houston was concentrated around the central business district of the market square and the courthouse square. The Thomas Flintoff painting of the St. Vincent de Paul Catholic Church illustrates how the gully on Caroline Street separated the east side of town from the business district and the church lay on the boundary between it and the residences of the Second Ward. The congregation was established very early in Houston's history when, in December, 1838, a Vincentian priest, the Rev. Jean Timon, arrived from New Orleans to establish a church. Father Timon reported to the Rt. Rev. Anthony

Blanc, Bishop of New Orleans, that about three hundred of Houston's 5,000 inhabitants were Roman Catholic[163].

Nevertheless, plans for the construction of a church began almost immediately. John Kennedy contributed funding to the first church building and donated lots for the cemetery. Construction was completed during the summer of 1842 and the first mass in the new church was celebrated by Bishop Jean Marie Odin on July 17, 1842. The St. Vincent de Paul Catholic Church, located on the west side of Caroline Street near the southwest corner with Franklin Avenue, was rectangular wooden structure with three large windows along the west side, a steeple on the front with a cross on the cupola. The small church measured fifty feet by twenty-five feet and it had twenty pews. In the steeple was a two hundred eighteen pound bell cast for the church by Schmidt and Wilson of Houston in early 1843. The Morning Star of February 18, 1843 reported that the bell was "the best piece of workmanship of the kind ever completed in the Republic" and it bore this inscription: "D. O. M. (To God, the best, the greatest) (cross) St. Vincenti, ora pro nobis (pray for us) Houston, Texas, 1843[164]."

The size of the congregation continued to grow and, by 1866, the two resident clergy were inadequate for the needs of the growing parish. Although the exact number of members of the church was not known, three services were held on Sundays and holidays to accommodate the parishioners. As a result of the increase in the Catholic population in Houston, the construction of Annunciation Church at 1618 Texas Avenue was started in 1867, and the first services were held in November, 1871[165].

After 1871, St. Vincent's became a subsidiary church which still served a few of the German parishioners, and was known as "the German church." The old church was renovated in 1888, and the building opened as a hospital annex to the St. Joseph Infirmary that had been built across the street on Franklin Avenue. Finally, in 1893, old St. Vincent's was torn down and a four story brick building replaced it[166].

The bell from the church was moved to St. Joseph's Church, a new church in the Sixth Ward. However, when the hurricane of 1900 destroyed the bell tower of St Joseph's, the damaged bell was discarded and forgotten. It lay buried beneath the church's rectory until 1940 when a young priest rediscovered the old bell. Eventually, the historic old church bell was relocated to Annunciation Church, where it remains today, inside the Crawford Street entrance[167].

Quality Hill

Although the Caroline Street gully was a natural, rather than an official, demarcation between the districts of the city, it functioned well to give the residents of the neighborhood a sense that they were away from the daily commercial activity of the town. This neighborhood which was centered on an area of high ground to the east of the courthouse became known as Quality Hill because a number of the city's early political leaders, merchants and entrepreneurs lived there. Quality Hill was not a platted subdivision, but it was generally defined as the area bounded by Buffalo Bayou on the north, Crawford Street on the east, Congress Avenue on the south, and Caroline Street on the west[168].

In the late 1840's, prominent citizens of Houston, those who formed the socially elite of the city, built large homes overlooking the bayou in Quality Hill. William J. Hutchins, the pioneer merchant and owner of Hutchins House lived at Franklin Avenue and LaBranch Street. John Dickinson, merchant, cotton factor and City Council member, lived across the street on La Branch Street. Jacob De Cordova, an early Texas real estate investor, surveyor and newspaper publisher, owned a home near the modern Minute Maid Park[169].

The architectural styles in Quality Hill ranged from the small, vernacular Gulf Coast cottages to large two-story Greek Revival homes. Charles S. Longcope, a steamboat captain, owned the most beautiful residence in the city at the time at 109 Chenevert Street. In early 1870's, he remodeled the house which was originally built by Michael Floeck in 1859. Longcope added stucco to the house's brick facade and imported cast filigree iron balconies from New Orleans which he placed across the front. Cornelius Ennis, a cotton merchant who came to Houston in 1839, built a house on Quality Hill, at 1618 Congress Avenue at Jackson Street, in 1871, that had features of the pre-Civil War Greek Revival and decorative elements of the Victorian period[170].

By the 1880's, Quality Hill was the silk stocking district in the Second Ward with great homes shaded by big oaks that lined the narrow thoroughfares and gardens of flowers screened by tall hedges. Rambling and turreted, mid-Victorian mansions had intricate gingerbread ornamentation, ornate railings and cupolas while cast-iron lions and other ingenious devices were used as hitching posts[171].

Eventually, though, commercial expansion and railroad construction began to squeeze out the residential area, and Quality Hill residents migrated farther south and west toward the edge of town. Fred Smith, whose residence occupied the entire block on Caroline Street between Commerce Avenue and Franklin Avenue, sold his home in 1889 and the site became part of the large International and Great Northern Railroad depot on Franklin Avenue[172].

Houston City Electric Street Railway

Throughout most of the nineteenth century, the block bordering the bayou between Austin Street and La Branch Street had no development on it other than a dwelling or two. However, when the Houston City Street Railway decided to introduce electric street cars to Houston, the company built its power generating facility there, on SSBB Block 7.

As early as 1868, mule drawn streetcars were introduced to Houston, but it was not until May, 1874 that the Houston City Street Railway marked the actual beginning of organized rail service. Electric streetcars promised to be a major improvement over the mule drawn cars, and on January 10, 1891, the Houston City Street Railway bought Block 7 and the improvements on the site from the Houston Gas Light Company for $15,000. In May, 1891, the machinery for the Houston City Street Railway's electric streetcars, including boilers and a 270 ton Corliss engine, arrived and was being set up in the new building on Commerce Avenue. The operation of electric streetcars began on June 12, 1891[173].

Public transportation was as difficult a business then as it is today, and the Houston City Street Railway went into receivership in 1896. The assets of the Houston City Street Railway was sold on the courthouse door by special commissioner John H. Kirby on May 5, 1896. The reorganized company became Houston Electric Railway, and the system's power house on Block 7 was upgraded to two dynamos and two 300 HP engines[174].

After a receivership in 1901, the new company, called the Houston Electric Company, fitted the electric power generating station for the streetcars with a dynamo room operating with a 1600 HP engine. Electric streetcar service operated several lines through the 1920's, but with competition from automobiles and motorized vehicles, the company introduced busses in 1924 to offer more flexibility to its ridership. Yet, the trend toward the automobile for transportation was overwhelming. From then on, the electric streetcar service went into decline due to the popularity of the personal automobile, and the Houston Electric Company made its last run in streetcars on June 9, 1940. The Houston Electric Company facility on Commerce Avenue was torn down after the company closed[175]. Block 7 remained a vacant lot during the 1950's and 1960's, but it found a new use in the early 1970's as a parking lot.

Houston Gas Works

Houston experienced a significant depression of economic activity during the years of the Civil War. With the war's end, the local business leaders sought to revive the once booming economy, and after less than a year, there was some sign that they would be successful. In May, 1866, the local newspaper reported a feeling of optimism in Houston because of surge of new business development in the town. By this time, both the Eureka Cotton Manufacturing Company and the Houston City Mills were under construction. Other new businesses, including the Houston Insurance Company and the Houston City Street Railway Company, uplifted the prospects for the city's future. In this environment, a promising new utility, the Houston Gas Light Company, was organized in September, 1866[176].

The Houston Gas Light Company set out to supplant kerosene as the primary fuel for house and street lighting, and thereby, provide a much safer product that would reduce to a minimum the dangers of fires caused by the use of oil for lamps. Manufactured coal gas is created by the simple process of heating coal which produces a flammable gas. That gas, a combination of carbon monoxide, hydrogen and other gases was stored in a holder or gasometer for later distribution[177].

The company's twenty-five year charter, granted by City Council on December 14, 1867, permitted it the right to build a gas manufacturing plant on the "Armory block bounded by Maple, Magnolia, Crawford and Jackson" streets (SSBB Block 108). The company must have found an adjacent tract more suitable since the gas plant was actually built in 1867 on SSBB Block 8 instead. The gas works began making coal gas in the spring of 1868[178].

The manufactured gas which the Houston Gas Light Company produced was a mixture of coal, oil and water. It had a low BTU content and gave off weak illumination, but it was suitable for street lights and home lighting. Although manufactured gas may have been a more convenient means of lighting, it was more expensive than the alternatives of kerosene and whale oil lanterns. The Houston Gas Light Company supplied gas under its exclusive charter without competition for nearly two decades. In the early 1880's, electricity for lighting was introduced by the Houston Electric Light and Power Company and the competition between the two light companies became fierce. Eventually, however, the Houston Gas Light Company acquired its rival, the Houston Electric Light and Power Company, on June 21, 1887. The Houston Electric Light and Power Company was then sold to the Citizens' Electric Light and Power Company on January 7, 1891[179].

The improved technology of manufactured gas and the company's successful operations enabled it to expand its plant and facilities on Block 8, along the bayou. Several buildings comprised the facility by 1896, including an office, an engineering shop, a purifying shop, a retorts room and two coal sheds. Two large, cylindrical gas holder tanks, called gasometers, were also located on the tract. By 1924, further expansions had encompassed the adjacent blocks to the east (SSBB Blocks 107 and 109) where the company, renamed the Houston Gas and Fuel Company, had two additional steel gasometers and other support structures[180].

Manufactured gas was produced from the early nineteenth century through the mid-twentieth century. The emergence of the oil industry in Texas brought natural gas to Houston in 1926 and it became available for both domestic and industrial uses. Between 1930 to mid-1950, companies began to convert to natural gas when it became more available as a fuel. In Houston, the Houston Gas and Fuel Company became the United Gas Corporation and it still maintained a warehouse on Block 8 although the gas plant and associated buildings were removed from the site by 1951. Today, a small, one story warehouse still sits on Block 8, and the sign on the fence says that it is the property of Center Point Energy[181].

Beth Israel Synagogue

The Handbook of Texas states that a Jewish house of worship was established in Frost Town by 1854[182]. That statement, however, appears to be an slight overstatement of the facts. There is no documentary evidence that a synagogue was ever located in the Frost Town Subdivision, the eight blocks laid out on the ten acres of land purchased by Jonathan B. Frost from the Allen brothers in 1837.

The common practice of many local historians to speak of Frost Town in the context of a much larger neighborhood has only compounded the problem. This "greater Frost Town area" has no specific boundaries, but, at times, includes areas south of the Frost Town Subdivision as far as what is now the George R. Brown Convention Center. It is in this area, south of Frost Town, an area that is more appropriately a part of the Second Ward, that there was, indeed, the center of Houston's Jewish community during the nineteenth century. This synagogue, built about 1869, was only two blocks south of Buffalo Bayou at the corner of Crawford Street and Franklin Avenue, but the story of the Jewish community in Houston begins much earlier[183].

The first Jewish settler in Houston has generally been recognized to be Eugene Joseph Chimene. Born in Bordeaux, France about 1820, Chimene and his brother immigrated to New Orleans. Eugene made his way to Texas and, according to many sources, fought at the Battle of San Jacinto (although he is not listed on the rosters of the San Jacinto Museum or other lists of members of the Texian Army)[184].

Several sources from the late nineteenth century and early twentieth century repeat the claims that Eugene Joseph Chimene settled "in Houston in 1835" (although the city did not start to take shape until December, 1836), fought at San Jacinto, and was one of Sam Houston's escorts on trip to plan Austin City. These claims seem to derive from a single common source which cites "family records" to document this information. One source also says that Eugene Chimene served in the Mexican War. Yet, without additional documentation of these events, the validity of the assertion that Chimene was Houston's first Jewish resident cannot be confirmed[185].

Eventually, however, Chimene did settle in the Houston. Working as a "peddler of notions," Chimene made enough money by 1847 to return to France and marry his sixteen year old third cousin Matilda Chimene. In 1850, Eugene Chimene returned to Houston with his bride and their young son Alfred who was born in 1848 while the couple was still in France. The young couple engaged in a variety of businesses, including a dairy, a fruit store and a restaurant, in order to support their growing family. Daughter Aleda was born in 1850 after their return to Houston. Alphonse came along in 1852, Caroline in 1853 and Leah in 1855. In October, 1860, Eugene J. Chimene worked as a carpenter and he was able to accumulate personal assets of $600. The Civil War, however, devastated Chimene's businesses and finances[186].

After the war, Chimene worked as a produce broker on Congress Avenue between Austin Street and LaBranch Street. His family continued to grow during the war with the birth of sons Ferdinand and Armand and afterwards with Albert, born in 1867, and Caliste, the last of their eight children who was born in 1869. By 1870, Eugene Chimene returned to the carpentry trade and, then, he opened an upholstering business on Congress Avenue. In 1873, Alfred Chimene joined his father in the business and worked as an upholsterer in the shop. They also began to sell furniture from the store[187].

Eugene Chimene died on October 4, 1875, and after his death, his widow Matilda and her sons operated the furniture store for several more years. Alfred Chimene opened a mattress factory on the southeast corner of Austin Street and Preston Avenue, and

Alphonse Chimene was the furniture dealer at the store on Congress Avenue[188].

By 1879, Alfred had established the Alfred Chimene Company at 19 Congress Avenue, then later at 73 Main Street, between Prairie Avenue and Preston Avenue, as a manufacturer and a wholesale and retail dealer in furniture and house furnishing goods. The company employed the whole family as the other Chimene brothers took roles in the business. Alphonse was the manager. Caliste Chimene was a collector for the company. Ferdinand Chimene was the cabinet maker and, later, the delivery clerk at the company, and Albert Chimene was the bookkeeper[189].

In 1886, the family company reorganized under the younger brother Albert. The Albert Chimene Company sold furniture and house furnishing goods from a location at 89 Congress Avenue between Main Street and Fannin Street. The eldest son Alfred worked for Albert Chimene, as did Alphonse and Caliste. Armand worked as a collector for the company. Ferdinand Chimene went on his own as a furniture mover[190].

The Albert Chimene and Company became a partnership between Albert and older brother Alfred in 1894 and they moved to a new building two blocks east at 1207 Congress Avenue. The business had expanded into carpets as well as furniture and house furnishings. They occupied all of the Jones Building and the third floor of the Shaw Building next door[191].

At a time when the Chimene business was prospering, they were caught up in one of the most tragic episodes in Houston's early history. On October 16, 1894, a fire began in a San Jacinto Street boarding house. The flames soon spread to other buildings on the block including the St. Joseph Infirmary and three new three story brick buildings facing Congress Avenue, the Shaw Building, the Jones Building and the Rich Building. The fire continued to spread despite the efforts of the fire brigade and ultimately, the fire damaged nearly every building on the block, including the store of W. L. Foley, a leading merchant[192].

In all, nine buildings were burned for loss of $103,000. The loss of furniture and merchandise stock totaled $270,000. The heaviest losses were those of W. L. Foley who had just received a shipment of new stock worth $150,000. The second largest loss from the fire was that of the Chimene store in which furniture stock valued at $60,000 was destroyed[193].

Far worse than the material goods lost was the death of two nuns at the infirmary. Although all of the patients at the infirmary were moved to safety, Sister Dolores and a novitiate Jennie Ellis lost their lives during the rescue attempts. This was the first loss of life in a fire in Houston in many years and the effect was shocking. Sadly, the initial reports were that the fire was believed to have been set by an incendiary in the San Jacinto boarding house[194].

The Chimene's regrouped after the fire and operated the furniture business as a family venture through the first years of the twentieth century. Ferdinand Chimene, however, branched out on his own and opened the Houston Moving and Storage Company in 1895, and by 1900, he was a dealer in coal, wood and kindling[195].

After the death of their mother about 1902, the family business began to fall apart and the brothers sought out individual business interests. Alphonse Chimene went to work as a railroad ticket broker and dealer in second hand furniture on Washington Avenue. Armand Chimene became an agent for the Southwestern Life Insurance Company, and later held similar positions with the New York Life Insurance Company and the Guarantee Life Insurance Company. Caliste Chimene became the head salesman for B. H. Greenberg and Son. Alfred Chimene became the manager of the Globe Furniture Company[196].

Albert Chimene became the manager of the William H. Opet Company in 1907. Opet was the father of Caliste Chimene's wife Flora and a furniture merchant in Yoakum, Texas. When the Opet Furniture Company, located at 514 Travis Street, was incorporated in 1909 with $10,000 of capital, James A. Breeding was the president and Albert Chimene was the secretary and treasurer of the enterprise[197].

By 1920, the Chimene family interests in furniture and home furnishings were over. The two youngest brothers were still employed, but not in the old business. Caliste I. Chimene was a traveling salesman, selling floor covering, while Albert J. Chimene worked as a salesman for insurance company[198].

Not surprisingly, Houston's potential for enterprise attracted large numbers of merchants and entrepreneurs in the late 1830's.

Among the most prominent was Jacob De Cordova, who successfully pursued business as a real estate investor, a surveyor and a
newspaper publisher. Born in Jamaica about 1808, De Cordova was
a devout Sephardic Jew, that is, a Jew who is of Spanish or Portu-
guese descent. He lived in Pennsylvania from about 1832 to 1836
before moving his family to Louisiana where they resided until
about 1838. He immigrated to Texas after that and received a third
class headright of 320 acres on December 12, 1839. De Cordova
was to play an important role in the Jewish community of Houston[199].

As an original member of the Houston Chamber of Commerce
when it formed in 1840, Jacob De Cordova became influential in
local politics and was elected a city alderman. In 1847, he was
elected as Harris County's representative to the state legislature. By
1850, De Cordova, at age 42, was living with his wife and five
children on the edge of the well to do neighborhood Quality Hill in
a house that was located on the site of today's Minute Maid Park. In
1852, however, De Cordova left Houston and moved to Austin[200].

It was through De Cordova's influence that a group of Jewish
immigrants came to Houston in the early 1840's. In 1844, these
Jews, bound together by religious belief into a community, purchased a tract of land on the San Felipe Road, just west of the City
Cemetery, for a Jewish Cemetery which is known today as the Beth
Israel Cemetery. With this core group of believers, Jacob De Cordova, in 1845, helped establish Houston's first local Minyon[201].

A minyon is a quorum of ten men required for the observance of
certain Jewish prayers. It derives from the biblical story of Sodom
and Gomorrah in which Abraham pleads for God to save the cities
from destruction if only ten just men could be found in them.
Considering the town's proliferation of saloons and it's reputation at
the time for gambling and other vices, the comparison may be apt[202].

In the census of 1850, there were seventeen Jewish adults,
eleven men and six women, in Houston, comprising about one
percent of the white population of 1,863 persons. The community
continued to grow and the Hebrew Congregation of Houston was
formed in 1854 and was chartered by the State Legislature on
December 28, 1859 with a membership of twenty-two adults, most
of whom came to Texas from western Europe. The Hebrew Congregation was an Orthodox congregation and it could be described as a

typical German Jewish community. Services were held in a room on Austin Street, between Texas Avenue and Prairie Avenue, until a frame building on La Branch Street and Prairie Avenue was built for their worship services[203].

By 1860, there were sixty-eight Jewish adults and forty children in Houston. Most of them came to Houston among the waves of German immigrants to Texas during the 1840's and 1850's. And, like many Germans, they settled in the Frost Town area and the Second Ward amid their German speaking neighbors. As observant Orthodox Jews, they generally tended to live within walking distance of their synagogue as prescribed by the tenets of their faith[204].

With the steady increase in the size of their congregation, the Jewish community planned for a prominent synagogue for their services. By 1869, the construction of a temple on the southeast corner of Crawford Street and Franklin Avenue had begun. The synagogue, facing Crawford Street, was an imposing gabled structure with a twenty-five foot ceiling. Five tall windows along the length of each side of the temple provided light to the main hall of the building[205].

The completion of this elegant and, at last, permanent place of worship in 1874 did not mean that the Hebrew Congregation was free of internal controversy. Many of the older German members of the congregation preferred a version of their faith that seemed more in accord with the style of life they had come to know in Houston, and by 1877, the congregation had begun a transformation to classical Reformed Judaism[206].

A group of new Eastern European immigrants, mostly from Russia and Poland, however, were opposed to reforms adopted by the congregation, and they broke away to form the Orthodox Congregation of Adath Yeshurun in 1889. They built a new brick synagogue and associated frame buildings a few city blocks south of Temple Beth Israel on land that became Union Station in 1910[207].

It may have been at this time of division in the Jewish community that the Hebrew Congregation of Houston began to identify itself more precisely as the Congregation Beth Israel. Although some historians say that the congregation called itself Beth Israel as early as 1854, the name does not become prominent in public documents until the early twentieth century when the synagogue is identified specifically as the Temple Beth Israel, perhaps to distinguish it from the Adath Yeshurun and the other congregations that subsequently arose, such as Congregation Adath Emeth on Houston Avenue in the Sixth Ward[208].

During the last decade of the nineteenth century, the Hebrew Congregation of Houston, more specifically, the Congregation Beth Israel, continued to flourish at its location at Franklin Avenue and Crawford Street. By 1885, a meeting hall for the congregation had been built on the lot south of the synagogue. This hall, constructed with a unique architectural design of its front facade, was named Montefiore Hall by 1896 in honor of Moses Montefiore, a prominent British Jew who supported the causes of the Jewish people around the world[209].

Moses Montefiore grew up in London, was very successful in business and retired in 1824 to devote himself to community affairs. His humanitarian interest in the poor and in the Jews in Eretz Israel resulted in him being knighted by Queen Victoria. One of Montefiore's favorite causes was Eretz Israel, "the Land of Israel", which refers to the area west of the Jordan River and south of present day Lebanon. Montefiore aided efforts to settle Jews in this land which was a part of Palestine at that time. He died a few months after his one hundredth birthday in 1885. The fulfillment of the dream of a Jewish homeland would not come for another sixty-three years, until 1948[210].

By the turn of the twentieth century, the Frost Town Subdivision, the Frost Town area and adjacent areas of the Second Ward had become a largely commercial and industrial district. The residential neighborhoods declined and were inhabited predominantly by low income families and the poor. Families with the financial means to do so followed the trend to move south of the downtown district, and their institutions relocated to these more prosperous areas of town. Congregation Beth Israel moved to a location on Lamar Avenue in 1908[211].

Subsequent shifts in residential patterns ensued as well. The congregation built a new temple farther south at Austin Street and Holman Avenue in 1925. And, today, the Congregation Beth Israel, which formally changed its name from the Hebrew Congregation of

Houston in 1945, is located in southwest Houston at 5600 N. Braeswood Boulevard[212].

By 1924, the former synagogue on the corner of Franklin Avenue and Crawford Street housed a blacksmith shop. The adjacent hall became a tent making business and electric motor repair operation. In 1951, the former location of the synagogue was a filling station owned by a predecessor of Exxon, and a tent and awning factory occupied the former hall. Today, the lots are vacant and offer an excellent view of the center field corner of Minute Maid Park[213].

Arsenal Block

At the end of Crawford Street, Buffalo Bayou makes a dramatic turn to the left and flows north, away from the downtown area. As you approach this turn from the direction of Allen's Landing, the view of the right bank is nothing extraordinary. The bank of the bayou at the turn is full of concrete fill and debris. The access ramps to the Elysian Viaduct rise gradually upwards from right to left, a few feet above the street level. Few people take note of this place because today it is totally unremarkable.

In historic times, however, the city block in this location was the site of the Arsenal of the Republic of Texas. The Houston Arsenal, or Armory, was established by the Army in 1837 to house the weapons of the Republic of Texas. Many of the items kept in the arsenal were rifles and arms captured from the Mexican army at the Battle of San Jacinto. In May, 1838, the Texas army contracted with Joseph Daniels, a Houston carpenter and contractor, to build an arsenal on the block at the north end of Crawford Street[214].

Initially, the arsenal was set up in a blacksmith shop since much of the work of the arsenal was the repair of the weapons used by members of the army. Daniels then built a special purpose, sturdy log structure on SSBB Block 108, Lots 1, 2 and 3. This building was 18 feet by 30 feet and made of nine inch hewn pine logs with a heavy oak door. By October, 1838, other buildings had been added to the complex to provide facilities for workshops, artillery sheds and a magazine. At its greatest extent, the arsenal was under the direction of a lieutenant with nine civilian employees, a master armorer, two armorers, a gunsmith and four laborers[215].

As the arsenal of the Republic, it was subject to the political policies of the day. When the capital of Texas was moved to Austin, the arsenal went with it. In February, 1840, most of the weapons stored at the Houston Arsenal were shipped to the new arsenal at Austin, and the armory facility on Block 108 closed[216].

Nevertheless, throughout the nineteenth century, that block retained the aura of the Republic's arsenal, and for decades, Block 108 was referred to in newspaper accounts and in deed records as "the Arsenal Block." Everyone at the time knew exactly where they meant when they said that. For example, in 1859, Peter Floeck transferred land nearby which he referenced as "the portion of land known as adjoining the Arsenal Block in the City of Houston." Such a shorthand name was probably made it easier for locals to identify the place instead of formally calling it the block "bounded by Maple, Magnolia, Crawford and Jackson" streets[217].

In the nineteenth century, when adventurous young men would actually swim in Buffalo Bayou, one of the most famous swimming holes on the bayou was the Arsenal Swimming Hole. As the name implies, the swimming hole was at the foot of La Branch Street and it lay in front of the Arsenal Block. Interestingly enough, the Arsenal Swimming Hole was very wide and very deep due to its location in the bend of the waterway where the currents are strong. This hole was for only the very best swimmers[218].

At the time of the founding of Houston in 1836, there were several large ravines that cut into the town blocks on the south side of the bayou. Block 108 was bisected by a deep gully crossing the tract from Jackson Street to Buffalo Bayou. The arsenal buildings were built along Magnolia Avenue (after about 1950, it is Ruiz Street) and occupied some of the only lots in the block not affected by the gully. The gully, which cut a diagonal across the block from the southeast corner to the bayou at the northwest corner, was quite large and deep. It prevented the full development of the block for decades, and even today the block is a storage lot and a parking lot[219].

A few months after Hurricane Ike in 2008 had churned up the waters and eroded some of the banks along the bayou, a long forgotten story of the Arsenal Block was revealed. As the flood waters associated with the storm receded, an old wooden wagon wheel was discovered on a sandbar at the Arsenal Block curve. The intricately hand-carved hub indicates that the wheel might date from the nineteenth century.

The wheel is fifty-six inches in diameter. The spokes are twenty-two inches in length. The hub appears to be hand carved and not turned on a lathe. The axle hole is approximately two inches in diameter and the outside measurements of the hub are ten inches long and eight inches in diameter. The outer rim surface of the felloe (the exterior rim or a segment of the rim of a wheel supported by the spokes) measures 1¼ inches and the rim is two inches thick. Judging from the small width of the wheel, it was a light duty carriage or wagon that may have served as a personal car for one of the many businessmen who lived in the upper Third Ward.

The question is: why was it here?

Prior to the introduction of the automobile in the early 1900's, carriages were a common means of personal transportation, and carriage factories and repair shops were found in town. In fact, there was a wagon wheel maker (Mosehart & Keller Company, Wagon and Carriage Factory) just south of the bayou at Caroline Street and Franklin Avenue operating in the late 1800's and early 1900's. Even closer, an existing building in the 100 block of Crawford Street, at Commerce Avenue, is the former Eller Wagon Works that dates from about 1910[220].

Another clue to the story comes from a newspaper article from the February 25, 1896 issue of the Galveston Daily News which says that in its regular weekly meeting, the Houston City Council passed a resolution that trash and garbage was allowed to be disposed of in the gully at the end of Crawford Street. That gully, which was just a block away from the Eller Wagon Works, is our Arsenal Block gully[221].

Seldom do we think about how the City handles the pick up of garbage and how it disposes of it today. But, the management of solid waste in Houston has gone through a number of phases since the City was founded. In many ways, the practice of garbage disposal in Houston mirrors the practices that were common in other cities in the country at the same time. While today, even though recycling is more common than ever, we dispose of a large percentage of our garbage in sanitary landfills.

For much of the nineteenth century, the City hired scavengers to collect household garbage and dispose of it. Scavenger contracts were competitively bid and highly sought after since the scavenger could keep anything of value that was collected. Much of the waste was then simply dumped in designated places, such as ravines. Within the city limits, the City Council authorized dumping of garbage in many of the ravines and gullies along Buffalo Bayou. Such was the case with the Arsenal Gully. In 1896, it became an authorized landfill site[222].

That brings us to the mystery of the wagon wheel. Perhaps the wheel had simply had worn out, and the owner brought his carriage to the wagon shop for a wheel replacement. The broken wheel was probably thrown away, or thrown into the gully, after 1896 when the City sanctioned the use of the gully for a trash dump. The carriage maker and repair shop could have been cleaning out their bin of replaced carriage wheels and simply tossed our wheel into the dump. Slowly, over time, the wheel settled to the bottom of the gully's mud, even after the gully was filled in. The wheel lay in the mud for a century until the rains of Hurricane Ike scoured the bottom mud of the bayou and released the wheel from its muddy bonds. It floated up and settled gently on the opposite bank as the water subsided. There it lay, waiting to tell its story.

And, like it or not, the garbage disposal practices of the late nineteenth century still impacting Buffalo Bayou today.

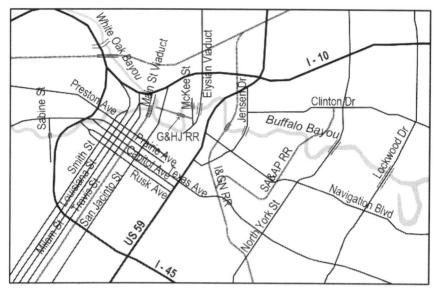

Map by Rachel A. Garcia

The Frost Town subdivision was establish outside of the city limits in 1838 near what we know today as McKee Street. Set in the "horseshoe-shaped" bend in Buffalo Bayou, Frost Town soon encompassed a larger neighborhood that extended along the south bank of the bayou from Crawford Street (at the end of the Elysian Viaduct) east to near the location of the International and Great Northern Railroad tracks.

Chapter 10
Frost Town

Floeck's Brewery

The place where Buffalo Bayou turns sharply to the left at the Arsenal Block, a tract of land makes a point of contact with the bayou. This point is the tip of a triangular lot that is formed with Maple Avenue on the south, McKee Street on the east and the former William F. Hodge property on the north. After Peter Gabel and Henry Schulte dissolved their brewery partnership in 1854, Schulte established a brewery on this site in partnership with F. P. Hoffman. The Schulte and Hoffman partnership dissolved in 1855 and Schulte built another brewery on San Jacinto Street.

Martin Floeck acquired the Hoffman and Schulte brewery in 1859, and he operated the brewery until 1867. This tract of land became associated with the Floeck and Settegast families for the remainder of the nineteenth century. During the twentieth century, the land was the focus of efforts to help the Mexican immigrant community through the settlement house movement and the public school programs centered at this location. But, the story begins with the Floeck family.

In 1847, Michael and Katarina Doetch Floeck immigrated to Texas from Mülheim near Coblenz with their seven children: Anna, Martin, Elizabeth, Peter, Carl, Michael and Nicolas. The family settled initially in northern Harris County on 150 acres on little Cypress Creek which Michael Floeck bought from Mark Shaben on August 3, 1847 for $85. About a year later, though, the Floeck family moved to Houston[1].

Michael Floeck and his family immigrated under the H. F. Fischer-Burchard Miller Colonization Contract prior to September 1, 1847. As a consequence, Floeck was issued Certificate No. 474 for 640 acres in McCulloch County on June 25, 1850. At that time,

Floeck was living in Harris County and did not intend to move to the Hill Country. Instead, he applied for the land grant in June, 1850 and then sold his rights to the land grant to Matthias D. Conklin for $75. Conklin patented the land in 1858. Floeck had chosen to make his home in Houston[2].

The Floeck family lived in the Second Ward and the oldest daughter Anna married Christopher Behler, a butcher from Germany. The fifty-five year old Michael listed his occupation as lumberman for the 1850 census, but he soon began to buy property in the Moody Addition and vicinity. On September 15, 1852, Floeck bought from Charles Stephanes the three-eighths of an acre in the Moody Addition, later, on March 1, 1853, he bought the Charles Stephanes homestead containing two lots or about one hundred square feet[3].

Michael Floeck died in late 1853, and on January 7, 1854, the family, led by Catherine (Katarina), agreed on the division of his estate among his wife and the children. Catherine received one third of the real and personal property while the remaining two thirds were divided equally among the children. Catherine Floeck, the widow, entered into the agreement for herself, as guardian for her minor children: Peter, Charles, Michael and Nicolas Floeck, and also for daughter Catherine Floeck who had remained in Europe. The older children, Martin Floeck and Anna Floeck Behler, represented themselves in the division of the Floeck estate[4].

By the end of the 1850's, the two oldest sons, Martin and Peter, were actively involved in the business and politics of the City. In 1857, Peter Floeck and his wife Elizabeth Schultz Floeck, after their marriage on February 28, 1857, combined their resources of $600 and opened a bakery, confectionery, restaurant and coffee house business. The place burned down at the end of the first year, but they rebuilt it and successfully operated the business for twenty years. Prior to the Civil War, Peter Floeck served two terms as Alderman from the Second Ward, but did not hold public office after the war[5].

Martin Floeck and Peter Floeck purchased the former Hoffman and Schulte Brewery in 1859. On July 1, 1859, F. P. Hoffmann sold the brewery property to them for $4,000 after a contentious end to his partnership with Henry Schulte. Schulte had begun his career as a brewer with Peter Gabel in 1850, and in 1854, he left the partnership with Gabel to form his own brewery with Hoffman. On June 30, 1854, Hoffman and Schulte bought the triangular tract of land adjoining the Arsenal Block which was bounded on the north by land originally sold to W. F. Hodge and on the south by land sold to J. W. Moody. The point of the triangle touched Buffalo Bayou. A sixty foot strip of land from the Hodge tract was added to this brewery tract by a conveyance from Peter Gabel to Henry Schulte on December 1, 1854[6].

The Hoffman and Schulte Brewery apparently had financial problems and the partnership dissolved about 1855. Hoffman filed a law suit in District Court against Schulte, and the court, on December 9, 1856, ordered a receiver to sell all of the property and improvements belonging to Hoffman and Schulte's Brewery at auction. An appeal of the judgment was upheld by the Texas Supreme Court on February 19, 1857, and on April 7, 1857, William L. Withers, the court appointed receiver, sold the property for the high bid of $3,000 which was placed by F. P. Hoffman himself. Hoffman then sold the brewery property to Martin and Peter Floeck[7].

In the fall of 1859, the Floeck brothers executed a couple of land transactions that would allow each them to establish their business interests in the City. On November 22, 1859, the brothers essentially made a land swap that gave Martin control of the brewery property. Peter Floeck relinquished his interest in the Hoffman and Schulte Brewery property that they acquired during the previous July, and Martin deeded to Peter a brick house he had built on Lots 8, 9 and 10 in Block 166 SSBB, property which he had purchased from W. R. Baker on February 17, 1859[8].

Peter Floeck sold the brick home at 109 Chenevert Street, on the corner with Commerce Avenue, to Charles S. Longcope, a Mississippi River steamboat captain, in 1865. The C. S. Longcope house was remodeled in the early 1870's. Stucco was added to its brick fascade and decorative New Orleans-type iron balconies were built across the front[9].

Martin Floeck then went into the brewery business and, by 1860, he employed four brewers who lived on the premises. The shortages of agricultural products during the Civil War, however, put a strain on the business. Martin even had to advertise for barley "at the highest price in either Confederate money or specie." After war, he ran into personal problems as a result of his conviction for man-slaughter in early 1867. Fortunately, Martin Floeck was granted a pardon by Governor Throckmorton on January 13, 1867, only a few days after his conviction. A final calamity occurred on June 20, 1867, when the well known brewery of Martin Floeck near the foot of Jackson Street caught fire. The building and its entire contents were destroyed for an uninsured loss of $20,000. The Floeck residence, which was adjacent to the brewery building, was saved[10].

Martin Floeck continued to live in the large house on the brewery tract. He and his wife Anna, known as Jennie, raised their children, Katie, William, Charlie, Robert, Adolph and Ameila in that house. In 1870, Martin Floeck was moderately successful and he reported assets of $18,000 in the census. On March 21, 1876, while serving as an Alderman, Martin Floeck died at his home in the Second Ward. The fifty year old Floeck had been ill for a week or two before passing away of hepatic cirrhosis. He was buried in Glenwood Cemetery on the following day from his home at the foot of Jackson Street in the triangular brewery tract[11].

Jennie Floeck, the widow of Martin, continued to reside at their home which, by 1886, was numbered as 9 Maple Street. Her son Adolph who worked as a produce commission merchant also lived at the family home with her until her death on September 5, 1887. In September, 1889, the Floeck children transferred their interests in the old family home to Julius J. Settegast, their brother in law. Julius Settegast had married Katie Floeck in 1867. He had extensive business enterprises in Houston including the family cattle business, a lumber yard, and a paint and hardware store. Settegast also owned over a hundred rent houses, and the large two story home on the brewery tract became one of those. By 1907, there were thirteen other dwellings besides the family home on the tract[12].

In 1902, the City built the Rusk School in the Second Ward. Located on the northwest corner of Commerce Avenue and Hamilton Street, the Rusk School was named for Thomas Jefferson Rusk, one of Texas' first U. S. Senators. About 1906, Sybil Campbell, a teacher at the school, persuaded the Woman's Club of Houston to build a free kindergarten and day nursery for working mothers. The first location of the free kindergarten was in a single story building on the southeast corner of Gable Street and Maple Place. In 1907, the free kindergarten moved across the street to the old Settegast home[13].

The education and social programs of the free kindergarten led to the establishment of the Houston Settlement Association in 1907, and the Women's Club turned over the kindergarten to the association. The settlement house movement, which began in the United States about 1889, enlisted single, college-educated women and older married women to perform charity work in voluntary associations. On May 5, 1909, the Houston Settlement Association opened their new home, the former Floeck/Settegast house on Maple Street. Named the Rusk Settlement House because of the kindergarten's affiliation with the Rusk School, the organization's programs emphasized education with the kindergarten and they taught cooking and sewing classes as well as English classes[14].

The Rusk School building, located about two blocks southeast of the Rusk Settlement House, caught fire in the evening of December 15, 1910 and was destroyed for a loss of $40,000. Temporary sheds were hastily constructed to house the students on the site. The City then bought the Settegast property as a location for a new school. The old Floeck house was then moved to the back of the lot on Gable Street. A modern, new reinforced concrete and brick school opened April 23, 1913 and became the new Rusk School. The building's outstanding feature was a large auditorium in the central section of the structure with twin stairs in the front[15].

As early as 1910, the Rusk Settlement House provided a range of social services to the Mexican immigrants who came to the City to work in the expanding industries along the ship channel. The Second Ward became the center of the Mexican community and the Rusk Elementary School soon became known as the "Mexican School." But, the services of the Rusk Settlement House extended to a wide array of newcomers to the City and by 1916, it was serving persons of twenty-three nationalities[16].

From the 1910's to the 1950's, the Rusk School was the primary educational institution for the Second Ward children, especially those of the Mexican community. However, by the mid-1950's, the area around the school was redeveloped for the construction of the Elysian Viaduct. The City bought the two story school and its 2.9

acres from the school district in 1955 for $208,819. It then took most of the playground for use as the right of way for the Elysian Viaduct[17].

The Rusk School Building was offered for sale by the City of Houston on May 23, 1956, and the school district replaced the Rusk Elementary School with new building on a new block in 1959. The building had no takers and eventually was torn down. The land became a part of the City of Houston Public Works Department, and today it was used as a repair shop and parking for the Sewer Division. The site bears little or no recognition of its long and storied history[18].

Gable Street Power Plant

Tucked away on a forgotten corner of Buffalo Bayou, the ghostly structure of the Gable Street Power Plant sat in quiet retirement for decades prior to its demolition in April, 2011. Once the throbbing electrical pulse of Houston, the plant had been decommissioned for over two decades. Yet, for over fifty years, this one facility provided a large percentage of the electricity that the city could consume.

Although the story of electric power in Houston begins in the early 1880's, at a time when candles and gas lights were much more common than electric lights, the story of the ten acres of land on which the plant sits takes us back to the earliest days of the Town of Houston.

In the aftermath of the Battle of San Jacinto, the Texas Army was disbanded over the period from May through the summer of 1836. Many of the young men who enlisted or who were recruited to come join the fight for Texas found themselves on the prairie of southeast Texas without land or homes. But, their future was promising. The rumors that Augustus C. Allen was planning to establish a new town in the area were widespread among those who remained. Allen was meeting with the Harris family near the ruins of Harrisburg and he also was communicating with William T. Austin in Columbia in an attempt to secure land for the new town[19].

Augustus C. Allen and his brother John K. Allen announced the founding of their town of Houston on August 30, 1836, and the new Congress voted to establish the seat of government of the Republic of Texas in Houston on November 30, 1836. The construction of homes and government buildings began in early 1837, and President Sam Houston wrote that, when he arrived in late April, 1837, there were about one hundred houses already built and approximately 1,500 people were engaged in various pursuits around town[20].

Many veterans came to the area to become a part of the new venture. They settled in and around the new town on Buffalo Bayou, and, it is highly possible that some of them had already been living in the area since the summer of 1836. Although the Allen brothers focused their attention on the sale of town lots, they also were willing to sell some tracts of land outside of the town limits. On April 13, 1837, two veterans of San Jacinto, William F. Hodge and Jonathan B. Frost, bought adjacent tracts of land along Buffalo Bayou downstream of town at $100 per acre. The deeds indicated that each man already had a residence on his tract at the time of the purchase[21].

William F. Hodge acquired ten acres of land that encompassed the south bank of Buffalo Bayou from the the first bend of the bayou downstream of Houston to a point that is approximately at the modern McKee Street bridge, then down a line that now parallels McKee Street to a point parallel to the origin, and then back to the beginning[22].

After the death of his thirty-two year old neighbor Jonathan Frost of congestive fever in September, 1837, Hodge was involved in the probate of the Frost estate. Hodge held the security bond for Samuel M. Frost who was appointed the administrator of Jonathan Frost's estate. The death of his friend and neighbor and Samuel Frost's intention to subdivide the Frost tract and sell lots may have motivated Hodge to pursue his opportunities elsewhere. While Samuel Frost acquired title to the Frost tract from his brother James Frost on May 5, 1838, William F. Hodge completed the sale of his land to fellow veteran John Beldin on May 8, 1838. Taking advantage of the rising value of land near the capitol, Hodge sold his land to Beldin for $3,000, reaping a $2,000 gain on the sale[23].

John Beldin was a more recognized veteran than either Hodge or Frost. Born in New York in 1812, Beldin enlisted in Captain William J. Cook's "New Orleans Greys" in October, 1835 and fought at the Storming and Capture of Bexar in December of that year. The twenty-three year old soldier sustained the loss of an eye while "spiking a cannon" and he was mustered out of the Texas Army in January, 1836 after convalescing in New Orleans. Yet, Beldin returned to Texas to join Amasa Turner's Company B at San Jacinto[24].

For his service to Texas, John Beldin received various grants of land. For his service in the Army in 1835, he received a certificate for three hundred twenty acres of land. It is said that he traded that certificate for a three year old grey mare. On December 18, 1837, he was granted a league of land in compensation for his permanent disability while serving in the Army. He later sold the certificate for that land to Buckman Canfield for $200 on July 10, 1840. On January 5, 1838, Beldin was issued a Headright Certificate for one third of a league of land. On October 25, 1838, Beldin was issues a Donation Certificate for six hundred forty acres for his participation at San Jacinto. This tract, surveyed near Brays Bayou, is now part of the City of Bellaire along Loop 610, a tract approximately bounded by Bellaire Boulevard on the north, South Rice Avenue on the west, Beechnut Street on the south and the Southern Pacific Railroad on the east[25].

Like many of the veterans who had been paid for their military service in land certificates, John Beldin instantly became a land speculator, whether it was his intention or not. It was probably while in this frame of mind that he purchased the Hodge land in 1838. Although he married Frances Bartlett on October 23, 1839, it is not likely that he planned to settle on the land he acquired from William F. Hodge. Within a year, on September 11, 1840, John Beldin sold the ten acres he bought from Hodge to Leonard S. Perkins and Levi Butler. As fate would have it, a year later, John Beldin, though still a young man, was struck down by one of the series of epidemics that were the scourge of Houston during the mid-1800's. He died of "congestive fever" in Houston on September 15, 1841 and was buried in the City Cemetery[26].

The partnership of Perkins, then thirty-one years old, and Butler did not exploit the ten acres tract in the way that was being done with the Frost tract and the adjacent Moody tract. While the neighboring land was subdivided into small home lots and sold to individuals, the Hodge tract remained undeveloped for over a decade. At some point during that time, Levi Butler obtained complete control of the land and, on June 1, 1853, Butler sold the entire property to a partnership of Peter Gabel and Henry Schulte[27].

The language of the property description used in the deed to Gabel and Schulte provides us with one of the earliest associations of this tract with the neighborhood in Houston that became known as Frost Town. "...Ten acres of land on the south side of Buffalo Bayou in the lower part of the City of Houston and part of what is called Frost Town..." The apparent success of Samuel Frost's sale of lots in the Frost Town Subdivision also attracted residents to the adjoining blocks of the Moody Addition and the Second Ward. A community developed and it encompassed an area larger than the eight blocks of the Frost's tract[28].

A year and a half later, on December 12, 1854, Henry Schulte deeded his one half interest in the property to Peter Gabel. Schulte, about ten years younger than Gabel, was a brewer who immigrated from Prussia. Although they dissolved their partnership in this tract of land, both men established successful breweries in downtown Houston[29].

Peter Gabel, in his early thirties at the time, arrived in Houston in the 1840's from Bavaria. By profession, he was a cooper, that is, a barrel maker, and he listed that as his occupation in the census of 1850. Shortly thereafter, however, Gabel began brewing beer. And, by 1857, his brewery had more than doubled in volume. Gabel became well established in the community and was a successful brewer, distiller and wine dealer. By 1866, he owned a brewery on the corner of Preston Avenue and Caroline Street and the Exchange Bar Room on Franklin Avenue, between Main Street and Travis Street[30].

From the time of his arrival in Houston, Peter Gabel showed a gregarious and socially active side of his personality. In January, 1854, Gabel hosted a meeting at his home on Preston Avenue in which ten young German men founded a club called the Houston Turn Verein. As a social organization dedicated to intellectual and athletic activities, the Turn Verein became a popular civic organization among the local German community, eventually reaching a membership of over 1,400 men. It was out of this group of men that the city's first fire-fighting company was established. Since many of these German men lived in the Frost Town area and the Second Ward, some historians have attributed the first fire-fighting company to Frost Town, whether that is wholly accurate, or not[31].

Peter Gabel himself never lived in Frost Town or on the tract of land along Buffalo Bayou. However, as a consequence of his long ownership of the property that had originally belonged to William F. Hodge, Gabel put his own stamp on the land. It became commonly known as the Gabel property, and the street along its eastern boundary became Gabel Street, with the spelling later Anglicized to "Gable" in almost all instances.

Unlike the Frost Town Subdivision across the street, the development of homes and businesses on the Gabel property proceeded slowly, and the Galveston and Houston Junction Railroad was built across the middle of the tract in 1865. By 1869, there were two houses on lots on the south half and a few scattered buildings in the north section of the tract. By 1873, there were three houses along Gabel Street and a couple outlying barn-like structures in the north section. The most significant and enduring development to the Gabel tract was to be the construction of the Citizens Electric Company Power Plant in 1890[32].

Gas lights were introduced in Houston shortly after the Civil War and were in widespread use in businesses and homes by 1880. The inventions by Thomas A. Edison in the late 1870's with the new source of energy of electricity were about to change the lives of Americans and Houstonians in particular. Edison's improvements to the incandescent light bulb and his development of an electric power distribution system led to the installation of the country's first incandescent light and power station for private consumers in New York City in 1882[33].

In the spring of that same year, Emmanuel Raphael obtained a franchise to build a plant utilizing Edison's concept of generating electrical current by means of a central dynamo, then distributing it in small quantities to thousands of homes and commercial buildings. Raphael received a charter for the Houston Electric Light and Power Company on May 20, 1882, and the company constructed its plant on Buffalo Bayou at the foot of Main Street near Commerce Avenue. Today, the site is a parking lot for the Spaghetti Warehouse Restaurant[34].

The difficulties of introducing a new technology to society and making it an economical and profitable business are monumental. The Houston Electric Light and Power Company had technical problems resulting in chronic low load conditions and financial problems caused by an inadequate rate structure. The company went into receivership in March, 1886 and was acquired by its rival, the Houston Gas Light Company, in 1887[35].

Sensing that there was still an opportunity in the Houston marketplace, investors chartered the Citizens' Electric Light and Power Company on July 29, 1889, and then purchased the franchise and the equipment of the Fort Wayne Jenny Electric Company. Citizens' Electric built its plant on Gabel Street, just north of the Galveston Houston and Henderson Railroad tracks. A rail siding provided access for coal to be piled on the south side of the coal fired plant which had two smoke stacks. A thirty-five foot tall, wooden water tower was located off the northwest corner of the facility[36].

The plant itself, a wooden structure that was sheathed in corrugated iron and covered with a tin roof, housed fifteen dynamos to provide electrical power. The power plant operated continuously, and, at any one time, the plant's seven horizontal tubular boilers and three engines, with a capacity of 720 horsepower, were driving ten arc dynamos which enabled the three bipolar power generators to produce a total capacity of 150 kilowatts[37].

Rather than compete for the electrical power market in Houston, the Houston Gas Light Company sold its interest in the Houston Electric Light and Power Company that it had acquired when the company went into receivership to Citizens' Electric in January, 1891. Citizens' Electric became the sole electric power provider for Houston[38].

Financial difficulties plagued the Citizens' Electric Light and Power Company, and the company went into receivership on January 7, 1898. The fortunes of the company suffered another blow a few weeks later. In the early evening of March 26, 1898, the No. 6 boiler at Citizens' Electric Gabel Street plant exploded. The force of the explosion toppled one of the smoke stacks causing it to break in two and fall across the GH&H trestle. The plant was destroyed and two men working at the plant died instantly. Another two men died within a week, and, miraculously two workmen survived[39].

The devastation of the power plant was compounded by a fire that was touched off the next day. A spark ignited the vapors in and around the facility, and hundreds of gallons of oil and solvents went up in flames. Fortunately, it does not appear that any of the ten homes that are depicted along the west side of Gabel Street in the 1891 "bird's eye" map were damaged by the explosion or fire[40].

The company struggled to survive the repercussions of the disaster. A new plant, constructed on the south side of the GH&H tracks to replace the Gabel Street plant destroyed by explosion, began operation in April, 1900. Nevertheless, in December, 1901, the court ordered the transfer of the Citizens' Electric assets to its creditors who reorganized the company as the Houston Lighting and Power Company[41].

The revitalized company made a commitment in 1905 to enhance the plant on Gabel Street with enough generating capacity to provide electricity to all the citizens of the city. By 1907, the plant consisted of an engine and dynamo room in the largest building, an adjacent office on the northeast corner of the structure, oil tanks off the northwest corner of the building, and other outlying buildings for storage[42].

In spite of the increase in industrial development in the area, the Gabel tract, by 1907, continued to have considerable residential development, as did the rest of Frost Town. Seventeen lots with dwellings lined the Gabel Street side of the south half of the tract and extended along the southern boundary as well. Nine lots with dwellings were on the north side of the tract lining the railroad tracks and extending northward along Gabel Street (which by this time is spelled "Gable"). A steel bridge across Buffalo Bayou at McKee Street connected Gable Street and Frost Town with the rail yards and commercial businesses on the north side of the bayou[43].

The electric utility attempted to keep up with the demand for electrical power service in Houston for the first quarter of the twentieth century. Industrialization of the local economy, the influx of population and the introduction of consumer appliances meant that the demand for electricity continued to rise in Houston. Construction on the Gable Street plant to improve the capacity took place at repeated intervals prior to the Depression with additions made to the facility in 1913, 1917, 1918 and 1921. However, by

1922, the Gable Street plant was considered inefficient since Buffalo Bayou was a shallow, narrow stream with minimal tidal action which resulted in circulating water temperatures in the cooling system that did not allow the generators to operate economically[44].

Although the major reconstruction of the power plant had been completed by 1924, the plant was unable to provide service to the whole Houston area. In August, 1924, the first unit of Houston Lighting and Power's Deepwater plant in Pasadena went online to share the load[45].

The physical plant and facilities at Gable Street, by 1924, began to take on the appearance of a modern industrial site. The area south of the railroad tracks, the south half of the Gabel tract, was almost completely occupied by the electric company facilities. The plant's main building contained the engine and dynamo room. Off to the northwest corner of the building there was a steel water tank on the ground, next to two oil tanks in underground concrete vaults. A water tank on a fifty foot tower stood adjacent to the west side of the main building, near the north corner[46].

Various outbuildings to the south of the main building included a supply warehouse, a bath house and general storage. The Houston Gas and Fuel Company had constructed a steel gasometer tank on Gable Street, south of the plant, where gas was stored near at normal pressure and temperature. The Settlement House, the former Settegast home, which had been moved to the far southern boundary of the Gabel property prior to the construction of the new Rusk School in 1912, seemed dangerously close to the volatile fuels and solvents of the plant[47].

In a similar pattern that mixed industrial fuel storage in close proximity to homes and residences, two large, steel oil storage tanks were located on the ground in the area north of the railroad tracks and adjacent to the homes along Kapner Street[48].

The residential development in the north half of the Gabel tract continued from 1907 to 1924. Isaac Kapner, a Polish immigrant from Austria, began buying properties in the Frost Town area about 1900 and by 1924, he had subdivided a large part of the part of the tract north of the railroad tracks into lots and small dwellings, most likely rental properties[49].

Kapner and his wife Sophia, both in their early twenties, had come to the United States about 1880 and lived for about five years in Arkansas before coming to Texas in 1885 or 1886. Kapner, who listed his occupation as a merchant, lived, in 1900, on the south side of Lyle Street in the Moody Addition, next to the GH&H Railroad tracks. He knew the neighborhood and the potential for providing low cost housing for the steady flow of immigrants to the city. In addition to the houses that existed in 1907, twenty-one new homes lined Kapner Street that branched west off Gable Street, north of Race Street by 1924[50].

Kapner continued to live in the area, and in 1920, he and his wife Sophia lived at 1902 Franklin Avenue, at the corner with Hamilton Street. By this time, at age 63, he considered himself retired. Sophia passed away in 1921, and by 1930, Isaac Kapner had remarried and lived with his wife Augusta, a German immigrant, at 1405 McGowen Street. Kapner died in 1945 at age eighty-eight and his son Charles filed his will for probate on October 8, 1945[51].

Additional construction and development of the Houston Lighting and Power Gable Street Plant occurred in 1939. And, by 1951, the main plant consisted of the boiler room, the engine room, the dynamo room and associated facilities. A separate oil pump house adjacent to Gable Street was built in 1950[52].

The complex extended across both sides of the GH&H tracks. The residential area along Kapner Street was removed and no houses remained on the north side of the railroad tracks by 1951. Instead, the HL&P facilities there include two cooling tower units, an oil storage facility with two tanks, a tile locker house on the south bank of the bayou, and other small buildings[53].

Security concerns related to the declaration of war with Germany may have prompted HL&P to erect a fence around the Gable Street plant. In particular, the fence separated the plant yard from the Settlement House on the far southern boundary of the property. The Settlement House was eventually razed in the mid-1950's for the construction of the Elysian Viaduct[54].

The Gable Street plant was finally decommissioned in 1983 as other, more efficient energy generation facilities became operational. The property has not, however, been abandoned. Recent additions and improvements to the electrical substation on the north part

Photo credit: Louis F. Aulbach

The remnants of the Gable Street Power Plant's cooling system lie in ruins along the banks of Buffalo Bayou even though the plant has been demolished and removed from the street level above.

of the tract to provide electric power service to the east side of downtown.

In 1993, the Gable Street Power Plant was considered for the site of a proposed energy museum, but that idea did not mature. The hull of the once prominent electrical generating facility stood remote and mysterious to passers-by on McKee Street, the new name of Gable Street, for decades. Seen from the bayou, the plant looked much as it did when it was functioning. In April, 2011, the fabulous old plant was demolished, and the lot at street level was cleared. Yet, the dock and bulkhead structures at water level along the bank are still visible, although, in disrepair. The large pipes of the cooling system lie in place among the scaffolds although many of the segments are broken and disconnected. Below the mowed lawn on the top of the bank, bayou vegetation and the indigenous undergrowth hides much of the former wharf structures that remind us of the time when boats and barges plied the waters of Buffalo Bayou this far into town.

G&HJ Railroad Bridge

Within sight of Minute Maid Park, the old railroad bridge, abandoned by the Missouri Kansas and Texas Railroad in the 1990's, is a reminder of the importance of rail transportation that made Houston an economic powerhouse by the beginning of the twentieth century.

At the approach of the Civil War, railroads in Houston were coming into their own. The Galveston, Houston and Henderson Railroad had rail service from Galveston to Houston, reaching a terminus at Rusk Avenue on the "far" eastern edge of Houston. The Houston and Texas Central Railway, with its maintenance yards on the north side of Buffalo Bayou, extended out of town along the north bank of Buffalo Bayou to the Brazos Valley.

In an attempt to capitalize on the economic efficiency of inter-connections, the Galveston and Houston Junction Railroad was chartered by the stockholders of the Galveston, Houston and Henderson Railroad on April 8, 1861 to link the Galveston, Houston and Henderson Railroad with the Houston and Texas Central Railway at Houston. Two miles of the Galveston and Houston Junction Railroad tracks were built in 1865 to connect the Galveston, Houston and Henderson Railroad at Rusk Avenue with the Houston and Texas Central Railway on the north side of Buffalo Bayou[55].

By 1865, the Galveston and Houston Junction Railroad had acquired land, laid tracks across the area known as Frost Town and built the first railroad bridge over Buffalo Bayou. By 1869, the Allen Station on the Galveston and Houston Junction Railroad was located on Commerce Avenue at West Broadway Street, now known as Hutchins Street. And, in December, 1871, the Galveston and Houston Junction Railroad was merged with the Galveston, Houston and Henderson Railroad[56].

Although there are reports that some residents of Frost Town had complained that the railroad company simply appropriated the right of way through the neighborhood for their tracks, the deed records show that the Galveston and Houston Junction Railroad did, indeed, acquire land in Blocks C, D and E in Frost Town during 1862.

F. and Joanne Steiner sold parts of Block D, Lots 6 and 7 to the Galveston and Houston Junction Railroad on May 8, 1862. H. D. Taylor sold parts of Block E, Lots 1 and 2 to Galveston & Houston Junction Railroad on May 10, 1862. M. Connelly's heirs sold Block C, Lots 1 and 2 to the Galveston and Houston Junction Railroad on May 30, 1862. H. and Mary Lahn sold parts of Block D, Lots 8 and 9 to the Galveston and Houston Junction Railroad on December 6, 1862. W. and Rosina Kwetton sold a fractional part of Block C, Lot 12 to the Galveston and Houston Junction Railroad on December 22, 1862[57].

There may have been, however, other lots in the Moody Addition and other tracts over which the two miles of track were laid in which the title to the land may have been in doubt. The creation of the Galveston and Houston Junction Railroad as a separate entity to build the connecting rail line may have been designed in such a way to shield the parent company, the Galveston, Houston and Henderson Railroad, from legal claims while land with uncertain titles on the right of way was acquired through the lengthy process of adverse possession, commonly known as squatter's rights. By 1871, any outstanding claims to land in the right of way would have been settled in favor of the Galveston and Houston Junction Railroad, so the railroad company was merged into the Galveston, Houston and Henderson Railroad[58].

The railroad bridge over the bayou today is a modern steel and concrete structure. Since it is a fixed bridge, rather than a draw bridge, it dates from after the time that shipping to Allen's Landing required moveable bridges over the bayou. This structure is, at least, the third or fourth bridge at this location. The original wooden draw bridge is depicted on the Wood map of 1869. A more substantial bridge appears to have been in place by the time it was represented on the bird's eye map of 1891[59].

In recent times, this descendant of the first railroad bridge over Buffalo Bayou, isolated from the bustle of Main Street and tucked away beyond a bend of the bayou in the deteriorating near east end of the central business district, appeared headed for the oblivion of forgotten history. However, the bridge and it's long history in Houston has been saved, and the bridge has become a part of the bikeways system of Houston, connecting the North Side of Buffalo Bayou with the Frost Town Historic Site.

Dickson Car Wheel Company

The tract of land on the north bank of Buffalo Bayou lying downstream of the GH&H Railroad bridge is vacant today and used as a parking lot. In the late nineteenth century, it was the site of a major industrial plant that was essential to the growth of railroads in Houston and Texas. The business was established by John F. Dickson in 1887. Dickson, who came to Houston from Marshall, Texas, planned to use iron from East Texas and Alabama to manufacture railroad car wheels and large centrifugal pumps. By 1896, the Dickson Car Wheel Company, located on Steam Mill Street, consisted of a main foundry building, a machine shop and a second, smaller foundry. Both foundries were serviced by rail sidings and loading platforms[60].

The success of the company prompted Dickson to expand his operations and by 1906, the Dickson Car Wheel Company had relocated its manufacturing facilities to the GH&SA railroad spur off Washington Avenue. The complex, set on a tract of land south of Washington Avenue and west of the railroad tracks, consisted of a main building, the foundry, and other buildings including the power house, a cork room, a sand bin and a sand shed. By 1913, the plant at 3115 Washington Avenue, was producing four hundred railroad car wheels per day[61].

Further alterations and additions to the wheel foundry were made in 1923. These modifications were designed by noted local architect Alfred C. Finn who had a long business relationship with Henry H. Dickson for whom he built a home in 1917 as well as other commercial structures[62].

The beginning of the end of the Dickson Car Wheel Company as a major Houston industry came on April 1, 1927 when the company was acquired by the Pullman Car and Manufacturing Corporation of Illinois. The Dickson Car Wheel Company became a subsidiary of the Pullman company in 1931. On December 26, 1934, the Dickson Car Wheel Company was liquidated and the

Certificate of Dissolution for the company became effective on March 1, 1935[63].

Raccoon Bend

The McKee Street exit from eastbound Interstate 10 has been opened as the gateway to the convention center, Minute Maid Park, the Toyota Center and other venues on the east side of downtown. What you may miss, however, if you speed along too quickly is the former bustling neighborhood of Frost Town. The McKee Street thoroughfare is designed to zip you quickly over Buffalo Bayou and past James Bute Park and the Reliant Energy substation. But, if you happen to stop for a moment at James Bute Park, you can see Raccoon Bend along the south bank of the bayou.

Raccoon Bend is formed as Buffalo Bayou makes a right hand turn about a half mile downstream from Main Street. A large sandbar is created on the south side of the bayou while a steep cut bank is found on the north side.

The name is not an official name, but it is the common name given to the place by the children of Frost Town during the 1930's and 1940's. Luz Vara, who was born in a home on Spruce Street at Bramble Street in Frost Town in 1937, recalls how she and her brothers had fun playing along the bayou near the bridge. As a community of Mexicans, many of whom were immigrants, they referred to Frost Town as El Barrio del Alacran -- the ward of the scorpion.

The brushy bank of the bayou, just upstream of the McKee Street bridge, was called Raccoon Bend, probably because the large trash dump, which was located in this section of the banks, attracted significant numbers of the mammalian scavenger and associated wildlife to earn the epithet. The site of the historic refuse dump on the south bank of Buffalo Bayou is officially recognized by the state with the archeological trinomial number 41HR621[64].

Crystal Ice Factory

Barely visible from the top of the bank and little noticed from the bayou when the vegetation growth is high, the ruins of the

Crystal Ice Works remind us of the vibrant industrial activity in the Frost Town area during the first one hundred years of Houston.

Set on the north bank of Buffalo Bayou on the west side of McKee Street, the Crystal Ice Works occupied the site that had been the home of Mrs. E. McKee as late as 1869. About 1880, the Houston Elevator Company built a grain elevator on the site that, by 1885, was leased to and operated by the Texas Star Flour Mills Grain Elevator Company. It had the capacity for the storage of 150,000 bushels of wheat in twenty-six wheat bins. However, by 1890, the Crystal Ice Works had taken over the facility from the Houston Elevator Company[65].

The Ice Factory of the Crystal Ice Works was a major industrial enterprise on the north bank of the bayou. It had a capacity of making forty tons of ice every twenty-four hours using an absorber process. The production of ice was dependent on water and the site on the bayou was chosen for this reason. The water supply for the factory was two fold. There was an artesian well on the lower part of the bank to tap the ground water and water from the bayou was pumped to the facility through a five inch suction pipe[66].

By 1907, the Crystal Ice Company had made improvements to its main building which included rooms for a freezing tank, a cold storage facility and a condenser room. A number of other out buildings were located on the property and a rail siding with a loading platform was on the north side of the plant. An additional rail siding extended along the bayou side of the plant. A steel truss, swing bridge had been constructed across Buffalo Bayou at McKee Street in 1904 to increase commercial traffic between the north side of the bayou and the City's East End. Business was expanding[67].

By this time, the Crystal Ice Company, situated adjacent to the Southern Pacific Railroad yard, became a supplier of ice to the local operations of the Pacific Fruit Express. The Pacific Fruit Express, established in 1906, was a joint venture between the Southern Pacific and the Union Pacific Railroads for refrigerator cars used for the rapid shipment of perishable fruits and vegetables. The brainchild of Edward H. Harriman of the Union Pacific Railroad, it became the world's largest owner and operator of refrigerated rail cars[68].

The Pacific Fruit Express supported the rise of irrigated agriculture in the West. Using a "follow the sun" strategy, it hauled potatoes from the Pacific Northwest in the fall, oranges from California in the winter, and fruit from the Southwest in the spring. In the peak year of service, the Pacific Fruit Express carried 465,000 rail car loads of fresh fruits and vegetables. The Pacific Fruit Express declined in the 1980's due to the decline in railroad service and competition brought by the deregulation of the trucking industry[69].

By 1924, the company became the Crystal Ice and Fuel Company, reflecting changing business conditions. The facility had rooms for an ice machine, a freezing tank, condensers, cold storage and a machine shop. The office was located in a separate building on the north side of building adjacent to the triangular concrete platform[70].

Economic conditions change, and the Crystal Ice and Fuel Company ceased operations about 1930. By 1951, the Crystal Ice Works facility and buildings were removed from the north bank of Buffalo Bayou. Only the substructures in the banks have survived the wrecking ball. Embedded in the clay and overgrown with vegetation, the concrete skeleton of the foundation of this once-thriving industrial plant whispers the story of its former prominence[71].

McKee Street Bridge

By far the most artistic bridge over Buffalo Bayou is the McKee Street Bridge near James Bute Park in the Warehouse District. Built by Houston City Engineer James Gordon McKenzie in 1932, the bridge is an unusual design of a reinforced concrete girder bridge. The peculiar feature of this bridge are the girders, which rise above the roadway to form two swooping curves[72].

This bridge replaced an earlier steel swing bridge at the same location. As the city's population grew in the Fifth Ward on the north side of Buffalo Bayou, the residents asked for another bridge to the south side. It was a long and circuitous route to go to San Jacinto Street where there was a bridge. Finally, the City Council voted for a new bridge in 1903. Construction began the following year, and in 1905, the McKee Street bridge was put in service. The McKee Street bridge was a motor-driven, steel truss swing bridge that illustrated the contemporary advancements in bridge design of the time[73].

The local prominence of the black steel structure rubbed off on the Frost Town community on the south bank where the bridge crossed the bayou. The neighborhood was called Blackbridge in the early twentieth century[74].

Nevertheless, after twenty years of service, the steel bridge was in serious need of repairs. Some repairs were finally made in 1927, but the structure was poorly built and sections of the bridge began to fall apart. The bridge was demolished in 1928[75].

The prospect of constructing a new bridge over the bayou gave City Engineer McKenzie the chance to complement the other recent bridges over the bayou with one of style, beauty and function. With assistance from engineers L. C. Wagner and H. D. Hilton, McKenzie designed a structure to provide clearance for the small boats that were navigating Buffalo Bayou at that time. The sharp angle of the bayou in this location presented a challenge for the design of the bridge. To compensate for the angle of the crossing, the McKenzie built the bridge on a twenty-three degree left forward skew with piers and abutments laid out with their downstream footings offset by arranging the floor beams over the supports at perpendicular angles[76].

The McKee Street bridge is a distinctive and unusual example of a reinforced concrete through-girder bridge. The partial through-girders rise beside the four lane roadway to form two parabolic curves. The curves rise as waves above the roadway and represent the reverse curve created by the intersection of two simple parabolas at a point of tangency fifteen feet out from the center of each support[77].

The thirty-eight foot roadway is surfaced with bricks, and the cantilevered concrete walkways are outlined with special design steel hand railing. At the time of construction, the McKee Street bridge had the longest main span of its type in the United States. It is the only known example of a reinforced concrete through-girder bridge in Texas. Built in 1932 by Don Hall Constructor, Inc., the McKee Street bridge cost about $122,000[78].

Until the 1980's, the bridge was abused through vandalism and graffiti. That was when artist Kirk Farris made it his pet project. He cleaned off the rust and urban decay, and applied the first coats of pastel paint. The flair of the bridge design has been described as representing either the waves of Buffalo Bayou below or perhaps a relative of the Loch Ness Monster, the globes on its light standards looking like multiple eyes[79].

The bridges of Houston owe a lot to artist Farris and photographer Paul Judice. During the time that Farris was an investigator for the Harris County Pollution Department in the 1970's, he realized that the bridges over Buffalo Bayou were monuments to the culture that built them and also told the story of the bayou and of Houston. In 1980, he received a grant from the Cultural Arts Council of Houston to prepare an exhibition about the bridges over Buffalo Bayou. In 1982, Farris and Judice created the exhibition called "Bridges over Buffalo Bayou" that was displayed at the Houston Public Library's downtown branch. That was when he decided to paint the McKee Street Bridge. With approval from the City, paint donated by the Bute Paint Company (originally located in the warehouse district at one end of the bridge - the buildings of which are now trendy lofts) and lighting supplied by the local Wholesale Electric Supply Company, Farris completed the revitalization of the McKee Street Bridge on "Bridge Day," July 19, 1985, and it remains as we see it today in all of its pastel glory[80]!

The original color scheme of shades of aquamarine, lavendar and purple conceived by artist Kirk Farris have been maintained in recent years by the City's Parks and Recreation Department. Permanent recognition of the uniqueness of the modern style of the McKee Street Bridge came in 2002 when the bridge was added to the National Register of Historic Places[81].

James Bute Park

In 1994, artist Kirk Farris convinced the Commissioners of Harris County to buy land adjacent to the McKee Street Bridge for James Bute Park. James Bute Park was named for the late James Bute IV, owner of Bute Paint Company, as well as for his grandfather James Bute I who founded the company and was a late nineteenth century contributor to the development of Houston[82].

James Bute Park consists of 12.5 acres around the Frost Town site, including the tract on the north bank of Buffalo Bayou where the Crystal Ice Factory stood and parts of the former Moody Addition. Farris and his Art and Environmental Architecture, a nonprofit group that promotes the nature and history of the area, hope to expand the park to include an additional twelve acres under the freeway system owned by the Texas Department of Transportation[83].

Frost Town -- The Frost Family Legacy

The events in Texas during the fall of 1835 set the course for revolution. General Martin Perfecto de Cos, Santa Anna's brother-in-law, led the Mexican army across the Rio Grande and captured San Antonio, making his headquarters there in September. However, the Texans and volunteers from the United States who gathered at Austin's "call to arms" confronted the Mexican army, laid siege to city, and, through a pattern of house-to-house, close-combat fighting, the Texans forced General Cos to surrender on December 10 and return to Mexico[84].

In the euphoria of this victory, the assembled militia disbanded, and the soldiers went back to their farms. The leaders of Texas, however, knew that Santa Anna would bring his forces back in the spring. The provisional government of the Texans, the Consultation, appointed Sam Houston as the Commander in Chief of the army, and on December 12, 1835, Sam Houston issued a Proclamation of the Army of Texas detailing the bounty payment of land for service in the army[85].

The terms of enlistment were fairly attractive -- 800 acres for a two year enlistment, 640 acres for an auxiliary volunteer for two years and 320 acres for a one year volunteer -- and the prospect of land appealed to many men in the southern states. This offer was particularly appealing to the Frost brothers of Tennessee. They came to Texas to serve in the army and, subsequently, became an important part of the history of Houston[86].

John M. Frost was born to Jonathan Frost and Mary Benson Frost on January 27, 1775 in South Carolina. His father, unfortunately, served on the Loyalist side during the American Revolution and after the war, his property was confiscated. The loss of his property caused the family to struggle in near poverty as John grew up. In 1802, John M. Frost, at age twenty-seven, married Rhoda Miles in South Carolina, and then, he moved his family to Tennessee, to an area known as Brentwood[87].

Brentwood, located ten miles south of Nashville, had been settled in the late 1700's by veterans of the Revolutionary War, and Frost established his home, known as Cottonport, on the Old Smyrna Road. The Frost homestead became the original site of business activity in the community, and the general store, the grist mill and the post office were located there[88].

In 1812, John M. Frost served as a captain in the War of 1812 under Andrew Jackson. Frost later served as a captain in the Tennessee militia. The military career of their father certainly inspired the adult Frost sons, as perhaps, did the wave of patriotism that the call from Texas inspired in many men in Kentucky and Tennessee. The reward of land, especially the large quantity of land offered for service in the Texas army, clinched the deal. Three of John M. Frost's sons, Jonathan, Samuel and James, set out for Texas[89].

Jonathan Benson Frost, the eldest son, left Fayette County, Tennessee on March 22, 1836 for Texas and joined the cavalry company of Captain James Smith, the Nacogdoches Mounted Volunteers, on April 11, 1836. The Nacogdoches Mounted Volunteers were organized on that day and the unit probably joined the army at the camp west of the Brazos opposite Groce's Plantation. During the twelve day stay at this camp, the army received reinforcements and supplies, including the famed Twin Sisters cannon, prior to crossing the Brazos on April 13 and making the week long march to San Jacinto and destiny[90].

Jonathan Frost served in the Texas army for three months until he was given an honorable discharge on July 12, 1836. Samuel Miles Frost also served three months in the Texas cavalry in 1836. But, it is unclear whether James Copeland Frost served. Although no record of his service or of a claim for a pension is available, it is believed that James C. Frost did come with his brothers. As the youngest of the brothers, James may have still been a minor when he came to Texas, and he may not been permitted to enlist in the regular army. While the Frost brothers were still in Texas, their father John M. Frost passed away on June 21, 1836 in Williamson County, Tennessee[91].

After his discharge, Jonathan Frost returned to Tennessee to bring his family back to Texas. Samuel and James appear to have returned as well. With the death of the family patriarch, Jonathan Frost organized the move of his whole household and his extended family to Texas. He brought his slaves, his household and his blacksmithing equipment to an area on Buffalo Bayou, about eight miles upstream of Harrisburg and about eight hundred yards east of the junction with White Oak Bayou. Within a couple of months, he was joined by his brothers Samuel Miles Frost and James Copeland Frost, his mother Rhoda Miles Frost, his sister and her husband, Mary Elizabeth and John B. Dunn, two minor children of his father, Rebecca S. Frost and Eislising B. Frost, and his father's slaves[92].

Many of the stories about the place where Frost chose to settle speak of a small community that dates from the earliest days of the Austin Colony. Attracted by Stephen F. Austin's promotions, settlers began arriving in this area by 1822. One of the most notable of these early settlers was Jane Mason Wilkins and her family.

Jane Wilkins, a widow, came to Texas with her daughters Jane and Mary in July or August, 1822 with a group of thirty persons from Florence, Alabama led by her father Robert Mason. Mason and his wife were elderly and they died from the hardships of the journey soon after reaching Texas. From this point, the story of Mrs. Wilkins is one of amazing events and extraordinary courage[93].

After Austin's advertisements for the Texas colony in 1821, the first Anglo-Americans began to come to Texas by boat from Louisiana. In early 1822, settlers chose home sites along the San Jacinto River estuary to take advantage of convenient waterways that drained prairies and forests of upper Galveston Bay. In May, 1822, a surveying party included Henry Smith Rider and John Iams James entered the area west of Galveston Bay that would become Harris County. The land was wild and devoid of any communities. John R. Harris would not arrive until 1823, the following year. The Mason party, traveling in a one hundred twenty foot keelboat, anchored near what is now Vince's Bayou. With the death of their leader and organizer, many in the group were uncertain about whether to proceed to the colony or abandon the venture[94].

The dispute ended when half of the group decided to return to Alabama. The dissident members sawed the keelboat in half and went back from whence they came. That the group came across the Gulf in a keelboat is remarkable. A keelboat is a river boat with a shallow draught and a keel but no sails. It was used to carry freight and was propelled by rowing, punting or towing. Navigation on the open Gulf must have been a challenge. Moreover, that they cut the boat in half seems to defy belief. However, many keelboats were designed for "one way" use. Often, after the cargo was delivered, the keelboat was broken up for scrap. It is not unreasonable that the boat could be partially dismantled and rebuilt as two boats. Nevertheless, the prospect of the untamed wilderness lay before those who would choose to remain. Mrs. Wilkins and her family stayed[95].

Fortunately, Mrs. Wilkins found that they were not alone. She and her family eventually joined with Dr. James A. E. Phelps and others who had come to Texas on the ship Lively. They made their way up the south side of Buffalo Bayou to a place about ten miles upstream from the modern Vince's Bayou where the fateful decision to remain had been made. The prairie in the vicinity of the modern Minute Maid Park and the George R. Brown Convention Center was settled by the Wilkins family, Dr. James A. E. Phelps and his wife Rosetta (sometimes listed as Rosalie) Abeline Yerby, Stephen Holston, John Austin and others as a small community grew up around the farmstead of Jane Wilkins. Although they could not claim legal ownership of the land, they erected tents and built cabins to provide shelter, and they made temporary accommodations for themselves in the new land[96].

The application for a grant of land in Spanish Texas was a bureaucratic process that could take a while. These first settlers on the land south of Buffalo Bayou did the best they could to survive until their time came. Eventually, though, the awards were made and the settlers could move on to their own land.

Dr. James A. E. Phelps had been recruited by Stephen F. Austin for his colony. In 1822, Phelps cultivated a farm in partnership with Stephen Holston until he received his grant of one sitio (4,428 acres) and two labors (177 acres each) in the modern Brazoria County on August 16, 1824[97].

On July 21, 1824, John Austin received a two league (4,428 acres each) survey on Buffalo Bayou. Austin purchased a cotton gin to be located on Buffalo Bayou in March, 1825, but by the summer, he had entered into a mercantile partnership with J. E. B. Austin, Stephen F. Austin's younger brother, in Brazoria and moved there[98].

The 1826 census of the Austin Colony listed twenty inhabitants in the area, including Jane Wilkins, most of whom listed their occupations as either farmers or stock raisers. Within a short time, however, Wilkins and her daughters had resettled in San Felipe de Austin and acquired town lots 117 and 82, where they operated a seamstress business and, at times, a boarding house. On May 26, 1827, Jane Wilkins, as one of Austin's Old Three Hundred, received a league of land located in what is now Fort Bend County, near US Highway 90A, the High Meadow and the New Territory Austin Ridge Subdivisions[99].

A number of twentieth century historians have claimed, or repeated the assertion, that in the ten years prior to the Battle of San Jacinto, German-speaking people began to arrive in the area along Buffalo Bayou, and the small settlement came to be called German-town. Unfortunately, no documents exist to support this claim. At the time of the Battle of San Jacinto, settlers had been pouring into Texas and many of them were scattered all over this section of the state. The population of this little community in 1836 has been estimated as between fifty and one hundred persons. Some of them probably were German. No contemporaneous records of the people or the community, however, have survived to give credence to these stories.

Stories also persist that prior to and after the battle of San Jacinto, the Allen brothers established their headquarters in the tiny hamlet upstream of Harrisburg. More likely, though, John K. Allen operated the business from their home in Nacogdoches, while Augustus C. Allen traveled to secure their business interests. In April, 1836, A. C. Allen was in New Orleans acquiring vessels to register under the flag of the cause of the Texian revolt. The Allen's owned vessels that were operating as privateers in the Gulf of Mexico and were providing supplies for the Texas army. They had a warehouse on Buffalo Bayou which they used as a staging area for materials and goods that were awaiting shipment, perhaps in partnership with William Tennant Austin, John Austin's brother. The existence of the Allen warehouse has been confirmed in the memoirs of George Bernard Erath. Two weeks after the battle of San Jacinto, Erath, leading his troops through the future location of Houston, noted "a single warehouse" near Buffalo Bayou belonging to the Allen brothers. The location of the Allen warehouse is generally thought to have been near the junction with White Oak Bayou, however, there is some evidence that suggests that the location may have been downstream, near the settlement on the bayou[100].

One other description of the area of Houston in its earliest days comes from Francis Lubbock. In his memoirs, published in 1900, Lubbock recounted a trip he took to the new town of Houston in late December, 1836. Leaving the steamer Laura and taking a yawl to scout the site of the town, Lubbock noted that "by close observation [we] discovered a road or street laid off from the water's edge. Upon landing we found stakes and footprints, indicating that we were in the town tract." He made his way up the bank of the bayou and along the freshly cleared street. There, he found a few small tents and another large one which was used as a saloon. Several houses were under construction and "logs were being hauled in from the forest for a hotel to be erected by Col. Benjamin Fort Smith." What Lubbock did not find was a warehouse[101].

Between these two firsthand accounts, we can surmise a few things. The Allen warehouse of 1836 did indeed exist, but it was not located at the new town site. The legend that the Allen's, or at least Augustus Allen, "lived" in the area that became Frost Town may have derived from the fact that the Allen warehouse was located downstream of White Oak Bayou near the future Frost Town area, and perhaps, near the natural landing at the foot of the modern La Branch Street.

The warehouse which the Allen brothers leased from William Austin would have been on the John Austin Survey. The southeast corner, and point of origin, of the John Austin Survey is located near the modern intersection of Franklin Avenue, Navigation Boulevard, Commerce Avenue and Hutchins Street all come together[102]. The Allen warehouse would be west of that point and near the bayou.

The warehouse also would most likely be near the San Felipe Road which passed near John Austin Survey point of origin. The road came directly over from Harrisburg to near the John Austin corner before skirting the forested area on the bayou by a route through the prairie to the modern West Dallas Avenue. The warehouse would not likely have been in the heavily wooded pine stands near the junction of White Oak Bayou, but it would more likely have been in the open prairie areas.

Each of these arguments is not conclusive in any one instance, but, taken together, they make a strong case for the location of the Allen warehouse of 1836 to be near the bend in Buffalo Bayou at La Branch Street, and perhaps on the adjacent block that a year later housed the Houston Arsenal.

Although A. C. Allen is known to have been in Columbia and in the area of the burned town of Harrisburg, there are no documents to indicate that he stayed in the village along Buffalo Bayou during the negotiations with Mrs. T. F. L. Parrott and William T. Austin in Brazoria for the purchase of the John Austin leagues or for the location of the site of the future town of Houston.

By the end of August, 1836, the Allen brothers had secured the purchase of one and one half leagues of John Austin's two leagues. They lobbied the Congress of the new Republic, and successfully established their new town of Houston as the new capital city. Builders, politicians, speculators and all sorts of other persons flocked to Houston to create a town out of the wilderness. Construction began in January in anticipation of the opening of the Congress on May 1, 1837. It was into this environment that Jonathan Frost brought his family and settled in the horseshoe bend of Buffalo Bayou, eight miles from Harrisburg, and about a half mile below the proposed town site of Houston[103].

Jonathan Frost built his home on land adjacent to William F. Hodge, who, like Frost, chose to establish a homestead near the new town. Lot sales and construction operations in the town occupied the Allen brothers in early 1837, but eventually, they came around to the settlers like Frost and Hodge to formalize the sale of the land on which they had constructed their homes. James S. Holman, a partner in the Houston Town Company, surveyed a fifteen acre tract bordering Buffalo Bayou on the north and lying adjacent to a ten acre tract on the west belonging to William F. Hodge. On the same day, April 13, 1837, in separate transactions, Augustus C. Allen and John K. Allen completed the sale of the fifteen acre tract to Frost and the ten acre tract to Hodge. Each tract sold for a price of $100 per acre. Thirteen days later, in a transaction that followed a similar pattern, the Allen's sold a fifteen acre tract adjoining Frost's land on both the south and the east to John W. Moody, the Auditor of Public Accounts for the Republic[104].

Few, if any considerations, were given by the Allen brothers to the civic infrastructure of their new town. Provisions for public drinking water and general sanitation were not made to any real extent. Those poor conditions promoted the outbreak of disease, and, in combination with the annual threat of yellow fever, the citizens of Houston were vulnerable to catastrophic epidemics and widespread death. Just as he was settling in and establishing his blacksmith shop, Jonathan B. Frost died at his home on September 16, 1837, at age thirty-two, of cholera. Frost was buried in the area that was later designated as the Frost Town cemetery[105].

Samuel M. Frost was appointed the administrator of the estate of Jonathan B. Frost on October 30, 1837 by Judge Andrew Briscoe. A security bond of $7,000 was placed with William F. Hodge, the neighboring farmer. There was some need to expedite the disposition of the estate since a number of debts existed, including the note for the purchase of the fifteen acres of land of the homestead. Samuel Frost asked the probate court, on March 26, 1838, to permit the sale of Jonathan Frost's land as sixteen lots of about one acre each. The plan was "to make each lot front the bayou and a street." The probate court ordered Samuel Frost to sell the personal property of Jonathan Frost before the court would approve the sale of the fifteen acres[106].

The inventory of the estate of Jonathan B. Frost filed by Samuel Frost in April, 1838 revealed the way the homestead was organized. Of the fifteen acres, only two lots of approximately one acre each had improvements. One of these lots contained a house and a blacksmith shop. Presumably, this was the home of Jonathan Frost. A second one acre lot also had a house which, possibly, was the residence of Samuel Frost since the deed of the subsequent sale of the property specifically mentioned that Samuel's residence was on the property[107].

In an attempt to reconcile the various interests of the five Frost heirs, a complex arrangement for the sale of the property was worked out between Samuel Frost and his brother James Frost. On April 28, 1838, Samuel M. Frost, as administrator of the estate, sold the fifteen acre tract to James C. Frost for $2000 after the land had been appraised by James S. Holman at $1950. Then, on the same day, James C. Frost deeded the fifteen acres to Samuel M. Frost for $2000 to finalize the deal[108].

After Samuel Frost obtained title to the fifteen acre tract, his plan for subdividing the land into lots changed. In June, 1838, Samuel M. Frost laid out a subdivision of eight blocks, lettered blocks A through H. The subdivision was two blocks wide and four blocks long. Each block had twelve lots in a pattern similar to that of the town of Houston. Each block had ten lots that were fifty feet by one hundred feet in size and two larger lots fifty feet by one hundred twenty-five feet. The main street of the subdivision was Spruce Street, a thirty foot wide lane running north-south between the two rows of blocks. The east-west cross streets were narrower than Spruce Street. Arch Street was eighteen feet wide, Race Street was twenty feet wide and Vine Street was eighteen feet wide. Two lots in Block H, numbers 7 and 8, were set aside for a cemetery since it is believed that Jonathan Frost was buried there[109].

On July 4, 1838, Samuel Frost sold Block A, lots 1, 2 and 4 to Henry Trott. This first transaction initiated the sales of lots, usually for $25 or $30 each, that would end up with sixty-six of the ninety-six lots sold by April, 1839[110].

Lots 7 through 12 in Block G were not sold in this first year of sales. That fact lends credence to historian L. W. Kemp's claim that the lots on Race Street at Pine Street were referred to as the Frost property as early as 1839, and it could have been the location of Jonathan Frost's home and his blacksmith shop. The Wood map of 1869 shows those lots to be vacant with the exception of a large house and one out building on lots 10 and 11. By that time, the property was owned by John W. Schrimpf[111].

County records indicate that the subdivision was platted as "Frost Town" and has always been spelled as two words on all manuscript documents. Auguste Girard, a retired Texas army officer, published a map of Houston in January, 1839 on which he included the Frost Town subdivision. However, he does not specifically name it. The first written reference to Frost Town was made in the September 11, 1839 edition of the Telegraph and Texas Register when four lots in "Frost town" were advertised for sale. The name referred specifically to the eight blocks of Frost's subdivision, but within a decade, the name Frost Town was associated with the neighborhood that developed around and near the Frost blocks. O. F. Allen, nephew of the city founders, writing in 1936, states that Frost Town referred to a large area of the Second Ward, commencing near Jackson Street and running parallel with Buffalo Bayou for about ten or twelve blocks along Runnels Street and Canal Street (formerly German Avenue) to about North Delano Street[112].

Samuel M. Frost had received a second class headright of 640 acres on June 6, 1838 as part of the land program in which second class headrights of 640 acres were awarded to single men who immigrated to Texas after the Declaration of Independence and prior to October 1, 1837. Yet, even though he had acquired the rural land, Frost was still in Houston in 1840. According to the tax rolls, in addition to his headright land, Frost owned other taxable property of three town lots in Houston, thirteen slaves and one watch. However, with the estate of his brother settled, Samuel Frost's concerns about the healthfulness of conditions in Houston convinced him to consider moving to the countryside[113].

On March 2, 1843, Samuel Miles Frost married Mrs. Harriet Harbert Hunter Head, a widow and the daughter of the pioneer settler Dr. Johnson C. Hunter of Fort Bend County. During the same year, Frost received a bounty land grant of 320 acres in Fort Bend County for his service of three months in the Texas army. He established a plantation on Oyster Creek and he expanded his operations by purchasing land up and down the Brazos River for cotton. With cattle ranches that his wife brought to the marriage, the Frost's became prominent landholders in the area around Hodge's Bend. Having sold his interests in the subdivision in Houston that bore the family name, Samuel Frost turned his attention to Fort Bend County and concentrated his efforts on farming and ranching along the Brazos River[114].

After sixteen years of marriage that produced eight children, five of whom were living at home, Samuel's wife Harriet died in child-birth on May 29, 1859. She was buried with her infant in the Dr. Johnson C. Hunter Cemetery (or Brick Church Graveyard) in Fort Bend County. The success and prosperity of their relationship was seen in the census record of 1860 which recognized Samuel Frost as a successful farmer in the Richmond area who, at age fifty-six, owned real estate valued at $76,510 and had personal assets of $99,975. Rhoda Frost, Samuel's mother, at age eighty-two, returned to her role of the lady of the household which included daughters Ada, age sixteen, Harriet, age three, and sons W. K., age thirteen, John Miles, age eight, and Franklin P., age five[115].

It appears that both Samuel Frost and his mother died sometime before 1870. At that time, the Frost household was headed by twenty-three year old daughter Ada B. Tabor who was either wid-owed or divorced. John M. Frost, age eighteen, and his brother Franklin, age fifteen, were attending school while living at the home in the Richmond area. But, it was not long before John Miles Frost took over the family ranching business and made a name for himself by importing Brahman cattle from India to Fort Bend County in 1885[116].

As the businesses in Fort Bend County prospered, John Miles Frost realized that greater opportunities existed in the city of Hous-ton which had become the economic center of southeast Texas. He was also attracted by other, more personal features of the city, and he married the twenty year old Rosa Bering on Sept 28, 1887. Rosa was the daughter of Theodore Bering, who was one of four Bering brothers who were prominent businessmen in Houston. Although August, Conrad and Charles Bering were well known in the lumber, wood products and hardware business, including the Bering Planing Mill on the southeastern edge of Frost Town, Theodore spent his career in the newspaper business as an agent and collector. In 1888, the Frost newlyweds built their two story, Victorian-style home at 406 Gray Avenue in Houston, not far from the homes of the many Bering family members nearby in what was euphemistically called "the Bering Settlement," and their son John Miles, Jr. was born on September 4th of that year[117].

About the turn of the century, Frost built a new home at 404 Gray Avenue, next to his first house, for his wife and their growing family. In addition to John Miles Frost, Jr., who was called by the playful nickname "Jaybird," son Henry was born in August, 1890, daughter Rosa was born in May, 1892, son Kenneth was born in June, 1894, son Clarence was born in September, 1896 and daughter Annie was born in November, 1899[118].

John M. Frost, at age 49, had become a successful real estate investor in Houston, however, he still considered himself primarily a rancher and farmer, and he was active in the operations of the Frost ranches along the Brazos River. In 1901, Frost was instrumental in the construction of the first rice canal to irrigate the crops as rice farming was introduced to Fort Bend County. He was the Treasurer of the Rice Canal at Clodine, and he also was the cattle commissioner for Houston[119].

As the children grew up, John M. Frost sought to keep the family close together and to prepare each of his children for the business world that he knew so well. Although John M., Jr. had married Julia Estelle Settegast, the daughter of prominent businessman J. J. Settegast on July 6, 1909, the young couple was still living at the family home on Gray Avenue in 1910, along with the other five children. In 1911, Vernon W. Frost was born, the seventh child of the fifty-nine year old John Miles Frost and his wife Rosa, age forty-three, and the new addition to the household may have prompted the oldest son and his wife to move on to their own home[120].

J. Miles, as the senior Frost was calling himself at the time, was a successful real estate agent, and he had both J. Miles, Jr. and Henry, the next eldest son, working with him as real estate agents. But, the farm and ranch business was still an important part of the family. By 1920, John M. "Jaybird" Frost, now thirty-one years old, considered himself a ranch manager, although he continued to live in Houston at 320 Sul Ross Street with his wife Julia and son John Miles III, age 5, and infant daughter Marion. Likewise, sons Henry, Kenneth and Clarence, while they each still lived at the family home on Gray Avenue, worked as cattlemen on the family ranches[121].

During the 1920's, as the discovery of oil in Texas was changing the economy of Houston and southeast Texas, the real estate expertise of Frost and his sons enabled them to take advantage of the new opportunities for leasing land for oil exploration. By the end of the decade, John M., Sr. and son Milo, the name John M., Jr. was going by, had become oil lease landmen, while Clarence M. "Pete" Frost was in the production side of the oil business[122].

The youngest Frost son, Vernon, also entered the oil business, but, he followed a path dictated by an unfortunate event. While still in high school, Vernon lost an eye in an accident, and he had to quit school. Due to various circumstances, including the advanced age of both parents, Clarence Frost filed for temporary guardianship of his brother Vernon W. Frost on February 11, 1929, who was a minor at that time. Clarence tutored Vernon and provided him with a job in an oil refinery doing clerical work. Eventually, the two brothers became partners in the oil business[123].

The elder John Miles Frost died in 1934 at age eighty-three. His namesake, John Miles Frost, Jr. died August 4, 1963 at age seventy-four. Both men found their fortune in the real estate dealings of the oil business and they both died in Houston, the center of the oil industry. Vernon Frost, however, returned to his roots in the Brazos valley. At age thirty-six, in 1945, he purchased a one thousand acre tract of land near Simonton where he established his Pecan Acres Ranch. The Pecan Acres Ranch was a wholesaler of pecans, and it established a reputation for producing prize winning Brahman cattle, the breed introduced to the area by his father over sixty years earlier[124].

Although Vernon Frost had moved out to the countryside, he never gave up his connection to the city. In 1952, Frost rode in the first Salt Grass Trail Ride, and he was a director of the Houston Fat Stock Show which evolved into the Houston Live Stock Show and Rodeo. He continued his association with the event until his death on July 11, 2000 at his ranch in Simonton at age eighty-nine. The passing of the last member of three generations of the Frost family brought to a close a chapter in the story of Houston that had its beginnings with the birth of the city, and followed the emergence, growth and maturity of the agriculture, cattle, real estate and oil industries of the area for over a hundred and sixty years[125].

From the Wood Map of 1869 in the author's collection.

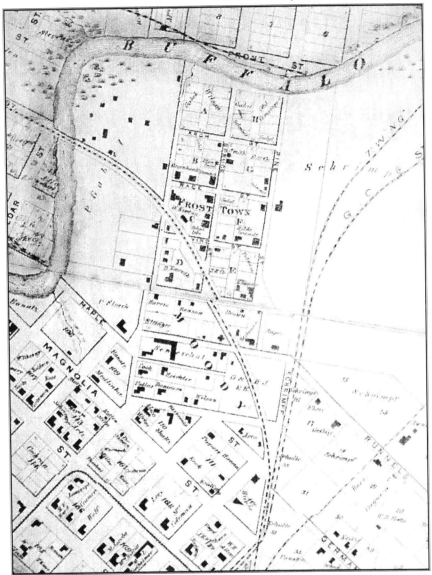

This map of the Frost Town Subdivision and the Moody Addition shows the ownership of lots in the neighborhood at the peak of the "German" period.

The German Immigrants

Although Samuel Frost decided that his future lay elsewhere than Frost Town, others welcomed the chance to live in the area. Within a year of the initial sale of lots in Frost Town, two thirds of the ninety-six lots had been sold. Although Frost Town was to become a largely German neighborhood, the buyers of the first lots were not German. They had typically Anglo-American names reflecting the cultural heritage of the majority of the first citizens of Houston.

Speculation in land and real estate was rampant in the first years of the Republic, and Houston, as the new capital of Texas, seemed to have more than its share of speculators and deal makers looking to make a quick buck. Few of the original purchasers of lots in Frost Town intended to build houses, and there was a relatively large amount of resale activity involving the lots.

One of the first, if not the first, German to buy a Frost Town lot was H. W. Carl, who, on November 5, 1838, bought one half of Frost Town Block E, Lot 5 from Q. N. Kinman. Carl himself seems to have been speculating in real estate, too, since there are a number of transactions in which he bought and sold lots in a short time. For example, he bought Frost Town Block H, Lots 1 and 2 from William W. Haygood on March 18, 1839, and he sold the lots to George Van Buren and Jonathan H. Hahn three months later on June 18, 1839. Although it is not clear that H. W. Carl ever lived on Block E, Lot 5 in Frost Town, his daughter Henrietta did marry John W. Schrimpf, on May 19, 1842, and she reigned as the "grande dame" of the Frost Town community for thirty years[126].

Starting in late 1839 and continuing through the 1840's, Germans began settling in the Frost Town area. By the late 1840's, there were about seventy-five German families and single men living in and near Frost Town. German colonists, passing through Houston and headed for the interior of Texas, often found friends and relatives in Frost Town and, instead of continuing on, chose to remain in the settlement near Houston. They blended easily with several Irish families who also came to the area to establish a community on the elevated and well-drained curve of Buffalo Bayou[127].

So common was the German language in the Frost Town neighborhood that the area was referred to as Germantown. At least, that is the story that has been told and retold for over a century. Although the story could possibly be true and the use of the name Germantown may have been common in the colloquial conversations of the day, there is no documented evidence of the use of the term Germantown for Frost Town. There may, however, have been some confusion among later writers with the Germantown that did exist. W. H. Sandusky filed a survey of the Germantown Subdivision, lying one and one half miles northwest of downtown Houston, on June 2, 1840. The location of this development was north of White Oak Bayou, near the modern intersection of North Main Street and Houston Avenue[128].

The Germans who came to Houston were only a small fraction of the large number of German immigrants who came to Texas in the 1840's and 1850's. What made them come in such large numbers? Why did Germans come to Texas more than persons from other countries?

Europe, in the aftermath of the Napoleonic wars, was undergoing profound and far reaching social changes. The decline of the guild system and the rise of industrialization and free trade laws created an economic crisis among the artisans and the handicraft industries. High population density and the scarcity of arable lands caused unrest and diminished opportunities for the agricultural communities while the potato famine that ravaged Ireland also struck the continent of Europe, including Germany. Popular unrest brought the specter of revolution, and when the German state governments sought to bolster their armies, many Germans immigrated to escape the military draft[129].

For all of these reasons, the flow of Germans into Texas surged during the 1840's. The prospect to gain the freedom to live without the social barriers of European society was very attractive to many Germans. Texas was perceived as a land of total freedom where one could live independently and have a better life. An overwhelming spirit of adventure and curiosity about Texas was inspired by German writers such as A. Korduel who wrote in his 1846 book that "there was a paradise on earth named Texas." And, to top it all off,

many German communities granted financial support to those wish-
ing to emigrate[130].

Each immigrant who settled in Frost Town had a unique story,
and it is possible to generalize too broadly. Nevertheless, the Germans who settled in Frost Town had a well deserved reputation as
an industrious, hard working, frugal and civic minded people. Many
of them were skilled tradesmen, craftsmen and working class laborers who went about their business each day and became the unher-
alded fabric of the city. In an attempt to provide a sense of these
people, the experience of the one German immigrant, Constantine
Fix, and his family may help to illustrate the character of the Frost
Town community from the 1840's to the 1880's.

Constantine Fix was born about 1804 in a small village in the
Black Forest region of the German state of Wuerttemberg, a region
also famous for the cities of Stuttgart and Heidelberg. He was one
of five surviving children of a master tanner of the village. Infant
mortality had claimed four other siblings. When Constantine came
of age, he chose to become a master potter since his older brother
had taken over the family tannery shop, and as a result of the decline
of the guilds, the shop could not support two master tanners[131].

At age thirty-seven, Fix married Teresa Farber and three years
later, in anticipation of brighter economic opportunities, they decided to immigrate to Texas with their two young children, age 2
and 9 months. The decision to leave Wuerttemberg was not taken
lightly, and the process of emigration was quite bureaucratic. Fix
had to submit an application for release of his German citizenship,
he had sign away his burgher rights, and he had to promise not to
wage war against the kingdom of Wuerttemberg. Furthermore, to
prevent a person from abandoning his financial obligations by
leaving town, a bondsman had to be hired to pay any outstanding
debts or obligations. On the other hand, the local municipality was
willing to provide support and assistance to Fix to enable him to
make the journey from his small village to the port city of Antwerp
and on to Texas[132].

The passage to America on a ship was a considerable undertaking in those days. The trip took about twelve weeks and the cost was
fifty Dutch florins, equivalent to about $600 today. A contract with
the shipping company was required by the passengers, and in Fix's

case, he contracted with the Society for the Protection and Transportation of Emigrants to America, a transportation business owned by F. Outendirk and Company. In addition to the fare, the passengers were required to bring enough food and supplies for each adult for the entire length of the voyage. Each adult had to bring: forty pounds of ship biscuit, ten pounds of bread, fifteen pounds of salted meat, six pounds of lard, forty-five pounds of flour, one hundred fifty pounds of potatoes, two pounds of salt and two quarts of vinegar[133].

The trip across the ocean was often difficult, at best. Storms and rough seas were common, and disease and epidemics frequently spread through the close quarters of the relatively small and crowded ships. Constantine Fix, his wife and 2 children set out from Antwerp for Houston in the spring of 1847. The two young children died either during the voyage or shortly after their arrival in Houston[134].

As was the case for many Germans coming to Houston, the Fix family found friends and acquaintances from the homeland in the Frost Town area. They settled among their friends and tried to establish themselves in their new home. After the loss of their first two children, Constantine and Teresa Fix were able to celebrate the birth of their first Texas child, Charles in 1851, four years after their arrival. Charles was baptized by the Lutheran Pastor Casper Braun, a minister who also came from Wuerttemberg. A certain Mr. Staehlen, a relative of the local official in their home village who had assisted them in the preparations for their trip, was the boy's the godfather. A second son, Conrad, was born two years later, in 1853[135].

On February 13, 1854, Constantine and Theresa Fix bought a lot in the Frost Town Subdivision. They purchased Block D, Lot 5 from L. and Maria Strauss, perhaps, with the intention of building a small house on the fifty by one hundred foot lot. However, about a year and a half later, the Fix's sold the lot to Johann Illig. It is unclear whether the sale was prompted by a sudden need to get cash, or whether Constantine's wages as a laborer were simply not sufficient to permit him to invest in a home. In 1860, the Fix family was living in the household of John W. Schrimpf, who had apartments which he rented to two other families, the Bonatz family and the Cunningham family, as well. After more than a decade in Houston, Fix, at age fifty-six, did not seem to be exceptionally prosperous since in the census of that year he listed no real assets and no personal assets[136].

Houston residents endured several episodes of yellow fever during the nineteenth century. Many of the epidemics were especially virulent and had a profound effect on Houston's population. Citizens of every social status were struck down as the fevers of the disease spread across the city in the late summer and early fall. In 1867, Houston endured a particularly deadly yellow fever outbreak that killed many in the city. Teresa Farber Fix, age 47, and son Charles, age 16, died in the yellow fever epidemic of 1867. The epidemic hit the residents of Frost Town very hard, and the gruesome stories of bodies of children lying unburied in the streets have been repeated many times. Those who died in Frost Town, including Teresa and Charles Fix, were probably buried in the Frost Town cemetery[137].

By 1870, the sixty-five year old Constantine Fix was probably nearing retirement after decades of working as a laborer in Houston. In an interesting sidelight, Constantine Fix listed his occupation on the census form as potter, perhaps indicating that in retirement, he was able to pursue his original craft. His son Conrad, age seventeen, was employed as a wood cutter. The extension of the East Texas piney woods along the north bank of Buffalo Bayou had provided jobs and hard work for young men since the founding of the city. Many worked in the timber lands of the Germantown survey of the northeast quadrant of the John Austin League to supply the raw materials for the local building trades[138].

It is believed that Constantine Fix died in 1872 or 1873, although no record of his death is available. He no longer appears in the city directories. Son Conrad, however, in his twenties, continued to work and live in Houston. On September 30, 1878, Conrad Fix, at age twenty-seven, married Mary E. Priest at the First German Evangelical Lutheran Church in Houston. The young couple lived on the very edge of Frost Town. Their residence was located on the northeast corner of Magnolia Street and Chenevert Street[139].

In 1884, Conrad Fix was a driver for Protection Hose Company Number One of the volunteer fire-fighting brigade, and he resided at 150 Texas Avenue between Fannin Street and San Jacinto Street. By 1886, Fix was employed as a laborer with J. G. Illig, owner of a confectionery and ice cream parlor located at 109 Fannin Street, between Texas Avenue and Capitol Avenue. Illig also rented a room to Fix at the business location. This is the last we know of Conrad Fix in Houston. However, his story does not end there. In fact, the Fix story has a strange twist[140].

Conrad Fix and his wife moved back to Germany in the late 1880's. Although neither he nor his father had ever been employed in high paying jobs or in any other way appeared to accumulate any material wealth, Conrad Fix returned to his father's homeland as a wealthy man and raised a family. He retained his United States citizenship until 1915, during World War I, and in 1983, his grandson Wolfgang Fix recounted the rest of the story on a trip to Houston to visit the birthplace and former Frost Town residence of his great grandparents and his grandfather who emigrated from Texas to Germany[141].

The seeds for the German community of Frost Town were sown during the two decades prior to the Civil War. By the mid-1840's, German immigrants had established themselves sufficiently in Houston that they were able to make investments in real estate and build homes. During this period, a number of deed transactions for Frost Town lots were recorded. Yet, interestingly, the percentage of German ownership of lots in Frost Town was still a fairly small percentage of the ninety-six lots.

Some of the names involved in the sale of Frost Town lots are familiar. John W. Schrimpf bought and sold lots in Blocks B, G and H during this period. Henry Scholibo bought a lot in Block C, Johann Klee also bought lots in Block C, George Dagenhart bought lots in Block B, J. Schroeder sold a lot in Block E to Henry Klepper, and Reinhardt Hildebrandt acquired lots in Block E. Others sales involved J. Rutersdorf in Block D, A. D. Duebner, L. Strauss, J. Buerking, F. Schmitt and Karl Priester for lots in Blocks D, F and G[142].

After 1850, Peter Gabel became very active in the acquisition of Frost Town lots. He bought several lots in Blocks A and H from Michael DeChaumes, an architect who designed an early county courthouse, in the six years prior to the Civil War. Gabel's intention appears to have been real estate speculation or income producing rental property since he was well established by this time in his residence on Preston Avenue[143].

Frost Town was a thriving German community by early 1854. German singing societies added to the cultural life of the city. The Houston Turn Verein had its beginnings at this time as well. The religious life of the German community supported the establishment and growth of Catholic, Lutheran and Methodist churches and a synagogue in the area surrounding the Frost Town area. Frederick Law Olmstead, passing through Houston, remarked that the majority of small tradesmen and mechanics in Houston were German. The Galveston, Houston and Henderson Railroad reached Frost Town area in 1853. The depot and train yards near Commerce Avenue and St. Emanuel Street made it convenient for those employed by the railroad to live nearby in homes in Frost Town[144].

The homes in Frost Town were modest and similar to many houses of the period. A typical Frost Town residence was a white frame cottage built of cypress as a square dog-trot with three rooms on each side of central hall and a roof sloping over the front porch. The roof had central dormer windows front and back to provide light to the loft, and there were separate buildings for the kitchen, a well house, a smokehouse, a wash house, a chicken house, a barn and a privy[145].

The homes were small, mostly clapboard houses, with flowering shrubs, gardens and animals, such as a cow, goats and chickens, to make a self-contained domestic unit. The gable-roofed cottages conveyed an elegance in their simplicity. Although the streets of Frost Town were narrow, like alleys, and covered with boards or wooden planks, as a neighborhood, Frost Town offered a convenient blend of a rural homestead in an urban environment[146].

The Civil War was a difficult time for Houstonians. The war time conditions included shortages of basic foods and materials as many items were diverted to support the war effort. In Frost Town, the major development of the war years was the construction of a railroad line across the neighborhood. The importance of rail transportation for the war effort probably permitted the use of locally scarce resources for the building of the two mile line linking the Galveston, Houston and Henderson Railroad terminus on Commerce Avenue with the Houston and Texas Central rail yards on the North Side of Buffalo Bayou at Allen Street.

The Galveston and Houston Junction Railroad Company, an enterprise chartered on April 8, 1861 by the same owners as the Galveston, Houston and Henderson Railroad, began buying right of way along an arching path from the terminus, through the Moody Addition, through Frost Town Blocks C, D and E, and across the Gabel tract and the bridge over the bayou to the Houston and Texas Central depot[147].

The Galveston and Houston Junction Railroad acquired lots and portions of lots in Frost Town Block C from W. and Rosina Kwetton and from the heirs of M. Connelly. Lots in Block D were acquired from Franz and Joanne Steiner and from H. and Mary Lahn. Lots in Block E were purchased from H. D. Taylor. Two of the five land owners were German, a proportion that reflects the overall percentage of land ownership in Frost Town by Germans at this time. With the land for the tracks acquired, the two miles of the Junction railroad that included the first railroad bridge across Buffalo Bayou were completed in 1865. The Galveston and Houston Junction Railroad merged with the Galveston, Houston and Henderson Railroad in 1871[148].

Following the Civil War, Houston attempted to recover its economic drive and its optimism that had made it a vigorous commercial center. This civic optimism is seen in the publication of the first City Directory in 1866. This booklet attempted to highlight what the city was all about and who were its citizens. Of special interest is the fact that it provided a listing of residents who lived in Frost Town and it identified each resident's occupation. With this information, we can get a good picture of the make up of the Frost Town community as a working class neighborhood.

Frost Town in the decade after the Civil War was the German community that has been described by twentieth century writers. The German immigrants who arrived in the 1840's and 1850's had established themselves and the community matured during the 1860's and 1870's. When the researchers in the 1930's interviewed the aged former residents of Frost Town, those residents recalled a pleasant, if not somewhat idealized, time in which they grew up in the close knit neighborhood. And, without a doubt, many of these

German residents were respected businessmen and citizens of Houston who felt that their lifelong values were formed by their youthful experiences in the small suburb.

The Wood Map of 1869 is the earliest record that identifies the specific locations of residences in Houston. As recorded on the Wood Map, there are a total of thirty houses and structures on the eight blocks of the Frost Town Subdivision. The two blocks along the south bank of Buffalo Bayou, Block A and Block H, have no houses. Frost Town's Old Cemetery was located in Lots 7 and 8 of Block H. Block B has five houses and Block G has four houses. Block C has six houses and Block F has five houses. Lastly, Block D has six houses and Block E has four houses. In all, there are thirty houses on the ninety-six lots of the Frost Town Subdivision. At this time, in 1869, only a third of the subdivision is developed. Those who lived here characterized the finest qualities of the neighborhood and their stories have come down to us today as the story of Frost Town[149].

Scholibo

Henry Scholibo arrived in Houston from Hesse Kassel in Germany about 1847 with his wife Catherine and their three children. On September 10, 1852, Scholibo purchased Lot 10 in Block C of the Frost Town Subdivision from Henry Sampson and there he built his home. The Scholibo house is located one lot north of the northwest corner of Vine Street (later called Bramble Street) and Spruce Street. By 1860, Henry Scholibo, at age forty-seven, was employed as a tinner. His real assets of $300, as indicated on the census of 1860, reflected the value of his lot and house in Frost Town. The household included his wife Catherine E. Scholibo, age fifty-one, and children Henry, age twenty, a carpenter, Charles, age fifteen, a baker, and Anna, age fourteen[150].

On May 5, 1866, William J. Settegast married Annie Elizabeth Scholibo, who was born November 1, 1846. They had eight children: Emma E., Sophia, Katie H., Mary E., Julius J., Charles Edward, Mary Blanche, and Charles Steward. By 1877, the Settegast family had moved to the home on Valentine Street in the Fourth Ward that the Settegast brothers had built for their two families.

Annie Scholibo Settegast died at Hot Springs, Arkansas on July 14, 1881[151].

Charles F. Scholibo, Annie's brother, arranged his own marriage in conjunction with the marriage of Annie and William Settegast. The double wedding ceremony in May, 1866 was accompanied by the special celebration of the shivaree that was a common practice in Frost Town at the time which reflected the cohesiveness of the neighborhood.

The shivaree was a raucous festivity provided to the bridal party by the local men. Derived from the French and established in the New Orleans area by 1805, the shivaree was common along and west of the Mississippi River during the 1800's. The participants would sing, shout and make outlandish noise in a mock serenade of the newlywed couple in hopes that they would pay the revelers to cease their activities. Sometimes the shiveree lasted for days[152].

Jules Bertrand, in the 1930's, recalled with distinct pleasure the shivaree of the Settegast and Scholibo weddings in 1866. Although Bertrand was only ten years old at the time, he remembered vividly his participation in the celebration of the dual ceremonies for these prominent families of Frost Town. The shivaree at his own wedding a decade later attested to the enduring practice of the shivaree through the years of the German Frost Town[153].

Charles and Mary Scholibo established their home in Frost Town. In 1870, Charles became a naturalized citizen of the United States and he was a prominent baker in Houston for over three decades. By 1900, Charles Scholibo had moved from the house at 83 Spruce Street in the Frost Town Subdivision, but he remained close by, living a few blocks south at 1704 Franklin Avenue with his wife and several of his grown children. Son Ed, age thirty-two, was a railroad clerk. Son Charles, age thirty-one, followed in his father's footsteps and continued in the bakery business, while daughter Emma, age twenty-one, was a house keeper. Frederick, at age eighteen, worked as a collector and the youngest child, Mable, age fourteen, lived at home. Son William Scholibo, age twenty-eight, had married about 1892, but he and his family lived nearby at 1714 Franklin Avenue. William was a paymaster with the railroad, and, in 1900, he and his wife Hattie, age twenty-six, had two children,

Joe A., born in September, 1893, and William, born in October, 1896[154].

The elder Charles Scholibo passed away between 1900 and 1910, yet, in 1910, his widow Mary continued to live at the home at 1704 Franklin Avenue. Son Frederick still lived there as well, and he was employed as a plumber. Daughter Emma had married about 1904, and she and her husband Ernest Newton Mills, age thirty-nine, lived in the family home with their daughters, Marie E., age five, Emma M., age four months and son Ernest N., age three[155].

By 1920, Ernest N. Mills, age forty-six, had become the head of the household at 1704 Franklin Avenue. He worked as a real estate manager, and the household included not only his wife Emma, thirty-nine, daughters Marie Elizabeth, fourteen, Emma May, ten, and sons Ernest Newton, twelve, Frederick Oliver, eight, but also his mother in law Mary Scholibo, age sixty-nine. In addition, the household also included the Scholibo daughter Mable McGaughey, age thirty-six, her daughter Julia May, age eleven, and son John L., age seven. Mable was employed as a chief clerk at the Houston Electric Company[156].

After the death of Mary Scholibo in 1929, the Mills family continued to live at the family home, while the Scholibo families moved away from Frost Town and the Second Ward to Montrose area neighborhoods. Ernest Mills was a successful investment broker by 1930. He and his wife Emma along with their twenty-one year old son Frederick, who worked as a real estate accounts collector, lived in the home on Franklin Avenue while their neighborhood was becoming home to large numbers of Mexican immigrants[157].

Dagenhart

On October 29, 1855, W. P. Hamblen sold to Lots 2, 3 and 5 in Block B of Frost Town to George Dagenhart (sometimes spelled Deigenhardt). In 1866, Dagenhart, born about 1816 in Prussia, listed his occupation as a drayman, or delivery man, but in the census of 1870, it was recorded that his product was milk, thus, he was a milkman. He lived in Frost Town with his wife Catherine, born about 1812, and daughter Annie who was born about 1849. The family immigrated to Texas from Prussia sometime after 1849. The

Dagenharts sold their Frost Town property, valued at $1000, to Catherine Kehoe on April 12, 1870, and they moved to the Third Ward[158].

Catherine Kehoe, who was born in September, 1838, was married to the thirty-five year old John Kehoe, a day laborer. They had immigrated to Texas from Ireland prior to 1862. In 1870, the Kehoe family included sons William, age 8, and Thomas, age 1, both of whom were born in Texas. During the 1870's, Mrs. Kehoe ran the boarding house on Gabel Street that catered to men who worked for the railroad[159].

After the death of John Kehoe, Catherine married a Mr. Anderson, and in 1900, she still lived with her son Thomas and his family at their home at 100 Gabel Street. Thomas Kehoe's wife was Susie and their children were Kattie M., born December, 1894, and Thomas R., born May, 1899. Kehoe worked as a cotton classer[160].

Thomas Kehoe was successful in the cotton business. By 1910, he was a manager at the cotton company. With prosperity, Kehoe chose to move the family from the declining neighborhood of Frost Town. The typical pattern was to move south or southwest as one's economic situation improved. The family bought a home at 212 Hawthorne Street in the Montrose area, near the modern intersection of Smith Street and Hwy 527 ramp off US 59. By 1930, Kehoe had become a cotton factor and had moved to the upscale neighborhood near Hermann Park and Brays Bayou at 2425 Calumet Street[161].

Klepper

The vitality of any community is seen in its ability to engage in social activities together. During the 1860's and 1870's, Frost Town's residents enjoyed the special entertainment of square dances at Henry Klepper's barn every Saturday night[162].

Henry Klepper purchased Lot 4 in Block E from J. and Mary Schroeder on June 3, 1846. He had immigrated from Hesse Kassel, and as a carpenter by trade he was able to make a good living. By 1860, the forty-six year old Klepper had acquired real assets of $1000 and personal assets of $100. His household on Lyle Street near the corner with Pine Street consisted of his wife Eliza, age thrity-six, and sons Henry, age ten, Louis, age eight, and August, age six. All of the children were born in Texas, and Henry's mother Julia, age seventy, also lived with them[163].

As was a common custom in those days, Henry Klepper took in boarders. One boarder in 1860 was A. Meyer, a twenty-seven year old man who was born in Hanover and worked as a cooper. The other boarder at the Klepper house was Anton Riesner. Riesner had immigrated with his family from Berlin, Germany in 1847 and settled in Brazoria where he worked as a cooper. Seeking better opportunities in Houston, Anton Riesner began working in Houston until he could finally bring his family to Houston from Brazoria in 1862. His son Benjamin A. Riesner later became a prominent businessman and City Alderman who was responsible for introducing the electric fire alarm system to Houston[164].

Henry Klepper and family continued to live on Lyle Street through the 1870's. His fourth son Alfred had been born in 1860, and his eighty-one year mother Julia still lived with them. On July 1, 1874, Klepper bought the south half of the adjacent Lot 5 from Charles W. Schrimpf. Beyond that date, however, little information of this family appears in the public records. By 1900, John Oberholz and his family lived in the home at 1825 Lyle Street. By 1930, Will Taylor and his wife rented the house for their residence. Taylor, an African-American cemetery laborer, was only one of the many blacks who moved into the Frost Town area during the 1930's[165].

Klee (Clay)

Johann Klee came to Texas about 1852 with his wife and two sons. Klee was born in Hesse Kassel about 1817, but lived in Prussia where his wife was born, about 1825, and they had their first two sons there prior to immigrating to America. On February 19, 1853, Johann Klee bought Lot 7 in Block C in the Frost Town Subdivision, on the southwest corner of Spruce Street and Race Street, from W. Braun and Christiana Buerking Braun. And, although he also purchased Lot 5 in Block C from Daniel and Jane H. Perry on March 18, 1855, Klee made his home on the corner lot[166].

Working as a laborer, Klee had real assets of $300 by 1860, indicating the value of his Frost Town property. The Klee household had grown to include wife Caroline, age thirty-five, the two oldest sons Adam, age twelve, and Amiel, age nine, and the Texas-born children John, age six, Antone, age three, and Anna, age one[167].

By 1866, Johann Klee had Anglicized his name to John Clay, and he was employed as a clerk. By 1870, the Clay family had grown with the addition of daughters Zetta in 1863 and Emma in 1866. Clay worked as a dray driver and value of his real property had increased to $800[168].

Later in the 1800's, Mary (Mrs. Anton) Clay operated a grocery in Frost Town on the corner of Spruce Street and Race Street called the "Anton Clay's Grocery[169]."

By 1900, the Clay family had moved away from the home and store at 95 Spruce Street in Frost Town. They leased the building to two enterprising merchants who had immigrated from Eastern Europe. These men operated a store on the site and identified themselves in the census record as peddlers. Finally, on November 4, 1909, Walter Clay deeded Lots 7 and 8 in Block C to Jacob Gaber. In 1930, the house and adjoining store was rented by John Garcia, an immigrant from Mexico, and his family and the Simon Duran family, also from Mexico. In 1952, the last operator of the grocery at 95 Spruce Street was Dave Martinez who leased the property from Mrs. Jacob Gabor. The property was acquired by the state for the right of way for the Elysian Viaduct which was built in 1954[170].

Klopp

Henry Klopp, a native of Hanover, and his wife, born in Prussia in June, 1831, arrived in Texas prior to 1854, the year their son Charles was born. On January 16, 1857, Klopp purchased Lots 1 and 2 in Block F in Frost Town from C. A. Priester. In 1860, the forty year old Henry Klopp was employed as a cooper, or barrel maker, and had real assets of $400 that reflected the value of his home and two lots[171].

The Klopp family was a popular fixture in the Frost Town community during the 1860's and 1870's as their family grew. Henry, Jr. was born on October 20, 1865. William F. was born in 1861. Edward was born on April 15, 1870, and John was born on July 29, 1871[172].

Difficult financial conditions seemed to plague the Klopp's. On August 1, 1874, they issued a deed of trust to Lot 2 Block F to F. A. Schafer for the use of Reinhardt Hildebrandt, their neighbor. Things appeared to improve a few years later, and on August 23, 1882, Caroline Hildebrandt sold Lot 2 Block F back to Louisa Klopp. Yet, within a year, on July 10, 1883, R. B. Talfer acquired Lots 1 and 2 in a sale by the Tax Collector. A year later, on May 30, 1884, R. B. Talfer released the tax lien on the title to William F. Klopp. The Klopp's did better financially for while, but a decade later, on May 1, 1895, the City of Houston filed a tax lien on Lots 1 and 2[173].

The Klopp family was an extraordinarily cohesive group, and through all of the financial difficulties, the family remained close. In fact, the 1900 census data, indicates that the widowed Louisa Klopp, the sixty-nine year old matriarch of the family, lived with the families of the three sons at the family home at 1813 Bramble Street (Lot 1, Block F), at the corner of Spruce Street[174].

A total of fourteen persons occupied Louisa Klopp's home. Edward Klopp and wife Riley had a ten month old son Willey, 10 months, born June 14, 1899. Henry Klopp and his wife Caroline had two sons, Henry, Jr., born October 23, 1889, and Paul, born July 19, 1891. The youngest son, John Klopp and his wife Emilia had their daughter Molley, born April 29, 1897, and her children from a prior marriage, Fredie Koenig, born Feb 2, 1887, Will Koenig, born Sept 13, 1890 and Sophia, born March 9, 1892[175].

Three of the four sons followed their father into the barrel-making trade, and as late as 1900, each of these sons was still employed as a cooper. William worked as a contractor building houses in the city, and that trade may have allowed William Klopp to prosper enough to leave the declining Frost Town neighborhood for the Fifth Ward[176].

By 1910, however, the Klopp's abandoned their home at 1813 Bramble Street. A comparison of the Sanborn insurance maps of 1907 and 1924 shows that the original house on Lots 1 and 2 was replaced a by a slightly larger house sometime before 1924. The original house may have been moved, razed or, perhaps, destroyed by fire. The eighty-three year old mother Louisa moved to a small house next door at 1815 Bramble Street, and, at this point, the children, now adults and with families of their own, began to find their own homes. John Klopp moved his family a few blocks to the west to a house at 1611 Maple Avenue in the old Floeck tract. Edward Klopp moved across Buffalo Bayou to 919 Clark Street at Nance Street in the Fifth Ward with his wife and daughter and son. He continued to work as a cooper for an oil refinery. William F. Klopp resided at 419 Boundary Street in the Fifth Ward (north of Quitman and the modern I-45) and was employed as a contractor building homes[177].

Delinquent taxes continued to cause problems for the Klopp's. The City filed a tax lien on Lots 1 and 2 Block F on October 23, 1907, and the City and the state filed additional tax liens on the property in 1911 and 1913 respectively. Ultimately, the various law suits involving the taxes and the Klopp property were resolved on March 24, 1920 when C. S. Settegast was deeded Lots 1 and 2 Block F to settle suits involving the Klopp heirs, William Klopp, John and Emilia Klopp, Henry and P. Klopp, and Edward Klopp[178].

In 1930, the house at 1813 Bramble Street was rented by Alberta Morgan, a forty year old black widow who had come to Texas from Mississippi. Morgan, who worked as a seamstress, paid $20.00 per month in rent for her family, which included her three daughters and one son[179].

Hildebrandt

As a young man in his mid-twenties, Reinhardt Hildebrandt and his wife Elizabeth, a native of Saxony, immigrated to Texas from Hesse Darmstadt in the mid-1840's. His work as a laborer was sufficient for Hildebrandt to purchase real estate and settle among the German community of Houston's Frost Town Subdivision. On August 7, 1849, Reinhardt Hildebrandt bought Lot 6 Block F in Frost Town from Adam and Johanna Buerking. He acquired Lot 12 Block F from John Fitzgerald on December 31, 1852, and on May 22, 1855, Hildebrandt purchased Lots 10 and 11 Block F from W. R. Baker to complete the assembly of a tract in Frost Town upon which he would build his homestead[180].

By 1869, the Hildebrandt family had two houses on their tract in Frost Town. One house was located on Lot 12, in the center of Block F along Vine Street (later named Bramble Street). The main house was on the southwest corner of Vine Street and Pine Street on Lots 10 and 11. The valuation of these real assets in 1860 was $800, but the economic effects of the Civil War are apparent in that, by 1870, the valuation of the same property was only $100[181].

Two children were born into the Hildebrandt family. Simon was born in 1854 and Margaret was born in 1858. Since Simon alone is listed in the census of 1870, it is presumed that Margaret died prior to 1870. Rhinehardt Hildebrandt was well known as a gardener, and he listed that as his occupation in 1870. The sixteen year old Simon worked at a brewery at that time[182].

After the death of Rhinehardt Hildebrandt, sometime after 1874, Simon and his family lived at the family home on Lots 10 and 11. By 1900, the address was designated as 1823 Bramble Street. Simon had married Anna Forsman, an immigrant from Sweden, in the early 1890's, and the family included her son John Forsman, their daughter Margarete and their son Reinhardt[183].

In 1910, the fifty-seven year old Simon Hildebrandt was employed as a tinner, and his stepson John also worked in a tin shop as a tinner. Sometime between 1910 and 1920, Simon died and, in 1920, only Anna Hildebrandt, 60, and her daughter Margaret lived at 1823 Bramble Street. By 1930, the house at 1823 Bramble Street, valued at $5000, had been sold to an Italian immigrant family[184].

Steiner

One of the often told stories of Frost Town is that of the Steiner dairy and its unorthodox system for the delivery of milk to homes in the community. School children were enlisted to take milk to customers in Frost Town, and as payment for this work, each child received a glass of milk to drink. The extent to which this system existed is unclear, but it is a charming story of life in German Frost Town that has become legend[185].

The proprietor of the dairy was Franz Steiner, an immigrant from Prussia who was born in 1809, immigrated to Texas with his wife Johanna, who was three years his senior, some time before 1853. On January 5, 1853, Steiner made a large investment in real estate when he purchased Lots 1, 2, 3, 4, 6, 12 and parts of Lots 9 and 11 in Block D in Frost Town from William and Mary Ferguson.

He added Lot 7 and other parts of 9 and 11 on March 9, 1860 which he bought from A. C. Smith. This gave Steiner the majority of the land in Block D, especially after the Galveston and Houston Junction Railroad set tracks across the north and west portions of the block in 1865[186].

Franz Steiner was a shoemaker by trade, and by 1860, his Frost Town property was worth $1000. The Civil War, however, appears to have brought difficult financial times to Steiner since he sold his property to John R. Neurath on May 23, 1867. On the Wood map of 1869, the Steiner property is shown as being owned by Neurath. However, Steiner's fortunes must have improved rapidly after the war since Steiner purchased Lot 12 and parts of Lots 3 and 9 from Henry Richter on May 11, 1868 and then reacquired his property from John R. and Mary A. Neurath two weeks later on May 26, 1868[187].

John R. Neurath was a young tailor from Frankfurt who, at age 34 in 1870, had a family that included his Texas-born wife was Mary, age 24, and son John, age four, and daughter Catherine, age two[188].

While still working as a shoemaker, by 1870, Frank (Anglicized from Franz) Steiner had personal assets of $700 to complement his property which was valued at $500. In addition, the sixty-one year old Steiner had married for a second time to Fredericka who was fifteen years younger and had come from Hesse Darmstadt via New York and Illinois. The Steiner family included Fredericka's children from her previous marriage. Amelia Souder was born in 1856 in New York, and the other siblings, born in Illinois, included Herman, age ten, Bertha, age seven, and Annie, age five[189].

During the 1870's, the Steiner family operated the dairy in Frost Town that gave the family its lasting fame. The bird's eye map of 1873 shows that there were four or five houses on the Steiner property, situated along Lyle Street and Gabel Street. The remaining portion of the property in the interior of Block D was vacant and could have provided the area necessary for the dairy cows. However, by 1891, when a second bird's eye map was drawn, the Steiner property on Block D had a house on every lot[190].

Fredericka Steiner celebrated her seventy-fifth birthday in December, 1900. She still lived at the family home at 1803 Lyle Street, in the second house from the corner with Gabel Street. By this time, however, she was residing with her daughter Bertha, son-in-law Carl Jantz and her granddaughter Ellie, born November, 1890. Jantz, born in September, 1862, had immigrated to Texas from Germany about 1881 when he was nineteen, and he married Bertha in 1888. Although he began working as a day laborer, Jantz eventually mastered the carpentry trade and was a building carpenter for most of his career. In all probability, he was responsible for the construction of the houses on the lots owned by the Steiners to take advantage of the growing demand for low cost housing during the 1890's and early twentieth century[191].

By 1910, it appears that Fredericka Steiner had died since only Carl and Bertha Jantz were listed at the address at 1803 Lyle Street. By 1920, Carl and Bertha Jantz had moved next door to the house on the corner with Gable Street at 1801 Lyle Street. According to the census records, the Jantz family owned that house while the other houses on the Steiner lots were rental property, suggesting that the Steiner/Jantz family owned the rental houses on their lots, including 1801, 1803, 1805, 1809 and 1811 Lyle Street and 64, 66, 72 and 74 Gable Street[192].

The demographic pattern of the Steiner property provides an insight into the way Frost Town's ethnic makeup had changed during the early part of the twentieth century. In 1920, the renters in the Steiner houses on Lyle Street consisted of twenty-two black families and adults, including the large rooming house at 1809 Lyle Street, and three Mexican families. Along Gable Street, there were four Mexican families and one black family.

By July, 1927, the Steiner/Jantz lots in Block D had become part of the MK&T Railroad Freight Terminal. The probate records indicate that the Jantz family had moved several blocks east into the Second Ward to a residence at 218 Hutcheson Street after the sale of their lots in Frost Town. Carl Jantz died about October, 1932 and his wife Bertha passed away about April, 1949[193].

Schrimpf

Undoubtedly, the most prominent family to live in Frost Town, besides the Frost family itself, was the Schrimpf family. On July 20,

1847, John W. Schrimpf purchased Lots 14 and 15 in Moody Square Number One from Richard Insall. The deed indicated that one of those lots was "now occupied as part of the residence of said John W. Schrimpf." Lots 14 and 15 of Moody Square One are located on the east side of the Frost Town Subdivision, opposite Frost Town Block G between Race Street and Arch Street[194].

Although the lots of Moody Square Number One are numbered 1 to 20 going north to south on both the Girard map of 1839 and the unnamed Houston map of 1900, a numbering of the lots in that order would place Lots 14 and 15 opposite Bramble Street. The Wood map of 1869 and the bird's eye map of 1873 however, clearly place homes in the location near Race Street. This suggests that the numbering of the lots in Moody Square Number One should be south to north, with lot number 1 being near Lyle Street. Then, Lots 14 and 15 will be opposite Frost Town Block G near Race Street.

Since Girard's map of 1839 displays questionable, and sometimes incorrect, numbering schemes for the Frost Town Subdivision as well as for the City blocks in Schrimpf's Field, there is a good chance that his map also inaccurately numbers the lots in Moody Square Number One. Both the Wood map and the bird's eye map of 1873 have good reputations for accuracy, and the location of the home of John W. Schrimpf opposite Race Street on those maps is probably accurate.

John E. Schrimpf married Fredericka Richter who lived nearby with her family on April 24, 1856. This prompted the Schrimpf's to look for another home. On May 29, 1857, John W. Schrimpf bought Lots 11 and 12 Block G in Frost Town from M. DeChaumes. Although the two Schrimpf brothers were partners in nearly all of their business transactions, it was John W. Schrimpf who made the deals. A second home was built on Lot 11 Block G for the other brother's family. Lot 11 Block G was on the corner of Race Street and Pine Street and was nearly opposite the home of his brother in the Moody Square Number One. There is a question, however, of which brother lived in which house[195].

The enumeration sequence of the Census of 1870 provides some clue to the answer of where each Schrimpf brother lived. The enumeration of dwellings was in this order: 175-Rhine Hildebrandt, 176-John E. Schrimpf, 177-Henrietta Schrimpf (John W.'s widow),

178-Jemima Reremo, 179-John Clay. This sequence corresponds to the sequence of homes along Pine Street as shown by the Wood map of 1869. The John E. Schrimpf home, listed second in order, is on the east side of Pine Street. John W. Schrimpf's home comes next in the sequence and is on Lot 11 Block G. The next two dwellings, for Jemima Reremo and John Clay are in the enumeration sequence as it turns west along Race Street[196].

About 1870, J. E. Schrimpf moved to a residence on Ann Street, a few blocks east of Frost Town, prior to his death shortly thereafter. Henrietta Schrimpf and her son Charles continued to live at their home in Frost Town until her death about 1873. After the death of his mother, Charles W. Schrimpf deeded the home on Lots 8, 11 and 12 Block G in Frost Town to W. J. and J. J. Settegast in a sale by the Tax Collector on April 8, 1877, and he settled the long running lawsuit with the Settegast brothers involving the lots of the John W. Schrimpf family home on July 30, 1879[197].

Although it was platted as a distinct subdivision outside of Houston, Frost Town was never separately incorporated. In 1840, the City set an arbitrary rectangular bound as the City limit that extended as far west as the modern Gillette Street and as far east as the modern North Velasco Street. Frost Town fell within these city limits at that time. A generation of German immigrants gave their character to Frost Town for a quarter of a century from the 1850's to the 1870's. The height of German Frost Town was the 1870's, but the generation that first settled in the area was on the wane, and the essential character of the community was in transition.

Many commentators have contended that Frost Town's decline began when the Galveston, Houston and Henderson Railroad was built through middle of the community in 1865. Although the tracks did separate the northern part of the Frost Town Subdivision from its lower blocks and the adjacent Moody Addition lots, it was the introduction of the railroads to the area, in a larger sense, that changed the course of Frost Town. The creation of a rail yard and the Galveston, Houston and Henderson Railroad, the International and Great Northern Railroad and the Texas Western Railway terminals near Commerce Avenue and Chartres Street, southeast of Frost Town, led to the rise of an industrial site on the east side of downtown which eventually included heavy industries around the perimeter of Frost Town Subdivision that included the Bering Planing Mill, the Kuhlman's Wood Yard and the Kuhlman's Hay and Feed Warehouse, the Hartwell Iron Works, the Meyers Spalti Manufacturing Company, the Citizens Electric Company (later Houston Light and Power Company), the National Biscuit Company, and other businesses.

Other changes in the community also indicated a neighborhood in transition, if not decline. Although Frost Town had mail delivered by letter carriers, and the first postmen were William Barell and a Mr. Phiffer, this privileged service was discontinued to the neighborhood in the 1880's. The Frost Town Cemetery, used during the yellow fever epidemic of 1867 and others, fell into disrepair in the 1880's, and ultimately it disappeared into the bayou. Even the private cemetery of the Schrimpf family, in which Henrietta Schrimpf and her brother-in-law J. E. Schrimpf were the only ones interred, was lost to the development of tenant houses on the Moody tract and Schrimpf's Field[199].

In 1873, during the "golden age" of the community, Frost Town had a total of thirty-four houses on its ninety-six lots. By 1891, there were forty-four houses on the Frost Town blocks. However, those early simple wood frame houses or log construction residences were described in 1890 as a "dreary huddle of shabby houses[200]."

The census data of 1900 indicate a shift in demographic patterns in the Frost Town Subdivision and the area known as Frost Town in general. Between 1870 and 1900, the neighborhood experienced a decline as a result of the differences in the social and economic status of those who lived in the area. Prosperity allowed many of the German and Irish families to move to more affluent neighborhoods which were developing on the city's perimeter to the south and southwest. Those who then moved into the area were at a lower level on the social and economic scale.

After the Civil War, former slaves arrived in Houston from the countryside. The emancipated blacks settled in areas around the city, especially in the Third Ward, in Freedmenstown on the outskirts of the Fourth Ward, and in the Frost Town area of the Second Ward. These lower income blacks were able to take advantage of the availability of housing in Frost Town, and by 1900, the once predominantly white subdivision had become racially mixed. The distribution of the one hundred forty-three families and single adults was 55.9% black, 44.1% white and none were Mexican[201].

A steel truss swing bridge was constructed over Buffalo Bayou at McKee Street in 1904, opening access to the industries on the north side of the bayou to workers living in Frost Town. This increased proximity to places of work enhanced the appeal of the area for the unskilled workers. In the period from 1891 to 1907, the number of houses on the Frost Town blocks more than doubled to a total of ninety-seven houses. This increase in the number of houses, mostly rental properties, was accompanied by a similar pattern of growth in the city blocks surrounding the old subdivision.

The population of Houston, and of Frost Town, continued to grow in the first decade of the twentieth century. Mexican immigrants began to move into Frost Town while white residents moved to other areas of town. The black population also increased significantly during this period. By 1910, of the one hundred eighty families and single adults living in Frost Town, 78.3% were black, 17.8% were white and 3.9% were Mexican[202].

Houston was in the upturn of an economic cycle as the 1920's began. Industrial development was spurred by the opening of the Ship Channel and its associated industries, by the rise of railroad transportation and by the advent of the oil industry. Workers for these businesses came to town and many of them found housing in Frost Town. The population of the Frost Town Subdivision rose to two hundred fifty-nine families and single adults at this time. The ethnic make up of Frost Town reflected the rise in the immigration of Mexicans to Houston as the population distribution in Frost Town in 1920 was 49.4% black, 20.1% white and 30.5% Mexican[203].

In the mid-1920's, a new, if different, sense of community was forming in Frost Town. The former subdivision not only had a total of one hundred two houses, but within the original blocks, there were seven stores and one church. Five of the stores were located in Block C and seemed to be clustered near the Houston Light and Power facility on the west side of Gable Street. The Lively Hope Colored Baptist Church was located on Lot 9 Block H near Buffalo Bayou.

In an ironic twist of history, the neighborhood came to be called Blackbridge, a named derived from the old black steel bridge at

McKee Street. Built in 1904, the bridge was in serious disrepair by this time. Sections of the bridge began to fall away from the structure, and, in 1928, it was demolished. Leona E. Walls, a black woman who lived on Lyle Street and on Arch Street recalled in 1992, that during the time she lived there, "she never heard of 'Frost Town[204].'"

The changing patterns of settlement continued throughout the first quarter of the twentieth century as Mexicans immigrated to Houston to fill the demand for workers in the emerging industries in the City. The white population of Frost Town declined sharply while the black population remained in the majority. By 1930, the distribution of families and single adults in the Frost Town Subdivision was 65.8% black, 10% white and 24.2% Mexican[205].

El Barrio del Alacran

The two decades from the 1930's to the 1950's was a time for the final generation of residents to live in Frost Town as a community. Along Spruce Street and the cross streets of Race Street and Bramble Street a close knit group of Mexican families lived where the neighborhood was equally mixed between Mexican and black families. At this time, many children played, went to school and grew up in the shadow of the downtown business center while the fathers worked to support the families and the mothers managed the meager resources and simple furnishings of the homes.

According to the 1930 census data, the occupations of the Mexican men living in Frost Town were those of a working class. Nearly every head of the household had a job and most of the older sons were employed in jobs that included shoe maker, biscuit company laborer, biscuit company baker, compress laborer, cafe cook, printer contractor, livery stable laborer, baker at a hotel, street construction laborer, cotton compress laborer, railroad machinist helper and plumbing contractor laborer.

Although a large number of the Mexican families had immigrated from Mexico, many of them, although of Mexican heritage, had come to Houston from other parts of Texas. Such was the case of the Vara family who lived on the southeast corner of Spruce Street and Race Street. Luz Coy Vara's family came from San

Antonio. They had arrived there in the 1730's as some of the earliest Spanish settlers in Texas and coming from Guerrero, Coahuila, Mexico. The Vara family came to Houston about 1934 and Luz, the youngest daughter was born on May 2, 1937 in the second story apartment of the clapboard, two story house at 72-1/2 Spruce Street, south of Bramble Street[206].

The Vara apartment in the house on Lot 6 Block E consisted of four rooms, three rooms upstairs and one room on the first level. A small porch on the front of the structure extended about two thirds of the way from the left side of the house, where the front door was, to the right. A one story lean to addition provided a room across the back of the structure. The house was built sometime before 1907 when it was shown on the Sanborn map in much the same form as it was in the 1950's. The house did not appear on the bird's eye map of 1873, but, it seems be represented on the bird's eye map of 1891[207].

The Vara's moved to the southeast corner of Spruce Street and Race Street and rented the house at 96 Spruce Street from Mr. Jacob Gaber. As a little girl, Luz was fascinated by Mr. Gaber as he would drive down Spruce Street in his convertible, stopping at each rent house that he owned to collect the rent[208].

Growing up in Frost Town during the 1940's was an experience like most children have. With many other kids in the neighborhood, they found places to play and things to do. Following the alley behind the Alice Emerson Meat Market and the Arthur Steves Lumber Company to the McKee Street bridge, the children had fun playing on the banks of the bayou, doing the things kids like to do, fishing, swimming and just playing around. They could meet up with the Campos kids who lived along the alley and make their way to the bridge. The concrete, fixed span bridge was built at McKee Street in 1932 to replace the old steel bridge, and the flowing curves of the new span captured the imagination and fascination of the young kids[209].

For years, garbage and trash from the homes in Frost Town was disposed of by throwing it into the bayou. At the bend in the bayou immediately upstream of the McKee Street bridge, the refuse pile was frequented by scavengers so that the place was known as

Raccoon Bend. The old bottle dump was subsequently registered as an archeological site with the state.

Luz's brother, who was twelve years her senior, played baseball with the boys in the neighborhood at a ball field on the edge of Frost Town. The houses that existed along the north end of McDonald Street (previously called Pine Street and later called Rains Street) had been torn down to build the Humble Oil and Refining Company Production Warehouse at the north end of Schrimpf Street. The pipe yard covered the vacant lots from Race Street to the bayou, but there was enough open space east of Rains Street at Arch Street for a ball field[210].

Luz Vara attended school at the Rusk School on McKee Street and Maple Avenue. Located on the tract that had been the home and the brewery of the Martin Floeck family during the 1800's, the Rusk School was only a few blocks from the homes in Frost Town and it was easily accessible by them. Many of the Mexican children in Frost Town and the surrounding area attended the school, and it became known as "the Mexican school," reflecting the tri-ethnic segregation of school children that was common at that time. The Texas Constitution of 1876 called for separate schools for "white" and "colored" children, but when large numbers of Mexican immigrants began coming to Texas and Houston, in particular, at the turn of the century, the segregation of Mexican children was enforced more by the patterns of settlement into neighborhoods like Frost Town in addition to the customs of the local school districts, than by any law. The matter was finally resolved in 1973 as the Houston Independent School District complied with court ordered plans for the desegregation of all students[211].

The curriculum at the Rusk School centered on variety of vocational skills, and the cooking program was exceptionally good according to Luz Vara. Although the Varas moved to a home on Canal Street before she finished her education at the Rusk School, Luz continued to go to the school and graduated from it in the early 1950's.

Although as a child in Frost Town during the 1940's, Luz Vara could remember how muddy the streets were, the lack of electricity in their home required them to come inside when it was late, and that served to shield her from the aspects of Frost Town after dark. Her older brother, however, knew that the neighborhood, the barrio, could be a wild and dangerous place. With some sense of irony, Frost Town was known to those who lived there during this time as "El Barrio del Alacran," the neighborhood of the scorpion.

The Alacran moniker appears to be a variation from the "shrimp" of Schrimpf Street which made a long arching curve away from Frost Town toward Buffalo Bayou along the path of the Galveston, Colorado and Santa Fe Railroad tracks. The transformation of the image from curling tail of the benign shrimp to the more sinister image of the scorpion may reflect the frustration and dissidence of some elements of the community[212].

The Ku Klux Klan held meetings in the two story house on the southwest corner of Bramble Street and Rains Street in 1939. Although the neighborhood was by this time, largely a mix of black and Mexican families, the Klan sought to provoke fear and intimidation among the Mexican residents as well as among the blacks. These were difficult times during the Depression and people were easily cowed. Many of the older persons who lived in Frost Town through these times still prefer to avoid mentioning that they had lived in this barrio because they felt oppressed and segregated there[213].

The cantina, located at 92 Gable Street, near the southeast corner with Race Street, was the place that provided the local night life. Usually, the excitement was generated by the accordion rhythms of "conjunto" music and other mild forms of revelry. However, on one night in 1948, the cantina burst with gunfire and became the scene of a shootout between Sabino Trevino and "El Blackie." In an episode that made a lasting impression on the eleven year old Luz Vara, the gun fight was likened to the "Tex Mex OK Corral." One man was killed, the tranquility of the neighborhood was shaken, and the local legend was born[214].

More than anything, though, life in Frost Town during the Alacran period was life among neighbors. The block of Spruce Street from Race Street to Bramble Street was the Vara's community. They knew the families up and down the street, and they shared the good times and bad. The Varas lived on the southeast corner of Spruce Street and Race Street. The neighborhood grocery was directly across the street in the old store formerly owned by the

Anton Klee family, and was last owned by Dave Martinez in 1952. The three houses to the south of the Vara's were the homes of the Villours family, "Cappie" and Luz's uncle Felix Vara. Luz's brother went off to Navy in 1942, and Johnny Villours joined the Army, but did not return. Johnny was killed in action in World War II[215].

Standing on her front steps, on the corner of Spruce Street and Race Street, in the heart of Frost Town, Luz Vara's childhood world lay before her as she looked up the street to the bayou to her right and down the street to her left. The familiar grocery store was across the street, and the families of her friends lived in either direction in her neighborhood. The Lopez family lived on the other corner. They had lived at 99 Spruce Street since before 1930, and during the 40's, Martin, Johnny and Josephine were part of the local youth.

One gentleman of the community had a problem handling alcohol and he was often drunk. On the days when he could not resist the urge to imbibe, he would stand in the intersection of Spruce Street and Race Street singing dedications to the women who lived in the homes on each corner. The community had a way of taking care of its own. When the inebriated crooner finally passed out, a group of the neighbors would drag him to the shade of a tree so he could sleep it off.

A few black families lived on Spruce Street and its cross streets in Frost Town, but many more lived along McDonald Street and its cross streets. On the south end of the subdivision, there was a tavern that catered to blacks on the northwest corner of Bramble Street and Rains Street (it was renamed from McDonald Street by this time). At the north end of Rains Street, the Lively Hope Missionary Baptist Church served the needs of the local black community, and sometimes, the Mexican inhabitants. One young girl, although she was a Catholic, would go to the church on Sunday just to hear the congregation of the Baptist church sing.

On the west side of Spruce Street, near the corner with Bramble Street, was a row of shotgun houses. The Ramirez family lived in the middle of the block. The Buendias family lived next door to them, and the Hernandez family lived on the corner at 79 Spruce Street. Several other Mexican families lived on Bramble Street, such as Garcia, Mesa and De la Cruz families, as well as farther north on Arch Street where Joe Borrita and the Borrita family lived. The

MKT Railroad tracks cut through Frost Town south of Bramble Street and formed the southern boundary of the community. Buffalo Bayou was the boundary to the north. And, as a whole, these families and numerous others formed the basis for a vigorous, though impoverished, community in the historic subdivision that was on its way to obscurity[216].

In 1951, there were a total of ninety-five houses in the Frost Town Subdivision. This number is slightly lower than the one hundred two houses that existed there in 1924. In some cases, new houses were built in Frost Town after 1924 such as the development at West Rains Street. West Rains Street was a small street, not much more than a driveway, in the middle of Frost Town Block F. The street extended west from Rains Street (formerly McDonald Street) for about one hundred feet. Along each side of the street were three duplex houses, each facing into the dead end street that was paved with bricks[217].

The six small duplex dwellings on West Rains Street (called West McDonald Street in the 1930 census) were small, one story frame houses with primitively carved porch columns. Each duplex had one large apartment and one smaller apartment. In 1930, the larger apartments rented for $18.00 per month while the smaller ones rented for $9.00 per month. Since the West Rains houses were relatively new, they were able to command a higher rate of rent. The older houses along Race Street and McDonald Street rented for $8.00 to $12.00 per month[218].

But, the construction of a few new houses were the exception, not the norm, during the this period between 1930 and 1950. Frost Town was becoming increasingly isolated as a residential community because of business and industrial development in the surrounding area. The Houston Light and Power Company plant on Gable Street expanded to the north side of the GH&H railroad tracks for the construction of its cooling tower complex which resulted in the removal of the thirty-five houses in the Kapner development on the west side of Gable Street. The north half of the Moody Square One lost twenty-two dwellings to the Humble Oil and Refining Company Warehouse and Pipe Yard by 1951[219].

Further adding to the deterioration of the neighborhood was the Hartwell Iron Works. Hartwell's was established on the south half of Moody Square Number One some time after 1896. By 1903, it was in operation and provided architectural iron work for many of the City's buildings. Fire had destroyed the plant some time prior to 1951 and the dilapidated ruins lay across the street from Frost Town, enclosed by a six foot wire fence[220].

Within the boundaries of Frost Town itself, there were significant encroachments on the residential nature of the community. In addition to the removal of all but five of the houses in the southern-most Moody Addition blocks, the construction of the Missouri Kansas and Texas Railroad Freight Terminal and the adjacent Builders Supply Warehouses in 1926 eliminated thirteen houses in Frost Town Block D. The Arthur Steves Lumber Company, on the east side of Gable Street, was situated on the west half Block A, the closed Arch Street and part of Block B. The Alice Emerson Meat Market was next door to the lumber company on McKee Street and occupied a large part of the west half of Block B. By 1951, five homes in Block E were lost to an auto repair business with a parking lot at the corner of Rains Street and Lyle Street[221].

The eight blocks of the original Frost Town Subdivision, by 1951, had become an isolated residential neighborhood. Industrial development encircled the community and industrial traffic along the widened McKee Street and the new McKee Street bridge had shifted the residential entrance to Frost Town to the corner of Rains Street and Bramble Street. While Spruce Street and Arch Street remained unpaved, Race Street was a shell road because it was used by trucks going from Gable Street to the oil company warehouse on the east side of the neighborhood. When columnist Sigman Byrd wrote about the site in 1952, he described Spruce Street as a narrow alley, only one car wide, that was full of pot holes and trash. An open sewer drained on each side of the road and a lone chinaberry tree stood on the east side near the high point from which Spruce Street, beyond Race Street, sloped gently down to Buffalo Bayou. He declared Frost Town to be one of Houston's worst slums[222].

The demise of Frost Town, however, was already in the works. The post-World War II economic boom led civic planners to envision automotive links across Buffalo Bayou from the northeast side of town. Elysian Street was to be connected by an elevated roadway through Frost Town to Crawford Street and U. S. Highway 59 was to be constructed over Schrimpf's Field and joined with the new highway route east of Jensen Drive on the north side of the bayou. The highway projects complemented the Clayton Homes urban renewal project of 1952 that replaced the slums of Schrimpf Alley. The two proposed highway projects would be the end of Frost Town as a residential neighborhood, and those who lived in Frost Town began relocating in the late 1940's and early 1950's.

Early in 1952, only a few residents remained in Frost Town. Dave Martinez owned the grocery at 95 Spruce Street, the same location in which Mrs. Anton Klee had operated a grocery in the 1880's. Across the street, Jimmy Carpio and his son Doroteo were planting roses in front of their house at 86 Spruce Street. In the next block, at 102 Spruce Street, Mrs. Albina Allen was preparing to leave her residence of over two decades, and the home which her husband Lorenzo had acquired more than fifty years prior[223].

Lorenzo W. Allen was born in August, 1861 in Michigan. He married his first wife Cora in 1882, and since she was a Texas native, they were probably in Texas and Houston at the time. Allen appears in the ownership records of Frost Town in 1894 when he was involved in a suit over Lots 1 and 2 of Block G. Various law suits on these lots continued until about 1911, but ultimately, Lorenzo Allen acquired title to the lots and the house on Lot 2[224].

In 1900, Lorenzo Allen, age 39, lived at 102 Spruce Street with Cora, age 37, and their son Vernon, age 15, who was born in March, 1885 in Texas. Lorenzo listed his occupation in 1900 as a mailman. His nephew Albert Allen, age 23, born in June, 1867 in Texas, lived with them and worked as a day laborer. The house was large enough that they also had a lodger, the twenty-one year old Florine Lora[225].

By 1910, Lorenzo W. Allen was working at his profession as a carpenter and building contractor. His son Vernon, age 24, still lived with them and worked as a general house carpenter. He remodeled the old frame house and expanded it to nine rooms. Allen jacked up the house and built a half basement of masonry and concrete. He also made improvements such as the installation of a septic tank system which was believed to be the only such system in Frost Town[226].

With the added space, he was able to rent the apartment to Manuel Gonzales, a thirty-four year old laborer whose parents had immigrated from Mexico, his wife Christine and their young sons Tony and Mike. Later, he rented to the Florez brothers, Cereeho and Francisco, who worked as day laborers for the railroad. In 1930, Lorenzo and his wife rented the apartment to a young, thirty-eight year old widow, Albina Perdue, who had married at age thirty-three, but had lost her husband. Albina helped to nurse Cora Allen through a long illness, and after Cora died in 1946, the elderly Lorenzo married Albina[227].

The Lorenzo and Albina Allen house reflected the special love and care that persons can show for a place they called their home. Lorenzo's craftsmanship showed in the detailed features of the gingerbread trim and the green shuttered windows. Albina's feminine touch was seen in the lace curtains at the windows. The house and yard were a veritable garden of vines clinging to the walls of the house, ferns hanging from the upper gallery and a broad display of colors in the roses, violets, phlox and geraniums growing in the inner courtyard[228].

After nearly sixty years as a resident of Frost Town, Lorenzo Allen died on December 13, 1951 at the age of ninety. In early 1952, Albina was preparing to leave her home in advance of the condemnation of the property for the right of way for the Elysian Viaduct. The new elevated roadway would curve out of downtown at Crawford Street, turning north over the intersection of Race Street and Spruce Street, and follow along the east side of Spruce Street to cross the bayou. The Allen home, on Lot 2 Block G, lay directly in this path and it was razed. Albina Allen died in late 1962 or early 1963 at age 70. Her will was filed for probate on January 16, 1963[229].

The Elysian Viaduct, a joint project of the City of Houston, Harris County and the State of Texas, was built in 1954. In 1955, there were still a few frame houses remaining from the 1860's and 1870's on lots lying outside the path of the viaduct. However, these old homes characterized by steep slanting roof lines, hand molded nails and quaint chimneys were not to survive as bulldozers clearing the area for the construction of U. S. Highway 59 took their toll on the last remaining gable-roofed cottages in Frost Town. In 1990, there were only six wood frame homes standing in Frost Town. Only one was left by 1995, and all were gone by 1999[230].

Epilogue

Just as Houston's first suburban subdivision seemed destined for the oblivion of forgotten history, the area's fortunes were rescued by a small group of dedicated individuals led by artist Kirk Farris. Farris petitioned the City to allow him to revive the drab, but historic McKee Street Bridge by painting it in shades of aquamarine, lavender and purple. With paint donated by the Bute Paint Company and with lighting provided by the Wholesale Electric Supply Company, the revitalized McKee Street Bridge was unveiled and celebrated on Bridge Day, July 19, 1985.

In 1985, Farris founded Art and Environmental Architecture, Inc., a nonprofit entity, to continue the rejuvenation of the McKee Street Bridge and to develop park around the environs. AEA operated a park under lease agreements with various property owners and promoted an arrangement to buy land for a park. Commissioner El Franco Lee was visionary enough to support the efforts of AEA, and in 1992, the process of acquiring the land began. In 1994, Harris County finalized the purchase of the land for James Bute Park, and Farris organized a group of volunteers to flatten the land into a sculpted green space.

James Bute Park consists of a little over twelve acres around the Frost Town site, including five and one half acres in Frost Town and the adjacent Schrimpf's Field owned by the Texas Department of Transportation (TxDOT). Farris hopes to fashion this green space into a park of luscious gardens at the McKee Street Bridge and to preserve the footprint of Frost Town. The goal envisioned for the James Bute Park/Frost Town Historic Site and Urban Gardens is to establish an interpretive historic site with visitation gardens as an anchor to the eastern edge of the Downtown District[231].

Farris was alerted to the archeological significance of the Frost Town site in 1985 when he found people digging up the area along the banks of the bayou at Raccoon Bend for bottles and artifacts. In 1990, highway construction crews uncovered two cisterns on Frost Town lots. The contractors took a few items from the cisterns and discarded other items, including a spoon from the settlement that Farris recovered, before covering the cisterns with soil. The episode made it clear that more cisterns and archeological features remained on the property.

In the fall of 2003, the Williams Brothers construction crews working on the new ramps to US 59 discovered two cisterns and a trash dump on the former Frost Town lots. According to Mike Solvay, the construction foreman, the sites were preserved as much as possible and were re-buried under about four feet of dirt. The locations of these sites were forwarded by Farris to TxDOT since they were on state property.

These nineteenth century cisterns were large, bell shaped underground structures built of brick and lined with plaster. The cisterns were built close to homes in order to collect rain water runoff from the roof. The cistern water was used for animals, gardens and household chores, but it was generally not potable. Drinking water came from artesian wells. The careful investigation of these features and their contents can add a tremendous amount of knowledge to our understanding of life in Houston during the nineteenth century.

Doug Boyd of Prewitt and Associates, Inc. of Austin, working as a subcontractor for Carter and Burgess in September, 2004, located remnants of cisterns and foundations of houses as a part of the investigations for the rebuilding of the Elysian Viaduct. Three intact cisterns and the substructure for three house footings were located in Block H, Lot 12 at 1813-1815 Arch Street, and in Block C, Lots 7, 8 and the edge of lot 9 at the intersection of Race Street and Spruce Street, the site of the historic Anton Klee grocery[232].

These recent demonstrations of the significance and value of the Frost Town site may finally awaken the community to the treasure that has been lying hidden in the shadow of the downtown skyscrapers. The Frost Town Historic Site is ready and waiting to happen. On May 22, 2010, an Official Texas Historical Marker for the Frost Town community was placed on the site to recognize the significance of Frost Town in Houston's history.

The Moody Addition - The Other Part of Frost Town

Access to a river or a stream is, and has been, a major consideration in the estimation of the value of a tract of land. In the early days of the Republic of Texas, settlers acquiring property in Texas sought land located on major streams, and many of those who bought land on the periphery of the town of Houston from the Allen brothers wanted land that fronted on Buffalo Bayou.

Today, the tree-lined south bank of Buffalo Bayou, sitting in relative obscurity less than a mile east of Main Street, shows little of the potential as prime real estate that it held for one of its earliest owners. A two hundred thirty-one foot segment of the south bank, now visually indistinguishable in the riparian vegetation along the bank, was part of a fifteen acre tract that John Wyatt Moody purchased from Augustus C. Allen and John K. Allen in 1837[233].

John Moody was born in Lunenburg County, Virginia, 65 miles southwest of Richmond, on June 10, 1776, and, as a teenager, he moved with his family to Iredell County, North Carolina in 1790. He married Mary Baldwin in Warren County, Ohio, on March 13, 1806, and after living in several places in Alabama, Moody finally moved his family to Wyumka in the Creek Indian territory in 1833. While there, he became interested in the settlement of Texas, and he came to Texas in May, 1835 with his wife Polly, his three sons Francis, John and William and daughter Dorinda. He settled first in Bastrop, but moved to La Grange in 1836[234].

Within a short time after his arrival, Moody became an active participant in the independence movement. On December 20, 1835, he was elected as the auditor of the Provisional Government. As the Texas Army was being formed, he was appointed to the Legion of Cavalry on January 9, 1836, with the rank of Major. After the victory at San Jacinto, Moody became the Auditor of Public Accounts for Texas, a position he held during the first two years of President Sam Houston's administration. He was in Houston in the spring of 1837 in an official capacity with the new government of the Republic of Texas as were many others who were drawn to the town by the convening of the Congress on May 1, 1837[235].

On April 26, 1837, A. C. and J. K. Allen sold to Moody fifteen acres of land "adjoining the City of Houston" and "adjoining the land of Frost," as described in the deed. Moody's property shared a common boundary with the fifteen acres of Jonathan Frost along both the south and east edges of the Frost tract. From the southeast corner of the Frost tract, the Moody property line went due north to Buffalo Bayou. The property line then followed the bayou east for two hundred thirty-one feet to the boundary of the land owned by Samuel M. Williams. The Moody property line followed the Williams property line due south for 1,534.5 feet to a stake in the prairie which is near the modern intersection of Canal Street and Chartres Street. From that stake, the boundary went due west "to a stake near a cluster of small post oak trees in the prairie," which is near the modern intersection of McKee Street and Chenevert Street, before returning to the origin near the Reliant Energy southern property line on McKee Street. The "backwards L" shape of Moody's tract locked in the Frost property, and the long, slender parcel on the east side of Frost's land gave Moody access to Buffalo Bayou[236].

The description of the Moody property in the deed gives us an idea of what the terrain was like in 1837. The expanse of land south of Buffalo Bayou was a coastal prairie. Clusters of small oak trees dotted the prairie, but the trees did not seem to be a dominant feature of the landscape. A riparian woodland was most likely found along the banks of the bayou.

The price that Moody paid for his land was $1,500, or $100 per acre. Both Jonathan Frost and William F. Hodge had purchased adjacent tracts of land two weeks earlier for the same price of $100 per acre. With these three transactions, the Allen brothers netted $4,500 for a fairly small portion of their 6,647 acres of the John Austin Survey that they had purchased in August, 1836 for $9,428, approximately $1.42 per acre. True to their profession as land speculators, the Allen brothers sought to sell the land around the town of Houston at more than fifty times what they paid for it[237].

During the boom town atmosphere that characterized Houston in the first few years of the Republic, everyone seemed to be a land speculator, or wanted to be. The deed records of the county are filled with the notations of land sales, and John Moody actively participated in this practice. It does not appear that Moody intended to live on the fifteen acres that he bought near Frost and Hodge. He owned other property in town and it appears that he lived there. Moody also acquired property and built a home north of Houston on Spring Creek, perhaps intending to make that his residence[238].

Early in 1838, Moody subdivided his fifteen acre tract, which became known as the Moody Addition, and began to sell lots. Between April 4, 1838 and May 15, 1839, he sold at least twenty pieces of property in the Moody Addition. After the death of Jonathan Frost, who had a home and a blacksmith facility on his property and clearly intended to live there, the Frost family decided to follow Moody's lead and subdivide their tract into lots, too. On March 26, 1838, Samuel Frost, the administrator of the Frost estate, petitioned the probate court to allow him to subdivide the land and sell lots in the Frost tract. Frost began selling his lots on July 4, 1838, and by April, 1839, sixty-six lots were sold[239].

The large number of lots that were sold within the year in both the Frost and Moody subdivisions indicate that the speculative ventures were successful. And, neither Moody nor Samuel Frost would choose to make their homes near Houston. Samuel Frost moved to Fort Bend County, near Hodge's Bend, soon afterward and was married there in March, 1843. Moody bought land for a farm on Spring Creek. Unfortunately, he died unexpectedly in Houston of congestive fever on August 21, 1839, at age sixty-three[240].

John W. Moody died intestate and Michael R. Goheen, a Captain of the army at San Jacinto and husband of Moody's daughter Dorinda, was appointed administrator the estate. The probate inventory filed in 1841 showed that Moody did not accumulate much personal wealth, despite his land deals. His personal assets included one silver watch, one four-horse wagon, one lot of cows and young cattle, and various pieces of household and kitchen furniture. His land holdings included a fractional interest in eight separate properties, including a one quarter interest in the headrights and bounty land of six individuals. Although he had an interest in over 6,300 acres of land, his partial interest in the parcels combined with the decline in the value of the land during the 1840's made it difficult to dispose of the his assets. The probate of Moody's estate dragged on for eighteen years until March, 1857[241].

The Frost and Moody subdivisions proved to be a popular residential location, especially for many of the German immigrants who began arriving in Houston in the early 1840's. Since the Frost subdivision and the Moody subdivision were linked both by their geographical location and the intent of their developers to simultaneously subdivide and sell lots, it seems natural that the name of the neighborhood encompassing both subdivisions would coalesce into a single name. The area became known simply as Frost Town.

The deed of July 20, 1847 conveying land from Richard Insall to John W. Schrimpf illustrates how the Moody Addition was absorbed into Frost Town. The deed states that Insall does "sell and release unto the said John W. Schrimpf the following described property in Frost Town, a suburb of the City of Houston,...Two lots of ground known and designated as lots number fourteen and fifteen in Moody's square number one now occupied as part of the residence of the said John W. Schrimpf...[242]"

By 1869, the Moody tract had a total of twenty-three houses. The tract on the east side of the Frost Town blocks contained only one house, however, the three blocks lying to the south of the Frost Town blocks were heavily developed and contained twenty-two residences. Although the Galveston and Houston Junction Railroad owned the large square tract of the Moody Addition through which the railroad tracks make a diagonal cut, many prominent citizens continued to live nearby. The Heitmann house was located on Runnels Street, east of the G&HJ railroad tracks. The Seneschal house was located on the southeast corner of Runnels Street and Gabel Street, and the Super family lived at the northwest corner of Runnels Street and Schrimpf Street which was on the eastern edge of the Moody tract. Other notable families residing in the Moody Addition were Harris, Benson, Brown, Ettinger, Cook, Reichter, Pallas, Wilson and Donaldson[243].

During the last two decades of the nineteenth century, the character of the Frost Town area, including its sister subdivision the Moody Addition, changed significantly. As second and third generation Houstonians found their place in society and prospered, they moved to other, more fashionable areas around Houston. They followed the trend of residential development to the south and west of the downtown district. The industrialization of the east side of downtown started with the construction of the Galveston, Houston and Henderson Railroad to Houston in 1859 and the subsequent connection of the GH&H railroad with the Houston and Texas Central Railway across Frost Town in 1865.

In 1877, the Texas Western Narrow Gauge Railway began operating from its depot on the edge of Frost Town at Chartres Street and Magnolia Avenue (modern Ruiz Avenue). Through this terminal, a spot situated today under the elevated freeway US 59, about three blocks northeast of Minute Maid Park, the TWNG railway brought agricultural products from the Brazos Valley near Pattison and Sealy to the International Press and Union Compress on the north side of Buffalo Bayou[244].

By 1885, the Gulf, Colorado and Santa Fe Railway had built tracks along the eastern edge of the Moody tract. Lying parallel to the Texas Western Narrow Gauge, the GC&SF tracks ran north across the bayou to the industrial plants on the north bank. The A. Bering and Brothers Planing Mill was built east of the GC&SF tracks between Runnels Street and German Street (modern Canal Street) to take advantage of the rail connections for the receipt of raw materials and the shipment of finished goods. Richardson's Grist Mill was located east of the GH&H tracks on Runnels Street on a site that, by 1896, became the Kuhlman's Wood Yard and the Kuhlman's Hay and Feed Warehouse[245].

Other industrial sites arose adjacent to the railroad tracks by 1907, including a mattress factory on North Hamilton Street. Hartwell's Iron Works, a foundry that made ornamental iron work for the local building industry, was established on the south half of the eastern block of the Moody tract[246].

As the residential quality of the neighborhood declined, the simple frame dwellings became tenant and low income housing for blacks and immigrants, many of whom were laborers in the east side industries. Yet, in spite of the industrial development in the area, the number of dwellings on the Moody tract continued to increase. By 1891, there were fifty-four dwellings, most of which were in the three Moody blocks south of the Frost blocks. The number of houses rose to eighty-one in 1907. Twenty-one dwellings were built on the northeast section of the Moody tract, north of Race Street. There were sixty houses in the southern blocks south of Lyle Street along with three small businesses and a school, the Women's Free Kindergarten[247].

The Women's Free Kindergarten, which was located on the southeast corner of Gabel Street and Maple Place, was a service of the Women's Club of Houston that provided educational opportunities for the children of poor working mothers in Houston's immigrant community. It's location on the narrow, unpaved Maple Place reflected the desire to place the school in close proximity to the people it served. The kindergarten program eventually expanded to provide social programs for adults in the evening, and it was eventually absorbed into the social programs of the Settlement House organization[248].

By 1924, the Moody tract had reached its high point in terms of housing density, and probably population, too. The number of houses in the section north of Race Street remained constant at twenty-two, but the dwellings and businesses in the south blocks, between Lyle Street and Maple Avenue increased to sixty-eight houses, eleven stores and three businesses[249].

The industrial development of the area continued as well. The Hartwell Iron Works plant expanded its facilities to include separate structures for a foundry with a coke oven, a pattern shop, a machine shop, a structural and sheet steel department, and other auxiliary buildings. Other businesses, such as the Stower's Furniture Company and the Lilienthal Brothers Company hay and grain storage and machine shop, located along the rail line[250].

The influence of the railroad industry in Houston was seen in the construction of Union Station at 501 Crawford Street and Texas Avenue in 1910. Significant developments by the rail companies in the mid-1920's would transform the east side of downtown, including the Moody Addition. By July, 1927, the Missouri, Kansas and Texas Railroad had completed construction of a large freight terminal on the section of the Moody Addition bounded by Lyle Street on the north, Gable Street on the west, Maple Avenue on the south and the GH&H tracks on the east. All of the homes and businesses on the tract were demolished to make room for this huge, modern facility. The MK&T Freight Terminal had separate warehouses set aside as a Motor Freight Station, an electric supplies warehouse and a beer warehouse. The eastern side of the terminal had rail sidings to serve warehouses for the Builders Supply Company for building materials, tile products and sand and gravel bins[251].

By mid-century, the residential nature of the Moody Addition had completely disappeared. The dwellings on the north end of tract, opposite the Hartwell Iron Works, were demolished. The Hartwell Iron Works itself lay in ruins, encircled by a six foot wire fence, after it was destroyed by a fire. Across the street, the Humble Oil and Refining Company established a Production Warehouse with a pipe yard in the north end of the Moody Addition from Race Street to the bayou[252].

The construction of the Eastex Freeway in the mid-1950's completed the transformation of the Moody Addition into the what we see today. The elevated freeway, US 59, and its associated off ramps and on ramps consume the bulk of Moody's original fifteen acres. Sections of the former MK&T Freight Terminal lie in ruins and vacant. The Star of Hope's Doris and Carloss Morris Men's Development Center, a social service facility at 1811 Ruiz Avenue offering sleeping quarters to the homeless, is the only remaining representation of the residential character of this once vibrant, but now forgotten, community[253].

Bayou City Compress

The last quarter of the nineteenth century saw the decline of the thriving residential community of Frost Town and the industrialization of the north bank of Buffalo Bayou, especially in the area immediately opposite from Frost Town.

The construction of a new cotton compress in the Fifth Ward was significant news for Houston as it re-established itself in the wake of the Civil War. Reconstruction had ended, and the City hoped to revive the business engines that drove its robust economy prior to the war. This new compress was operational by late October, 1875, and it would play a major role during the next three decades when cotton was king in Houston[254].

The cotton enterprise started slowly, but by 1877, the new facility for cotton was organized as the Buffalo Warehouse and Compress Company. Development on the north bank of the bayou had not spread as far as the modern McKee Street so the address of the compress was simply indicated as "east of GH&H freight depot." Everyone knew where that was[255].

The Buffalo Compress had a substantial management team of prominent local businessmen, including A. J. Burke as President, W. D. Cleveland as Vice President and F. A. Rice as the company's Secretary and Treasurer. James G. Timmins, an experienced cotton warehouseman, was the plant superintendent. Burke was an early merchant in Houston and a partner with Benjamin A. Shepherd until

1855. Burke, later, became mayor of Houston in January, 1879. William D. Cleveland had been in the grocery business for over a decade and was expanding his enterprises as a commission merchant with the cotton compress. Frederick Allyn Rice was William Marsh Rice's younger brother who joined him in business in Houston. Fred Rice later married Charlotte Allen's daughter[256].

The economic conditions at the time, however, were difficult for the new compress company, and, despite the experienced management, the Buffalo Compress went bankrupt. On February 6, 1878, the Buffalo Compress, one of the finest warehouse and compress facilities in the state, was sold at public auction to W. D. Cleveland who held a lien of $26,000 on the property. The cotton compress was then re-organized, in 1879, as the Bayou City Compress Company with Cleveland as President, Rice as Secretary and Treasurer, and Timmins as the superintendent. By 1882, W. D. Cleveland left to establish his own compress company, and S. K. McIlhenny took his place as the President of the Bayou City Compress Company. The other officers of the company remained the same[257].

By 1885, the Union Compress and Warehouse Company had built a facility in the same area as the Bayou City Compress. The two complexes were separated by the switch track of the Houston and Texas Central Railway. The Bayou City Press Cotton Warehouse was on the north side of the tracks while the Union Compress Warehouse Company buildings lay south of the tracks, between the tracks and the bayou. Loading platforms along the railroad tracks provided access to the cotton sheds on each side of the tracks. The Union Compress was the larger of the two compresses with ten cotton sheds. Although most of the cotton transfers took place from the rail platforms, a small loading dock and platform with "slides" did provide access from the Union Compress warehouses to vessels on Buffalo Bayou[258].

The Bayou City Compress Company was acquired by the Union Compress and Warehouse Company on January 28, 1887 as there was some consolidation of the compress companies in Houston. A little over a year later, on May 7, 1888, W. D. Cleveland was elected as a director of the Union Compress and Warehouse Company. The facility at this location on Buffalo Bayou retained the name Bayou City Compress and through the 1890's and early twentieth century, it was one of the major cotton operations in the City. The production levels reached extraordinary levels due to the state of the art, Morse Press with an eighty-four inch cylinder[259].

The Depression of the 1930's brought changes to Houston's cotton industry. The processing of cotton moved closer to the place where the crops were grown. The High Plains of Texas emerged as the state's primary cotton growing region, and by late 1937, new cotton warehouses and compresses were built in and around the city of Lubbock. The Union Compress Company abandoned its Bayou City plant and opened cotton warehouses and compresses in Lubbock, Lamesa, Brownfield, Plainview, Slaton and Littlefield. By 1951, only a few small, scattered structures remained on the former Union Compress and Warehouse Company tract east of the McKee Street bridge and on the north bank of Buffalo Bayou. Today, the tract is a vacant lot, awaiting development, and graced only with weeds and the north side segment of the East End Bike Trail along the top line of the bank[260].

Elysian Viaduct

The popularity of the personal automobile in the economic boom after World War II brought significant changes to both the Frost Town neighborhood south of the bayou and the industrial zone to the north. In 1954, the local governments of Houston and Harris County sought to improve automobile access to the downtown center with the construction of the Elysian Viaduct. This mile and a half long, elevated roadway was built through the middle of Frost Town and the center of the former Bayou Compress site on the north side and has played a major role in the decline of both Frost Town and the Near North Side neighborhood[261].

The proposal by the Texas Department of Transportation in 2004 to rebuild and expand the four lane Elysian Viaduct has resurrected the controversy over the bridge and the roadway. If the viaduct is replaced with a ground level boulevard, the disruption of James Bute Park and the historic remnants of Frost Town will be complete. An alternate proposal made by the County Commissioner to rehabilitate the roadway as a viaduct would preserve the parkland and the historic Frost Town site. The initial TxDOT plan was halted by the downturn in the economy in 2008, but eventually a decision on the Elysian Viaduct will resurface. At that time, the nature of this historic near east side area will be determined[262].

Schrimpf's Field - A Story of Two German Families

The tree lined south bank, as you canoe downstream beyond the Elysian Viaduct, gives no indication that you are passing beyond Frost Town, the bayou frontage of the Moody Addition and Schrimpf's Field.

The boundary between Moody's tract and Schrimpf's Field is also the boundary between John Austin's two league grant of 1824 and one of the eleven leagues of land granted to Samuel May Williams in 1828. Schrimpf's Field encompassed the northwestern tip of Williams' league, and it was bounded by Buffalo Bayou in its course along the eastern half of the horseshoe bend downstream of Main Street. Its most prominent feature is the massive concrete architecture of the US 59 overpass complex that rises majestically from the former cow pasture. With some measure of elegance, the highway structure is quite impressive when it is viewed by boaters from the little-traveled bayou. Automotive travelers riding the lanes high above the bayou scarcely realize that they are traversing the historic land and commercial waterway so important to nineteenth century Houston.

Schrimpf's Field is a tract of land that is approximately thirty-five acres in size. It is bounded on the west by the survey line which separates the John Austin league from the Samuel M. Williams league, running from Buffalo Bayou on the north to near Runnels Street on the south. Today, US 59 lies on this line. The boundary of the tract then follows Runnels Street east to the International and Great Northern Railroad tracks that lie west of the Alexan Lofts, the former Myers-Spalti Manufacturing Company. Then, it follows the railroad tracks north to the bayou and back to the origin along the course of the bayou. The field was named for the Schrimpf family, a prominent German family living in the Second Ward during the middle of the nineteenth century, and this tract of land is the center-piece of an epic story of two German families of historic importance to the city[263].

The story of Schrimpf's Field begins within three years of the establishment of the town when the two Schrimpf brothers, Johann Wilhelm Schrimpf and Johann Ernst Schrimpf, immigrated to Houston from Frankfurt am Main, Germany. It is possible that the Schrimpf men were among the three hundred families that arrived in October and December, 1839, but certainly, they had come by the fall of 1840 since Johann Wilhelm Schrimpf is listed among the founding members of the German Society of Texas on November 29, 1840[264].

The similarity of the brothers' names, with the same first name and distinguishing middle names, has caused some confusion among later historians who failed to recognize that there were two individuals and their families living and working in the Frost Town area during the mid-1800's. The brothers used the names John W. and John E. in some instances, while identifying themselves as J. W. and J. E. Schrimpf at other times. Further ambiguity has arisen because they worked together in their butcher business and lived with their families in adjacent homes prior to 1870.

When they arrived in 1840, John W., at about age twenty-eight, was three years older than his brother John E. Schrimpf. John W. also seemed to be more outgoing than his younger brother, and he soon became actively involved in the local German community, as mentioned above. He married Henrietta Carl, the daughter of Henry W. Carl, an early Frost Town resident, on May 19, 1842. And, as evidence of his gregarious nature and his involvement in local politics, John W. Schrimpf was one of two aldermen from the Second Ward in 1843[265].

Although Houston had suffered an economic downturn when the capital was moved to the small hamlet of Austin in 1839, the placement of the capital of the republic near the western frontier may have benefited Houston more than its residents realized at the time. Large land grants encouraged the colonization of Texas, and the prospect of statehood overcame the fears brought on by the prospect of war with Mexico. Settlers looked to the lands on the frontier, and the easiest route to this territory was through Houston via the port of Galveston.

Texas was particularly attractive to the German-speaking peoples of Europe. Hundreds of Germans had arrived in Houston by

1840, and by the end of the decade, the tally of German immigrants would number several thousand. Carl, Prince of Solms-Braunfels, as Commissioner-General of the Adelsverein, was a principal figure in the settlement of Germans in Texas. On July 3, 1844, Prince Carl arrived in Houston to begin a year long survey of Texas in order to establish a colony for German immigrants[266].

John W. Schrimpf was visited by Prince Carl on October 7, 1844. On that day, the Prince attended a dinner prepared by August Senechal at the home of Major Robert S. Neighbors (who later became the Indian Agent to the Lipan and Tonkawa tribes) with the mayor of Houston Horace Baldwin, local merchants and other local dignitaries. Afterwards, he visited the City Arsenal, before stopping at Schrimpf's where he looked at pictures of old friends and familiar places in Frankfurt. Prince Carl then spent the evening in discussions with B. Owen Payn, the Captain of Ordnance[267].

The relationship between Schrimpf and Prince Carl appears to have been more personal than business. These two men in their mid-thirties seemed to share a common vision of the opportunities that Texas presented. The town of Solms is less than fifty miles north of the city of Frankfurt. They were able to relax amid the intense business negotiations involved in the Prince's work for the Adelsverein and discuss the mundane topics of their common homeland in Hessen.

On his final trip through Houston, on Sunday, May 25, 1845, Prince Carl of Solms spent the evening at Schrimpf's home in Frost Town. The Prince noted in his journal that he ate sausage while awaiting the arrival of the steamer to Galveston. After a year of hard travel and difficult circumstances, it was just one final, relaxing evening with his German friend before wrapping up the business of the Adelsverein and returning to Germany via New York. Within a year, the influx of German immigrants to Texas and the colony in the Hill Country began a transformation of Texas and its people, a heritage that is with us even today[268].

The Schrimpf brothers operated a butcher shop and the success of that business allowed John W. to pursue investments in other areas. In July, 1847, John W. Schrimpf made two significant purchases of land. On July 20, he acquired from Richard Insall two lots, designated in the deed as "in Frost Town," that were located in

Square One of the Moody Addition. The deed indicated that part of his residence occupied portions of these two lots. Four days later, John W. purchased about three hundred thirty-seven acres of the Samuel M. Williams league east of the Houston city limits from Mangus J. Rodgers[269].

Included in the Rodgers transaction was a 31.1 acre tract that became known as Schrimpf's Field. The original deed for Schrimpf's Field describes the bounds of the tract as "...31 & 1/10 acres according to said plan bounded on the north by Buffalo Bayou, on the east by Lot No. 1, on the south by Ann Street and on the west by the line of the S. M. Williams original survey...[270]"

Also included in the purchase were three other tracts of land that ensured Schimpf's control over the large areas of growth along Buffalo Bayou east of town. The first tract included twenty-two lots on the near east side of the City on the south bank of Buffalo Bayou and lying on both sides of Runnels Street. Two other tracts, one of slightly more than one hundred sixteen acres and the other slightly more than one hundred twenty-one acres, consisted of land extending from Buffalo Bayou to Canal Street, and bound on the east by the modern North Milby Street and the west by the modern North Super Avenue[271].

Numerous land transactions during the decade of the 1840's reveal that John W. Schrimpf not only ran a successful butcher and meat market business with his brother John E., but he also capitalized on the heady economic activity of Houston through land speculation. By the end of the decade, his wealth was estimated at approximately $20,000. With assets of that amount, John W. Schrimpf was among the top three percent of the population of Harris County. His wealth and assets compared favorably with other young men in the county whose names are more familiar to us today, including William Marsh Rice, Paul Bremond, Benjamin A. Shepherd and Thomas W. House. Schrimpf was the wealthiest German in Houston in 1850[272].

John W. Schrimpf's personal life prospered during the decade as well. His marriage to Henrietta had produced three children by 1850, including their five year old son Augustus, three year old Carl and their infant daughter Anna. After ten years in Houston, John W.

Schrimpf had achieved a good measure of financial success and he was poised for further gains in the decade prior to the Civil War[273].

In spite of one's plans, events over which one has no control often occur which change the outcome of a person's destiny. During the 1850's, a number of events happened in Houston which greatly affected the fortunes of the Schrimpf family in later decades. One such event was the arrival of the Settegast family in Houston in 1851[274].

Maria William Settegast, his wife and four children came to Houston from their home in Koblenz, Germany. John W. Schrimpf often welcomed newcomers, especially those from Germany, to Houston and frequently provided them with the means to get settled and to establish a foothold in their new home. Within a year of his arrival, Settegast bought about thirty-five acres of land along Buffalo Bayou from Schrimpf. In all probability, this was the land which became known as Schrimpf's Field. Schrimpf had purchased it in 1847, but he sold it four years later. Only a quirk of fate would intervene so that this tract retained the name of Schrimpf[275].

The epidemics of yellow fever stuck Houston frequently during the nineteenth century, often changing the course of history when the prominent and powerful of society died in equal measure with the anonymous common people. In 1853, yellow fever reappeared in Houston with its usual devastating results. In particular, the Settegast family was decimated by the epidemic, and all of the members of the Settegast family died except for sons William, age seven, and Julius, age five. John W. Schrimpf took responsibility for the orphaned young boys, placed them in the home of his brother and put them to work in the butcher market to learn a trade[276].

Business was good. Houston had prospered during the 1850's and the Schrimpf brothers expanded their business accordingly. The meat market developed into a large scale slaughterhouse and meat packing operation by 1860. By that time, John W. Schrimpf owned real estate valued at $75,000 with personal assets of $5,000, nearly four times his wealth of a decade earlier. His younger brother John E. also prospered and had real assets of $15,000[277].

The approach of war, however, posed problems for John W. Schrimpf. According to the census of 1860, his household included only his wife Henrietta and his son Charles. His other children,

Augustus and Anna, did not survive, and it is possible that they may have fallen victim to the same epidemic that took the lives of the Settegast family. As the war between the states grew imminent, the prospect that his only remaining child, a young man of fourteen at the beginning of the war, could be lost in military service may have prompted him to send is son Charles to Germany for schooling. His efforts to shelter his family, however, proved futile. John W. Schrimpf, in his mid-50's, is reported to have died on a trip to Germany to visit his son in the mid-1860's. The City Directory of 1867 lists Mrs. Henrietta Carl Schrimpf, indicating that she was a widow at this time. Charles Schrimpf, her twenty year old son, lived with her[278].

After thirty years in Texas, the first generation of the Schrimpf family was fading from the scene. With the death of John W., the family lost its patriarch and its leader. John E. Schrimpf, the younger brother, had never showed the type of drive and leadership that his older brother had. At age fifty-five, in 1870, John E. Schrimpf endured the difficulties of the Civil War with only a slight diminishment of his assets which stood at $10,500. He continued to live to the east of Frost Town on Ann Street with his teenage son William and daughter, but, having listed his occupation on the census form as "none," he appears to have retired. He is not listed in the City Directory after 1871 and is presumed to have died about that time. Henrietta Schrimpf, John W.'s widow, retained the assets of her husband which amounted to $50,000 in 1870, and she contin-ued to live in the Frost Town home until her death sometime around 1872. It is believed that both Henrietta and John E. Schrimpf, her brother-in-law, were buried on the Schrimpf's Field property, how-ever, the location of the family cemetery has never been confirmed[279].

Charles Schrimpf, John W. and Henrietta's son, was twenty-four years old in 1872, and as the surviving member of the family, should have been in line to manage the Schrimpf businesses for the next generation. Charles, however, did not have the charisma and busi-ness acumen of his father. In addition, he was challenged by the two orphaned boys that his father had accepted into his household in 1853.

William Joseph Settegast and Julius J. Settegast, both now in their late twenties, had worked in the Schrimpf family businesses since they were children, and they had become successful butchers in their own right. With the passing of all of the elder Schrimpf's, persons for whom they may have held strong sentiments of gratitude for their upbringing, the Settegast brothers felt that they should have shared equally with Charles Schrimpf in the wealth created during the previous twenty years. When Charles Schrimpf began to sell parcels of the family estate, the Settegasts filed suit in 1872 and obtained an injunction to prevent the further sale of property. The Settegast claimed, in at least two suits, compensation for $90,000. They based their claim on the fact that they had not been fairly compensated for their work in the family businesses and that the thirty-five acre tract, known as Schrimpf's Field, had been bought by their father before his death, but the land had been kept and used by John W. Schrimpf since 1853[280].

The suit progressed slowly through the Harris County District Court for two years. Finally, on July 30, 1879, an agreement was reached between the two parties. The court documents provided that the terms of the agreement were sealed. However, with the single transaction of the sale of Frost Town Block E, Lot 5, south half to W. J. Settegast and J. J. Settegast, all of their claims against Charles W. Schrimpf were dropped. Ironically, the sale of one half of a lot which usually sold for about $25 closed a deal worth over $100,000, and it propelled the Settegast family into ranks of the prominent businessmen of Houston[281].

After the settlement, the Schrimpf name faded from history in Houston. Charles Schrimpf left town and no Schrimpf's appeared in the City Directory of 1880. Eventually, he made his way to San Antonio. By 1900, Charles W. Schrimpf, at age 52, was a widower. He lived at boarding house of Ella White at 816 Avenue B in San Antonio, and he was employed as a cattle buyer. Schrimpf remarried in 1904 and, in 1910, he was living with his wife Eugenia, age 54, at the boarding house of Oscar R. Schultz at 817 Nolan Street in San Antonio. Shrimpf continued to work as a sheep stockman as his circumstances were obviously modest and seemed to be a far removed from the life of wealth of his youth. He died some time prior to 1920[282].

Julius Settegast turned twenty-one in 1867 and that year he married Katie Floeck, the seventeen year old daughter of Frost Town brewer Martin Floeck. Julius showed he had learned the lessons of business well and, by 1870, the J. J. Settegast and Company was his own meat market on Commerce Avenue, between Chenevert Street and Hamilton Street, on the south edge of Frost Town. Older brother William, similarly, followed the lead of Julius, and, by 1873, William Joseph Settegast had moved from the Frost Town neighborhood where they had grown up and had established his butcher shop across town near the San Felipe Road[283].

The boys had grown into men, and they were ready and willing to assume the mantle from of the first generation. After they had successfully sued for their share of the Schrimpf estate, they bought cheap grazing land for their cattle, opened a small dairy, built their butcher businesses and, through Julius, found themselves to be among the largest landowners in Houston[284].

During the 1870's, William and Julius Settegast bought a large tract of land across from the Fairgrounds on the south end of town. About 1877, they built a rectangular two-story, white house with a front porch at each level. The house was large enough for both families. And, following a pattern of migration that persists even today, the succeeding generation in Houston moved from their in town neighborhood to the more affluent and elegant suburban neighborhoods south and west of downtown[285].

The Settegast's house was located at what is now 2218 Valentine Street, between Hadley Street and McGowen Street. Julius and Katie had ten children, and, in time, each child worked in the family businesses which included the cattle business, a lumber yard, a paint and hardware store and hundreds of rent houses[286].

William J. Settegast died at his home in 1895 at age fifty-one. Julius' family remained close, and in addition to those children still living at home, several of the married children and their families resided in nearby in a house at 2218 Bagby Street. In an ironic turn of events that seems to tie together in a strange way, the founders of Frost Town and the German families that made Frost Town a dynamic neighborhood for over a half a century, John Miles Frost, Jr., grandson of Samuel Miles Frost who platted the Frost Town

Subdivision, married Julia Estelle Settegast, daughter of J. J. Settegast, on July 6, 1909[287].

In 1910, Julius J. Settegast moved the family home from its original site a couple blocks to 102 McGowen Street and remodeled it. The family lived at 2404 Bissonnet Street during the renovations, but Julius, Katie and the unmarried children returned to the home and continued to live in the house on McGowen Street into the 1930's. Katie Settegast died in 1924, and Julius died in 1933 at age 88. So undeniable was the impact of the Settegast family on the Second Ward of Houston and the east end that in 1919, when the U. S. Geological Survey was mapping Houston, the agency named the 7-1/2 minute quadrangle map that covers the east side of Houston the "Settegast Quadrangle[288]."

For most of the nineteenth century, Schrimpf's Field was used for grazing cattle in support of the Schrimpf family butcher and meat market operations. Situated on a "splendid hill," to use the description of Jesse Ziegler who grew up in the area during the late 1800's, Schrimpf's Field was a well-drained grassland that served as an excellent pasture. The first development on the property was the laying of tracks during the post-Civil War railroad building boom. By 1869, two railroads crossed diagonally across the field to connect the warehouse and compress facilities on the north bank of Buffalo Bayou with the Union Depot near the east end of Commerce Avenue at St. Emanuel Street. The Texas Western Narrow Gauge Railway ran parallel to the standard gauge tracks of the Gulf Colorado and Santa Fe Railroad as both sets of tracks spanned the bayou near where the modern US 59 highway does[289].

By the 1880's, the Frost Town area was a residential neighborhood in decline. The original families that settled in the neighborhood were dying out and their children moved to more attractive and affluent neighborhoods. Industrial sites, such as the Bering Planing Mill on the south side of Runnels Street opposite Schrimpf's Field, were built in proximity to the rail lines, and the character of the area was becoming more industrial than residential. The housing that was in the area tended to be rental houses and dwellings for low income workers. By 1890, a row of about ten small houses, the first structures constructed on the otherwise vacant Schrimpf's Field, lined the north side of Runnels Street. Maps of the time indicate that these houses were occupied by black families[290].

Early in the twentieth century, the industrialization of the area accelerated. In addition to the recently-expanded Bering Mills, the Hartwell Iron Works was built on the western edge of Schrimpf's Field in the Moody Addition between Schrimpf Street and Pine Street. The J. C. Carpenter Fig Company Canning Factory was located southeast of the corner of Runnels Street and Schrimpf Street, and the Tofte Boiler and Sheet Iron Works was the first plant built on Schrimpf's Field along the east side of Schrimpf Street, north of the narrow lane known as Schrimpf Alley. The need for housing for immigrants and plant workers was prompting development on the field. Chartres Street was extended north of Runnels Street to the cross street of Schrimpf Alley. By 1907, small houses lined these new streets, and the Sanborn insurance maps showed Schrimpf's Field consisting of forty-eight houses, one store and nine frame buildings[291].

The emergence of Houston as a commercial, industrial and transportation center during the first quarter of the twentieth century continued the transformation of Schrimpf's Field. Vacant land so near to town and the rail lines would not stay idle for long. By 1924, the Anderson Lumber Company comprising two structures, a lumber shed and a planing mill, was located at the north end of Schrimpf's Field on the west side of the GC&SF railroad tracks near the banks of Buffalo Bayou. Schrimpf Street was extended north in a curving fashion parallel to the railroad tracks and it was lined on the east side with twenty-eight simple dwellings. A mostly Mexican neighborhood, famous for conjunto (accordion) players, the street dead ended in a curving pattern of shotgun houses along the end of Schrimpf Street which suggested both the curl of a shrimp tail and the stinger of a scorpion. The Mexican immigrants who lived there and in Frost Town, with some sense of amusement and, perhaps, cynicism, called their neighborhood El Barrio del Alacran (the community of the scorpion)[292].

In the south half of Schrimpf's Field, the number of houses doubled in the first two decades of the century. Chartres Street extended farther north into the field and it sprouted three side streets, Schrimpf Alley, Chartres Alley and Settegast Alley. A total of one hundred six houses clustered along this maze of alley ways which also included three small stores and one business. At the north end of Charters Street stood the St. Ollie Colored Baptist Church which served the residents of this part of the neighborhood[293].

Few major changes had occurred to Schrimpf's Field by mid-century. The lumberyard near the bayou was replaced by the Humble Oil and Refining Company Production Warehouse and pipe yard. The South Texas Stone Company's stone cutting facility, and it neighbor, the Gooch Monument Company were on the east side of Schrimpf Street at Lyle Street. And, the number of small houses along the narrow streets of Kaiser (formerly Chartres) Alley, Schrimpf Alley and Settegast Alley was essentially the same as it had been twenty-five years earlier. However, the wear and tear of a quarter of a century on the neighborhood had produced the old Schrimpf Alley slum. During the 1930's and 1940's, Schrimpf Alley was a wild and lawless slum ridden with vice, gambling and prostitution. In 1952, it was regarded as the worst slum in the city[294].

The blight, however, was too blatant to ignore. Susan Vahn Clayton, wife of Will Clayton, the co-founder of Anderson, Clayton and Company, a large cotton exporting firm, purchased the twenty-three acre tract, about two-thirds of Schrimpf's Field, that contained Schrimpf Alley, and she donated it to the Houston Housing Authority for the Clayton Homes project. This public housing project, completed 1952, was designed to transform the slum into a healthy neighborhood. The remaining one third of Schrimpf's Field was purchased by the state in the mid-1950's for the construction of US 59[295].

Forty-six years later, in 1998, the Clayton Homes public housing project was renovated and replaced by low income housing in a mix of styles for rental or ownership. Three hundred of the original three hundred thirty-two apartments were torn down, and in their place, one hundred sixty new town homes were constructed on the site at 1919 Runnels Street. Although located within a half mile of Minute Maid Park and just east of the affluent loft and town home development of the Alexan Lofts, the Clayton Homes project remains a rough neighborhood rife with drugs and crime. Only time will tell if the revitalization of the Second Ward will ultimately recreate the long sought after neighborhood that beckons back to first decades of Houston[296].

Texas Western Narrow Gauge Railway Bridge

As one paddles past the Elysian Viaduct bridge, an enormous expanse of concrete and auto traffic lies ahead. The spaghetti bowl of main lanes, entrance ramps and exit ramps is U. S. Highway 59. Thousands of cars per day drive across the bridge and the elevated roadway, and few of those traveling there even imagine the nineteenth and early twentieth century stories of Houston that took place below them. Before the first US 59 bridge was built in the late 1950's, the land and the bayou here were crossed by two railroads. These railroads brought agricultural products from the western farming regions to the city warehouses while returning finished goods to the rural locales. They were part of the large network of rail lines that provided the economic growth of Houston's commercial hub.

The first bridge one would encounter was the bridge of the Texas Western Narrow Gauge Railway. Although the bridge was abandoned in the early twentieth century, remnants of railroad ties and rail fasteners found on the north bank in 2008 suggest that the location of the TWNG bridge was near the westernmost edge of the US 59 ramps. This also coincides with the placement of the bridge on maps of the period.

As early as 1870, the Western Narrow Gauge Railway was promoted by Houston investors I. S. Roberts, Thomas W. House, Thomas H. Scanlan and Eugene Pillot. In fact, the tracks of the railroad appear on the Wood map of Houston of 1869, perhaps in anticipation of the construction of the railroad which planned to run from Houston to San Antonio via Bellville, La Grange and New Braunfels. The railroad was chartered on August 4, 1870 as the first narrow gauge railroad chartered in Texas. The financing of the project, however, was slow to materialize, and it was not until January 18, 1875 that the railroad was chartered as the Texas Western Narrow Gauge Railway with financing from Abram Morris Gentry[297].

Construction on the railroad began in early 1875, and the initial ten miles of track opened on July 3, 1875. A second ten miles opened in 1876, and the entire forty-two miles to Pattison were opened on April 23, 1877. The train began shipping cotton from the Brazos Valley to Houston that same year with two locomotives, fifteen freight cars and one passenger car. Nevertheless, the economics of the enterprise were difficult and the railroad was forced into receivership in 1880. It was reorganized and re-chartered on April 28, 1881 as the Texas Western Railway Company[298].

In 1882, the Texas Western Narrow Gauge was extended four miles to the west side of the Brazos River to serve the towns of San Felipe and Sealy. For a number of years, the railroad operated successfully, if not profitably. Yet, the competition in the railroad industry at this time was demanding. In 1890, the Missouri, Kansas and Texas Railroad was built as far as the town of Katy. The MKT line's entry into Houston led to the decline and demise of the TWNG Railway. The Texas Western Narrow Gauge Railway ceased operations in 1896. It's tracks were abandoned by 1899 and they were pulled up by 1900[299].

In terms of the railroad industry of Houston, the Texas Western Narrow Gauge was a minor player. Its thirty year existence was notable for its grandiose plans and its disappointing results. The dominance of the standard gauge track in the railroad industry was overwhelming for the narrow gauge lines. After the demise of the company and the removal of the TWNG tracks at the beginning of the twentieth century, there are few visible remains of the existence of the railroad.

At its crossing of Buffalo Bayou to the rail yards on the north bank, we can only surmise the location of the TWNG bridge from old maps. These same maps show us the southerly route of the rail. From the depot at St. Emanuel Street and Commerce Avenue, the tracks went down St. Emanuel Street to McIlhenny Street, then they angled southwest to a point near LaBranch Street and Holman Avenue. The tracks then went west on Holman Avenue to Fannin Street where they curved to connect with Alabama Street. The Texas Western Narrow Gauge right of way then went due west until it was joined by the modern Westheimer Road west of the Galleria and Sage Road. From there the TWNG railroad followed the modern route of Westheimer Road to Barker Reservoir where it angled northwest toward Katy, Pattison and Sealy. The remarkably straight alignment of Westheimer Road to Highway 6 is the City's legacy from the long forgotten Texas Western Narrow Gauge Railway[300].

Strauss Bascule Bridge

Once you have paddled your canoe or kayak under the full canopy of the Highway 59 overpass complex and adjusted your hearing to the remarkable din of the vehicular traffic above, you realize that there is something peculiar here. There is a drawbridge under the highway!

The drawbridge, which is the classical drawbridge style with a leaf hinged on the north bank of the bayou that lowers to the base on the south side, is a bascule bridge built in 1912 for the Houston Belt and Terminal Railway Company. The bridge was designed by Joseph Strauss, the owner of the Strauss Bascule Bridge Company of Chicago, and built by the Wisconsin Bridge and Iron Company[301].

A bascule bridge is a moveable bridge with a counterweight that continuously balances the span throughout the entire upward swing. The term bascule comes from the French word for seesaw. A bridge of this design requires very little energy to operate. The fixed trunnion bascule design rotates around a large axle (the trunnion) to raise. The axle with its large gears is on the north bank. The enormous counter weight for the bridge has been moved from the bridge mechanism and rests a short distance east of the bridge, several yards away. Bridges of this type are sometimes called a "Chicago bascule" since the design was developed and perfected by Joseph Strauss of Chicago and used for many of that city's bridges[302].

Joseph Baermann Strauss was born January 7, 1870 in Cincinnati and he graduated from University of Cincinnati in 1892. Ten years later, he established his firm. The bascule bridge in Houston is one of about four hundred bascule bridges that Strauss had completed by 1916. In that year, the City of San Francisco solicited ideas for a bridge across the bay, and Joseph Strauss responded with a large scale proposal that included a massive cantilever on each side and a central suspension segment. Strauss spent more than a

Photo credit: Linda Gorski

The Strauss Bascule bridge under US 59 is a typical "Chicago style" drawbridge that Strauss made famous. The large pivot gear is on the turret on the north bank (right).

decade gathering support for his design for the Golden Gate bridge[303].

The city officials required that Strauss consult with other experts on the engineering design of the bridge, and although Strauss was the chief engineer of the Golden Gate bridge, the graceful suspension design was that of Leon Moisseiff of NewYork, and the principal engineer was Charles Alton Ellis who did the technical and theoretical work. Neither Moissieff nor Ellis received the recognition at the time that they deserved. Construction began on January 5, 1933, and the Golden Gate bridge was completed by April, 1937. The Golden Gate Bridge was truly Strauss's life work. Strauss died May 16, 1938 in Los Angeles, a little more than a year after the completion of the bridge[304].

The renovation of the US 59 overpass and access ramps in 2003 called for the restoration of this historic drawbridge. The bridge is permanently locked in the down position since the roadbed will become part of the bikeway system under construction along Buffalo Bayou. The Strauss Bascule Bridge will provide access for hikers and bikers to the trails on both sides of the bayou.

International and Great Northern Railroad Bridge

As you continue downstream and move out from under the Highway 59 overpass, Buffalo Bayou opens to a wide channel as it makes a right hand turn. To the left, on the north bank, is a large, vacant field. To the right is the Clayton Homes development. Ahead lies a substantial railroad bridge where the bayou, again, makes another turn, this time to the left. This rail right of way dates to the early 1870's and it was the main route of one of the major rail lines of Houston, the International and Great Northern Railroad.

On October 22, 1866, the Houston and Great Northern Railroad was chartered to build a road from Houston to the Red River. The principal organizers of this railroad were Houston businessmen Ebenezer B. Nichols, William Marsh Rice, W. J. Hutchins, H. D. Taylor, B. A. Shepherd and Moses Taylor of New York City[305].

Reconstruction delayed the initial progress on the construction of the rail lines, but, in 1870, the company purchased eighty acres on the north side of Buffalo Bayou. The first construction contract for tracks was issued on December 14, 1870, and in 1871, the Houston and Great Northern Railroad completed fifty-five miles of track from Houston to New Waverly[306].

In 1872, work began on improvements necessary for the railroad. A drawbridge over Buffalo Bayou was built which connected the tracks on the north bank to the depot on the south side of the bayou at Allen Station. The Great Northern iron drawbridge was the only structure of its kind in Texas when it was built, and it was described as "a beautiful and symmetrical structure" when the draw swung out from its place of rest on the great piers. In the same year, the Great Northern Wharves were built in place of the former Schrimpf's Landing which had fallen into disuse about 1870. The goal of the Houston and Great Northern Railroad was to branch out from Huntsville to the cotton counties of East Texas to provide access to the Houston and Galveston markets for those crops[307].

On September 27, 1873, the Houston and Great Northern Railroad stockholders met to consider the consolidation with the International Railroad Company. The Houston and Great Northern Railroad transferred its 253.1 miles of track to the new International and Great Northern Railroad Company which became a major component of the Missouri Pacific Railroad in Texas. Through the remainder of the nineteenth century and the first decades of the twentieth century, the I&GN Railroad was a significant transportation provider on the east side of Houston[308].

By 1907, in addition to the freight depot in downtown on Commerce Avenue, the I&GN built a cotton warehouse facility on the north side of Buffalo Bayou, west of its tracks. These cotton sheds were leased to companies such as the American Cotton Company and, in the 1920's, M. H. Wolf and Company. After the decline of the cotton industry in Houston, the I&GN warehouses were leased to other companies, such as Morris-Sewall and Company, Inc. Wholesale Grocers[309].

In 1956, International and Great Northern Railroad was merged into the reorganized Missouri Pacific Railroad Company. In 1980, the Union Pacific, the Missouri Pacific and the Western Pacific railroads filed merger applications with the Interstate Commerce Commission which were approved on December 22, 1982. On January 1, 1997, the Missouri Pacific Railroad was formally merged into the Union Pacific Railroad which became the surviving corporation. Today, the Union Pacific trains still rumble across the bridge over Buffalo Bayou[310].

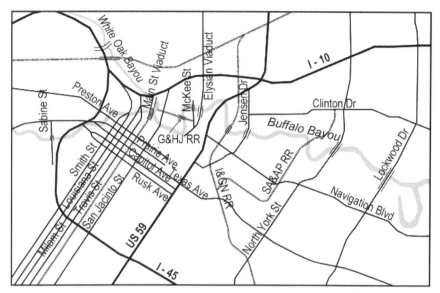

Map by Rachel A. Garcia

Although the Second Ward extended from Main Street east along the south bank of Buffalo Bayou, the community that developed in the Second Ward was east of what is today US 59 and it was centered near what is now Jensen Drive at Navigation Boulevard. The Fifth Ward community also developed on the north bank around the street that is now Jensen Drive.

Chapter 11
The Second Ward

Myers Spalti Manufacturing Company

The large brick building at the I&GN Railroad tracks is the Alexan Lofts, one of the recent developments that are transforming the Second Ward neighborhood in the twenty-first century. The railroad line and its adjacent siding is not important to the modern residential building, but the siding was responsible for the post-Civil War industrial zone that grew up alongside the railroad tracks. This particular building that we see today is the factory of the Myers Spalti Furniture Manufacturing Company. The story of manufacturing on that site, however, goes back to the 1890's when the Lottman brothers established their mattress manufacturing operations on the site.

Carl Albert Lottman and his wife Charlotte, both natives of Hamburg, Germany, arrived in Texas about 1852 when he was about thirty-four years old and she was six years younger. They began their family in Texas with their first son Albert who was born in April, 1855. Clement followed 1858, Herman in 1859 and the final Lottman son Charles was born in April, 1862. In 1870, the Lottman's lived in Bastrop where the elder Lottman was a moderately prosperous rancher and a farmer[1].

The Lottman brothers established a mattress making firm in 1878, although they probably were operating in Bastrop at that time. By 1882, the twenty-three year old Herman Lottman had moved to Houston. Although he listed his occupation as the company's agent, he was on the look out for opportunities in the big city. During this time, Herman lived at a popular boarding house run by the widow Mrs. Paulina Rosenfield. The boarding house was located at 141 and 143 Congress Avenue on the northwest corner with Caroline Street, and it provided a location, only one block east of the courthouse in the business district, from which Lottman could evaluate the business opportunities in Houston. Herman Lottman must have believed the location to be a good one. By 1884, he brought his brothers Albert and Charles to Houston and they established the Lottman Brothers Houston Machine Mattress Manufactory at 140-142 Congress Avenue, across the street from the boarding house, on the southwest corner at Caroline Street[2].

In early 1885, the Lottman brothers began to expand their operations with the construction of a new factory at the foot of Rusk Avenue near Buffalo Bayou. However, there was a minor setback on March 29, 1885 when the structure, which was being built on the slope of a hill, collapsed with a tremendous crash and fell into a shattered and twisted mass of wood. Undeterred, the Lottman brothers completed the factory, and by November, they were actively seeking to hire six first class mattress makers[3].

This business venture brought the Lottman brothers to Houston and it brought their mother Charlotte, a widow by 1886, to the City from Bastrop, as well. The factory was located at 54 Rusk Avenue, on the south side of Rusk Avenue between Brazos Street and Bagby Street while their showroom and office was at 104 Main Street, between Texas Avenue and Capitol Avenue. Albert C. Lottman, the eldest son, established his home at 58 Rusk Avenue, on the corner with Brazos Street. Charlotte, their mother, lived with him, as did his younger brother Charles. Herman Lottman, however, lived at 35 Webster Street between Caroline Street and Austin Street[4].

The Lottman brothers found a ready market for their high quality mattresses and bed springs, but the business was not without its difficulties. On December 6, 1892, a fire alarm was pulled for the Lottman Brothers mattress factory at 1:00 pm, but the fire was put out before the fire engines arrived. The conditions that led to that hazard were not resolved, however, and disaster struck five weeks later. The Lottman Brothers mattress factory complex caught fire on the evening of January 14, 1893 and burned to the ground. The mattress factory, the bed spring factory, a two story building, the warehouse, a storage warehouse and one or two small houses at the factory were destroyed. The lack of water pressure to fight the fire that was whipped by a strong wind resulted in a total loss of the factory buildings. Several neighboring residences near the factory also suffered complete or partial damage from the fire[5].

The loss of the factory did not defeat the Lottman brothers. Within six weeks, they started construction on a large mattress factory in the Second Ward, on the site of the old Timmons place, which was east of the International and Great Northern Railroad, on the south side of Buffalo Bayou. The Lottman's purchased the tract which had a cotton warehouse built by Dr. D. F. Stuart in 1880 and converted the warehouse into a factory to produce mattresses, spring beds, woven wire mattresses, bedsteads, cots and bedding. On July 8, 1893, the Lottman Brothers Manufacturing Company of Houston was chartered by Albert C., Charles F. and Herman W. Lottman with capital of $100,000. The company was incorporated on the following day, July 9, 1893, as the successor to Lottman Brothers of Houston[6].

The factory that was built on the east side of the I&GN tracks was one of the most sophisticated of its type. Separate warehouses housed a mattress factory and a woven wire mattress factory. The mattress factory building housed a sewing room. The woven wire mattress factory had seven excelsior machines and a section set aside for a cotton picker area. A third warehouse, near the bayou and connected to the rail siding by a platform, had basement storage for items treated with a japanning process in the japanning oven situated adjacent to the warehouse[7].

These modern facilities contained the latest equipment for quality mattress and furniture manufacture. The japanning process was the application of a heavy varnish or lacquer in heat-dried layers which were then polished to give a smooth, glossy finish. As a specialized tool, the japanning oven was heated to the desired temperature, 100 to 400 degrees Fahrenheit, while being able to remain hermetically sealed to prevent dust, soot or dirt from entering to mar the beauty and luster of the object being japanned or enameled. The top grade products were then packed in excelsior produced by the seven excelsior machines which made the fine, hair-like wood shavings used for packing material[8].

From the time that the Lottman's established their business, they felt that they had an advantage in the market because of their expertise and innovations in mattress and furniture manufacturing techniques. As early as 1887, the Lottman brothers patented inventions in their business. Charles F. Lottman was issued a patent for a new and improved process of curing Spanish moss to shorten the curing time, to obtain a larger percentage of higher grade fiber and to obtain any desired grade of fiber. In the same year, Albert C. Lottman was awarded a patent for a new and improved mosquito net frame which could be disassembled frequently without damaging the frame members[9].

Throughout the decade of the 1890's, their inventiveness continued as Albert Lottman was awarded two more patents. The first was another patent for improvements in mosquito-net frames which are simple, durable and easily attached or detached from any bedstead. The second was a patent for improvements in tightening devices for spring bed bottoms to provide a simple and inexpensive means of tightening or adjusting the bed bottoms and securely holding the adjustment without needing special tools[10].

The management of the Lottman Brothers Manufacturing Company was closely held by the brothers. Albert Lottman, the eldest son, was the president of the company. Charles Lottman was the vice-president and Herman Lottman, handled the dual role of secretary and treasurer of the corporation. The company was very successful and its owners were well regarded in the local community[11].

By 1899, a subtle change in the Lottman company's management structure occurred when Albert Lottman went on his own as a wholesale dealer and manufacturer of spring beds, cots, mattresses and his patented bar frames. Albert opened his business operations at 206 Milam Street. The youngest brother Charles Lottman remained as vice president of the Lottman Brothers Manufacturing Company and also assumed the role of general manager of the factory operations. Herman Lottman retained his role as secretary and treasurer[12].

This peculiar management arrangement among the brothers continued for another few years. Although there appears to have been fractures in the cohesion of the family business operations, only minor changes took place until 1903. A reorganization of the company took place in 1903, the year after Charlotte Lottman, the family matriarch, passed away. Herman Lottman took over as the president of the Lottman Brothers Manufacturing Company, while Charles Lottman continued as vice president[13].

A more significant management change occurred in 1904 which suggests some of the turmoil among the brothers. Albert Lottman appears to have bought out his brothers in a move to gain control of the business. Then, on June 9, 1904, Albert Lottman joined with William S. Myers of Dallas and J. A. Grieves of Houston to incorporate the Lottman-Myers Manufacturing Company with $100,000 in capital stock. William Myers became the president and Albert Lottman was the vice president of the new venture that planned to use the factory on the I&GN tracks to manufacture all grades of bedding supplies and to be jobbers of fine furniture. Myers was a principal of the Olive and Myers Manufacturing Company, established in 1899 in Dallas, and the Houston operation would be a regional center for its quality household furniture[14].

After the sale of the company, Charles F. Lottman established his own manufacturing operations for mattresses and cots. The location of his office and factory was 2411 Washington Avenue in the Sixth Ward. This location was next door to his home at 2409 Washington Avenue, and he also had another facility at the corner of Foote Street and Bremond Street in the Fifth Ward, on the north bank of Buffalo Bayou opposite the former family factory. Charles Lottman operated this small mattress company in the 1920's. His sons Carl and Edwin joined him as partners in the company making spring beds, woven wire mattresses, cots and bedding[15].

Herman W. Lottman opened the H. W. Lottman Furniture Company at 210-212 Milam Street. His company was a dealer in furniture and also manufactured spring beds, mattresses, pillows, cots, patent mosquito net frames, brass and iron bedsteads. In the summer of 1910, the H. W. Lottman Furniture Company was forced into involuntary bankruptcy. On September 20, 1913, W. A. Monteith was selected by the bankruptcy court as the trustee to oversee the sale of assets of the company. Herman Lottman worked as an accountant at the shipyards in the early 1920's before his retirement[16].

In 1907, Albert Lottman sold the remaining Lottman interest in the mattress and furniture factory at 2115 Runnels Street to Myers and his partner from Dallas, H. E. Spalti. By the next year, the Lottman-Myers Manufacturing Company was managed with W. S.

Myers as president and H. E. Spalti as vice president. The name was changed by 1910 to the Myers-Spalti Manufacturing Company, and it was advertised as the successor to the Lottman Myers Manufacturing Company, manufacturing a similar line of products, including furniture, mattresses, spring beds, lawn swings and window shades[17].

The Myers-Spalti Manufacturing Company expanded the 2115 Runnels Street factory in 1909, in 1923, 1926 and, again, in 1928, on its way to becoming one of the largest the furniture manufacturers in the Southwest, producing quality household furniture and mattresses for nearly sixty years. The familiar five story facade that we see from the bayou was among the last of the structures built, in 1928, and it represents the factory at the peak of its manufacturing activity[18].

On December 28, 1955, the Olive-Myers-Spalti Manufacturing Company announced plans for a new manufacturing plant in Athens, Texas. A modern furniture manufacturing plant was built on fifty-seven acres and the company began, in 1957, to close its regional plants and warehouses in order to consolidate its operations at the new facility in Athens. At this time, the Houston plant was closed[19].

George Curtis Mathes, an early Texas manufacturing pioneer in electronics and air conditioning, purchased a majority interest in Olive-Myers-Spalti in 1957 and renamed the company the Curtis Mathes Manufacturing Corporation, combining furniture and electronics for hi-fi's and televisions. The brand became well known for its high fidelity entertainment systems, but eventually the company declined as the market changed. The Curtis Mathes Manufacturing Corporation ceased operations at the Athens plant on July 31, 1982. Curtis Mathes was acquired by Enhanced Electronics Corporation in 1993 and took the name, a year later, as Curtis Mathes Holding Corporation. In 1998, Curtis Mathes became uniView Technologies Corporation, a company that today is a hybrid broadband systems integrator and internet company providing e-business solutions[20].

For nearly thirty years, the Myers-Spalti Manufacturing Company buildings were vacant. Then, in the early 1980's, the factory complex was converted to international theme shopping mall called El Mercado del Sol. Although the building was transformed into a commercial center based on Mexican theme, the original structural design of the structures, including handmade bricks and wood fixtures, were retained. In 1997, the property, although it had been severely vandalized, was bought by developer Alan J. Atkinson and the Transamerica Group Ltd. The Transamerica Group called their development of loft apartments and offices The Americas, but in 2001, the Trammell Crow Residential company acquired the property and renamed it the Alexan Lofts. The Alexan Lofts opened in 2003 with 244 loft apartments. Perry Homes acquired the 3 acres next to the Alexan Lofts and built seventy-three town homes on the site adjacent to the former factory[21].

The Myers-Spalti buildings, now the Alexan Lofts, stand as visible reminders of the industries that lined the banks of Buffalo Bayou to the east of the city. Factories and businesses were established in this area as early as the 1860's, but most of the structures from those earlier enterprises are now gone. Here and there, some remnants remain, but mostly, the land is now clear or modern warehouses have been built on the older sites.

For a little over four miles, from the I&GN Railroad bridge to the Turning Basin, Buffalo Bayou flows nearly due east. Its channel has been widened and straightened over time, especially when ship and barge traffic to the City Wharves at Main Street was common in the nineteenth century. The outlying areas of town, both in the Second Ward south of the bayou and in the Fifth Ward north of the bayou, provided a good location for factories, compresses, mills and other commercial and civic ventures. The industrial nature of this segment of Buffalo Bayou continues to dominate the use of the land, however, as seen with the Alexan Lofts and the Perry Homes developments, the area east of downtown is showing a significant amount of residential development as well.

The south bank of the bayou from the I&GN tracks to Jensen Drive shows evidence of the area's early development. A rail spur was laid along the bank in the early years of the twentieth century as far as the modern Jensen Drive. In the 1920's, the Texas Company established an oil depot on the site with oil tanks aligned along the railroad tracks. Closer to Jensen Drive, the Zero Ice Factory was built in 1921[22].

Wade Hampton Irvin founded the Sanitary Ice Cream Company in 1917, and a few years later, he acquired the Zero Ice Company.

In the era before refrigeration, manufactured ice was a household commodity that was stored in the proverbial ice box. Commercial ice dealers, such as Zero Ice, had extensive operations with freezing tanks and ice storage vaults to provide ice to its customers on a regular basis. It was a lucrative business in the 1920's. Nevertheless, Wade Irwin liquidated all of his ice and ice cream interests in 1928 in order to concentrate on his Citizens State Bank which he founded in 1919. The Zero Ice Company ceased operations after the advent of refrigerators in the home, and by 1951, the structure associated with the ice plant at Jensen Drive were vacant. The building was demolished after 1981 during the construction of Guadalupe Plaza Park[23].

The land for Guadalupe Plaza Park was acquired by the City in 1986. The Hispanic-styled plaza park at 2311 Runnels Street was dedicated on October 15, 1988 by Mayor Kathy Whitmire. It occupies 6.46 acres and consists of a community center as well as park space along the bayou. Stairs lead down from the pavilion at the top of the bank to a concrete bulkhead and boat landing at the water's edge[24].

Jensen Drive Bridge

The growth of Houston on the north bank of Buffalo Bank resulted in the creation of the Fifth Ward in 1866. For many years after that, the residents petitioned City Council to improve the access to the downtown district from the Fifth Ward by building a bridge across Buffalo Bayou. That request was granted in January, 1883 with an order for the construction of the San Jacinto Street bridge[25].

Almost immediately, the Fifth Ward residents then began to ask for another bridge farther downstream. After ten years of citizen requests, on October 4, 1895, the Houston City Council considered the proposal to build a bridge at Hill Street to connect the Second and Fifth Wards. The appropriate approvals were obtained from the United States government and a contract was issued to the Indiana Bridge Company for the construction of a new bridge over Buffalo Bayou. On May 24, 1896, work was set to begin on the new bridge which would link Hill Street on the north side of the bayou with

Marsh Street on the south. The bridge was known as the Hill Street Bridge and it played an essential role in connecting the cotton warehouse district north of the bayou with the downtown business district[26].

The bridge at Hill Street was a steel draw bridge that would allow ship and barge traffic to navigate upstream to the wharves at Main Street. Wooden approaches to the bridge were built on both sides. The total span of the bridge was three hundred four feet, and, at the time it was built, the bridge was the longest highway bridge of its kind in the South. The whole structure was painted a brilliant Venetian red color[27].

The completion and final inspection of the new bridge was held on on February 3, 1897. After the inspection by the city officials was done, the bridge was "baptized with a keg of beer and solid refreshments[28]."

By the 1930's, the Hill Street bridge was one of the oldest bridges in Houston. The flood of 1935 severely damaged the bridge, and although repairs were made, the bridge needed to be replaced. Finally, on August 11, 1937, the Hill Street bridge was closed so that it could be demolished in favor a new bridge[29].

The South Jensen Drive bridge, previously known as the Hill Street Bridge, was designed by J. G. McKenzie, the City bridge engineer, and built by Russ Mitchell, Inc. in 1938 at a cost of $230,000. The bridge is one of a small number of steel multi-girder span bridges in Texas, and it is noteworthy for the length of its main span, its special steel handrail and concrete parapet approach walls. Its steel multi-girder technology provides one hundred forty-three feet of horizontal clearance and sixty-two feet of vertical clearance over the bayou for ships[30].

As a combination steel and concrete superstructure, the five hundred foot long bridge crests the bayou on three steel fabricated girder spans balanced on tall concrete piers. A forty foot wide roadway handles four lanes of traffic with concrete sidewalks on each side that are provided by steel cantilever framing. A heavy steel handrail outlines the roadway over the bayou. The approaches to the main spans are constructed of reinforced concrete girder and slab spans erected over concrete bents and abutments[31].

Today, this bridge is an integral part of vehicular access to the revitalized Second Ward, and it is known, simply, as the Jensen Drive bridge.

St. Vincent's Cemetery

Less than two blocks south of the Jensen Drive bridge is the historic Saint Vincent's Cemetery. Located on the east half of the block bounded by Navigation Boulevard (formerly Runnels Street), Jensen Drive (formerly Marsh Street), Ann Street and St. Charles Street (formerly Buffalo Street), St. Vincent's Cemetery is Houston's oldest Roman Catholic burial ground. The cemetery, which is less than an acre in size, was established in 1852 on lots donated by Houston businessman John Kennedy, parishioner of St. Vincent's Church[32].

Although many of Houston's early German and Irish settlers are buried at the cemetery, the most notable burial is that of Lt. Richard William Dowling, the hero of the Battle of Sabine Pass. Dick Dowling died of yellow fever in 1867 at age twenty-nine, and he was buried in St. Vincent's Cemetery along with many other victims of the epidemic[33].

Another prominent person interred in the cemetery is Samuel Paschall, a veteran of the Battle of San Jacinto and one of Houston's earliest residents. He settled in Houston's Second Ward where he worked as a cabinet maker and carpenter. Paschall married Bridget O'Reilly on September 21, 1839 and they had three children. After Paschall's death on June 6, 1874, he was buried in St. Vincent's Cemetery[34].

In May, 1871, the City of Houston condemned St. Vincent's Cemetery as a burial ground. Little attention was paid to maintenance of the cemetery, and the hurricanes of 1900 and 1915 displaced markers, broke fences enclosing family lots and blew down trees on the lot. The headstones and monuments lay in disarray and decay, and it was hard to identify St. Vincent's Cemetery as a burial place. Eventually, though, funds were raised to restore and beautify the cemetery. Today, St. Vincent's Cemetery is maintained by the Archdiocese of Galveston-Houston, and the Church of Our Lady of Guadalupe, at 2405 Navigation Boulevard, adjoins it to the west[35].

Geiselman Tannery

About one hundred fifty yards downstream from the Jensen Drive bridge, the concrete slab of a demolished warehouse complex on the south bank of the bayou marks the site of one of the earliest industrial ventures along this segment of the Buffalo Bayou. It was on this tract of land in early 1862 that Samuel Geiselman established a tannery for the production of leather products[36].

In 1857, Samuel Geiselman, age twenty-five, and his older brother Jacob, age twenty-nine, both moved with their respective families to Houston from Maryland. By 1860, the two brothers had become merchants in Houston and the young families lived next door to each other in the Third Ward. The decline of commercial activity as a result of the Civil War in 1861 left many of the City's merchants without stock for their stores. This situation led merchants like the Geiselman's to open other businesses. Samuel Geiselman acquired a tract of land in the Second Ward at the end of Buffalo Street (the modern St. Charles Street), and in the spring of 1862, he built a tannery[37].

The Geiselman tannery consisted of one large building for the tannery and two storehouses, one for hides and one for bark. The main building had twenty-nine tanning vats in operation. A fulling mill with seven heavy hammers was used to soften the hides before they were processed in the currying room and the finishing room[38].

A large boiler was fired up for extracting the tannin from roots, weeds such as camomile, and oak bark. The tannin was then fed into two large liquor vats. All of this machinery was powered by a twelve horsepower engine. By May, 1862, the thirty workmen employed at the tannery were producing three hundred sides of leather per week to supply the Houston market with harnesses, shoe soles and upper leathers of all varieties[39].

After the Civil War, Samuel Geiselman continued to operate the tannery, and he also opened a saddlery and leather goods shop on Travis Street between Franklin Avenue and Commerce Avenue. In the post war year of 1866, both Samuel and his brother Jacob served as aldermen from the wards in which they lived, the Second and the Third, respectively[40].

By 1870, Samuel Geiselman was operating both a tannery and a beef packing business. His finished leather goods were of sufficient quality that he won an award at the 1871 Texas State Fair in the Best Dozen Texas Upper Leather, Tanned category. Nevertheless, Geiselman focused more on the food business during the 1870's, and for the next twenty-five years, he operated a meat market in one of the stalls at the City Market[41].

It was during the early years of his business in the City Market that Samuel Geiselman made his most significant contribution to Houston's history. About 1867, Geiselman, a devout member of the Presbyterian Church, initiated a plan to not open the market on Sunday morning in observance of the commandment to keep the Lord's Day holy. As a result, many businesses in the City Market did not open on Sunday morning, but instead, the market opened on Saturday evening and created a tradition that was particular to Houston for over thirty years[42].

Samuel Geiselman died at his family home on March 29, 1895, at age sixty-two. During the thirty-eight years that he lived in Houston, Geiselman introduced the local implementation of the blue law movement to Houston. In the nineteenth century, blue laws were enacted in Texas and many other western states. Blue laws were laws designed to enforce religious standards, especially the observance of Sunday as a day of worship and rest where shopping is restricted. Needless to say, the enforcement of such laws was very controversial at the time, and the laws often went unheeded[43].

Nevertheless, blue laws stayed on the books well into the twentieth century. Eventually, in 1961, the U. S. Supreme Court upheld the right of states to enact blue laws as long as the purpose was not religious. The Texas blue law prohibiting the sale of forty-two items on consecutive Saturdays and Sundays was repealed by the Legislature in 1985. Yet, even today, Texas blue laws include provisions that car dealerships must remain closed on either Saturday or Sunday at the option of the dealer[44].

After the turn of the century, the Houston White Brick Company built a brick works on the former Geiselman property at the end of Buffalo Street. The Houston White Brick Company was incorporated on September 8, 1904 with $80,000 of capital stock. The principals of this new company were J. M. Rockwell, McClure

Kelly, Luda Jones, Edgar Watkins and Frank C. Jones of Houston, and E. D. Steger of Bonham[45].

By 1907, the company had constructed a two story brick manufacturing facility which housed three brick machines in the main building. These machines were powered by a one hundred fifty horsepower engine. The steam cylinder ovens or kilns were in a single story structure attached to the south side of the main building. A small office was attached to the east side of the main building[46].

The era in which paving bricks were used for streets and roadways was in decline due to the growing use of asphalt. The Houston White Brick Company faced significant financial difficulties during its short existence. On June 19, 1908, L. C. McBride, the receiver for the Western Bank and Trust filed a suit for foreclosure on Houston White Brick Company's mortgage note of $20,000. The charter for the Houston White Brick Company was forfeited for non-payment of the state franchise tax on July 2, 1909[47].

In the early 1920's, the Dedman Iron Works took over and expanded the facility that had formerly housed the Houston White Brick Company. The company was founded in 1914 by Henry W. Dedman who set up shop in a small building near his home on Spring Street. As Dedman's business grew, he had to move to larger facilities in 1918, and again, in 1922, to the Buffalo Street location where he installed the iron and brass foundries[48].

With the addition of the foundries, Dedman renamed his business the Dedman Foundry and Machine Company, and continued to expand his operations. On July 26, 1925, the Dedman Foundry and Machine Company was issued a building permit for $10,000 to construct a large steel factory building on the site. When they moved in on November 1, 1925, the plant complex consisted of a two story office building, a garage, an iron and brass foundry, a machine shop, a pattern storage warehouse, a pattern shop for welding and blacksmithing, and a sheet metal shop. The Dedman Foundry buildings were equipped with the most modern tools and technology available, including engine lathes, boring mills, radial drills and three hundred ton hydraulic press. From its location on Buffalo Bayou, the plant employed two electric cranes and hoisting equipment to load materials and machinery from barges in the ship channel to the back of the machine shop[49].

From its location on the upper end of the Houston Ship Channel, the Dedman Foundry also offered a service that was extraordinary at the time. It maintained a floating barge plant with all of the necessary equipment that could be moved to any location along the ship channel for repair work on vessels. The Dedman Foundry specialized in building and repairing cotton compresses, pumps and oil mill machinery[50].

The development from a small machine shop to a large scale industrial service company required a reorganization of the company and the inclusion of financial backers. On April 19, 1928, Henry W. Dedman transferred his various property holdings, including the two acres in Lot 70 of the S. M. Williams Survey where the foundry was situated, to the Dedman Foundry and Machine Company for $1 and other considerations. The following day, Dedman, C. E. Newton and A. E. Ammerman chartered the Dedman Investment Company with $190,000 and the Dedman Foundry and Machine Company with $160,000. Henry Dedman became the president and general manager of the foundry while C. E. Newton served as the Assistant General Manager and Auditor[51].

After nearly a decade of this partnership and the business environment of the Great Depression, Henry Dedman chose to re-acquire the assets of the Dedman Foundry and Machine Company. On August 7, 1936, he bought back the property assets of the firm for $64,000. As a result, his operation was well positioned to contract with the government during World War II for marine contracts for rudder stocks and other "essential war work[52]."

In 1944, the Dedman Foundry and Machine Company was purchased by the Federal Steel Products Corporation of Houston. Henry Dedman, although he was in his early sixties, continued to work as the plant's manager. During the difficult times of the steel worker's strike of 1946, the Dedman Foundry was one of only two firms in the nation that tried to continue operations[53].

A fire on January 20, 1948 destroyed the cleaning plant of the Federal Steel Products Corporation for a complete loss of $175,000. A new and expanded plant was built on the site by 1951, and the Federal Steel Products Corporation complex included a mold room, a bath room, pattern storage, the cleaning department, the core room, the foundry and the machine shop. On April 24, 1956, the

United Stockyards Corporation, a national chain of stockyards, acquired a controlling interest in the Federal Steel Products Corporation of Houston as part of their diversification policy[54].

The steel industry in the United States saw domestic production and services decline in the 1970's and 1980's as foreign steel production increased. Local operations such as the plant on Buffalo Bayou eventually closed. The vacant facility and warehouses were demolished after 2004, and the barren concrete floor is all that remains, now, to remind us of the long industrial history of the site at the foot of Buffalo Street (now known as St. Charles Street).

W. D. Cleveland Compress

The north bank of Buffalo Bayou at Jensen Drive saw industrial development in the early 1890's. William D. Cleveland had been active in both the wholesale grocery trade and the cotton business since the end of the Civil War. His participation in the Buffalo Compress and the Union Compress led him to establish his own compress company, and in 1894, Cleveland built the Cleveland Compress and Warehouse on the east side of Hill Street. The Cleveland Compress was an impressive complex of cotton warehouses, classing sheds and loading platforms with an inclined ramp to a wharf at the bayou. In the era when cotton was king, this was one of the city's finest facilities for processing cotton[55].

Misfortune, however, descended upon the Cleveland Compress in 1912. In the early morning hours of February 21, 1912, as a strong cold front moved through the city bringing with it brisk north winds, a fire broke out in the Fifth Ward and swept rapidly across about forty city blocks, destroying everything in its path. The largest single loss in the fire was the Cleveland Compress with damage to goods and facilities totally $1.9 million. In 1912, that was an enormous sum[56]!

Called the Great Fire of 1912, the conflagration was the most devastating fire in Houston's history at that time. It is believed that the fire began in a vacant house on Hardy Street near its intersection with Opelousas Street. This location is about two blocks northwest of the modern site of the Saint Arnold's Brewing Company on Interstate 10. The abandoned building once housed the Mad House

Saloon. The two story building was near the rail yards and had become a shelter for hobos who hopped the trains. Vagrants in the building were suspected of starting the fire in an attempt to keep warm[57].

At half past midnight, the fire was discovered. Fanned by thirty-eight mile per hour winds, the flames raced like a prairie fire across the city, leaping from block to block, according to eye witnesses. By 2:00 am, the burn area was between the Southern Pacific Railroad tracks, Hardy Street and Opelousas Street. The three story brick Star and Crescent Hotel, located at 1208 Hardy Street on the northeast corner with Conti Street, only a block from where the fire started, was among the first structures destroyed. Two blocks of residences were burning with more structures expected to burn. The local fire department worked heroically to stop the flames[58].

Thousands of people were driven from their homes due to the fire. Many dashed from their homes with only the night clothes they were wearing. Relief efforts got underway immediately. The fire crew and local community leaders organized a relief committee that provided food and clothing to those displaced by the fire. Much of the effort to care for the victims was lead by Nat Q. Henderson, a forty-five year old teacher in the local public school and a respected member of the African American community[59].

Nathaniel Q. Henderson was one of the earliest graduates of Prairie View State Normal and Industrial College. Henderson, his wife Mamie and their six children lived a few blocks east of the fire at 3019 Nance Street. As soon as he was able, Henderson began to organize the relief efforts after the fire, and, as a result, "there was comparatively little suffering" by those affected by the disaster[60].

Henderson was the principal of Blanche Bruce Elemetary School in the Fifth Ward from 1909 to 1942. Because of his service to the community and his actions during the Great Fire of 1912, he was called the "Mayor of Fifth Ward." After his death in 1949, Henderson's career in education was honored when the Nat Q. Henderson School, at 701 Solo Street, was named for him in 1956[61].

The Great Fire, blown south to Buffalo Bayou by the north winds, traveled more than one and a half miles in a path that was a quarter of a mile wide and it incinerated every structure in its path. The fire even jumped across Buffalo Bayou to warehouses in the

Second Ward. The glow from the flames could be seen by passengers on a train thirty-five miles away[62].

When the final tally was made, the Great Fire of 1912 had consumed thirteen industrial plants, eight stores, twenty-nine two-story dwellings, ninety frame cottages, the St. Patrick Church and school, nine oil tank cars, one hundred sixteen boxcars and at least 48,000 bales of cotton. The devastation totaled an estimated $7 million in damages to residential and business property. Miraculously, no one was killed or seriously injured[63].

The losses to businesses along the bayou were staggering. The Cleveland Compress suffered the worst damage, estimated at $1.9 million. Nearly 32,000 bales of cotton were burned in its sheds and adjoining railroad yards. The Southern Pacific Railroad lost twenty-one loaded rail cars and the International and Great Northern Railroad lost a whole train of cars. The Hudson Lumber Company, pencil manufacturers located on the north bank at the I&GN bridge, had a $40,000 loss. Businessman John Lyons, a fixture in the Fifth Ward since the 1870's, suffered a $40,000 loss[64].

Businesses on the south side of the bayou were damaged as well. The fire engulfed the McFadden Southern Compress and Warehouse Company in the Second Ward, causing an estimated $1 million loss. The Standard Compress Company had a total loss of the plant and 16,000 bales of cotton, estimated at $992,000. Further down stream, the Houston Packing Company had a portion of its facility burned for a $7,000 loss[65].

Ironically, a similar fire occurred in the Fifth Ward about twenty years earlier. On May 20, 1891 at 5:30 pm, a fire started in the shaving room of the Phoenix Lumber Mills at corner of Providence Street and Maffitt Street. This location is about two blocks southeast of where the fire of 1912 started. The fire department was promptly on the scene, but the water pressure and the water supply was entirely inadequate to fight the fire. The 1891 fire progressed rapidly northward due to a south wind. In addition to a number of businesses, the fire consumed several residences and cottages, a boarding house and St. Patrick's Church at corner of Conti Street and Maury Street along with its two story rectory and the parish school. The Fire of 1891 was one of the top three fires in Houston's history to that date. Only the fire that destroyed the International Compress in 1884 and the burning of the Morris Block in 1877 were greater[66].

The loss of St. Patrick's Church to both fires, in 1891 and in 1912, and the rebuilding of the church each time reflects the resilience and persistence of the Irish community of Houston. In 1870, out of the four hundred ninety-seven households in the Fifth Ward, twenty-five of those were immigrant families from Ireland. St. Patrick's Church was established by the Diocese of Galveston in 1880. The church's location on the southeast corner of Conti Street and Maury Street was selected to serve the Catholic Irish immigrants who settled in the Fifth Ward[67].

After the fire of 1891, St. Patrick's Church was rebuilt on the southeast corner of Maury Street and Conti Street. After the Great Fire of 1912, the reconstruction of the church began with a new chapel at 1103 Maury Street on the corner with Providence Street in 1913. A new church and school building was then built at 1105 Maury Street. St. Patrick's Church is currently located at 4918 Cochran Street, about thirty blocks north of its original location[68].

John Lyons, whose businesses suffered significant damage in the 1912 fire, was a leading resident of the Fifth Ward for over forty years. Lyons immigrated to Houston in 1871 from his native Ireland when he was eighteen years old. Within a few of years, Lyons had established his residence and a store along the Liberty Road on the east side of International and Great Northern Railroad tracks. His store sold groceries and provisions, wines, liquors and cigars[69].

By 1879, Lyons had added a boarding house to his property at the corner of Liberty Road and Carr Street which ran beside the railroad tracks. The Lyons House advertised that it was "conveniently located for all classes of workingmen," especially those who worked in the rail yards and factories of the Fifth Ward. Catering to the basic needs of these men, the Lyons House was situated "in connection [with] a neat little bar" with groceries, wines, liquors, cigars and "fresh beer always on draught[70]."

When the City assigned street numbers, about 1886, the Lyons House and Saloon was to be found at 43-45 Liberty Road. By 1892, the City renamed Liberty Road in honor of Bishop Jean M. Odin, and the Lyons House and Saloon was designated as 2501-2503 Odin Avenue at corner with Carr Street. Jean Marie Odin, born in France in 1800, was named as the first bishop of the new Diocese of Galveston on May 4, 1847. He served as bishop until 1861 when he became the archbishop of New Orleans. Odin died in France on May 25, 1870. Then, as now, the naming of streets for prominent figures of the community was a recognition that was well appreciated by the local residents[71].

About 1908, John Lyons expanded his business operations with the acquisition of the nearby Star and Crescent Hotel. The Star and Crescent Hotel, built about 1907 and owned by Harry A. Schaffer, was a three story brick building at at 1208-1210 Hardy Street on the northeast corner with Conti Street. The hotel occupied the second and third floors of the building while the first floor consisted of a store on the corner, a Lunch and Dining Room and a kitchen off to the rear[72].

By 1912, John Lyons' enterprises included both the Lyons House on Odin Avenue and the Star and Crescent Hotel on Hardy Street. Business in the Fifth Ward was good, and Lyons promoted his lodgings with the slogan that "Electric street cars pass the door every five minutes." The dreadful blaze of February 21, 1912, however, changed the Irishman's luck. One of the first buildings lost to the fire was the brick Star and Crescent Hotel. Additional losses to Lyons' businesses totaled about $40,000 and he faced certain financial difficulties. A year later, on March 8, 1913, John Lyons, proprietor of the Lyons House, owner of Star and Crescent Hotel and a prominent merchant, filed a voluntary bankruptcy petition in Federal court[73].

Lyons was determined to turn his businesses around. With the help of his friends, such as Hugh Hamilton, Lyons was able to reopen his businesses. Hamilton bought the Star and Crescent Hotel from the bankruptcy trustee and, on May 6, 1914, he sold the hotel back to John Lyons for a small cash down payment and a note for $61,172. Before his financial recovery could be competed, however, Lyons passed away. John Lyons died on January 26, 1915 at his home at 2501 Odin Avenue. His funeral was attended by many notable Houstonians, including former mayor John T. Browne and W. L. Foley, both of whom served as pallbearers[74].

Thomas C. Lyons, John's younger brother, took over as the manager of the Lyons House after the death of his brother. He managed the boarding house for the family until he passed away in the 1920's. In 1917, the recognition of John Lyons' contributions to the City and to the Fifth Ward was made by renaming a segment of Odin Avenue as Lyons Avenue. Eventually, the whole length of the former Liberty Road and Odin Avenue became Lyons Avenue, as it is today, in honor of the Irishman who lived and worked in the Fifth Ward for over forty years[75].

After the destruction of the Cleveland Compress in the Great Fire of 1912, the tract of land where it stood was redeveloped as a cotton compress and warehouse complex by the Shippers Compress Company. The Shippers Compress Company was incorporated on October 23, 1913 with capital stock of 100,000 by J. M. Dorrance, H. Roberts, J. W. Sanders. By 1924, the Shippers Compress complex consisted of several large sheds on both sides of a I&GN Railroad spur. The decline of the cotton business brought new tenants to the large warehouse facility. By May, 1940, warehouses were leased by the Clinton Warehouse Company to Montgomery Ward and Company for furniture and paint storage, building materials, and mail order merchandise. Another compress company, the Ship Channel Compress Company also built warehouses on the tract immediately east of the Clinton Warehouse. The I&GN Railroad spur ran between the two cotton complexes[76].

Montgomery Ward and Company acquired the warehouse complex from the Clinton Warehouse Company on February 13, 1990. Real estate investor Curtis Michael Garver bought the property on October 11, 2001, and he transferred the 11.6 acre tract with warehouses to his commercial real estate company, CG 7600 LP, on June 30, 2004. The tenants of the warehouse facility currently include Alpha Used Tire, Inc. and DSI Logistics, a refrigerated warehouse and storage company[77].

The commercial warehouse on the former Ship Channel Compress Company site is currently owned by Kellogg Brown and Root LLC. In addition to this 9.64 acre tract, KBR owns the bulk of the land from here to Hirsch Road and from Clinton Drive to Buffalo Bayou. Several warehouses and structures can be seen along the north bank of the bayou although the KBR facility has been mostly inactive in recent years[78].

Pritchard Rice Milling Company

A small warehouse on the KBR property, the third structure east of Jensen Drive at the end of Meadow Street, is on the former site of the Pritchard Rice Milling Company, an agricultural processing plant dating from the first decade of the twentieth century. The Pritchard mill was one of the first rice mills in Texas and it was the successor to the Lane Rice Mill that began in the late nineteenth century[79].

The Pritchard Rice Milling Company was incorporated in 1907 with capital stock of $100,000. W. B. Dunlap of Beaumont was the president of the company. G. W. Collier was the vice-president, and Paul F. Pritchard was the secretary. Pritchard also served as the manager of the plant[80].

Ground breaking for the Pritchard plant took place on May 15, 1907. The original plant included a warehouse made of artificial stone and a mill constructed of reinforced concrete. A seventy-five foot tall grain elevator with a capacity of 100,000 bushels was situated south of the mill house and it stood near the bayou. Expansion of the plant in the 1920's included the addition of a "rough rice" warehouse to the west of the mill. Belt conveyors to the bayou were installed to transfer grain between the elevator and barges on Buffalo Bayou[81].

The Pritchard Rice Milling Company mill and warehouse was destroyed by fire on July 8, 1936. Losses totaled $115,000. The plant was rebuilt and operated into the 1960's, before it was acquired by Brown and Root[82].

Houston Shell and Concrete

A most interesting site along this stretch of Buffalo Bayou is found opposite the warehouses on the north bank east of Jensen Drive. From your perspective in a boat on the water, mysterious towers rise above the edge of the high bank. Four concrete silos can be clearly seen from the bayou, standing as if they were the fortifications of some ancient castle. Nonetheless, the silos are neither ancient nor parts of some kind of fortifications.

Photo credit: Linda Gorski

The gravel silos of the former Houston Shell and Concrete facility cast a mysterious spell over this section of the bayou.

During the post-WWII economic expansion in Houston, the Houston Shell and Concrete Company establish a materials yard on the south bank of Buffalo Bayou near the end of North St. Charles Street. Some time in the 1950's, the company opened another yard a few blocks downstream at the end of North Live Oak Street. Between 1964 and 1973, the silos which stored various grades of gravel were added to the facility. The site also has a number of aggregate bins which appear to date prior to the silos. Houston Shell and Concrete was a local provider of ready mixed concrete, shell, sand and gravel[83].

In general, the bayou frontage along the south bank here has been little developed, even well into the twentieth century. Around 1920, there was some residential housing along Pless Street (modern North Live Oak Street) that extended toward the bayou, but then, as now, the land has been used for storage by companies such as Houston Shell and Concrete and the Parker Brothers and Company, a supplier of shell and other building materials[84].

About 2003, the Buffalo Bayou Partnership acquired the 2.3 acres east of the foot of North St. Charles Street. The BBP picked up another 1.4 acres at the end of North Nagle Street from C. M. Garver in 2004 to make a pocket park in connection with the hike and bike trail that runs along the top of the bayou's bank from Jensen Drive to Lockwood Drive. Garver had purchased the property from the Parker Brothers in 1997[85].

Between North Nagle Street and Middle Street lies the Factory Addition. The Factory Addition was platted in 1867 for working class Houstonians, and the subdivision is characterized by narrow streets and small homes set close to the street, a feature indicative of the days of horse drawn carriages and wagons. In 2007, the Pinto East End LLC acquired the two blocks of the Factory Addition nearest to Buffalo Bayou. Presumably, this part of the Second Ward will see more upscale residential development in the next economic cycle[86].

Oddly enough, the initial development of the Factory Addition came in the economic upturn in Houston after the depressing days of the Civil War. Just downstream of the Factory Addition lies the site, now occupied by the bare ground from which a warehouse has been recently removed, where one of the first post war factories in Houston was built in 1866. This enterprise was the Houston City Mills.

Houston City Mills

Despite the defeat of the Confederacy, business leaders in Houston were determined to reinvigorate the local economy. The war had brought the once booming commercial activity of the Port of Houston to a trickle. The optimism of the entrepreneurial spirit of Houston's business community looked forward to the recovery from the war, and almost right away, there was a surge of new business development. By the late spring of 1866, new factories and businesses had come to Houston, including the Eureka Cotton Manufacturing Company, the Houston Gas Works, the Street Railway Company and the Houston City Mills[87].

The Houston City Mills was organized in the spring of 1865 to manufacture plain cotton goods. By May, 1866, the buildings for the textile mill were under construction on the banks of Buffalo Bayou east of town. The major stockholders initially capitalized the company with $75,000, but they soon increased that to $100,000. These stockholders, among the most influential businessmen of the time and well known to us even today, included W. J. Hutchins, T. W. House, R. S. Willis of Galveston, Benjamin A. Shepherd, W. R. Baker, William Marsh Rice, Alexander Sessums, T. M. Bagby, John T. Brady and Alexander McGowen. B. A. Shepherd was the president of the company[88].

The construction of the Houston City Mills was completed by early 1869, and operations began for the production of a variety of cotton fabrics including sheetings, shirtings, stripes, hickory, ticking, checks, cottonades and family jeans. Although many of the cloths that were made are not familiar to us today, they were utilitarian cotton cloths of the time. The most popular of these specialty fabrics were Cheviot, Hickory and Osnaberg. Cheviot, made from the wool of the Cheviot sheep, is a rugged and harsh fabric with an uneven surface that does not hold a crease and it sags with water. It is a twill weave for coats and suits and is sold as tweed. Hickory cloth is a twill weave of cotton known for excellent durability. Hickory is warp striped, comes in a variety of colors and is used for work clothes. Osnaberg, a medium to heavy weight fabric known for strength and durability, is a course cloth that varies in color and print and, today, is used for draperies and covers[89].

The overall quality of the goods produced at the mill was very good. At the State Fair, held in Houston in May, 1872, James F. Dumble, the agent for the Houston City Mills, accepted the awards for "best display in cotton goods made anywhere" and "best five pieces of sheeting[90]."

The main building of the Houston City Mills was an imposing three story brick structure with a tower that rose at the center of the front side of the large and spacious factory that was situated at the back of the tract, near Buffalo Bayou. The building extended lengthwise from west to east and there was a wing on the east end that went back north toward the bayou to form an "L" shape. At the north end of the building was the Cotton Room, the place where the raw cotton began its journey through the manufacturing process. Bales of cotton were shipped to the mill near Buffalo Bayou and loaded from a wharf to back of the factory for the first stage of the process. By March, 1874, the Houston City Mills were going through four bales of cotton per day, approximately 115,000 pounds of cotton a day[91].

In the cotton room, the raw cotton was sorted and made ready for the two pickers. Pickers were large machines through which the cotton was run and cleaned of dirt, dust and foreign substances. The cotton then was passed over fluted rollers to create large rolls for the carders[92].

Carding is the process in which the unorganized clumps of cotton fibers are broken up and the individual fibers are aligned more or less parallel to each other. The card clothing of a carder has wire pins embedded in a rubber backing to comb the fibers into batting. The Houston City Mills had thirty-two carding machines on the second floor of the building. Rolls of cotton batting were transferred to the carders on an elevator and the batting was made into continuous rolls before it was sent to the speeders[93].

Speeders were complicated machines which combined two cotton rolls through drawing frames, spinning frames and warpers to draw out the fibers spun into threads to make the warp. The warp was then twisted and wound on spools, bobbins and shuttles. This thread was then sent to the seventy-one looms of the factory. There were separate looms for sheetings, jeans and ticking, and the operation produced cloth at a rate of 3,400 yards per day[94].

All of the machinery of the mill was driven by a single twenty-four horsepower Corliss steam engine. The Corliss engine was patented by American engineer George Henry Corliss in 1849, and because of the engine's increased efficiency over the conventional steam engine, it became the state of the art stationary engine to provide mechanical power to line shafting in factories and mills. The Houston City Mills' engine had a fifteen foot flywheel and a twenty inch cylinder having a stroke of four feet. It took four cords of wood per day to keep the engine operating[95].

The Houston City Mills employed eighty-three workers and two thirds of them were women and girls. The usual work day was eleven hours, and there was a significant disparity among the wage rates. Men earned $1.25 to $3 per hour. Women earned from $20 to

$25 per month, and children were paid from fifteen cents to ninety cents per day[96].

Nevertheless, there were benefits to employment at the textile mill. The company built eight or nine tenements and cottages for the use of workers at the factory. About nineteen families of employees lived in the houses that surrounded the Houston City Mills, and the rent was nearly free. The grounds of the factory were landscaped and quite appealing. Areas of the fifteen acre tract were cultivated and planted with trees, shrubbery, flowers and green grass. The superintendent of factory, C. H. Robinson, lived on site in a two story house "with every convenience." Overall, the Houston City Mills was cited as an example of a successful investment and evidence of the new prosperity of Houston[97].

In June, 1875, production at the Houston City Mills was at an all time peak. The Eureka Mills, its competitor located on the west side of town, had idled many of its looms because of the high price of cotton. Many of those workers moved to work at the Houston City Mills. The quantities produced in the first week of June were some of the largest ever, including 1,000 yards of Osnaberg, 26,240 yards of shirting, 6,615 yards of drilling, 19,880 yards of lowells, 3,600 yards of ticking and 6,887 yards of cottonade. The mill also shipped 2,800 pounds of knitting cottons and spun yarns[98].

With productivity at a high level and the business outlook optimistic, disaster struck the east side plant. On August 7, 1875, between two and three o'clock in the afternoon, a fire began in the drying room on the third floor of the Houston City Mills. The alarm was sounded from the bell in the Market Tower, but by the time the firemen arrived, the whole building was in flames. Work for the day had stopped only a few minutes earlier. Within ten minutes of the watchman passing on his rounds, the fire erupted. The room filled so quickly with smoke that it could not be entered and a fire extinguisher was ineffective. The factory of the Houston City Mills was destroyed within thirty minutes[99].

Only a few items, including some machinery and manufactured goods, could be salvaged from the fire. The loss was estimated at between $150,000 and $200,000. The Houston City Mills had been only minimally insured for about $7,000, and the investors and principals owners were the biggest losers. About one hundred employees were put out of work, including about ninety factory workers, who supported families totaling about three hundred persons[100].

The economic impact of the loss of the textile mill was significant. The local press called for a reconstruction of the mills as soon as possible, but the investment losses were too great. An aggressive campaign to encourage the rebuilding of the mills as a matter of civic pride failed, and the remaining assets of the Houston City Mills were sold. The land remained vacant for two decades before a new enterprise occupied the site[101].

In September, 1895, the construction of the compress and warehouses of the Standard Compress Company was completed. William C. Robards of San Antonio was the president of the Standard Compress Company and M. E. Andrews served as its secretary and treasurer. The company chose the tract of land at the foot of Middle Street because it was considered to be the most desirable location for a compress with a long frontage "on a deep stretch of water" near the San Antonio and Aransas Pass Railway bridge over Buffalo Bayou. A loading wharf on the bayou connected with the loading platforms along the railroad siding[102].

The compress complex consisted of four warehouse units under one roof. At the north end of the warehouses was the press room which had a Morse press. The Morse cotton press, initially patented by Edmund L. Morse of St. Louis in 1878, became the standard press of the cotton industry because of the machine's simplicity, productivity and durability. Housed in a sixty foot tower, the Morse press could compress a bale of cotton from a plantation press from four feet thick to one foot thick[103].

The success of the Standard Compress Company was abruptly shattered on the night of February 21, 1912. The flames from the Great Fire of 1912 jumped Buffalo Bayou and caught the Standard Compress on fire. The building and the 16,000 bales of cotton stored in the warehouses were totally destroyed for a loss of $992,000[104].

In the aftermath of the devastation of the Great Fire of 1912, many businessmen where unable to rebuild their businesses. William D. Cleveland, the owner of the Cleveland Compress, suffered the largest loss during the fire when his compress on the north bank burned. Yet, Cleveland marshaled his resources and set out to rebuild his compress business, and in 1912, he acquired the Merchants Compress Company[105].

The Merchants Compress Company had been incorporated in April, 1910 by William Bartlett Chew, who served as the company's president. J. W. Sanders was the vice president and K. E. Womack was the secretary-treasurer. Initially, the Merchants Compress was located near the Merchants and Planters Oil Mill on the north bank of Buffalo Bayou, at foot of Kansas Street at Roanoke Street (modern Bringhurst Street and Clinton Drive)[106].

The unexpected death of William D. Cleveland, Sr. on Christmas Eve of 1912 did not derail the take over of the Merchants Compress Company. William B. Chew retired as the president of the Merchants Compress Company in 1913, and the Cleveland interests proceeded to construct a new cotton compress facility on the former site of the Standard Compress Company. Thirteen warehouse buildings were erected in 1913, and by 1915, the Merchants Compress Company was operating with A. Sessums Cleveland serving as president, John T. Scott as vice president, Austin W. Pollard as secretary-treasurer and Leon H. Bullard as the plant superintendent[107].

On July 3, 1923, the assets of the Merchants Compress Company were divided and the company was split into two companies. The entity that retained the former name was headed by A. S. Cleveland. The offshoot became the Exporters Compress and Warehouse Company and it had A. A. Bath as president. Nevertheless, the Merchants Compress added additional warehouses to the site on Middle Street in 1924, 1925 and 1929. The company declined, however, during the Depression, and by 1945, the warehouse complex had been taken over by the Feld-Reynolds Warehouse Corporation[108].

During the 1950's, the Feld-Reynolds Warehouse leased the seventeen warehouses to a variety of clients, including the Pollock Paper Corporation, the Houston Central Warehouse Company and the Southern Warehouse Corporation. The Pinto East End LLC, acquired the warehouse complex from the Feld Warehouse Company on December 4, 2007[109].

Pinto East End is a real estate investment company that was incorporated on October 18, 2007. It is associated with the Cockrell

Investment Partners LP and Robert K. Hatcher. Hatcher is the President and CEO of the Cockrell Interests, Inc. and its associated businesses. He joined the firm in 2001 and is an adjunct professor at the Jones Graduate School of Business at Rice University[110].

The former site of the Houston City Mills has recently been cleared of the old warehouses and its twenty-one acres are vacant commercial land.

North Velasco Street

Beyond the Houston City Mills site, the south bank is covered with trees and brush. At times, it is possible to make out the hike and bike trail near the top of the bank, but the terrain above the bank appears to be heavily wooded. An old ravine, called Deek Gully on early maps, cuts through the area to drain into Buffalo Bayou where a foot bridge of the hike and bike trail can be seen from the bayou. This location consists of the northern most blocks of the Weisenbach Addition, and those blocks, numbers 10 and 11, are owned by Pinto East End LLC. The eastern boundary is North Velasco Street, and from 1840 until 1903, the city limits crossed Buffalo Bayou near the foot of North Velasco Street[111].

After 1900, the City began to change the way it handled the disposal of trash and solid waste. During the nineteenth century, trash and garbage was collected by the city scavenger, under a contract managed by the City Health Officer, and dumped in designated ravines and gullies around the city. Later, incinerators were installed near many of the city dump sites to burn the trash. An incinerator was established in the Fifth Ward in 1916, and by 1930, there were eight incinerators throughout the Houston, burning three hundred eighty-two tons of waste per day. An incinerator was opened on North Velasco Street in 1925[112].

A new incinerator was built on North Velasco Street in 1947 on 1.6 acres in Block 6 of the Weisenbach Addition. Although the City's use of incinerators began to decline in the late 1930's, the Velasco Street Incinerator continued operating into the 1950's. Eventually, sanitary landfills became the standard for garbage disposal, and the incinerator was closed. The incinerator facility was

Photo credit: Louis F. Aulbach

The brick chimneys of the North Velasco Street incinerator are all that remain of this solid waste disposal unit of the City.

dismantled after 1981, but the two brick chimneys still remain today and they can be seen in the trees and brush along the railroad tracks[113].

The Southern Pacific Railroad right of way along North Velasco Street occupies nearly twelve acres between Navigation Boulevard and Buffalo Bayou. Recent improvement to the railroad grade indicate that the rail spur is still in use. These tracks were originally built about 1890 as a part of the San Antonio and Aransas Pass Railway line into Houston, and for over a century, a steel draw bridge spanned the bayou at this point[114].

San Antonio and Aransas Pass Railway

The San Antonio and Aransas Pass Railway (the SA&AP) was one of the many railroad lines that were built in Texas during the last quarter of the nineteenth century. Although the Galveston, Harrisburg and San Antonio Railway (the GH&SA) reached San Antonio in 1877, businessmen in that city still wanted a more direct route to a deepwater port, namely, to the Aransas Pass waterway. The SA&AP, deriving its name from the intended location of the railroad, was incorporated on August 7, 1884. In March, 1885, the SA&AP was reorganized and Corpus Christi businessman Uriah Lott became its president. The railroad's general offices were located in San Antonio while its operational center was established in Yoakum[115].

On May 18, 1885, construction began on the SA&AP's first line from San Antonio to Rockport, near Aransas Pass, but the company lacked the financial resources to reach Rockport, so Lott decided to terminate the line at Corpus Christi in 1886. With the financial backing of Mifflin Kenedy, the SA&AP built a line from the town of Kenedy to Houston during 1887 and 1888. The first freight was delivered to Houston on February 21, 1889, and regular service commenced on October 1, 1889. In 1890, the SA&AP extended its line a short distance from the Houston depot on Polk Avenue to the Texas and New Orleans Railroad (the T&NO) line in the Fifth Ward. The SA&AP bridge across Buffalo Bayou was built at this time[116].

The rapid expansion of the railroad created financial problems that forced the SA&AP into receivership on July 14, 1890. The SA&AP emerged from receivership when the Southern Pacific Railroad acquired the line on June 16, 1892. The Texas Railroad Commission forced the Southern Pacific to give up control of the SA&AP in March, 1903, but the Southern Pacific reacquired the line in 1924. The SA&AP was leased to the Southern Pacific controlled GH&SA Railway on April 8, 1925, and on June 30, 1934, the SA&AP and the GH&SA were merged into the T&NO Railroad[117].

During the reorganization of the nation's railroad systems in the last part of the twentieth century, the traffic on the former SA&AP line in this part of Houston declined significantly. In 1992, the Southern Pacific sold the Houston to Eagle Lake line of the former SA&AP Railway along the Westpark corridor to Houston Metro. The tracks were abandoned in 2001. The old SA&AP bridge over Buffalo Bayou was removed by 2002[118].

Remnants of this relatively minor railroad line still exist. The bulkhead of the SA&AP right of way on the north bank of Buffalo Bayou is visible at the water line. The concrete barriers that stabilized the right of way boundary on the north bank have been repaired to prevent further bank erosion. As of May, 2011, the downstream barrier had been removed while the upstream one is still in place.

Merchants and Planters Oil Company

The primary beneficiary of the SA&AP connection across Buffalo Bayou in the 1890's was the Merchants and Planters Oil Mill on the north side of the bayou. The Merchants and Planters Oil Company was incorporated on April 11, 1889 by T. W. House, W. D. Cleveland, E. A. Sewall, T. H. Scanlan, T. J. Boyles, J. S. Price and James A. Baker with capital stock of $125,000. Although William Marsh Rice was not listed among the original stockholders in the company, James A. Baker may have been representing Rice's investment in the venture. After Rice's marriage in 1867, he moved back to New York, but over the next twenty three years, Rice resided at times in both New York and Houston and he actively oversaw his Texas investments. As late as 1895, William Marsh Rice maintained a residence on the third floor of the Rice Building on the north east corner of Texas Avenue and Travis Street. Rice's ownership of the Merchants and Planters Oil Company dates from 1894, at the very least[119].

By mid July of 1889, the Merchants and Planters Oil Mill was under construction. The site lay on the eastern edge of the city in a location that was relatively inaccessible, requiring the contractors to build a floating bridge across Buffalo Bayou to haul materials to the site. On September 14, 1889, the construction of the Merchants and Planters Oil Mill was completed and the plant was ready to begin making oil[120].

The Merchants and Planters Oil Mills employed eighty men and the mill had a crushing capacity of one hundred thirty-five tons of cottonseeds per day, or over 20,000 tons of seeds per year. This capacity ranked the mill third among the cottonseed oil mills in Houston at the time. The Southern Oil Mills had a capacity for crushing 45,000 tons of cottonseed annually, while the largest local mill, the National Oil Mills, had a capacity for crushing 60,000 tons of seed annually while producing three million gallons of cottonseed oil[121].

The products made at the Merchants and Planters Mill were cottonseed oil, oil cake, meal and linters, the fine, silky fibers which adhere to the seeds of the cotton plant after ginning. The company also experimented with the use of cottonseed hulls to fatten cattle, and as early as 1892, it had shipped twenty five car loads of fat stock to Chicago. Cottonseed oil was used to manufacture soap and glycerine, and after the improvements in the refining process for cottonseed oil, the mill began to manufacture a line of food grade oils and shortening. The brand names of the Merchants and Planters Oil Company retail products were "M&P butter oil," "Planto" and "Polar White" lard[122].

In 1900, a series of dramatic events involving the Merchants and Planters Oil Company took place which have had a lasting effect on the City of Houston. On September 16, 1900, a week after the hurricane that destroyed Galveston, a fire was discovered about noon in the refinery while the employees were at lunch. The fire raged out of control and burned the whole afternoon, sending a column of black smoke that seemed to connect with the clouds. The Merchants and Planters Oil Mill was completely destroyed and losses to mill, one of the most prosperous businesses in the region, were between $350,000 and $400,000[123].

William Marsh Rice, the eighty-four year old owner of the mill, was living in New York at the time that he received the news of the fire. He immediately authorized the expenditure of $200,000 to rebuild the plant. This decision prompted his valet Charles F. Jones and his New York attorney Albert T. Patrick to put their scheme to kill Rice into action. Their plan was to obtain the bulk of his fortune through a forged will. W. M. Rice was murdered in his hotel room on September 23, 1900. Only through the persistent efforts Rice's Houston attorney and friend James A. Baker, Sr. was the plot revealed and the criminals brought to justice. The wealth of Rice's estate was then used to establish the William Marsh Rice Institute for the Advancement of Literature, Art and Science (now Rice

University), which opened in 1912 and remains as one of the most prestigious universities in the United States to this day[124].

After William Marsh Rice's death in 1900, Benjamin Botts Rice, the youngest son of Rice's brother Frederick A. Rice, became vice president and general manager of the Merchants and Planters Oil Company. B. B. Rice began work at the Merchants and Planters Oil Company in 1894 as the company's cashier and bookkeeper, and by 1895, he was the assistant manager. Two years later, B. B. Rice became the secretary and treasurer. B. B. Rice's rise in the company, especially after 1900, represented the interest of the Rice family and, subsequently, the Rice Institute in the Merchants and Planters Oil Company. Benjamin B. Rice managed those interests through his role as the general manager, "a position he held until the company's demise in 1941[125]."

The plant of the Merchants and Planters Oil Company at 3800 Clinton Drive caught fire on December 2, 1940. The company had survived the Great Depression, but a fire in the cottonseed storage and equipment warehouse put the company out of business[126].

Brown and Root

The dramatic end of a company that had operated in Houston for fifty years provided an opportunity for an up and coming company that would become a mainstay in Houston for the next seventy years. The Brown and Root construction company obtained the former Merchants and Planters property and built three new warehouses on the site by the end of 1942[127].

Brown and Root, Inc. had its beginning in 1919 when Herman Brown received financial backing from his brother in law Dan Root and formed a construction company which he named Brown and Root. Younger brother George Brown joined the firm in 1922 after graduating from the Colorado School of Mines. After the death of Dan Root in 1929, Herman Brown and George Brown purchased Root's interest and incorporated the firm as Brown and Root, Inc[128].

The big break for Brown and Root came in 1936 when the company was awarded the the contract for the Marshall Ford Dam, which today is the Mansfield Dam that forms Lake Travis near Austin, a project that showed the company could handle very large construction projects. That experience paved the way for several government contracts during World War II. By the end of the war, Brown and Root was a major construction firm in the United States[129].

By 1951, the Brown and Root site on Clinton Drive had buildings housing the company's engineering division and other general offices. Separate structures included a sheet metal works and warehouse, a machine shop, a truck maintenance and equipment storage facility, and a tractor, machinery and pipe yard. In the mid 1950's, the company added a tank manufacturing plant and nine hundred fifty feet of steel sheet pile bulkhead and wharf along Buffalo Bayou[130].

Herman Brown's declining health in the early 1960's led the Brown's to find a buyer for the company, and they turned to the Halliburton Company with whom they had a long standing business relationship. After Herman's death in 1962, George Brown completed the sale of Brown and Root to Halliburton. For the next three decades, Brown and Root tackled some of the largest construction projects in the world. In 1998, the M. W. Kellogg Company merged with Brown and Root to form Kellogg Brown and Root (KBR), a wholly owned subsidiary of the Halliburton Company. In 2007, KBR was separated from Halliburton to become a stand-alone company. Today, KBR, Inc. employs more than 35,000 people globally and is one of the world's premier engineering, construction and services companies[131].

After the merger with M. W. Kellogg in 1998, the corporate offices were consolidated at the Kellogg corporate headquarters at 601 Jefferson Street in Houston. Business activity at the Brown and Root facilities on Clinton Drive dwindled, and the site appears to be unused today. The KBR property of over one hundred acres along Clinton Drive, between Jensen Drive and Hirsch Road, includes two high rise office buildings, seven low rise office buildings and twenty-four warehouses and is awaiting its next phase of development[132].

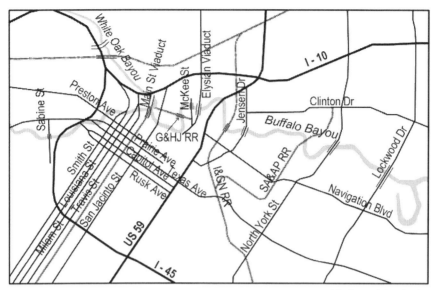

Map by Rachel A. Garcia

During the nineteenth century, a large German community lived in the eastern end of the Second Ward where German cultural events, such as the Volksfest, took place. Both sides of Buffalo Bayou, from the San Antonio and Aransas Pass Railroad to Lockwood Drive, were home to businesses that were significant contributors to the history and the enterprises of Houston.

Chapter 12
Volksfest Park

Volksfest Association

Between the SA&AP Railroad right of way and the North York Street bridge, Buffalo Bayou makes a long "U" shaped curve. The north bank is the KBR property, and the south bank consists of three tracts beginning at the railroad right of way and ending at North York Street. From the bayou, two metallic warehouses can be seen on the first two tracts of land. The third tract, which is about the same size as the combined tract with the warehouses, is vacant land bordering the bayou.

During the last third of the nineteenth century, these large lots were owned by two organizations formed by members of the German community in Houston. The tracts were the site of major public festivals and social events for the city and surrounding communities. Public festivals were not particularly common in Houston prior to the Civil War, but the devastation of the local economy and public spirit after the war prompted the a German fraternal society to do something to revive the sense of community. The end of the Civil War brought the military occupation of the cities in Texas, including Houston. The civilian government was a contentious combination of reformed Confederates, former Union supporters and carpetbaggers. The Reconstruction period was a difficult time of transition for the citizens of Houston, especially the businessmen who were trying to return the City to its former level of commercial activity. The Houston Turn Verein originated the idea of having a Volksfest to bring people together and promote fraternal feelings among all people in the community[1].

The Houston Turn Verein was organized January 14, 1854, and later incorporated on December 1, 1871, as a gymnastic society, but it also had social, intellectual and benevolent goals. Ten young

Germans met at home of Peter Gabel to form the society whose object was the physical and mental training of members and the advancement of social and literary entertainment of their friends[2].

The Houston Turn Verein was the second such society in Texas as a manifestation of the turnverein movement which was brought to the United States by political refugees from Germany around 1848. The term "turnverein" means a gymnastic or athletic club, and these men were practitioners of the gymnastic system begun by Fredriech Ludwig Jahn in 1811. The first American Turn Verein was established in Cincinnati in 1848 and another started in New York City in the same year. The first Texas turnverein was established in Galveston in 1851, and others soon followed in New Braunfels in 1855, in San Antonio in 1855, and in Comfort in 1860[3].

One of the first actions of the Houston Turn Verein was to establish the first volunteer fire department in the City. Houston's Turners also cared for the sick and needy, established schools and provided dramatic and musical entertainment. Although the turnvereins in Texas were divided on issues of slavery and secession, many members volunteered for the South in the Civil War. After the war, the clubs survived and focused on gymnastics, local interests and good fellowship. It was with this in mind that Houston Turn Verein members organized the first Volksfest in Texas in 1869, a festival that was celebrated annually until 1897 and was the City's most prominent public festival in which the entire population participated[4].

The Volksfest Association was initially formed as early as June, 1860, but the events of the spring of 1861 caused the festival plans to be delayed by the Civil War and Reconstruction until 1869. Germans knew of the benefits of popular festivals and celebrations from their European heritage. A Volksfest had been held in New Orleans as early as 1856, and that may have been the inspiration for a similar "people's festival" in Houston[5].

Houston's First German Volksfest was held at Lubbock's Grove on June 7 and 8, 1869. Lubbock's Grove was located in the Second Ward near the southeast corner of Buffalo Street (modern North St. Charles Street) and Commerce Avenue. A grand procession from Courthouse Square to Lubbock's Grove began the Volksfest. Led by Grand Marshal, the three quarter mile procession had a band and a color guard displaying the German and American colors -- "the German flag displaying the colors black, red and gold, without the eagle." Numerous floats, wagons and men on foot made up the rest of the procession to the grounds where refreshments at the grove awaited[6].

The wagons and floats of the Volksfest parade were often elaborately decorated. Prizes were awarded for the three best decorated wagons, and competition was often intense. One wagon, in particular, was a standard feature of each procession, and that was the wagon bearing the Hall of King Gambrinus. King Gambrinus was the legendary King of Flanders and unofficial patron saint of beer brewing, and, without a doubt, many toasts to the king were made during the two day event. At this very first Volksfest, however, the first prize for the most original and best decorated wagon went to the wagon of Louis Hillendahl of Spring Branch upon which were four little girls dressed in white and each was holding a plow, a hoe, a rake or other farm implements[7].

The German citizens of the city established the festival to bring people together without regard to politics in order to renew friendships and form new ones. The event was a celebration designed solely for amusement and recreation. Uplifting orations were given in the afternoon in both English and German, but political speeches were strictly prohibited. Amusements, games, concerts and music for dancing all day and into the evening made for a day of fun and enjoyment. The grove was brilliantly illuminated in the evening with two hundred Chinese transparencies for the dance crowd of three thousand ladies, gentlemen and children. Fireworks at 10 pm capped off the event in spectacular fashion[8].

The success of the first Volksfest planted the seed for the State Fair held in Houston. As a complementary event to the Volksfest, the Agricultural, Mechanical and Blood Stock Association of Texas held a four day exposition in 1870 with the support of local businesses. Farm products, machinery and industrial products were exhibited and the competitions awarded hundreds of prizes. Just as with the Volksfest, the State Fair was an outstanding success and the City reportedly profited about $250,000 from the event. That allowed the Agricultural, Mechanical and Blood Stock Association, in 1871, to acquire a fairgrounds on Main Street at the edge of town near Webster Street on which they built a grandstand, a one mile race track and exhibition halls for the annual State Fair[9].

The Volksfests were held at Lubbock's Grove from 1869 to 1873, but the general success of the annual Volksfest and the expansive grounds and facilities at the Fairgrounds enticed the Volksfest Association to move their event to the Fairgrounds in 1874. The Volksfests would continue at the Fairgrounds until 1886. In 1887, the Volksfest Association moved the event to its own grounds in the Second Ward at the north end of Sampson Street, along Buffalo Bayou[10].

The Fairgrounds was such a popular venue for civic events and recreation that, on May 17, 1876, the City Council leased the Fairgrounds from the State Fair Association for five years as a public park. Up to that time, there had not been a public park in Houston and it would be another twenty-three years before the City purchased land for its first city park, Sam Houston Park[11].

The Eighth Annual Texas State Fair was held at the Fairgrounds for five days in late May, 1877. Awards were given for nearly every industry in the state, including field crops, farm products, cigars, wines, malt liquors, soaps, candles, paints and other categories of agricultural and industrial goods. About nine thousand people attended the State Fair that year and it was a commercial success. However, the event was marred by the presence of numerous pickpockets working the crowd and the usually peaceful festival was disrupted by a homicide at the park. The following year, in 1878, the State Fair ran into bad weather. There was a yellow fever scare that year, as well, and the citizens lost interest in the fair. The financial results were disastrous, and the Texas State Fair in Houston came to an end that year[12].

The Volksfest, on the other hand, continued to thrive. The annual celebration of traditional German food and drink accompanied by games, contests, amusements, dancing, gymnastics and shooting demonstrations was popular with nearly everyone. The wagon decoration competition of the Volksfest parade often produced some ingenious displays. In fact, some of the best displays were created for the Second Volksfest in 1870. The Houston Schuetzen Verein ("shooting club") platform wagon was arranged as a woodland with a party of German hunters singing national

Courtesy of the Harris County Archives

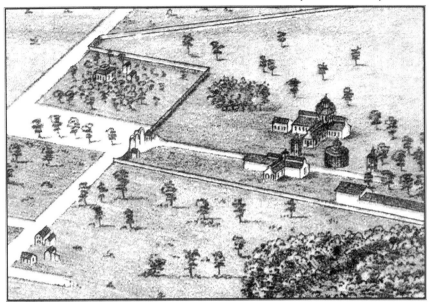

For several years, the Volksfest was held at the Fairgrounds, located on the out-skirts of town, southwest of the corner of Main Street and McGowen Street. The facilities of the park are shown in this excerpt from the Bird's Eye Map of Houston, 1873.

songs and "refreshing themselves with good lager." Wine merchant Peter Gabel's wagon was outfitted as a wine vault that was adorned with allegorical and mythological figures. The Houston City Mills wagon was decorated with an assortment of their own manufactured cloths. A more patriotic and cultural theme was found in a wagon carrying the elegant beauties portraying the two great societies, Frauelein Germania and Mademoiselle Columbia[13].

The opening day of the Volksfest always began with a sunrise artillery salute at Courthouse Square by one of the local militia units or shooting clubs. Then, at 10 am, the grand procession paraded from the Courthouse through several blocks of the main business district before heading out to the grounds where the event was to be held. In the early years, that was out Congress Avenue to Lubbock's Grove in the Second Ward. Then, the parade marched down Main Street to the Fairgrounds for several years, before finally, in later years, the procession went out Commerce Avenue to the Volksfest Park in the Second Ward. The city streets were often crowded with people. Businesses closed, and the stores and businesses had bunting draped everywhere in colors of the United States and the German Empire[14].

Each year, the Grand Marshal of the Volksfest led the procession to festival grounds. Sometimes it was simply the Grand Marshal in the lead followed by the color bearers on horseback, the bands and the rest of the parade. But, in other years, the figurehead of the Volksfest could put on quite a show. Such was the case in 1894 when J. J. Settegast was the Grand Marshal. Settegast divided his corps of marshals into two divisions marching behind his lead. In the first division, each man wore a full dress suit, a black Prince Albert coat, black pants, a silk hat and a white sash. The men in the second division were attired with a soft black hat turned up on one side and held by Texas star. They wore a black coat, white pants and vest, and a red, white and blue sash. It was certainly an impressive display[15].

On the festivals grounds, the amusements offered games and contests for children and families. At the first Volksfest, to encourage attendance and participation, ladies and children were admitted to the festival for free while men paid a fifty cents admission fee. Even the youngest boys and girls could enter the sack races, foot races and molasses licking contests. The gymnastics of the horizontal bar was presented by Turners, and other popular entertainments included fantasy reenactments from the Middle Ages. At festivals during the early 1870's, mock battles of medieval knights in armor with helmets and swords were staged to the delight of the crowds -- much like the events seen at the modern Renaissance Festival. The national pastime was also represented at the Volksfest. As early as 1872, baseball games were played as a part of the regular event schedule[16].

Refreshments and food were available on the grounds of the Volksfest that enabled families to spend the whole day at the park. Japhet's lager booth, which was elegantly decorated and used as a saloon, was especially popular with the beer drinkers. Other booths sold lemonade, ice cream, venison and pies for those who preferred other varieties of food and drink during the festival[17].

The Houston Volksfest was generally successful each year from the time of its founding in 1869. The Volksfest that was held in

May, 1881 cleared $1,000, and that brought the association's fund balance from previous events to $8,600. As a consequence of these accomplishments, the organization decided that it needed a formal structure and on November 23, 1881, the Houston Volksfest Association filed for a state charter. The incorporation allowed the Volksfest Association to deal with other issues related to the management of the festival[18].

The ongoing celebration of the annual Volksfest was not without its challenges. In 1880, heavy rains forced the postponement of the two day event for one week. The Volksfest of 1882 was characterized by a parade that was thought to be below par. There was only a very limited number of wagons and the decorations very not very elaborate. It seemed that the enthusiasm for the Volksfest had waned. The 1884 German Volksfest was only a one day event held in August and "the attendance was rather meager." A more traditional festival was held at the Fairgrounds in 1885, but the Volksfest of May 30, 1886 was, again, only a one day event[19].

To counteract this decline, the Volksfest Association held a membership drive in November, 1886 to revitalize the organization. The group advertised that membership was encouraged for "any white male person of twenty-one years and over." It cost twenty-five cents to register and dues were twenty-five cents a year[20].

In addition, the City's lease of the Fairgrounds on Main Street had expired and the Volksfest needed to secure another location for its future events. The Volksfest of 1886 was the last one held at the Fairgrounds on Main Street. Early the next year, the Volksfest Association purchased a thirty-four and one half acre tract of land adjoining the western edge of Merkel's Grove from George Hermann and J. J. Settegast. Both Hermann and Settegast were members of the Volksfest Association and, in his well known spirit of philanthropy, Hermann donated five percent of the sales price back to the association. The ownership of Volksfest Park permitted the association to begin improvements that would make the park "the most attractive pleasure resort on the suburbs of Houston[21]."

The Houston Volksfest Park was located at the north end of Sampson Street on the south bank of Buffalo Bayou, and it adjoined Merkel's Grove, the home of the Houston Schuetzen Verein. The popularity of the Volksfest caused the city street car company to create a street car route to the new Volksfest grounds. The Volksfest Line went out from Main Street at Franklin Avenue to Hutchins Street, to Commerce Avenue to Sampson Street, then to Engelke Street and on to Volksfest Park. The street car system allowed people from all of the districts of Houston to get across town to Volksfest Park with relative ease. It is hard to imagine today that Houston was among the most sophisticated cities in the United States for urban mass transit in the nineteenth century[22].

The membership drive and the acquisition of the festival park seemed to revive the Volksfest. The festival of 1887 was heavily promoted in Houston and the surrounding area. Flags of the United States and the Republic of Texas lined the city streets and throngs of people watched the magnificent Volksfest parade. The new Volksfest grounds enabled everyone to have a glorious time[23].

On May 12, 1890, the Houston Volksfest completed its four day event which was attended by a large number of people, and the festival was considered a great success. The purchase of the Volksfest Park as the festival site seemed even more significant since, on July 5, 1890, the Texas State Fair Association of Houston sold the Fairgrounds property to the Galveston and Houston Investment Company for $75,000. Within a year, the Fairgrounds Addition had been platted and lots were being sold. By October, 1891, two new residences were under construction in the new subdivision[24].

The Volksfest of 1892 was well promoted and immense crowds showed up. Many businesses on the principal streets of town were decorated from the first floor to the roof with flags and banners, and the festival was one of the most successful ever held. Nevertheless, financial problems plagued the Volksfest Association and a lawsuit challenging the ownership of Volksfest Park put the future of the organization doubt. On October 14, 1892, the Houston Volksfest Association advertised the entire thirty-four and one half acre Volksfest Park for sale. The advertisement stated that "the most beautiful magnolia grove" in Houston could be divided into one hundred home lots and it also included seven acres of bayou frontage for manufacturing purposes[25].

The Volksfest Association held a meeting on January 8, 1893 to settle the fate of the park grounds. Some members were in favor of forming a stock company to pay off indebtedness of $10,000 without requiring the sale of the park. But, ultimately, the majority of members decided to sell the park. The uncertainty created by the financial problems and the pending legal actions forced the association to cancel the Volksfest in 1893. A Volksfest was held at Volksfest Park in 1894 as a joint event with the Houston Saengerbund ("singing club")[26].

On January 26, 1895, the Volksfest Association members met and accepted the offer of $15,000 from J. J. Settegast and Louis M. Rich for thirty-four and one half acres of Lot 68 of the S. M. Williams original grant, known as Volksfest Park. At a special meeting of the Volksfest Association in March, a committee was formed to determine whether to hold a Volksfest celebration in 1895. A large number of Germans representing the community were in favor of it, and J. J. Settegast offered the use of the park for the event. Nevertheless, on April 14, 1895, the members of the Volksfest Association voted to disband the organization and each was given a sum of $44.40 as a disbursement of the funds remaining after the association's indebtedness was paid[27].

In lieu of a Volksfest, the members of the various German societies of Houston, including the Turn Verein, the Saengerbund, the Deutsche Gesellschaft, the Houston Schuetzen Verein, the Frohsinn, the Sons of Hermann and the Foresters, met at Turner Hall and decided to hold a German Day celebration at Volksfest Park on October 6, 1895. On November 11, 1895, a meeting was held at Turner Hall to reorganize the Volksfest Association, and the new association agreed to revive the grand celebration as in the past[28].

In an attempt to broaden the appeal of the Volksfest and make it a patriotic celebration, the festival was planned to coincide with San Jacinto Day. The Twenty-fifth Volksfest was held at Forest Park, also known as Coombs Park, on April 21, 1896. As in the past, the Volksfest began with a parade through the business district, but this time, instead of marching to the festival grounds, the participants disbanded and made their way to Forest Park in Houston Heights at Heights Boulevard and 4th Avenue[29].

Forest Park/Coombs Park was an amusement park was built by the Coombs family on land they owned in Houston Heights, north of White Oak Bayou. Eden L. Coombs was a broker of stocks and bonds, as well as a dealer in watches, diamonds and jewelery at his store at 312 Main Street. The Coombs mansion was located south of the bayou on an elevated area known as Coombs Terrace. Coombs Park and the natatorium opened to the public on April 12, 1895, and it could be reached by street car route Number 8[30].

The success of the the 1896 Volksfest prompted the finance committee of the Volksfest Association to immediately commence preparations for the Twenty-sixth Volksfest. The festival, again, was planned for San Jacinto Day, April 21, 1897, but subsequent considerations caused the event to be held on Independence Day. For the second year, the Volksfest took place at Forest Park, and the schedule of events was patterned after the Volksfest of old. Since the Fourth of July fell on a Sunday, however, there was no morning street parade in deference to those who wanted to attend church services[31].

The Twenty-sixth Annual Volksfest was opened with a sunrise salute of forty-eight guns by the Houston Light Guard. A grand promenade concert was held during the afternoon, as were speeches in German and a reading of the Declaration of Independence. Competitive drills by military companies, bicycle races, children's foot races, exercises by the Turner class and other contests rounded out the day time activities. Despite the wide variety of amusements and entertainment, the festival was only moderately attended. Some blamed the low attendance on the street car strike then in effect. Yet, whatever the reason, the Volksfest of 1897 was the last Houston Volksfest[32].

For a quarter of a century, the German community of Houston hosted a light hearted event for all classes of people to come together in a spirit of togetherness. But, like all civic events on such a grand scale, they run their course and leave the stage for the next great festival idea. The Houston Volksfest Association still had seventeen members in 1900, but the association faded away after that[33].

After the sale of the Volksfest Park, the property was available for commercial development. On March 4, 1897, a group of investors lead by John Finnegan of New York announced a plan to erect the largest packery in the South on the former Volksfest grounds. This enterprise was the Houston Packing Company and it was one of the Second Ward's first large industrial plants. The company was incorporated in January, 1897 with capital stock of $60,000, and the company officers included Robert E. Paine as president, John Finnegan as vice-president, and Tharon H. Thompson as treasurer[34].

The Houston Packing Company, located northwest of the intersection of Engelke Street and North York Street, was a slaughterhouse and wholesale dealers in dressed meats and packing house products. The plant also operated a ice manufacturing facility. The initial phase of construction in 1897 included the main building on the west side of the rail spur that serviced the tract. Three smaller buildings were built in a row along the east side of the spur[35].

The main building of the Houston Packing Company was a four story structure. A city sales room was located on the first floor on the north end of the building. Coolers and a wash room occupied the central part of the first floor while a cutting room was on the second floor, a sausage kitchen and the bone room was on the third floor, and a canning room was on the fourth floor. A two story structure was attached to the south end of the main building which housed the condenser and dynamo room. Ice was produced in that section of the plant where there were ice tanks and an ice storage room[36].

Southwest of the main building, there were two hog pens and three cattle pens. A ten foot deep pond was on the southeast corner of the tract. The company's general offices were in a one story building situated near the railroad siding and south of the main building[37].

The three buildings on the east side of the railroad siding handled aspects of the production supplies, packaging and shipments of goods from the packing house. The south most building housed a small cotton seed oil refinery with adjacent storage tanks. The middle building was a three story building for the processing and storage of lard. The third building, on the north end, was a platformed warehouse for the storage of barrels, cans and box materials[38].

The Houston Packing Company was designed for the efficient, large scale operation of a meat packing facility. The initial construction was completed by 1907, and with this assembly line layout, the company operated the plant successfully for several years. The Great Fire of 1912 damaged the packing plant when the flames jumped across Buffalo Bayou from the Fifth Ward and caused

$7,000 damage. But, the repairs were made, and the plant continued to operate as usual[39].

In 1922, an expansion of the slaughterhouse increased the production capacity and other processes were streamlined. A new, four story abattoir was built to the east of the original main building. Chutes from the cattle pens ushered the animals to the killing room on the fourth floor. From there, the carcasses were forwarded to the cutting rooms of the attached original main building -- pork on the third floor and beef on the second floor. In the new abattoir building, workers processed the meat in the casing room on the third floor and the sausage and canning room on the second floor. Additional ice production capacity and cold storage was also included in the 1922 additions to the plant. Minor additions were made to the packing and shipping areas of the plant in the 1940's, but the industrial packing house complex, designed at the turn of the century, worked efficiently and profitably into the 1950's[40].

Butchers have played an important role in the City since its very earliest days, and many prominent citizens of Houston were butchers by trade, including George Baker, Sam Geiselman, the Schrimpf brothers and the Settegast brothers. The Houston Packing Company brought industrial production practices to a business that in the nineteenth century was a trade where individuals owned and operated the shops.

Sometime between 1964 and 1973, the Houston Packing Company plant was demolished and the former Volksfest site was cleared. By 1981, a new warehouse on the west side of the Houston Packing Company site, and by 2002, a second warehouse was constructed to the east of the first warehouse. Both warehouses are still in use today. The west side warehouse, a 238,125 square foot commercial property, was acquired by AN/WRI Partnership Ltd on December 7, 1999 from Weingarten Realty who bought it from the Navigation Business Park Venture on January 2, 1988. The AN/WRI Partnership Ltd is a subsidiary of Weingarten Realty Investors. The easternmost warehouse is owned by the Navigation Realty Company, Ltd of Brooklyn, NY, and it is a 206,443 square foot commercial warehouse[41].

Merkel's Grove and the Houston Schuetzen Verein

The south bank of Buffalo Bayou lying east of the two ware-houses on the former Houston Packing Company tract is vacant commercial land. Old buildings at the south end of the tract, near Navigation Boulevard and along North York Street remain from late twentieth century industrial plants located here. For the greater part of the nineteenth century, this land was owned by Joseph Merkel and it was the site of Merkel's Grove. Merkel's Grove was a private recreational park and beer garden, but more importantly, for over thirty years, it was the home of the Houston Schuetzen Verein, a "shooting club" organized by members of Houston's German community. The story of Merkel's Grove and the Houston Schuetzen Verein are closely intertwined with the story of Joseph Merkel[42].

In September, 1846, Johan Merkel, at age forty-eight, came to Texas from Koblenz, Germany with his family of five children of whom Joseph, at age fifteen, was the oldest. They arrived at the port at Galveston and soon made their way to Houston where, in 1847, Johan Merkel purchased a forty acre tract of land from Charlotte and A. C. Allen. Merkel and his son Joseph raised cattle and operated a butcher business like many Germans who lived in the Second Ward. The Merkel home was on Buffalo Street (modern North St. Charles Street) in the block southeast of the corner with Commerce Avenue, one block south of the Lubbock home at Lubbock's Grove[43].

Johan Merkel's oldest son Joseph caught "gold fever" in 1849, and the eighteen year old headed for California to seek his fortune. Joseph returned to Houston in 1852 without success in the mining fields. But, once back in Houston, Joseph Merkel settled down. On December 20, 1855, he married the fifteen year old Caroline Krieger[44].

Johan Merkel died unexpectedly in August, 1858. His body was found five miles from Cane Island (modern Katy) where he apparently had died from sun stroke a few days prior to August 11, 1858. Each of the Merkel sons, trained in the father's butcher trade, took up the family business. Anton Merkel, the youngest son, lived with brother John Merkel and his family in the Third Ward. Joseph Merkel bought the property along Buffalo Bayou that would be associated with his name for the remainder of the nineteenth century[45].

On August 13, 1860, Joseph R. Merkel and his wife Caroline purchased 101 acres in Lot 67 of the Samuel May Williams Survey, including a home, from Samuel and Mary Baron for $3,000. The land was a mile and a half east of downtown on the south bank of Buffalo Bayou. Merkel then built a five bay Gulf Coast Cottage on the tract for his wife and four children. This homestead became the center of his cattle ranch for livestock for his butcher business. Merkel operated a small stall in the city market on Market Square while raising cattle at his Second Ward ranch[46].

The Civil War was a pivotal time for Joseph Merkel. The Houston Guards was a unit of volunteers from the local German community that was organized at a meeting at the Turn Verein Hall on October 12, 1861. Merkel enlisted as a 4th sergeant in the Houston Guards. The unit soon performed the sad duty of escorting the casket of Captain Benjamin Terry in December, 1861 on its return to Houston. Later during the war, Merkel went to Mexico to look after a mining scheme, and that may have been the action that prompted his wife Caroline to leave him and take their children in 1863[47].

On May 21, 1867, a jury trial in the divorce of Caroline W. Merkel and Joseph Merkel granted the divorce because of Joseph Merkel's adultery and the abandonment of his wife. The land purchased from the Barron's was equally divided between them with Joseph Merkel receiving the west half of the tract and Caroline Krieger Merkel the east half. There were six hundred head of cattle on the land at that time bearing the brands "UM" and "TS." The cattle were equally divided between Joseph and his ex-wife, and custody of the four children was awarded to Caroline Merkel[48].

After the divorce, Caroline Merkel married William Bohlae in January, 1868, and they moved to Washington County. Joseph Merkel married Henrietta Schultz and they lived in the house that he had built in the west half of the original tract of land. Joseph and Henrietta went on to have three children[49].

In the late 1860's, Joseph Merkel established a suburban summer resort at his home that he called Merkel's Grove. In 1869, Peter Floeck, a member of the Houston Guards and a relative of Joseph

Merkel by marriage, joined with other former members of the Houston Guards to found the Houston Schuetzen Verein. The Houston Schuetzen Verein leased three acres of the Merkel property for $10 per year. The lease included the improvements on the property including a bar operated by Joseph Merkel, a ten pin bowling alley and a rifle range. The Merkel house was included in the lease, too, but it remained Merkel's residence. In reality, there was a special relationship between Merkel and the Schuetzen Verein. The club met in his house and he maintained the beer garden for the club. The Houston Schuetzen Verein used specialized rifles in their competitive marksmanship contests, and eventually they added their rifle targets and ranges to the grounds[50].

For a number of years, the Houston Schuetzen Verein met at Merkel's Grove on the first Sunday of each month. Beginning in 1887, the regular meetings were changed to the second Sunday in the months of January, April, July and October. Special events, such as the twelfth anniversary of the Houston Schuetzen Verein, held on February 22, 1880, were held at other times. A dance pavilion had been added to the grounds, and the twelfth anniversary was celebrated with speeches, shooting contests, promenade concert and singing and an evening grand ball at the brightly illuminated grounds[51].

The annual state shoot was hosted by the Houston Schuetzen Verein at Merkel's Grove on May 14, 1892. Representatives from shooting clubs from around the state came to the event, including shooters from clubs in San Antonio, New Braunfels and West Texas. Targets were designed with the standard bull's eye and ranges had targets set at 100, 150 and 225 yards[52].

Membership in the Houston Schuetzen Verein Garden fluctuated between fifty and one hundred members annually. During the peak of the club's popularity, it had one hundred members in 1886. The membership numbers stayed in the fifties during the 1890's, and the last recorded count was thirty members in 1900[53].

On January 3, 1896, Joseph Merkel died suddenly at his home just before noon. His death, at age sixty-three, was attributed to tuberculosis, and he was buried in the family plot in Evergreen Cemetery on Altic Street. Henrietta Merkel, Joseph's widow, took over as the proprietress of Merkel's Grove and the Houston

Photo credit: Louis F. Aulbach

The Joseph Merkel House is the last remaining structure of Merkel's Grove and the Houston Schuetzen Verein.

Schuetzen Verein Garden at the north end of Hutcheson Street, two blocks north of Engelke Street, and her son Fritz managed the place. The family also continued to live at the house on the property. Between 1896 and 1899, Joseph Merkel's heirs subdivided and platted the property into Merkel's First, Second and Third Additions. Shortly after 1900, Merkel's Grove closed[54].

Henrietta Merkel continued to live at the Merkel house until 1912. At that time, she built a new house directly across Hutcheson Street from the old home, and she lived in the new house until her death in 1920, at age sixty-nine. The new Merkel house was demolished in the widening of North York Street in the 1960's. The original Joseph Merkel House survives today and is located at 416 North Hutcheson Street, near the modern intersection of York Street, Sampson Street and Navigation Boulevard. It is a 1-1/2 story, wood frame house on a pier and beam foundation with a gable roof and a full width inset porch. Three equally spaced gable roof dormers, located in the upper half story, were probably added during remodeling about 1923. The house is one of the few extant examples of Gulf Coast Cottage style in Houston, and it is all that remains of Merkel's Grove[55].

The Texas Company acquired the seventeen acre tract east of the Houston Packing Company by 1917. The land was undeveloped until the Trinity Portland Cement Company established a construction materials plant on the site in the late 1920's.

In 1929, the Portland Cement Association recognized the perfect safety record of the Trinity Portland Cement Company plant in Houston with the award of the organization's "Safety Follows Wisdom" monument. The award also was given to the Houston plant in 1945, 1947 and 1950. The monument can still be seen near the entrance to the plant on North Hutcheson Street.

In 1982, Canadian Cement Lafarge Ltd. (CCL) acquired General Portland, Inc., the second largest cement producer in the United States. A year later, Canadian Cement Lafarge became the Lafarge Corporation, headquartered in Dallas. A portion of the former Merkel's Grove site was acquired by the Buffalo Bayou Partnership from the Lafarge Corporation on March 21, 2001[56].

The North York Street bridge crosses Buffalo Bayou just ahead. Built between 1957 and 1964, the bridge connects North York Street, cutting through the Merkel Subdivision, with Hirsch Road on the north side[57].

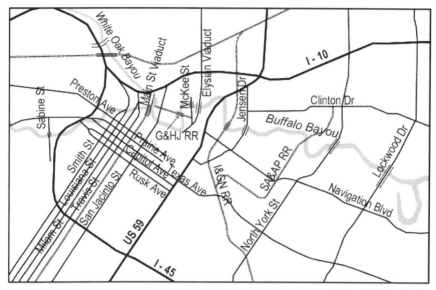

Map by Rachel A. Garcia

Industrial development along both sides of Buffalo Bayou from the North York Street bridge (above) to Wayside Drive flourished in the twentieth century. Much of this development, above and below Lockwood Drive, was a result of the expansion of the Houston Ship Channel and the Port of Houston that was established at the Turning Basin (below) in 1914.

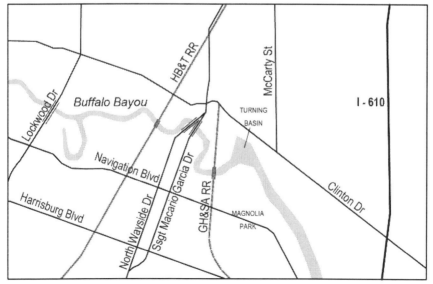

Map by Rachel A. Garcia

Chapter 13
Lockwood Drive

Tony Marron Park

On the east side of the North York Street bridge and across the bayou from Ingraham Gully and Japhet Creek is Tony Marron Park. The City acquired this 19.07 acre park, located at 806 North York Street, in 1987, and for a decade, it was known as North York Park. The park was renamed for Antonio "Tony" Marron, Sr. on Sunday, March 29, 1998[1].

Tony Marron was an immigrant from Mexico who settled in Houston in 1926. He served as the president of the East End Civic Club for many years, and he was instrumental in the renovation of Hidalgo Park in the Magnolia Park neighborhood, about two miles downstream from this point. Marron died in 1996 at the age of seventy-five[2].

The park was renovated in 2003 and developed into five soccer fields, hiking trails, a playground, a pavilion and picnic areas. There are restrooms and ample parking for using this park as a base for exploring the bayou hike and bike trail which extend along the bank at the north end of the park. The bayou trail on the south bank goes as far west as Guadalupe Plaza and the I&GN Railroad bridge near Jensen Drive and as far east as Lockwood Drive. The future plans by the Buffalo Bayou Partnership are to extend the trail as far east as Buffalo Bend Nature Park and Hidalgo Park. The development of the North York Boat Launch, immediately upstream of the park, will enhance the recreational access to Buffalo Bayou for canoes and kayaks[3].

The Buffalo Bayou Partnership's boat dock and storage facility is adjacent to the Tony Marron Park's east boundary. The BBP uses the former warehouses at 723 North Drennan Street as a place to store and maintain its fleet of tour boats and trash pick up boats that operate to beautify and clean the bayou each day. The south bank hike and bike trail passes through the property as the path continues to Lockwood Drive[4].

Only one other commercial tract is located along the south bank of the bayou before you get to Lockwood Drive. The Dan-Loc Bolt and Gasket Company has a manufacturing facility to the east of the BBP facility. The Dan-Loc company, founded in 1961, was acquired from DL Industries, LP in March, 2007 in a management buyout financed by the equity firm of Laud Collier and Company. Dan-Loc makes quality stud bolts and metal ring joint gaskets for the energy industry[5].

The Texas Land and Cattle Company and its partners own most of the fifty-five acre tract of undeveloped land between Dan-Loc and the Lockwood bridge. Among the other owners with undivided interests in the tract are the DeBakey Medical Foundation, founded by Dr. Michael E. DeBakey, and the Methodist Hospital System. Texas Land and Cattle Company president J. N. Taub stated in 2002 that the land, which has never been lived on, is mostly forested and used for grazing cattle. It is held as an investment, not for development. The City of Houston Parks and Recreation Department owns a fifty foot wide strip of park land along the south bank of Buffalo Bayou that was created from the Texas Land and Cattle Company tract[6].

The Lockwood Drive bridge, just ahead, was completed in December, 1928. Originally, the bridge was called the Adams Street bridge since it connected Adams Street on the south side with the north side of Buffalo Bayou. The style of the bridge was a lift span type or a vertical lift bridge. Towers on each side of the span were used to raise the span high enough to allow passage under the span. The Lockwood Drive bridge had a span of 409 feet and a vertical lift of sixty-five feet[7].

During the 1930's, the Lockwood Drive bridge displayed a sign proclaiming the popular slogan: "Houston, where 17 railroads meet the sea." In the early 1960's, a large barge towed by tug boats from the Brown and Root construction site, destined for Mexico, was one of the last times the Lockwood Drive bridge was raised. The drawbridge was removed in 1983 and replaced with a fixed bridge[8].

Ingraham Gully

As you float under the bridge at North York Street, you enter a short, half mile segment of the bayou between this bridge and the Lockwood Drive bridge. The vegetation along the north bank surrounds and helps to conceal two drainages flowing into Buffalo Bayou. The two drainages are only about two hundred feet apart, and neither one flows along a very extensive course. Nevertheless, each one is a little pocket of history from Houston's early days.

The first drainage downstream of the North York bridge is the Ingraham Gully. The gully starts near Lyons Avenue and flows south, past the Kellogg Brown and Root site and into the bayou. The gully has been replaced with culverts in recent years and the only open part of the tributary lies between Clinton Drive and Buffalo Bayou.

Ingraham Gully is believed to be named for Robert C. Ingraham, an immigrant from Ireland and an early settler in Houston who was involved in real estate speculation as early as 1842. By trade, Ingraham was a boot and shoe maker who had a shop on Liberty Road, and he lived in the Irish neighborhood of the Fifth Ward until the early 1870's. On November 10, 1860, R. C. Ingraham was among the prominent citizens of Harris County called to meet and consult on what measures should be adopted by Texas in view of the election of Abraham Lincoln. Nevertheless, time has erased the traces of this man from our memory in Houston's history, and only this small creek remains to remind us of him. He probably made excellent boots[9].

Japhet Creek

A short distance downstream along the north bank is a small, but more prominent, drainage which is referred to in modern times as the Japhet Creek. The Japhet family owned a home on the east side of the creek, just south of the modern Clinton Drive, but the Japhet businesses in downtown were well known throughout the last half of the nineteenth century.

Isidor P. Japhet was born in 1842 and he immigrated from Prussia to Texas after the Civil War. By 1870, Japhet had established himself in Houston. He was a partner with John D. Usener in the firm of Usener and Japhet, working as the bookkeeper for the Metropolitan Beer Saloon while living at the Dissen House. The Dissen House, owned by William Dissen, was a popular hotel among the German immigrants to the City and many stayed at the Third Ward establishment until they could find permanent accommodations. Located at 28 Preston Avenue, on the south side of Preston Avenue between Main Street and Fannin Street, the Dissen House was just around the corner from Japhet's place of work. The Metropolitan Saloon was in the Gray's Building on Fannin Street between Congress Avenue and Preston Avenue[10].

By 1877, Isidore Japhet had taken over the Metropolitan Saloon and expanded its selection of beverages to include the best straight liquors and western beer. The saloon also sold Havana cigars, a product which was a specialty of the house. William Dissen and John D. Usener had formed a partnership, called Dissen and Company, which sold wholesale wines, liquors and cigars. They were also agents for the E. Anheuser and Company Brewing Association of St. Louis[11].

Within two years, Japhet had either acquired the Dissen and Company or had successfully modeled his own enterprise on a similar business plan since, as the proprietor of the Metropolitan Saloon, he was selling liquors and imported pilsner beer as well as operating as a wholesale dealer in imported and domestic cigars. William Dissen's only business was as the proprietor of the Dissen House, and John Usener was manager of the Solo Saloon[12].

By 1880, Japhet and Company was operating out of two locations. The Metropolitan Saloon was located at 50 and 52 Fannin Street, while the wholesale liquor business was next door at 46 and 48 Fannin Street. At this same time, Japhet moved into a home at 129 Prairie Avenue. Two years later, Isidore Japhet was one of the local investors for the American Brewing Association of Houston. Japhet became the vice president of the beer venture brought to Houston in 1882 by Adolphus Busch of St. Louis. About a year later, Japhet moved his wholesale liquor business into a new, two story building at 39 Commerce Avenue on the northwest corner with Main Street[13].

In addition to his successful businesses, Isidore Japhet participated in several of the City's social organizations as well. He joined
the Houston Turn Verein soon after his arrival in Houston and
served as the society's treasurer in 1877. He was a member of the
International Order of Odd Fellows, and he served as the secretary
of the Industrial Art School on Main Street. In the mid-1870's,
Japhet provided the lager beer booth at the annual Volksfest celebration. These were only a few of the many groups he was involved
with during his time in Houston[14].

Japhet was active in the real estate market, too. One transaction,
in particular, was especially profitable for him. On March 24, 1890,
Isidore Japhet sold eight hundred acres near the Merchants and
Planters Oil Mill for $75,000 which he purchased only a few years
prior for $8,000. With the windfall from this sale, Japhet decided to
move out of the downtown district. In April, 1890, he bought a tract
of farm land on the north side of Buffalo Bayou one half mile east
of the city limits where he built a large home for his family[15].

Isidore Japhet had married Ida Wipprecht of New Braunfels
about 1871. Ida Wipprecht was born in Texas in 1857 to Rudolph
and Julie Wipprecht who immigrated from Prussia, just as Isidore
Japhet had done. Isidore and Ida Japhet had seven children who
survived to adulthood and, by 1892, they had moved to the farm[16].

About 1894, Isidor Japhet's twenty-one year old son Daniel A.
Japhet joined him at Japhet and Company. For a decade, the company had prospered while following the same formula of selling
wholesale liquors, wines and cigars, and operating as agents for
Schlitz Milwaukee bottled beer. The business location remained the
same, but the street address was updated to 919 Commerce Avenue[17].

Daniel Japhet had only a short time to learn the family business
before events caused him to take on the responsibility for the family
business. Isidore Japhet suffered a stroke in late December. He lay
on a coma for about four days before he passed away on December
25, 1895 at the family home beyond the eastern city limits on the
north side of Buffalo Bayou. Isidore Japhet was only fifty-three
years old, and he was buried in Glenwood Cemetery. His wife and
children would have to continue the business themselves[18].

The will of Isidore Japhet was filed in the Harris County Clerk's
Office on January 19, 1896. Mrs. Ida Japhet was appointed as

executrix by the probate court. Half of his estate went to his widow and the other half was to be divided among his children[19].

Daniel Japhet took over as the manager of Japhet and Company after the death of his father. About 1902, he moved the warehouse and offices from the corner of Commerce Avenue and Main Street to 817-819 Commerce Avenue, one block west to the northwest corner of Commerce Avenue and Travis Street. Japhet and Company was incorporated on January 1, 1907 with capital stock of $250,000. Daniel A. Japhet was the company's president, Mrs. Ida Japhet was vice president and Thomas W. Wilson was secretary-treasurer[20].

The Japhet and Company wholesale liquor business was effected by the coming of Prohibition, as were all other businesses selling or producing alcoholic beverages. The company closed in 1918. Fortunately, the Japhet sons had each pursued other occupations, and by 1920, each son had business interests outside of the liquor business. Daniel Japhet was an independent oil producer for a short time before becoming the vice president of the State Bank and Trust, which later became the State National Bank. William E. Japhet became the district engineer for the Humble Oil and Refining Company. Gustav Japhet began working as a wholesale produce merchant around 1900, and operated his business at 917 Commerce Avenue until about 1922 when he became president of Houston Loan and Investment Company. Mrs. Ida Japhet continued to live at the rural home on the south side of Market Street Road (later modern Clinton Drive) with her son Alfred K. Japhet. Alfred Japhet farmed at the family home in the early 1920's and developed a poultry business on the farm. Five poultry houses on the tract, south of the main house[21].

After Alfred Japhet moved to San Antonio and Emile Japhet went to East Elmira, New York, Ida Japhet remained at the farm on her own. Mrs. Japhet decided to liquidate the farm property and consolidate the homestead to the single block on which she lived, Block 28. On March 21, 1927, she sold Blocks 14 to 23 and Block 29 in Japhet Addition to W. G. Fraser for $16,700[22].

Sadly, Ida Japhet began to suffer from the effects of mental illness in her early seventies, and by 1930, she was a patient at the Greenwood Sanitarium. Dr. James Greenwood established the sanitarium in 1912 to treat nervous and mental diseases, as well as alcohol and drug addiction. The hospital was located on the west side of Old Main Street Road (modern Fannin Street, between Brays Bayou and Old Spanish Trail), one mile south of the William M. Rice Institute. With new buildings and all of the modern conveniences, the Greenwood Sanitarium was a first class facility. Ida Wipprecht Japhet died in May, 1942 and was buried in Glenwood Cemetery on May 21, 1942[23].

The Japhet homestead was acquired by James M. Ohmart on July 13, 1988 from C. P. Irby, Sr. who had owned it since 1984. Two houses are on the ten lots of Block 28. A house, at 4510 Inman Street, was built in 1905 and is a square design with a hipped roof around a central chimney. It has floor space of 1,529 square feet. The other house facing Emile Street is smaller at 1,040 square feet and was built in 1925[24].

In November, 2004, Jim Ohmart and his wife Eileen Hatcher started the Japhet Creek Restoration Project in hopes of restoring the wildlife habitat of the drainage. Over the years, cleanup projects have removed over 2,000 pounds of scrap metal, about two hundred tires, and numerous bags of trash from the creek. With the ongoing support of civic groups such as the Buffalo Bayou Partnership and the Japhet Creek Community Association, Japhet Creek will again be the native habitat for migrating songbirds, aquatic turtles, swamp rabbits and red tail hawks[25].

Proler International

Shortly after the Japhet's had moved to their rural home just beyond the city limits, industrial development followed them to the far reaches of the north side of Buffalo Bayou. In 1895, the Union Compress and Warehouse Company sold an undivided 5/8 interest in fifty-five acres in the lower portion of the Harris and Wilson Survey to the Inman Compress Company[26].

The Inman Compress Company, incorporated in 1883, was one of the first large cotton compresses to be built in Houston. Under the leadership of company president Samuel K. Dick, the Inman Compress Company established its compress on the north side of the Houston and Texas Central Railway near the western city limits.

Twenty years later, though, Inman wanted to expand their capacity with a new warehouse and compress east of the city. In 1895, the Inman Compress built its "new" press on Blocks 17, 18 and 19 of the Harris and Wilson Survey, about about two miles northeast of downtown. The new compress was adjacent to the Japhet land and just southeast of the homestead[27].

For Samuel Dick, the construction of the Inman Compress near the Japhet land was the final achievement of his long and successful career in the cotton business. Dick retired from the firm of Inman and Company in Houston, as well as from the S. M. Inman and Company of Atlanta and Inman, Sanders and Company of Bremen, Germany, on August 31, 1896. Dick's association with the Japhet's must have been especially cordial and friendly since, when the Japhet Addition was platted, two of the streets were named Inman Street and Dick Street. The two additional streets, which completed the four the boundaries of the block where the Japhet home was situated, were Ida Street and Emile Street -- named for Mrs. Ida Japhet and her son Emile[28].

The Inman Compress Company operated the New Press for about fifteen years until economic conditions forced the closure of the company. On March 24, 1910, the Inman Compress Company filed a certificate of dissolution of the corporation. The trustees of the company conveyed the compress property to the Merchants Compress Company's Exporters Compress and Warehouse on April 25, 1910[29].

The Merchants Compress, one of the six cotton compresses in Houston, operated the compress until 1923 when the firm was split into two companies. On July 3, 1923, the Merchants Compress was divided into the Merchants Compress Company, headed by A. S. Cleveland, and the Exporters Compress and Warehouse Company with Albert A. Bath as president. As a part of the transaction, the Merchants Compress Company conveyed the Clinton Drive compress property to the Exporters Compress and Warehouse Company[30].

Through the 1920's and 1930's, the Exporters Compress and Warehouse Company, Inc. participated in the commercial warehouse business, advertising the benefits of their "eighteen acres under roof." The years of the Second World War, however, proved difficult for the company, and the warehouse complex was acquired by the Coffield Warehouse Company in the late 1940's[31].

By the mid-1950's, the Coffield Warehouse Company, with 650,000 square feet of floor space and a dock along the Buffalo Bayou supported by a six hundred foot steel retaining wall, was an important component of Houston's upper ship channel industries. Located conveniently between the Port of Houston and the City at 15 Japhet Street, Coffield's major tenants were Gulf Oil, General Electric, the American Can Company and Brown and Root[32].

By the 1990's, however, the business had declined and the warehouse facility was acquired by Proler Southwest. Proler Southwest dates from the company started by Ben Proler in 1925. Ben's son Israel Proler was CEO of Proler International until his death in 1985, and his sons Bill and Ronny Proler started Proler Southwest in 1992. Proler Southwest became a leading recycler of industrial ferrous scrap and other scrap metals. On August 29, 1997, Proler Southwest merged with Metals Management, Inc. of Chicago. A decade later, in 2008, the Sims Group Ltd of Australia and Metals Management, Inc. merged to create the largest metals and electronics recycler in the world. The company was renamed Sims Metal Management Limited, and its daily recycling operations provide a colorful industry along Buffalo Bayou[33].

American Bag Company

Immediately downstream of the metal recycling facility is a small warehouse complex located at the south end of Japhet Street. These buildings house the American Bag Company, but the story of the site dates to the first decades of the twentieth century.

This tract of land was owned by the Lowry Bale Storage and Warehouse Company as early as 1912 when a portion of it was conveyed to the Exporters Compress and Warehouse Company for the construction of their cotton compress. By 1929, the Lowry Warehouse Company had constructed a small, single story warehouse for cotton storage near the end of Japhet Street. The warehouse closed in the 1930's, and in 1938, the Kelley Manufacturing moved into the former cotton warehouse[34].

The Kelley Manufacturing Company began in 1937 when Edward W. Kelley bought the Tennison Brothers Sheet Metal Company of Mt. Pleasant, Texas and renamed it the Kelley Manufacturing Company. From the Japhet Street warehouses, Kelley Manufacturing made stove pipes, roof ventilators, water tanks, flues and other sheet metal products. During World War II, Kelley Manufacturing produced tanks and shoulder carriers for chemical warfare, porthole screens and scoops for naval ships[35].

In 1946, after Edward Kelley's death in May, 1946 at age 49, his wife became company president for over a decade until her son Edward W. Kelley, Jr. took over the company in June 1959. The younger Edward Kelley was president and CEO of Kelley Manufacturing from 1959 until he sold the company in 1981. He was a graduate of Rice University and served on its board for 10 years. In 1995, Edward W. Kelley, Jr. was recognized by Rice University as a Distinguished Alumnus[36].

The Wang Association, headed by Jason Wang, purchased the 8.25 acre tract of land from Kelley Manufacturing in 1988 for its American Bag Company. The American Bag Company, established in 1985, is a producer and importer of high quality custom polyethylene and polypropylene products for the grocery and specialty retail industries[37].

North Side Sewage Treatment Plant

The last tract of land on the north bank of Buffalo Bayou before you come to the Lockwood Drive bridge is the site of the City's North Side Sewage Treatment Plant, a remnant of the first wastewater treatment system established by Houston at the beginning of the twentieth century. If one looks closely, the old pump house can be seen just beyond the brush along the bank. Between this point and the 69th Street facility near Wayside Drive, the story of Houston's wastewater management is told in the fields and processing plants built along this part of Buffalo Bayou.

Houston's first sewage treatment plan was written in 1866 by Colonel William H. Griffin, a civil engineer, for the City's Board of Health. The plan called for three main sewer lines draining into Buffalo Bayou. Two drainage ditches were completed right away, and the Caroline Street underground brick sewer, the first underground sewer in the state, was completed in 1874, but Griffin's comprehensive sewer plan was not implemented[38].

By the 1880's, with the new water supply system providing water to buildings and households, there was a need for a comprehensive sewage system to remove the water and wastes. Although five public mains and some private lines served the downtown area, residents relied primarily on private cesspools. Flooded cesspools, privy vaults and ditches were common. The city lacked a system of surface or underground drainage for storm water and households had no outlet for waste water except city ditches[39].

In 1889, Mayor Daniel C. Smith and Council agreed to plan a citywide sewage system after many complaints about the inadequate sewerage system, and the city debated whether to establish a combined or separate system of sewer pipes, one for storm water and one for household waste. City engineer C. W. Jarvis developed a wastewater plan which included establishing districts and constructing sewer lines in several wards, but implementation of the plan was incomplete and many residents were left with makeshift sewage systems or none at all[40].

The situation reached a crisis when, in 1895, after a request to the federal government for help in deepening Buffalo Bayou, Major A. M. Miller of the U. S. Army Corps of Engineers inspected the ship channel and said that it must be cleaned up before any federal monies would be spent to deepen the channel. In order the protect the ship channel development and the economic lifeline of the city, City Council authorized $250,000 for the construction of a lift station sewer system designed by Alexander Potter[41].

The Willow Street Pumping Station was the central pumping station for this filter bed type sewage treatment system. The Willow Street plant forced sewage through a twenty-four inch pipe to the filter beds four and a half miles away in the Fifth Ward. There the heavy matter stayed on the surface and was raked away, while the rest of the wastewater was filtered through layered beds of broken stone, gravel, coke and sand before flowing to a canal to Buffalo Bayou. These filter beds were on the site lying to the west of the modern Lockwood Drive bridge[42].

Almost from the time the new system was completed in 1902, its maintenance was neglected. There was no storm sewer component to the system and storm waters often overloaded the system. Many citizens, also, were not connected to the system. Thus, by 1905, the sewage treatment system was considered to be non-functional[43].

A survey done in 1911 found that the sewer system in Houston was inadequate for a city of its size. The system did not cover the entire municipality, and where sewer mains did exist, the requirement for businesses and residents to connect to the sewer mains was not enforced. There were a large number of surface closets, numerous cesspools and makeshift sewers in use without regard to the city's sanitary regulations. Mayor Ben Campbell, in 1916, estimated that seventy to eighty percent of the city's sewage was untreated and polluted the waterways. There were, in fact, thirty-five private sewers draining directly into Buffalo Bayou[44].

With new state laws prohibiting the dumping of untreated sewage into Texas waterways, Houston chose to install the new technology of activated sludge treatment for its wastewater system, and the North Side Disposal Plant was built and placed in operation in May, 1917. Designed by Edward Emmett Sands, Houston's city engineer from 1913 to 1918, the North Side Disposal Plant was the largest activated sludge sewage treatment plant then in existence. It replaced the old style filter beds of the city's first system with a ten acre open lagoon method of activated sludge treatment. The plant was capable of processing 5.5 million gallons of wastewater per day[45].

Located at the end of Japhet Street, off of the 4800 block of the modern Clinton Drive, the North Side Disposal Plant and the associated fertilizer manufacturing facility sat above the top line of a twenty foot deep "slush pit" that extended about three hundred yards toward the bayou. An electrified sewer pump house powered an air compressor at the north end of the lagoon to assist with the flow and aeration of the sewage[46].

By January, 1926, the North Side activated sludge plant was overloaded, so the facility was enlarged in 1928, and then, again, in 1937. The pump house in the lower end of the lagoon, near the bayou, was added in 1928. Yet, further improvements to the system were delayed during the Depression years and the Second World War. But, in 1949, the City transformed the existing sludge disposal system into a modern, heat drying process to produce a marketable fertilizer, called Hou-Actinite, at sixty tons per day. The North Side site was expanded to add lagoons north of the fertilizer manufacturing plant, and a new pump house was built south of the concrete slush pits, near to 1928 pump house. The enlargement of the North Side treatment plant, in conjunction with the Simms Bayou plant, provided a combined capacity of fifty-six million gallons per day which was estimated, at the time, to be sufficient for the city until 1970[47].

Construction of an expansion of the North Side plant on land on the east side of Lockwood Drive was underway by 1964. The population of Houston in 1970 was 1,233,000, and the city operated two sludge disposal plants which processed one hundred seventy-two million gallons of wastewater per day and produced one hundred twenty tons of fertilizer per day. By 1977, the North Side Wastewater and Sludge Treatment Plant was handling only about forty percent of the city's wastewater, and more capacity was need. Groundbreaking for a new plant at 69th Street and Clinton Drive was held in December, 1977. Additional facilities for the plant would be built along the north bank of Buffalo Bayou from Lockwood Drive to 69th Street. The enormous new sewage treatment plant was completed in 1983[48].

The 69th Street Wastewater Treatment Plant employs a four step process: preliminary treatment, a two stage activated sludge process, effluent filtration and disinfection. Wastewater enters the plant through a one hundred forty-four inch diameter trunk sewer and goes to the preliminary treatment area where the sewage flows through four mechanically cleaned bar screens for the removal of trash. Grit removal chambers remove sand and similar particles. The wastewater then flows through the two stage activated sludge process where pure oxygen is used. The pure oxygen also alleviates odor and air pollution problems. Filtration, the third step, separates out finely divided particles not settled out in the clarifiers. Finally, the flow is disinfected with chlorine, and after chlorination, the flows enter Buffalo Bayou through an outfall structure located a short distance upstream of the old 69th Street bridge[49].

The 69th Street Wastewater Treatment Plant is the centerpiece of Houston's award winning wastewater system, and with over 6,300 miles of sanitary sewers, forty treatment plants and four hundred twenty lift pump stations, over two hundred million gallons of sewage per day can be treated and released back into Buffalo Bayou[50].

Parker LaFarge

Downstream of the Lockwood Drive bridge, the south bank of Buffalo Bayou is an industrial development of concrete and asphalt companies, warehouses and other shipping businesses. The land between Lockwood Drive and the Houston Belt and Terminal Railroad bridge, about a mile downstream, was open rural land until the 1930's, even as the City of Houston grew eastward and the Magnolia Park and Central Park subdivisions developed around the Turning Basin in the early years of the twentieth century. The Houston Belt and Terminal Railroad tracks, built about 1912 in conjunction with the opening of the Ship Channel at the Turning Basin, form the western boundary of Central Park, and the rail right of way seems to have prevented the residential encroachment on the land to the west.

The extension of Navigation Boulevard to the City Wharves at the Turning Basin was completed by 1928, and by 1940, several companies had established operations along the bayou, especially in the large, southward bend in the bayou known as Turkey Bend. Industrial Way provided vehicular access to the area and the San Antonio and Aransas Pass Rail spur also serviced the area. The Houston Barge Terminal Warehouse and the warehouses of the Libby Warehouse Company and the Bargier Warehouse were built at the south end of Turkey Bend. The Continental Supply Company occupied the east side of Turkey Bend, and Baker Oil Tools, the National Supply Company and the Reed Roller Bit Company established facilities along Industrial Way[51].

By 1951, Parker Brothers and Company, Inc. had located its Building Materials and Concrete Mining Plant near the southwest end of Turkey Bend. In the mid-1950's, the channel of Buffalo Bayou had been cut through at the top of Turkey Bend to improve navigation toward downtown. An oxbow lake was formed from the former bend by 1957 as the easternmost arm of the bend was partially filled in and Parker Brothers took the thirty acres of new land, formerly in the bend, for their concrete plant[52].

In June, 1990, the Lafarge Corporation of Reston, Virginia formed an aggregate and asphalt company from assets purchased from the Parker Brothers of Houston and named it Parker Lafarge, Inc. On May 19, 1994, Cemex's Sunbelt Acquisitions, Inc. purchased a fifty-two percent interest in Parker Lafarge, Inc. and then established the Sunbelt Asphalt and Materials Company on a six and one half acre tract of vacant land along the east side of Lockwood Drive. Today, Parker Lafarge continues to operate its concrete and asphalt plant on the Turkey Bend land and Cemex operates its Concrete Crushing Facility nearby[53].

The land on the east side of the Turkey Bend Oxbow is largely vacant, although its owner, General Stevedores, Inc. has a warehouse on 19.6 acres on the south bank of Buffalo Bayou. General Stevedores, Inc., organized on December 7, 1945 by Guy D. Graves, handles and warehouses waterborne cargoes. The company's main office is located at 5807 Navigation Boulevard. The company also operates an outside storage facility at 6125 Industrial Way on a 6.3 acre tract east of the H. B. Fuller Company tract which lies between the two General Stevedores tracts on the south bank of the bayou[54].

The H. B. Fuller Company owns a warehouse at 6012 Industrial Way on a 4.6 acre tract east of North Greenwood Street on the south bank of Buffalo Bayou. The company was founded in 1887 by Harvey Benjamin Fuller who developed adhesives such as wallpaper paste. Today, the H. B. Fuller Company, based St. Paul, Minnesota, employs 4,500 people worldwide and is a provider of adhesives, sealants and coatings used in manufactured goods[55].

The remainder of the south bank to the Houston Belt and Terminal Railroad bridge is owned by Cemex, Inc. and its subsidiaries. Cemex acquired the property from Gulf Coast Portland Cement in 1995 and 1996, and it operates a manufacturing facility at 6200 Industrial Way on a 2.9 acre tract east of General Stevedores. The remaining 38.9 acre tract, extending to the railroad right of way, is a concrete products facility at 6203 Industrial Way owned by Transenergy Grinding, a subsidiary of Cemex, Inc[56].

The Houston Belt and Terminal Railroad bridge, since 1998, has been the reference point for all downstream drawbridges on Buffalo Bayou. With twenty-four hours notice the bridge will be opened for traffic on the bayou. The drawbridge is a swing bridge with an enormous pivot gear on the pillar in the bayou channel. It reminds us of the importance of ship traffic on this upper section of the ship channel and the former days of commercial shipping to the city wharves at Main Street when all of the bridges across the bayou were drawbridges[57].

Downstream of the HB&T bridge, Buffalo Bayou makes a short, but winding mile long path to the Turning Basin of the Port of Houston. In the first bend of the extended S-turn of the channel, the main plant of the 69th Street Wastewater Treatment facility releases its treated water back into the bayou. The Central Park Subdivision lies on the south bank of the bayou at this point as the bayou flows under the remnants of the former 69th Street bridge and its replacements, the modern Wayside Drive and SSgt Macario Garcia Drive bridges.

SSgt Macario Garcia Drive is named in honor of SSgt Macario Garcia, a recipient of the Medal of Honor during World War II and a champion of struggles faced by Hispanics in the mid-twentieth century.

Macario Garcia was born on January 2, 1920, in Villa de Castaño, Mexico. In 1923, his family moved to Texas and eventually settled in Sugar Land. Drafted into the army on November 11, 1942, Garcia served in Germany in late 1944 where he fought with the extraordinary courage and bravery that earned him the Medal of Honor. He was awarded the Medal of Honor on August 23, 1945, by President Harry S. Truman. Garcia also received the Purple Heart, the Bronze Star, and the Combat Infantryman's Badge, as well[58].

In September, 1945, shortly after his return to Texas, Macario Garcia was denied service at a restaurant in Richmond simply because he was Hispanic. Outraged that he was treated like a second class citizen, Garcia fought with the owner and was arrested and charged in the incident. His case immediately became a cause célèbre, symbolizing not only the plight of Hispanic soldiers, but that of the Hispanic community as a whole. Eventually, all charges against Garcia were dropped[59].

Macario Garcia died on December 24, 1972, in a car crash and was buried in the National Cemetery in Houston. At the graveside ceremonies, an honor guard from Fort Sam Houston in San Antonio performed the military rites. In 1981, the Houston City Council officially changed the name of Sixty-ninth Street to SSgt Macario García Drive[60].

Immediately after SSgt Macario Garcia Drive, the bends sharply to the right along the shoreline of the new Buffalo Bend Nature Park on the south bank. Buffalo Bend Nature Park is a scenic ten acre waterfront parcel on the south bank of Buffalo Bayou that has been set aside for the restoration of wetland habitat[61].

Located at 2300 SSgt Macario Garcia Drive, the Buffalo Bend tract was an industrial site owned by S&B Engineers and Constructors Ltd during the 1980's. It was later transferred to S&B Neuco Ltd in 1993. Thomas P. and Peggy J. Davidson acquired the property on February 5, 2002, and they sold it to the Trust for Public Land on July 15, 2004[62].

On Wednesday, December 8, 2004, the Buffalo Bend Nature Park was formally transferred from the Trust for Public Land to Harris County, Precinct 2. Of the $1.7 million in funds for the purchase of the park, $700,000 came from the National Oceanic and Atmospheric Administration's Coastal and Estuarine Land Protection program. The remainder of the funding came from Harris County, the Flood Control District and the Buffalo Bayou Partnership[63].

In addition to providing wetland restoration, wildlife habitat, water quality improvements and natural flood control, Buffalo Bend Nature Park will have a canoe and kayak launch and it will be connected by hike-and-bike trails to the nearby Hidalgo Park, Tony Marron Park and the North York Boat Launch[64].

A only a couple of outlying warehouses can be seen on the banks of Buffalo Bayou beyond Buffalo Bend Nature Park, but otherwise, the land, owned by the Port of Houston, is vacant and wooded. After one more sharp, hairpin curve, the bayou sweeps past the Magnolia Park neighborhood and its Hidalgo Park before passing under the Southern Pacific Railroad bridge that marks the boundary of the Turning Basin and the Houston Ship Channel.

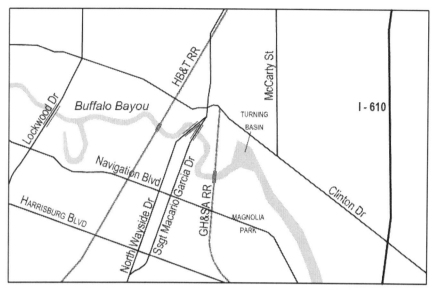

Map by Rachel A. Garcia

In the 1890's, John T. Brady developed a recreational area, which he called Magnolia Park, near Constitution Bend (now, the Turning Basin). His proposed Port Houston industrial site for a deep water port included wharves along the south bank of Buffalo Bayou from the Turning Basin to Brays Bayou.

Chapter 14
Magnolia Park

The story of the modern Port of Houston is best told at the place known as Magnolia Park. From the beginning of its existence, the City of Houston's reason for being was the waterway that brought ships from the Gulf to its wharves at Main Street. But, travel up Buffalo Bayou was never easy, and business interests in Houston worked continually to keep the waterway open. By the time of the Civil War, many felt that the upper reaches of the ship channel were too shallow, too winding and too narrow for the large vessels sailing the oceans. The transfer of goods to and from shallow draft paddle steamers which could reach the wharves in downtown was too much of an expense to bear. These factions wanted a deep water port somewhere downstream of Main Street[1].

John T. Brady, a young attorney who had served the Confederacy on ships on Buffalo Bayou, emerged from the Civil War with an idea of where the deep water port should be. On April 18, 1866, Brady purchased a tract of two thousand acres on Buffalo Bayou from Robert Lockhart, and he spent the next twenty-five years trying to establish a new port for ocean going ships on the site. Fifteen years after Brady's death, his vision was affirmed by the establishment of the Port of Houston Turning Basin at the location where it exists today[2].

John Thomas Brady was born on October 10, 1830 in Charles County, Maryland to John and Mary Brady. The Brady family had settled in Maryland in 1634, and the elder Brady was a farmer. The young John was the oldest of four children and he received a good education. In 1847, at age seventeen, John T. Brady began teaching school while studying privately for the legal profession. He passed the bar at age twenty-one in 1851[3].

In 1853, Brady moved to Westport Missouri near Kansas City and worked for a time as a journalist, but, in 1856, moved to Texas to practice law in Houston while living in Harrisburg. Brady married Caledonia Tinsley, the daughter of Isaac T. Tinsley, a wealthy planter in Brazoria County, on March 31, 1858. By 1860, John Brady and his wife Callie were living in Houston's Third Ward. John's younger brother William had come to Houston, as well, and was staying with them[4].

When the war came, John Brady served the Confederacy on the staff of General John B. Magruder. In 1863, he was an aide to Commodore Leon Smith on the cotton-clad steamer Bayou City in the capture of the Harriet Lane at the Battle of Galveston. Later that year, he was elected to the State Legislature and re-elected in 1866[5].

After the war, during the summer of 1865, John Brady and his younger brother William went into business as commission merchants with offices in Houston on Commerce Avenue and in Galveston on the Strand. While William Brady focused on the mercantile business, John Brady espoused grand enterprises. In the early 1870's, John Brady originated the idea of the Texas State Fair and served as the state fair's first president. He establish a brick yard in the Second Ward and operated it for several years. John T. Brady was elected to the State Senate in 1878, and he ran for U. S. Congress in 1880, but was defeated by Roger Q. Mills. Brady also served as a director of the Houston Gas Light Company. John Brady's most ambitious enterprise, however, was his idea of a deep water port near Harrisburg[6].

Brady's plans for a deep water port began shortly after the Civil War. On April 18, 1866, John T. Brady acquired two thousand acres of land from Robert Lockhart and others. This tract had frontage on Buffalo Bayou from Brays Bayou upstream to near the location of the modern Wayside Drive. In December, 1866, Brady conveyed the two thousand acres to W. P. Hamblen who was acting as the trustee for Isaac T. Tinsley and his associates, including John Brady and his brother William Brady. This group intended to lay out a town site on the land which would be called New Houston, and they formed a company called the New Houston City Company[7].

The second step in Brady's plan was to provide a means to transport goods to and from the new port to the City of Houston. Through the efforts of John Brady, the Texas Transportation Company was chartered on September 6, 1866 and incorporated on

September 23, 1866 with John T. Brady as president and W. P. Hamblen as secretary. The company's charter authorized it to construct a railroad along the south side of Buffalo Bayou from Houston to a point near Bray's Bayou. Brady also unsuccessfully introduced a bill in the Legislature to make Constitution Bend the terminus of bayou navigation, thus creating a rival port to the city of Houston[8].

In September, 1867, John Brady was in New York to try to secure funding of the ship channel projects. Hamblen wrote to him that he should seek about $300,000 in funds since the City Engineer had calculated the cost of dredging a channel thirteen feet deep to Constitution Bend would be about $170,500. On October 15, 1867, the Texas Transportation Company solicited subscriptions for stock in order to open a canal on both Red Fish Bar and Clopper's Bar (also referred to as Morgan's Point), but Hamblen reported to Brady that he was unable to convince even the stockholders of the New Houston City Company to invest in the enterprise due to uncertainties caused by yellow fever, Reconstruction, the Radical Republicans and state politics. Some construction was done on the Texas Transportation Company railroad, but the backers of the project were unable to complete the construction of the rail line. The project that Brady had envisioned languished for several years[9].

Clopper's Bar was a sand bar at the entrance to San Jacinto Bay that was named for Nicholas Clopper, an early settler to Texas who bought the peninsula between Galveston Bay and San Jacinto Bay in 1826. In 1834, Clopper sold the land to James Morgan, a Phildelphia-born merchant who came to Texas in 1830. Morgan established the New Washington community on the peninsula that became known as Morgan's Point. Clopper's Bar was a barrier to navigation up Buffalo Bayou, and efforts to improve the channel to Harrisburg and to Houston centered on opening a passage through the sand bar with a canal across the tip of Morgan's Point[10].

Others besides Brady and his associates were interested in the ship channel, and on January 23, 1869, the Buffalo Bayou Ship Channel Company was organized. It was incorporated on July 28, 1870, and the company undertook the task of straightening out Buffalo Bayou to Morgan's Point. About this time, Charles Morgan, a Connecticut-born shipping magnate operating throughout the Gulf from New Orleans, noticed that small craft could easily navigate Buffalo Bayou up to Houston. Morgan began to investigate the possibility of navigating his ocean going vessels to a point near Houston, and some work on a canal through Morgan's Point had been started about 1870, but it was unfinished[11].

In the summer of 1874, the Buffalo Bayou Ship Channel Company contracted with Charles Morgan to complete the passage through Morgan's Point. Morgan's crew began in September, 1874 to cut a canal through the peninsula that would be one hundred eighty feet wide and eighteen feet deep. The goal of the dredging work was to provide sufficient depth for Morgan's ocean going vessels to go as far upstream on Buffalo Bayou as Constitution Bend where connections by rail would be made to Houston. When Charles Morgan began his contract with the Buffalo Bayou Ship Channel Company in 1874, he had no interest in that company, but by February, 1875, Morgan had acquired a significant stockholder investment in the company[12].

The federal government also had appropriated funds for improvements to the ship channel, and in February, 1875, government dredges were working to cut a nine foot deep channel through Red Fish Bar and to clear the channel at the mouth of the San Jacinto River. By the end of 1875, there was a line of navigation nine feet deep from Bolivar Roads to the San Jacinto River and a minimum of thirteen feet from there to Constitution Bend, the place on Buffalo Bayou where, in 1837, the famous warship Constitution had to turn around because it was unable to navigate all the way to the foot of Main Street. With the success of these channel improvements, the Buffalo Bayou Ship Channel Company sought bids for wharf pilings to be delivered to the Long Reach section of the channel, between Harrisburg and Constitution Bend[13].

Charles Morgan, a steamship line owner who had been shipping to Texas since before it was a republic, had his own substantial resources and a habit of doing things his own way. Although the Buffalo Bayou Ship Channel Company sought to open the ship channel to ocean going vessels as far as the Long Reach wharves, where John Brady owned land, Morgan decided to take a different approach[14].

By early 1876, Charles Morgan had acquired enough of the stock in the Texas Transportation Company to gain control of it. The Texas Transportation Company had rights to build a rail line from Houston to near Brays Bayou, but Morgan used its charter to build an eight mile line from Clinton to Houston along the north side of Buffalo Bayou. Morgan selected his terminus for the channel at the mouth of Sims Bayou, about two miles downstream from Harrisburg, and he constructed new wharves extending eleven hundred feet along the bayou in front of the mouth of Sims Bayou. He dredged a basin two hundred fifty feet across and sixteen feet deep at the mouth of Sims Bayou for turning his steamers, and on April 21, 1876, the first vessel to use the new channel, ironically named the Clinton, arrived with construction materials for the railroad. The rail line was completed in September, 1876, and its seven mile track ran to the Fifth Ward near McKee Street from the Sims Bayou wharves. Morgan had no intention of extending the ship channel to Constitution Bend as favored by John Brady and the New Houston City Company[15].

Charles Morgan died on May 8, 1878, in New York City. After Morgan's death, his transportation system passed to other hands and the company focused on the deep water port at Galveston. The old Clinton terminal was abandoned by the company's ocean going vessels. The last Morgan vessel navigated Buffalo Bayou to Clinton on July 26, 1884. Between 1883 and 1885, Morgan's Louisiana and Texas Railroad and Steamship Company was absorbed into the Southern Pacific system[16].

Although the Morgan Lines gave up on a deep water port for Houston, the local business community did not. By the end of the 1880's, John Thomas Brady was ready to present his most ambitious plan for a port. Brady's development, which he called Port Houston, included a wharf and warehouse facilities at Long Reach on Buffalo Bayou with space for factories along the north bank of Brays Bayou, a railroad connecting the 1,374 acre development to downtown Houston, a residential area and a large, well landscaped public park. The park was called Magnolia Park, and with the 3,750 magnolia trees that Brady had planted there, it became the centerpiece for the promotion of his enterprise[17].

On May 23, 1889, the Sunday School children of Beth Israel Congregation became one of the first groups to use Magnolia Park as they held a picnic in the park at the invitation of John Brady. Magnolia Park, laid out in 1889 on three hundred acres, was designed with meandering drives and areas for picnicking among the magnificent grove of magnolia trees. Situated along the south bank of the bayou at Constitution Bend, Magnolia Park also provided recreational access to the waters of Buffalo Bayou. By 1890, the park had a pavilion-type clubhouse and docking facilities for pleasure boats. Houston residents flocked to Magnolia Park for picnics and outdoor events[18].

The second phase of the Port Houston project was the construction of a railroad to the site. On April 2, 1889, Houston Belt and Magnolia Park Railway Company was incorporated with John Brady as president and Charles H. Milby as secretary. By August, 1890, Brady's large crew of thirty teams totaling seven hundred men were at work grading the line of the Houston Belt and Magnolia Park Railway. Service was established in 1890, and the line's six miles of track ran from its depot at Fannin Street and Commerce Avenue to Brady station near Constitution Bend. Its principal business was carrying passengers to and from Magnolia Park[19].

John Brady took every opportunity to tout his Port Houston concept. When a Deep Water Meeting was held at Galveston in 1890, Brady arranged for the businessmen who attended the meeting to stop for lunch at Magnolia Park on their return to Houston, and he conducted them through the development. By the summer of 1891, the Houston Belt and Magnolia Park Railway was nearly finished, the harbor and wharves were almost complete and the beautification of the park was progressing well. Brady was hosting an inspection tour of Port Houston and Magnolia Park when, on the evening of June 25, 1891, he was overcome by heat and returned to Houston in very critical condition. John T. Brady died the next day, June 26, 1891[20].

The funeral of John Thomas Brady took place on June 30, 1891 at Annunciation Church. His pall bearers included Leon Smith, his commodore during the Battle of Galveston, his law partner Henry F. Ring, and business associates T. W. House, J. A. Baker and the

From the collection of the author

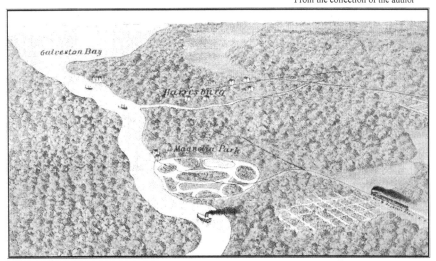

This detail of Magnolia Park from the Houston Bird's Eye Map of 1891 shows the essential features of John Brady's new park, including the curving lanes along the waterfront, which is connected to Houston by Brady's railroad line. Note that the distance to Galveston Bay is not to scale.

Honorable W. P. Hamblen. Brady was buried at Glenwood Cemetery beside his first wife[21].

William Brady arrived from New York on July 2, 1891, and began to review his brother's projects, including the railroad, Magnolia Park and the proposed Port Houston. For the next four years or so, the management of Magnolia Park tried to maintain the resort in first class shape. Band concerts, picnics and other celebrations were held at the park, as usual. A passing track was built midway between Houston and Magnolia Park so that the trains could run between the park and downtown every fifteen or twenty minutes. Nevertheless, without the leadership of John Brady, the enterprise faltered[22].

On November 3, 1891, the Houston Belt and Magnolia Park Railway went into receivership. One of the railway's directors, T. D. Cobbs, filed suit against the Port Houston Land and Improvement Company, the owner of Magnolia Park, and other creditors soon joined in the suit. In the fall of 1895, the court ordered the sale of the property of the Port Houston Land and Improvement Company. Through a series of negotiations and transactions, the creditors were paid and the assets of the Port Houston Land and Improvement Company, including Magnolia Park, were acquired by the Magnolia Park Company. The Magnolia Park Company had been incorporated on March 25, 1896 by Houston businessmen E. F. Hamblen, H. E. Ring and L. W. Craig to purchase, sell and subdivide real property in towns, cities and their suburbs[23].

The Houston Belt and Magnolia Park Railway was conveyed to the Houston Land and Trust Company on April 26, 1893, and the rail line was used by the Galveston, LaPorte and Houston Railway as an entrance to Houston during 1895. The railroad was sold to Herbert E. Fuller under court order on November 1, 1898. The Houston, Oaklawn and Magnolia Park Railway was chartered on May 16, 1899 to acquire the property of the former Houston Belt and Magnolia Park Railway Company from Herbert E. Fuller. The International and Great Northern Railroad Company bought the Houston, Oaklawn and Magnolia Park Railway on December 27, 1903 in order to acquire waterfront property near the Turning Basin, and the rail line became a valuable industrial track[24].

The advantages of having a deep water port at Houston became evident during the mid 1890's, and in 1897, Congress approved the concept of dredging the ship channel to a depth of twenty-five feet with a terminus at Long Reach. The plan, authorized, in 1899, called for cuts in the ship channel through Irish Bend, Clinton Bend and Harrisburg Bend. Dredging finally began in March, 1905 and by 1908, the Houston Ship Channel was eighteen feet deep and it had a turning basin at Long Reach. The dredging operations in 1907 to straighten the Harrisburg Bend in Buffalo Bayou formed an island near Harrisburg, and this island was named Brady's Island in tribute to the man who championed the deep water channel[25].

In the summer of 1907, a large part of the Magnolia Park Addition was purchased by Galveston businessmen James R. Cheek and Moritz O. Kopperl. Both men were on the board of the Merchants National Bank in Galveston where Kopperl was the president of the bank and Cheek was vice president. They chartered and incorporated the Magnolia Park Land Company with Cheek as president and Kopperl as vice president, and they set up the company's home office at 912 Travis Street in Houston. Cheek claimed that they bought the Magnolia Park land because it was a bargain. They believed that it would be desirable residential property[26].

Two years later, on June 1, 1909, the Magnolia Park Land Company began offering lots in Magnolia Park for sale. The four hundred thirty-one acre tract of generally sloping, high and well drained woodlands, which was clothed with a magnificent forest of pine, oak, magnolia and bay trees, was subdivided into a residential area called the Magnolia Park Addition, and the trees of Magnolia Park were cut down when roads were built and the lots were prepared for the subdivision's modest homes[27].

The sales of lots were brisk. With easy terms of $5 down and $5 a month, approximately three thousand lots were sold in the first six weeks. Magnolia Park was considered to be a great investment since it occupied a strategic position between Houston and Harrisburg and the Houston Harbor, the head of ocean navigation. But, it was also destined to be the home to thousands of employees working at the wharves, factories, elevators, storehouses on the waterfront[28].

As a suburb of Houston, Magnolia Park had a lot going for it in 1909. The Harrisburg Road, which extended along the south side of Magnolia Park, was one of the best macadamized shell roadways in Texas. In addition, street car service from Houston to Magnolia Park in 1909 was a fifteen minute ride costing fifteen cents. The population of the community grew quickly, and in 1909, Magnolia Park became an independent municipality. Two years later, on August 2, 1911, the citizens of Magnolia Park met to call for elections to create an independent school district for the one hundred fifty school children living in Magnolia Park[29].

The growth of the population of Magnolia Park soon led to a shortage of available land for housing. A large tract of vacant land to the west of the Magnolia Park Addition offered a solution to the problem. Robert C. Duff, a Houston attorney, formerly of Beaumont, with ties to the International and Great Northern Railroad, had acquired the tract, called Central Park, through his Central Park Land Company. By early 1911, Duff had done little to develop his property. The most significant event that occurred on the property was the encampment of the First Brigade of the U. S. Army on the land on June 1, 1911. The one night encampment came during maneuvers of the four thousand man brigade as they marched from Galveston to Houston for a parade through the city[30].

Shortly after the encampment, Robert C. Duff sold the Central Park land to the Magnolia Park Land Company, and then he dissolved the Central Park Land Company. Capitalizing on its experience with Magnolia Park, the Magnolia Park Land Company began advertising lots in Central Park on May 1, 1912, offering the same easy terms. Lots in Central Park went for $800 ($10 down, $10 a month) and $400 ($5 down, $5 a month). After only a month, lots sales exceeded expectations, and it was anticipated that the whole area would be rapidly settled[31].

The initial residents of Magnolia Park were Anglos, but Mexican Americans soon began to move into the area. Arriving from South Texas, these Mexican Americans found the affordable housing in the nearby neighborhood a convenience to their jobs in the ship channel industries. Many of them worked as laborers for the railroads, loaded ships with cotton or helped construct the ship channel. A few years later, immigrants from Northern Mexico came to the area. Attracted to Magnolia Park by employment opportunities and the chance to escape the turmoil to the Mexican revolution, Mexicans established new homes in the community[32].

By 1915, Magnolia Park had become a Mexican-American barrio. Residents fostered the Mexican cultural life. Clubs, fraternal organizations, theatrical groups, and mutual aid organizations such as the Sociedad Mutualista Benito Juárez, founded in 1919, provided a strong sense of community identity. The barrio had its own business district of Mexican-owned firms, and a Mexican chamber of commerce looked after the community's interests[33].

Magnolia Park was annexed by the City of Houston in October, 1926, and along with the annexation came a ten acre tract of land along the banks of the Houston Ship Channel which had served as a landfill for the City of Magnolia Park. The residents of the neighborhood raised money to purchase the land for a city park which they named in honor of Miguel Hidalgo y Costilla whose proclamation of 1810 inspired Mexico to liberate itself from Spain. The Mexican American community of Magnolia Park viewed Hidalgo Park, located at 7000 Avenue Q, as a hub in their community where announcements, entertainment and speeches were held[34].

Photo credit: Linda Gorski

The GH&SA Railway tracks, running along the eastern boundary of Hidalgo Park, separated the Central Park Addition from the Magnolia Park Addition in 1913. Today, the railroad's swing drawbridge across Buffalo Bayou marks the upstream boundary of the Turning Basin and the Houston Ship Channel. The bridge pivots on the large turret near the south bank (right).

The formal dedication of Hidalgo Park took place during a three day festival which began on September 14, 1934 to coincide with the celebration of the Hidalgo proclamation and the opening of the new park. Included in these celebrations was the dedication of the Hidalgo Park Quiosco, a twenty-five foot by twenty-five foot octagonal-shaped gazebo[35].

The Hidalgo Park Quiosco has a unique appearance in which its features, such as its concrete columns and railings, are designed to look like tree trunks. The hand-molded textured concrete pillars resemble tree trunks with different bark textures representing Oak trees. Atop the roof is a flag pole made to look like a tree branch, and the hand railing around the floor of the quiosco appears to be tree branches fastened together. On the steps leading up to the stage floor is an inscription that reflects the sentiment of the community with pride for their home, "Houston Mexicans to Their City, V. Lozano[36]."

Vidal Lozano, the designer and builder of the gazebo, was born on October 4, 1888 in Mexico. He immigrated to Laredo, Texas with his parents in 1892, and by 1918, he had moved to Houston's near north side. An iron works molder and pipe fitter, Lozano developed a reputation as a sculptor of the artwork style, Faux Bois

(False Wood). The Hidalgo Park Quiosco is the only known public example of Lozano's artwork[37].

Between 1920 and 1930, the Mexican population in Houston increased from about 6,000 to 14,500. While the Second Ward became predominantly Mexican, Magnolia Park became Houston's largest Mexican neighborhood. By 1990, the community was a working class neighborhood of 14,000 people. It remains, today, one of the largest Mexican-American communities in Houston[38].

The Port of Houston

From the Turning Basin, Buffalo Bayou follows a relatively straight course for about two miles until it comes to the junction with Brays Bayou and the historic town site of Harrisburg. This section of the ship channel, historically known as the Long Reach because of its straight course, is lined with the docks, wharves and warehouses of the Port of Houston, a deep water port serving ocean going vessels from all over the world.

On November 10, 1914, Sue Campbell, the young daughter of Houston Mayor Ben Campbell, tossed a bouquet of white roses on the new Ship Channel to signal its opening. The U. S. Army Corps of Engineers had deepened the fifty mile channel to twenty-five feet from the Gulf to the Turning Basin, and the first deep water vessel to dock at the new Port of Houston was the S. S. Saltillo[39].

The commitment by the federal government to maintain the deep water port for Houston allowed the City to build the Municipal Wharves on the south bank of the Turning Basin. The private development of the ship channel was also encouraged, and in 1923, Anderson, Clayton and Company had built docks on the south side of the bayou at Long Reach. By the early 1940's, the full length of the south bank of Buffalo Bayou between the Turning Basin and Brays Bayou was industrialized[40].

The Port Authority attempted to acquire the Long Reach docks in 1953, but failed. In 1965, the Port did acquired the Long Reach docks, but as it built more docks on the north side of the channel, the Long Reach facilities fell into disrepair. The City docks on the south bank had deteriorated so much by 1987 that the only ships that routinely berthed there were military ships[41].

The Port began to rehabilitate two berths and re-establish a railroad connection in 1998. The city docks, which had been idle for more than fifteen years, re-opened in January, 2000 as the Empire Stevedoring company started using the four docks on the south side of the Turning Basin. Today, large vessels are a common sight at the docks on both sides of the channel from the Turning Basin to Brays Bayou[42].

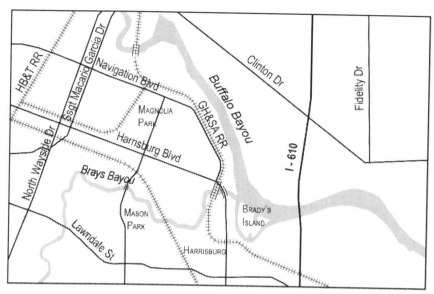

Map by Rachel A. Garcia

John R. Harris found that Buffalo Bayou was navigable as far upstream as Brays Bayou. In the mid-1820's, Harris established the town of Harrisburg and began shipping operations between his wharf and ports along the Gulf of Mexico. Harrisburg prospered through the mid-nineteenth century, but the town declined after the dredging of a deep water ship channel in the late 1800's bypassed the "Harrisburg Bend" and created Brady's Island.

Chapter 15
Harrisburg

Beyond the last Navigation District warehouse and the scrap metal recycling yard of Derichebourg S. A. of France on the south bank, the main course of the Ship Channel moves off to the left. On the right, the mouth of Brays Bayou flows into Buffalo Bayou and the original channel of Buffalo Bayou goes straight ahead to the former town site of Harrisburg. The original course of Buffalo Bayou made a sharply crooked bend that was bypassed when the deep water channel was dredged in 1907. The dredging of the "cut off" created Brady's Island[1].

The name of Brays Bayou, sometimes spelled as Bray's, with an apostrophe, dates from the earliest days of the Austin Colony. Although the name Brays Bayou was in common use by 1828, it is believed to have been called by that name as early as 1824 when the land grants were issued to the settlers in the Austin Colony along the San Jacinto River basin. A man named Bray arrived in March, 1822 accompanied by his son-in-law (and perhaps his son, too), and they settled on the bayou that now bears his name. Nevertheless, another source claims that the bayou was named for a Frenchman named DuBraize, but no other information about this man is provided[2].

The south bank of Buffalo Bayou, south of Brays Bayou, is the site of the historic town of Harrisburg. Harrisburg was founded by John Richardson Harris, a native of East Cayuga, New York. Born in 1790, the twenty-two year old Captain John R. Harris served in the War of 1812 in the regiment in which his father was a colonel. John Harris married Jane Birdsall on May 7, 1813 and they settled near Waterloo, New York where sons DeWitt Clinton Harris and Lewis Birdsall Harris were born. By 1819, the Harris family was living in St. Genevieve, Missouri where daughter Mary Jane Harris was born in 1819, and son John Birdsall Harris was born in 1821. During this time in St. Genevieve, Harris met Moses Austin and decided to go to Texas. He moved the family back to New York until he could settle in Texas, and a little over a year later, he set out for Texas[3].

When John R. Harris sailed from New Orleans on his own vessel in 1823, he visited several sites before selecting one at the junction of Brays Bayou and Buffalo Bayou for a trading post. Harris built a house on the peninsula between Brays Bayou and Buffalo Bayou and a store and warehouse along Buffalo Bayou. Like many of the families who responded to Stephen F. Austin's advertisements, Harris wrongly assumed that the San Jacinto estuary was part of the Austin grant. Merchants and boatmen, however, remained in the area because it was the best transportation system in Texas[4].

Mexico gave Stephen F. Austin special permission to issue titles to those already settled along Buffalo Bayou, the San Jacinto River and Cedar Bayou, and in July, 1824, land commissioner Baron de Bastrop was authorized to issue twenty-nine titles to the settlers. On August 16, 1824, John R. Harris was granted a league of land, totaling 4,428.4 acres, that was nearly a mile wide and more than six miles long on the western side. The John R. Harris grant extends from Brays Bayou on the north to the modern Belfort Boulevard on the south, and about one half mile on either side of the modern Broadway Street[5].

After the Buffalo Bayou area became part of Austin Colony in 1824, it was possible to use the waterway through Galveston Bay and up Buffalo Bayou for a short overland trip to San Felipe. John R. Harris had explored the coast extensively and had followed Buffalo Bayou for most of its length. He was satisfied that his settlement was at the head of navigation. The route from Harris's settlement along the San Felipe Road soon became the principal route into the interior of the Austin Colony[6].

With the success of the trade through his settlement, Harris decided to lay out a town site on the village of about twenty log cabins that were scattered among the trees and not situated according to any plan. In 1826, he hired Francis W. Johnson to survey the town which he named Harrisburg in honor of Harrisburg, Pennsylvania which had been founded by his great-grandfather[7].

John R. Harris had grand ambitions for his fledgling commercial enterprise. He brought machinery for a grist mill and a sawmill to

Harrisburg, and he established a blacksmith shop and carpenter shop. With his brothers David Harris and William Plunkett Harris, along with his partner Robert Wilson, the Harris family sloops and schooners sailed to New Orleans and Mexican ports. The thriving port of Harrisburg became the commercial and shipping center for the region[8].

An inventory of Harris's Harrisburg store included ready-made clothing, bolts of cloth, candles, shoes, soap, spices, books, lace, gilt buttons, and silk vests. He accepted payment in cotton, sugarcane and hides. Jared Groce delivered cotton to Harris at Harrisburg from his plantation near Hempstead. Lumber made from pine trees rafted directly to the Harris saw mill was shipped in his ships to Tampico and Vera Cruz[9].

In 1829, John R. Harris began assembling the first steam saw-mill in Texas. In August, 1829, Harris sailed on one of his ships to New Orleans to buy belting for the mill. At that time, there was a yellow fever epidemic in the city and Harris contracted the disease. John R. Harris died in New Orleans on August 21, 1829, shortly before his thirty-eighth birthday[10].

Although John R. Harris died before completing the steam saw mill project, his brothers William P. Harris and David Harris, along with Robert Wilson, completed the mill and operated it until 1833. As might be expected of such a prosperous enterprise, the property of John R. Harris went into litigation after his death. William P. Harris and his partner Robert Wilson presented their claims against the estate of John R. Harris. In addition, Jane Harris, John's widow, and their son DeWitt C. Harris arrived in Texas in 1833 to assert their interests[11].

Jane Harris accused Robert Wilson of fraudulently claiming much of her late husband's business as his own, and the Harris estate became mired in legal actions for several years. At this time, the brothers John K. Allen and Augustus C. Allen, land speculators from Nacogdoches, had approached the heirs of John R. Harris with an offer to buy all or part of the Harris family's interest in the town. Because the estate was so involved in complex litigation, the pro-posal by the Allen brothers was impossible to consider. By the time the suit against Wilson was settled in 1838, the town of Harrisburg had been burned to the ground by Santa Anna's troops and the Allen brothers had dropped plans to develop the Harrisburg site. They founded the town of Houston instead[12].

The Harris family rebuilt Harrisburg after the Battle of San Jacinto and they attempted to revitalize their commercial interests by forming the Harrisburg Town Company in 1839. Harrisburg was incorporated June 5, 1837, and it was consolidated with Hamilton, a town on the opposite bank of Buffalo Bayou on June 23, 1839. In July, 1839, the town of Harrisburg was laid out, again, by F. Jacob Rothaas, and it had a population of about 1,400. Even after the founding of Houston, Harrisburg continued to serve as a port for passengers and freight. Many vessels preferred Harrisburg as a more convenient port until after the Civil War[13].

Jane Birdsall Harris rebuilt her home after the Battle of San Jacinto with help of Mexican prisoners of war and operated it as an inn that was well patronized by the travelers through Harrisburg. Her son-in-law Andrew Briscoe began dealing in cattle after his term as the Chief Justice of Harrisburg County ended in 1839, and he also promoted a railroad from Harrisburg to the Brazos River. In 1840, Briscoe wrote a paper entitled "California Railroad" in which he envisioned a plan for building a railroad from Harrisburg to San Diego, California by way of Richmond, Austin and El Paso[14].

Andrew Briscoe organized a private venture of the Harrisburg and Brazos Railroad in 1840 and then, in 1841, he received a charter for the Harrisburg Railroad and Trading Company. This was an attempt by Briscoe and the Harris family to build a railroad from Harrisburg to the Brazos River in order to handle the commerce of the rich plantations of the Brazos Valley. The company graded two miles of track, but the company failed and the track was abandoned[15].

In 1847, a group headed by General Sidney Sherman acquired the railroad holdings and the town site of Harrisburg. Andrew Briscoe moved his family to New Orleans in the spring of 1849 and gave up the idea of a railroad in Texas. Briscoe died in New Orleans on October 4, 1849, at age thirty-nine, but Sidney Sherman continued to pursue the railroad, and on February 11, 1850, he received a charter for the Buffalo Bayou, Brazos and Colorado Railway. Construction of the rail line began in Harrisburg in 1851, and the first passengers to ride a train in Texas went from Harrisburg to Thomas Point, three miles to the west, on April 21, 1853. Regular operations of the Buffalo Bayou, Brazos and Colorado Railway began in August, 1853 after tracks were laid to Stafford's Point from its terminal in Harrisburg[16].

The opening of the first railroad in Texas seemed to bring Harrisburg back to the prominence that it once held in Texas. The railroad stretched across the county to Stafford's Point and facilitated the shipment of cotton and sugar to ports of the world. Harrisburg had its train, while Houston, in 1853, still had only ox teams and creaking wagons. The town had a steam sawmill, several stores, three good hotels and a railroad terminal with shops and yards. Harrisburg was in its heyday[17].

One of those good hotels in Harrisburg was the Harris House. Located a few hundred feet from the new railroad station, machine shops and railway yards, it was near the busy docks and just off the dusty main road to Houston. Jane Harris had converted her home into a hotel where railroad officials and other prominent men were entertained by a hospitable tavern keeper. The Harris House was at the crossroads of rail, water and overland traffic, and Jane Harris operated the inn until her death on August 15, 1869[18].

Sidney Sherman faired less well during the 1850's. His sawmill in Harrisburg burned, his residence burned, and the railroad office where he was living burned. Having lost most of his fortune to a series of separate fires, he moved to Galveston in 1855 and ran the Island City Hotel until 1861. Sidney Sherman died in Galveston on August 1, 1873 at age sixty-eight[19].

The decade after the Civil War was one of decline for the town of Harrisburg. The Buffalo Bayou, Brazos and Colorado Railway suffered substantial losses during Reconstruction. The railroad was sold on January 24, 1870, and reorganized as the Galveston, Harrisburg and San Antonio Railway. The 1875 hurricane covered the railroad tracks at Harrisburg and ruined the wharf. The railroad and its shops were moved to Houston and Harrisburg's population was sharply reduced almost over night. Many of the railroad employees tore their houses down, carried the materials to Houston in wagons, and rebuilt them in the neighborhood of the Southern Pacific shops. In December, 1876, Thomas Peirce moved the headquarters of the Galveston, Harrisburg and San Antonio Railway to Houston[20].

In July, 1870, the U. S. government designated Houston as a "port of delivery" and assigned a customs officer to the city. Houston merchants deepened and straightened the bayou so that larger ships could unload farther upstream. The importance of Harrisburg as a port diminished significantly as Houston's port development proceeded. By 1890, the population of Harrisburg had declined to four hundred thirty-one persons. In December, 1926, Harrisburg was annexed by Houston[21].

Twin Sisters

The Civil War effected Harrisburg about the same as it did to any Texas community. Harrisburg, however, was a rail center and that did focus the activity of troop and equipment movements through the town. At the end of the war, the federal troops occupied Harrisburg and used the railroads to collect cannons and other Confederate armaments for shipment by boat to federal arsenals. This activity resulted in what can only be described as one of the most enduring mysteries of Texas -- the location of the Twin Sisters cannons that were used at the Battle of San Jacinto.

The Twin Sisters were two cannons donated to the Texas cause by sympathetic citizens of Cincinnati, Ohio in 1836. When the shipment of the cannon arrived at Galveston, the nine year old twin daughters of Dr. C. C. Rice, Elizabeth and Eleanor, who were also on the ship, were drafted to do a presentation of the cannons, and the name Twin Sisters was suggested for the cannons. At the Battle of San Jacinto, the Twin Sisters played a significant role in the defeat of the Mexican army[22].

The cannons were shipped to the Texas arsenal in Austin in 1840 and used only for ceremonial occasions. By 1845, the Twin Sisters were historical relics with little military value, and they were taken to the U. S. arsenal in Baton Rouge under the terms of the annexation of Texas[23].

At the outset of the Civil War, the Texas Secession Commission asked the state of Louisiana for the return of the Twin Sisters. The cannons had been sold to a foundry in Baton Rouge as scrap iron. One was still at the foundry, and the other had been sold to a private citizen in Iberville Parish. Nevertheless, the Louisiana Legislature purchased and repaired the Twin Sisters and presented them to Texas on April 20, 1861 -- 25 years after their original firing[24].

The Twin Sisters were used by the Confederate forces in the Battle of Galveston in January, 1863, and in February, 1864, the cannons were sent to San Antonio. After the surrender of the Confederacy, M. A. Sweetman, a Union soldier stationed in Houston, saw them near Market Square on July 30, 1865. Sweetman recognized them by the presentation plaques attached to them by Louisiana in 1861. The next, and last, time that the Twin Sisters were seen was in Harrisburg, about August 15, 1865[25].

Among the former Confederate soldiers lingering in Harrisburg while waiting for transportation back to their homes was a small group of young men who noticed that among the stockpile of Confederate cannons along side the railroad were the fabled Twins Sisters. Vowing to prevent these relics of the Republic of Texas from being taken by the federal government, the men returned at night and stole the cannons. Led by the nineteen year old Henry North Graves, four other former soldiers and Graves' black servant took the woodwork of the cannons apart and burned it. Then, they threw the carriages into the bayou and rolled the Twin Sisters several hundred yards into the woods to be buried. The men dug a shallow grave for the Twin Sisters, covered the grave with leaves and branches to conceal it, and marked the nearby trees to identify the burial place[26].

In 1888, Henry N. Graves returned to Harrisburg to retrieve the Twin Sisters, but the town had changed and only two of his markers remained. Graves was confused by the landscape and was unable to locate the burial place of the Twin Sisters. Graves visited Harrisburg several times over the next thirty years in an attempt to find where he had buried the cannons, but without success[27].

A number of other historians, explorers and treasure hunters have tried to follow the clues left by Graves in the search for the Twin Sisters. It seems that every thirty years or so there is a concerted effort to find the buried cannons. In 1982, in conjunction with the Texas Sesquicentennial Celebration, Lynn Ashby of the Houston Post promoted a prize of $50,000 for the person who could find the Twin Sisters. The prize went unclaimed, but for a few years thereafter, the last major search for the Twin Sisters took place. As yet, the mystery of the location of the Twin Sisters remains[28].

Glendale Cemetery

The resting place of many of the early pioneers of Harrisburg, most notably Jane Birdsall Harris, is Glendale Cemetery. Located at 8315 East Magnolia Street, Glendale Cemetery is the oldest burial ground in Houston. The six acre cemetery was established some time after Harrisburg was laid out in 1826, and when it was created, the cemetery looked out over the main channel of Buffalo Bayou. With that view in mind, General Sidney Sherman built his magnificent residence adjacent to the cemetery, and a granite monument along the fence line, erected in 1936, marks the site. Today, Glendale Cemetery is tucked away on the old channel of the bayou opposite Brady Island[29].

Sidney Sherman Bridge

Beyond the Glendale Cemetery, Buffalo Bayou flows under the Interstate 610 bridge. The towering bridge was opened to ten lanes of traffic on March 2, 1973. With a main span of six hundred feet, and a vertical clearance of one hundred thirty-five feet, the bridge allows large vessels on the Ship Channel to navigate to the Port of Houston. The bridge was named for Sidney Sherman in 1974[30].

The Sidney Sherman Bridge serves as a marker for the end of our story about Houston and Buffalo Bayou. Although the Houston city limits lie about two miles downstream, our story gives way at this point to the story of Pasadena, the Ship Channel industries and the San Jacinto Battleground. And, that is the subject of another book.

Notes

Chapter 1: The Headwaters of Buffalo Bayou

1. "Buffalo Bayou." The Handbook of Texas Online. <http://www.tshaonline.org/ handbook/online/articles/rhb28> [Accessed August 03, 2011].
2. Barwis, Susan DeVries. "A history of Katy, Texas." KatyTexas.com <http:// www.katytexas.com/katyhistory.cfm> [Accessed August 03, 2011].
3. "Katy." Texas Historical Commission. Atlas. <http://atlas.thc.state.tx.us/shell-site.htm> [Accessed August 03, 2011].
Von-Maszewski, Wolfram M. Voyage to North America 1844-45, Prince Carl of Solms's Texas Diary of People, Places, and Events. Denton: German-Texas Heritage Society, 2000. Page 150.
4. Barwis, Susan DeVries. "A history of Katy, Texas." KatyTexas.com <http:// www.katytexas.com/katyhistory.cfm> [Accessed August 03, 2011].
5. "Wood Creek Reserve Project History." Wood Creek Reserve. <http:// www.woodcreekreserve.com/project_news_history.htm> [Accessed August 03, 2011].
6. Grayson Lakes. <http://www.graysonlakes.com> [Accessed July 2, 2002].
Bivins, Ralph. "National commercial market slowdown to miss Houston." Houston Chronicle, 02/03/2001. Section: Business. <http://www.chron.com/CDA/archives/archive.mpl?id=2001_3278856> [Accessed August 03, 2011].
7. Horton, Tom. "A Prairie Called Katy." Land & People. Spring, 1998. Trust for Public Lands. <http://www.tpl.org/publications/land-and-people-magazine/archive/landpeople-spring-1998/a-prairie-called-katy.html> [Accessed August 03, 2011].
8. Bivins, Ralph. "Cinco Ranch grows in size, suburban dominance." Houston Chronicle, Wednesday, 07/17/2002. Section: B, Page 1, 3 Star Edition.
9. Feser, Katherine. "Cinco Ranch amenities draw buyers." Houston Chronicle, Sunday, 06/08/1997. Section: Business, Page 10, 2 Star Edition.
10. Hassell, Greg. "Wortham's firm grew along with Bayou City." Houston Chronicle, Tuesday, 03/13/2001. Section B, Page 1, 3 Star Edition.
11. Bivins, Ralph. "Fast-growing Cinco Ranch gets commercial venture." Houston Chronicle, Sunday, 11/11/2001. Section: D, Page 8, 2 Star Edition.
12. "You're not in Texas anymore." Shark.com. <http://www.shark.com/experience/ travel/> [Accessed July 10, 2002].
13. Ensor, H. Blaine. Cinco Ranch Sites, Barker Reservoir, Fort Bend County. College Station: Texas A & M University, Archeological Research Laboratory, 1987.

Chapter 2: Barker Reservoir

1. Lezon, Dale. "Coyotes are at the door in some suburban areas." Houston Chronicle, Tuesday, 01/02/2001. Section State & Local.

2. Ensor, H. Blaine. Cinco Ranch Sites, Barker Reservoir, Fort Bend County. College Station: Texas A & M University, Archeological Research Laboratory, 1987.
3. "Peak Streamflow for Texas. USGS 08074000 Buffalo Bayou at Houston, TX." <http://waterdata.usgs.gov/tx/nwis/peak> [Accessed August 6, 2002].
4. "Barker Reservoir." The Handbook of Texas Online. <http://www.tshaonline.org/handbook/online/articles/rob03> [Accessed August 04, 2011].
5. "Addicks and Barker Reservoirs." U. S. Army. Corps of Engineers. Galveston District. "Harris County Precinct 3." Houston Chronicle, Wednesday, 06/14/00. This Week Section, Page 11, 2 Star Edition.
6. Ensor, H. Blaine.
7. Campbell, Thomas N. "Akokisa Indians." The Handbook of Texas Online. <http://www.tshaonline.org/handbook/online/articles/bma17> [Accessed August 04, 2011].
8. Ensor, H. Blaine.
9. Ladd, Kevin. "El Orcoquisac." The Handbook of Texas Online. <http://www.tshaonline.org/handbook/online/articles/hve49> [Accessed August 04, 2011].
10. Ensor, H. Blaine.
11. "The Ant-Hills." West Houston Cycling Club. <http://www.khfweb.com/greg/default.htm> [Accessed November 29, 2000].
12. "Habermacher Settlement, Harris County, Texas." U. S. Department of the Interior. National Park Service. National Register of Historic Places. 1997.
Von-Maszewski, Wolfram M. Voyage to North America 1844-45, Prince Carl of Solms's Texas Diary of People, Places, and Events. Denton: German-Texas Heritage Society, 2000. Page 81.
13. Harris, Dilue Rose. Life in Early Texas, the Reminiscences of Mrs. Dilue Harris. n.p. Page 23.
14. "Habermacher Settlement, Harris County, Texas." U. S. Department of the Interior. National Park Service. National Register of Historic Places. 1997.
15. Soergel, Alwin H. A Sojourn in Texas, 1846-47. San Marcos, TX: German-Texan Heritage Society, n. d. Pages 36-39.
16. Russell, Marie. 1850 Census Harris County, Texas with added genealogical notes. Baytown: n.p., 1981.
17. "Habermacher Settlement, Harris County, Texas."
18. "Quinan Community, Site of." Texas Historical Commission. Atlas. <http://atlas.thc.state.tx.us/scripts/>. [Accessed January 12, 2001].
19. Sizemore, Deborah Lightfoot. The LH7 Ranch, in Houston's Shadow. The E. H. Marks' Legacy from Longhorns to the Salt Grass Trail. Dennison: University of North Texas Press, n.d.
20. "Habermacher Settlement, Harris County, Texas."
21. Reed, S. G. A History of Texas Railroads. Houston: St. Clair Publishing Co., ?. p. 478-479.
Kirkland, Hayes and Waqar Fazlani. "Texas Narrow Gauge Railroad." Houston: unpublished paper, 1997.
22. Reed, S. G.
23. "Texas' First Narrow Gauge Railway Depot." Texas Historical Commission. Atlas. <http://atlas.thc.state.tx.us/scripts/>. [Accessed September 13, 2002].
24. "Seven Families of Texas Longhorns." Longhorn Network. <http://www.longhornnetwork.com/family.html> [Accessed August 19, 2002].
25. Sizemore, Deborah Lightfoot.
26. Lightfoot, D. J. "Queries that worked: Successful Query Letters and Synopses." Deborah Lightfoot Sizemore. <http://users2.ev1.net/~djls/myquery.html> [Accessed August 19, 2002].

27. "Maud Smith Marks." Harris County Public Library. <http://www.hcpl.lib.tx.us/branchinfo/mm/mminfo.htm> [Accessed July 10, 2002].

28. Sizemore, Deborah Lightfoot. "LH7 Ranch." The Handbook of Texas Online. <http://www.tshaonline.org/handbook/online/articles/aplts> [Accessed August 04, 2011].

29. Ibid.

30. "Addicks and Barker Reservoirs." U. S. Army. Corps of Engineers. Galveston District.

Chapter 3: Addicks

1. Edwards, Margaret Hopkins. "Addicks, Texas." The Handbook of Texas Online. <http://www.tshaonline.org/handbook/online/articles/hla04> [Accessed August 03, 2011].

2. Beazley, Julia. "Harris, John Richardson." The Handbook of Texas Online. <http://www.tshaonline.org/handbook/online/articles/fha85> [Accessed July 27, 2011].

3. Jones, C. Anson. "Early history of Harris County, Texas." Genealogical Record. Houston. December, 1984. p. 141-144. and March, 1985. p. 17-21.

4. "Valentine Bennet Scrapbook by Miles S. Bennet." McKeehan, Wallace L. Sons of DeWitt Colony Texas. <http://www.tamu.edu/ccbn/dewitt/bennetscrap.htm> [Accessed December 31, 2000].

First Settlers of the Republic of Texas. Volume 1: Headright grants which were reported...January, 1840. Austin: Cruger & Wing, 1841.

5. Solms-Braunfels, Carl, Prince of. Texas 1844 - 1845. Houston: Anson Jones Press, 1936. Page 39.

Ferdinand Roemer. Texas. Houston?: German-Texas Hertiage Society, 1983. Page 73.

Russell, Marie. 1850 Census Harris County, Texas with added genealogical notes. Baytown: n.p., 1981.

6. Sizemore, Deborah Lightfoot. The LH7 Ranch, in Houston's Shadow. The E. H. Marks' Legacy from Longhorns to the Salt Grass Trail. Dennison: University of North Texas Press, n.d.

7. Addicks Site Report. Houston: Museum of Natural Science, 1947.

8. Bivins, Ralph. "Out of the Loop / Local real estate market finds success in small, thrifty, suburban homes." Houston Chronicle, Sunday, 05/07/1995. Section: Business, Page 1, 2 Star Edition.

Feser, Katherine. "Fleetwood is quiet, yet accessible." Houston Chronicle, 10/24/1997. <http://www.chron.com/content/chronicle/business/homedata/f/fleetwood.html> [Accessed December 31, 2001].

9. Feser, Katherine. "Briarhills has wide selection of home styles." Houston Chronicle, 11/03/1996.
<http://www.chron.com/content/chronicle/business/homedata/b/briarh.html> [Accessed December 31, 2001].

10. Feser, Katherine. "Guarded gate gives residents secure feeling." Houston Chronicle, Sunday, 03/16/1997. Section: Business, Page 10, 2 Star Edition.

11. Hill, Steve. "Texas A & M honors Houston's Hershey, Bryan's Blackburn." Texas A & M University. Ag News. <http://agnews.tamu.edu/dailynews/stories/RPTS/hershey.html> [Accessed September 13, 2002].

12. Chandrupatla, Archana. "Hershey Park hike-and-bike trail to lengthen." Houston Chronicle, Wednesday, 08/09/00. This Week Section, Page 1, 2 Star Edition.

13. "The Ant-Hills." West Houston Cycling Club. <http://www.khfweb.com/greg/default.htm> [Accessed November 29, 2000].

14. "Eldridge, William Thomas." The Handbook of Texas Online. <http://www.tshaonline.org/handbook/online/articles/fel33> [Accessed August 03, 2011].

15. Feser, Katherine. "Thornwood's mature feel called 'homey'." Houston Chronicle, Sunday, 04/18/1999. Section: Business, Page 6, 2 Star Edition.

16. Feser, Katherine. "Nottingham Forest drawing young families." Houston Chronicle, Sunday, 07/06/1997. Section: Business, Page 9, 2 Star Edition.

17. Feser, Katherine. "Schools, events attract families to Westchester." Houston Chronicle, 07/31/1994. <http://www.chron.com/content/chronicle/business/homedata/w/westchester.html> [Accessed December 31, 2001].

18. "Growth patterns of Houston and the Katy Prairie." University of Texas. <http://www.utexas.edu/depts/grg/ustudent/gcraft/fall96/ngo/projects/spring97/kprairie/patterns.html> [Accessed December 12, 2001].

19. Hazlewood, Claudia. "Alief, Texas." The Handbook of Texas Online. <http://www.tshaonline.org/handbook/online/articles/hja04> [Accessed August 03, 2011].

20. Kleiner, Diana J. "Satsuma, Texas." The Handbook of Texas Online. <http://www.tshaonline.org/handbook/online/articles/hrs18> [Accessed August 03, 2011].

21. Addicks Site Report. Houston: Museum of Natural Science, 1947.

22. Feser, Katherine. "Ashford South homes attract young families." Houston Chronicle, Sunday, 04/30/2000. Section Business, Page 8, 2 Star Edition.

23. Feser, Katherine. "Nottingham Forest drawing young families." Houston Chronicle, Sunday, 07/06/1997. Section: Business, Page 9, 2 Star Edition.

24. Feser, Katherine. "Lots of options in subdivision built in 70's." Houston Chronicle, Sunday, 09/03/2000. Section Business, Page 10, 2 Star Edition.

25. Zook, Jim. "Homeowners file suit over Kirkwood project." Houston Chronicle, Saturday, 02/22/1992. Section: A, Page 26, 2 Star Edition.

26. Mintz, Bill. "Homeowners hit Memorial road project." Houston Chronicle, Saturday, 04/16/1988. Section: 1, Page 16, 2 Star Edition.

"Buffalo Bayou preservation group plans tour of three sites / River Oaks Garden Club sponsors event." Houston Chronicle, Wednesday, 11/01/2000. Section This Week, Page 3, 2 Star Edition.

27. "Variety of Buffalo Bayou featured on Nov. 12 tour." Houston Chronicle, Saturday, 11/04/2000. Section Houston, Page 6, 2 Star Edition.

28. "Lakeside Country Club - Private." <http://sports.yahoo.com/pga/golfcourses/texas/houston/3706.html> [Accessed September 29, 2000].

"Houston to have first new private, country club community in almost half a century inside city limit." Royal Oaks Country Club. <http://www.royaloakscc.com/newrevs/pressroom/releases/pr051199.html> [Accessed January 4, 2002].

29. Auliff, Lily. "Greener greens." Citizens' Environmental Coalition. <http://www.cechouston.org/newsletter/nl_08-01/greenergreens.html> [Accessed January 4, 2002].

30. Feser, Katherine. "Great values can be found in Nottingham." Houston Chronicle, Sunday, 09/02/2001. Section: Business, Page 6, 2 Star Edition.

"Wilchester and Wilchester West." Houston Chronicle. <http://www.chron.com/content/chronicle/business/homedata/w/wilches.jpg> [Accessed December 31, 2001].

31. Feser, Katherine. "Wilchester skips cycle of decline." Houston Chronicle, Sunday, 12/18/1994. Section Business, Page 8, 2 Star Edition.

Feser, Katherine. "Neighborhoods share it all, and families love it." Houston Chronicle, Sunday, 04/18/2004. Section: Business, Page 6, 2 Star Edition.

32. Feser, Katherine. "Renovations up property values in Gaywood." Houston Chronicle, Sunday, 12/14/1997. Section: Business, Page 12, 2 Star Edition.

33. Feser, Katherine. "Memorial Glen uses outdoors to great effect." Houston Chronicle, Sunday, 06/24/2001. Section D, Page 6, 2 Star Edition.

34. Feser, Katherine. "Memorial Glen uses outdoors to great effect." Houston Chronicle, Sunday, 06/24/2001. Section D, Page 6, 2 Star Edition.

Feser, Katherine. "Rustling Pines sees its share of renovations." Houston Chronicle, Sunday, 01/20/2002. Section: Business, Page 6, 2 Star Edition.

35. Feser, Katherine. "Homeowners enjoy isolation, wooded setting." Houston Chronicle, Sunday, 01/19/2003. Section: Business, Page 6, 2 Star Edition.

Feser, Katherine. "Range of styles, continuity keep Estates on map." Houston Chronicle, Sunday, 02/01/1998. Section: Business, Page 10, 2 Star Edition.

36. Feser, Katherine. "Focusing on family and schools." Houston Chronicle, Sunday, 08/06/1995. Section: Business, Page 6, 2 Star Edition.

37. Vara, Richard. "Down but not out / Membership declining at county's oldest church." Houston Chronicle, Saturday, 10/09/93. Religion Section, Page 1.

38. "Bauer Family." Fayette County Texas Heritage. ?: Curtis Media, Inc., 1996. Pages 26-27.

39. Luthe, William J. "The Story of St. Peter Church, 1848-1948." Journal. Austin: German-Texas Heritage Society. Volume XII, Number 1 (Spring, 1990), Pages 46-50.

40. Tveten, John and Gloria Tveten. "Audubon cabin a state landmark." Houston Chronicle, Friday, 02/14/97. Houston Section, Page 3.

"Moore Log House." Texas Historical Commission. Atlas. <http://atlas.thc.state.tx.us/scripts/>. [Accessed January 12, 2001].

41. Clark, Gary. "Sanctuary provides escape from busy city / Wonders of Nature." Houston Chronicle, Friday, 08/25/00.

Parks, Louis B. "Houston's hidden haven." Houston Chronicle, Thursday, 04/23/87. Weekend Preview Section, Page 1, 2 Star Edition.

42. Feser, Katherine. "Memorial neighborhood sticks together." Houston Chronicle, Sunday, 05/12/1996. Section: Business, Page 10, 2 Star Edition.

43. Feser, Katherine. "Briargrove Park has consistent flavor and value." Houston Chronicle, Sunday, 12/02/2001. Section: D, Page 8, 2 Star Edition.

44. Feser, Katherine. "Houston homes / Million dollar neighborhoods." Houston Chronicle, Sunday, 04/08/2001. Section: Business, Page 9, 2 Star Edition.

45. AAA Street Map of Houston. San Jose, CA: H. M. Gousha Co., 1975.

46. Kleiner, Diana J. "Bunker Hill Village, Texas." The Handbook of Texas Online. <http://www.tshaonline.org/handbook/online/articles/hgb12> [Accessed August 04, 2011].

47. Feser, Katherine. "Bunker Hill Village keeps prestige image." Houston Chronicle, Sunday, 01/21/2001. Section D, Page 8, 2 Star Edition.

48. "Exploring the Works of Frank Lloyd Wright." Sideways.com. <http://www.sideways.com/fllw/thaxton.htm> [Accessed July 26, 2002].

"Texas." All-Wright Site. Frank Lloyd Wright Building Guide. <http://www.geocities.com/SoHo/1469/flw_tx.html> [Accessed July 26, 2002].

49. Feser, Katherine. "Homes offer an alternative to buying new." Houston Chronicle, Sunday, 11/17/1996. Section: Business, Page 10, 2 Star Edition.

50. Feser, Katherine. "Sandalwood elaborately refurbished." Houston Chronicle, Sunday, 12/17/1995. Section Business, Page 6, 2 Star Edition.

51. Leland, Stephen B. Sam Houston Area Council. Boy Scouts of America. Houston, TX. Personal communication to Mark Andrus. February 11, 2002.

Chapter 4: Piney Point

1. Bivins, Ralph. "New investment firm will check out hotels to buy cheap." Houston Chronicle, Sunday, 09/02/2001. Section: D, Page 6, 2 Star Edition.

2. "Station 08074000 Buffalo Bayou at Houston, TX." U. S. Geological Survey. Texas Water Information Home Page. <http://tx.water.usgs.gov/>

3. "Valentine Bennet Scrapbook by Miles S. Bennet." McKeehan, Wallace L. Sons of DeWitt Colony Texas.
<http://www.tamu.edu/ccbn/dewitt/bennetscrap.htm> [Accessed December 31, 2000].

4. Solms-Braunfels, Carl, Prince of. Texas 1844 - 1845. Houston: Anson Jones Press, 1936. Page 39.

5. Peterson, Melissa M. The Road to Piney Point. Piney Point Village, TX: Piney Point Village Historic Committee, 1994. Pages 23-29.

6. Soergel, Alwin H. A Sojourn in Texas, 1846-47. San Marcos, TX: German-Texan Heritage Society, n.d. p.36-39.

7. Sommer, C. von. Bericht ueber meine Reise nach Texas in Jahre 1846. Bremen: Druck und Verlag von Johann Georg Heyse, 1847. Pages 78, 79.

8. Peterson, Melissa M.

9. Ibid.

10. Kleiner, Diana J. "Taylor, John D." The Handbook of Texas Online. <http://www.tshaonline.org/handbook/online/articles/fta21> [Accessed August 04, 2011].

11. Peterson, Melissa M.

12. Ibid.

13. "Houston Morning Star Death Notices, 1844 - ." Marilyn Hoye. <http://files.usgwarchives.org/tx/harris/obits/houobi44.txt> [Accessed August 04, 2011].

14. Peterson, Melissa M.

15. Sommer, C. von.

16. Peterson, Melissa M.

17. "Texas. Harris County. Geneology. Marriages [1837-1847]." Our Lost Family.
<http://www.maxpages.com/ourlostfamily2/Marriages_Part_One> [Accessed January 3, 2001].
Russell, Marie. 1850 Census Harris County, Texas with added genealogical notes. Baytown: n.p., 1981.

18. Peterson, Melissa M.

19. Ibid.

20. Ibid.

21. Ibid.

22. Kleiner, Diana J. "Piney Point Village, Texas." The Handbook of Texas Online. <http://www.tshaonline.org/handbook/online/articles/hgp06> [Accessed August 04, 2011].

23. Ibid.

24. Feser, Katherine. "Piney Point richest town in all of Texas." Houston Chronicle, Sunday, 05/05/2002. Section: Business, Page 9D, 2 Star Edition.

25. Feser, Katherine. "Young couples are flocking to old subdivision." Houston Chronicle, Sunday, 07/22/2001. Section: Business, Page 8, 2 Star Edition.

26. Feser, Katherine. "Renovations all the rage in Charnwood." Houston Chronicle, Sunday, 01/17/1999. Section: Business, Page 6, 2 Star Edition.

27. Santangelo, Susan H. "Kinkaid School." The Handbook of Texas Online. <http://www.tshaonline.org/handbook/online/articles/kbk05> [Accessed August 04, 2011].

28. Huber, Kathy. "Kinkaid Garden redefines open classroom concept / Natural resources." Houston Chronicle, Saturday, 10/13/2001. Section: Houston, Page 1, 2 Star Edition.

29. Rich, Jan. "City makes state's 'best, worst' water polluters list." Houston Chronicle, Friday, 11/15/1985. Section: 1, Page 1, 3 Star Edition.

30. Zuniga, Jo Ann. "Water commission 'forgave' authority's penalties." Houston Chronicle, Friday, 06/24/1988. Section: 1, Page 18, 2 Star Edition.

31. Tutt, Bob. "Storms hasten erosion along Buffalo Bayou." Houston Chronicle, Sunday, 06/27/1993. Section: C, Page 1, 2 Star Edition.

32. "Regatta makes waves on Saturday." Houston Chronicle, Friday, 04/06/1990. Section: Weekend Preview, Page 1, 2 Star Edition.

33. Parks, Louis B. "Make waves with regatta competitions." Houston Chronicle, Friday, 05/21/1993. Section: Weekend Preview, Page 1, 2 Star Edition.

34. Evans, Everett. "Make waves with fun times on the bayou." Houston Chronicle, Thursday, 05/02/2002. Section: Preview, Page 15, 2 Star Edition.

35. "Hunters Creek Village, Texas." The Handbook of Texas Online. <http://www.tsha.utexas.edu/handbook/online/articles/> [Accessed January 31, 2000].

36. Feser, Katherine. "Close in, but with room to roam." Houston Chronicle, Sunday, 04/16/1995. Section: Business, Page 6, 2 Star Edition.

37. "From our files. October 29, 1901." Houston Chronicle, 04/06/2001. <http://www.chron.com/cs/CDA/story.hts/first100/1900/869533> [Accessed November 11, 2001].

Houston, A History and A Guide. Houston: Anson Jones Press, 1942. Page 219.

38. Johnston, Marguarite. Houston, The Unknown City, 1836-1946. College Station: Texas A & M University Press, 1991. Page 141.

39. "Houston Country Club." Houston City Search. <http://houston.citysearch.com/> [Accessed January 4, 2002].

40. Houghton, Dorothy K. H. Houston's Forgotten Heritage. Houston: Rice University Press, 1991. Page 293.

41. Feser, Katherine. "Tanglewood's tale had a slow start." Houston Chronicle, Sunday, 10/02/1994. Section: Business, Page 6, 2 Star Edition.

42. Williams, John. "Council balks at giving cash to settle suit." Houston Chronicle, Thursday, 05/14/1992. Section: A, Page 27, 2 Star Edition.

43. Sophie Network. Network of Sacred Heart Schools. <http://www.sofie.org/SOFIEfiles/network/Network.htm> [Accessed November 11, 2001].

"General Information." Duchesne Academy of the Sacred Heart. <http://www.duchesne.org/> [Accessed November 5, 2001].

44. Kientz, Renee. "Memories spring from historic community." Houston Chronicle, Sunday, 08/08/99. Lifestyle Section, Page 4, 2 Star Edition.

Kleiner, Diana J. "Spring Branch, Texas." The Handbook of Texas Online. <http://www.tshaonline.org/handbook/online/articles/hrsrj> [Accessed August 04, 2011].

Hornburg, David. Personal communication, February 3, 2008.

45. "Vehlein, Joseph." The Handbook of Texas Online. <http://www.tshaonline.org/handbook/online/articles/fve03> [Accessed August 04, 2011].

46. "Bauer Family." Fayette County Texas Heritage. ?: Curtis Media, Inc., 1996. Pages 26-27.

47. Luthe, William J. "The Story of St. Peter Church, 1848-1948." Journal. Austin: German-Texas Heritage Society. Volume XII, Number 1 (Spring, 1990), Pages 46-50.

48. Ibid.

49. "Early Texas German Churches." Journal. Austin: German-Texas Heritage Society. Volume X, Number 1 (Spring, 1988), Pages 69ff.

50. Kientz, Renee. "Memories spring from historic community."

51. Luthe, William J.

52. Ibid.

53. Vara, Richard. "Down but not out / Membership declining at county's oldest church." Houston Chronicle, Saturday, 10/09/93. Religion Section, Page 1.

Luthe, William J.

54. Kientz, Renee. "Memories spring from historic community."
Luthe, William J.

55. Ibid.

56. Houston, A History and A Guide. Page 188.

57. Brunsman, Steve. "145-year old German church celebrates proud heritage, Spring Branch group traces roots to 1848." Houston Post, Saturday, 10/09/93. Local Section, Page E2, Final Edition.

58. "Bauer Family."

59. Luthe, William J.

60. Russell, Marie. 1850 Census Harris County, Texas.

61. Kientz, Renee. "Once upon a time / Tiny cemetery on busy Long Point last trace of Hillendahl family farm." Houston Chronicle, Sunday, 08/08/99. Lifestyle Section, Page 1, 2 Star Edition.

62. Ibid.

63. Freedenthal, Stacey. "Parking lot's family plot / Strip shopping centers grew up around old graveyard, but relatives want it to stay put." Houston Chronicle, Monday, 06/15/97. Section 1, Page 10, 2 Star Edition.

64. Kientz, Renee. "Memories spring from historic community."

65. González, Aníbal A. "St. Mary's Seminary." The Handbook of Texas Online. <http://www.tshaonline.org/handbook/online/articles/kbs63> [Accessed August 05, 2011].

66. Chapman, Betty T. "Architectural gems of Briscoe, Sullivan cover local landscape." Houston Business Journal, October 27-November 2, 2000.

67. "Old Road Maps of Houston." Texas Freeway. <http://www.texasfreeway.com/historic/road_maps/houston_road_maps.shtml> [Accessed February 19, 2002].

68. Authentic Road Guide of Harris County. 1916.

69. Bivins, Ralph. "Twenty is plenty at luxury condo project." Houston Chronicle, Saturday, 09/01/2001. Section: C, Page 1, 3 Star Edition.

70. Sallee, Rad. "Happy Trails / Nature has help taking its course." Houston Chronicle, Saturday, 04/09/2005. Section: 1, Page 3, 3 Star Edition.

71. Tyre, Brad. Personal communication, 5/31/2002.

72. Bivins, Ralph. "Surrounded by developments, Sacks finally sells house." Houston Chronicle, Saturday, 03/18/2001. Section D, Page 8, 2 Star Edition.

73. Miller, Ray. Ray Miller's Houston. Houston: Cordovan Press, 1984. Page 192.

74. Sallee, Rad. "Park's tiny land swap a big deal." Houston Chronicle, Saturday, 03/09/2002. Section: A, Page 33, 3 Star Edition.

75. "Buffalo Bayou Loop." World Nature Trails. <http://www.worldnaturetrails.com/birding_trails/buffalo_bayou_loop.htm> [Accessed August 7, 2001].

76. "Houston Arboretum and Nature Center." Texas Hiker. <http://www.texashiker.com/Houston_Arboretum_&_Nature_Center.html> [Accessed November 28, 2002].

77. "Trees of Central Texas by Robert A. Vines." UT Press. University of Texas. <http://www.utexas.edu/utpress/books/vincep.html> [Accessed November 28, 2002].
Emmott, Sarah H. Memorial Park, a priceless legacy. Houston: Herring Press, 1992. Pages 9-11.

78. "Buffalo Bayou Loop." World Nature Trails.

79. "Nature Center to dedicate birding walkway." Houston Chronicle, Wednesday, 11/08/00. This Week Section, Page 2, 2 Star Edition.

80. "Houston Heights, 1922. 7.5 Minute Quadrqangle." U. S. Geological Survey. Topographic Maps.

81. "Houston Railroads, 1997." Houston Rail Fan. <http://houston.railfan.net/map.html> [Accessed January 7, 2002].

Chapter 5: Memorial Park

1. Emmott, Sarah H. Memorial Park, a priceless legacy. Houston: Herring Press, 1992. Pages 9-11.

Henson, Margaret Swett. "Long, Jane Herbert Wilkinson." The Handbook of Texas Online. <http://www.tshaonline.org/handbook/online/articles/flo11> [Accessed August 05, 2011].

2. Glass, James L. Replica Chart of the Galveston-Houston Area circa 1836. Houston: Kelvin Press, 1986.

3. Emmott, Sarah H.

4. Ibid.

"Von Roeder, Ludwig." San Jacinto Museum. <http://www.sanjacinto-museum.org/ Herzstein_Library/Veteran_Biographies/San_Jacinto_Bios/biographies/ default.asp?action=bio&id=3540> [Accessed August 05, 2011].

5. Emmott, Sarah H.

"'Oldest House' well preserved; built in early 30's by John Reinermann." Houston Chronicle, Wednesday, 08/04/1915.

6. "Texas. Harris County. Geneology. Marriages [1837-1847]." Our Lost Family. <http://www.maxpages.com/ourlostfamily2/Marriages_Part_One> [Accessed January 3, 2001].

Russell, Marie. 1850 Census Harris County, Texas with added genealogical notes. Baytown: n.p., 1981.

7. Emmott, Sarah H.

Moore, Roger G., William E. Moore and David S. Pettus. An Archeological Survey of Nine Land Units Within Memorial Park in Houston (Harris County), Texas. Houston: Moore Archeological Consulting, 1989.

8. Quesnell, Carl Wilhelm Adolph, 1829 - 1890. From tyranny to Texas (A German Pioneer in Harris County). San Antonio, TX: Naylor, 1975. Pages 60-61.

Emmott, Sarah H.

9. Ibid.

Moore, Roger G., William E. Moore and David S. Pettus.

Quesnell, Carl Wilhelm Adolph.

10. "'Oldest House' well preserved; built in early 30's by John Reinermann."

Mercer, Linda. Personal communication, August 22, 2005.

11. Wood, W. E. City of Houston, Harris County, Texas [map]. Houston, 1869.

Koch, Augustus (1840 - ?). Bird's Eye View of the City of Houston, Texas 1873. Madison, WI: J. J. Stoner, 1873.

Westyard, A. L. (attributed). Houston, Texas (Looking South) [Bird's Eye] 1891. Chicago: D. W. Ensign, Jr., 1891.

12. Miller, Ray. Ray Miller's Houston. Houston: Cordovan Press, 1984. Page 129.

13. Johnston, Marguarite. Houston, The Unknown City, 1836-1946. College Station: Texas A & M University Press, 1991. Pages 240, 256.

14. Emmott, Sarah H.

15. Miller, Ray. Page 221.

16. Wall, Lucas. "Squabble over urban gem. Nature-lovers, recreationists clash on Memorial Park use." Houston Chronicle, Sunday, 09/15/2002. Section: A, Page 37, 4 Star Edition.

17. Tuley, Aaron. "Presentation of Buffalo Bayou Master Plan to Houston Canoe Club meeting, 7/10/2002." Buffalo Bayou Partnership. Houston, TX.

18. Sallee, Rad. "Happy Trails / Nature has help taking its course." Houston Chronicle, Saturday, 04/09/2005. Section: 1, Page 3, 3 Star Edition.

19. Miller, Ray. Page 129.

20. "From our files. April 2, 1936." Houston Chronicle, 01/09/2001. <http://www.chron.com/cs/CDA/story.hts/first100/1930/790669> [Accessed November 12, 2001].

"University of Houston History - A Timeline." Library. University of Houston. <http://info.lib.uh.edu/speccoll/finding/uhtime.html> [Accessed December 20, 2002].

Johnston, Marguarite. Page 309.

21. Wall, Lucas.

22. Memorial Park Golf Course. Houston City Search. <http://houston.citysearch.com/> [Accessed January 4, 2002].

23. Memorial Park Golf Course. Official Web Site, City of Houston. <http://www.ci.houston.tx.us/municipalgolf/memorial/> [Accessed December 9, 2002].

24. Memorial Park Golf Course. Houston City Search.

25. Memorial Park Golf Course. Official Web Site, City of Houston.

26. Auliff, Lily. "Greener greens." Citizens' Environmental Coalition. <http://www.cechouston.org/newsletter/nl_08-01/greenergreens.html> [Accessed January 4, 2002].

27. Auliff, Lily.

28. Moore, Roger G., William E. Moore and David S. Pettus.

Hazlewood, Claudia. "Camp Logan." The Handbook of Texas Online. <http://www.tshaonline.org/handbook/online/articles/qcc26> [Accessed August 05, 2011].

29. Moore, Roger G., William E. Moore and David S. Pettus.

30. Ibid.

"World War I Story of Cpl. Paul B. Hendrickson." JimGill.net <http://www.jimgill.net/gill/wwipages/index.html> [Accessed May 23, 2008].

31. Moore, Roger G., William E. Moore and David S. Pettus.

32. Ibid.

33. Ibid.

34. Ibid.

35. Ibid.

36. Haynes, Robert V. "Houston Riot of 1917." The Handbook of Texas Online. <http://www.tshaonline.org/handbook/online/articles/jch04> [Accessed August 05, 2011].

37. Ibid.

38. "History." 33rd Infantry Division Association, Inc. <http://www.33rdinfantrydivision.org/history.htm> [Accessed August 05, 2011].

Rinaldi, Richard A. The United States Army in World War I, Orders of Battle. [n. p.: Tiger Lily Publications, 2004.]

39. Houston, A History and A Guide. Houston: Anson Jones Press, 1942. Page 326.

Moore, Roger G., William E. Moore and David S. Pettus.

40. Johnston, Marguarite. Pages 234, 416 #1, 235, 257, 418.

41. "Clayton, William L., Summer House." Texas Historical Commission. Atlas. <http://atlas.thc.state.tx.us/scripts/>. [Accessed January 12, 2001].

42. Kleiner, Diana J. "River Oaks, Houston." The Handbook of Texas Online. <http://www.tshaonline.org/handbook/online/articles/hpr01> [Accessed August 05, 2011].

43. River Oaks Country Club. Houston City Search. <http://houston.citysearch.com/> [Accessed January 4, 2002].

"Houston: The top private courses." Houston Chronicle. Golf Guide 2001. <http://www.chron.com/cs/CDA/story.hts/sports/glf/guide01/849818> [Accessed January 4, 2002].

44. Auliff, Lily.

45. Scott, La Quencis Gibbs. "Reynolds, Allen C." The Handbook of Texas Online. <http://www.tshaonline.org/handbook/online/articles/frels> [Accessed August 05, 2011].

46. Ibid.

47. Ibid.

48. Schooler, Lionel M. "Westheimer, Mitchell Louis (1831-ca. 1906)." The Handbook of Texas Online. <http://www.tshaonline.org/handbook/online/articles/fwets> [Accessed August 05, 2011].

49. Ibid.

50. Johnston, Marguarite. Page 227.

51. Price, Gary. "Ball, Thomas Henry [1859-1944]." The Handbook of Texas Online. <http://www.tshaonline.org/handbook/online/articles/fba48> [Accessed August 05, 2011].

52. Kleiner, Diana J. "River Oaks, Houston."

53. "History of Bayou Bend." About Bayou Bend. University of Houston. <http://www.bayoubend.uh.edu/about/history.html> [Accessed January 4, 2003].

54. Kleiner, Diana J. "River Oaks, Houston."

55. Houghton, Dorothy K. H. Houston's Forgotten Heritage. Houston: Rice University Press, 1991. Page 158

56. Kleiner, Diana J. "River Oaks, Houston."

57. Chapman, Betty T. "Architectural gems of Briscoe, Sullivan cover local landscape." Houston Business Journal, October 27-November 2, 2000.

"Clayton, William L., Summer House." Texas Historical Commission. Atlas. http://atlas.thc.state.tx.us/scripts/>. [Accessed January 12, 2001].

58. Ibid.

59. "Sewall, Cleveland Harding House." Texas Historical Commission. Atlas. <http://atlas.thc.state.tx.us/scripts/> [Accessed January 12, 2001].

60. Ibid.

61. Fox, Stephen. "Bayou Bend." The Handbook of Texas Online. <http://www.tshaonline.org/handbook/online/articles/lbb01> [Accessed August 06, 2011].

62. Johnston, Marguarite. Page 256.

63. Houston, A History and A Guide. Pages 121-122.

Feser, Katherine. "Thriving in shadows of River Oaks." Houston Chronicle, Sunday, 03/12/1995. Section Business, Page 6, 2 Star Edition.

Kleiner, Diana J. "River Oaks, Houston."

64. Tutt, Bob. "Storms hasten erosion along Buffalo Bayou." Houston Chronicle, Sunday, 06/27/1993. Section: C, Page 1, 2 Star Edition.

65. Urban, Jerry. "Group opposes plan for upscale housing." Houston Chronicle, Thursday, 06/18/1992. Section: A, Page 36, 2 Star Edition.

Oeser, Michael D. "Crestwood Acres loses battle with city planners." Houston Chronicle, Friday, 06/19/1992. Section: A, Page 28, 4 Star Edition.

66. Bivins, Ralph. "Inner Loop projects slated / Land for homes becoming scarce inside 610." Houston Chronicle, Sunday, 03/04/1990. Section: Business, Page 6, 2 Star Edition.

67. Feser, Katherine. "City evolution, history shown in Glen Cove." Houston Chronicle, Sunday, 10/07/2001. Section: D, Page 6, 2 Star Edition.

68. Memorial Cove Lofts. <http://www.memorialcovelofts.com> [Accessed December 26, 2002].

69. Fox, Stephen. "Bayou Bend." The Handbook of Texas Online. <http://www.tshaonline.org/handbook/online/articles/lbb01> [Accessed August 09, 2011].

70. "Life of Ima Hogg: Her Legacy." The Collectors. College of Education. University of Houston. <http://www.fm.coe.uh.edu/comparisons/ima4a.html> [Accessed August 09, 2011].

71. Cotner, Robert C. "Hogg, James Stephen." The Handbook of Texas Online. <http://www.tshaonline.org/handbook/online/articles/fho17> [Accessed August 09, 2011].

72. "James Hogg's Ancestry - recent information." The Hogg Family. <http://members.fortunecity.com/gadevilgrl/hogg/id13.html> [Accessed January 3, 2003].

73. Cotner, Robert C. "Hogg, James Stephen."
"Life of Ima Hogg: Her Legacy."

74. Cotner, Robert C. "Hogg, James Stephen."
Lefevre, Arthur, Jr. "Hogg, William Clifford." The Handbook of Texas Online. <http://www.tshaonline.org/handbook/online/articles/fho20> [Accessed August 09, 2011].

75. Ibid.

76. Ibid.
"Life of Ima Hogg: Her Legacy."

77. Lefevre, Arthur, Jr. "Hogg, William Clifford."

78. "Life of Ima Hogg: Her Legacy."

79. Bernhard, Virginia. "Hogg, Ima (1882 - 1975)." The Handbook of Texas Online. <http://www.tshaonline.org/handbook/online/articles/fho16> [Accessed August 09, 2011].

80. Ibid.

81. Fox, Stephen. "Bayou Bend."

82. Bernhard, Virginia. "Hogg, Ima (1882 - 1975)."

83. Lefevre, Arthur, Jr. "Hogg, William Clifford."

84. Ibid.
Holtzman, Wayne H. "Hogg Foundation for Mental Health." The Handbook of Texas Online. <http://www.tshaonline.org/handbook/online/articles/vrh01> [Accessed August 09, 2011].

85. Long, Christopher. "Jim Hogg State Historical Park." The Handbook of Texas Online.
<http://www.tshaonline.org/handbook/online/articles/gkj02> [Accessed August 09, 2011].

86. "History of Bayou Bend." About Bayou Bend. University of Houston. <http://atlantis.coe.uh.edu/webscapes/bayoubend/about/history.htm> [Accessed August 09, 2011].
"Frederic Remington: The Hogg Brothers Collection of the Museum of Fine Arts, Houston." Princeton University Press. Princeton University. <http://www.pup.princeton.edu/titles/6791.html> [Accessed January 5, 2003].

87. "History of Bayou Bend."

88. Ibid.

89. Fox, Stephen. "Bayou Bend."

90. Bernhard, Virginia. "Hogg, Ima (1882 - 1975)."

91. "Life of Ima Hogg: Her Legacy."

92. "History of Bayou Bend."

93. Ibid.

94. Ibid.

95. Ibid.

96. "Bayou Bend. Collection and Gardens." Houston: Houston Museum of Fine Arts.
"History of Bayou Bend."

97. "History of Bayou Bend."

98. Ibid.

99. "Life of Ima Hogg: Her Legacy."

100. "Bayou Bend. Collection and Gardens."

"History of Bayou Bend."

101. "Winedale Historical Center: An inventory of the collection, 1961-1993." Library. University of Texas. <http://www.lib.utexas.edu/taro/utaaa/00086/aaa-00086.html> [Accessed August 09, 2011].

102. "History of Bayou Bend."

103. Ibid.

104. Ibid.

105. Ibid.

106. Ibid.

107. Ibid.

108. Sheridan, Mike. "More than 200 condos posted for foreclosure." Houston Chronicle, Thursday, 10/15/1987. Section: Business, Page 1, 2 Star Edition.

109. Fox, Stephen. "Briscoe, Birdsall Parmenas." The Handbook of Texas Online. <http://www.tshaonline.org/handbook/online/articles/fbrbw> [Accessed August 09, 2011].

110. Ibid.

111. "Clayton, William L., Summer House." Texas Historical Commission.

112. Chapman, Betty T. "Architectural gems of Briscoe, Sullivan cover local landscape." Fox, Stephen. "Bayou Bend."

Fox, Stephen. "Briscoe, Birdsall Parmenas."

113. Rainbow Lodge. <http://www.rainbow-lodge.com/> [Accessed December 23, 2002].

114. "History." Rainbow Lodge. <http://www.rainbow-lodge.com/History.asp> [Accessed August 09, 2011].

115. Emmott, Sarah H. Memorial Park, a priceless legacy.

116. Zheng, Chunhua Zen. "Proposed retail strip center springs woman into action." Houston Chronicle, Thursday, 09/13/2001. Section: This Week, Page 32, 2 Star Edition.

117. Sarnoff, Nancy. "Land sale squeezes out longtime restaurant." Houston Business Journal, July 13-19, 2001. Page 1.

118. Huber, Kathy. "Garden Design / Masterson's touch in Rienzi's gardens." Houston Chronicle, Sunday, 02/21/1999. Section Texas Magazine, Page 4, 2 Star Edition.

Huber, Kathy. "Azalea Trail preparations herald annual rite of spring." Houston Chronicle, Saturday, 02/24/2001. Section D, Page 1, 2 Star Edition.

119. Huber, Kathy. "Garden Design / Masterson's touch in Rienzi's gardens."

120. "Newest star in Houston's galaxy of museums." Kaleden. <http://www.kaleden.com> [Accessed February 16, 2003].

"Rienzi." MFAH Destinations. Houston Museum of Fine Arts. <http://www.mfah.org/> [Accessed December 19, 2002].

121. "Newest star in Houston's galaxy of museums." Kaleden.

122. Huber, Kathy. "Garden Design / Masterson's touch in Rienzi's gardens."

123. "Newest star in Houston's galaxy of museums." Kaleden.

Huber, Kathy. "Garden Design / Masterson's touch in Rienzi's gardens."

124. "Newest star in Houston's galaxy of museums." Kaleden.

125. "Buffalo Bayou preservation group plans tour of three sites / River Oaks Garden Club sponsors event." Houston Chronicle, Wednesday, 11/01/2000. Section This Week, Page 3, 2 Star Edition.

126. Sarnoff, Nancy. "Land sale squeezes out longtime restaurant."

127. Freemantle, Tony. "Carl Detering, 96; prominent builder." Houston Chronicle, Friday, 05/11/2001. Section: Metro, Page 44, 3 Star Edition.

128. Ibid.

"About our company." Detering Company. <http://www.detering.com/> [Accessed January 3, 2003].

129. Karbari, Barbara. "House of history." Houston Chronicle, Sunday, 06/30/2002. Section: E, Page 2, 2 Star Edition.

Beazley, Julia and Eldon S. Branda. "Groce, Leonard Waller." The Handbook of Texas Online. <http://www.tshaonline.org/handbook/online/articles/fgr71> [Accessed August 09, 2011].

130. Karbari, Barbara. "House of history."

131. Ibid.

132. "History." Liendo Plantation. <http://www.liendo.org/plantation.html> [Accessed August 09, 2011].

133. "Clear Creek (Waller County)." The Handbook of Texas Online. <http://www.tshaonline.org/handbook/online/articles/rbcfj> [Accessed August 09, 2011].

Karbari, Barbara. "House of history."

134. Beazley, Julia. "Liendo Plantation." The Handbook of Texas Online. <http://www.tshaonline.org/handbook/online/articles/ccl01> [Accessed August 09, 2011].

135. Cutrer, Emily F. "Ney, Elisabet." The Handbook of Texas Online. <http://www.tshaonline.org/handbook/online/articles/fne26> [Accessed August 09, 2011].

136. Ibid.

137. Beazley, Julia. "Liendo Plantation."

138. Ibid.

"History." Liendo Plantation.

139. Huynh, Dai. "Homespun hospitality enlivens Liendo's Restaurant." Houston Chronicle, 11/09/2001. <http://www.chron.com/cs/CDA/story.hts/dining/1123960> [Accessed November 9, 2001].

140. "History." Liendo Plantation.

141. Bivins, Ralph. "Real Estate: Old bayou apartments to be a stormy memory." Houston Chronicle, Sunday, 08/03/2003. Section: Business, Page 6, 2 Star Edition.

142. "Historic Neighborhood Council, April 2003." Greater Houston Preservation Alliance.

Feser, Katherine. "Rice Military an eclectic 'urban center'." Houston Chronicle, Sunday, 01/12/2003. Section: Business, Page 6, 2 Star Edition.

143. Feser, Katherine. "Rice Military an eclectic 'urban center'."

144. Lezon, Dale. "Mary Milkovisch, co-creator of Houston's Beer Can House." Houston Chronicle, Thursday, 03/21/2002. Section: A, Page 35, 3 Star Edition.

145. Ibid.

146. Sloan, Anne. Personal communication. Feb 23, 2003.

147. Feser, Katherine. "Rice Military an eclectic 'urban center'."

148. Byars, Carlos. "Who says there's no life in Buffalo Bayou." Houston Chronicle, Sunday, 07/24/1988. Section: Texas Magazine, Page 6, 2 Star Edition.

"HPARD Land Inventory, 3-5-08." Parks and Recreation Department. City of Houston. <http://www.houstontx.gov/parks/pdfs/inventory.pdf/> [Accessed January 5, 2009].

149. Thompson, Tommy. "Homeplace quietly builds quality." Houston Chronicle, Sunday, 10/19/1986. Section: Business, Page 10, 2 Star Edition.

150. Houston, A History and A Guide. Page 330.

151. Kleiner, Diana J. "DePelchin, Kezia Payne." The Handbook of Texas Online. <http://www.tshaonline.org/handbook/online/articles/fdekt> [Accessed August 09, 2011].

152. Ibid.

153. Ibid.

Houston City Directory, 1866. Dallas: R. L. Polk & Co, 1866.

154. Kleiner, Diana J. "Bayland Orpahns' Home for Boys." The Handbook of Texas Online. <http://www.tshaonline.org/handbook/online/articles/ynb01> [Accessed August 09, 2011].

155. DePelchin Children's Center. <http://www.depelchin.org/history.html> [Accessed January 3, 2003].

156. Bivins, Ralph. "Historic building purchased." Houston Chronicle, Saturday, 09/22/2001. Section: C, Page 1, 2 Star Edition.

157. Johnston, Marguarite. Page 100.

158. DePelchin Children's Center.

159. Bivins, Ralph. "Historic building purchased."
Sarnoff, Nancy. "No place like home: Old Midtown orphanage to undergo conversion." Houston Business Journal, September 21-27, 2001. Page 12.

160. Johnston, Marguarite. Pages 286, 304.
DePelchin Children's Center.

161. Kleiner, Diana J. "DePelchin, Kezia Payne."

162. DePelchin Children's Center.

163. Davis, Burton. "Houston history recalled by opening of new modern bridge at 'Shepherd's Dam'." Galveston Daily News, November 5, 1922. Page 3.
"Harris County 1870 Census Page." Rootsweb.com <http://www.rootsweb.com/~txharri2/harcen.html>. [Accessed January 7, 2002].
Houston City Directory, 1866.

164. Davis, Burton. "Houston history recalled by opening of new modern bridge at 'Shepherd's Dam'."

165. "City of Houston, Texas." Houston Title & Guaranty Co., 1917.
Ziegler, Jesse A. Wave of the Gulf. San Antonio: Naylor Co., 1938. Page 135.

166. Davis, Burton. "Houston history recalled by opening of new modern bridge at 'Shepherd's Dam'."

167. Ziegler, Jesse A. Page 135.

168. Davis, Burton. "Houston history recalled by opening of new modern bridge at 'Shepherd's Dam'."
Houston Street Guide. n.p.: J. M. Kelsen, 1913.

169. Ziegler, Jesse A. Page 135.
Davis, Burton. "Houston history recalled by opening of new modern bridge at 'Shepherd's Dam'."

170. Armstrong. Robert M. Sugar Land Texas and the Imperial Sugar Company. Sugar Land, TX: R. M. Armstrong, 1991.

171. Brazos River Authority. <http://www.brazos.org/ORGANIZATION/history.htm> [Accessed May 19, 2003].

172. Houston Street Guide. n.p.: J. M. Kelsen, 1913.

173. "Map of Houston, Texas." Fantham & Fantham, [March, 1928].

174. Ashburn, J. Foster. Ashburn's Map of Houston, Texas. 1942.

175. "Humble Oil Roadmap, 1952". Old Road Maps of Houston. Texas Freeway. <http://www.texasfreeway.com/> [Accessed Mon January 5, 2004].

176. Hinton, Marks and Aaron Howard." The colorful stories behind Houston's historic street names." Inside Houston Magazine. <http://www.insidehoustonmag.com/feature/> [Accessed January 8, 2002].

177. "Shepherd History." City of Shepherd, Texas. <http://www.shepherdtx.org/cityofshepherd/history.htm> [Accessed March 30, 2002].
Ziegler, Jesse A. Page 291.

178. Ibid. Page 292.

179. Hinton, Marks and Aaron Howard.

Potter, Charline. Houston and the surrounding area. Curriculum Bulletin Number 58CBM34. Houston: Houston Public Schools, 1958.

"Benjamin A. Shepherd to A. W. Noble, January 29, 1851." Deed Records. Harris County, Texas. Vol. O, Page 425.

180. Russell, Marie. 1850 Census Harris County, Texas with added genealogical notes.

181. Ziegler, Jesse A. Page 293.

182. "Census Images on CD. The 1860 Harris County, Texas, Census Images." Rootsweb.com <http://www.rootsweb.com/~usgenweb/tx/harris/census/1860/0000read.html>. [Accessed June 6, 2001].

183. Ziegler, Jesse A. Page 293.

184. Ibid.

185. Ibid. Page 293-294.

186. "Eureka Manufacturing Company." Texas Historical Commission. Atlas. <http://atlas.thc.state.tx.us/scripts/>. [Accessed December 2, 2000].

187. Ziegler, Jesse A. Page 294.

188. Rust, Carol. "How Buffalo Speedway got its name ... and other street stories." Houston Chronicle, Sunday, 03/02/97. Lifestyle Section, Page 1, 2 Star Edition.

Houston, A History and A Guide. Page 259.

189. Houston City Directory, 1866.

"Harris County 1870 Census Page." Rootsweb.com.

190. Wooster, Robert. "Shepherd, Texas" The Handbook of Texas Online. <http://www.tshaonline.org/handbook/online/articles/hjs14> [Accessed August 10, 2011].

"Landmarks and Monuments. Old Houston. "Houston History. <http://www.houstonhistory.com/preservation/landmarks/history9a.htm> [Accessed August 10, 2011].

191. Ziegler, Jesse A. Page 295.

"Dollars for the Endowment. A Grave Tradition of Fundraising." Rice University. Library. Friends of Fondren Library. <http://ruf.rice.edu/~fofl/Flyleaf47.3/glenwood.html> [Accessed January 26, 2002].

192. Smith, Gary. "Shepherd School: Making Music Central to Learning." Rice University. Shaping a Century: Essays by Rice Deans. <http://www.ruf.rice.edu/~opa/shaping_a_century/shaping_a_century12.html> [Accessed March 30, 2002].

193. "City of Houston, Texas." Houston Title & Guaranty Co., 1917.

194. Johnston, Marguarite. Pages 418 note 8.

195. "Peak Streamflow for Texas. USGS 08074000 Buffalo Bayou at Houston, TX." <http://nwis.waterdata.usgs.gov/tx/nwis/peak?search_site_no=08074000> [Accessed August 10, 2011].

196. "Station 08074000 Buffalo Bayou at Houston, TX." U. S. Geological Survey. Texas Water Information Home Page. <http://tx.water.usgs.gov/> [Accessed August 9, 2002].

197. "Hugh Potter's and the Hogg Brothers' River Oaks." River Oaks Property Owners. Inc. <http://www.ropo.org/neighbor.html> [Accessed August 10, 2011].

198. Winningham, Geoff. "Photographer traces Buffalo Bayou history, character." Houston Chronicle, Sunday, 02/09/2003. Section: Texas Magazine, Page 1.

199. "Historic Photos of the Houston Area." Texas Freeway. <http://www.texasfreeway.com/houston/historic/photos/houston_historic_photos.shtml> [Accessed February 9, 2003].

200. Squyres, Roland E. Personal communication. February 5, 2002.

201. "Clean Rivers." Houston-Galveston Area Council. <http://www.hgac.cog.tx.us/resources/crp/watersheds.html> [Accessed August 1, 2002].

202. Chapman, Betty T. "Female physician put Houston on map in fight against disease." Houston Business Journal, October 26-November 1, 2001. Page 27.

203. "General correspondence: Tuberculosis Hospital." Houston: City of Houston Treasury Department, 1945.

204. Ibid.

"Houston, 1924-1948. Volume 5, Sheet 501." Sanborn maps, 1867-1970: Texas. [Ann Arbor, Mich.] : Bell & Howell Information and Learning, c2001.

205. "Guide to the James Lockhart Autry papers, 1834-1922." Texas Archival Resources Online. Library. University of Texas. <http://www.lib.utexas.edu/taro/ricewrc/00002/rice-00002.html> [Accessed August 10, 2011].

206. "General correspondence: Tuberculosis Hospital."

207. "Houston, 1924-1948. Volume 5, Sheet 501." Sanborn maps, 1867-1970: Texas.

208. Chapman, Betty T. "Female physician put Houston on map in fight against disease."
"Houston, 1924-1948. Volume 5, Sheet 501." Sanborn maps, 1867-1970: Texas.

209. "Houston, 1924-1948. Volume 5, Sheet 501." Sanborn maps, 1867-1970: Texas.

210. "General correspondence: Tuberculosis Hospital."

211. Chapman, Betty T. "Female physician put Houston on map in fight against disease."
"Houston/Harris County TB Cases at 26-Year Low". Texas Medical Center News, Vol. 22, No. 6 (April 1, 2000).

212. "General correspondence: Tuberculosis Hospital."

213. Horswell, Cindy. "Military cuts threaten Houston's air defense." Houston Chronicle, Monday, 04/21/2003. Section: A, Page 1, 3 Star Edition.

214. Ibid.

215. Ibid.

216. "General correspondence: Tuberculosis Hospital."

217. Center Serving Persons with Mental Retardation. <http://www.cri-usa.org/> [Accessed July 28, 2003].

218. Feldman, Claudia. "Mending chairs - and lives / Cullen Caners take pride in their accomplishments." Houston Chronicle, Thursday, 07/03/2003. Section: Houston, Page 1, 2 Star Edition.

219. Lamb, R. E., C.S.B. "St. Thomas High School." The Handbook of Texas Online. <http://www.tshaonline.org/handbook/online/articles/kbs60> [Accessed August 10, 2011].

220. "St. Thomas High School." Texas Historical Commission. Atlas. <http://atlas.thc.state.tx.us/scripts/> [Accessed January 12, 2002].
Lamb, R. E., C.S.B. "Basilian Fathers." The Handbook of Texas Online. <http://www.tshaonline.org/handbook/online/articles/ixb03> [Accessed August 10, 2011].

221. Houston, A History and A Guide. Page 329.

222. "St. Thomas High School." Texas Historical Commission. Atlas.

223. Houston, A History and A Guide. Page 329.

224. Ibid. Page 330.
"St. Thomas High School." Texas Historical Commission. Atlas.
Chapman, Betty T. "Architectural gems of Briscoe, Sullivan cover local landscape."

225. "'Brummer.' Harris County 1870 Census Page." Rootsweb.com <http://www.rootsweb.com/~txharri2/harcen.html> [Accessed January 7, 2002].

226. Chapman, Betty T. "Brunner suburban development now home to inner-city growth." Houston Business Journal, October 6-12, 2000, page 30A.

227. Houston City Directory, 1866.

228. "'Brummer.' Harris County 1870 Census Page." Rootsweb.com.

229. "Von Roeder, Ludwig." San Jacinto Museum.
Emmott, Sarah H. Memorial Park, a priceless legacy.

230. Emmott, Sarah H. Memorial Park, a priceless legacy.

231. Houston City Directory, 1866.

232. "'Brummer.' Harris County 1870 Census Page." Rootsweb.com.
Emmott, Sarah H. Memorial Park, a priceless legacy.
233. Chapman, Betty T. "Brunner suburban development now home to inner-city growth."
234. Ibid.
235. Kleiner, Diana J. "Brunner, Texas." The Handbook of Texas Online. <http://www.tshaonline.org/handbook/online/articles/hrbrw> [Accessed August 10, 2011].
236. Chapman, Betty T. "Brunner suburban development now home to inner-city growth."
237. "Postmasters and Post Offices of Harris County, Texas, 1846 - 1930." Rootsweb.com. <http://www.rootsweb.com/~txpost/harris.html> [Accessed August 10, 2011].
238. "Shepherd Drive Methodist Church." Texas Historical Commission. Atlas. <http://atlas.thc.state.tx.us/scripts/> [Accessed January 12, 2001].
239. Houston, A History and A Guide. Page 162.
240. Kleiner, Diana J. "Brunner, Texas."
241. Chapman, Betty T. "Brunner suburban development now home to inner-city growth."
242. Washington On Westcott Roundabout Initiatve. <http://www.wowroundabout.org> [Accessed August 1, 2002].
243. Chapman, Betty T. "Brunner suburban development now home to inner-city growth."
244. Rothrock, W. P. Completion Report of Camp Logan, Houston, Texas. [Houston? Tex. : s.l., 1918?] [on file at Houston Public Library]
245. Unless otherwise noted, the information in this story about the Houston Riot of 1917 comes from the following sources:
Haynes, Robert V. Night of Violence: the Houston riot of 1917. Baton Rouge: LSU Press, 1976.
"Houston Riot of 1917." The Handbook of Texas Online. <http://www.tshaonline.org/handbook/online/articles/jch04> [Accessed August 14, 2011].
Kennedy, Tom. "The Camp Logan Riot of 1917." Badge and Gun, [vol ? (2005?)]. Manuscript in author's possession.
Zoch, Nelson. "Lest We Forget." Badge and Gun, Volume XXXII, No. 5 (May, 2006).
246. "Butcher, George, 1910 Census, Series T624, Roll 1560, Page 269" and "Butcher, George, 1920 Census, Series T625, Roll 1812, Page 58". Heritage Quest Online. ProQuest Information and Learning Company. <http://www.heritagequestonline.com/> [Accessed June 23, 2006].
247. "Smith, Eli H, 1910 Census, Series T624, Roll 1559, Page 93". Heritage Quest Online. ProQuest Information and Learning Company. <http://www.heritagequestonline.com/> [Accessed June 23, 2006].
248. "Burkett, William, 1920 Census, Series T625, Roll 1813, Page 262". Heritage Quest Online. ProQuest Information and Learning Company. <http://www.heritagequestonline.com/> [Accessed June 23, 2006].

Chapter 6: Buffalo Bayou Park

1. Ashburn, J. Foster. Ashburn's Map of Houston, Texas. 1942.
"Bayou Park Village Apartments." <http://yp.yahoo.com/> [Accessed May 11, 2004].
"Houston, 1924-1951. Volume 7, Sheet 738 and 739." Sanborn maps, 1867-1970: Texas. [Ann Arbor, Mich.] : Bell & Howell Information and Learning, c2001.

2. "HPARD Land Inventory, 3-5-08." Parks and Recreation Department. City of Houston. <http://www.houstontx.gov/parks/pdfs/inventory.pdf/> [Accessed January 5, 2009].

3. "City of Houston, Texas." Houston Title & Guaranty Co., 1917.

"Subdivision Price Trends: Vicks Park Subdivision." Houston Association of Realtors. <http://www.har.com/> [Accessed June 16, 2003].

4. Emmott, Sarah H. Memorial Park, a priceless legacy. Houston: Herring Press, 1992. Pages 9-11.

5. "Houston, 1924-1951. Volume 7, Sheet 740." Sanborn maps, 1867-1970: Texas.

6. Sarnoff, Nancy. "Real Estate Roundup." Houston Business Journal, July 27-August 2, 2001. Page 10.

Bivins, Ralph. "Finger's high-rise apartment tower gets first tenants." Houston Chronicle, Wednesday, 10/06/2002. Section: Business, Page 6, 2 Star Edition.

"School Histories. Cleveland Elementary School." Houston Independent School District. <http://www.hisd.org/> [Accessed December 27, 2010].

"Jackson Hill, Account number 1223760010001." Harris County Appraisal District. <http://www.hcad.org/> [Accessed December 27, 2010].

7. Houghton, Dorothy K. H. Houston's Forgotten Heritage. Houston: Rice University Press, 1991. Page 58.

8. "Star Engraving Company Building." Texas Historical Commission. Atlas. <http://atlas.thc.state.tx.us/scripts/> [Accessed December 2, 2000].

9. "San Felipe Courts Historic District." Texas Historical Commission. Atlas. <http://atlas.thc.state.tx.us/scripts/> [Accessed December 2, 2000].

10. Prather, Patricia Smith. "Exhibit honors former slaves who emerged as pathfinders." Houston Chronicle, Sunday, 02/08/87. Lifestyle Section, Page 1, 2 Star Edition.

11. Houghton, Dorothy K. H. Houston's Forgotten Heritage. Houston: Rice University Press, 1991. Page 256.

12. Chapman, Betty T. "Educational, spiritual legacy of Jack Yates remains clear." Houston Business Journal, February 2-8, 2001, Page 33.

13. Houghton, Dorothy K. H. Page 256.

"Houston, 1924-1948, Volume 5, Sheet 502." Sanborn maps, 1867-1970: Texas. [Ann Arbor, Mich.?] : Bell & Howell Information and Learning, c2001.

14. Johnston, Marguarite. Houston, The Unknown City, 1836-1946. College Station: Texas A & M University Press, 1991. Page 418, note 6.

15. Lezon, Dale. "Big Plans for preservation." Houston Chronicle, Thursday, 05/29/2008. Section: B, Page 1, 3 Star Edition.

16. "Adath Emeth." Rootsweb.com. <http://freepages.geneology.rootsweb.com/~prsmith/alpha_cem_a-f.htm> [Accessed December 21, 2003].

17. Tutt, Bob. "City cemetery a forgotten, torn eyesore." Houston Chronicle, Sunday, 04/02/89. Section C, Page 1, 2 Star Edition.

"3605 West Dallas Ave., Account number 0442170000005, Facet 5357C1." Harris County Appraisal District. <http://www.hcad.org/> [Accessed August 11, 2011].

Liebrum, Jennifer. "Cemetery cleanup set this weekend." Houston Chronicle, Friday, 04/10/92. Section A, Page 34, 2 Star Edition.

18. Marshall, Thom. "Community spirit saved a cemetery." Houston Chronicle, Wednesday, 02/10/93. Section A, Page 15, 2 Star Edition.

Rodrigues, Janette. "Once eyesore, graveyard tells a historic tale." Houston Chronicle, Saturday, 08/02/2003. Section: A, Page 1, 3 Star Edition.

"Historical Marker Detail for Sessums, John, Jr." Harris County Historical Commission. <http://www.historicalcommission.hctx.net/markerDetail.aspx?marker=9886> [Accessed August 14, 2011].

19. Liebrum, Jennifer. "Cemetery cleanup set this weekend."

"Houston, 1924-1948, Volume 5, Sheet 501." Sanborn maps, 1867-1970: Texas.

20. Tutt, Bob. "City cemetery a forgotten, torn eyesore."

Liebrum, Jennifer. "Cemetery cleanup set this weekend."

Rodriquez, Lori. "Cemetery work teaches youths history, respect." Houston Chronicle, Saturday, 02/01/97. Section A, Page 1, 3 Star Edition.

21. "Historical Marker Detail for Sessums, John, Jr." Harris County Historical Commission.

22. Barr, Alwyn. "The Black Militia of the New South: Texas as a Case Study." The Journal of Negro History, Vol. 63, No. 3 (July, 1978), Pages 209-219.

23. Ibid.

24. "Houston Happenings." Galveston Daily News, Saturday, January 3, 1880, Issue 246, column F.

"Sessums, John, 1880 Census, Series T9, Roll 1309, Page 300." Heritage Quest Online. ProQuest Information and Learning Company. <http://www.heritagequestonline.com/> [Accessed May 20, 2008].

"Paid for their grounes[sic]." Galveston Daily News, Friday, June 25, 1886, page 3, Issue 61, column A.

Barr, Alwyn.

25. "From Houston." Galveston Daily News, Saturday, November 24, 1883, Issue 247, column H.

"Inventory of Adjutant General's Department Texas Volunteer Guard Military Rolls at the Texas State Archives, 1880-1903." Texas Archival Resources Online. Library. University of Texas. <http://www.lib.utexas.edu/taro/tslac/30079.xml> [Accessed May 20, 2008].

"Over the State. Houston" Galveston Daily News, Sunday, September 24, 1882, Issue 160, column F.

"Davis Rifles' Uniforms." Galveston Daily News, Tuesday, June 1, 1886, page 3, Issue 37, column A.

"John Sessums's Company." Galveston Daily News, Tuesday, April 20, 1886, page 3, Issue 360, column A.

"Davis Rifles to the Front." Galveston Daily News, Friday, April 8, 1887, page 3, Issue 347, column A.

26. Blacklock-Sloan, Debra. "John Sessums." Application for an Official Texas Historical Marker. Harris County Historical Commission. August 29, 2008. On file at the Harris County Archives.

Young, Samuel Oliver. A thumb-nail history of the city of Houston, Texas, from its founding in 1836 to the year 1912. Houston, Tex.: Press of Rein, 1912. Pages 123-124.

27. "John Sessums Jailed." Galveston Daily News, Tuesday, July 6, 1886, page 3, Issue 72, column A.

Young, Samuel Oliver. Page 125.

28. Ibid. Page 125, 129.

"Light Guard Day." Galveston Daily News, June 8, 1889, Issue 42, column D.

29. "First in the new armory." Galveston Daily News, Saturday, January 23, 1892, page 3, Issue 305, column A.

Blacklock-Sloan, Debra.

30. "Town Notes." Galveston Daily News, Wednesday, May 21, 1890, page 3, Issue 23, column A.

"Zouave." Wikipedia. <http://en.wikipedia.org/> [Accessed July 3, 2008].

"Day at Houston." Galveston Daily News, Wednesday, August 29, 1894, page 3, Issue 159, column A.

"Pickaninny Soldiers." Galveston Daily News, Friday, October 11, 1895, page 3, Issue 201, column A.

31. "Town Notes." Galveston Daily News, Wednesday, May 21, 1890, page 3, Issue 23, column A.

"Houston Headlight Flashes." Galveston Daily News, Monday, July 24, 1893, page 3, Issue 123, column C.

"Day at Houston." Galveston Daily News, Sunday, September 1, 1895, Issue 161, column A.

"For Atlanta." Galveston Daily News, Saturday, August 17, 1895, page 3, Issue 146, column A.

"Negro Zouave Company." Dallas Morning News. 9/5/1898, page 4.

32. "Colored Military Officers." Galveston Daily News, Wednesday, January 8, 1890, page 3, Issue 256, column A.

"John Sessums' New Company." Galveston Daily News, Thursday, September 11, 1890, page 3, Issue 135, column A.

Barr, Alwyn.

33. "Afro-American Fair." Galveston Daily News, Sunday, August 2, 1896, page 4, Issue 131, column A.

"State Capital. Department Notes." Dallas Morning News. 8/11/1896.

Raines, Cadwell Walton. Year Book for Texas. Austin: Gammel-Statesman Publishing Co., 1903.

"Afro-American Drill Scores." Galveston Daily News, Saturday, October 17, 1896, page 5, Issue 207, column D.

34. "Twice a week drills." Galveston Daily News, Sunday, January 17, 1897, page 4, Issue 299, column A.

Barr, Alwyn.

35. "Militia Act of 1903." Wikipedia. <http://en.wikipedia.org/wiki/Militia_Act_of_1903> [Accessed August 12, 2011].

Barr, Alwyn.

36. Blacklock-Sloan, Debra.

37. "Adath Emeth." Rootsweb.com.

Houston, A History and A Guide. Houston: Anson Jones Press, 1942. Page 189.

Maas, Elaine H. "The Jews in Houston Today." Houston History. <http://www.houstonhistory.com/erhnic/history1jews.htm> [Accessed January 27, 2005].

38. Houston, A History and A Guide. Page 261.

"3500 Allen Parkway, 5357A9, 5357A10." Harris County Appraisal District. <http://www.hcad.org/> [Accessed May 11, 2004].

39. Maas, Elaine H.

40. "Rochow, Charles, 1870 Census, Series M593, Roll 224, Page 437." Heritage Quest Online. ProQuest Information and Learning Company. <http://www.heritagequestonline.com/> [Accessed May 23, 2004].

"Rochow, Carl, 1900 Census, Series T623, Roll 387, Page 205." Heritage Quest Online. ProQuest Information and Learning Company. <http://www.heritagequestonline.com/> [Accessed May 23, 2004].

41. Ibid.

42. "Rochow, Robert, 1910 Census, Series T624, Roll 330, Page 180." Heritage Quest Online. ProQuest Information and Learning Company. <http://www.heritagequestonline.com/> [Accessed May 23, 2004].

43. "Houston, 1924, Volume 5, Sheet 502." Sanborn maps, 1867-1970: Texas. [Ann Arbor, Mich.?] : Bell & Howell Information and Learning, c2001.

"Houston, 1924-1951, Volume 5, Sheet 502." Sanborn maps, 1867-1970: Texas.

44. "Rochow, Robert G., 1930 Census, Series T626, Roll 2349, Page 253." Heritage Quest Online. ProQuest Information and Learning Company. <http://www.heritagequestonline.com/> [Accessed May 23, 2004].

"Rochow, Carl O., 1930 Census, Series T626, Roll 2349, Page 253."

"Rochow, Max P., 1930 Census, Series T626, Roll 2349, Page 253."

45. Snyder, Mike. "Distinctive 75-year-old structure razed for apartments." Houston Chronicle, Thursday, 05/17/2001. Section: Metro, Page 1, 3 Star Edition.

Bivins, Ralph. "Tower may replace 72-year-old building on Allen Parkway." Houston Chronicle, 10/05/00.

Alfred C. Finn: Builder of Houston. Houston: Houston Public Library, 1983.

46. "Houston, 1924-1951. Volume 5, Sheet 502." Sanborn maps, 1867-1970: Texas.

"Star Engraving Company Building." Texas Historical Commission. Atlas.

47. "Rochow Subdivision." Houston Association of Realtors. <http://www.har.com/> [Accessed June 18, 2004].

"Rochow Subdivision, 5357C2, 5357A10." Harris County Appraisal District. <http://www.hcad.org/> [Accessed June 18, 2004].

48. Snyder, Mike. "Distinctive 75-year-old structure razed for apartments."

"3333 Allen Parkway." Simmons Vedder and Company. <http://www.simmonsvedder.com/PA/allenparkway/apsum.htm> [Accessed June 18, 2004].

Sarnoff, Nancy. "Central City fights parking plans." Houston Chronicle, Sunday, 01/09/2005. Section: D, Page 3, 2 Star Edition.

49. "Houston National Cemetery, Houston, Harris County, Texas." Interment.net. <http://www.interment.net/data/us/tx/harris/housnat/houston_rocroq.htm> [Accessed June 18, 2004].

50. "Star Engraving Company Building." Texas Historical Commission. Atlas.

51. Ibid.

52. Ibid.

53. Ibid.

"Texas - Harris County." National Register of Historic Places. <http://www.nationalregisterofhistoricplaces.com/> [Accessed January 9, 2004].

54. "Houston, 1924-1951, Volume 5, Sheet 503." Sanborn maps, 1867-1970: Texas.

55. "A look back at American General." Houston Chronicle, Tuesday, 03/13/2001. Section B, Page 1, 3 Star Edition.

56. Mackey, Jim. "Bats on the bayou." Newsletter. White Oak Bayou Association. Houston, TX. Issue 49 (Fall, 2003).

Rust, Carol. "Houston has street sense (and nonsense as well)." Houston Chronicle, Wednesday, 04/16/97. Houston Section, Page 1, 2 Star Edition.

Leatherwood, Carl. "Going Batty." Houston Press, Jun 10, 2004. <http://www.houstonpress.com/> [Accessed June 18, 2004].

"Bayou Briefs. July, 2005." Buffalo Bayou Partnership. Houston, TX.

Karkabi, Barbara. "Bats come out at night at Buffalo Bayou." Houston Chronicle, Tuesday, 11/15/2005. Section: E, Page 1, 2 Star Edition.

57. Ibid.

Holtcamp, Wendee. "Houston's Bat Bridge." Texas Parks and Wildlife Magazine, May, 2006. P. 13.

58. "Bayou Briefs. July, 2005."

59. "Bayou Briefs. August, 2006."

60. "Wortham Fountain." Glass Steel and Stone. Houston. <http://www.glasssteelandstone.com> [Accessed July 14, 2007].

61. "American General Corporation." The Handbook of Texas Online. <http://www.tshaonline.org/handbook/online/articles/dja02> [Accessed July 15, 2007].

62. "Houston, 1924. Volume 5, Sheet 503." Sanborn maps, 1867-1970: Texas.

63. "Houston, 1924-1951. Volume 5, Sheet 503." Sanborn maps, 1867-1970: Texas.

64. "Magnolia Cemetery and the American General Center - 5357A12, 5357A12, 5357C4" Harris County Appraisal District. Harris County Appraisal District. <http://www.hcad.org/> [Accessed July 15, 2007].

65. "Wortham, Gus Sessions." The Handbook of Texas Online. <http://www.tshaonline.org/handbook/online/articles/fwo34> [Accessed July 14, 2007].

66. "Order Number 01-0820. Acquisition of American General Corporation by American International Group, Inc." Official Order of the Commissioner of Insurance of the State of Texas. Texas Dept of Insurance. <http://www.tdi.state.tx.us/orders/index.html/> [Accessed July 14, 2007].

"American International Group." <http://en.wikipedia.org/wiki/American_International_Group> [Accessed July 14, 2007].

67. "Wortham, Gus Sessions." The Handbook of Texas Online.

68. Hassell, Greg. "Wortham's firm grew along with Bayou City." Houston Chronicle, Tuesday, 03/13/2001. Section B, Page 1, 3 Star Edition.

Leimer, ChrisTina. "Magnolia Cemetery." The Tombstone Traveller's Guide. <http://home.flash.net/~leimer/magnolia.htm> [Accessed October 8, 2001].

69. "Magnolia Cemetery." Marker. Historic Texas Cemetery, 2002.

70. Ibid.

71. Ibid.

Leimer, ChrisTina. "Magnolia Cemetery."

72. Ibid.

"Wortham, Elizabeth Lyndall Finley." The Handbook of Texas Online. <http://http://www.tshaonline.org/handbook/online/articles/fwo37> [Accessed September 25, 2000].

"Wortham, Gus Sessions." The Handbook of Texas Online.

73. "Vick, 1900 Census, Series T623, Roll 1642, Page 312." Heritage Quest Online. Pro-Quest Information and Learning Company. <http://www.heritagequestonline.com/> [Accessed May 15, 2004].

74. "1900 Census, Series T623, Roll 1642, Page 311-312."

75. Whitty, P. "Houston, January, 1906 [map]." 1906.

76. Chapman, Betty T. "Brunner suburban development now home to inner-city growth." Houston Business Journal, October 6-12, 2000, page 30A.

Justman, Dorothy E. German Colonists and their Descendants in Houston Including Usener and Allied Families. Wichita Falls: Nortex Offset Publications, Inc., 1974.

"City of Houston, Texas." Houston Title & Guaranty Co., 1917.

77. Ibid.

"Vick, Tobe S., 1910 Census, Series T624, Roll 1561, Page 14." Heritage Quest Online. ProQuest Information and Learning Company. <http://www.heritagequestonline.com/> [Accessed May 15, 2004].

78. "Vick, Andrew J., 1910 Census, Series T624, Roll 1532, Page 154."

79. "City of Houston, Texas." Houston Title & Guaranty Co., 1917.

80. "Subdivision Price Trends: Vicks Park Subdivision." Houston Association of Realtors. <http://www.har.com/> [Accessed June 16, 2003].

"Waugh Drive, Heights Blvd., 5357A3, 5357A4, 5357A7, 5357A8." Harris County Appraisal District. <http://www.hcad.org/> [Accessed May 16, 2004].

81. "Galveston, Harrisburg and San Antonio Railway." The Handbook of Texas Online. <http://www.tshaonline.org/handbook/online/articles/eqg06> [Accessed September 28, 2001].

82. "Brevities." Galveston Daily News, Saturday, March 6, 1880, Issue 300, Column F.

"Brevities." Galveston Daily News, Sunday, May 16, 1880, Issue 47, Column E.

83. "Cottonseed Industry." The Handbook of Texas Online. <http://www.tshaonline.org/handbook/online/articles/drc04> [Accessed November 27, 2008].

84. "Over the state." Galveston Daily News, Sunday, May 6, 1883, Issue 45, Column E.

"Over the state." Galveston Daily News, Friday, August 10, 1883, Issue 141, Column E.

"Cotton-Compress Industry." The Handbook of Texas Online. <http://www.tshaonline.org/handbook/online/articles/drc02> [Accessed December 1, 2008].

85. "Big blaze in Houston." Galveston Daily News, Sunday, August 29, 1886, page 5, Issue 126, Column E.

"Bayou City's Budget." Galveston Daily News, Monday, August 30, 1886, page 3, Issue 127, Column A.

86. "New Oil Mill." Galveston Daily News, Tuesday, March 15, 1887, page 5, Issue 323, Column E.

"History of Wesson Oil and Snowdrift Company, Inc." Journal of the American Oil and Chemists Society, Vol. 37 (February, 1960), page 4.

"Bayou City Budget." Galveston Daily News, Tuesday, April 5, 1887, page 3, Issue 344, Column A.

"Bayou City Budget." Galveston Daily News, Saturday, May 7, 1887, page 3, Issue 11, Column A.

"Southern Oil Cotton Mill." Galveston Daily News, Sunday, October 9, 1887, page 3, Issue 166, Column A.

87. "Bayou City Budget." Galveston Daily News, Friday, August 26, 1887, page 3, Issue 122, Column A.

88. "Oil Mills." Galveston Daily News, Sunday, January 31, 1892, page 6, Issue 313, Column F.

89. Ibid.

"Cottonseed Industry." The Handbook of Texas Online.

90. Ibid.

91. Ibid.

"Cotton. Uses." Info Comm. UNCTAD. <http://r0.unctad.org/infocomm/anglais/cotton/uses.htm/> [Accessed November 27, 2008].

"History of Wesson Oil and Snowdrift Company, Inc."

"Biographies: David Wesson." Journal of the American Oil and Chemists Society, Vol. 10, No. 3 (March, 1933), pages 56-57.

Hixon, H. C., "The Rise of the American Cottonseed Oil Industry." The Journal of Political Economy, Vol. 38, No. 1 (Feb., 1930), pages 73-85.

92. "Cottonseed Oil Comeback Tour." National Cottonseed Products Association. <http://www.cottonseedoiltour.com/facts/> [Accessed November 26, 2008].

"Cottonseed Industry." The Handbook of Texas Online.

"History of Wesson Oil and Snowdrift Company, Inc."

93. "Houston, 1896, Sheet 74." Sanborn maps, 1867-1970: Texas. [Ann Arbor, Mich.?] : Bell & Howell Information and Learning, c2001.

"Houston, 1907, Volume 2, Sheet 74." Sanborn maps, 1867-1970: Texas. [Ann Arbor, Mich.?] : Bell & Howell Information and Learning, c2001.

94. Book of Houston: a brief sketch of its history, educational facilities...[Houston, TX?]: [s. n.], 1915. Page 38.

95. "Houston, 1907, Volume 2, Sheet 74." Sanborn maps, 1867-1970: Texas.

"Charters filed." Dallas Morning News. 1/30/1902, page 5.

"First sack of new rice." Dallas Morning News. 8/3/1902, page 23.

Texas Civil Appeals Reports: Cases Argued and Determined in the Courts of Civil Appeals of the State of Texas. Austin: State of Texas, 1908. Page 522.

96. "Charters Filed." Dallas Morning News. 7/23/1905, page 23.

"Houston, 1896, Sheet 73." Sanborn maps, 1867-1970: Texas.

"Houston, 1907, Volume 2, Sheet 69." Sanborn maps, 1867-1970: Texas.

97. "Houston, 1907, Volume 2, Sheet 63." Sanborn maps, 1867-1970: Texas.

98. Morrison & Fourmy Directory of the City of Houston, 1907. Houston: Morrison & Fourmy, 1907.

"Cotton-Compress Industry." The Handbook of Texas Online.

99. "Galveston, Harrisburg and San Antonio Railway." The Handbook of Texas Online.

"Houston, 1924-1948, Volume 2, Sheet 203." Sanborn maps, 1867-1970: Texas.

100. "Cottonseed Industry." The Handbook of Texas Online.

"Houston, 1924-1951, Volume 2, Sheet 225." Sanborn maps, 1867-1970: Texas. [Ann Arbor, Mich.?] : Bell & Howell Information and Learning, c2001.

101. Beberdick, Frank H. "Pullamn Timeline." Pullamn Virtual Museum. <http://www.eliillinois.org/30108_87/timeline.html> [Accessed April 14, 2005].

"Houston, 1924-1951, Volume 2, Sheet 225." Sanborn maps, 1867-1970: Texas.

102. Houghton, Dorothy K. H. Houston's Forgotten Heritage. Page 319.

History of Houston Fire Department, 1875-1880. <http://www.maxmcrae.com/> [Accessed August 17, 2005].

Bivins, Ralph. "Memorial Heights, site of old rice silos, rapidly filling up." Houston Chronicle, Sunday, 03/25/2001. Section: Business, Page 6, 2 Star Edition.

Bivins, Ralph. "Last parcel sold from silo acreage." Houston Chronicle, Friday, 05/31/2002. Section: Business, Page 2C, 3 Star Edition.

103. Sarnoff, Nancy. "Odds are two lots to turn into homes." Houston Chronicle, Thursday, 09/30/2004. Section: D, Page 1, 2 Star Edition.

104. "About Sears. Opening retail stores." Sears, Roebuck and Company. <http://www.sears.com/sr/misc/sears/about/public/history/history_1925.html> [Accessed December 1, 2003].

105. Sarnoff, Nancy. "History yields to present on Allen Parkway." Houston Chronicle, Sunday, 11/19/2006. Section: D, Page 3, 2 Star Edition.

"Houston's Most Endangered, November 19, 2001". Greater Houston Preservation Alliance. <http://www.ghpa.org/houston_s_most_endangered_buil.html> [Accessed December 28, 2001].

Houston History. <http://houstonhistory.com/decades/timeline/5i1tl.htm> [Accessed August 15, 2011].

106. Sarnoff, Nancy. "History yields to present on Allen Parkway." Houston Chronicle, Sunday, 11/19/2006. Section: D, Page 3, 2 Star Edition.

107. Ashburn, J. Foster. Ashburn's Map of Houston, Texas. 1942.

Miller, Ray. Ray Miller's Houston. Houston: Cordovan Press, 1984. Page 153.

108. Sarnoff, Nancy. "History yields to present on Allen Parkway."

Sarnoff, Nancy. "A home with history / Old warehouse, once a Sears and a Med School, could get a new life as apartments." Houston Chronicle, Sunday, 08/08/2004. Section: Business, Page 3, 2 Star Edition.

109. Sarnoff, Nancy. "Odds are two lots to turn into homes."

"Foundation buys Montrose parcel." Houston Chronicle, Thursday, 11/16/2006. Section: D, Page 1, 3 Star Edition.

110. Ibid.

Vara, Richard. "A place of gathering / Ismaili muslims open new cultural center, national offices in Sugar Land." Houston Chronicle, Saturday, 06/22/2002. Section: Religion, Page 1, 2 Star Edition.

111. "Speech by His Highness the Aga Khan." Aga Khan Development Network. <http://www.akdn.org/speeches/texas.html> [Accessed November 16, 2006].

112. "About Houston: Rosemont Bridge." City of Houston. <http://www.houstontx.gov/abouthouston/rosemontbridge.html> [Accessed August 11, 2011].

Rosson, Rachel. "New 'Tolerance' sculptures along Buffalo Bayou." Houston Real Estate Blogoshpere. <http://www.har.com/Houston-Real-Estate-Blogs/17372/New-%22Tolerance%22-Sculptures-along-Baffalo-Bayou> [Accessed August 11, 2011].

113. "Dedication ceremony for Jaume Plensa sculptures, Tolerance." Houston Arts Alliance. <http://www.houstonartsalliance.com/news/dedication-ceremony-for-jaume-plensa-sculptures-tolerance/> [Accessed August 11, 2011].

Rosson, Rachel. "New 'Tolerance' sculptures along Buffalo Bayou."

114. Sarnoff, Nancy. "Flood damage sinks old Allen Park Inn." Houston Business Journal, December 21, 2001. <http://houston.bizjournals.com/houston/stories/2001/12/24/story3.html> [Accessed December 15, 2008].

115. "What's That?" Houston Chronicle, Sunday, 10/16/2005. Section: D, Page 3, 2 Star Edition.

Dawson, Jennifer. "Apartments continue to rise on Allen Parkway." Houston Business Journal, May 24, 2004. <http://houston.bizjournals.com/houston/stories/2004/05/24/newscolumn4.html> [Accessed December 15, 2008].

"Finalists." Houston Business Journal, April 27, 2007. <http://buffalo.bizjournals.com/houston/stories/2007/04/30/focus15.html> [Accessed December 15, 2008].

116. Wagner, J. K., and Company, Inc. "Archival Research Lot 39, Part Lot 40 O. Smith Survey A-696, Houston, Harris County, Texas." HISD Gregory Lincoln / HSPVA Archeological Testing Project #99714. July, 2005.

Muir, Andrew Forest. "Kesler's Arcade." MSS 17-33.6. Papers. Woodson Research Center. Rice University. Houston, TX.

Houston, A History and A Guide. Page 212.

117. Gill, Dee. "Fourth Ward's poor wary of grand redevelopment plan / Residents fear they'll face the streets." Houston Chronicle, Sunday, 08/12/1990. Section: A, Page 1, 2 Star Edition.

"Temple Terrace, 5357B9." Harris County Appraisal District. <http://www.hcad.org/> [Accessed December 16, 2008].

118. Bivins, Ralph. "Home builders are looking for land inside the Loop." Houston Chronicle, Sunday, 03/31/1996. Section: Business, Page 10, 2 Star Edition.

"Townes of Buffalo Bayou." House Almanac. <http://www.housealmanac.com/> [Accessed December 15, 2008].

119. "KHOU-TV." Wikipedia. <http://en.wikipedia.org/> [Accessed Dec 3, 2008].

Miller, Ray. Ray Miller's Houston. Pages 16-17.

120. "KHOU-TV." Wikipedia.

"Peak Streamflow for Texas. USGS 08074000 Buffalo Bayou at Houston, TX." <http://waterdata.usgs.gov/tx/nwis/peak> [Accessed August 6, 2002].

121. "Service Corporation International." Wikipedia. <http://en.wikipedia.org/wiki/Service_Corporation_International> [Accessed August 16, 2011].

"Welcome to Heights Funeral Home." Dignity Memorial. <http://www.dignitymemorial.com/2091/Printable.aspx> [Accessed December 17, 2008].

122. Wagner, J. K., and Company, Inc.

123. Ibid.

124. "Sam Houston to Lewis A. Levy, November 11, 1845." Deed Records. Harris County, Texas. Vol. I, Page 104.

125. "Lewis A. Levy to George Baker, October 10, 1845." Deed Records. Harris County, Texas. Vol. J, Page 578.

126. "Sam Houston to Lewis A. Levy, November 11, 1845."

127. Wagner, J. K., and Company, Inc.

"Sam Houston Ranch, 5357D1, 5357D5." Harris County Appraisal District. <http://www.hcad.org/> [Accessed December 17, 2008].

128. Baker, Colette. Personal communication, September 30, 2007.

129. "HPARD Land Inventory, 3-5-08."

130. "Historic Photos of the Houston Area." Texas Freeway. <http://www.texasfreeway.com/houston/historic/photos/houston_historic_photos.shtml> [Accessed February 9, 2003].

131. Johnson, Patricia C. "Officers memorial takes shape / Sculptor Moroles uses landscape as a guide for his design." Houston Chronicle, Sunday, 11/08/92. Zest Section, Page 13, 2 Star Edition.

Byars, Carlos. "Last full measure of devotion / Memorial dedicated to police killed in line of duty." Houston Chronicle, Friday, 11/20/92. Section A, Page 21, 2 Star Edition.

132. Huber, Kathy. "Pruning stimulates growth after freeze." Houston Chronicle, Saturday, 03/16/2002. Section: Houston, Page 1, 2 Star Edition.

133. "Henry Moore at Kew." Royal Botanical Gardens, Kew. <http://www.kew.org/henry-moore/> [Accessed May 25, 2008].

134. "Public Art Collection." Official Web Site, City of Houston. <http://www.ci.houston.tx.us/municipalart/> [Accessed February 2, 2004].

135. Chapman, Betty T. "Tranquility Park took off in turmoil after lunar landing." Houston Business Journal, June 1-7, 2001. Page 29.

136. "Public Art Collection."

137. "Henry Moore." Wikipedia. <http://en.wikipedia.org/wiki/Henry_Moore> [Accessed August 16, 2011].

138. "Henry Moore at Kew."

139. "Previous Scenic Houston Annual Gala Dinner Award Winners." Scenic Houston. <http://www.scenichouston.org/prior-gala/> [Accessed January 10, 2009].

"Eleanor Tinsley Papers, 1965-1995." Library. University of Texas. <http://www.lib.utexas.edu/taro/houpub/00032/00032-P.html/> [Accessed January 10, 2009].

Bernstein, Alan. "Eversole, Tinsley clash in Pct. 4 commissioner race." Houston Chronicle, Sunday, 10/28/1990. Section: Voter's Guide, Page 1, 2 Star Edition.

140. Wagner, J. K., and Company, Inc.

Historical records search and archeological subsurface testing for the Jefferson Davis Hospital site at 1801 Allen Parkway Drive, Houston, Harris County, Texas. Houston: Moore Archeological Consulting, 1999. Page 4.

"Old Sixth Ward - History & Housing." Old Sixth Ward Neighborhood Association. <http://www.old6ward.org/> [Accessed December 19, 2008].

Morrison and Fourny's Revised Map of the City of Houston, Texas. ?: ?, 1882.

141. "Shady Grove Plaza." Dedication plaque. City of Houston.

"Downtown Houston. Public Art Attractions." Houston Arts Alliance. <http://sonjakramer.com/images/haa_brochure_v2.pdf/> [Accessed January 10, 2009].

"Future Projects." Justice for All. <http://www.jfa.net/projects.html/> [Accessed January 10, 2009].

142. "City of Houston Municipal Art Collection." City of Houston. <http://www.houstonmunicipalart.org/> [Accessed December 28, 2008].

"Downtown Public Art Tour." Houston Downtown. <http://www.houstondowntown.com/Home/Lifestyle/WhatToDo/PerformingandCulturalA/PublicArt/DowntownPublicArtTour/Downtown%20Public%20Art%20Tour.PDF> [Accessed January 6, 2009].

"Solid Waste Management Facility." Public Art Online. <http://www.publicartonline.org.uk/casestudies/collaboration/solidwaste/biog_glatt.php> [Accessed January 6, 2009].

143. Fake, Kyle W. "Tapping into nature / Nonprofit puts bayou back into city." Houston Chronicle, Thursday, 03/11/2004. Section: This Week, Page 1, 2 Star Edition.

144. "Tapley Tributary." Buffalo Bayou Partnership. <http://www.buffalobayou.org/tapley.html> [Accessed January 12, 2009].

145. Fake, Kyle W. "Tapping into nature / Nonprofit puts bayou back into city."

146. Chapman, Betty T. "Tranquility Park took off in turmoil after lunar landing." Harman, Greg. "Dateline. Who's Bayou?" Texas Observer. June 2, 1006. <http://www.texasobserver.org/> [Accessed June 20, 2006].

Warren, Susan. "UH Downtown headquarters getting dramatic new look." Houston Chronicle, Monday, 07/22/85. Section 1, Page 10, No Star Edition.

147. Gish, Theodore G. "Germans in Houston Today." Houston History. <http://www.neosoft.com/~sgriffin/houstonhistory/> [Accessed September 9, 2000].

Mistrot, Bernice. Secretary of the Washington Cemetery Historic Trust. September, 2002. "History of Washington Cemetery, Houston, Texas." Journal. Austin: German-Texas Heritage Society. Volume VIII, Number 2 (Summer, 1986).

"Bayou City Budget." Galveston Daily News, February 9, 1887, Page 3, Issue 289, column A.

148. "Welcome to the Old Sixth Ward."

149. Gish, Theodore G. "Germans in Houston Today."

"History of Washington Cemetery, Houston, Texas."

Justman, Dorothy E.

150. Sher, Len. "Lost Civil War manuscript may be somewhere in Houston." Houston Chronicle, Sunday, 01/26/2003. Section: Texas Magazine.

151. Cecil, Paul F. "Seelye, Sarah Emma Evelyn Edmundson." The Handbook of Texas Online. <http://www.tshaonline.org/handbook/online/articles/fse16> [Accessed August 17, 2011].

152. Sher, Len. "Lost Civil War manuscript may be somewhere in Houston."

153. Cecil, Paul F. "Seelye, Sarah Emma Evelyn Edmundson."

154. Ibid.

Sher, Len. "Lost Civil War manuscript may be somewhere in Houston."

Houston, A History and A Guide. Pages 328-329.

155. Mistrot, Bernice. Secretary of the Washington Cemetery Historic Trust. September, 2002.

Mitchell, Doug. "Cemetery of the famous." City Savvy. Vol. 5, No. 2, Spring 2000.

"Washington-Glenwood Cemeteries, 5357B1, 5357B2, 5357B5, 5357B6." Harris County Appraisal District. <http://www.hcad.org/> [Accessed December 18, 2008].

156. "Wynns, Archibald." The Handbook of Texas Online. <http://www.tshaonline.org/handbook/online/articles/fwy05> [Accessed August 17, 2011].

Peterson, Dorothy Burns. Daughters of Republic of Texas. Nashville: Turner Publishing Co., 1995. Page 303.

"John Wynns." Neighbors. Sally's Family Place. <http://www.sallysfamilyplace/Neighbors/wynnsj.htm/> [Accessed December 19, 2008].

"Old Sixth Ward - History & Housing."

157. "Wynns, Archibald." The Handbook of Texas Online.

Cutrer, Thomas W. "Lawrence, William." The Handbook of Texas Online. <http://www.tshaonline.org/handbook/online/articles/fla56> [Accessed August 17, 2011].

Looscan, Adele B. "Harris County, 1822-1845." Southwestern Historical Quarterly Online. Volume 19, No. 1, Page 57. <http://www.tsha.utexas.edu/publications/journals/shq/online/v019/n1/0190010057> [Accessed May 22, 2005].

158. Russell, Marie. 1850 Census Harris County, Texas with added genealogical notes. Baytown: n.p., 1981.

"Wynns, M. A. 1860 Census, Series M653, Roll 1296, Page 376." Heritage Quest Online. ProQuest Information and Learning Company. <http://www.heritagequestonline.com/> [Accessed November 4, 2005].

159. "Surnames beginning with 'W' - the Daughters of the Republic of Texas." Ancestry. <http://boards.ancestry.co.uk/topics.lost-family-and-friends/37128/mb.ash/> [Accessed December 19, 2008].

"Wynns, M. A. 1860 Census, Series M653, Roll 1296, Page 376."

Houston City Directory, 1866. Dallas: R. L. Polk & Co, 1866. Page 54.

Peterson, Dorothy Burns.

160. "Old Sixth Ward - History & Housing."

"Mayoral History." City of Houston. <http://www.houstontx.gov/mayor/history1800.htm> [Accessed September 6, 2005].

"King, WM H. 1860 Census, Series M653, Roll 1296, Page 428."

Wood, W. E. City of Houston, Harris County, Texas [map]. Houston, 1869.

"King, Mary. 1870 Census, Series M593, Roll 1589, Page 618."

Chapman, Betty T. "Working on the railroad made Sixth Ward early 'uptown' hub." Houston Business Journal, August 25-31, 2000.

161. "Houston Cemetery Company." Application for an Official Texas Historical Marker. Harris County Historical Commission, November, 2008. On file at the Harris County Archives.

"New Cemetery." Houston Daily Telegraph, October 26, 1871.

"Houston Happenings." Galveston Daily News, July 18, 1879, Issue 100, column C.

162. Gibbens, Pam. "Here lies Houston's history." Greater Houston Weekly, October 25, 2005.

Houghton, Dorothy K. H. Page 29.

"Whitaker, A. 1860 Census, Series M653, Roll 1296, Page 394."

"Whitaker, Alfred. 1870 Census, Series M593, Roll 1589, Page 622."

163. Gammel, Hans Peter. The Laws of Texas, 1822-1897. Volume 6. Austin: Gammel Book Co., 1898. Pages 323-325.

Gibbens, Pam. "Here lies Houston's history."

164. "New Cemetery."

"Houston Cemetery Company."

165. "From Houston." The Galveston News, Friday, June 14, 1872.

"Houston Cemetery Company."

"Dollars for the Endowment. A Grave Tradition of Fundraising." Rice University. Library. Friends of Fondren Library. <http://ruf.rice.edu/~fofl/FLyleaf47.3/glenwood.html>. [Accessed January 26, 2002].

Houston, A History and A Guide. Page 289.

166. "Houston Local Items." Galveston Daily News, Tuesday, January 20, 1874, Issue 39, column B.

Chapman, Betty T. "Working on the railroad made Sixth Ward early 'uptown' hub."

167. "Houston Local Items." Galveston Daily News, August 22, 1875, Issue 192, column D.

"Topics in the Interior." Galveston Daily News, July 16, 1878, Issue 98, column C.

168. "Bayou City Locals." Galveston Daily News, Tuesday, November 4, 1884, Page 3, Issue 195, column C.

"Bayou City Locals." Galveston Daily News, October 12, 1884, page 3, Issue 172, column C.

169. "Bayou City Locals." Galveston Daily News, April 8, 1885, page 3, Issue 349, column A.

"Bayou City Locals." Galveston Daily News, September 3, 1885, page 3, Issue 23, column A.

"Bayou City Locals." Galveston Daily News, Sunday November 1, 1885, page 3, Issue 191, column A.

"Easter in Houston." Galveston Daily News, Monday, April 11, 1887, page 3, Issue 350, column A.

"Blue and the Gray." Galveston Daily News, Friday, May 31, 1889, page 2, Issue 34, column A.

"Bayou City Budget." Galveston Daily News, May 31, 1890, page 3, Issue 33, column A.

"Houston Happenings." Galveston Daily News, June 11, 1891, page 3, Issue 79, column A.

170. "Day at Houston." Galveston Daily News, May 31, 1895, page 3, Issue 68, column A.

"Day at Houston." Galveston Daily News, February 19, 1896, page 3, Issue 332, column A.

"Day at Houston." Galveston Daily News, February 21, 1896, page 3, Issue 334, column A.

171. "Day at Houston." Galveston Daily News, February 28, 1896, page 3, Issue 341, column A.

"Day in Houston." Galveston Daily News, March 27, 1896, page 3, Issue 3, column A.

"Day at Houston." Galveston Daily News, April 19, 1896, page 4, Issue 26, column A.

"Day at Houston." Galveston Daily News, April 21, 1896, page 7, Issue 28, column A.

"Day at Houston." Galveston Daily News, April 24, 1896, page 3, Issue 31, column A.

"Tilt over Tombs." Galveston Daily News, Sunday, April 26, 1896, page 7, Issue 33, column A.

172. "Graveyard Trust." Daily Picayune (New Orleans, LA), May 22, 1896, page 7, Issue 119, column B.

"Day at Houston." Galveston Daily News, May 24, 1896, page 4, Issue 61, column A.

"Day at Houston." Galveston Daily News, August 14, 1896, page 5, Issue 143, column A.

"Day at Houston." Galveston Daily News, September 18, 1896, page 5, Issue 178, column A

173. "Decoration Day in Houston." Galveston Daily News, May 31, 1897, page 3, Issue 68, column A.

"Houston Cemetery Company."

Mitchell, Doug. "Cemetery of the famous."

174. "Houston Cemetery Company."

175. History of Houston Fire Department.

176. Ibid.

Mitchell, Doug. "Cemetery of the famous."

177. Mistrot, Bernice. Secretary of the Washington Cemetery Historic Trust. September, 2002.

"Washington-Glenwood Cemeteries, 5357B1, 5357B2, 5357B5, 5357B6."

178. Davenport, Harbert. "Fannin and His Men." Texas State Historical Association. <http://www.tsha.utexas.edu/supsites/fannin/hd_home.html> [Accessed June 6, 2003].

White, Gifford, ed. They Also Served, Texas Service Records from Headright Certificates. Nacogdoches: Ericson Books, 1991.

Historical records search and archeological subsurface testing for the Jefferson Davis Hospital site at 1801 Allen Parkway Drive, Houston, Harris County, Texas. Page 4.

Muir, Andrew Forest. "Phineas Jenks Mahan." MSS 17-35.9. Papers. Woodson Research Center. Rice University. Houston, TX.

179. Muir, Andrew Forest. "Phineas Jenks Mahan."

Houston City Directory, 1866. Page 35.

180. "Brown, Reuben R." The Handbook of Texas Online. <http://www.tsha.utexas.edu/handbook/online/articles/view/> [Accessed August 21, 2000].

Muir, Andrew Forest. "Phineas Jenks Mahan."

Historical records search and archeological subsurface testing for the Jefferson Davis Hospital site at 1801 Allen Parkway Drive, Houston, Harris County, Texas. Pages 5-6.

181. Ibid. Page 23.

182. Ibid.

"Groesbeck, Texas." The Handbook of Texas Online. <http://www.tsha.utexas.edu/handbook/online/articles/GG/hgg6.html> [Accessed December 30, 2008].

183. Historical records search and archeological subsurface testing for the Jefferson Davis Hospital site at 1801 Allen Parkway Drive, Houston, Harris County, Texas. Page 6.

"Multiple Classified Advertisements." Galveston Daily News, September 8, 1881, Issue 145, column F.

184. Historical records search and archeological subsurface testing for the Jefferson Davis Hospital site at 1801 Allen Parkway Drive, Houston, Harris County, Texas. Pages 6, 24.

185. "Multiple Classified Advertisements." Galveston Daily News, April 25, 1887, Issue 364, column C.

"Factories." Galveston Daily News, January 31, 1892, page 6, Issue 313, column G.

"Daily Houston Budget." Galveston Daily News, June 29, 1897, Page 3, Issue 97, column A.

Historical records search and archeological subsurface testing for the Jefferson Davis Hospital site at 1801 Allen Parkway Drive, Houston, Harris County, Texas. Page 7.

186. Ibid. Page 9.

Johnston, Marguarite. Pages 129, 141.

187. Historical records search and archeological subsurface testing for the Jefferson Davis Hospital site at 1801 Allen Parkway Drive, Houston, Harris County, Texas. Page 9.

188. Ibid. Page 13.

"Houston, 1924. Volume 5, Sheet 505." Sanborn maps, 1867-1970: Texas.

189. Historical records search and archeological subsurface testing for the Jefferson Davis Hospital site at 1801 Allen Parkway Drive, Houston, Harris County, Texas. Page 14.

190. Ibid. Page 15.

191. "Cornerstone for City-County hospital laid in 1936." Houston Post, Saturday, 07/19/86. Local Section, Page 4B, Final Edition.

Gray, Lisa. "The noble salvage." Houston Chronicle, Sunday, 07/10/2005. Section: Zest, Page 12.

Houston, A History and A Guide. Page 323.

192. "Houston, 1924-1951. Volume 5, Sheet 505." Sanborn maps, 1867-1970: Texas.

193. Martinez, John F. "Jefferson Davis Hospital." The Beat. Volume 7, Issue 2 (March 2006). Houston: Harris County Hospital District.

"Detailed Chronology of the Texas Medical Center." Texas Medical Center. <http://www.tmc.edu/tmc-chronology.html/> [Accessed May 24, 2004].

Historical records search and archeological subsurface testing for the Jefferson Davis Hospital site at 1801 Allen Parkway Drive, Houston, Harris County, Texas. Page 17.

Byars, Carlos. "A piece of medical history shattered / 15 blasts bring an end to Jeff Davis Hospital." Houston Chronicle, Sunday, 05/16/99. Section A, Page 29 MetFront, 4 Star Edition.

194. Ibid.

Bivins, Ralph. "Olajuwon adds to holdings." Houston Chronicle, 07/14/2000. <http://www.chron.com/disp/story.mpl/business/603475.html> [Accessed January 2, 2009].

195. "Federal Reserve Bank, Houston, Texas, Petroleum-Impacted Site Renaissance." U. S. EPA. <http://www.epa.gov/Region06//6sf/pdffiles/fedreservebanksuccess2007.pdf/> [Accessed January 2, 2009].

Bivins, Ralph. "Olajuwon adds to holdings."

Sarnoff, Nancy. "Real Estate Roundup." Houston Business Journal, July 27-August 2, 2001. Page 10.

"Remarks by Vice Chairman Roger W. Ferguson, Jr., October 16, 2002." Federal Reserve Board. <http://www.federalreserve.gov/boarddocs/speeches/2002/200210162/default.html/> [Accessed January 2, 2009].

196. "Federal Reserve Bank sets the standard for facilities nationwide." Houston Business Journal, April 28, 2006. <http://houston.bizjournals.com/houston/stories/2006/05/01/focus9.html> [Accessed December 27, 2008].

Pugh, Clifford. "Graves new world." Houston Chronicle, Sunday, 11/06/2005. Section: Zest Magazine, Page 14.

"Kent Ullberg's sculpture 'The Guardian' bound for new Federal Reserve." Design News. <http://designtaxi.com/> [Accessed January 2, 2009].

197. Sarnoff, Nancy. "That city to the north may not stay on sign." Houston Chronicle, Saturday, 05/21/2005. Section: D, Page 1, 3 Star Edition.

198. Johnson, Laurie. "Swedish artist sculpts American tribute." KUHF-FM. <http://www.kuhf.org/> [Accessed January 2, 2009].

"Kent Ullberg's sculpture 'The Guardian' bound for new Federal Reserve." Design News. <http://designtaxi.com/> [Accessed January 2, 2009].

"Fed opens new Houston Branch building." Federal Reserve Bank of Dallas. <http://www.dallasfed.org/news/releases/2005/nr051027b.html/> [Accessed January 2, 2009].

199. Historical records search and archeological subsurface testing for the Jefferson Davis Hospital site at 1801 Allen Parkway Drive, Houston, Harris County, Texas. Pages 18-19.

Beverly, Trevia Wooster. "12. Allen Parkway Village Cemetery." At Rest: A Historical Directory of Harris County, Texas, Cemeteries (1822-2001). Houston: Tejas Publications & Research, 2001.

200. "Houston Wrought Up." Dallas Morning News. 1/4/1891, page 16.

201. "Bayou City Budget." Galveston Daily News, Tuesday, April 14, 1891, page 3, Issue 21, column A.

202. Historical records search and archeological subsurface testing for the Jefferson Davis Hospital site at 1801 Allen Parkway Drive, Houston, Harris County, Texas. Page 22.

203. Ibid. Page 12, 13, 20, 21.

204. Beverly, Trevia Wooster. "12. Allen Parkway Village Cemetery."

Makeig, John. "Records rebut activist in APV graves dispute." Houston Chronicle, Tuesday, 07/16/96. Section A, Page 20, 3 Star Edition.

205. "Allen Parkway Village Cemetery." "Cemeteries of Harris." <http://www.cemeteries-of-tx.com/Etx/Harris/cemetery/allenb.htm> [Accessed August 17, 2011].

Beverly, Trevia Wooster. "12. Allen Parkway Village Cemetery."

206. Passey, M. Louise. Freedmantown: the evolution of a black neighborhood in Houston, 1865-1880. Thesis (M. A.). Rice University, 1993. Page 79.

207. Blandin, Isabella Margaret Elizabth, Mrs. History of Shearn Church, 1837-1907. Houston: Shearn Auxiliary, 1908.

Wagner, J. K., and Company, Inc. "Archival Research Lot 39, Part Lot 40 O. Smith Survey A-696, Houston, Harris County, Texas."

"Clement R. Hopson to Garrett S. Hardcastle, May 6, 1857." Deed Records. Harris County, Texas. Vol. P, Page 749.

208. Wagner, J. K., and Company, Inc. "Archival Research Lot 39, Part Lot 40 O. Smith Survey A-696, Houston, Harris County, Texas."

209. "Five Points. Some of the Lower Quarters of Houston. The acrid abodes of Vinegar Hill. The smokey rows of Smokeyville, Freedmantown and Chapmansville." Houston Daily Telegraph, July 25, 1874.

Barr, Alwyn and Cary D. Wintz. "Allen, Richard." The Handbook of Texas Online. <http://www.tshaonline.org/handbook/online/articles/fal24> [Accessed August 17, 2011].

210. Mackey, Thomas C.. "Thelma Denton and associates: Houston's Red Light Reservation and a question of Jim Crow." Houston Review. Volume 14, No. 3 (1992). Houston: Houston Library Board, 1992.

Wagner, J. K., and Company, Inc. "Archival Research Lot 39, Part Lot 40 O. Smith Survey A-696, Houston, Harris County, Texas."

211. "San Felipe Courts Historic District." Texas Historical Commission. Atlas. <http://atlas.thc.state.tx.us/scripts/> [Accessed December 2, 2000].

212. "Freedmen's Town Historic District." Texas Historical Commission. Atlas. <http://atlas.thc.state.tx.us/scripts/> [Accessed December 26, 2005].

213. "Jim Mozola Memorial DGC (Bayou Course)." DG Course Reveiw. <http://www.dgcoursereview.com/course.php?id=1397> [Accessed January 10, 2009].

"What is Disc Golf?" Disc Golf Association. <http://www.discgolfassoc.com/> [Accessed January 25, 2009].

214. Manning, Tom. "Supporters push for centrally located skate park." Houston Chronicle, Thursday, 01/20/2005. Section: This Week Z11, Page 7, 2 Star Edition.

Crowe, Robert. "Skaters are eager to flip, spin and slide." Houston Chronicle, Friday, 02/08/2008. Section: B, Page 4, 3 Star Edition.

215. "Central Skatepark." Houston Parks Board. <http://www.hpbinc.org/downtown_skatepark.htm> [Accessed March 2, 2006].

216. Elliott, Chris. "A big push to get rolling." Houston Chronicle, Wednesday, 06/20/2007. Section: C, Page 1, 3 Star Edition.

Crowe, Robert. "Skaters are eager to flip, spin and slide." Houston Chronicle, Friday, 02/08/2008. Section: B, Page 4, 3 Star Edition.

217. A. L. Westyard (attributed). Houston, Texas (Looking South) 1891. Chicago: D. W. Ensign, Jr., 1891.

"Sabine Street Bridge." Texas Historic Bridge Inventory. Texas. Department of Transportation. August 30, 2005.

218. Ibid.

219. Ibid.

220. Snyder, Mike. "Bridging the City and nature. Supporters hope the $15 million Sabine-to-Bagby Promenade jump-starts more efforts to develop city's signature waterway." Houston Chronicle, Sunday, 06/04/2006. Section: B, Page 1, 4 Star Edition.

"Sabine Street Bridge over Buffalo Bayou." National Register of Historic Places. Registration Form. US Dept of the Interior. National Park Service.

Chapter 7: The Sabine Promenade

1. Wood, W. E. City of Houston, Harris County, Texas [map]. Houston, 1869.

2. Himmel, Richard L. "Jones, Mary Smith." The Handbook of Texas Online. <http://www.tshaonline.org/handbook/online/articles/fjo93> [Accessed August 18, 2011].

"Woodruff, John." Republic Claims Search Results. Texas State Library and Archives Commission. <http://www2.tsl.state.tx.us/trail/> [Accessed December 5, 2005].

"Jones, Mary (Mrs. Anson), Letters, 1858-1900." Library. University of Houston. <http://www.lib.utexas.edu/taro/uhsc/00034/hsc-00034.html> [Accessed August 18, 2011].

"Mrs. Mary Anson Jones is dead." Houston Daily Post. January 1, 1908.

"Samuel W. Punchard to John Woodruff, March 30, 1839." Deed Records. Harris County, Texas. Vol. D, Page 59.

3. "Allen's reminiscences of Texas, 1838-1842." Volume 18, Numnber 3, Southwestern Historical Quarterly Online, Page 287-304. <http://www.tsha.utexas.edu/publications/journals/shq/online/v018/n3/article_3_print.html> [Accessed April 3, 2006].

"Woodruff, John." Republic Claims Search Results.

4. "Obedience Smith to R. C. Campbell, December 27, 1842." Deed Records. Harris County, Texas. Vol. K, Page 197.

Wagner, J. K., and Company, Inc. "Archival Research Lot 39, Part Lot 40 O. Smith Survey A-696, Houston, Harris County, Texas. HISD Gregory Lincoln / HSPVA Archeological Testing Project #99714. July, 2005.

"Robert C. Campbell to Justin Castanie, July 3, 1846." Deed Records. Harris County, Texas. Vol. K, Page 431.

Wood, W. E. City of Houston, Harris County, Texas [map]. Houston, 1869.

5. "James S. Holman to Clement R. Hopson and John J. Cain, June 5, 1843." Deed Records. Harris County, Texas. Vol. I, Page 404.

"John Stein to C. R. Hopson, April 6, 1846." Deed Records. Harris County, Texas. Vol. K, Page 271.

"Robert C. Campbell to Justin Castanie, July 3, 1846." Deed Records. Harris County, Texas. Vol. K, Page 431.

"George Stevens and Elizabeth Stevens to Clement R. Hopson, May 1, 1857." Deed Records. Harris County, Texas. Vol. P, Page 749.

Givens, Murphy. "Beef packing houses once dotted the coast." Corpus Chrisit Caller-Times, December 19, 2007. <http://www.caller.com/news/2007/dec/19/beef-packing-houses-once-dotted-the-coast/> [Accessed March 14, 2009].

"Clement R. Hopson to Garrett S. Hardcastle, May 6, 1857." Deed Records. Harris County, Texas. Vol. P, Page 749.

6. "Ancient Order of Pilgrims TX6127." Historical Markers. Texas Historical Commission. <http://www.historicalmarkers.com/> [Accessed January 22, 2008].

7. "Freedmen's Town Historic District." Texas Historical Commission. Atlas. <http://atlas.thc.state.tx.us/scripts/>. [Accessed December 26,l 2005].

Slotboom, Erik. Houston Freeways. Houston: Oscar F. Slotboom, 2003.

8. "City asked for cemetery." Houston Chronicle, Tuesday, 02/09/99. Section A, Page 14, 3 Star Edition.

9. Ibid.

10. Sallee, Rad. "Enhancements will put maze of bridges, ramps in new light." Houston Chronicle, Tuesday, 07/18/00. Section A, Page 17, 3 Star Edition.

11. McCurdy, Bill. "A brief history of baseball in Texas." Texas Baseball Hall of Fame. <http://www.tbhof.org/features/feature-20051028> [Accessed December 29, 2005].

"Major League Baseball." Wikipedia. <http://en.wikipedia.org/wiki/Major_League_Baseball> [Accessed August 18, 2011].

12. "Top 100 Teams." Minor League Baseball. <http://www.minorleaguebaseball.com/app/history/> [Accessed December 29, 2005].

13. Ibid.

14. Ibid.

"Houston, 1907. Volume 1, Sheets 39 and 86." Sanborn maps, 1867-1970: Texas. [Ann Arbor, Mich.?] : Bell & Howell Information and Learning, c2001.

"Play Ball! March 31, 2008" Bayou City History. Houston Chronicle. <http://blogs.chron.com/bayoucityhistory/> [Accessed April 4, 2008].

15. "Top 100 Teams."

16. McCurdy, Bill. "A brief history of baseball in Texas."

17. Ibid.

18. "Houston Astros. History. Astros Timeline." Major League Baseball. <http://houston.astros.mlb.com/NASApp/mlb/hou/history/timeline1.jsp> [Accessed December 30, 2005].

19. Hamm, Madeleine McDermott. "These old houses / Structures from bygone days, forgotten sites keep city's past alive in Sam Houston Park." Houston Chronicle, Sunday, 06/01/97. Lifestyle Section, Page 1, 2 Star Edition.

Mitchell, Doug. "Relax in Sam Houston Park." City Savvy. Vol. 5, No. 3, Summer 2000.

Houghton, Dorothy K. H. Houston's Forgotten Heritage. Houston: Rice University Press, 1991. Page 43.

20. Houghton, Dorothy K. H. Houston's Forgotten Heritage. Page 74.

McComb, David G. Houston: A History. Austin: University of Texas, 1981. Page 17.

21. "Kellum, N. K. 1860 Census, Series M653, Roll 1295, Page 277." Heritage Quest Online. ProQuest Information and Learning Company. <http://www.heritagequestonline.com/> [Accessed April 15, 2009].

Kellum, Nathaniel. Reverse Index to Deed Records. Harris County, Texas. Vol. 9, Page 215.

Perry, John. "Houston heritage has a home in city park." City Savvy. Quarterly newsletter published for City of Houston employees. Vol. 10, No. 1 (Winter 2005). Houston: City of Houston.

"Marriage Notices from the Houston Morning Star Newspaper, April, 1839-1844." US-GenWeb. <http://files.usgwarchives.org/tx/harris/vitals/marriages/marrhous.txt> [Accessed August 18, 2011].

22. Holman, James J., to Nathaniel K. Kellum, February 9, 1844. Deed Records. Harris County, Texas. Vol. J, Page 223.

Bagby, Thomas M., to Nathaniel K. Kellum, May 16, 1844. Deed Records. Harris County, Texas. Vol. I, Page 394.

Lubbock, F. R., to Nathaniel K. Kellum, November 22, 1845. Deed Records. Harris County, Texas. Vol. J, Page 609.

"Nathaniel K. Kellum to Benjamin A. Shepherd, October 13, 1849." Power of Attorney. Deed Records. Harris County, Texas. Vol. O, Page 280.

Glass, James L. Personal communication, March 27, 2006.

Pierce, Gerald S. Texas Under Arms. Austin: Encino Press. 1969. p. 68-69.

23. Hamm, Madeleine McDermott. "These old houses / Structures from bygone days, forgotten sites keep city's past alive in Sam Houston Park."

Houston, A History and A Guide. Houston: Anson Jones Press, 1942. Page 281.

24. "Nathaniel K. Kellum to Benjamin A. Shepherd, October 13, 1849." Power of Attorney. Deed Records. Harris County, Texas. Vol. O, Page 280.

"Benjamin A. Shepherd to A. W. Noble, January 29, 1851." Deed Records. Harris County, Texas. Vol. O, Page 425.

25. "Grimes County, TX. 1850 Federal Census." US GenWeb. <http://www.usgwcensus.org/cenfiles/tx/grimes/1850/pg00770.txt/> [Accessed April 25, 2009].

Valenza, Janet. Taking the waters of Texas. Austin: University of Texas Press, 2000. Page 173-174.

"Texas News Items." Galveston Daily News, July 29, 1879, Issue 109, column B.

26. Valenza, Janet. Taking the waters of Texas. Page 173-174.

27. "Piedmont Springs Resort Site." Grimes County , Texas Historical Markers Page. Rootsweb.com <http://www.rootsweb.ancestry.com/~txgrimes/GrimesHistorical.html> [Accessed April 25, 2009].

28. Wheat, Jim. "Postmasters and Post Offices of Grimes County, Texas, 1846 - 1930." Rootsweb.com <http://www.rootsweb.com/~txpost/grimes.html> [Accessed April 25, 2009].

"Kellum, N. K. 1860 Census, Series M653, Roll 1295, Page 277."

"Kellum Springs." Houston Tri-Weekly Telegraph, August 11, 1862. Page 2, Column 2. <http://www.uttyler.edu/vbetts/houston_tri-w_telegraph_jul-dec_62.htm/> [Accessed April 25, 2009].

29. Valenza, Janet. Taking the waters of Texas. Page 174.

"Kellum, Nathan. 1870 Census, Series M593, Roll 1588, Page 324." Heritage Quest On-line. ProQuest Information and Learning Company. <http:// www.heritagequestonline.com/> [Accessed April 25, 2009].

"State News, Anderson County." Galveston Daily News, August 29, 1877, Issue 136, column B.

"Texas News Items." Galveston Daily News, July 29, 1879, Issue 109, column B.

30. "Sunday at Houston." Galveston Daily News, July 9, 1894, Page 3, Issue 108, column A.

"Joint Debate." Galveston Daily News, August 29, 1896, Page 6, Issue 158, column D.

31. "Noble." Family Stories. Rootsweb.com. <http:// freepages.geneology.rootsweb.ancestry.com/~sorters/stories.html> [Accessed April 15, 2009].

"Our Southern Roots." Family Stories. Rootsweb.com. <http:// freepages.geneology.rootsweb.ancestry.com/~sorters/pafg02.htm> [Accessed April 20, 2009].

Houghton, Dorothy K. H. Houston's Forgotten Heritage. Page 255.

Houston, A History and A Guide. Page 281.

32. Karkabi, Barbara. "Student of history / Betty Trapp Chapman passes on lessons of Houston's past." Houston Chronicle, Wednesday, 09/16/98. Houston Section, Page 1, 2 Star Edition.

Hamm, Madeleine McDermott. "These old houses / Structures from bygone days, forgotten sites keep city's past alive in Sam Houston Park."

33. "Noble, A. W.", 1860 Census, Series M653, Roll 1296, Page 428."

"Noble." Family Stories. Rootsweb.com.

"Our Southern Roots." Family Stories. Rootsweb.com.

Houghton, Dorothy K. H. Houston's Forgotten Heritage. Page 255.

34. Houghton, Dorothy K. H. Houston's Forgotten Heritage. Page 43.

Mitchell, Doug. "Relax in Sam Houston Park."

35. Houston, A History and A Guide. Page 313-314.

Hamm, Madeleine McDermott. "These old houses / Structures from bygone days, forgotten sites keep city's past alive in Sam Houston Park."

Perry, John. "Houston heritage has a home in city park."

36. Soils Map Harris County. The U. S. Department of Agriculture Bureau of Soils Field Operations. A. Hoen & Co. Lithography, Baltimore, MD, 1922. <http://www.hctx.net/ RecordsManagement/Img.aspx?img=9> Accessed June 19, 2009].

37. Glass, James L. The Houston Municipal Wharf 1836-1840. Otherwise known as "Allen's Landing" Circa 1967. A Reconstruction by James L. Glass, March, 2007. [unpublished manuscript]

Russell, Marie. 1850 Census Harris County, Texas with added genealogical notes. Baytown: n.p., 1981.

"Stanly [Stanley], L. C. 1860 Census, Series M653, Roll 1296, Page 429."

"Stanley, Lardner C. 1870 Census, Series M593, Roll 1589, Page 615."

38. Evans, H., to S. W. Young, June 23, 1866. Deed Records. Harris County, Texas. Vol. 3, Page 187-188.

"Ellen W. Fuller and husband J. L. Fuller to Samuel W. Young, February 3, 1869." Deed Records. Harris County, Texas. Vol. 7, page 237.

"Houston Local Items." Galveston Daily News, October 29, 1875, Issue 250, column C.

"Bayou City Budget." Galveston Daily News, January 7, 1891, page 3, Issue 252, column A.

39. "Houston, 1896. Sheet 48." Sanborn maps, 1867-1970: Texas. [Ann Arbor, Mich.?] : Bell & Howell Information and Learning, c2001.

40. Wolf, George E., Jr. "Masonic Cemetery." Cemeteries of Harris County, Texas. <http://www.usgennet.org/usa/tx/topic/cemeteries/Etx/Harris/cemetery/masonic.htm> [Accessed August 20, 2011].

History of Texas Together with a Biographical History of the Cities of Houston and Galveston. Chicago: Lewis Publishing Co., 1895. Pages 567-569.

Johnston, Marguarite. Houston, The Unknown City, 1836-1946. College Station: Texas A & M University Press, 1991. Page 312.

"Benjamin A. Shepherd to A. W. Noble, January 29, 1851." Deed Records. Harris County, Texas. Vol. O, Page 425.

41. Houston, A History and A Guide. Page 282.

"Richardson, Stephen." The Handbook of Texas Online. <http://www.tshaonline.org/handbook/online/articles/fri09> [Accessed August 20, 2011].

42. Cutrer, Thomas W. "Baker, Moseley" The Handbook of Texas Online. <http://www.tshaonline.org/handbook/online/articles/fba37> [Accessed August 20, 2011].

43. Houston, A History and A Guide. Page 282.

44. Wolf, George E., Jr. "Masonic Cemetery."

45. Historical records search and archeological subsurface testing for the Jefferson Davis Hospital site at 1801 Allen Parkway Drive, Houston, Harris County, Texas. Houston: Moore Archeological Consulting, 1999. Pages 18-19.

Johnston, Marguarite. Houston, The Unknown City, 1836-1946. Pages 312, 422 note 13.

46. Wagner, Janet. Personal communication. December 14, 2005.

47. "Neuhaus Fountain (Three Coyotes)." Houston Municipal Art. <http://www.houstonmunicipalart.org/> [Accessed October 22, 2007].

48. Johnston, Marguarite. Houston, The Unknown City, 1836-1946. Page 312.

"Benjamin A. Shepherd to A. W. Noble, January 29, 1851."

Wood, W. E. City of Houston, Harris County, Texas [map]. Houston, 1869.

Houghton, Dorothy K. H. Houston's Forgotten Heritage. Page 138.

"Houston, 1896. Sheet 19." Sanborn maps, 1867-1970: Texas.

49. "DeGeorge, Michal, 1900 Census, Series T623, Roll 1642, Page 109." Heritage Quest Online. ProQuest Information and Learning Company. <http://www.heritagequestonline.com/> [Accessed May 31, 2009].

50. "About Us." DeGeorge Real Estate Services, Inc. <http://degeorgerealestate.com/aboutus.html> [Accessed June 2, 2009].

"Thomas H. Monroe House." Landmark Designation Report. Archaeological and Historical Commission. City of Houston. April 29, 2008.

51. "DeGeorge, Michele, 1910 Census, Series T624, Roll 1559, Page 258." Heritage Quest Online. ProQuest Information and Learning Company. <http://www.heritagequestonline.com/> [Accessed May 31, 2009].

"Houston, 1907. Volume 1, Sheet 21." Sanborn maps, 1867-1970: Texas.

52. "Houston, 1924. Volume 1, Sheet 37." Sanborn maps, 1867-1970: Texas. [Ann Arbor, Mich.?]: Bell & Howell Information and Learning, c2001.

"About Us." DeGeorge Real Estate Services, Inc.

"DeGeorge, Rosalie, 1930 Census, Series T626, Roll 2349, Page 194." Heritage Quest Online. ProQuest Information and Learning Company. <http://www.heritagequestonline.com/> [Accessed May 31, 2009].

53. Houghton, Dorothy K. H. Houston's Forgotten Heritage. Page 138.

"Houston, 1924-1951. Vol. 1. Sheet 37." Sanborn maps, 1867-1970: Texas. [Ann Arbor, Mich.?]: Bell & Howell Information and Learning, c2001.

54. Manning, Tom. "Pedestrian bridge to access hike, bike trails / Pathway over Buffalo Bayou to link downtown destinations." Houston Chronicle, Thursday, 12/15/2005. Section: This Week, Page 3, 2 Star Edition.

55. "Our History." Antioch Missionary Baptist Church. <http://www.antiochhouston.org/History.htm.> [Accessed Jul 18 16:35:00 US/Central 2002].

Chapman, Betty T. "Educational, spiritual legacy of Jack Yates remains clear." Houston Business Journal, February 2-8, 2001, Page 33.

56. Wood, W. E. City of Houston, Harris County, Texas [map]. Houston, 1869.

"Happenings at Houston." Galveston Daily News, May 15, 1892, Page 3, Issue 52, column A.

"Houston, 1896. Sheet 20." Sanborn maps, 1867-1970: Texas.

"Houston, 1924. Volume 1, Sheet 37." Sanborn maps, 1867-1970: Texas.

57. "Houston, 1924-1951. Vol. 1. Sheet 37." Sanborn maps, 1867-1970: Texas.

Johnston, Marguarite. Houston, The Unknown City, 1836-1946. Page 258.

58. "Houston says able to care for Democrats." Dallas Morning News. 1/15/1928, page 10.

Tutt, Bob. "Echoes of Sam Houston Coliseum / Venue hosted political events, concerts, revivals and more." Houston Chronicle, Sunday, 06/07/98. Section A, Page 29 MetFront, 2 Star Edition.

59. "1928 Democratic National Convention." Wikipedia. <http://en.wikipedia.org/wiki/1928_Democratic_National_Convention> [Accessed August 19, 2011].

60. Tutt, Bob. "Echoes of Sam Houston Coliseum / Venue hosted political events, concerts, revivals and more."

61. Ibid.

"Houston, 1924-1951. Vol. 1. Sheet 37." Sanborn maps, 1867-1970: Texas.

62. Tutt, Bob. "Echoes of Sam Houston Coliseum / Venue hosted political events, concerts, revivals and more."

"Historic Photos of the Houston Area." Texas Freeway. <http://www.texasfreeway.com/houston/historic/photos/houston_historic_photos.shtml> [Accessed February 9, 2003].

63. Pugh, Clifford. "Hobby Center (almost) a work of art." Houston Chronicle, Friday, 05/10/2002. Section: A, Page 1, 3 Star Edition.

Pugh, Clifford. "A stellar debut." Houston Chronicle, Friday, 05/10/2002. <http://www.chron.com/cs/CDA/story.hts/ae/theater/1395004> [Accessed May 10, 2002].

Pugh, Clifford. "The Hobby Center at a glance." Houston Chronicle, Friday, 05/10/2002. <http://www.chron.com/cs/CDA/story.hts/ae/theater/1395007> [Accessed May 10, 2002].

64. "Untitled." Houston Chronicle, Friday, 09/06/2002. Section: D, Page 4, 2 Star Edition.

65. Pugh, Clifford. "A stellar debut."

Pugh, Clifford. "The Hobby Center at a glance."

66. "Houston, Tex." Stone & Webster Public Service Journal. Volume 16 (Jan-Jun 1915). Page 216, 306.

67. Radowick, Pete. "Standing the test of time." City Savvy. Vol. 5, No. 4, Fall 2000.

"Sweeney Clock." Civic Center Marker. City of Houston.

68. "Houston, 1896. Sheet 20." Sanborn maps, 1867-1970: Texas.

69. Russell, Marie. 1850 Census Harris County, Texas with added genealogical notes. Houghton, Dorothy K. H. Houston's Forgotten Heritage. Pages 26, 329 note 62.

70. "Stanley, J. H. S. 1860 Census, Series M653, Roll 1296, Page 429." Houston City Directory, 1866. Dallas: R. L. Polk & Co, 1866. Page 47.

71. "Stanley, J. H. Stephen. 1870 Census, Series M593, Roll 1589, Page 593."

72. "Houston Local Items." Galveston Daily News, March 14, 1874, Issue 58, column C. "Houston Local Items." Galveston Daily News, January 16, 1876, Issue 218, column E. "Scientists in Texas." Galveston Daily News, September 13, 1877, Issue 149, column B.

73. "Vasmer, Elizabeth H, 1880 Census, Series T9, Roll 1309, Page 148." Heritage Quest Online. ProQuest Information and Learning Company. <http://www.heritagequestonline.com/> [Accessed June 26, 2009].
"Houston Cotton Quotations." Galveston Daily News, June 23, 1882, Issue 80, column G.

74. "Day at Houston." Galveston Daily News, May 2, 1895, Page 3, Issue 39, column A.

75. Ibid.
"Day at Houston Local Items." Galveston Daily News, June 16, 1895, Page 3, Issue 84, column A.
"Day at Houston Local Items." Galveston Daily News, September 13, 1895, Page 3, Issue 173, column A.
"Jail Building." Galveston Daily News, June 30, 1896, Issue 98, column D.
Houston, A History and A Guide. Page 243.

76. "Courthouses of Eugene Heiner (1852-1901)." Texas Escapes. <http://www.texasescapes.com/TexasCourthouses/Courthouses-of-Eugene-T-Heiner.htm> [Accessed June 28, 2009].
"Day at Houston Local Items." Galveston Daily News, September 13, 1895, Page 3, Issue 173, column A.

77. Ibid.

78. Houston, A History and A Guide. Page 243, 284.
Radowick, Pete. "Old oak witnesses history." City Savvy. Vol. 6, No. 1, Winter 2001.

79. Ibid.
"Full list of manuscripts." Woodson Research Center. Fondren Library. Rice University. <http://www.rice.edu/> [Accessed Sep 25 16:01:00 US/Central 2004].

80. Nissimov, Ron. "Bayou Place." Houston Chronicle, Wednesday, 12/01/2004. Section: B, Page 1, 3 Star Edition.
Walden, Jim. "Bayou Place complex to double in size / Council OKs lease agreement." Houston Chronicle, Wednesday, 01/24/2001. Section This Week, Page 06, 2 Star Edition.
"Planet relocates headquarters to Houston's Bayou Place." Reuters. <http://www.reuters.com/articlePrint?articleId=US131706%2B12-Dec-2007%2BBW20071212/> [Accessed June 25, 2009].

81. "Old Hanging Oak." Civic Center Marker. City of Houston.

82. Famous Trees of Texas. Texas Forest Service. <http://famoustreesoftexas.tamu.edu/explore-Period.aspx> [Accessed August 19, 2011].

83. "Execution." Telegraph and Texas Register, Saturday, March 31, 1838.
Winningham, Geoff. Along forgotten river: photographs of Buffalo Bayou and the Houston Ship Channel, 1997-2001. Austin: Texas Historical Association, 2003.

84. Muir, Andrew Forest, ed. "Diary of a Young Man in Houston, 1838." Southwestern Historical Quarterly. Volume 53, Number 3 (January, 1950), Pages 299-301 .

85. Hardin, Stephen L. Texian Macabre. College Station: Texas A&M University Press, 2007.

86. Muir, Andrew Forest, ed. "Diary of a Young Man in Houston, 1838." Page 300, note 116.

87. "Advertisement." Telegraph and Texas Register, February 13, 1839.

"Survey for John W. N. A. Smith, by Henry Trott, March 26, 1839." Harris County Surveyors' Records, Vol. A, Page 289.

88. Glass, James L. Personal communication, June 28, 2009.

"Mary O'Brien to Miss Emma Blake, March 2, 1841." Deed Records. Harris County, Texas. Vol. H, Page 206-207.

"James and Jane Wells to Auguste Girard, Charles J. Hedenberg and Philip V. Vedder, January 1, 1840." Deed Records. Harris County, Texas. Vol. E, Page 378.

89. "Houston Local Items." Galveston Daily News, January 28, 1874, Issue 19, column F.

"Houston Local Items." Galveston Daily News, August 12, 1876, Issue 122, column C.

"Houston Local Items." Galveston Daily News, June 17, 1877, Issue 74, column E.

90. "Justice is done." Galveston Daily News, August 5, 1893, Page 3, Issue 135, column A.

Young, S. O. True stories of old Houston and Houstonians. Galveston: Oscar Springer, 1913. Page 8.

91. "Bayou City Budget." Galveston Daily News, August 23, 1887, Page 3, Issue 119, column A.

92. "Obedience Smith to John Stine [Stein], February 17, 1843." Deed Records. Harris County, Texas. Vol. H, Page 387-388.

A. L. Westyard (attributed). Houston, Texas (Looking South) [Bird's Eye] 1891. Chicago: D. W. Ensign, Jr., 1891.

Pocket Map of the City of Houston. Houston: Wm. W. Thomas & Co., 1890.

Young, S. O. True stories of old Houston and Houstonians. Page 8.

93. Radowick, Pete. "Old oak witnesses history."

Houston, A History and A Guide. Page 284.

Miller, Ray. Ray Miller's Houston. Houston: Cordovan Press, 1984. Page 196.

"Old Hanging Oak." Civic Center Marker. City of Houston.

94. Looscan, Adele B. "The Beginnings of Houston." in Houston, a nation's capital 1837 - 1839. Houston: Harris County Historical Society, 1985. Pages 2-7.

Kleiner, Diana J. "Beauchamps Springs, Texas." The Handbook of Texas Online. <http://www.tshaonline.org/handbook/online/articles/hvbce> [Accessed August 19, 2011].

95. O'Donohoe, Steve. "The Houston Water System, 1878-1981." Public Works Department. City of Houston. [unpublished manuscript], 1981.

Smyer, Susan. "History of the City of Houston's Drinking Water Operations." City of Houston. <http://documents.publicworks.houstontx.gov/documents/divisions/utilities/history_of_drinking_water_operations.pdf> [Accessed September 25, 2008].

96. O'Donohoe, Steve. "The Houston Water System, 1878-1981."

97. McComb, David G. Houston: A History. Page 89.

Johnston, Marguarite. Houston, The Unknown City, 1836-1946. Pages 96, 116.

"Houston, 1890. Sheet 20." Sanborn maps, 1867-1970: Texas. [Ann Arbor, Mich.?] : Bell & Howell Information and Learning, c2001.

Smyer, Susan. "History of the City of Houston's Drinking Water Operations."

98. Ibid.

"Houston, 1924-1948. Volume 2, Sheet 213." Sanborn maps, 1867-1970: Texas. [Ann Arbor, Mich.?] : Bell & Howell Information and Learning, c2001.

99. Ibid.

O'Donohoe, Steve. "The Houston Water System, 1878-1981."

"Part of Houston submerged as Buffalo Bayou surges over banks." Galveston Daily News, December 9, 1935. Page 2.

Mitchell, Doug. "Water at the center of Central." City Savvy. Vol. 5, No. 1, Winter 2000.

100. Muir, Andrew Forest. "Swimming Holes." Papers. MS17, Box 34.1. Woodson Research Center. Rice University. Houston, TX.

101. Houghton, Dorothy K. H. Houston's Forgotten Heritage. Page 20.

Muir, Andrew Forest. "Indians." MSS 17-33.6. Papers. Woodson Research Center. Rice University. Houston, TX.

"Chief John Bowles and the Texas Cherokee are rarely remembered." Smoky Mountain News. Mountain Voices, 02/28/01. <http://www.smokymountainnews.com/issues/2_01/2_28_01/> [Accessed March 7, 2004].

102. Glass, James L. Personal communication. February 8, 2004.

103. Moore, Roger G. and Allan D. Meyers. Data recovery excavations for the Sesquicentennial Park Project, Stage II, Houston, Harris County, Texas. (Texas Antiquities Permit No. 987). Houston: Moore Archeological Consulting, 2000. Page 7.

104. McAshan, Marie Phelps. On the corner of Main and Texas, a Houston legacy. Houston: Hutchins House, 1985. Page 44.

Glass, James L. Personal communication. February 8, 2004.

105. Washington On Westcott Roundabout Initiatve. <http://www.wowroundabout.org> [Accessed August 1, 2002].

Turner, Allan. "Shaping up style on Washington Avenue." Houston Chronicle, Sunday, 04/10/2005. Section: B, Page 1, 3 Star Edition.

106. Book of Houston: a brief sketch of its history,...[Houston, TX?]: [s. n.], 1915. Page 74-75.

"Houston, August, 1885. Sheet 14." Sanborn maps, 1867-1970: Texas. [Ann Arbor, Mich.?] : Bell & Howell Information and Learning, c2001.

107. Houston, A History and A Guide. Page 153.

"Texas. Harris County. Geneology. Marriages [1837-1847]." Our Lost Family. <http://www.maxpages.com/ourlostfamily2/Marriages_Part_One> [Accessed January 3, 2001].

Worm, Jeri & John. "Harris County, Texas - Founder's Memorial Park." USGENWEB. <http://files.usgwarchives.net/tx/harris/cemeteries/founders.txt> [Accessed August 20, 2011].

Russell, Marie. 1850 Census Harris County, Texas with added genealogical notes.

"Stockbridge, E., 1860 Census, Series M653, Roll 1296, Page 421."

"Stockbridge, Elam, 1870 Census, Series M593, Roll 1608, Page 77."

108. Ibid.

"Stockbridge, Judge, 1880 Census, Series T9, Roll 1331, Page 125."

109. Houghton, Dorothy K. H. Houston's Forgotten Heritage. Page 32.

Campbell, Robert. Lone Star Confederate: a gallant and good soldier of the 5th Texas Infantry. College Station: Texas A&M Press, 2003. Page 142.

110. Houston City Directory, 1866. Page 46.

"Simpson, Benj, 1870 Census, Series M593, Roll 1589, Page 616."

"Simpson, Benj C, 1880 Census, Series T9, Roll 1308, Page 12."

Courtney, John L. Personal communication, January 24, 2006. Owner of a State Fair prize medallion.

111. Campbell, Robert. Lone Star Confederate: a gallant and good soldier of the 5th Texas Infantry. Page 142.

"Houston, 1896. Sheet 46." Sanborn maps, 1867-1970: Texas.

Whitty, P. "Houston, January, 1906 [map]." 1906.

"Houston, 1924-1948. Volume 2, Sheet 214." Sanborn maps, 1867-1970: Texas.

Johnson, Patricia C. "Bayou Artpark opening set." Houston Chronicle, Friday, 02/28/92. Weekend Preview Section, Page 4, 2 Star Edition.

Johnson, Patricia C. "Art commission votes to relocate artpark." Houston Chronicle, Friday, 04/21/95. Houston Section, Page 12, 2 Star Edition.

112. History of Houston Fire Department. <http://www.maxmcrae.com/> [Accessed June 23, 2003].

Reyes, Raul, Asst. Chief. "Explore HFD history at fire museum." Houston Chronicle, Thursday, 06/19/2003. Section: This Week, Zone 11, Page 8, 2 Star Edition.

113. Schwartz, Matt and Rachel Graves. "Council approves lease for Landry's aquarium center." Houston Chronicle, 03/08/2001. Section: State & Local.

114. Houston, A History and A Guide. Page 286.

115. Chapman, Betty T. "Farmers' Market: Shopping hub served as public center." Houston Business Journal, June 15-21, 2001. Page 26.

116. Ibid.

Houston, A History and A Guide. Page 285.

117. Ibid.

Chapman, Betty T. "Farmers' Market: Shopping hub served as public center."

118. Ibid.

Houghton, Dorothy K. H. Houston's Forgotten Heritage. Page 319.

119. Laird, Cheryl. "Houston landmarks etched into our minds." Houston Chronicle, Sunday, 11/05/95. Lifestyle Section, Page 16, 2 Star Edition.

"Wortham Center. General information." City of Houston. <http://www.houstontx.gov/worthamcenter/general.htm> [Accessed January 10, 2010].

120. Ibid.

Laird, Cheryl. "Houston landmarks etched into our minds."

121. "Sesquicentennial Park. General information." City of Houston. <http://www.houstontx.gov/sqpark/generalinfo.htm> [Accessed December 31, 2009].

Pugh, Clifford and Patricia C. Johnson. "A point of pride / Bayou park supporters celebrate downtown destination." Houston Chronicle, Sunday, 05/03/98. Zest Section, Page 8, 2 Star Edition.

122. "Sesquicentennial Park. General information."

Johnson, Patricia C. "PBS show spotlights downtown." Houston Chronicle, Sunday, 04/23/2006. Section: Zest, Page 5, 2 Star Edition.

Asher, Ed. "Fire on the water / Sparkling downtown park opens with a splash, bash." Houston Chronicle, Sunday, 05/10/98. Section A, Page 1, 4 Star Edition.

123. "Civic Art." Landscape Online. <http://www.landscapeonline.com/lolpages/editorial/projects/streetscapes/9910civicart.htm> [Accessed August 18, 2002].

"Mel Chin: Do Not Ask Me." Artshound. <http://www.artshound.com/event/detail/520> [Accessed June 28, 2009].

124. "Sesquicentennial Park. General information."

Olson, Bradley. "Downtown statue to honor Baker." Houston Chronicle, Sunday, 12/27/2009. Section: B, Page 5, 3 Star R. O. Edition.

Johnson, Patricia C. "A floating gallery tour." Houston Chronicle, Sunday, 06/02/2002. Section: Zest, Page 13.

125. "Civic Art." Landscape Online.

126. Johnson, Patricia C. "A floating gallery tour."

127. "James A. Baker Monument: A magnificent American." James A. Baker Statue Fund. <http://www.bakermonument.com/> [Accessed December 31, 2009].

Olson, Bradley. "Downtown statue to honor Baker." Houston Chronicle, Sunday, 12/27/2009. Section: B, Page 5, 3 Star R. O. Edition.

Turner, Allan. "Statue stands tall for ex-Secretary of State James A. Baker." Houston Chronicle, Tuesday, October 26, 2010. <http://www.chron.com/news/houston-texas/article/Statue-stands-tall-for-ex-Secretary-of-State-1716578.php> [Accessed August 21, 2011].

128. Moore, Roger G. and Allan D. Meyers. Data recovery excavations for the Sesquicentennial Park Project, Stage II, Houston, Harris County, Texas. Pages 8-9.

129. Ibid.

130. Houghton, Dorothy K. H. Houston's Forgotten Heritage. Pages 24, 71.

131. Johnston, Marguarite. Houston, The Unknown City, 1836-1946. Page 73.

Moore, Roger G. and Allan D. Meyers. Data recovery excavations for the Sesquicentennial Park Project, Stage II, Houston, Harris County, Texas. Pages 1, 12.

"Houston, 1924. Volume 1, Sheet 7." Sanborn maps, 1867-1970: Texas.

132. "Houston, 1924-1948. Volume 1, Sheet 7." Sanborn maps, 1867-1970: Texas.

133. Moore, Roger G. and Allan D. Meyers. Data recovery excavations for the Sesquicentennial Park Project, Stage II, Houston, Harris County, Texas. Pages 13.

134. Ibid. Page 1.

135. Pugh, Clifford and Patricia C. Johnson. "A point of pride / Bayou park supporters celebrate downtown destination."

"Civic Art." Landscape Online.

136. Ibid.

137. Turner, Allan. "Bush receives monumental honor." Houston Chronicle, Friday, 12/03/2004. Section: B, Page 3, 2 Star Edition.

Hodge, Shelby. "Monument to honor former President Bush." Houston Chronicle, Monday, 11/24/2003. Section: Houston, Page 3, 3 Star Edition.

Foster, Charles C. and David B. Jones. "Clip and save: A Baedeker to a new Bush Monument." Houston Chronicle, Saturday, 12/04/2004. Section: B, Page 9, 3 Star Edition.

138. Ibid.

Smith, Frank C., Jr. "Letters: Mitchell even greater icon." Houston Chronicle, Friday, 05/20/2005. Section: B, Page 8, 2 Star Edition.

139. Foster, Charles C. and David B. Jones. "Clip and save: A Baedeker to a new Bush Monument."

Chapter 8: The Historic Downtown

1. "Franklin Avenue Bridge." Bridge plaque. City of Houston.

2. History of Texas Together with a Biographical History of the Cities of Houston and Galveston. Chicago: Lewis Publishing Co, 1895. Pge 378.

McComb, David G. Houston: A History. Austin: University of Texas, 1981. Page 44.

3. Ziegler, Jesse A. Wave of the Gulf. San Antonio: Naylor Co., 1938. Page 21.

4. "State Fair." Houston Tri-Weekly Telegraph, May, 1872, third week.

5. Ziegler, Jesse A. Wave of the Gulf. Page 22.

6. Wilson, Ann Quin. Native Houstonian, a collective portrait. Norfolk, VA.: Donning Co., 1982. Page 49.

"History of the State Fair of Texas." BigTex.com. <http://www.bigtex.com/aboutus/history/> [Accessed August 29, 2005].

7. Houston, A History and A Guide. Houston: Anson Jones Press, 1942. Page 287.

8. "Five Points. Some of the Lower Quarters of Houston. The acrid abodes of Vinegar Hill. The smokey rows of Smokeyville, Freedmantown and Chapmansville." Houston Daily Telegraph, July 25, 1874.

9. E-Newsletter. Historic Neighborhoods Council. August, 2004. Greater Houston Preservation Alliance. <http://www.ghpa.org/>

McComb, David G. Houston: A History. Page 106.

"Houston, 1907. Volume 2, Sheet 52." Sanborn maps, 1867-1970: Texas. [Ann Arbor, Mich.?] : Bell & Howell Information and Learning, c2001.

10. Houston, A History and A Guide. Houston: Anson Jones Press, 1942. Page 287.

Hornburg, David. Personal communication. November 1, 2005.

11. "Houston local items." Galveston Daily News, March 22, 1874, Issue 65, column E.

"One nuisance less." Galveston News. 8/4/1869, page 3.

"Police Court, July 30." Flake's Bulletin (Galveston, Texas). 08/01/1868, page 5.

12. "Local news." Flake's Bulletin (Galveston, Texas). 05/26/1870, page 5.

"Houston local items." Galveston Daily News, April 23, 1874, Issue 92, column E.

13. "One nuisance less." Galveston News. 8/4/1869, page 3.

14. Green, Charles D. Fire Fighters of Houston, 1838-1915. Houston: [s.n.], 1915. Pages 137-139.

Justman, Dorothy E. German Colonists and their Descendants in Houston Including Usener and Allied Families. Wichita Falls: Nortex Offset Publications, Inc., 1974. Page 88.

"Five Points. Some of the Lower Quarters of Houston. The acrid abodes of Vinegar Hill. The smokey rows of Smokeyville, Freedmantown and Chapmansville."

15. "Houston local items." Galveston Daily News, March 22, 1874, Issue 65, column E.

Justman, Dorothy E. German Colonists and their Descendants in Houston Including Usener and Allied Families. Pages 88-89.

Green, Charles D. Fire Fighters of Houston, 1838-1915. Pages 137-139.

16. Ibid.

Houston, A History and A Guide. Page 287.

"Houston local items." Galveston Daily News, March 22, 1874, Issue 65, column E.

17. Ibid.

"Houston local items." Galveston Daily News, April 23, 1874, Issue 92, column E.

18. "Five Points. Some of the Lower Quarters of Houston. The acrid abodes of Vinegar Hill. The smokey rows of Smokeyville, Freedmantown and Chapmansville."

Green, Charles D. Fire Fighters of Houston, 1838-1915. Pages 137-139.

"Houston local items." Galveston Daily News, July 26, 1877, Issue 107, column F.

"Vinegar Hill. Died suddenly." Houston Architecture Information Forum. <http://www.houstonarchitecture.com/haif/topic/7147-vinegar-hill-and-tin-can-alley/page__hl__vinegarroon> [Accessed January 16, 2010].

19. "Houston local items." Galveston Daily News, February 24, 1877, Issue 289, column G.

"Houston happenings." Galveston Daily News, March 23, 1879, Issue 313, column E.

20. "Houston happenings." Galveston Daily News, June 7, 1879, Issue 65, column F.

21. Wood, W. E. City of Houston, Harris County, Texas [map]. Houston, 1869.

Ziegler, Jesse A. Wave of the Gulf. Page 22.

"Geronimo at Fort Sam Houston." Army Medical Department Regiment. Fort Sam Houston. San Antonio Texas. <http://ameddregiment.amedd.army.mil/fshmuse/geronimo.pdf> [Accessed February 29, 2008].

22. Werner, George C. "Houston and Texas Central Railway." The Handbook of Texas Online. <http://www.tshaonline.org/handbook/online/articles/eqh09> [Accessed August 21, 2011].

Houston, A History and A Guide. Page 287.

"Houston, 1896. Sheet 46." Sanborn maps, 1867-1970: Texas.

23. "Houston, 1890. Sheet 19." Sanborn maps, 1867-1970: Texas.

Houston, A History and A Guide. Page 102.

"Houston, 1896. Sheet 46." Sanborn maps, 1867-1970: Texas.

Bivins, Ralph. "Developers moving in at old hotel / Tennison being turned into apartments, offices." Houston Chronicle, Wednesday, 11/04/98. Business Section, Page 1, 3 Star Edition.

"Hotels Houston." Historic Texas Postcards from the George Fuermann City of Houston Collection. University of Houston Libraries. <http://info.lib.uh.edu/speccoll/exhibits/texpost/houhotel.htm> [Accessed December 28, 2001].

24. Bivins, Ralph. "Developers moving in at old hotel / Tennison being turned into apartments, offices."

"Joshua Tennison and his descndants." Tennitex.com. <http://www.tennitex.com/> [Accessed February 12, 2010].

25. Johnston, Marguarite. Houston, The Unknown City, 1836-1946. College Station: Texas A & M University Press, 1991. Pages 300, 421 note 13.

"What's that half-finished building?" Houstonist.com. <http://houstonist.com/2007/02/14/ask_houstonist_6.php> [Accessed February 12, 2010].

History of Houston Fire Department. <http://www.maxmcrae.com/> [Accessed June 23, 2003].

26. Houston, A History and A Guide. Page 287.

"Houston, 1924-1951. Volume 2, Sheet 218." Sanborn maps, 1867-1970: Texas.

27. Houston, A History and A Guide. Page 287.

28. Ibid. Page 286.

"Houston, 1924-1951. Volume 2, Sheet 218." Sanborn maps, 1867-1970: Texas.

29. Johnston, Marguarite. Houston, The Unknown City, 1836-1946. Page 300.

30. Borden, G. and T. H.. Borden. Plan of the City of Houston. Surveyed by G. & T. H. Borden, 1836. [Altered and presented on January 18, 1837.]

31. Wood, W. E. City of Houston, Harris County, Texas [map].

"Houston, August, 1885. Sheet 11." Sanborn maps, 1867-1970: Texas.

32. "Houston, 1890. Sheet 2." Sanborn maps, 1867-1970: Texas.

"Woman's charred remains." Dallas Morning News. 02/22/1894, page 2.

33. Ibid.

"Accidentally shot / Foot mashed." Dallas Morning News. 12/18/1892, page 4.

34. "Woman's charred remains."

35. Ibid.

36. "Houston, 1896. Sheet 55." Sanborn maps, 1867-1970: Texas.

"Day at Houston." Galveston Daily News, Tuesday, June 16, 1896, page 5, Issue 84, column A.

37. "Mortuary. Charles W. Boyle." Galveston Daily News, Sunday, November 15, 1896, page 2, Issue 236, column B.

Sister M. Agatha. History of the Houston Heights. Houston: Premier Printing, 1956. <http://community.rice.edu/focusresources/books/agatha/chapter1.html> [Accessed June 27, 2008].

"Short talks and personals." Galveston Daily News, Friday, February 26, 1897, page 8, Issue 339, column D.

"Hotel was burned." Dallas Morning News. 10/20/1901, page 7.

38. "Woman jumps from roof." Dallas Morning News. 11/29/1908, page 32.

39. "Three men burn to death when flames raze Houston hotel." Dallas Morning News. 12/13/1928.

40. Moore, Roger G. and Allan D. Meyers. Data recovery excavations for the Sesquicentennial Park Project, Stage II, Houston, Harris County, Texas. (Texas Antiquities Permit No. 987). Houston: Moore Archeological Consulting, 2000.

Boyd, Douglas K., Cory Julian Broehm and Amy Dase. Archeological investigations for Elysian Viaduct from Quitman Street to Commerce Street in Houston, Harris County, Texas. Austin: Prewitt and Associates, Inc., 2005.

41. Houston, A History and A Guide. Page 95.

42. Muir, Andrew Forest. "Notes on Young's True Stories of Old Houston and Houstonians." MSS 17-34.2. Papers. Woodson Research Center. Rice University. Houston, TX.

43. "Plans for New Bridge Work." Houston Post, August 30, 1912.

44. Ibid.

45. "Houston, Tex." Stone & Webster Public Service Journal. Volume 16 (Jan-Jun 1915). Page 216, 306.

"Houston monument is plan." Galveston Daily News, January 19, 1915. Page 5.

46. Book of Houston: a brief sketch of its history, educational facilities...[Houston, TX?]: [s. n.], 1915. Page 75.

"Houston monument is plan." Galveston Daily News, January 19, 1915. Page 5.

"Bridge in Bloom." American City. Volume XIII, No. 2 (February, 1921). Pittsfield, MA: Buttenheim Pub. Corp. Page 130.

47. "Plan monster bridge to relieve congestion." Dallas Morning News. 11/29/1922, page 2.

48. "Plan to improve bayou at Houston." Galveston Daily News, Friday, April 6, 1923. Page 3.

49. "Smith Street Bridge 'Open for business'." Daily Court Review, August 7, 1925. Page 3.

50. "City employees busy Sunday clearing up flood debris; municipal damage $200,000." Galveston Daily News, June 3, 1929. Page 3.

"Franklin Avenue Bridge." Bridge plaque. City of Houston.

51. "Deaths mount as Houston's flood passes." Galveston Daily News, December 11, 1935. Page 1.

Tutt, Bob. "Old building awaits new life." Houston Chronicle, Saturday, 05/07/94. Section A, Page 33, 2 Star Edition.

"Part of Houston submerged as Buffalo Bayou surges over banks." Galveston Daily News, December 9, 1935. Page 2.

52. Shields, Mitchell J. "Houston's new home for dance." Houston Ballet. <http://www.houstonballet.org/CenterforDance/More_about_the_New_Home_For_Dance/> (Accessed April 7, 2010).

53. "Downtown Public Art Tour." Houston Downtown. <http://www.houstondowntown.com/Home/Lifestyle/WhatToDo/PerformingandCulturalA/PublicArt/DowntownPublicArtTour/Downtown%20Public%20Art%20Tour.PDF> [Accessed January 6, 2009].

54. Vivian, Julia L. "Donnellan, Thurston John." The Handbook of Texas Online. <http://www.tshaonline.org/handbook/online/articles/fdo15> [Accessed August 22, 2011].

55. Ibid.

56. White, Gifford. 1840 Citizens of Texas, Volume 2, Tax Rolls. Austin: Gifford White, 1984.

57. Dermot H. Hardy & Ingham S. Roberts, Historical Review of Southeast Texas, Vol. I, p. 237-238 (Chicago, Lewis Pub. Co., 1910), quoted by Adele B. Looscan in "Harris County, 1822-1845," Vol. 19 (1916), No. 1, Southwestern Historical Quarterly Online, footnote 64, <http://www.tsha.utexas.edu/publications/journals/shq/online/v019/n1/article_4 .html> [Accessed March 12, 2007].

58. "Caution." The Civilian and Galveston City Gazette, Saturday, January 28, 1843, p. 3 c. 3, and Wednesday, February 22, 1843, p. 3 c. 4. [Accessed March 12, 2007 at GenealogyBank.com].

59. Marriage Records, Harris County, Texas, Book A, p. 117: Timothy Donnellan and Emilie De Ende, married Sunday, May 11, 1841 by I. N. Moreland, County Justice, Harris County.

60. "Benjamin Franklin Donnellan, born April 15, 1841, baptized July 20, 1841, godfather Algernon Sidney Thruston." St. Vincent de Paul Catholic Church (Houston, Texas) Parish registers, FHL Film #25180, Baptisms (1880-1957), #18.

61. Death certificate. Emily Donnelan, d. 18 Jun 1911, Harris Co, # 13558.

62. "Thruston John Donnellan, born July 6, 1845, 4½ a.m., baptized November 21, 1846." St. Vincent de Paul baptism register, #110.

63. Wolf, George E. Jr. "Donnellan Grave Vault." <http://www.freewebs.com/graveyardwolf/donnellangravevault.htm> [Accessed June 10, 2007].

64. Russell, Marie. 1850 Census Harris County, Texas with added genealogical notes. Baytown: n.p., 1981.

65. "E. De Ende Donnellan." 1850 Census, Houston, Harris County, TX, roll M432-911, Page 6A.

66. "Dwyer." Heritage Quest Online. ProQuest Information and Learning Company. <http://www. heritagequestonline.com/> [Accessed Jan 24, 2007].

67. Houston City Directory, 1866. Dallas: R. L. Polk & Co, 1866, Page 20.

68. "Francis Dwyer m. Emily De Ende, December 24, 1856." St. Vincent de Paul Catholic Church (Houston, Texas) Parish registers, FHL Film #25182, Marriages (1840-1914), #62.

69. "Mary Frances Dwyer, born 1859, baptized September 8, 1865." St. Vincent de Paul baptism register, #1018. [but age 2 in 1860 census.]

70. "F. Dwyer," 1860 Census, Houston, Ward 1, Harris County, TX, roll M653-1296, Page 394A.

71. "Frank Beauregard Dwyer, born August 21, 1861, baptized September 17, 1865." St. Vincent de Paul baptism register, #1021.

72. Wood, W. E. City of Houston, Harris County, Texas [map]. Houston, 1869.

73. Houston City Directory, 1866, Page 20.

74. "Tinsmith." Wikipedia. <http://en.wikipedia.org/wiki/Tinsmith> [Accessed August 23, 2011].

75. "Dwyer..." The Galveston News, Wednesday, January 18, 1860, p. 1 c. 2. [Accessed March 12, 2007 at NewspaperArchive.com]

76. "F. Dwyer..." The Galveston News, Wednesday, January 18, 1860, p. 2 c. 9.

77. "Meeting of Mechanics and Working Men." The Galveston News, Wednesday, July 12, 1865, p. 2, c. 4-5.

78. "Henry D. Donnellan, Co. B, 2nd Texas Infantry." Compiled Service Record, NARA microfilm M323-265, #738 [at George Library, Richmond, TX].

79. "Mrs. Jessamine Donnellan, widow of Thurston John Donnellan." Widow's Application for Pension, #37680, approved November 7, 1921 [copy from Texas State Archives].

80. "The Great Reunion. Reunion of the Second Texas Infantry." Dallas Morning News, Saturday, May 25, 1895, p. 6 c. 1 & c. 6. [Accessed March 12, 2007 at GenealogyBank.com]

81. "Rev. L. C. Littlepage..." The Galveston News, Wednesday, May 17, 1865, p. 2 c. 1.

82. Fitzhugh, Lester Newton. "Walker's Texas Division." The Handbook of Texas Online. <http://www.tshaonline.org/handbook/online/articles/qkw01> [Accessed August 23, 2011].

83. Houston City Directory, 1866. Page 19.

84. Ibid.

85. Ibid., Page 42.

86. "Richer." 1860 Census, Jefferson County, Texas, roll M653-1300, Page 474. Heritage Quest Online. [Accessed January 15, 2007].

87. "Estate Frank Dwyer." Probate Records, Harris County, Texas, Book F, Page 23.

88. "Notice." Houston Daily Telegraph, Tuesday, February 26, 1867, Volume XXXII, No. 285, Page 5, Column 1.

89. "Fatal accident." Galveston Daily News, Tuesday, February 12, 1867, page 2, column 3.

90. Houston, A History and A Guide. Page 74 .

91. Young, Dr. S. O. "Relics of the War." True Stories of Old Houston and Houstonians. Galveston: Oscar Springer, 1913. Pages 131-133.

92. "Fatal accident." Galveston Daily News, Tuesday, February 12, 1867, Page 2, Column 3.

93. "Notice." Houston Daily Telegraph, Tuesday, February 26, 1867, Volume XXXII, No. 285, Page 5, Column 1.

94. "Notice." Houston Daily Telegraph, Sunday, March 3, 1867, Volume XXXII, No. 290, Page 6, Column 6.

95. "Estate Henry D. Donnellan." Probate Records, Harris County, Texas, Book F, Page 65.

96. Houston City Directory, 1866. Page 19.

97. "Estate Henry D. Donnellan." Probate Records, Harris County, Texas. Book F, Page 72.

98. Wolf, George E., Jr., "Donnellan Grave Vault."

99. "Minors Mary and Frank Dwyer." Probate Records, Harris County, Texas, Book S, Page 441.

100. Ibid. Book F, Page 307.

101. "Donnellan." 1870 Census, Houston, Ward 1, Harris County, TX, Roll M593-1589, Page 519A. Heritage Quest Online. [Accessed August 30, 2004].

102. "Donnellan." 1880 Census, Houston, Subdivision No. 1, Harris County, TX, Roll T9-1308, Page 6C. Heritage Quest Online.

103. "Donnellan, Thurston John." The Handbook of Texas Online.

104. "Capt. Chas. Bickley's play..." The Tri-Weekly Union, Saturday, February 5, 1870.

105. "Local Items." Houston Daily Union, Wednesday, April 6, 1870.

106. "From Houston." The Galveston News, Friday, June 14, 1872.

107. Allen, O. F. The City of Houston from Wilderness to Wonder. Temple, TX: O. F. Allen, 1936. Pages 1-35.

108. "Donnellan, Thurston John." The Handbook of Texas Online.

109. Marriage Records, Harris County, Texas. Book G, Page 109: T. J. Donnellan and Jesamine Hawthorne, married December 31, 1873 by J. R. Hutchinson, Minister.

110. "Mrs. Donnellan, Wife of Artist, Dies in Houston." Galveston Daily News, Sat., August 14, 1937, p. 7, c. 4.

111. "Houston local items." Galveston Daily News, Wednesday, November 21, 1877, p. 4, c. 3.

112. "Observance of Decoration Day." Galveston Daily News, Saturday, April 7, 1888, p. 3, c. 1.

113. "Houston, August 1885, Sheet 2." Sanborn maps, 1867-1970, Texas.

114. "Houston, October, 1890, Sheet 21." Sanborn maps, 1867-1970, Texas.

115. "Houston, 1896, Sheet 55." Sanborn maps, 1867-1970, Texas.

116. "Donnellan." 1900 Census. Houston, Ward 4, Harris County, TX, Roll T623-1642, Page 109B. Heritage Quest Online.

117. "Mary Francis Treadway m. William Maurice Anderson, Jan. 4, 1882." IGI, Batch M591995.

118. "Houston, August 1885, Sheet 2." Sanborn maps, 1867-1970: Texas.

119. "Houston, 1907, Volume 2, Sheet 4." Sanborn maps, 1867-1970: Texas.

120. "Bodies Recovered." Galveston Daily News, Wednesday, December 4, 1901. Also "Donnelon,
3 bodies, Dec 2, 1901, Old Strangers Rest grave #407." per Glenwood Cemetery records.

121. "Flowers for Remembrance." Houston Chronicle, April 26, 1906; (essentially a reprint of the December 18, 1899 and June 1, 1898 lists in the Houston Post).

122. "Houston 1924-1951, Volume 1, Sheet 5." Sanborn maps, 1867-1970: Texas.

123. "Donnellan, Thurston John." The Handbook of Texas Online.

124. "Funeral of Miss Donnellan." Galveston Daily News, Tuesday, June 20, 1911, p. 4, c. 2.

125. Glenwood Cemetery records: Miss Emily Donnellan, OSR-316; T. J. Donnellan, OSR-291; Mrs. Jessamine Donnellan OSR-419.

126. "Mrs. Donnellan, Wife of Artist, Dies in Houston."

127. "F. B. Dwyer, buried June 28, 1937, lot F-16 SW", from Washington Cemetery records.

128. Industrial advantages of Houston, Texas and environs. Houston: Akehurst Publishing Co., 1894. Pages 61-62.

129. "Warm Beer." Kegerators.com. <http://www.kegerators.com/warm-beer.php> [Accessed May 7, 2010].

130. Ibid.

131. Woolrich, Willis R. and Charles T. Clark. "Refrigeration." The Handbook of Texas Online. <http://www.tshaonline.org/handbook/online/articles/dqr01> [Accessed August 23, 2011].
Briley, George C. "A history of refrigeration." National Insulation Association. <http://www.insulation.org/articles/article.cfm/> [Accessed May 4, 2010].

132. "Great Exhibition. The Machinery Hall Display." New York Times, Wednesday, August 22, 1876, page 2.
"Warm Beer." Kegerators.com.

133. Mooney & Morrison's directory of the city of Houston for 1877-78. Houston: Mooney & Morrison, 1877. Page 216.

134. Ibid. Page 109.

135. Morrison & Co.'s general directory of the city of Houston for 1879-80. Houston: C. D. Morrison & Co., 1879. Page 123.

136. Ibid. Page 245.

137. Ibid. Page ix.

138. Ibid. Page 194.

139. Ibid. Page xxv.

140. "Capitalist and inventor will be buried this week." Mexia Evening News, Monday, August 7, 1922, page 2.
Morrison & Co.'s general directory of the city of Houston for 1879-80. Page 245.
Morrison & Fourmy's general directory of the city of Houston for 1880-81. Houston: Morrison & Fourmy, 1880. Page 151.

141. "Capitalist and inventor will be buried this week."

142. Morrison & Fourmy's general directory of the city of Houston for 1880-81. Pages xxx, 151, 218.

143. "Plot D-47. Juila Wickham Cleary, Hugh Hamilton." Washington Cemetery Book. [Houston: Washington Cemetery Association, nd.]

144. Morrison & Fourmy's general directory of the city of Houston, 1889-90. Galveston: Morrison & Fourmy, 1889. Page 237.

Morrison & Fourmy's general directory of the city of Houston for 1884-85. Houston: Morrison & Fourmy, 1884. Page 137.

Morrison & Fourmy's general directory of the city of Houston for 1887-88. Houston: Morrison & Fourmy, 1887. Page 338.

145. Morrison & Fourmy's general directory of the city of Houston for 1884-85. Page 69.

146. Morrison & Fourmy's general directory of the city of Houston for 1882-83. Houston: Morrison & Fourmy, 1882. Page 25.

147. Morrison & Fourmy's general directory of the city of Houston, 1889-90. Page 121.

Morrison & Fourmy's general directory of the city of Houston for 1886-87. Houston: Morrison & Fourmy, 1886. Page 35.

148. Morrison & Fourmy's general directory of the city of Houston, 1889-90. Page 20.

"Christian Moerlein." Ohio History Central. <http://www.ohiohistorycentral.org/entry.php?rec=276/> [Accessed May 3, 2010].

149. "Capitalist and inventor will be buried this week."

"Houston." Texas Breweries.Com. <http://ns2.ktc.com/~jeffh/houston.htm> [Accessed August 10, 2001].

Houston, A History and A Guide. Page 98.

150. "Brewery History." Magnolia Ballroom. <http://www.magnoliaballroom.com/> [Accessed April 9, 2010].

Industrial advantages of Houston, Texas and environs. Page 61.

151. Ibid.

"Houston Ice and Brewing Co. [advertisement]." Houston Daily Post, February 25, 1894.

"Houston." Texas Breweries.Com.

152. Turner, Allan. "Magnolia Ballroom becomes Houston's first protected landmark." Houston Chronicle, Tuesday, 10/10/2006. Section: B, Page 1, 3 Star Edition.

"Houston, 1907. Volume 2, Sheet 4." Sanborn maps, 1867-1970: Texas.

153. Turner, Allan. "Magnolia Ballroom becomes Houston's first protected landmark."

"Brewery History." Magnolia Ballroom.

Bivins, Ralph. "Some of city's oldest buildings attract developers' interest." Houston Chronicle, Sunday, 04/04/99. Business Section, Page 6, 2 Star Edition.

154. "Brewery History." Magnolia Ballroom.

155. "Warm Beer." Kegerators.com.

"Brewers of Texas are up for hearing." Galveston Daily News, August 10, 1915, page 8.

155a. Smith, Russ. "Book Review: Last Call." Wall Street Journal, Saturday/Sunday, May 8-9, 2010, Page W8.

Bailey, Richard. "Sheppard, John Morris." The Handbook of Texas Online. <http://www.tshaonline.org/handbook/online/articles/fsh24> [Accessed August 24, 2011].

Kerr, K. Austin. "Prohibition." The Handbook of Texas Online. <http://www.tshaonline.org/handbook/online/articles/vap01> [Accessed August 24, 2011].

156. "Transform brewery into sugar refinery." Galveston Daily News, Wednesday, April 16, 1919, page 4.

"Magnolia Dairy Products Co. [ad]." Galveston Daily News, April 20, 1919, page 7.

"Magnolia Dairy Products Co. [ad]." Galveston Daily News, June 18, 1920, page 10.

"Hamilton, Hugh." 1920 Census, Series T625, Roll 1813, Page 163. Heritage Quest Online. ProQuest Information and Learning Company. <http://www.heritagequestonline.com/> [Accessed May 3, 2010].

"Houston, 1924-1948." Sanborn maps, 1867-1970: Texas.

157. "Capitalist and inventor will be buried this week."

"Funeral of Hugh Hamilton." Galveston Daily News, October 1, 1911, page 17.

158. "Transform brewery into sugar refinery." Galveston Daily News, Wednesday, April 16, 1919, page 4.

"Houston, 1924. Volume 1, Sheet 5." Sanborn maps, 1867-1970: Texas.

"New hotel to be open by the first of next month." Galveston Daily News, March 8, 1925, page 33.

159. Alfred C. Finn: Builder of Houston. Houston: Houston Public Library, 1983.

160. "Great bond issue urged in Houston." Galveston Daily News, December 12, 1925. Page 1.

161. "Warm Beer." Kegerators.com.

Turner, Allan. "Magnolia Ballroom becomes Houston's first protected landmark."

162. Ibid.

Tamborello, Charles J. "Reconstruction of Franklin Street Bridge at Buffalo Bayou." Tamborello Engineering Corporation. [1996?].

Johnson, Patricia C. "Get a peek inside 5 historical industrial structures on tour." Houston Chronicle, Sunday, 03/25/2001. Section: Zest, Page 28, 2 Star Edition.

"Manfred Jachmich BA '69." Houston Baptist University. <http://www.hbu.edu/hbu/ Manfred_Jachmich.asp?SnID=2> [Accessed June 5, 2010].

"Historic Magnolia Ballroom. Historic Information." Magnolia Ballroom. <http:// www.magnoliaballroom.com/historic_information.html> [Accessed January 20, 2002].

163. "Houston Nightclubs." Houston.com <http://www.houston.com/nightlife/ nightclubs.html> [Accessed June 5, 2010].

164. Bivins, Ralph. "Entertainment zone could mean big fun on the bayou." Houston Chronicle, Sunday, 09/01/96. Business Section, Page 4, 2 Star Edition.

165. Texas Historic Bridge Inventory. Texas. Department of Transportation. August 30, 2005.

166. McAshan, Marie Phelps. On the corner of Main and Texas, a Houston legacy. Houston: Hutchins House, 1985. Pages 3-4.

Houston, A History and A Guide. Page 139.

167. Glass, James L. Personal communication. February 8, 2004.

Red, Ellen Robbins. Early Days on the Bayou, 1838-1890. The Life and Letters of Horace Dickinson Taylor. Waco: Texian Press, 1986. Front dust cover image.

Moore, Roger G. and Allan D. Meyers. Data recovery excavations for the Sesquicentennial Park Project, Stage II, Houston, Harris County, Texas. Page 7.

168. Glass, James L. Personal communication. February 8, 2004.

Ziegler, Jesse A. Wave of the Gulf. Page 10.

Augustus Koch (1840 - ?). Bird's Eye View of the City of Houston, Texas 1873. Madison, WI: J. J. Stoner, 1873.

169. "Kennedy Bakery." Texas Historical Commission. Atlas. <http://atlas.thc.state.tx.us/ scripts/>. [Accessed January 30, 2001].

Justman, Dorothy E. German Colonists and their Descendants in Houston Including Usener and Allied Families. Page 53.

Johnston, Marguarite. Houston, The Unknown City, 1836-1946. Page 83.

Russell, Marie. 1850 Census Harris County, Texas with added genealogical notes.

170. McComb, David G. Houston: A History. Page 17.

Houston, A History and A Guide. Page 74.

171. Walker, John C. "Reconstruction in Texas." Galveston Daily News, Sunday, November 15, 1896, page 9.

Young, Dr. S. O. "Relics of the War."

172. "Digging up bombshells." Laredo Times, January 31, 1906, page 4, column 2.

173. "Houston local items." Galveston Daily News, Wednesday, November 21, 1877, page 4, column 3.

174. "Digging up bombshells."

175. Ibid.

176. Texas Historic Bridge Inventory.

"Civil War blockade runner lies near heart of Houston." Amarillo Globe-Times, Friday, June 21, 1968, page 10.

177. "Sunken Confederate Ship [Harris County]." Texas Historical Marker File. Texas Historical Commission. Austin, TX.

178. Ibid.

179. "Civil War blockade runner lies near heart of Houston."

180. "Sunken Confederate Ship [Harris County]."

181. Ibid.

182. "Sunken Confederate Ship, Site of." Texas Historical Commission. Atlas. <http://atlas.thc.state.tx.us/scripts/> [Accessed March 31, 2002].

"Sunken Confederate Ship [Harris County]."

183. "'Live' Confederate cannonballs found." Brownsville Herald, July 24, 1968, page 16.

"Civil War blockade runner lies near heart of Houston."

184. Hodge, Shelby. "Architectural rebirth." Houston Post, Wednesday, December 10, 1975, Section AA, page 1.

185. "Houston, 1907. Volume 1, Sheet 1." Sanborn maps, 1867-1970: Texas.

186. Mooney & Morrison's directory of the city of Houston for 1877-78. Houston: Mooney & Morrison, 1877. Pages 54 and 220.

187. Morrison & Co.'s general directory of the city of Houston for 1879-80. Houston: C. D. Morrison & Co., 1879. Page 51.

Morrison & Fourmy's general directory of the city of Houston for 1880-81. Houston: Morrison & Fourmy, 1880. Page 366.

188. "Hotel Arrivals." Galveston Daily News, December 21, 1877, page 6, Issue 234, Column F.

Morrison & Co.'s general directory of the city of Houston for 1879-80. Page 199.

Morrison & Fourmy's general directory of the city of Houston for 1880-81. Page 313.

189. Morrison & Fourmy's general directory of the city of Houston for 1882-83. Houston: Morrison & Fourmy, 1882. Page 303.

190. Morrison & Fourmy's general directory of the city of Houston for 1884-85. Houston: Morrison & Fourmy, 1884. Page 161.

Morrison & Fourmy's general directory of the city of Houston for 1887-88. Houston: Morrison & Fourmy, 1887.

Page 283.

"Houston, August, 1885. Sheet 11." Sanborn maps, 1867-1970: Texas. [Ann Arbor, Mich.?]: Bell & Howell Information and Learning, c2001.

191. "Houston Business Directory." Galveston Daily News, October 1, 1889, page 6.

Morrison & Fourmy's general directory of the city of Houston, 1889-90. Galveston: Morrison & Fourmy, 1889. Page 325.

Morrison & Fourmy's general directory of the city of Houston for 1886-87. Houston: Morrison & Fourmy, 1886.

Page 265.

192. "Houston Business Directory."

"Hides and Wool." Galveston Daily News, Friday, April 10, 1891, page 3, Issue 17, Column F.

"Houston, 1896. Sheet 1." Sanborn maps, 1867-1970: Texas.

193. "Firm History." Abraham, Watkins, Nichols, Sorrels, Agosto and Friend. <http://www.abrahamwatkins.com/Firm-History.shtml> [Accessed June 9, 2010].

"Houston, 1907. Volume 1. Sheet 1." Sanborn maps, 1867-1970: Texas.

"[Graves Dry Goods...]" Home Furnishings Review, Volume 26 (1906), No. 12, Page 908.

"Building Being Planned at Houston." Galveston Daily News, June 23, 1922, page 3.

"Rice University-Campanile Yearbook-Class of 1927." E-Yearbook.Com <http://www.e-yearbook.com/yearbooks/Rice_University_Campanile_Yearbook/1927/Page_353.html/> [Accessed July 2, 2010].

194. "Siewerssen, E, 1910 Census, Series T624, Roll 1560, Page 141." Heritage Quest Online. ProQuest Information and Learning Company. <http://www.heritagequestonline.com/> [Accessed June 9, 2010].

"Siewerssen, Emile, 1920 Census, Series T625, Roll 1813, Page 122."

"Siewerson [Siewerssen], Lillia, 1930 Census, Series T626, Roll 2347, Page 65."

"Wool and Hides [Adveriesement]." Brookshire Times, June 27, 1930. Page 7.

"Siewerssen Lily." Probate Court Inquiry System. County Clerk. Harris County, Texas. <http://www.cclerk.hctx.net/> [Accessed June 9, 2010].

195. "Houston, 1924-1951. Volume 1, Sheet 1." Sanborn maps, 1867-1970: Texas.

196. Hodge, Shelby. "Architectural rebirth." Houston Post, Wednesday, December 10, 1975, Section AA, page 1.

"Firm History."

"Abraham Frank T Trust, Account 0010160000007." Harris County Appraisal District. <http://www.hcad.org/> [Accessed June 9, 2010].

197. Mooney & Morrison's directory of the city of Houston for 1877-78. Houston: Mooney & Morrison, 1877. Page 119.

"Houston, August, 1885. Sheet 3." Sanborn maps, 1867-1970: Texas.

"For Sale." Dallas Morning News. 7/11/1886, page 3.

198. "Houston, 1907. Volume 2, Sheet 4." Sanborn maps, 1867-1970: Texas.

199. "Houston, 1924. Volume 2, Sheet 220." Sanborn maps, 1867-1970: Texas.

"Houston, 1924-1951. Volume 2, Sheet 220." Sanborn maps, 1867-1970: Texas.

200. "Project Update" Trail Way, Vol 2, No. 2 (Aug-Oct, 1999). Houston: City of Houston Department of Public Works.

201. "University of Houston Downtown - Academic Building." ArtsHound.com. <http://www.artshound.com/venue/detail/2375/University_of_Houston_Downtown_Academic_Building> [Accessed August 25, 2011].

202. Morrison & Co.'s general directory of the city of Houston for 1879-80. Page xxv.

Morrison & Fourmy's general directory of the city of Houston for 1882-83. Page 25.

203. Ibid.

Daily Cougar. Online. Volume 61 (Fall 1995-Summer 1996), Issue 81 (January 25, 1996). <http://www.uh.edu/campus/cougar/index.html> [Accessed June 16, 2003].

204. "Houston." Texas Breweries.Com.

205. Daily Cougar.

206. Ibid.

"Houston, 1924. Volume 2, Sheet 220." Sanborn maps, 1867-1970: Texas.

207. Houston, A nation's capital 1837-1839. Houston: Harris County Historical Society, 1985. Page 71.

Frantz, Joe B. "Borden, Gail, Jr.." The Handbook of Texas Online. <http://www.tshaonline.org/handbook/online/articles/fbo24> [Accessed August 25, 2011].

Henson, Margaret Swett. "Harris County." The Handbook of Texas Online. <http://www.tshaonline.org/handbook/online/articles/hch07> [Accessed August 25, 2011].

Williams, Amelia W. "Allen, Augustus Chapman." The Handbook of Texas Online. <http://www.tshaonline.org/handbook/online/articles/fal17> [Accessed August 25, 2011].

Houston, A History and A Guide. Page 41.

208. Ibid. Pages 25, 312-322.

Worm, Jeri and John Worm. "Harris County, Texas - Founder's Memorial Park." Rootsweb.com <http://ftp.rootsweb.com/pub/usgenweb/tx/harris/cemeteries/founders.txt>. [Accessed October 14, 2003].

Gonzales, J. R. "Ceremony at the cemetery." Houston Chronicle, 08/26/2007. Bayou City History.

Russell, Marie. 1850 Census Harris County, Texas with added genealogical notes.

209. Houston, A History and A Guide. Page 49.

Williams, Amelia W. "Allen, Augustus Chapman."

Worm, Jeri and John Worm. "Harris County, Texas - Founder's Memorial Park."

210. Williams, Amelia W. "Allen, Augustus Chapman."

211. Ibid.

Urban, Jerry. "A kinship with history. The Houston area is home to hundreds of descendants from three of the most notable families in Texas' past." Houston Chronicle, Sunday, 10/08/2005. Section: Texas Magazine, Page 8, 2 Star Edition.

212. History of Texas Together with a Biographical History of the Cities of Houston and Galveston. Page 469.

Allen, O. F. The City of Houston from Wilderness to Wonder. Page 12.

213. Miller, Aragorn Storm. "Allen, Henry R." The Handbook of Texas Online. <http://www.tshaonline.org/handbook/online/articles/falba> [Accessed August 25, 2011].

Palmquist, Peter E. and Thomas R. Kailbourn. Pioneer photographers from the Mississippi to the continental divide. San Francisco: Stanford University Press, 2005. Page 71.

214. Worm, Jeri and John Worm. "Harris County, Texas - Founder's Memorial Park."

215. Russell, Marie. 1850 Census Harris County, Texas with added genealogical notes.

History of Texas Together with a Biographical History of the Cities of Houston and Galveston. Page 639-640.

Leimer, ChrisTina. "Founder's Memorial Park." The Tombstone Traveller's Guide. <http://home.flash.net/~leimer/founder.html> [Accessed February 8, 2000].

216. Russell, Marie. 1850 Census Harris County, Texas with added genealogical notes.

217. "Allen, S L, 1860 Census, Series M653, Roll 1296, Page 397." Heritage Quest Online. ProQuest Information and Learning Company. <http://www.heritagequestonline.com/> [Accessed July 22, 2010].

"Allen, H H, 1860 Census, Series M653, Roll 1296, Page 369."

"Allen, H R, 1860 Census, Series M653, Roll 1296, Page 428."

218. "Allen, Samuel L, 1870 Census, Series M593, Roll 1589, Page 627." Heritage Quest Online. ProQuest Information and Learning Company. <http://www.heritagequestonline.com/> [Accessed July 22, 2010].

"Allen, Henry R, 1870 Census, Series M593, Roll 1589, Page 590."

Worm, Jeri and John Worm. "Harris County, Texas - Founder's Memorial Park."

219. "Allen, Charlotte, 1870 Census, Series M593, Roll 1589, Page 605."

220. Morrison & Fourmy's general directory of the city of Houston for 1880-81. Page 64.

221. Miller, Aragorn Storm. "Allen, Henry R."

"Special Austin Correspondence. Austin, October 23, 1871." Houston Daily Union, October 28, 1871, page 2.

History of Texas Together with a Biographical History of the Cities of Houston and Galveston. Page 640.

Morrison & Co.'s general directory of the city of Houston for 1879-80. Page 45.

"Sam Allen & Co.'s Lumber Mills [ad]." Galveston Daily News, September 1, 1882, page 15.

222. "Allen, M A, 1880 Census, Series T9, Roll 1309, Page 135." Heritage Quest Online. ProQuest Information and Learning Company. <http://www.heritagequestonline.com/> [Accessed July 22, 2010].

"Allen, Mrs A C, 1880 Census, Series T9, Roll 1309, Page 133."

"Houston, August, 1885. Sheet 3." Sanborn maps, 1867-1970: Texas.

"Houston, October, 1890. Sheet 22." Sanborn maps, 1867-1970: Texas.

223. "Day at Houston." Galveston Daily News, January 3, 1895, page 3.

Houston, A History and A Guide. Page 98.

Miller, Ray. Ray Miller's Houston. Houston: Cordovan Press, 1984. Page 72.

"Samuel L. Allen." Marker. Glenwood Cemetery, Houston, Texas.

224. "Long Standing Litigation." Galveston Daily News, October 27, 1901, page 7.

Urban, Jerry. "A kinship with history. The Houston area is home to hundreds of descendants from three of the most notable families in Texas' past."

225. "Houston, 1896. Sheet 56." Sanborn maps, 1867-1970: Texas.

226. "Houston, 1907. Volume 2. Sheet 5." Sanborn maps, 1867-1970: Texas.

"Houston, 1907. Volume 2, Sheet 4." Sanborn maps, 1867-1970: Texas.

"Houston, 1924. Volume 2, Sheet 220." Sanborn maps, 1867-1970: Texas.

227. Houston, A History and A Guide. Page 117.

"Texas - Harris County." National Register of Historic Places. <http://www.nationalregisterofhistoricplaces.com/> [Accessed January 9, 2004].

228. "Houston, 1924-1951. Volume 2, Sheet 220." Sanborn maps, 1867-1970: Texas.

229. Warren, Susan. "UH Downtown headquarters getting dramatic new look." Houston Chronicle, Monday, 07/22/85. Section 1, Page 10, No Star Edition.

230. Ibid.

"UHD History." University of Houston Downtown. <http://www.uhd.edu/about/history.html/> [Accessed July 15, 2010].

231. "Texas - Harris County." National Register of Historic Places.

Warren, Susan. "UH Downtown headquarters getting dramatic new look."

232. Ibid.

233. Seay, Gina. "Cruise to highlight bayou improvements." Houston Chronicle, Sunday, 10/09/1988. Section: Lifestyle, Page 8, 2 Star Edition.

"Outdoors Waterfront Festival makes a splash." Houston Chronicle, Friday, 10/21/1988. Section: Weekend Preview, Page 15, 2 Star Edition.

Davidian, Geoff and Bob Tutt. "Longtime councilman Goyen dies / He was the voice of UH football." Houston Chronicle, Monday, 12/16/1991. Section: A, Page 1, 3 Star Edition.

234. "Houston merchant dies at his home." Galveston Daily News, August 9, 1934, page 3.

Field, William Scott. Last of the Past, Houston Architecture: 1847 to 1915. Houston: GHPA, 1980. Page 90.

235. "Hipp acquires produce firm." Brownsville Herald, December 27, 1940, page 9.

"Houston merchant dies at his home."

236. Shey, Brittanie. "Texas Traveler: Spaghetti Warehouse." Houston Press. <http://blogs.houstonpress.com/hairballs/2009/10/texas_traveler_spaghetti_wareh.php> [Accessed August 25, 2011].

"Spaghetti Warehouse." Answers.com. <http://www.answers.com/topic/spaghetti-warehouse> [Accessed August 25, 2011].

237. Ibid.

238. "Spaghetti Warehouse." Wikipedia. <http://en.wikipedia.org/wiki/Spaghetti_Warehouse> [Accessed August 25, 2011].

239. Frandeli Group. <http://www.frandeligroup.com> [Accessed August 14, 2010].

"Spaghetti Warehouse." Wikipedia.

240. "Heavy Rains Roll Through Houston Area Overnight, Some Missing in Flood Waters, White Oak and Buffalo Bayous Very High Downtown." Trip to the Outhouse.

<http://triptotheouthouse.wordpress.com/2009/04/28/heavy-rains-pound-houston-area-overnight-lots-of-flooded-ramps-and-exits-white-oak-and-buffalo-bayous-very-high-in-downtown-houston/> [Accessed August 25, 2011].
241. Beck, Bill. At your service: an illustrated history of Houston Lighting & Power Company. Houston: Gulf Publishing Co., 1990. Page 22.
"Edison, Thomas Alva. The Incandescent Lamp." Encarta. <http://encarta.msn.com/encyclopedia_761563582_2/Thomas_Edison.html> [Accessed April 13, 2005].
242. Beck, Bill. At your service: an illustrated history of Houston Lighting & Power Company. Pages 9, 12.
Chapman, Betty T. "Electric power surged after sputtering start in Houston." Houston Business Journal, September 7-13, 2001. Page 26.
243. Beck, Bill. At your service: an illustrated history of Houston Lighting & Power Company. Pages 19-20.
244. "Magnolia City Mention." Galveston Daily News, August 6, 1889, page 3, Issue 101, column A.
Beck, Bill. At your service: an illustrated history of Houston Lighting & Power Company. Page 22.
245. Tutt, Bob. "Flooding clashes with decor." Houston Chronicle, Saturday, 03/07/92. Section B, Page 11, 2 Star Edition.

Chapter 9: Allen's Landing

1. "This week's contract news." Municipal journal and engineer, Volume 25 (July-Dec., 1908). NY: Swetland Pub. Co., 1925. Page 882.
"City Beautiful movement." Wikipedia. <http://en.wikipedia.org/City_Beautiful_movement> [Accessed December 3, 2010].
2. "Begin last important job on Main Street Viaduct." Galveston Daily News, October 14, 1912, page 5.
3. Texas Historic Bridge Inventory. Texas. Department of Transportation. August 30, 2005.
4. Ibid.
"Sabine Street Bridge over Buffalo Bayou." National Register of Historic Places. Registration Form. US Dept of the Interior. National Park Service.
Technologies of power: essays in honor of Thomas Parke Hughes and Agatha Chipley Hughes. Cambridge: MIT Press, 2001. Pages 141-142.
"142. Deformed Bars." Cyclopedia of Architecture, Carpentry, and Building, Volume 4-6. American Technical Society, 1912. ChestofBooks.com <http://www.chestofbooks.com/Cyclopedia-Carpentry-Building-4-6/142-Deformed-Bars.html> [Accessed November 29, 2010].
Cox, Ronald C. and Michael H. Gould. Civil Engineering Heritage: Ireland. London: Thomas Telford Publications, 1998. Page 138.
5. Texas Historic Bridge Inventory. Texas. Department of Transportation. August 30, 2005.
"Houston's new street car ordinance." Galveston Daily News, August 27, 1912, page 9.
6. "Important events on San Jacinto Day." Galveston Daily News, April 22, 1913, page 10.
7. Book of Houston: a brief sketch of its history, educational facilities...[Houston, TX?]: [s. n.], 1915. Page 75.
"Raze San Jacinto Street Bridge." Galveston Daily News, June 17, 1913, page 3.
8. Texas Historic Bridge Inventory. Texas. Department of Transportation. August 30, 2005.

Wall, Lucas. "Main Street light rail." Houston Chronicle, Thursday, 01/01/2004. Section: A, Page 1, 3 Star Edition.

9. Lubbock, Francis Richard. Six decades in Texas or Memoirs of Francis Richard Lubbock. Austin: Ben C. Jones & Co. Printers, 1900. Pages 45-47.

10. Houston, A History and A Guide. Houston: Anson Jones Press, 1942. Page 36.

Allen, O. F. The City of Houston from Wilderness to Wonder. Temple, TX: O. F. Allen, 1936. Page 1.

11. Henson, Margaret Swett. The History of Galveston Bay Resource Utilization. Publication GBNEF-39. Galveston: Galveston Bay National Estuary Program, 1993. Pages 22, 25.

12. Glass, James L. "The Original Book of Sales of Lots of the Houston Town Company from 1836 Forward." Houston Review. Volume XVI, No. 3 (1994). Houston: Houston Library Board, 1994.

Glass, James L. The Houston Municipal Wharf 1836-1840. Otherwise known as "Allen's Landing" Circa 1967. A Reconstruction by James L. Glass, March, 2007. [unpublished manuscript]

"Ports of the World: US, Texas, Houston." The Maritime Heritage Project. <http://www.maritimeheritage.org/ports/usTexas.html/> [Accessed December 6, 2010].

Sibley, Marilyn M. "Houston Ship Channel." The Handbook of Texas Online. <http://www.tshaonline.org/handbook/online/articles/rhh11> [Accessed August 25, 2011].

Looscan, Adele B. "Harris County, 1822-1845." Vol 019 No 1 Page 057. Southwestern Historical Quarterly Online.<http://www.tsha.utexas.edu/publications/journals/shq/online/v019/n1/0190010057> [Accessed May 22, 2005].

13. Henson, Margaret Swett. The History of Galveston Bay Resource Utilization. Page 30.

14. Houston, A History and A Guide. Pages 53, 132.

Carlson, Shawn Bonath. A subsurface survey of Allen's Landing Park, City of Houston, Harris County, Texas. Houston: Moore Archeological Consulting, 1998.

Sibley, Marilyn M. "Houston Ship Channel."

15. Henson, Margaret Swett. The History of Galveston Bay Resource Utilization. Page 33.

16. Sibley, Marilyn McAdams. Port of Houston: a history. Austin: Univ of Texas Press, 1968. Page 70.

Henson, Margaret Swett. The History of Galveston Bay Resource Utilization. Pages 35-36.

17. Ibid. Page 37.

Sibley, Marilyn M. "Houston Ship Channel."

Sibley, Marilyn McAdams. Port of Houston: a history. Page 128.

18. Sibley, Marilyn M. "Houston Ship Channel."

Henson, Margaret Swett. The History of Galveston Bay Resource Utilization. Page 38.

Scardino, Barrie and Bruce Webb. Ephemereal City: Cite looks at Houston. Austin: Univ of Texas Press, 2003. Page 26.

19. Henson, Margaret Swett. The History of Galveston Bay Resource Utilization. Pages 38, 40.

Sibley, Marilyn M. "Houston Ship Channel."

20. Price, Gary. "Ball, Thomas Henry [1859-1944]." The Handbook of Texas Online. <http://www.tshaonline.org/handbook/online/articles/fba48> [Accessed August 26, 2011].

Henson, Margaret Swett. The History of Galveston Bay Resource Utilization. Page 40.

21. "Houston-Galveston Navigation Channel Project." US Army Corps of Engineers. Galveston District. <http://www.swg.usace.army.mil/items/hgnc/> [Accessed December 6, 2010].

22. "Parks." Buffalo Bayou Partnership. Houston, TX. <http://www.buffalobayou.org/parks.html> [Accessed August 19, 2005].

Snyder, Mike. "Buffalo Bayou back on center stage." Houston Chronicle, October 27, 2000, Section A, Page 31 Metfront, 3 STAR Edition.

Glass, James L. The Houston Municipal Wharf 1836-1840.

Glass, James L. "The Original Book of Sales of Lots of the Houston Town Company from 1836 Forward."

Gray, Lisa. "Peering into Allen's Landing's Murky History." Houston Chronicle, Thursday, 08/21/2008. Section: E, Page 1, 3 Star Edition.

23. "Redevelopment begins." Houston Chronicle, Saturday, 10/28/00. Section A, Page 37, 3 Star Edition.

24. Elder, Laura Elizabeth. "No-tsu-oh backers bid to resurrect bygone bash." Houston Business Journal, July 8, 1996.

"King Nottoc has crowned his queen." Galveston Daily News, November 11, 1909, Page 3.

25. "No-Tsu-Oh invitation, 1910." Museum of Houston. <http://www.museumofhouston.org> [Accessed October 22, 2007].

"Tek Ram calls you!" Bayou City History. Houston Chronicle. <http://blogs.chron.com/bayoucityhistory/> [Accessed October 22, 2007].

26. Sibley, Marilyn M. "No-Tsu-Oh." The Handbook of Texas Online. <http://www.tshaonline.org/handbook/online/articles/lln01> [Accessed August 26, 2011].

27. "Tek Ram calls you!"

28. Werner, George C. "Houston and Texas Central Railway." The Handbook of Texas Online. <http://www.tshaonline.org/handbook/online/articles/eqh09> [Accessed August 26, 2011].

Henson, Margaret Swett. "Harris County." The Handbook of Texas Online. <http://www.tshaonline.org/handbook/online/articles/hch07> [Accessed August 26, 2011].

29. Young, Nancy Beck. "Galveston and Houston Junction Railroad." The Handbook of Texas Online. <http://www.tshaonline.org/handbook/online/articles/eqgvg> [Accessed August 26, 2011].

Kleiner, Diana J. "Brown, Aaron B." The Handbook of Texas Online. <http://www.tshaonline.org/handbook/online/articles/fbr79> [Accessed August 26, 2011].

30. Werner, George C. "Houston and Texas Central Railway."

31. Andrews, Alfred. Memorial. Genealogy, and Ecclesiastical History [of First Chruch, New Britain, Conn.]. Berlin, CT: A. H. Andrews, 1867. Page 351.

"Letters written by Elijah Burritt." Elihu Burritt Archives. <http://library.ccsu.edu/about/departments/spcoll/burritt/burr25.html> [Accessed December 13, 2007].

32. Andrews, Alfred. Memorial. Genealogy, and Ecclesiastical History. Page 351.

"Letters written by Elijah Burritt."

"Atlas of the Heavens Charts. Elijah Hinsdale Burritt, 1835." George Glazer Gallery. <http://www.georgeglazer.com/maps/celestial/burritt/burritt.html/> [Accessed December 13, 2007].

33. "Burritt's Universal Multipliers." New England Review (Hartford, CT). Monday, August 30, 1830, Issue 129, Column A.

Carroll, H. Bailey. "Texas Collection." Volume 48, Number 3. Southwestern Historical Quarterly Online. <http://www.tsha.utexas.edu/publications/journals/shq/online/v048/n3/contrib_DIVL6564.html> [Accessed December 13, 2007].

"Letters written by Elijah Burritt."

34. "Atlas of the Heavens Charts. Elijah Hinsdale Burritt, 1835."
"Celestail Maps - Burritt." Filling the Sky. <http://www.fillingthesky.com/burritt.html> [Accessed December 13, 2007].
"Burritt, Elijah Hinsdale; Engravings, Celestial Charts." Prices 4 Antiques. <http://www.prices4antiques.com/itemsummary/391893.htm> [Accessed December 13, 2007].
35. "Letter from Elijah Burritt to Ann W. Burritt, August 30, 1837." from Elihu Burritt Library. Central Connecticut State University. <http://library.ccsu.edu/help/spcoll/burritt/elijahletters.php>.
36. Carroll, H. Bailey. "Texas Collection."
"Letter written by Elijah Burritt to Ann W. Burritt, October 8, 1837." Transcribed by Louis F. Aulbach and Linda Gorski. Buffalo Bayou. <http://www.epperts.com/lfa/BB71.html> [Accessed August 10, 2008], from Elihu Burritt Library. Central Connecticut State University.
Glass, James L. Personal communication, July 30, 2008. The date Burritt arrived in Houston was October 3, 1837.
37. Gammel, Hans Peter. The Laws of Texas, 1822-1897. Volume 1. Austin: Gammel Book Co., 1898. Pages 76-77.
38. "Letter written by Elijah Burritt to Ann W. Burritt, October 8, 1837."
39. Girard, A. City of Houston and its vicinity [map]. [Houston?]: [n.p.], January, 1839.
40. "Letter written by Elijah Burritt to Ann W. Burritt, October 8, 1837."
41. "Brig." Wikipedia. <http://en.wikipedia.org/wiki/Brig> [Accessed August 26, 2011].
42. "Letter written by Elijah Burritt to Ann W. Burritt, October 8, 1837."
43. Ibid.
44. "Letter written by Elijah Burritt to Ann W. Burritt, October 12, 1837." Transcribed by Louis F. Aulbach and Linda Gorski. Buffalo Bayou. <http://www.epperts.com/lfa/BB71.html> [Accessed August 10, 2008], from Elihu Burritt Library. Central Connecticut State University.
"1837 Racer's Storm." Wikipedia. <http://en.wikipedia.org/> [Accessed Dec 13, 2007].
"Galveston Police Department." Galveston Police Department. <http://www.galvestonpd.com/> [Accessed December 13, 2007].
45. "Letter written by Elijah Burritt to Ann W. Burritt, October 12, 1837."
46. "Ezekiel Andrews, Jr." Family History Research. <http://www.tqsi.com/genealogy/> [Accessed December 16, 2007].
Cornwall, Edward Everett. William Cornwall and his Descendants: A Geneological History of the Family. New Haven: Tuttle, Morehouse and Taylor Co., 1901. Page 55.
"Estate of Elijah H. Burritt." Probate Records. Harris County, Texas. Book A, Pages 113-121, Book B, Pages 247-250.
Glass, James L. "The Original Book of Sales of Lots of the Houston Town Company from 1836 Forward." Page 127. See Deed Records of Harris County, Texas. Volume A, Pages 232, 203, 513.
Carroll, H. Bailey. "Texas Collection."
47. "Estate of Elijah H. Burritt."
48. Ibid.
49. Werner, George C. "Houston and Brazos Rail Road." The Handbook of Texas Online. <http://www.tshaonline.org/handbook/online/articles/eqhet> [Accessed August 26, 2011].
"Houston - a modern city." [Bird's Eye map.] [Houston]: Hopkins and Motter, 1912.
50. Feibel, Carolyn. "Bayous are flush with fecal bacteria." Houston Chronicle, 12/19/2007. <http://www.chron.com/disp/story.mpl/front/5389411.html> [Accessed December 19, 2007].

51. "Improving Water Quality in the Houston Area." Total Maximum Daily Load Program. Texas Commission on Environmental Quality. October, 2007.

52. Melosi, Martin V. Effluent America: Cities, Industry, Energy and the Environment. Pittsburgh: Univ of Pittsburgh Press, 2001. Pages 173-174.

53. Bivins, Ralph. "Some of city's oldest buildings attract developers' interest." Houston Chronicle, Sunday, 04/04/99. Business Section, Page 6, 2 Star Edition.
"Willow Street Pump Station." <http://www.ghpa.org/awards/2005/willow.html> [Accessed December 18, 2007].

54. "Houston, 1907. Volume 2, Sheet 5." Sanborn maps, 1867-1970: Texas. [Ann Arbor, Mich.?]: Bell & Howell Information and Learning, c2001.
"Willow Street Pump Station." <http://www.ghpa.org/awards/2005/willow.html>.
Weber, Rick. "UH-Downtown seeks more campus space." Houston Chronicle, Tuesday, 12/19/00. Section: West U/Bellaire/Meyerland/West News.

55. "Houston, 1885. Sheet 3." Sanborn maps, 1867-1970: Texas.
"Houston, 1890. Sheet 22." Sanborn maps, 1867-1970: Texas.
"Houston, 1896. Sheet 57." Sanborn maps, 1867-1970: Texas.

56. Smyer, Susan. "City of Houston Wastewater History." City of Houston. Public Works and Engineering Department. <http://documents.publicworks.houstontx.gov/documents/utilities/history_waste_water_operations.pdf/> [Accessed June 18, 2011].

57. "Willow Street Pump Station." Houston Architecture Info. <http://houstonarchitecture.info/> [Accessed December 18, 2007].
"Willow Street Pump Station." National Register of Historic Places. <http://nrhp.focus.nps.gov/natregsearchresult.do?fullresult=true&recordid=0> [Accessed August 26, 2011].

58. Robinson, James. "Delays plague park that isn't a park / Waterfront nature spot awaits reality." Houston Chronicle, Saturday, 09/16/95. Section A, Page 29, 3 Star Edition.

59. Morrison & Fourmy Directory of the City of Houston, 1907. Houston: Morrison & Fourmy, 1907. Page 153.

60. "Port of Houston." Democratic Telegraph and Texas Register (Houston, TX), Volume 16, Number 12, Edition 1, Friday, March 21, 1851, Page 3, Column 3.

61. Muir, Andrew Forest. "Rice, William Marsh." The Handbook of Texas Online. <http://www.tshaonline.org/handbook/online/articles/fri03> [Accessed August 26, 2011].
Turner, Allan. "Rice's mysterious murder revisited 100 years later." Houston Chronicle, 09/16/00.
Wood, W. E. City of Houston, Harris County, Texas [map]. Houston, 1869.

62. Beazley, Julia. "Nichols, Ebenezar B." The Handbook of Texas Online. <http://www.tshaonline.org/handbook/online/articles/fni01> [Accessed August 26, 2011].
"Cotton factor." Wikipedia. <http://en.wikipedia.org/wiki/Cotton_factor> [Accessed December 23, 2010].

63. Muir, Andrew Forest. "Rice, William Marsh."
"Rice, WM M, 1860 Census, Series M653, Roll 1296, Page 402." Heritage Quest Online. ProQuest Information and Learning Company. <http://www.heritagequestonline.com/> [Accessed August 26, 2011].

64. "Colbert County, Alabama. Letters left in the Tuscumbia Post Office." Rootsweb.com <http://www.rootsweb.ancestry.com/~alcolber/news-letters-3.htm> [Accessed December 13, 2010].
"Lauderdale County, AL. 1830 Federal Census Index P-S. Pages 0198A, 0198B." U. S. Census. <http://www.us-census.org/image-index/al/lauderdale/1830/p-s.htm/> [Accessed December 13, 2010].
"Brick House." Democratic Telegraph and Texas Register (Houston), Volume 11, Number 46, Edition 1, Monday, November 16, 1846, page 4.

Russell, Marie. 1850 Census Harris County, Texas with added genealogical notes. Baytown: n.p., 1981.

65. "Dickenson, J, 1860 Census, Series M653, Roll 1296, Page 402." Heritage Quest Online. ProQuest Information and Learning Company. <http://www.heritagequestonline.com/> [Accessed December 23, 2010].

"Dickinson, John, 1870 Census, Series M593, Roll 1589, Page 529." Heritage Quest Online. ProQuest Information and Learning Company. <http://www.heritagequestonline.com/> [Accessed December 23, 2010].

"Dissolution." Democratic Telegraph and Texas Register (Houston, TX), Volume 12, Number 47, Edition 1, Thursday, November 25, 1847, Page 4, Column 6.

"Abstract of Imposts." Galveston Civilian, February 18, 1843, page 3.

[Ads.] "John Dickinson." Democratic Telegraph and Texas Register (Houston, TX), Volume 12, Number 47, Edition 1, Thursday, November 25, 1847, Page 3, Column 5.

66. "Dissolution of copartnership." Galveston News, August 16, 1856, page 1.

"John Dickinson." Galveston News, January 17, 1857, page 4.

67. "Finances of Houston." Galveston Weekly News, January 20, 1857, page 1.

[News. Houston and Brazoria Tap road.] Galveston Civilian and Gazette, July 28, 1857, page 2.

68. "Dickenson, J, 1860 Census, Series M653, Roll 1296, Page 402." Also, for William J. Hutchins.

"Rice, WM M, 1860 Census, Series M653, Roll 1296, Page 402."

69. Historical records search and archeological subsurface testing for the Jefferson Davis Hospital site at 1801 Allen Parkway Drive, Houston, Harris County, Texas. Houston: Moore Archeological Consulting, 1999. Page 26.

Muir, Andrew Forest. "Rice, William Marsh."

"Dickinson, John, 1870 Census, Series M593, Roll 1589, Page 529." Also, for William J. Hutchins.

70. Houston City Directory, 1866. Dallas: R. L. Polk & Co, 1866. Page 36.

"Dickinson, John, 1870 Census, Series M593, Roll 1589, Page 529."

"In bankruptcy." Houston Union, July 14, 1871. Page 4.

71. "Remains of John Dickinson." Houston Union, December 16, 1871. Page 3.

"Dickinson." Glenwood Cemetery. <http://www.glenwoodcemetery.org/search/> [Accessed December 23, 2010].

72. "Dissolution of copartnership." Galveston News, August 16, 1856, page 1.

"Cleveland funeral to be held Wednesday." Dallas Morning News. 12/24/1912.

73. Ibid.

"1850 Census Austin County, Texas." USGenWeb. <http://files.usgwarchives.org/tx/austin/census/1850/1850.txt/> [Accessed December 14, 2010].

"Cleveland funeral to be held Wednesday."

74. "Genealogy Data Page 225 (Descendancy Pages)." Southern Grace.com <http://www.southerngrace.com/bornnbred/html/d_e0.html> [Accessed December 18, 2010].

"Rev. Davis Sessums." Maryland Sun, April 15, 1891.

75. "Sessums, A, 1860 Census, Series M653, Roll 1296, Page 439." Heritage Quest Online.

"William Davis Cleveland." Find a Grave Memorial. <http://www.findagrave.com/cgi-bin/fg-cgi?page=gr&GRid=54639133> [Accessed December 11, 2010].

"Cleveland funeral to be held Wednesday."

"Roster of Company B, 10th Texas Infantry." Scott McKay. <http://members.aol.com/SMckay1234/Roster/Co-B.htm> [Accessed April 22, 2004].

76. "Cleveland funeral to be held Wednesday."

Houston City Directory, 1866. Page 115.

"New advertisements." Galveston Daily News, August 31, 1867, page 2.

77. "Sessums, Alexr, 1870 Census, Series M593, Roll 1586, Page 239." Heritage Quest Online.

"[Announcements - A. Sessums, Powell & Co.]." Galveston Daily News, March 20, 1872, page 4.

Murray's City Directory for 1870-71. Houston: W. Murray, 1870. Page 49.

78. "Death of A. Sessums." Galveston News, Sunday, February, 2, 1873, page 2, column 1.

"Sessums." Burial Records. Glenwood Cemetery, Houston, TX.

79. "Notice." Galveston Tri-Weekly Civilian, May 16, 1873, page 2.

"Auction sale of office furniture." Galveston Daily News, May 25, 1873, page 2.

80. "Rev. Davis Sessums."

81. Ibid.

"Sessums, Davis." USGenWeb <http://files.usgwarchives.net/la/orleans/bios/s-000011.txt.html> [Accessed December 18, 2010].

"Bishop Davis Sessums Tenth Anniversary..." New Orleans Times-Picayune, June 25, 1901, page 3.

"Sessums, Davis." The National Cyclopedia of American Biography. Volume 11. New York: James T. White & Co., 1901. Page 343.

82. "Sessums, David Rev, 1910 Census, Series T624, Roll 523, Page 175." Heritage Quest Online.

"Sessums, Davis, 1920 Census, Series T625, Roll 623, Page 114." Heritage Quest Online.

83. "Cleveland funeral to be held Wednesday."

Houston, A History and A Guide. Page 259.

84. Mooney & Morrison's directory of the city of Houston for 1877-78. Houston: Mooney & Morrison, 1877. Pages iv, 13, 70.

"Houston Local Items." Galveston Daily News, February 6, 1878, page 7.

Morrison & Co.'s general directory of the city of Houston for 1879-80. Houston: C. D. Morrison & Co., 1879. Page 53.

85. "Brevities." Galveston Daily News, Saturday, March 6, 1880, Issue 300, Column F.

Morrison & Fourmy's general directory of the city of Houston for 1880-81. Houston: Morrison & Fourmy, 1880. Page 9.

Glass, James L. The Houston Municipal Wharf 1836-1840.

86. "Houston, October, 1890. Sheet 22." Sanborn maps, 1867-1970: Texas. [Ann Arbor, Mich.?]: Bell & Howell Information and Learning, c2001.

"Cleveland funeral to be held Wednesday."

87. Houston, A History and A Guide. Page 92.

"Real Estate Transfers." Galveston Daily News, January 28, 1887, page 5.

"Houston Compress Officials." Dallas Morning News. 5/9/1888, page 2.

"Capital Cullings." Dallas Morning News. 4/12/1889, page 2.

88. "Heavy loss in Houston." Galveston Daily News, Saturday, April 8, 1893, page 2.

89. "Houston, 1896. Sheet 2." Sanborn maps, 1867-1970: Texas.

Parks, Louis B. "Bayou plan would bring Allen's Landing back to life." Houston Chronicle, Monday, 08/27/2007. Section: 1, Page 1, 3 Star Edition.

90. "Wm. D. Cleveland & Co. [ad]." Galveston Daily News, Saturday, May 6, 1894, page 1.

"Houston, 1896. Sheet 2."

91. "Cleveland funeral to be held Wednesday."

"Lombardi, Caesar, 1910 Census, Series T624, Roll 72, Page 87." Heritage Quest Online.

"Lombardi, Joseph, 1870 Census, Series M593, Roll 520, Page 612." Heritage Quest Online.

Morrison & Fourmy's general directory of the city of Houston for 1894-95. Galveston: Morrison & Fourmy, 1894. Page 158.

92. "Lombardi, Maurice E, 1900 Census, Series T623, Roll 144, Page 272." Heritage Quest Online. ProQuest Information and Learning Company. <http://www.heritagequestonline.com/> [Accessed December 26, 2010].

"Lombardi, Caesar, 1910 Census, Series T624, Roll 72, Page 87." Heritage Quest Online.

93. "Cleveland funeral to be held Wednesday."

"Cleveland, Alex S., 1910 Census, Series T624, Roll 1560, Page 18." Heritage Quest Online.

94. "W. D. Cleveland & Co. Assign." Mexia Evening News (Ledger), Volume 5, No. 107, August 11, 1899, page 1.

"Into voluntary bankruptcy." Dallas Morning News. 8/11/1899, page 2.

95. "W. D. Cleveland & Co." San Antonio Daily Express, September 9, 1899, page 4.

96. Morrison & Fourmy Directory of the City of Houston, 1907. Houston: Morrison & Fourmy, 1907. Page 153.

"Wm. D. Cleveland & Co. [ad]." Galveston Daily News, Saturday, May 6, 1894, page 1.

"Houston, 1896. Sheet 02." Sanborn maps, 1867-1970: Texas.

Glass, James L. The Houston Municipal Wharf 1836-1840.

Parks, Louis B. "Bayou plan would bring Allen's Landing back to life."

"Sunset Coffee [ad]." San Antonio Light and Gazette, December 19, 1909, page 21.

97. "150 years of firefighting / The history of the Houston Fire Department." Houston Chronicle, Sunday, 08/14/88. Texas Magazine, Page 8, 2 Star Edition.

"Houston fire area to be rebuilt soon." Dallas Morning News. 2/23/1912, page 1.

"Our first 100 years / Looking back / Downtown up in a blaze from 1912 fire." Houston Chronicle, Sunday, 03/25/2001. Section A, Page 39, 4 Star Edition.

"William Davis Cleveland." Find a Grave Memorial.

"W. D. Cleveland's body laid to rest." Dallas Morning News. 12/26/1912, page 8.

98. "Cleveland funeral to be held Wednesday."

"Pioneer firm plans to quit." Dallas Morning News. 3/21/1930, page 2.

99. "W. D. Cleveland, Wholesale Grocer, Houston, 1924-1951. Volume 1. Sheet 02." Sanborn maps, 1867-1970: Texas. [Ann Arbor, Mich.?]: Bell & Howell Information and Learning, c2001.

100. Parks, Louis B. "Bayou plan would bring Allen's Landing back to life."

Turner, Allan. "Let the critics cringe, David Adickes' sculpture is BIG STUFF and more is on the way - Beatles heads, anyone?" Houston Chronicle, Sunday, 05/16/2004. Section: Texas Magazine, Page 6, 2 Star Edition.

Adickes, David. Personal communication, September 18, 2009. Adickes said that he invested $25,000 in the club.

101. Hickey, Dennis. "Love Street Light Circus and Feel Good Machine." <http://www.faculty.missouristate.edu/d/DennisHickey/lovestreet.htm/> [Accessed June 12, 2008].

"Sorcerer's Apprentice Project: Talking Shop with David Adickes." TheGardenArtForum.Com. <http://www.thegardenartforum.com/> [Accessed June 12, 2008].

102. "Allen's Landing." Wikipedia. <http://en.wikipedia.org/> [Accessed June 12, 2008].

103. Warren, Susan. "Concrete Cowboy: Sculptor of Tall Art Sets Sights Higher." Wall Street Journal, January 18, 2006. Section: A, Page 1.

"About the Artist - David Adickes." Sam Houston Statue. <http://www.samhoustonstatue.org/david-adickes.htm> [Accessed June 8, 2008].

"Mount Rush Hour Revisited." Off the Kuff. <http://www.offthekuff.com/mt/archives/011666.html> [Accessed June 8, 2008].

104. "About the Artist - David Adickes."

Warren, Susan. "Concrete Cowboy: Sculptor of Tall Art Sets Sights Higher."

105. Parks, Louis B. "Bayou plan would bring Allen's Landing back to life."

106. "FotoFest 2002 - Georges Rousse at Barbara Davis Gallery." FotoFest. News & Reviews. <http://www.fotofest.org/> [Accessed July 17, 2002].

Parks, Louis B. "Bayou plan would bring Allen's Landing back to life."

107. "Harris County Jails." Houston Chronicle, Wednesday, 11/09/2005. Section: B, Page 4, 3 Star Edition.

108. Glass, James L. The Houston Municipal Wharf 1836-1840.

109. Houston, A History and A Guide. Page 223.

110. Morrison & Fourmy's general directory of the city of Houston for 1884-85. Houston: Morrison & Fourmy, 1884. Page 278.

"Star Bottling Works Company." Galveston Daily News, June 8, 1884, page 6.

111. "Soft drink." Wikipedia. <http://en.wikipedia.org/wiki/Soft_drink> [Accessed January 7, 2011].

112. "Ginger ale." Wikipedia. <http://en.wikipedia.org/wiki/Ginger_ale> [Accessed January 3, 2011].

"Inventors. Introduction to Pop." About.com <http://inventors.about.com/od/sstartinventions/a/soft_drink.html> [Accessed January 3, 2011].

"Root beer." Wikipedia. <http://en.wikipedia.org/wiki/Root_beer> [Accessed January 3, 2011].

113. Morrison & Fourmy's general directory of the city of Houston for 1880-81. Page 106.

"Cotter, Robert, 1870 Census, Series M593, Roll 1589, Page 601." Heritage Quest Online.

Houston City Directory for 1867-68. Houston: Gray, Smallwood, 1867. Page 20.

Morrison & Co.'s general directory of the city of Houston for 1879-80. Pages iii, 78.

Murray's City Directory for 1870-71. Houston: W. Murray, 1870. Page 31.

114. Morrison & Fourmy's general directory of the city of Houston for 1882-83. Houston: Morrison & Fourmy, 1882. Page 269.

Morrison & Fourmy's general directory of the city of Houston for 1884-85. Page 278.

"Star Bottling Works Company." Galveston Daily News, June 8, 1884, page 6.

115. Morrison & Co.'s general directory of the city of Houston for 1879-80. Page 53.

Morrison & Fourmy's general directory of the city of Houston for 1880-81. Page 73.

"[August Baumbach]." Galveston Daily News, April 20, 1885, page 16.

"Chambers County Courthouse." Texas Escapes. <http://www.texasescapes.com/TexasGulfCoastTowns/Anahuac-Texas-Chambers-County-Courthouse.htm> [Accessed January 3, 2011].

"Marlin." Galveston Daily News, August 21, 1886, page 10.

"[August Baumbach]." Galveston Daily News, October 30, 1889, page 6.

"Addition to Truck House." Galveston Daily News, September 14, 1894, page 3.

116. "Inventors. Introduction to Pop."

"Writ of injunction prayed for." Galveston Daily News, February 10, 1887, page 14.

"Moxie Nerve Food Co v. Baumbach and others." OpenJurist <http://openjurist.org/32/f1d/205> [Accessed January 1, 2011]. Pages 201, 205.

"Injunction sustained." Galveston Daily News, July 12, 1887, page 15.

117. Morrison & Fourmy's general directory of the city of Houston, 1889-90. Galveston: Morrison & Fourmy, 1889. Page 335.

118. Morrison & Co.'s general directory of the city of Houston for 1879-80. Page 59.

"Bonner, Aug, 1880 Census, Series T9, Roll 1308, Page 6." Heritage Quest Online. Pro-Quest Information and Learning Company. <http://www.heritagequestonline.com/> [Accessed January 3, 2011].

Morrison & Fourmy's general directory of the city of Houston for 1880-81. Page 81.

Morrison & Fourmy's general directory of the city of Houston for 1886-87. Houston: Morrison & Fourmy, 1886.

Page 80.

Morrison & Fourmy's general directory of the city of Houston, 1890-91. Galveston: Morrison & Fourmy, 1890. Page 380.

Morrison & Fourmy's general directory of the city of Houston, 1892-93. Galveston: Morrison & Fourmy, 1892. Page 433.

"Smilax regelii." Wikipedia. <http://en.wikipedia.org/wiki/Smilax_regelii> [Accessed January 3, 2011].

119. Morrison & Fourmy's general directory of the city of Houston, 1895-96. Galveston: Morrison & Fourmy, 1895. Page 100.

"An Easy Way to Die." Galveston Daily News, August 22, 1896, page 5.

"Fatal dose." Galveston Daily News, August 21, 1896, page 4.

120. "County Court." Galveston Daily News, January 27, 1897, page 3, Issue 309, column A.

Morrison & Fourmy's general directory of the city of Houston, 1897-98. Galveston: Morrison & Fourmy, 1897. Page 269.

Morrison & Fourmy's general directory of the city of Houston, 1900-01. Galveston: Morrison & Fourmy, 1900. Page 311.

Morrison & Fourmy's general directory of the city of Houston, 1902-03. Galveston: Morrison & Fourmy, 1902. Page 413.

Morrison & Fourmy's general directory of the city of Houston, 1903-04. Galveston: Morrison & Fourmy, 1903. Page 407.

Morrison & Fourmy's general directory of the city of Houston, 1908-09. Galveston: Morrison & Fourmy, 1908.

Page 15.

"Navarro, Tony, 1910 Census, Series T624, Roll 1559, Page 27." Heritage Quest Online.

"Star Bottling Works." Directory of the City of Houston, 1911-12. Houston: Texas Publishing Co., 1911.

121. Morrison & Fourmy Directory of the City of Houston, 1913. Houston: Morrison & Fourmy, 1913. Page 16.

"Star Bottling Building." LoopNet <http://www.loopnet.com/Listing/15540479/> [Accessed January 1, 2011].

"Houstonian killed on porch of home." Galveston Daily News, June 25, 1932, page 2.

"Navarro, Joseph, 1930 Census, Series T626, Roll 2341, Page 159." Heritage Quest Online. ProQuest Information and Learning Company. <http://www.heritagequestonline.com/> [Accessed January 9, 2011].

Lane, Bob and Alice Lane. Early Houston Sodas. [Houston: n.p.], 1973.

122. "Houston, 1924-1951. Volume 1, Sheet 2." Sanborn maps, 1867-1970: Texas.

123. Houston, A History and A Guide. Page 93.

124. "Letter to Editor about new bridge and the Houston City Mills Consumed." Houston Daily Telegraph, August 10, 1875.

Texas Historic Bridge Inventory.

Moore, Roger G., et. al. Archeological Monitoring at the METRO Multi-Use Facility, Houston, TX. Houston: Moore Archeological Consulting, 1995. Page 5.

125. Gillette, Halbert Powers. "Design and construction of the San Jacinto St. reinforced concrete bridge, Houston, Texas." Engineering & Contracting, Volume 59, Issues 2-6 (Jan-June, 1914). Chicago: Myron C. Clark Pub. Co., 1914. Pages 492-495. Texas Historic Bridge Inventory.

126. "Raze San Jacinto Street Bridge." Galveston Daily News, June 17, 1913, page 3. Texas Historic Bridge Inventory.

Gillette, Halbert Powers. "Design and construction of the San Jacinto St..."

127. Texas Historic Bridge Inventory.

128. Ibid.

Gillette, Halbert Powers. "Design and construction of the San Jacinto St..."

129. Texas Historic Bridge Inventory.

130. "Interpretive guide to Monument Hill/Kreische Brewery State Historic Sites." Texas Parks and Wildlife Department. <http://www.tpwd.state.tx.us/publications/pwdpubs/media/pwd_br_p4505_0048v.pdf> [Accessed August 28, 2011].

131. "Death Roll. Peter Gabel." Houston Post, 01/08/1896.

History of Texas Together with a Biographical History of the Cities of Houston and Galveston. Chicago: Lewis Publishing Co, 1895. Pages 356-357.

132. "Death Roll. Peter Gabel." Houston Post, 01/08/1896.

History of Texas Together with a Biographical History... Pages 357-358.

133. Ibid. Page 359.

Hornburg, David. Personal communication, August 26, 2005.

"Fifty Years Ago." Galveston Daily News, March 21, 1921.

134. "Houston locals." Galveston Tri-Weekly News, March 29, 1871, page 4.

Russell, Marie. 1850 Census Harris County, Texas with added genealogical notes.

"Henry Schulte." Galveston Daily News, November 29, 1877, page 1.

135. Houston, A History and A Guide. Page 154.

"Houston locals." Galveston Tri-Weekly News, March 29, 1871, page 4.

History of Texas Together with a Biographical History... Page 358.

"Death Roll. Peter Gabel." Houston Post, 01/08/1896.

"Old Land Mark." Galveston Daily News, July 3, 1897.

136. History of Texas Together with a Biographical History... Page 358.

"Houston". Texas Breweries.Com. <http://ns2.ktc.com/~jeffh/houston.htm> [Accessed August 10, 2001].

Morrison & Co.'s general directory of the city of Houston for 1879-80. Page ix.

"Houston locals." Galveston Tri-Weekly News, March 29, 1871, page 4.

137. Tiling, Moritz. History of the German Element in Texas. Houston: Moritz Tiling, 1913. Pages 163-175.

"Houston Volksfest." Flake's Bulletin (Galveston, Texas). June 10, 1870, page 1.

"Houston locals." Galveston Tri-Weekly News, March 29, 1871, page 4.

"Death Roll. Peter Gabel." Houston Post, 01/08/1896.

"Old Land Mark." Galveston Daily News, July 3, 1897.

138. "Heinrich Schulte to Peter Gabel, December 12, 1854." Deed Records. Harris County, Texas. Book P, Page 476.

"Houston locals." Galveston Tri-Weekly News, March 29, 1871, page 4.

139. "Henry Schulte." Galveston Daily News, November 29, 1877, page 1.

"Shulte, Gerhard, 1870 Census, Series M593, Roll 1589, Page 534." Heritage Quest Online.

"Fire yesterday." Flake's Bulletin (Galveston, Texas). 05/09/1868, page 5.

Houston City Directory for 1867-68. Page LI.

"Porter (beer)." Wikipedia. <http://en.wikipedia.org/wiki/Porter_(beer)> [Accessed January 21, 2011].

140. "Advertisement." Flake's Bulletin (Galveston, Texas). 11/21/1866, page 2.

"Advertisement." Flake's Bulletin (Galveston, Texas). 03/15/1868, page 3.

"Henry Schulte." Galveston Daily News, November 29, 1877, page 1.

"Advertisement." Galveston Tri-Weekly News, March 7, 1873, page 4.

"Dissolution notice." Galveston Daily News, July 13, 1873, page 4.

141. "Henry Schulte." Galveston Daily News, November 29, 1877, page 1.

142. Morrison & Co.'s general directory of the city of Houston for 1879-80. Page 194.

143. Mooney & Morrison's directory of the city of Houston for 1877-78. Page 177.

Morrison & Fourmy's general directory of the city of Houston for 1882-83. Page 241.

144. Morrison & Fourmy's general directory of the city of Houston for 1884-85. Page 319.

"Houston, August, 1885. Sheet 9." Sanborn maps, 1867-1970: Texas. [Ann Arbor, Mich.?] : Bell & Howell Information and Learning, c2001.

145. "Houston Society News." Galveston Daily News, March 20, 1898, page 21.

"Schulte, Annie, 1900 Census, Series T623, Roll 1642, Page 330." Heritage Quest Online.

"For lease." Galveston Daily News, August 21, 1901, page 7.

"Schulte House." Morrison & Fourmy's general directory of the city of Houston, 1908-09.

146. Schuhmacher, Henry C. The Schuhmacher Family. [Houston?]: [n.p.],[1968?] Pages 2-3.

147. Ibid

Cox, Hildegard Streithoff. Personal communication. Hildegard Cox (1892-1993) is the author's maternal grandmother.

148. "Schuhmacher, John, 1900 Census, Series T623, Roll 1634, Page 79." Heritage Quest Online.

Schuhmacher, Henry C. The Schuhmacher Family. Page 7.

Morrison & Fourmy Directory of the City of Houston, 1912. Houston: Morrison & Fourmy, 1912. Page 55.

149. Morrison & Fourmy's general directory of the city of Houston, 1908-09. Galveston: Morrison & Fourmy, 1908. Page 10.

Morrison & Fourmy Directory of the City of Houston, 1912. Page 587.

Morrison & Fourmy Directory of the City of Houston, 1910-11. Houston: Morrison & Fourmy, 1910. Page 708.

Morrison & Fourmy Directory of the City of Houston, 1913. Houston: Morrison & Fourmy, 1913. Page 1.

150. Reports of the Tax Court of the United States, Volume 8. Washington, DC: USGPO, 1947. Page 453.

Schuhmacher, Henry C. The Schuhmacher Family. Page ii.

Sloane, Story Jones III. Houston in the 1920s and 1930s. Charleston: Arcadia Press, 2009.

Advertising and selling, Volume 41, Issues 1-6. Page 62.

151. Schuhmacher, Henry C. The Schuhmacher Family. Page 3.

"San Jacinto Street, Account number 0010050000004." Harris County Appraisal District. <http://www.hcad.org/> [Accessed December 30, 2010].

152. Glass, James L. The Houston Municipal Wharf 1836-1840.

Girard, A. City of Houston and its vicinity [map]. [Houston?]: [n.p.], January, 1839.

153. "Houston, 1896. Sheet 57." Sanborn maps, 1867-1970: Texas.

"North San Jacinto Street, Account number 0031220000001." Harris County Appraisal District. <http://www.hcad.org/> [Accessed December 30, 2010].

154. Farrar, R. M. The Story of Buffalo Bayou and the Houston Ship Channel. Houston: Chamber of Commerce, 1926.

155. Kleiner, Diana J. "Peden, Edward Andrew." The Handbook of Texas Online. <http://www.tshaonline.org/handbook/online/articles/fpe14> [Accessed January 24, 2011].

Honl, Samantha. "Houston spares two buildings for now." Preservation. <http://www.preservationnation.org/magazine/2009/todays-news/houston-spares-two-buildings.html> [Accessed January 24, 2011].

"North San Jacinto Street, Account number 0031210000001." Harris County Appraisal District. <http://www.hcad.org/> [Accessed December 30, 2010].

Brewer, Steve. "Court complex to have starring role downtown." Houston Chronicle, Sunday, 07/14/2002. Section: A, Page 31, 4 Star Edition.

156. Ibid.

Brewer, Steve. "Firm is hired to stem erosion." Houston Chronicle, Wednesday, 05/01/2002. Section: Metro, Page 21A, 3 Star Edition.

Snider, Mike. "Picnicers may share Buffalo Bayou with inmates." Houston Chronicle, Wednesday, 10/10/2007. Section: A, Page 1, 3 Star Edition.

157. Brewer, Steve. "Firm is hired to stem erosion."

"San Jacinto Street, 5457A7." Harris County Appraisal District. <http://www.hcad.org/> [Accessed December 29, 2010].

"Kegans (HM)." Texas Department of Criminal Justice. <http://www.tdcj.state.tx.us/stat/unitdirectory/hm.htm/> [Accessed May 15, 2010].

158. "New Corrections Initiative for Texas." Texas Department of Criminal Justice. <http://www.tdcj.state.tx.us/publications/state-jail/SJD-new-corrections-initiative.PDF/> [Accessed May 15, 2010].

159. Ziegler, Jesse A. Wave of the Gulf. San Antonio: Naylor Co., 1938. Page 35.

160. Glass, James L. Personal communication, March 18, 2006.

Glass, James L. "The Original Book of Sales of Lots of the Houston Town Company from 1836 Forward." Houston Review. Volume XVI, No. 3 (1994). Houston: Houston Library Board, 1994.

161. Ziegler, Jesse A. Wave of the Gulf. Page 35.

Houghton, Dorothy K. H. Houston's Forgotten Heritage. Houston: Rice University Press, 1991. Page 20.

McAshan, Marie Phelps. On the corner of Main and Texas, a Houston legacy. Houston: Hutchins House, 1985. Page 36.

162. Johnston, Marguarite. Houston, The Unknown City, 1836-1946. College Station: Texas A & M University Press, 1991. Page 73.

"Houston, 1924. Volume 1, Sheet 4." Sanborn maps, 1867-1970: Texas. [Ann Arbor, Mich.?] : Bell & Howell Information and Learning, c2001.

163. "Catholic Church." Houston Review. Volume 8, No. 3. Houston: Houston Library Board.

Tutt, Bob. " Hopes are high for digging deep into Houston history." Houston Chronicle, Sunday, 05/28/89. Section C, Page 4, 2 Star Edition.

Houston, A History and A Guide. Page 186.

164. "Kennedy Bakery." Texas Historical Commission. Atlas. <http://atlas.thc.state.tx.us/scripts/>. [Accessed January 30, 2001].

Taylor, William H, et. al. The Archeology and History of Block 12, South Side of Buffalo Bayou (41HR787), Houston, Harris County, Texas. Houston: BC & AD Archeology, Inc., 1998. Page 261.

Houston, A History and A Guide. Pages 187, 262.

"Catholic Church." Houston Review.

McComb, David G. Houston: A History. Austin: University of Texas, 1981. Page 17.

165. Houston City Directory, 1866. Dallas: R. L. Polk & Co, 1866. Page 113.

"History." Annunciation Catholic Church. <http://www.eldersforlife.org/annunciationcc/history.html/> [Accessed February 1, 2011].

Houston, A History and A Guide. Page 188.

166. Ibid. Pages 264, 303.

167. "History of St. Vincent de Paul Parish in Houston." St. Vincent de Paul Catholic Church. <http://www.stvincentcatholicchurch.org/> [Accessed February 1, 2011].

168. "Historic Neighborhoods Council, August 2003." Greater Houston Preservation Alliance.

Ziegler, Jesse A. Wave of the Gulf. Page 35.

169. Houghton, Dorothy K. H. Houston's Forgotten Heritage. Page 70.

"Dickinson, Block 26." Wood, W. E. City of Houston, Harris County, Texas [map]. Houston, 1869.

"Historic Neighborhoods Council, August 2003."

170. Ibid.

Ziegler, Jesse A. Wave of the Gulf. Page 276.

Houghton, Dorothy K. H. Houston's Forgotten Heritage. Pages 116, 247.

171. Houston, A History and A Guide. Page 96.

172. Ziegler, Jesse A. Wave of the Gulf. Page 277.

173. Houston, A History and A Guide. Page 88.

"Real estate transfers." Galveston Daily News, January 10, 1891, page 5.

"Electric machinery arrives." Galveston Daily News, May 5, 1891, page 5.

History of Houston Fire Department. <http://www.maxmcrae.com/> [Accessed June 23, 2003].

174. McCurdy, Bill. "A short ride on Houston's first rail system." Pecan Park Eagle. <http://bill37mccurdy.wordpress.com/2010/01/28/a-short-ride-on-houstons-first-rail-system/> [Accessed January 24, 2011].

"Town notes." Galveston Daily News, May 3, 1896, page 4.

"Houston, 1896. Sheet 07." Sanborn maps, 1867-1970: Texas.

175. McCurdy, Bill. "A short ride on Houston's first rail system."

"Houston, 1907. Volume 1. Sheet 9." Sanborn maps, 1867-1970: Texas.

176. "Remarks on the market." Houston Daily Telegraph, May, 1866.

Beck, Bill. At your service: an illustrated history of Houston Lighting & Power Company. Houston: Gulf Publishing Co., 1990. Page 2.

177. Justman, Dorothy E. German Colonists and their Descendants in Houston Including Usener and Allied Families. Wichita Falls: Nortex Offset Publications, Inc., 1974. Page 84.

Casteneda, Christopher. "Manufactured and natural gas industry." EH.net Encyclopedia. <http://www.eh.net/encyclopedia/article/casteneda.gas.industry.us/> [Accessed February 4, 2011].

178. "Gas company franchise." Galveston Daily News, December 16, 1896, page 5.

Chapple, Joe Mitchell, editor. National Magazine, Volume 31 (October, 1909). [Washington, DC?]: Chapple Publishing Company, Ltd., 1909. Page 108.

Wood, W. E. City of Houston, Harris County, Texas [map]. Houston, 1869.

179. Beck, Bill. At your service... Pages 2, 20, 22.

180. "Houston, 1896. Sheet 7." Sanborn maps, 1867-1970: Texas.

"Houston, 1924. Volume 1. Sheet 04." Sanborn maps, 1867-1970: Texas.

181. McComb, David G. Houston: A History. Page 80.

Casteneda, Christopher. "Manufactured and natural gas industry."

"Houston, 1924-1951. Volume 1. Sheet 04." Sanborn maps, 1867-1970: Texas.

182. Clark, Gladys E. "Frostown, TX." The Handbook of Texas Online. <http://www.tshaonline.org/handbook/online/articles/hvf61> [Accessed August 29, 2011].

183. Wood, W. E. City of Houston, Harris County, Texas [map]. Houston, 1869.

184. Maas, Elaine H. "The Jews in Houston Today." Houston History. <http://www.houstonhistory.com/erhnic/history1jews.htm> [Accessed January 27, 2005]. History of Texas Together with a Biographical History... Page 533.

185. Cohen, Rev. Henry. "Settlement of the Jews in Texas." Publications of the American Jewish Historical Society, Issues 1-2. NY: American Jewish Historical Society, 1893. Pages 150-151.

186. History of Texas Together with a Biographical History... Page 533. "Chimene, J., 1860 Census, Series T653, Roll 1296, Page 412." Heritage Quest Online.

187. Houston City Directory, 1866. Page 16. "Chimene, Carl, 1910 Census, Series T624, Roll 1560, Page 143." Heritage Quest Online. "Chimene, Albert J., 1920 Census, Series T625, Roll 1813, Page 212." Heritage Quest Online. Murray's City Directory for 1870-71. Page 30. Houston City Directory for 1873. Houston: Tracey and Barker, 1873. Page 26.

188. History of Texas Together with a Biographical History... Page 533. Mooney & Morrison's directory of the city of Houston for 1877-78. Page 76.

189. Morrison & Co.'s general directory of the city of Houston for 1879-80. Page 72. Morrison & Fourmy's general directory of the city of Houston for 1884-85. Page 107.

190. Morrison & Fourmy's general directory of the city of Houston for 1886-87. Page 97. Morrison & Fourmy's general directory of the city of Houston, 1892-93. Page 146.

191. Morrison & Fourmy's general directory of the city of Houston for 1894-95. Page 151. Morrison & Fourmy's general directory of the city of Houston, 1899. Galveston: Morrison & Fourmy, 1898. Page 58. "Houston blaze." Dallas Morning News. 10/17/1894.

192. Ibid.

193. Ibid.

194. Ibid.

195. Morrison & Fourmy's general directory of the city of Houston, 1895-96. Page 120. Morrison & Fourmy's general directory of the city of Houston, 1899. Page 58.

196. Morrison & Fourmy's general directory of the city of Houston, 1903-04. Page 123. Morrison & Fourmy Directory of the City of Houston, 1905-06. Houston: Morrison & Fourmy, 1905. Page 117. Morrison & Fourmy Directory of the City of Houston, 1907. Page 107. Morrison & Fourmy's general directory of the city of Houston, 1908-09. Page 117.

197. Morrison & Fourmy Directory of the City of Houston, 1907. Page 107. "Chimene, Albert J., 1920 Census, Series T625, Roll 1813, Page 212." Heritage Quest Online. Morrison & Fourmy's general directory of the city of Houston, 1908-09. Page 315. Morrison & Fourmy Directory of the City of Houston, 1910-11. Page 53.

198. "Chimene, Caliste I., 1920 Census, Series T625, Roll 1813, Page 128." Heritage Quest Online. "Chimene, Albert J., 1920 Census, Series T625, Roll 1813, Page 212." Heritage Quest Online.

199. Russell, Marie. 1850 Census Harris County, Texas with added genealogical notes.

"First Setters of the Republic of Texas. Volume 1: Headright grants which were reported...January, 1840. Austin: Cruger & Wing, 1841.

200. Maas, Elaine H. "The Jews in Houston Today."

Russell, Marie. 1850 Census Harris County, Texas with added genealogical notes.

"Historic Neighborhoods Council, August 2003." Greater Houston Preservation Alliance.

Moore, Roger G. and Allan D. Meyers. Data recovery excavations for the Sesquicentennial Park Project, Stage II, Houston, Harris County, Texas. (Texas Antiquities Permit No. 987). Houston: Moore Archeological Consulting, 2000.

Natalie Ornish, "De Cordova, Jacob Raphael," Handbook of Texas Online <http://www.tshaonline.org/handbook/online/articles/fde03> [Accessed August 29, 2011].

201. Houston, A History and A Guide. Page 170.

202. "Question 9.12: What is the reason for a 'minyon' (a quorum of 10 men required for certain prayers)?" FAQS.org <http://www.faqs.org/faqs/judaism/FAQ/05-Worship/section-13.html> [Accessed January 25, 2005].

203. Maas, Elaine H. "The Jews in Houston Today."

Barnette, Mic. "Beth Israel nearing its 150th year." Houston Chronicle, Saturday, 10/18/2003. Section: Houston, Page 7, 2 Star Edition.

Houston City Directory, 1866. Page 83.

204. Maas, Elaine H. "The Jews in Houston Today."

205. Wood, W. E. City of Houston, Harris County, Texas [map]. Houston, 1869.

Augustus Koch (1840 - ?). Bird's Eye View of the City of Houston, Texas 1873. Madison, WI: J. J. Stoner, 1873.

206. Barnette, Mic. "Beth Israel nearing its 150th year."

Sealy, Margaret. "A grave undertaking / Take a tombstone tour for Halloween." Houston Chronicle, Thursday, 10/31/1985. Section: Weekend Preview, Page 1, No Star Edition.

Maas, Elaine H. "The Jews in Houston Today."

207. Houston, A History and A Guide. Pages 189, 261.

208. Maas, Elaine H. "The Jews in Houston Today."

209. "Houston, August, 1885. Sheet 8." Sanborn maps, 1867-1970: Texas.

Montefiore, Sir Moses." Jewish Virtual Library. <http://www.jewishvirtuallibrary.org/jsource/biography/montefiore.html> [Accessed December 23, 2004].

"Houston, 1896. Sheet 8." Sanborn maps, 1867-1970: Texas.

210. Montefiore Orthodox Synagogue. <http://montefiore.torah.org/> [Accessed December 23, 2004].

Montefiore, Sir Moses." Jewish Virtual Library.

211. Maas, Elaine H. "The Jews in Houston Today."

212. Barnette, Mic. "Beth Israel nearing its 150th year."

"Congregation Adath Emeth." Switchboard.com. <http://www.switchboard.com/> [Accessed October 7, 2003].

213. "Houston, 1924. Volume 1, Sheet 31." Sanborn maps, 1867-1970: Texas.

"Houston, 1924-1951. Volume 1, Sheet 31." Sanborn maps, 1867-1970: Texas.

214. Glass, James L. Personal communication. February 8, 2004.

Nance, Joseph Milton. After San Jacinto. Austin: UT Press, 1963. Pages 43-43. <http://www.tsha.utexas.edu/supsites/nance/jn_r005.html> [Accessed September 30, 2007].

Pierce, Gerald S. Texas Under Arms. Austin: Encino Press. 1969. Pages 68-69.

215. Glass, James L. Personal communication. February 8, 2004.

Pierce, Gerald S. Texas Under Arms. Pages 68-69.

216. Ibid.

217. "Peter Floeck to Martin Floeck, November 22, 1859." Deed Records. Harris County, Texas. Book V, Page 758.

218. Ziegler, Jesse A. Wave of the Gulf. Page 28.

Muir, Andrew Forest. "Swimming Holes." Papers. MS17, Box 34.1. Woodson Research Center. Rice University. Houston, TX.

219. Augustus Koch (1840 - ?). Bird's Eye View of the City of Houston, Texas 1873.

220. "Houston, 1907. Volume 1, Sheet 9." Sanborn maps, 1867-1970: Texas.

"Eller Wagon Works Building." Venue Directory. ArtsHound.com. <http://www.artshound.com/venue/detail/985/Eller_Wagon_Works_Building> [Accessed August 30, 2011].

221. "Day at Houston." Galveston Daily News, Tuesday, February 25, 1896, page 3, Issue 338, column A.

222. "Needed sanitation for Houston." Galveston Daily News, May 4, 1881, Issue 36, column B.

Melosi, Martin V, and Joseph A. Pratt. Energy Metropolis: An Environmental History of Houston and the Gulf Coast. Pittsburgh: Univ of Pittsburgh Press, 2007. Page 124.

Chapter 10: Frost Town

1. Hornburg, David. Personal communication. September 4, 2008.

Mark Shaben to Michael Flick [Floeck]. August 3, 1847. Deed Records. Harris County, Texas. Book M, Page 197.

History of Texas Together with a Biographical History of the Cities of Houston and Galveston. Chicago: Lewis Publishing Co, 1895. Page 521.

2. "Michael Floeck, Original Grantee. File Number 001636." Texas. General Land Office. Land Grant Search. <http://www.glo.texas.gov/cf/land-grant-search/index.cfm> [Accessed March 10, 2011].

3. Michael Floeck estate, division among heirs. January 7, 1854. Deed Records. Harris County, Texas. Book R, Page 293.

Russell, Marie. 1850 Census Harris County, Texas with added genealogical notes. Baytown: n.p., 1981.

"Charles Stephanes to Michael Floeck, September 15, 1852." Deed Records. Harris County, Texas. Book P, Page 229.

Catherine Floeck to Charles Floeck. August 1, 1854. Deed Records. Harris County, Texas. Book R, Page 293.

4. Michael Floeck estate, division among heirs. January 7, 1854. Deed Records. Harris County, Texas. Book R, Page 293.

5. History of Texas Together with a Biographical History... Pages 521-522.

6. F. P. Hoffmann to Martin and Peter Floeck. July 1, 1859. Deed Records. Harris County, Texas. Book V, Page 478.

"Houston locals." Galveston Tri-Weekly News, March 29, 1871, page 4.

Hoffman and Schulte, by receiver, to F. P. Hoffman. April 7, 1857. Deed Records. Harris County, Texas. Book S, Page 778.

7. Ibid.

"Supreme Court." Galveston Daily News, February 24, 1857, page 3.

F. P. Hoffmann to Martin and Peter Floeck. July 1, 1859.

8. "Peter Floeck to Martin Floeck, November 22, 1859." Deed Records. Harris County, Texas. Book V, Page 758.

"Martin Floeck to Peter Floeck, November 22, 1859." Deed Records. Harris County, Texas. Book V, Page 759.

9. Houghton, Dorothy K. H. Houston's Forgotten Heritage. Houston: Rice University Press, 1991. Pages 73, 247.

10. "Flock, M, 1860 Census, Series M653, Roll 1296, Page 401." Heritage Quest Online. ProQuest Information and Learning Company. <http://www.heritagequestonline.com/> [Accessed August 30, 2011].

"Wanted." Houston Telegraph, August 26, 1864.

"Letter from Sioux." Galveston Daily News, January 13, 1867, page 2.

"Fire at Houston." Flake's Bulletin (Galveston, Texas). 06/20/1867.

11. Mooney & Morrison's directory of the city of Houston for 1877-78. Houston: Mooney & Morrison, 1877. Page 97.

Clark, Gladys. Files, 1986. "Letter to Mrs. Anderson." No date. Copy in author's possession.

"Floeck, Martin, 1870 Census, Series M593, Roll 1589, Page 538." Heritage Quest Online.

"Houston Local Items. Death of an Alderman." Galveston Daily News, March 22, 1876, Issue 274, column G.

12. Morrison & Fourmy's general directory of the city of Houston for 1886-87. Houston: Morrison & Fourmy, 1886. Page 131.

Morrison & Fourmy's general directory of the city of Houston for 1884-85. Houston: Morrison & Fourmy, 1884. Page 137.

Clark, Gladys. Files, 1986. "Letter to Mrs. Anderson."

"Magnolia City Mention." Galveston Daily News, September 8, 1889, page 3, Issue 135, column A.

Kaplan, David. "The Settegasts." Houston Style. January, 1986. Houston, TX: Houston Style Pub. Co.

History of Texas Together with a Biographical History... Page 565.

"Houston, 1907. Volume 1, Sheet 90." Sanborn maps, 1867-1970: Texas. [Ann Arbor, Mich.?]: Bell & Howell Information and Learning, c2001.

13. "School Histories: the stories behind the names." HISD. <https://www.houstonisd.org/HISDConnectDS/v/index.jsp?> [Accessed March 4, 2011].

"Houston, 1907. Volume 1, Sheet 10." Sanborn maps, 1867-1970: Texas.

Chapman, Betty T. "Settlement houses: Havens of help in early Houston." Houston Business Journal, December 29, 2000-January 4, 2001.

14. Ibid.

Martin, Betty. "Neighborhood Centers boosting people's lives." Houston Chronicle, Thursday, 08/18/2005. Section: This Week, Z11, Page 1, 2 Star Edition.

"Settlement House Opened." Galveston Daily News, May 5, 1909, page 9.

15. "Summary of news." Galveston Daily News, December 16, 1910, page 1.

Gunter, Jewel Boone Hamilton. Committed, the official 100-year history of the Woman's Club of Houston, 1893-1993. Houston: D. Armstrong, Inc., c1995.

"New Rusk School opens." Galveston Daily News, April 23, 1913, page 3.

"Houston, 1924. Volume 1, Sheet 29." Sanborn maps, 1867-1970: Texas.

16. "Mexicans in Houston Today." Houston History. <http://www.houstonhistory.com/> [Accessed January 25, 2005].

Chapman, Betty T. "Settlement house in Second Ward relieved problems of overcrowding." Houston Business Journal, March 14-20, 1997.

17. "Birthday, a lecture, a magazine." Bayou City History. Houston Chronicle. <http://blogs.chron.com/bayoucityhistory/> [Accessed August 21, 2008].

18. Ibid.

"School Histories: the stories behind the names." HISD.

"Account 0400010000022, Map 5457A8." Harris County Appraisal District. <http://www.hcad.org/> [Accessed December 17, 2004].

19. Dittman, Ralph E. Allen's Landing: the authentic story of the founding of Houston. Houston: AC & JK Allen Pub., c1986.

20. Houston, A History and A Guide. Houston: Anson Jones Press, 1942. Pages 38, 131. "West Columbia, Texas." The Handbook of Texas Online. <http://www.tsha.utexas.edu/handbook/online/articles/WW/hgw3.html> [Accessed December 30, 2006].

21. "A. C. and J. K. Allen to William F. Hodge, April 13, 1837." Deed Records. Harris County, Texas. Book A, Page 405.

"A. C. and J. K. Allen to Jonathan B. Frost, April 13, 1837." Deed Records. Harris County, Texas. Vol. A, Pages 453-454.

22. "A. C. and J. K. Allen to William F. Hodge, April 13, 1837."

23. Clark, Gladys. Files, 1986. "Old Germantown." Copy in author's possession.

"Estate of Jonathan B. Frost, 1837." Probate Records. Harris County, Texas. Vol. A, Pages 228-230.

"J. C. Frost to S. M. Frost, May 5, 1838." Deed Records. Harris County, Texas. Vol. A, Pages 475-476.

"William F. Hodge to John Beldin, May 9, 1838." Deed Records. Harris County, Texas. Book A, Page 407.

24. "Belden, John." San Jacinto Museum. <http://www.sanjacinto-museum.org/Herzstein_Library/> [Accessed April 12, 2005].

"Frances Emmaline Bartlett." Rootsweb.com <http://homepages.rootsweb.com/~bartlett/bartlett-frances-emmaline.html>. [Accessed April 12, 2005].

"Officers and Enlisted Men Battle of San Jacinto 21st April 1836." McKeehan, Wallace L. Sons of DeWitt Colony Texas. <http://www.tamu.edu/ccbn/dewitt/> [Accessed December 11, 2004].

25. "Belden, John." San Jacinto Museum.

Whitty, P., Surveyor. Map of Harris County, Texas. Houston: Houston Map Co., Inc., 1908.

26. "Frances Emmaline Bartlett." Rootsweb.com.

"John Beldin to Leonard D. Perkins and Levi Butler, September 11, 1840." Deed Records. Harris County, Texas. Book F, Page 517.

27. "Levi Butler to Peter Gabel and Henry Schulte, June 1, 1853." Deed Records. Harris County, Texas. Book P, Page 327.

28. Ibid.

29. "Heinrich Schulte to Peter Gabel, December 12, 1854." Deed Records. Harris County, Texas. Book P, Page 476.

30. Houston, A History and A Guide. Page 154.

31. Gish, Theodore G. "The Germans in Houston. The beginnings." Washington Cemetery Centennial Book. Houston: Concerned Citizens for Washington Cemetery Care, 1988.

32. Wood, W. E. City of Houston, Harris County, Texas [map]. Houston, 1869. Augustus Koch (1840 - ?). Bird's Eye View of the City of Houston, Texas 1873. Madison, WI: J. J. Stoner, 1873.

Beck, Bill. At your service: an illustrated history of Houston Lighting & Power Company. Houston: Gulf Publishing Co., 1990. Page 23.

33. "Edison, Thomas Alva. The Incandescent Lamp." Encarta. <http://encarta.msn.com/encyclopedia_761563582_2/Thomas_Edison.html> [Accessed April 13, 2005].

34. Chapman, Betty T. "Electric power surged after sputtering start in Houston." Houston Business Journal, September 7-13, 2001. Page 26.

Beck, Bill. At your service... Page 9.

35. Ibid. Page 19-20.

36. "Capital City Chat." Galveston Daily News, August 1, 1889, Issue 96, column B.

"Magnolia City Mention." Galveston Daily News, August 6, 1889, page 3, Issue 101, column A.

"CenterPoint Energy Historical Timeline." Center Point Energy. <http://www.centerpointenergy.com/cda/print/1,3220,100431,00.html> [Accessed April 16, 2005].

"Houston, 1896. Sheet 58." Sanborn maps, 1867-1970: Texas.

37. Beck, Bill. At your service... Page 33.

38. "CenterPoint Energy Historical Timeline."

39. Ibid.

Chapman, Betty T. "Electric power surged after sputtering start in Houston."

Beck, Bill. At your service... Pages 23-24.

40. Ibid.

A. L. Westyard (attributed). Houston, Texas (Looking South) [Bird's Eye] 1891. Chicago: D. W. Ensign, Jr., 1891.

41. Beck, Bill. At your service... Page 44.

"CenterPoint Energy Historical Timeline."

42. Chapman, Betty T. "Electric power surged after sputtering start in Houston."

"Houston, 1907. Volume 1, Sheet 89." Sanborn maps, 1867-1970: Texas.

43. Ibid.

44. "Houston, 1924-1951. Volume 1, Sheet 25." Sanborn maps, 1867-1970: Texas.

Beck, Bill. At your service... Page 65.

45. Ibid.

46. "Houston, 1924. Volume 1, Sheet 25." Sanborn maps, 1867-1970: Texas.

47. "Houston, 1924. Volume 1, Sheets 25 and 26." Sanborn maps, 1867-1970: Texas.

48. "Houston, 1924. Volume 1, Sheet 25." Sanborn maps, 1867-1970: Texas.

49. "Kapner, Isaac. 1900 Census, Series T623, Roll 1642, Page 13." Heritage Quest Online.

Clark, Gladys. Files, 1986. "Frostown-Moody Ownership Map, 1946." Copy in author's possession.

50. "Kapner, Isaac. 1900 Census, Series T623, Roll 1642, Page 13." Heritage Quest Online.

"Houston, 1924. Volume 1, Sheet 25." Sanborn maps, 1867-1970: Texas.

51. "Kapner, I. 1920 Census, Series T625, Roll 1812, Page 43." Heritage Quest Online.

"Kapner, Isac. 1930 Census, Series T626, Roll 2346, Page 148." Heritage Quest Online.

"Kapner." Probate Court Inquiry System. County Clerk. Harris County, Texas. <http://www.cclerk.hctx.net/> Accessed April 20, 2005].

52. "Houston, 1924-1951. Volume 1, Sheet 25." Sanborn maps, 1867-1970: Texas.

53. Ibid.

54. Beck, Bill. At your service... Page 67.

55. Young, Nancy Beck. "Galveston and Houston Junction Railroad." The Handbook of Texas Online. <http://www.tshaonline.org/handbook/online/articles/eqgvg> [Accessed August 31, 2011].

56. Ibid.

Wood, W. E. City of Houston, Harris County, Texas [map]. Houston, 1869.

57. "Frost Town. Lot sales, 1840-1880." Abstracts. Stewart Title. Houston, TX. Copy in author's possession.

58. Young, Nancy Beck. "Galveston and Houston Junction Railroad."

59. Wood, W. E. City of Houston, Harris County, Texas [map]. Houston, 1869.

A. L. Westyard (attributed). Houston, Texas (Looking South) [Bird's Eye] 1891. Chicago: D. W. Ensign, Jr., 1891.

60. McComb, David G. Houston: A History. Austin: University of Texas, 1981. Page 76.

"Additional Notes." Galveston Daily News, January 31, 1892, page 7, Issue 313, column D.

"Houston, 1896. Sheet 60." Sanborn maps, 1867-1970: Texas.

61. Whitty, P. "Houston, January, 1906 [map]." 1906.

"Houston, 1907. Volume 2, Sheet 69." Sanborn maps, 1867-1970: Texas.

Book of Houston: a brief sketch of its history, educational facilities...[Houston, TX?]: [s. n.], 1915. Page 38.

62. "Alfred C. Finn: An inventory of his records at the Houston Metropolitan Research Center, Houston Public Library." Library. University of Texas. <http://www.lib.utexas.edu/taro/houpub/00024/hpub-00024.html> [Accessed April 14, 2005].

63. Beberdick, Frank H. "Pullman Timeline." Pullman Virtual Museum. <http://www.eliillinois.org/30108_87/timeline.html> [Accessed April 14, 2005].

64. Farris, Kirk. Personal communiation, July 3, 2005.

65. Wood, W. E. City of Houston, Harris County, Texas [map]. Houston, 1869.

"Houston, August, 1885. Sheet 5." Sanborn maps, 1867-1970: Texas.

"Houston, 1890. Sheet 28." Sanborn maps, 1867-1970: Texas.

66. Ibid.

67. "Houston, 1907. Volume 2, Sheet 8." Sanborn maps, 1867-1970: Texas.

"McKee Street Bridge by Years." The North Side of Houston. [City of Houston report.] Houston[?]: [?], 1931.

68. "Pacific Fruit Express." Reviews. Signature Press. <http://www.signaturepress.com/pferev.html> [Accessed January 21, 2005].

69. Ibid.

70. "Houston, 1924. Volume 3, Sheet 304." Sanborn maps, 1867-1970: Texas.

71. Glass, James L. Letter to Anna Fisher, May 16, 1989. Harris County, Precinct One, Texas. Copy in possession of the author.

"Houston, 1924-1951. Volume 3, Sheet 304." Sanborn maps, 1867-1970: Texas.

72. Texas Historic Bridge Inventory. Texas. Department of Transportation. August 30, 2005.

73. "McKee Street Bridge by Years."

"Sabine Street Bridge over Buffalo Bayou." National Register of Historic Places. Registration Form. U.S. Dept of the Interior. National Park Service.

74. "Frosttown: the vision and the nightmare." Houston Press, 2/26/1952.

75. Glass, James L. Letter to Anna Fisher, May 16, 1989. Harris County, Precinct One, Texas.

76. "McKee Street Bridge: The Engineering Record." Art & Environmental Architecture, Inc. <http://www.frosttownhistoricsite.org/bridge.html> [Accessed April 28, 2003]. Texas Historic Bridge Inventory.

77. Ibid.

78. "McKee Street Bridge: The Engineering Record."

"Form over function." Houston Chronicle, Friday, 01/14/00. Section A, Page 29 Met-Front, 3 Star Edition. Texas Historic Bridge Inventory.

79. Williams, John. "Park vs. concrete / Downtown boom spurs return of old debate." Houston Chronicle, Sunday, 12/06/98. Section A, Page 37 MetFront, 2 Star Edition.

80. "McKee Street Bridge: The Engineering Record."

81. "Texas - Harris County." National Register of Historic Places. <http://www.nationalregisterofhistoricplaces.com/> [Accessed January 9, 2004].

82. "Historic Frost Town." Art & Environmental Architecture, Inc. <http://www.frosttownhistoricsite.org/> [Accessed January 10, 2003].

83. Ibid.

84. Fehrenbach, T. R. Lone Star, a history of Texas and Texans. New York: American Legacy Press, 1983. Pages 191-203.

85. Ibid.

"Proclamation of Sam Houston, A Call for Volunteers, December 12, 1835." Texas State Library and Archives Commission. <http://www.tsl.state.tx.us/treasures/republic/proclamation-houston.html> [Accessed June 14, 2005].

86. Ibid.

87. "Selected Families and Individuals." Tripod Family Tree. <http://members.tripod.com/beejay1/pafg469.html> [Accessed May 23, 2005].

"History." Frost Family History Project. <http://frostfamilyhistory.com/FFHOL/history.php> [Accessed May 23, 2005].

88. Ibid.

"City of Brentwood, TN." <http://www.brentwood-tn.org/> [Accessed July 3, 2005].

89. "History." Frost Family History Project.

90. "Frost, Jonathan B." Republic Claims Search Results. Texas State Library and Archives Commission. <http://www2.tsl.state.tx.us/trail/> [Accessed July 3, 2005].

"Smith, James." Maxey, H. David. Index to the Military Rolls of the Republic of Texas, 1835-1845. <http://www.mindspring.com/~dmaxey/rep_mil7.htm> [Accessed July 3, 2005].

Stevens, L. L. "Smith, James." The Handbook of Texas Online. <http://www.tshaonline.org/handbook/online/articles/fsm25> [Accessed August 31, 2011].

Winkler, E. W. "The 'Twin Sisters' Cannon, 1836-1865." V21, No1. SW Historical Quarterly Online. Texas State Historical Assn. <http://www.tsha.utexas.edu/publications/journals/shq/online/v021/n1/021001061.html> [Accessed March 28, 2003].

91. "Frost, Jonathan B." Republic Claims Search Results.

Clark, Gladys E. "Frostown, Texas." The Handbook of Texas Online. <http://www.tshaonline.org/handbook/online/articles/hvf61> [Accessed September 01, 2011].

"Selected Families and Individuals." Tripod Family Tree.

92. Clark, Gladys E. "Frostown, Texas."

Clark, Gladys. Files, 1986. "Frostown." Copy in author's possession.

Clark, Gladys. Files, 1986. "Old Germantown."

93. Parmelee, Deolece M. "Wilkins, Jane Mason." The Handbook of Texas Online. <http://www.tshaonline.org/handbook/online/articles/fwi14> [Accessed September 01, 2011].

94. Ziegler, Jesse A. Wave of the Gulf. San Antonio: Naylor Co., 1938. Page 25.

Kennedy, Elizabeth W. "Houston - the way we were." Genealogical Record, June 1986. Pages 79-87.

Parmelee, Deolece M. "Wilkins, Jane Mason."

95. "Arkansas River Historical Timeline, 1800-1900." Arkansas River Historical Society. <http://www.tulsaweb.com/port/history2.htm> [Accessed July 3, 2005].

96. Weir, Merle. "Phelps, James Aeneas E." The Handbook of Texas Online. <http://www.tshaonline.org/handbook/online/articles/fph02> [Accessed September 01, 2011].

Clark, Gladys E. "Frostown, Texas."

Clark, Gladys. Files, 1986. "Frostown."

97. Weir, Merle. "Phelps, James Aeneas E."

"Phelps, James, Brazoria County, Patent Number 446." Land Grant Search. Texas. General Land Office. <http://www.glo.texas.gov/cf/land-grant-search/LandGrantsWorklist.cfm> [Accessed September 01, 2011].

98. Muir, Andrew Forest. "Frosttown." Papers. MS17, Box 34.1. Woodson Research Center. Rice University. Houston, TX.

"Austin, John, Harris County, Patent Number 200." Land Grant Search.

Muir, Andrew Forest. "Frosttown."

"Founding of Brazoria." Brazoria County Historical Museum. <http://www.bchm.org/Austin/panel26.html> [Accessed October 1, 2003].

99. Index to the First Census of Texas. Rootsweb.com <http://www.rootsweb.com/~txjackso/Index_First_Census.html> [Accessed August 12, 2003].

Clark, Gladys E. "Frostown, Texas."

Marek, Marianne. "The Long-neglected site of the first capital of colonial Texas: Investigations at San Felipe de Austin (51AU2), Austin County, Texas. Current Archeology in Texas. Volume 7, Number 1 (April, 2005). Austin: Texas Historical Commission.

Parmelee, Deolece M. "Wilkins, Jane Mason."

"79(R) SB1820." Texas Legislative Office. <http://www.capitol.state.tx.us/tlo/79R/billtext/SB01820E.HTM> [Accessed May 21, 2005].

100. Bartholomew, Ed Ellsworth. The Houston Story; a chronicle of the city of Houston and the Texas frontier from the Battle of San Jacinto to the War Between the States, 1836-1865. Houston, Frontier Press of Texas, 1951.

Glass, James L. Personal communication. February 8, 2004.

Glass, James L. "The Original Book of Sales of Lots of the Houston Town Company from 1836 Forward." Houston Review. Volume XVI, No. 3 (1994). Houston: Houston Library Board, 1994.

101. Lubbock, Francis Richard. Six decades in Texas or Memoirs of Francis Richard Lubbock. Austin: Ben C. Jones & Co. Printers, 1900. Pages 45-47.

Houston, A History and A Guide. Page 41.

102. "Facet Map 5457A12." Harris County Appraisal District. <http://www.hcad.org/> [Accessed September 1, 2011].

103. Muir, Andrew Forest. "Founding of Houston." MSS 17-33.6. Papers. Woodson Research Center. Rice University. Houston, TX.

History of Texas Together with a Biographical History... Page 262.

104. "A. C. and J. K. Allen to William F. Hodge, April 13, 1837."

"A. C. and J. K. Allen to Jonathan B. Frost, April 13, 1837."

"A. C. and J. K. Allen to John W. Moody, April 26, 1837." Deed Records. Harris County, Texas. Book D, page 260.

105. "History." Frost Family History Project.

Clark, Gladys. Files, 1986. "Old Germantown."

Clark, Gladys Engbrock. "A vision of hope for Frost-Town." Genealogical Record. Houston. June, 1985. p. 52-56.

106. "Estate of Jonathan B. Frost, 1837." Probate Records. Harris County, Texas. Vol. A, Pages 228-230.

"Estate of J. B. Frost, 1838." Probate Records. Harris County, Texas. Vol. A, Pages 361-365.

107. Ibid.

108. Ibid.

"J. C. Frost to S. M. Frost, May 5, 1838." Deed Records. Harris County, Texas. Vol. A, Pages 475-476.

109. Muir, Andrew Forest. "Frosttown."

Clark, Gladys Engbrock. "A vision of hope for Frost-Town."

Wood, W. E. City of Houston, Harris County, Texas [map]. Houston, 1869.

110. Muir, Andrew Forest. "Frosttown."

111. Phelps, Marie Lee. "Visit to Frost Town." Houston Post, 05/27/1955.

Wood, W. E. City of Houston, Harris County, Texas [map]. Houston, 1869.

112. Girard, A. City of Houston and its vicinity [map]. [Houston?]: [n.p.], January, 1839.

Muir, Andrew Forest. "Subdivisions." MSS 17-33.8. Papers. Woodson Research Center. Rice University. Houston, TX.

Allen, O. F. The City of Houston from Wilderness to Wonder. Temple, TX: O. F. Allen, 1936. p. 1-35.

113. First Settlers of the Republic of Texas. Volume 1: Headright grants which were reported...January, 1840. Austin: Cruger & Wing, 1841.

White, Gifford. 1840 Citizens of Texas. Volume 2. Tax Rolls. Austin: Gifford White, 1984.

114. "Timeline re: Mary Martha (Harbert) & Johnson C. Hunter family." Hunter Cemetery. <http://www.home.earthlink.net/~huntercemetery> [Accessed May 23, 2005].

Clark, Gladys. Files, 1986. "Frostown."

"History." Frost Family History Project.

115. "Timeline re: Mary Martha (Harbert) & Johnson C. Hunter family."

"Frost, S. M., 1860 Census, Series M653, Roll 1294, Page 380." Heritage Quest Online.

116. "Frost, John M., 1870 Census, Series M593, Roll 1585, Page 553." Heritage Quest Online.

"Timeline re: Mary Martha (Harbert) & Johnson C. Hunter family."

117. Wallingford, Sharon. The Vernon Frost Story. [Richmond ?]: [n. p.], [1996 ?].

"The City." Houston Daily Telegraph, June ??, 1878.

"Bering, Theordore, 1870 Census, Series M593, Roll 1589, Page 606." Heritage Quest Online.

118. "Frost, John M., 1900 Census, Series M623, Roll 1642, Pages 179-180." Heritage Quest Online.

119. "History of Fort Bend County." Sugar Land Town Square. <http://www.sugarlandtownsquare.com/images/fbHistory.pdf> [Accessed May 23, 2005].

"History." Frost Family History Project.

120. Wallingford, Sharon. The Vernon Frost Story.

"Frost, J. Miles, 1910 Census, Series T624, Roll 1559, Page 205." Heritage Quest Online.

"Frost, John M., 1920 Census, Series T625, Roll 1813, Page 245." Heritage Quest Online.

121. Ibid.

"Frost, Jaybord Jr., 1920 Census, Series T625, Roll 1814, Page 37." Heritage Quest Online.

122. "Frost, Rosa L., 1930 Census, Series T626, Roll 2348, Page 12." Heritage Quest Online.

"Frost, J. Milo, 1930 Census, Series T626, Roll 2348, Page 152." Heritage Quest Online.

"Frost, Clarence, 1930 Census, Series T626, Roll 2348, Page 41." Heritage Quest Online.

123. "Livestock show director Vernon W. Frost dies." Houston Chronicle, Wednesday, 07/12/2000. Section: A, Page 23, 3 Star Edition.

"Frost." Probate Court Inquiry System. County Clerk. Harris County, Texas. <http://www.cclerk.hctx.net/> [Accessed May 28, 2005].

124. Wallingford, Sharon. The Vernon Frost Story.

"Livestock show director Vernon W. Frost dies."

125. Ibid.

126. "Frost Town." Clark, Gladys E. Notes. [no date].

"Texas. Harris County. Geneology. Marriages [1837-1847]." Our Lost Family. <http://www.maxpages.com/ourlostfamily2/Marriages_Part_One> [Accessed January 3, 2001].

127. Clark, Gladys. Files, 1986. "Frostown."

128. Gish, Theodore G. "Germans in Houston Today." Houston History. <http://www.neosoft.com/~sgriffin/houstonhistory/> [Accessed September 19, 2000].

Tutt, Bob. "Frost Town wasn't Germantown, and who was Martha Hermann?" Houston Chronicle, Saturday, 10/24/1987. Section: 2, Page 11, 2 Star Edition.

Muir, Andrew Forest. "Subdivisions."

129. Justman, Dorothy. "Ein Texas-Deutscher aus Deutschland." Genealogical Record, December 1983. Pages 140-144.

"Metternich and the New Social Order 1815-1848." Western New England College. <http://mars.acnet.wnec.edu/~grempel/cources/germany/lectures/06metternich.html>. [Accessed July 10, 2005].

130. Kordul, A. Der sichere fuehrer nach und in Texas. Rottweilam Neckar: I. P. Setzersche buch handlung, 1846.

Justman, Dorothy. "Ein Texas-Deutscher aus Deutschland."

131. Ibid.

132. Wolf, George, Jr. "Frost-town Cemetery." Cemeteries and History of Harris Co., TX. <http://community-2.webtv.net/herronhistory/CEMETERIESHISTORYOF/> [Accessed May 11, 2000].

Justman, Dorothy. "Ein Texas-Deutscher aus Deutschland."

133. Ibid.

134. Ibid.

135. "Schrimpf, J. W., 1860 Census, Series M653, Roll 1296, Page 400." Heritage Quest Online.

Justman, Dorothy. "Ein Texas-Deutscher aus Deutschland."

136. "Frost Town." Clark, Gladys E. Notes.

"Schrimpf, J. W., 1860 Census, Series M653, Roll 1296, Page 400." Heritage Quest Online.

137. Wolf, George, Jr. "Frost-town Cemetery."

Clark, Gladys. Files, 1986. "Letter to Mrs. Anderson."

138. "Fix, Constantine, 1870 Census, Series M593, Roll 1589, Page 539." Heritage Quest Online.

139. Wolf, George, Jr. "Frost-town Cemetery."

Von-Maszewski, Wolfram M. Personal communication, 3/9/2005.

"Frost Town." Clark, Gladys E. Notes.

140. Ibid.

141. Justman, Dorothy. "Ein Texas-Deutscher aus Deutschland."

142. "Frost Town. Lot sales, 1840-1880." Abstracts. Stewart Title. Houston, TX.

143. Ibid.

144. Gish, Theodore G. "Germans in Houston Today."

145. Taylor, William H, et. al. The Archeology and History of Block 12, South Side of Buffalo Bayou (41HR787), Houston, Harris County, Texas. Houston: BC & AD Archeology, Inc., 1998.

146. Mead, Fannie Mae, Sr. [sic: Wead]. "Frost Town." Genealogical Record, June 1984. Pages 64-67.

147. Young, Nancy Beck. "Galveston and Houston Junction Railroad." The Handbook of Texas Online. <http://www.tshaonline.org/handbook/online/articles/eqgvg> [Accessed August 26, 2011].

148. "Frost Town. Lot sales, 1840-1880." Abstracts. Stewart Title. Houston, TX.

Young, Nancy Beck. "Galveston and Houston Junction Railroad."

149. Wood, W. E. City of Houston, Harris County, Texas [map]. Houston, 1869.

150. "Sholibo, H., 1860 Census, Series M653, Roll 1296, Page 400." Heritage Quest Online.

"Frost Town. Lot sales, 1840-1880." Abstracts. Stewart Title. Houston, TX.

151. History of Texas Together with a Biographical History... Page 565.

Houghton, Dorothy K. H. Houston's Forgotten Heritage. Page 122.
152. "Shivaree." American Heritage Dictionary of the English Language. <http://www.bartleby.com/61/27/S0352700.html> [Accessed February 13, 2006].
153. "Bertrand, Julius, 1870 Census, Series M593, Roll 1589, Page 539." Heritage Quest Online.
Mead, Fannie Mae, Sr. [sic: Wead]. "Frost Town." Genealogical Record, June 1984. Pages 64-67.
154. "Scholibo, Chas F., 1900 Census, Series T623, Roll 1642, Page 336." Heritage Quest Online.
155. "Scholibo, Mary, 1910 Census, Series T624, Roll 1559, Page 95." Heritage Quest Online.
156. "Scholibo, Mary, 1920 Census, Series T625, Roll 1812, Page 45." Heritage Quest Online.
157. "Scholibo." Probate Court Inquiry System. County Clerk. Harris County, Texas. <http://www.cclerk.hctx.net/> [Accessed August 7, 2005].
"Mills, Earnest N., 1930 Census, Series T626, Roll 2346, Page 160." Heritage Quest Online.
158. "Frost Town. Lot sales, 1840-1880." Abstracts. Stewart Title. Houston, TX.
Clark, Gladys. Files, 1986. "Frost-Town Notes: Miscellaneous."
"Dagenhart, George, 1870 Census, Series M593, Roll 1589, Page 574." Heritage Quest Online.
159. "Kehoe, John, 1870 Census, Series M593, Roll 1589, Page 540." Heritage Quest Online.
"Kehoe, Thomas, 1900 Census, Series T623, Roll 1642, Page 12." Heritage Quest Online.
"Forgotten Frost Town, City's first suburb, really was 'Papa' of Houston by 11 years." Houston Press, 12/11/1936.
160. "Kehoe, Thomas, 1900 Census, Series T623, Roll 1642, Page 12." Heritage Quest Online.
161. "Kehoe, Thomas, 1910 Census, Series T624, Roll 1560, Page 39." Heritage Quest Online.
"Kehoe, Thomas, 1930 Census, Series T626, Roll 2348, Page 46." Heritage Quest Online.
162. Phelps, Marie Lee. "Visit to Frost Town." Houston Post, 05/27/1955.
Gish, Theodore G. "Germans in Houston Today."
163. "Frost Town. Lot sales, 1840-1880." Abstracts. Stewart Title. Houston, TX.
"Klepper, Henry, 1860 Census, Series M653, Roll 1296, Page 404." Heritage Quest Online.
164. Ibid.
History of Texas Together with a Biographical History... Page 389.
165. "Frost Town. Lot sales, 1840-1880." Abstracts. Stewart Title. Houston, TX.
Hornburg, David. Personal communication, August 22, 2005.
"Taylor, Will, 1930 Census, Series T626, Roll 2346, Page 116." Heritage Quest Online.
166. "Klay, John, 1860 Census, Series M653, Roll 1296, Page 400." Heritage Quest Online.
Wead, Jimmy. Personal communication, January 31, 2006. Wead is a descendant of the Klee family.
"Frost Town. Lot sales, 1840-1880." Abstracts. Stewart Title. Houston, TX.
167. "Klay, John, 1860 Census, Series M653, Roll 1296, Page 400." Heritage Quest Online.
168. Clark, Gladys. Files, 1986. "Frost-Town Notes: Miscellaneous."

"Clay, John, 1870 Census, Series M593, Roll 1589, Page 539." Heritage Quest Online.
169. Mead, Fannie Mae, Sr. [sic: Wead]. "Frost Town." Genealogical Record, June 1984. Pages 64-67.
170. "Frost Town. Lot sales, 1840-1880." Abstracts. Stewart Title. Houston, TX.
Vara, Luz. Personal communication. October 10, 2004.
"Frosttown: the vision and the nightmare." Houston Press, 2/26/1952.
171. "Klopp, Henry, 1860 Census, Series M653, Roll 1296, Page 400." Heritage Quest Online.
"Frost Town. Lot sales, 1840-1880." Abstracts. Stewart Title. Houston, TX.
172. "Klapp, William F., 1910 Census, Series T624, Roll 1560, Page 59." Heritage Quest Online.
"Klopp, Ed, 1910 Census, Series T624, Roll 1560, Page 203." Heritage Quest Online.
"Klopp, John, 1910 Census, Series T624, Roll 1559, Page 97." Heritage Quest Online.
"Klopp, Henry, 1910 Census, Series T624, Roll 1559, Page 97." Heritage Quest Online.
173. "Frost Town. Lot sales, 1840-1880." Abstracts. Stewart Title. Houston, TX.
174. "Klopp, Henry, 1900 Census, Series T623, Roll 1642, Page 11." Heritage Quest Online.
175. Ibid.
176. Ibid.
"Klapp, William F., 1910 Census, Series T624, Roll 1560, Page 59." Heritage Quest Online.
177. "Klapp, William F., 1910 Census, Series T624, Roll 1560, Page 59." Heritage Quest Online.
"Klopp, Ed, 1910 Census, Series T624, Roll 1560, Page 203." Heritage Quest Online.
"Klopp, John, 1910 Census, Series T624, Roll 1559, Page 97." Heritage Quest Online.
"Klopp, Henry, 1910 Census, Series T624, Roll 1559, Page 97." Heritage Quest Online.
178. "Frost Town. Lot sales, 1840-1880." Abstracts. Stewart Title. Houston, TX.
179. "Morgan, Alberta, 1930 Census, Series T626, Roll 2346, Page 115." Heritage Quest Online.
180. "Frost Town. Lot sales, 1840-1880." Abstracts. Stewart Title. Houston, TX.
"Hildebrant, R., 1860 Census, Series M653, Roll 1296, Page 405." Heritage Quest Online.
181. Wood, W. E. City of Houston, Harris County, Texas [map]. Houston, 1869.
"Hildebrant, R., 1860 Census, Series M653, Roll 1296, Page 405." Heritage Quest Online.
"Hildebrand, Rhine, 1870 Census, Series M593, Roll 1589, Page 539." Heritage Quest Online.
182. Ibid.
183. "Hildabrand, Simon, 1910 Census, Series T624, Roll 1559, Page 114." Heritage Quest Online.
184. Ibid.
"Hildebrand, Enna, 1920 Census, Series T625, Roll 1812, Page 26." Heritage Quest Online.
"Frost Town. Lot sales, 1840-1880." Abstracts. Stewart Title. Houston, TX.
185. "Allens lived in village when San Jacinto was fought." Houston Press [newspaper]. December, 1936.
186. "Steiner, Frank, 1860 Census, Series M653, Roll 1296, Page 400." Heritage Quest Online.
"Frost Town. Lot sales, 1840-1880." Abstracts. Stewart Title. Houston, TX.
187. "Steiner, Frank, 1860 Census, Series M653, Roll 1296, Page 400." Heritage Quest Online.

"Frost Town. Lot sales, 1840-1880." Abstracts. Stewart Title. Houston, TX.

188. "Newrath, John R., 1870 Census, Series M593, Roll 1589, Page 542." Heritage Quest Online.

189. "Steiner, Frank, 1870 Census, Series M593, Roll 1589, Page 538." Heritage Quest Online.

190. Augustus Koch (1840 - ?). Bird's Eye View of the City of Houston, Texas 1873. A. L. Westyard (attributed). Houston, Texas (Looking South) [Bird's Eye] 1891.

191. "Stiner, Fredicka, 1900 Census, Series T623, Roll 1642, Page 13." Heritage Quest Online.

192. "Jantz, C. B., 1910 Census, Series T624, Roll 1559, Page 116." Heritage Quest Online.

"Jantz, Carl, 1920 Census, Series T625, Roll 1812, Page 28." Heritage Quest Online.

193. "Jantz." Probate Court Inquiry System. County Clerk. Harris County, Texas. <http://www.cclerk.hctx.net/> [Accessed August 7, 2005].

194. "Richard Insall to John W. Schrimpf, July 20, 1847." Deed Records. Harris County, Texas. Book M, Page 116.

195. "Frost Town." Clark, Gladys E. Notes. [no date].

"Frost Town. Lot sales, 1840-1880." Abstracts. Stewart Title. Houston, TX.

196. "Schrimpf, John, 1870 Census, Series M593, Roll 1589, Pages 538-539." Heritage Quest Online.

197. "Frost Town." Clark, Gladys E. Notes. [no date].

"Frost Town. Lot sales, 1840-1880." Abstracts. Stewart Title. Houston, TX.

198. Mead, Fannie Mae, Sr. [sic: Wead]. "Frost Town." Genealogical Record, June 1984. Pages 64-67.

199. Chapman, Betty T. "James Bute Park: An early oasis of urban green space." Houston Business Journal, July 14-20, 2000.

200. "Historic Frost Town." Art & Environmental Architecture, Inc. <http://www.frosttownhistoricsite.org/> [Accessed January 10, 2003].

201. Analysis of the census data for the Frost Town blocks by the author.

202. Ibid.

203. Ibid.

204. Clark, Gladys. Files, 1986. "Letter from Leona E. Walls, October 21, 1992."

205. Analysis of the census data for the Frost Town blocks by the author.

206. Vara, Luz. Personal communication. October 10, 2004.

207. "Houston, 1907. Volume 1, Sheet 89." Sanborn maps, 1867-1970: Texas.

208. Vara, Luz. Personal communication. October 10, 2004.

209. Ibid.

210. Ibid.

211. "Mexicans in Houston Today." Houston History. <http://www.houstonhistory.com/> [Accessed January 25, 2005].

212. Rosales, F. Arturo. "Mexicans in Houston: The struggle to survive, 1908-1975." Houston Review. Volume 3, No. 2 (Summer 1981). Houston: Houston Library Board, 1981. Pages 224-248.

213. Vara, Luz. Personal communication. October 10, 2004.

214. Ibid.

215. Ibid.

216. Ibid.

217. "Houston, 1924. Volume 1, Sheets 25, 26." Sanborn maps, 1867-1970: Texas.

"Houston, 1924-1951. Volume 1, Sheets 25, 26." Sanborn maps, 1867-1970: Texas.

218. "Houston, 1924-1951. Volume 1, Sheet 26." Sanborn maps, 1867-1970: Texas.

"1930 Census, Series T626, Roll 2346, Page 122." Heritage Quest Online.

219. "Houston, 1924-1951. Volume 1, Sheets 25, 26." Sanborn maps, 1867-1970: Texas.

220. "Houston, 1924-1951. Volume 1, Sheet 26." Sanborn maps, 1867-1970: Texas.

"First Ward." Historic Neighborhoods Council. March 2005. Greater Houston Preservation Alliance.

221. "Houston, 1924-1951. Volume 1, Sheets 25, 26." Sanborn maps, 1867-1970: Texas.

222. Byrd, Sigman. "'The Houston Story': Notes on a bookman and his book." Houston Press, 04/12/1951.

223. "Frosttown: the vision and the nightmare." Houston Press, 2/26/1952.

224. "Allan, Lonrezo. 1900 Census, Series T623, Roll 1642, Page 12." Heritage Quest Online.

"Frost Town. Lot sales, 1840-1880." Abstracts. Stewart Title. Houston, TX.

225. "Allan, Lonrezo. 1900 Census, Series T623, Roll 1642, Page 12." Heritage Quest Online.

226. "Frosttown: the vision and the nightmare." Houston Press, 2/26/1952.

227. "Allen, L. W., 1910 Census, Series T624, Roll 1559, Page 114." Heritage Quest Online.

"Allen, Louis W., 1920 Census, Series T625, Roll 1812, Page 27." Heritage Quest Online.

"Allen, Lorenzo, 1930 Census, Series T626, Roll 2346, Page 114." Heritage Quest Online.

228. "Frosttown: the vision and the nightmare." Houston Press, 2/26/1952.

229. "Allen." Probate Court Inquiry System. County Clerk. Harris County, Texas. <http://www.cclerk.hctx.net/> [Accessed August 29, 2005].

230. "Who we are." Preservation Texas. <http://www.preservationtexas.org/about/index.htm> [Accessed August 29, 2005].

231. Chapman, Betty T. "James Bute Park: An early oasis of urban green space."

"Historic Frost Town." Art & Environmental Architecture, Inc.

232. Boyd, Douglas K., Cory Julian Broehm and Amy E. Dase. Archeological investogations for Elysian Viaduct from Quitman Street to Commerce Street in Houston, Harris County, Texas. Austin: Prewitt and Associates, 2005.

233."A. C. and J. K. Allen to John W. Moody, April 26, 1837."

234. "Lunenburg County, Virginia - Biographical Notes on John Wyatt Moody." Rootsweb.com <http://ftp.rootsweb.ancestry.com/pub/usgenweb/va/lunenburg/bios/jwmoody.txt> [Accessed September 1, 2011].

235. Ibid.

"John Wyatt Moody of Texas." MSS 181. John Wyatt Moody Biographical Papers, 1964-1967. Woodson Research Center. Rice University. Houston, TX.

236. "A. C. and J. K. Allen to John W. Moody, April 26, 1837."

237. Houston, A History and A Guide. Page 37.

238. "Ancestry of Helen Foster Snow." MSS 181. John Wyatt Moody Biographical Papers, 1964-1967. Woodson Research Center. Rice University. Houston, TX.

239. "John Wyatt Moody of Texas." MSS 181. John Wyatt Moody Biographical Papers, 1964-1967. Woodson Research Center. Rice University. Houston, TX.

Muir, Andrew Forest. "Frosttown."

240. "Ancestry of Helen Foster Snow."

"Lunenburg County, Virginia - Biographical Notes on John Wyatt Moody."

241. "Letter: W. Broadus Smith to Helen Foster Snow, May 25, 1967." MSS 181. John Wyatt Moody Biographical Papers, 1964-1967. Woodson Research Center. Rice University. Houston, TX.

"Ancestry of Helen Foster Snow."

"Lunenburg County, Virginia - Biographical Notes on John Wyatt Moody."

242. "Richard Insall to John W. Schrimpf, July 20, 1847." Deed Records. Harris County, Texas. Book M, Page 116.

243. Wood, W. E. City of Houston, Harris County, Texas [map]. Houston, 1869.

244. Reed, S. G. A History of Texas Railroads. Houston: St. Clair Publishing Co., ?. Pages 478-479.

Kirkland, Hayes and Waqar Fazlani. "Texas Narrow Gauge Railroad." Houston: unpublished paper, 1997.

245. "Houston, August, 1885. Sheets 5 and 7." Sanborn maps, 1867-1970: Texas.

"Houston, 1896. Sheet 70." Sanborn maps, 1867-1970: Texas.

246. "Houston, 1907. Volume 1, Sheets 89 and 90." Sanborn maps, 1867-1970: Texas.

247. Ibid.

A. L. Westyard (attributed). Houston, Texas (Looking South) [Bird's Eye] 1891.

248. Martin, Betty. "Neighborhood Centers boosting people's lives."

249. "Houston, 1924. Volume 1, Sheet 29." Sanborn maps, 1867-1970: Texas.

250. "Houston, 1924. Volume 1, Sheets 26 and 30." Sanborn maps, 1867-1970: Texas.

251. Houston, A History and A Guide. Page 261.

"Houston, 1924-1951. Volume 1, Sheet 29." Sanborn maps, 1867-1970: Texas.

252. "Houston, 1924-1951. Volume 1, Sheet 26." Sanborn maps, 1867-1970: Texas.

253. "Doris and Carloss Men's Development Center." Star of Hope Mission. <http://www.sohmission.org/esMens.html> [Accessed May 15, 2005].

254. "Houston Local Items." Galveston Daily News, September 3, 1875, page 4.

"Houston Local Items." Galveston Daily News, October 29, 1875, page 4.

255. Mooney & Morrison's directory of the city of Houston for 1877-78. Page 70.

256. Ibid. Pages 13 and 70.

Ziegler, Jesse A. Wave of the Gulf. Page 292.

Houston, A History and A Guide. Page 90.

Historical records search and archeological subsurface testing for the Jefferson Davis Hospital site at 1801 Allen Parkway Drive, Houston, Harris County, Texas. Houston: Moore Archeological Consulting, 1999. Page 26.

257. "Houston Local Items." Galveston Daily News, February 6, 1878, page 7.

Morrison & Co.'s general directory of the city of Houston for 1879-80. Houston: C. D. Morrison & Co., 1879.

Page 53.

Morrison & Fourmy's general directory of the city of Houston for 1882-83. Houston: Morrison & Fourmy, 1882. Page 91.

258. "Houston, August, 1885. Sheet 5." Sanborn maps, 1867-1970: Texas.

259. "Real Estate Transfers." Galveston Daily News, January 28, 1887, page 5.

"Houston Compress Officials." Dallas Morning News. 5/9/1888, page 2.

"Houston, 1890. Sheet 28." Sanborn maps, 1867-1970: Texas.

260. "Building Cotton Warehouses Now Popular Outdoor Sport." Lubbock Morning Avalanche, December 1, 1937, page 3.

"Houston, 1924-1951. Volume 3, Sheet 307." Sanborn maps, 1867-1970: Texas.

261. Manning, Tom. "Proposed new viaduct draws debate." Houston Chronicle, Thursday, 12/02/2004. Section: This Week Z10, Page 1, 2 Star Edition.

"Who we are." Preservation Texas.

262. Manning, Tom. "Proposed new viaduct draws debate."

263. Kaplan, David. "The Settegasts."

"M. J. Rodgers to Jno. W. Schrimpf, July 24, 1847." Book M, Page 99. Deed Records. Harris County, Texas.

264. Muir, Andrew Forest. "German Union." MSS 17-34.2. Papers. Woodson Research Center. Rice University. Houston, TX.

"Frost Town." Clark, Gladys E. Notes. [no date].

265. "Schrimpf, 1860 Census, Series M653, Roll 1296, Page 400." Heritage Quest Online.

Texas. Harris County. Geneology. Marriages [1837-1847]." Our Lost Family. <http://www.maxpages.com/ourlostfamily2/Marriages_Part_One> [Accessed January 3, 2001].

Looscan, Adele B. "Harris County, 1822-1845." Vol 019 No 1 Page 057. Southwestern Historical Quarterly Online.<http://www.tsha.utexas.edu/publications/journals/shq/online/v019/n1/0190010057> [Accessed May 22, 2005].

266. Lich, Glen E. and Günter Moltmann, "Solms-Braunfels, Prince Carl of," Handbook of Texas Online. <http://www.tshaonline.org/handbook/online/articles/fso03> [Accessed September 04, 2011].

Von-Maszewski, Wolfram M. Voyage to North America 1844-45, Prince Carl of Solms's Texas Diary of People, Places, and Events. Denton: German-Texas Heritage Society, 2000. Page 35.

267. Ibid. Pages 81, 89-90.

268. Ibid. Page 151.

269. "Richard Insall to John W. Schrimpf, July 20, 1847." Deed Records. Harris County, Texas. Book M, Page 116.

"M. J. Rodgers to Jno. W. Schrimpf, July 24, 1847." Book M, Page 99. Deed Records. Harris County, Texas.

270. Ibid.

271. Ibid.

272. Russell, Marie. 1850 Census Harris County, Texas with added genealogical notes. Baytown: n.p., 1981.

273. Ibid.

274. Kaplan, David. "The Settegasts."

275. Ibid.

276. History of Texas Together with a Biographical History... Pages 564-565.

277. Houston, A History and A Guide. Page 154.

"Schrimpf, J. W., 1860 Census, Series M653, Roll 1296, Page 400." Heritage Quest Online.

278. Ibid.

Mead, Fannie Mae, Sr. [sic: Wead]. "Frost Town."

"Frost Town." Clark, Gladys E. Notes. [no date].

279. "Schrimpf, John, 1870 Census, Series M593, Roll 1589, Page 539." Heritage Quest Online.

Mead, Fannie Mae, Sr. [sic: Wead]. "Frost Town."

"Shrimp's Field Cemetery." Cemeteries of Texas. Harris [County]. <http://www.cemeteries-of-tx.com/Etx/Harris/cemetery/shrimp.htm> [Accessed September 6, 2011].

280. Kaplan, David. "The Settegasts."

"District Court." Houston Daily Telegraph, April 4, 1872.

281. "Frost Town. Lot sales, 1840-1880." Abstracts. Stewart Title. Houston, TX.

282. "Schrimpf, Chas W., 1900 Census, Series T623, Roll 1611, Page 97." Heritage Quest Online.

"Schrimpf, Chas W., 1910 Census, Series T624, Roll 1531, Page 144." Heritage Quest Online.

283. Kaplan, David. "The Settegasts."

"Frost Town." Clark, Gladys E. Notes. [no date].

284. Kaplan, David. "The Settegasts."

285. Houghton, Dorothy K. H. Houston's Forgotten Heritage. Page 31.

286. Ibid. Page 122.

Kaplan, David. "The Settegasts."

287. Houghton, Dorothy K. H. Houston's Forgotten Heritage. Page 122.

"Settegast, Edward C., 1900 Census, Series T623, Roll 1642, Page 177." Heritage Quest Online.

"History." Frost Family History Project.

288. Houghton, Dorothy K. H. Houston's Forgotten Heritage. Page 122.

"Settegast, Julius J., 1910 Census, Series T624, Roll 1569, Page 191." Heritage Quest Online.

Kaplan, David. "The Settegasts."

"Settegast Quadrangle, 7-1/2 minute quadrangle." U. S. Geological Survey. Topographic Maps. 1919.

289. Ziegler, Jesse A. Wave of the Gulf. Page 26.

Wood, W. E. City of Houston, Harris County, Texas [map]. Houston, 1869.

290. "Houston, 1890. Sheet 16." Sanborn maps, 1867-1970: Texas.

291. "Houston, 1907. Volume 1, Sheets 89, 91, 96." Sanborn maps, 1867-1970: Texas.

292. "Houston, 1924. Volume 1, Sheets 26 and 27." Sanborn maps, 1867-1970: Texas.

293. "Houston, 1924. Volume 1, Sheet 28." Sanborn maps, 1867-1970: Texas.

294. "Houston, 1924-1951. Volume 1, Sheet 28." Sanborn maps, 1867-1970: Texas.

Farris, Kirk. Personal communication. August 17, 2003.

295. "Public Housing Debate: Houston's public housing fight of the 1940's - 50's." Texas Housing. Texas Low Income Housing Information Service. <http://www.texashousing.org/txlihis/phdebate/past 113.htm> [Accessed August 7, 2001].

Snyder, Mike. "Public housing, private hopes / City planners look to project as a catalyst." Houston Chronicle, Sunday, 10/25/1998. Section: A, Page 33, 2 Star Edition.

"US 59 proposed route across Buffalo Bayou, 1955." <http://www.texasfreeway.com/Houston/historic/road_maps/images/> [Accessed August 29, 2005].

296. Snyder, Mike. "Public housing, private hopes..."

297. Werner, George C. "Texas Western Railway." The Handbook of Texas Online. <http://www.tshaonline.org/handbook/online/articles/eqtpg> [Accessed September 06, 2011].

Geiser, Samuel Wood. "Gentry, Abram Morris." The Handbook of Texas Online. <http://www.tshaonline.org/handbook/online/articles/fge02> [Accessed September 06, 2011].

298. Reed, S. G. A History of Texas Railroads.

Geiser, Samuel Wood. "Gentry, Abram Morris."

299. Terneny, Tiffany T. Archeological survey of the proposed George Bush Hike and Bike Trail, Harris County, Texas. Houston: Moore Archeological Consulting, 2002.

Hilton, George Woodman. American Narrow Gauge Railroads. Stanford: Stanford University Press, 1990. Page 528.

"History Timeline." Fort Bend Model Railroad Club. <http://www.fbmrrc.com/history_timeline.html> [Accessed June 18, 2004].

300. "Houston, 1896. Sheet 0b." Sanborn maps, 1867-1970: Texas.

301. "Buffalo Bayou Bridge for Houston Belt & Terminal Railway Co. - 1912." Bridge Plaque. (located on the bridge)

302. "Bascule bridge." Wikipedia. <http://en.wikipedia.org/Bascule_bridge> [Accessed December 3, 2010].

303. "Joseph Baermann Strauss." Structurae. <http://www.structurae.de/> [Accessed January 9, 2004].

"Golden Gate Bridge." Wikipedia. <http://en.wikipedia.org/wiki/Golden_Gate_Bridge> [Accessed April 13, 2011].
304. Ibid.
"Joseph Baermann Strauss." Structurae.
305. Young, Nancy Beck. "Houston and Great Northern Railroad." The Handbook of Texas Online. <http://www.tshaonline.org/handbook/online/articles/eqh08> [Accessed April 10, 2011].
306. Ibid.
Houston, A History and A Guide. Page 145.
307. "Schrimpf's Landing." Houston Weekly Telegraph, December 12, 1872.
308. "[Advertisements]." Galveston Daily News, September 18, 1873, page 1.
Werner, George C. "International - Great Northern Railroad." The Handbook of Texas Online. <http://www.tshaonline.org/handbook/online/articles/eqi04> [Accessed September 06, 2011].
309. "Houston, 1907. Volume 2, Sheet 76." Sanborn maps, 1867-1970: Texas.
"Houston, 1924. Volume 3, Sheet 308." Sanborn maps, 1867-1970: Texas.
"Houston, 1924-1951. Volume 3, Sheet 308." Sanborn maps, 1867-1970: Texas.
310. Werner, George C. "International - Great Northern Railroad."
"Missouri Pacific, Predecessors & Subsidiaries Chronological History." Missouri Pacific Historical Society. <http://www.mopac.org/history.asp> [Accessed April 13, 2011].

Chapter 11: The Second Ward

1. "Carl A. Lottman." Family Tree Maker Online. <http://familytreemaker.genealogy.com/users/w/a/l/Roy-E-Walker-TX/WEBSITE-0001/UHP-0816.html> [Accessed April 23, 2011]
"Lottmann, C. A., 1870 Census, Series M593, Roll 1574, Page 427." Heritage Quest Online. ProQuest Information and Learning Company. <http://www.heritagequestonline.com/> [Accessed August 30, 2011].
2. Morrison & Fourmy's general directory of the city of Houston for 1882-83. Houston: Morrison & Fourmy, 1882. Pages 7, 249, 294.
Morrison & Fourmy's general directory of the city of Houston for 1884-85. Houston: Morrison & Fourmy, 1884. Page 205.
3. "Bayou City Locals." Galveston Daily News, March 29, 1885, page 5.
"[Advertisements]." Galveston Daily News, November 20, 1885, page 9.
4. Morrison & Fourmy's general directory of the city of Houston for 1886-87. Houston: Morrison & Fourmy, 1886. Page 201.
5. "Town Notes." Galveston Daily News, December 6, 1892, page 3.
"Big Blaze in Houston." Galveston Daily News, January 15, 1893, Page 3, Issue 297, column A.
6. "Town Notes." Galveston Daily News, February 26, 1893, page 3.
"Myers-Spalti Manufacturing Plant - Houston, Harris County, Texas." 9Key.com. <http://www.9key.com/markers/marker_detail.asp?atlas_number=5201012976> [Accessed April 15, 2011].
"At the State Capital." Galveston Daily News, July 9, 1893, page 3.
"Houston Business Directory." Galveston Daily News, July 19, 1893, page 3.
7. "Houston, 1896. Sheet 57." Sanborn maps, 1867-1970: Texas. [Ann Arbor, Mich.?]: Bell & Howell Information and Learning, c2001.
8. "Japanning." Wikipedia. <http://en.wikipedia.org/wiki/Japanning> [Accessed April 23, 2011].

Brown, William N. A handbook on Japanning. New York: Van Nostrand Company, 1913. Page 10.

9. Lottman, Charles F. "Process of Curing Moss. Patent number 363,150, dated May 17, 1887." U. S. Patent Office.

Lottman, Albert C. "Mosquito-net frame. Patent number 367,151, dated July 26, 1887." U. S. Patent Office.

10. Lottman, Albert C. "Mosquito-net frame. Patent number 442,486, dated December 9, 1890." U. S. Patent Office.

"List of patents." Fort Worth Morning Register, October 17, 1899, page 2.

Lottman, Albert C. "Tightening device for spring bed-bottoms. Patent number 634,531, dated October 10, 1899." U. S. Patent Office.

11. Morrison & Fourmy's general directory of the city of Houston, 1897-98. Galveston: Morrison & Fourmy, 1897. Page 193.

"Saengerbund meeting." Galveston Daily News, June 21, 1897, page 3.

12. Morrison & Fourmy's general directory of the city of Houston, 1899. Galveston: Morrison & Fourmy, 1898. Page 184.

13. Morrison & Fourmy's general directory of the city of Houston, 1902-03. Galveston: Morrison & Fourmy, 1902. Page 281.

Morrison & Fourmy's general directory of the city of Houston, 1903-04. Galveston: Morrison & Fourmy, 1903. Page 286.

14. "Myers-Spalti Manufacturing Plant - Houston, Harris County, Texas."

"Austin News." Galveston Daily News, June 10, 1904, page 5.

Morrison & Fourmy Directory of the City of Houston, 1905-06. Houston: Morrison & Fourmy, 1905. Page 264.

15. Ibid.

"Lottmann, Charles F., 1910 Census, Series T624, Roll 1560, Page 264." Heritage Quest Online.

"Lottmann, Charles F., 1920 Census, Series T625, Roll 1815, Page 65." Heritage Quest Online.

16. Morrison & Fourmy Directory of the City of Houston, 1910-11. Houston: Morrison & Fourmy, 1910. Page 394.

"Lottman Bankruptcy Statement." Galveston Daily News, September 1, 1910, page 8.

"Bankruptcy Matters." Galveston Daily News, September 21, 1910, page 5.

"Lottmann, Herman W., 1920 Census, Series T625, Roll 1815, Page 33." Heritage Quest Online.

17. Richardson, Robin. "Industrial tour gives look at unseen buildings." Houston Chronicle, Wednesday, 03/28/2001. Section: This Week, Page 1, 2 Star Edition.

Morrison & Fourmy's general directory of the city of Houston, 1908-09. Galveston: Morrison & Fourmy, 1908. Page 269.

Morrison & Fourmy Directory of the City of Houston, 1910-11. Page 449.

18. Johnson, Patricia C. "Get a peek inside 5 historical industrial structures on tour." Houston Chronicle, Sunday, 03/25/2001. Section: Zest, Page 28, 2 Star Edition.

"Houston, 1924-1951. Volume 4, Sheet 401." Sanborn maps, 1867-1970: Texas.

19. "Work begins Jan. 4 on new Athens plant." Waco News-Tribune, December 29, 1955, page 18.

Waters, Glenn. "The Official Vintage Curtis Mathes site by Glenn Waters." <http://curtismathes.webs.com/apps/blog/show/4490378...> [Accessed April 15, 2011].

"[Advertisements]." San Antonio Light, March 10, 1957, page 44.

"Myers-Spalti Manufacturing Plant - Houston, Harris County, Texas."

20. Mathes, W. Michael. "Mathes, George Curtis." The Handbook of Texas Online. <http://www.tshaonline.org/handbook/online/articles/fmahd> [Accessed April 23, 2011].

"History." uniView Technologies. <http://www.nathanwebster.com/uniview/company/history.html> [Accessed April 15, 2011].

Waters, Glenn. "The Official Vintage Curtis Mathes site by Glenn Waters."

21. Evans, Marjorie. "Touring the bayou / Event highlights historic buildings." Houston Chronicle, Wednesday, 08/09/00. This Week Section Zone 11, Page 2, 2 Star Edition.

Perez, Danny. "Tour tells of history of Second Ward area." Houston Chronicle, Wednesday, 02/07/01. Section This Week, Page 6, Zone 11, 2 Star Edition.

Perez, Danny. "Trammell Crow opens Alexan Lofts / Former Meyers-Spalti Manufacturing building set to receive Texas Historical Commission designation." Houston Chronicle, Thursday, 09/25/2003. Section: This Week, Page 5, 2 Star Edition.

Richardson, Robin. "Industrial tour gives look at unseen buildings."

Bivins, Ralph. "Real Estate. Developer tackles two communities at once." Houston Chronicle, Sunday, 05/04/2003. Section: Business, Page 6, 2 Star Edition.

Bivins, Ralph. "El Mercado gets a new lease on life." Houston Chronicle, Friday, 12/21/2001. Section: C, Page 1, 3 Star Edition.

22. "Houston, 1924. Volume 4, Sheet 401." Sanborn maps, 1867-1970: Texas.

23. "Did you know? Houston's Ice King." Historic Neighborhoods Council. July 2005. Greater Houston Preservation Alliance.

"Houston, 1924. Volume 4, Sheet 401." Sanborn maps, 1867-1970: Texas.

"Houston, 1924-1951. Volume 4, Sheet 401." Sanborn maps, 1867-1970: Texas.

"Houston, Texas, 1981." Historic Aerials. <http://www.historicaerials.com/> [Accessed May 2, 2011].

24. "Parks." Buffalo Bayou Partnership. Houston, TX. <http://www.buffalobayou.org/parks.html> [Accessed August 19, 2005].

"New plaza for Houston." Houston Chronicle, Sunday, 10/16/1988. Section: A, Page 30, 3 Star Edition.

25. Kever, Jeannie. "Pride lives on in city's six historical wards." Houston Chronicle, Tuesday, 09/07/2004. Section: E, Page 5, 2 Star Edition.

Houston, A History and A Guide. Houston: Anson Jones Press, 1942. Page 93.

26. "Bridge at Hill Street." Galveston Daily News, October 4, 1895, page 3.

"Hill Street Bridge." Galveston Daily News, May 25, 1896, page 3.

27. "Daily Houston Budget." Galveston Daily News, February 9, 1897, page 3, Issue 322, column A.

28. Ibid.

"Day in the Bayou City." Galveston Daily News, February 3, 1897, page 3, Issue 316, column A.

29. "Council orders Hill Street bridge shut." Daily Court Review, August 11, 1937. Page 4.

30. Texas Historic Bridge Inventory. Texas. Department of Transportation. August 30, 2005.

31. Ibid.

32. Houston, A History and A Guide. Page 288.

"Our History." Catholic Cemeteries. Archdiocese of Galveston - Houston. <http://ccadgh.org/aboutus_histry.php> [Accessed May 3, 2011].

"Kennedy Bakery." Texas Historical Commission. Atlas. <http://atlas.thc.state.tx.us/scripts/> [Accessed January 30, 2001].

33. Houston, A History and A Guide. Page 289.

34. "Paschall, Samuel." San Jacinto Museum. <http://www.sanjacinto-museum.org/kemp/v631.html> [Accessed January 9, 2001].

35. Houston, A History and A Guide. Page 288-289.

36. Ibid. Page 74.

"Geiselman's Tannery." Houston Tri-Weekly Telegraph, May 19, 1862, page 2, column 2.

37. "Samuel Geiselman." Galveston Daily News, March 29, 1895, page 3.

"Geiselman, S., 1860 Census, Series M653, Roll 1296, Page 410." Heritage Quest Online.

Houston, A History and A Guide. Page 74.

38. "Geiselman's Tannery." Houston Tri-Weekly Telegraph, May 19, 1862, page 2, column 2.

39. Ibid.

40. Houston City Directory for 1867-68. Houston: Gray, Smallwood, 1867. Page 48.

Houston City Directory, 1866. Dallas: R. L. Polk & Co, 1866. Page 57.

41. "Texas State Fair. Department." Galveston Tri-Weekly News, June 2, 1871, page 1.

42. "Sunday closing." Galveston Daily News, November 7, 1897, page 4.

"Samuel Geiselman." Galveston Daily News, March 29, 1895, page 3.

43. Ibid.

"Blue law." Wikipedia. <http://en.wikipedia.org/wiki/Blue_law> [Accessed April 6, 2011].

"Blue laws." Galveston Daily News, July 18, 1872, page 4.

"State press." Galveston Daily News, August 6, 1879, page 5.

"Persistent intolerance." Galveston Daily News, October 29, 1883, page 4.

"Reformer says proposed 'Blue Sunday' movement will never be enforced." Galveston Daily News, December 4, 1920, page 7.

44. Roth, Michael P. Crime and punishment: A history of the criminal justice system, 2nd edition. Belmont, CA: Cengage Learning, 2010.

"24-Year Texas blue law ends." New York Times, Wednesday, September 3, 1985.

"Blue law." Wikipedia.

45. "Charters Filed." Dallas Morning News, 9/9/1904, page 7.

46. "Houston, 1907. Volume 1, Sheet 96." Sanborn maps, 1867-1970: Texas.

47. "L. C. McBride files suit against Houston White Brick Company." Galveston Daily News, June 20, 1908, page 3.

Biennial report of the Secretary of State of Texas, 1910. Austin: Austin Printing Co., 1911. Page 111.

48. "Dedman Foundry and Machine firm does all varieties of heavy work; company maintains floating plant." Houston Post, October 29, 1926, page 12.

49. "Building permits." Galveston Daily News, July 26, 1925, page 11.

"Dedman Foundry and Machine firm does all varieties of heavy work; company maintains floating plant."

50. Ibid.

"[Advertisement]." Dallas Morning News. April 23, 1926, Part 2, page 24.

51. "Transfer of Real Estate." Daily Court Review, April 20, 1928. Page 1.

"Late charter filings." Daily Court Review, April 20, 1928. Page 4.

52. "Deeds filed show $100,000 transfer of property." Daily Court Review, August 7, 1936. Page 1.

"Help wanted." Brookshire Times, July 14, 1944. Page 10.

53. "Federal Steel Products buys Dedman Foundry." World Oil, Volume 113 (1944). Houston: Gulf Publishing Company, 1944. Page 78.

"Dedman, Henry W, 1930 Census, Series T626, Roll 2345, Page 221." Heritage Quest Online.

"Texas Steel Firms Hopeful." San Antonio Light, February 17, 1946, page 4.

54. "Steel company's plant destroyed by fire in Houston." Mexia Daily News, January 20, 1948, page 6.

"Houston, 1924-1951. Volume 4, Sheet 402." Sanborn maps, 1867-1970: Texas.

"Stockyards buy interest in steel." Twin Falls Times News, April 24, 1956, page 8.

55. Morrison & Fourmy's general directory of the city of Houston for 1894-95. Galveston: Morrison & Fourmy, 1894. Page 158.

"Houston, 1896. Sheet 76." Sanborn maps, 1867-1970: Texas.

56. "Houston fire area to be rebuilt soon." Dallas Morning News. 2/23/1912, page 1.

57. "Our first 100 years / Looking back / Downtown up in a blaze from 1912 fire." Houston Chronicle, Sunday, 03/25/2001. Section A, Page 39, 4 Star Edition.

Houston Firefighters' Relief and Retirement Fund. <http://www.hfrrf.org/> [Accessed June 20, 2003].

58. "Our first 100 years / Looking back / Downtown up in a blaze from 1912 fire."

"Big fire burning in the Bayou City." Galveston Daily News, February 21, 1912, page 14.

59. "Houston, Tex., swept by fire causes loss estimated at six million..." Salt Lake Telegram, February 21, 1912, page 8.

Marshall, Thom. "Mayor has knack for getting it done." Houston Chronicle, Wednesday, 08/15/2001. Section: A, Page 21, 3 Star Edition.

"Negroes also hold rally." Dallas Morning News. June 6, 1911, page 3.

"Henderson, Q Nat, 1910 Census, Series T624, Roll 1560, Page 175." Heritage Quest Online.

60. "School Histories. Nathaniel Q. Henderson Elementary School." Houston Independent School District. <http://www.hisd.org/> [Accessed May 9, 2011].

"Houston, Tex., swept by fire causes loss estimated at six million..."

61. "School Histories. Nathaniel Q. Henderson Elementary School."

Marshall, Thom. "Mayor has knack for getting it done."

"Contact us." Houston Independent School District. <http://es.houstonisd.org/hendersones/contact.html> [Accessed May 9, 2011].

62. "Our first 100 years / Looking back / Downtown up in a blaze from 1912 fire."

63. Chapman, Betty T. "Fifth Ward: Ethnic melting pot and industrial business district." Houston Business Journal, August 18-24, 2000.

History of Houston Fire Department. <http://www.maxmcrae.com/> [Accessed June 23, 2003].

"150 years of firefighting / The history of the Houston Fire Department." Houston Chronicle, Sunday, 08/14/88. Texas Magazine, Page 8, 2 Star Edition.

"Our first 100 years / Looking back / Downtown up in a blaze from 1912 fire."

64. "Houston fire area to be rebuilt soon."

"Our first 100 years / Looking back / Downtown up in a blaze from 1912 fire."

65. Ibid.

"Houston fire area to be rebuilt soon."

"Great fire at Houston causes $7,000,000 damages." Dallas Morning News. 2/22/1912, page 1.

66. "Houston's Great Fire." Dallas Morning News. May 21, 1891.

67. "Census Results, 1870 and 1880 Census, Harris County, Texas." Heritage Quest Online.

"St. Patrick Church." Archdiocese of Galveston-Houston. <http://www.archgh.org/> [Accessed May 9, 2011].

Morrison & Fourmy's general directory of the city of Houston for 1882-83. Page 60.

68. Morrison & Fourmy's general directory of the city of Houston, 1892-93. Galveston: Morrison & Fourmy, 1892. Page 50.

Morrison & Fourmy Directory Co. Houston City Directory, 1923-1924. Houston: R. L. Polk & Co., 1924. Page 47.

"St. Patrick Church."

69. "Lyons, Jno, 1900 Census, Series T623, Roll 1642, Page 108." Heritage Quest On-line.

Mooney & Morrison's directory of the city of Houston for 1877-78. Houston: Mooney & Morrison, 1877. Page 139.

70. Morrison & Co.'s general directory of the city of Houston for 1879-80. Houston: C. D. Morrison & Co., 1879. Page 149.

Morrison & Fourmy's general directory of the city of Houston for 1884-85. Page 63.

71. Morrison & Fourmy's general directory of the city of Houston for 1886-87. Page 202.

Morrison & Fourmy's general directory of the city of Houston, 1892-93. Page 316.

Foley, Patrick. "Odin, Jean Marie." The Handbook of Texas Online. <http://www.tshaonline.org/handbook/online/articles/fod02> [Accessed May 9, 2011].

72. Morrison & Fourmy's general directory of the city of Houston, 1908-09. Page 382.

Morrison & Fourmy Directory of the City of Houston, 1907. Houston: Morrison & Fourmy, 1907. Page 359.

"Houston, 1907. Volume 2. Sheet 21." Sanborn maps, 1867-1970: Texas.

73. Morrison & Fourmy Directory of the City of Houston, 1912. Houston: Morrison & Fourmy, 1912. Page 453.

Morrison & Fourmy's general directory of the city of Houston, 1908-09. Page 272.

"Big fire burning in the Bayou City."

"Houston, Tex., swept by fire causes loss estimated at six million..."

"Houston fire area to be rebuilt soon."

"Bankruptcy petition filed." Fort Worth Star-Telegram, March 9, 1913, part 2, page 35.

74. "Hotel sells for $61,172." Galveston Daily News, May 7, 1914, page 8.

Houston City Directory, 1915. Houston: Morrison & Fourmy, 1915. Page 644.

"[Obituaries:] Lyons." Galveston Daily News, January 28, 1915, page 5.

75. Houston City Directory, 1915. Page 644.

"Lyons, Thomas, 1920 Census, Series T625, Roll 1814, Page 241." Heritage Quest On-line.

Bernstein, Alan. "Attempt to honor Leland clashes with history." Houston Chronicle, Thursday, 05/23/2002. Section: Metro, Page 1.

Morrison & Fourmy Directory Co. Houston City Directory, 1917. Houston: R. L. Polk & Co., 1917. Page 264.

76. "Express Company Chartered in Austin." Dallas Morning News. 1/23/1913, page 3.

"Houston, 1924. Volume 3, Sheet 310." Sanborn maps, 1867-1970: Texas.

"Houston, 1924-1951. Volume 3, Sheet 310." Sanborn maps, 1867-1970: Texas.

77. "2800 Clinton Drive, 5457B6, Account numbers 0422160010002, 0422160010003, 0351560000001." Harris County Appraisal District. <http://www.hcad.org/> [Accessed May 15, 2011].

"Alpha Used Tire Inc." Company Profiles. Cortera. <http://start.cortera.com/> [Accessed May 16, 2011].

"DSI Logistics." Company Profiles. Cortera. <http://start.cortera.com/> [Accessed May 16, 2011].

78. "2800 Clinton Drive, 5457B6, Account numbers 0422160010002, 0422160010003, 0351560000001."

"4100 Clinton Dr., 5457B7, 5457B8, Account numbers 0372030000001, 0362560000001, 0351630000001, 0421530000016, 0421530000001, 0421530000082." Harris County Appraisal District. <http://www.hcad.org/> [Accessed May 15, 2011].

79. "Pritchard Rice Mill Records." Library. University of Louisiana, Lafayette. <http://library.louisiana.edu/Spec/COL/047.shtml> [Accessed May 17, 2011].

80. Houston City Directory, 1915. Page 100.

81. "Houston, 1907. Volume 2, Sheet 75." Sanborn maps, 1867-1970: Texas.
"Houston, 1924. Volume 3, Sheet 311." Sanborn maps, 1867-1970: Texas.
82. "$115,000 Houston fire razes mill; 2 overcome." Dallas Morning News. 7/9/1936, page 3.
"Pritchard Rice Mill Records."
"2800 Clinton Drive, 5457B6, Account numbers 0422160010002, 0422160010003, 0351560000001."
83. "Houston, 1924-1951. Volume 4, Sheet 402." Sanborn maps, 1867-1970: Texas.
"Upper Channel Industrial Development." Houston Port Book, Volume 35 (Spring), 1957, page 71.
"Houston, Texas, 1973." Historic Aerials. <http://www.historicaerials.com/> [Accessed May 2, 2011].
84. "City of Houston, Texas." Houston Title & Guaranty Co., 1917.
"E-Newsletter." Historic Neighborhoods Council. May, 2004. Greater Houston Preservation Alliance.
"Upper Channel Industrial Development."
85. "400 Jensen Drive, 5457B6, 5457B10, Account numbers 0371110000019, 0372040000031, 0372040000002, 0371690000001, 0131700000001." Harris County Appraisal District. <http://www.hcad.org/> [Accessed May 15, 2011].
86. Wood, W. E. City of Houston, Harris County, Texas [map]. Houston, 1869.
"E-Newsletter." Historic Neighborhoods Council. May, 2004. Greater Houston Preservation Alliance.
"400 Jensen Drive, 5457B6, 5457B10, Account numbers 0371110000019, 0372040000031, 0372040000002, 0371690000001, 0131700000001."
87. "[Eureka Mills]." Houston Daily Telegraph. May [?], 1866. Copy in author's possession.
88. Houston City Directory, 1866. Pages 115-116.
89. "Houston City Mills." Houston Daily Telegraph, Friday, April 24, 1874.
"Product of the Houston City Mills Manufacturing Company for June." Houston Daily Telegraph, Sunday, June 11, 1875.
"All-About-Fabrics." All-About-Fabrics.com <http://www.all-about-fabrics.com/> [Accessed December 31, 2006].
90. "State Fair." Houston Tri-Weekly Telegraph, May, 1872, third week.
91. Wood, W. E. City of Houston, Harris County, Texas [map]. Houston, 1869.
"Houston City Mills." Houston Daily Telegraph, Friday, April 24, 1874.
92. Ibid.
93. Ibid.
94. Ibid.
95. Ibid.
"Corliss steam engine." Wikipedia. <http://en.wikipedia.org/wiki/Corliss_steam_engine> [Accessed May 20, 2011].
96. "Houston City Mills." Houston Daily Telegraph, Friday, April 24, 1874.
97. Ibid.
98. "Product of the Houston City Mills Manufacturing Company for June."
99. "Destructive Fire. Houston City Mills Consumed." Houston Daily Telegraph, August 8, 1875.
100. Ibid.
101. "City Mills." Houston Daily Telegraph, August 10, 1875.
"Rebuild the City Mills." Houston Daily Telegraph, Thursday, September 9, 1875.
102. Morrison & Fourmy's general directory of the city of Houston, 1895-96. Galveston: Morrison & Fourmy, 1895. Pages 2, 317.

103. "Houston, 1896. Sheet 76." Sanborn maps, 1867-1970: Texas.

Morse, Edmund L. "Cotton-press. Patent number 258,246, dated May 23, 1882." U. S. Patent Office.

Morris, John and F. W. Wilkinson. The elements of spinning. London: Longmans, 1897. Pages 45-47.

104. "Houston fire area to be rebuilt soon."

105. "Pioneer firm plans to quit." Dallas Morning News. 3/21/1930, page 2.

"New Texas Charters." Dallas Morning News. 5/30/1912, page 14.

106. Directory of the City of Houston, 1911-12. Houston: Texas Publishing Co., 1911. Pages 78, 839.

107. "W. B. Chew, Houston, Dies in Colorado." Dallas Morning News. 8/19/1932, page 6.

"Houston, 1924. Volume 4. Sheet 405." Sanborn maps, 1867-1970: Texas.

Houston City Directory, 1915. Page 679.

108. "Merchants Compress is divided into companies." Galveston Daily News, July 4, 1923, page 3.

"Houston, 1924-1951. Volume 4, Sheet 405." Sanborn maps, 1867-1970: Texas.

"[Advertisements]." Engineering news-record, Volume 134 (1945). NY: McGraw-Hill. Page 186.

109. "Houston, 1924-1951. Volume 4, Sheet 405." Sanborn maps, 1867-1970: Texas.

"4100 Clinton Dr., 5457B7, 5457B8, Account numbers 0372030000001, 0362560000001, 0351630000001, 0421530000016, 0421530000001, 0421530000082."

110. "Pinto East End LLC." Company Profiles. Corporationwiki. <http://www.corporationwiki.com/Texas/Houston/pinto-east-end-llc/37966851.aspx> [Accessed May 16, 2011].

"Cip Gp, LLC." Company Profiles. Corporationwiki.

"Robert K. Hatcher." Jones Graduate School of Business. Rice University. <http://business.rice.edu/Robert_Hatcher_Biography.aspx> [Accessed May 16, 2011].

111. Houston 1904 Street Guide. Houston: P. Whitty, Surveyor, 1904. <http://www.hctx.net/archives/Img.aspx?Img=1> [Accessed May 16, 2011].

"4100 Clinton Dr., 5457B7, 5457B8, Account numbers 0372030000001, 0362560000001, 0351630000001, 0421530000016, 0421530000001, 0421530000082."

"Map of Houston, Texas." Fantham & Fantham, [March, 1928].

112. Melosi, Martin V, and Joseph A. Pratt. Energy Metropolis: An Environmental History of Houston and the Gulf Coast. Pittsburgh: Univ of Pittsburgh Press, 2007. Page 124-125.

113. Ibid. Page 126.

"500 North York, 5457B11, 5457B12, 5457D3, Account numbers 0362520000001, 0371990000045, 0371990000049, 0371990000001." Harris County Appraisal District. <http://www.hcad.org/> [Accessed May 15, 2011].

"Houston, 1924-1951. Volume 4, Sheet 407." Sanborn maps, 1867-1970: Texas.

114. "500 North York, 5457B11, 5457B12, 5457D3, Account numbers 0362520000001, 0371990000045, 0371990000049, 0371990000001."

115. San Antonio and Aransas Pass Railway. <http://saap.tonrr.com/> [Accessed May 21, 2011].

116. Ibid.

117. Ibid.

118. Ibid.

"Houston, Texas." Historic Aerials. <http://www.historicaerials.com/> [Accessed May 21, 2011].

119. "Capital Cullings." Dallas Morning News. 4/12/1889, page 2.

Historical records search and archeological subsurface testing for the Jefferson Davis Hospital site at 1801 Allen Parkway Drive, Houston, Harris County, Texas. Houston: Moore Archeological Consulting, 1999. Pages 26-27.
Morrison & Fourmy's general directory of the city of Houston, 1895-96. Page 288.
"Merchants and Planters Oil Company records (MS260)." Woodson Research Center. Rice University. <http://library.rice.edu/collections/WRC/finding-aids/manuscripts/0260/> [Accessed May 23, 2011].
120. "Bayou City Budget." Galveston Daily News, Thursday, September 12, 1889, page 3, Issue 139, column A.
"Town Notes." Galveston Daily News, Tuesday, July 16, 1889, page 3, Issue 80, column A.
121. Morrison & Fourmy's general directory of the city of Houston, 1892-93. Page 5.
122. Ibid. Page 337.
"Cotton." Wikipedia. <http://en.wikipedia.org/wiki/Cotton> [Accessed May 24, 2011].
"Large cattle shipment." Galveston Daily News, Thursday, February 11, 1892, page 2, Issue 324, column E.
Houston City Directory, 1915. Page 679.
123. Johnston, Marguarite. Houston, The Unknown City, 1836-1946. College Station: Texas A & M University Press, 1991. Page 119.
"Houston Oil Mill Burned." Dallas Morning News, 9/17/1902, page 4.
124. Johnston, Marguarite. Houston, The Unknown City, 1836-1946. Page 119.
"William Marsh Rice." Wikipedia. <http://en.wikipedia.org/wiki/William_Marsh_Rice> [Accessed September 13, 2011].
125. "Merchants and Planters Oil Company records (MS260)."
Morrison & Fourmy's general directory of the city of Houston for 1894-95.
Morrison & Fourmy's general directory of the city of Houston, 1895-96. Page 288.
Morrison & Fourmy's general directory of the city of Houston, 1897-98. Page 45.
126. History of Houston Fire Department.
"Merchants and Planters Oil Company records (MS260)."
127. "4100 Clinton Dr., 5457B7, 5457B8, Account numbers 0372030000001, 0362560000001, 0351630000001, 0421530000016, 0421530000001, 0421530000082."
128. "Brown, Herman." The Handbook of Texas Online. <http://www.tshaonline.org/handbook/online/articles/fbr86> [Accessed May 21, 2011].
"Kellogg Brown & Root, Inc." Funding Universe. <http://www.fundinguniverse.com/company-histories/Kellogg-Brown-amp;-Root-Inc-Company-History.html> [Accessed May 21, 2011].
129. Ibid.
130. "Houston, 1924-1951. Volume 3. Sheet 376." Sanborn maps, 1867-1970: Texas.
"Upper Channel Industrial Development." Houston Port Book, Volume 35 (Spring), 1957, page 71.
131. "Kellogg Brown & Root, Inc." Funding Universe.
"History." KBR. <http://www.kbr.com/About/History/> [Accessed May 25, 2011].
132. "4100 Clinton Dr., 5457B7, 5457B8, Account numbers 0372030000001, 0362560000001, 0351630000001, 0421530000016, 0421530000001, 0421530000082."

Chapter 12: Volksfest Park

1. Fehrenbach, T. R. Lone Star, a history of Texas and Texans. New York: American Legacy Press, 1983. Pages 393-442.
"Forty years since the Houston Turn Verein was founded." Galveston Daily News, January 15, 1894, page 3, Issue 298, column A.

2. Tiling, Moritz. History of the German Element in Texas. Houston: Moritz Tiling, 1913. Pages 163-175.

Morrison & Fourmy's general directory of the city of Houston for 1884-85. Houston: Morrison & Fourmy, 1884. Page 348.

3. LeCompte, Mary Lou. "Turnverein Movement" The Handbook of Texas Online. <http://www.tshaonline.org/handbook/online/articles/vnt02> [Accessed September 14, 2011].

4. Gish, Theodore G. "The Germans in Houston. The beginnings." Washington Cemetery Centennial Book. Houston: Concerned Citizens for Washington Cemetery Care, 1988.

Tiling, Moritz. History of the German Element in Texas.

5. McWhorter, Thomas. "From Das Zweiter to El Segundo, A Brief History of Houston's Second Ward." Houston History, Volume 8, Number 1 (Fall 2010). Page 40.

"Volksfest" New Orleans Times, May 7, 1866, page 1.

6. "New advertisements." Houston Union, June 2, 1869. Page 4.

Mooney & Morrison's directory of the city of Houston for 1877-78. Houston: Mooney & Morrison, 1877. Page 139.

"Volksfest at Houston." Flake's Bulletin (Galveston, Texas). June 12, 1869, page 4.

7. Ibid.

"New advertisements." Houston Union, June 2, 1869. Page 4.

"Gambrinus." Wikipedia. <http://en.wikipedia.org/wiki/Gambrinus> [Accessed June 2, 2011].

8. "Volksfest at Houston." Flake's Bulletin (Galveston, Texas). June 12, 1869, page 4.

9. "Houston Volksfest." Flake's Bulletin (Galveston, Texas). June 10, 1870, page 1.

McComb, David G. Houston: A History. Austin: University of Texas, 1981. Page 44.

Wilson, Ann Quin. Native Houstonian, a collective portrait. Norfolk, VA.: Donning Co., 1982. Page 49.

10. "[Advertisement]. Third German Volksfest." Houston Union, April 28, 1871. Page 3.

"From Houston." Galveston Tri-Weekly News, June 14, 1872, page 2.

"Houston Volksfest." Galveston Tri-Weekly News, May 9, 1873, page 4.

"Houston Local Items." Galveston Daily News, March 25, 1874, Issue 67, column C.

"Bayou City's Budget." Galveston Daily News, May 20, 1886, Page 3, Issue 25, column A.

"Houston's Great Holiday." Galveston Daily News, May 6, 1887, Page 4, Issue 11, column F.

11. "Houston Local Items." Galveston Daily News, May 17, 1876, Issue 47, column D.

12. "Eighth Texas State Fair." Galveston Daily News, April 13, 1877, Issue 18, column A.

"Texas State Fair." Galveston Daily News, May 26, 1877, Issue 55, column B.

McComb, David G. Houston: A History. Page 44.

Wilson, Ann Quin. Native Houstonian, a collective portrait. Page 49.

13. "Houston Volksfest." Flake's Bulletin (Galveston, Texas). June 10, 1870, page 1.

14. "Houston Ninth Annual German Volksfest." Galveston Daily News, May 8, 1877, Issue 39, column G.

"New advertisements." Houston Union, June 2, 1869. Page 4.

"Volksfest at Houston." Galveston Daily News, May 13, 1892, page 3, Issue 50, column A.

15. "Houston Volksfest." Galveston Weekly News, May 20, 1878, page 2.

"Volksfest Circular." Galveston Daily News, May 4, 1894, page 3, Issue 42, column A.

16. "New advertisements." Houston Union, June 2, 1869. Page 4.

"Houston Volksfest." Galveston Tri-Weekly News, May 9, 1873, page 4.

"Daily Houston Budget." Galveston Daily News, July 5, 1897, page 3, Issue 103, column E.

McComb, David G. Houston: A History. Page 43.

17. "Southern Culture." A History in Progress. <http://trojanowski.no-frills.net/index.html> [Accessed December 7, 2003].

"Houston Volksfest." Flake's Bulletin (Galveston, Texas). June 10, 1870, page 1.

McComb, David G. Houston: A History. Page 43.

18. "Texas Topics." Dallas Weekly Herald, June 2, 1881, page 7.

"State Specials." Dallas Weekly Herald, December 1, 1881, page 7.

19. "Houston Fest." Galveston Weekly News, May 27, 1880, page 2.

"Over the State." Galveston Daily News, May 5, 1882, Issue 38, column G.

"Bayou City Locals." Galveston Daily News, August 11, 1884, Issue 121, column A.

"Bayou City Locals." Galveston Daily News, May 2, 1885, Page 3, Issue 8, column A.

"Bayou City's Budget." Galveston Daily News, May 20, 1886, Page 3, Issue 25, column A.

20. "Bayou City Budget." Dallas Morning News. November 12, 1886, page 2.

21. Morrison & Fourmy's general directory of the city of Houston for 1887-88. Houston: Morrison & Fourmy, 1887. Page 54.

McWhorter, Thomas. "From Das Zweiter to El Segundo, A Brief History of Houston's Second Ward."

22. Morrison & Fourmy's general directory of the city of Houston for 1882-83. Houston: Morrison & Fourmy, 1882. Page xv.

23. "Houston's Great Holiday." Galveston Daily News, May 6, 1887, Page 4, Issue 11, column F.

24. "Bayou City." Dallas Weekly Times Herald. May 17, 1890, page 3.

"Bayou City Budget." Galveston Daily News, July 11, 1890, Page 3, Issue 74, column A.

"Bayou City Budget." Galveston Daily News, May 1, 1891, Page 3, Issue 38, column A.

"Yesterday in Houston." Galveston Daily News, October 8, 1891, Page 3, Issue 198, column A.

25. "Volksfest at Houston." Galveston Daily News, May 13, 1892, page 3, Issue 50, column A.

"Multiple classified advertisements." Galveston Daily News, October 14, 1892, page 3, Issue 204, column G.

McWhorter, Thomas. "From Das Zweiter to El Segundo, A Brief History of Houston's Second Ward."

26. "Bayou City Budget." Galveston Daily News, Janaury 4, 1893, page 3, Issue 286, column A.

"Volksfest finances." Galveston Daily News, January 9, 1893, page 3, Issue 291, column A.

"Volksfest Association." Galveston Daily News, January 16, 1893, page 3, Issue [298], column A.

"Grown weary of living." Galveston Daily News, April 17, 1893, Page 3, Issue 24, column A.

"Hebrew installation." Galveston Daily News, October 3, 1893, Page 3, Issue 194, column A.

"Teachers' Institute." Galveston Daily News, November 13, 1893, Page 3, Issue 235, column A.

"People's Festival." Dallas Morning News. May 12, 1894, page 8.

27. "Day at Houston." Galveston Daily News, January 26, 1895, page 3, Issue 309, column A.

"Day at Houston." Galveston Daily News, February 7, 1895, page 3, Issue 321, column A.

"Sunday at Houston." Galveston Daily News, March 4, 1895, page 3, Issue 345, column A.

"Day at Houston." Galveston Daily News, March 9, 1895, page 3, Issue 350, column A.

"Day at Houston." Galveston Daily News, April 14, 1895, page 3, Issue 21, column A.

28. "Day at Houston." Galveston Daily News, August 26, 1895, page 3, Issue 155, column A.

"Day at Houston." Galveston Daily News, November 11, 1895, page 3, Issue 232, column F.

29. "Day at Houston." Galveston Daily News, April 22, 1896, page 3, Issue 29, column E.

Morrison & Fourmy's general directory of the city of Houston, 1897-98. Galveston: Morrison & Fourmy, 1897. Page 129.

30. "Coombs Park and Heights Natatorium." Houstorian. <http://houstorian.wordpress.com/page/3/> [Accessed May 26, 2011].

Morrison & Fourmy's general directory of the city of Houston, 1897-98. Pages 102, 129.

Complete Guide to Houston, Texas. No. 2, April, 1895. Houston: Dealy & Baker, 1890, 1895. Page 50.

31. "Day at Houston." Galveston Daily News, May 11, 1896, page 3, Issue 48, column E.

"Daily Houston Budget." Galveston Daily News, July 4, 1897, page 4, Issue 102, column A.

"Daily Houston Budget." Galveston Daily News, July 5, 1897, page 3, Issue 103, column E.

32. Ibid.

33. Morrison & Fourmy's general directory of the city of Houston, 1900-01. Galveston: Morrison & Fourmy, 1900. Page 416.

"[Volksfest, Houston, 1900-1910]" Geneology Bank. <http://www.geneologybank.com/gbnk/newspapers/> [Accessed May 26, 2011].

34. "Daily Houston Budget." Galveston Daily News, March 4, 1897, page 3, Issue 345, column D.

McWhorter, Thomas. "From Das Zweiter to El Segundo, A Brief History of Houston's Second Ward."

Morrison & Fourmy's general directory of the city of Houston, 1897-98. Pages 44, 162.

35. Ibid. Page 162.

Houston 1904 Street Guide. Houston: P. Whitty, Surveyor, 1904. <http://www.hctx.net/archives/Img.aspx?Img=1> [Accessed May 26, 2011].

36. "Houston, 1907. Volume 1, Sheet 101." Sanborn maps, 1867-1970: Texas. [Ann Arbor, Mich.?] : Bell & Howell Information and Learning, c2001.

37. Ibid.

38. Ibid.

39. "Houston fire area to be rebuilt soon." Dallas Morning News. 2/23/1912, page 1.

40. "Houston, 1924. Volume 4, Sheet 407." Sanborn maps, 1867-1970: Texas.

"Houston, 1924-1951. Volume 4, Sheet 407." Sanborn maps, 1867-1970: Texas.

41. "Houston, Texas." Historic Aerials. <http://www.historicaerials.com/> [Accessed May 21, 2011].

"500 North York, 5457B11, 5457B12, 5457D3, Account numbers 0362520000001, 0371990000045, 0371990000049, 0371990000001." Harris County Appraisal District. <http://www.hcad.org/> [Accessed May 15, 2011].

"Weingarten Realty Investors." SEC Info. <http://www.secinfo.com/dP9fr.11e.8.htm> [Accessed May 16, 2011].

42. McWhorter, Thomas. Director, Historic Neighborhoods Council, Greater Houston Preservation Alliance. Personal communication. Spetember 24, 2003.

43. Ibid.

"E-Newsletter." Historic Neighborhoods Council. May, 2004. Greater Houston Preservation Alliance.

Wood, W. E. City of Houston, Harris County, Texas [map]. Houston, 1869.

44. "Day at Houston." Galveston Daily News, January 4, 1896, page 3.

"Joseph Merkel House." Protected Landmark Designation Report. Archeological and Historical Commission. City of Houston. January 20, 2008.

45. "[Mr. John Merkel; Cane Island]." Houston Weekly Telegraph, August 11, 1858.

"Merkel, John, 1860 Census, Series M653, Roll 1296, Page 423." Heritage Quest Online. ProQuest Information and Learning Company. <http://www.heritagequestonline.com/> [Accessed June 6, 2011].

46. Stewart Abstract and Title Company. "Abstract of Title to the Shannon Addition to the City of Houston. Prepared October 12, 1909." No. 4/3571. Page 34.

"Joseph Merkel House." Protected Landmark Designation Report.

47. Ibid.

McWhorter, Thomas. "From Das Zweiter to El Segundo, A Brief History of Houston's Second Ward."

"Day at Houston." Galveston Daily News, January 4, 1896, page 3.

48. Stewart Abstract and Title Company. "Abstract of Title to the Shannon Addition..." Page 36.

49. "Joseph Merkel House." Protected Landmark Designation Report.

50. "Day at Houston." Galveston Daily News, January 4, 1896, page 3.

"Joseph Merkel House." Protected Landmark Designation Report.

51. Morrison & Fourmy's general directory of the city of Houston for 1884-85. Page 348.

Morrison & Fourmy's general directory of the city of Houston for 1887-88. Page 51.

"Houston Happenings." Galveston Daily News, February 22, 1880, page 7.

52. "Fun still goes on second day of the Volksfest at Houston." Galveston Daily News, May 14, 1892, page 3, Issue 51, column A.

53. Morrison & Fourmy's general directory of the city of Houston for 1886-87. Houston: Morrison & Fourmy, 1886. Page 51.

Morrison & Fourmy's general directory of the city of Houston, 1895-96. Galveston: Morrison & Fourmy, 1895. Page 59.

Morrison & Fourmy's general directory of the city of Houston, 1900-01. Page 407.

54. "Day at Houston." Galveston Daily News, January 4, 1896, page 3.

"Joseph Merkel House." Protected Landmark Designation Report.

Morrison & Fourmy's general directory of the city of Houston, 1897-98. Page 208.

McWhorter, Thomas. "From Das Zweiter to El Segundo, A Brief History of Houston's Second Ward." Page 41.

"E-Newsletter." Historic Neighborhoods Council. May, 2004. Greater Houston Preservation Alliance.

Johnston, Marguarite. Houston, The Unknown City, 1836-1946. College Station: Texas A & M University Press, 1991. Page 172.

55. "Joseph Merkel House." Protected Landmark Designation Report.

56. "City of Houston, Texas." Houston Title & Guaranty Co., 1917.

Ashburn, J. Foster. Ashburn's Map of Houston, Texas. 1942.

"Houston, 1924-1951. Volume 4, Sheet 409." Sanborn maps, 1867-1970: Texas.

"Lafarge Corporation." Funding Universe. <http://www.fundinguniverse.com/company-histories/Lafarge-Corporation-Company-History.html> [Accessed May 16, 2011].

"500 North York, 5457B11, 5457B12, 5457D3, Account numbers 0362520000001, 0371990000045, 0371990000049, 0371990000001."

57. "Houston, Texas." Historic Aerials. <http://www.historicaerials.com/> [Accessed May 21, 2011].

Chapter 13: Lockwood Drive

1. "Parks." Buffalo Bayou Partnership. Houston, TX. <http://www.buffalobayou.org/parks.html> [Accessed August 19, 2005].

"500 North York, 5457B11, 5457B12, 5457D3, Account numbers 0362520000001, 0371990000045, 0371990000049, 0371990000001." Harris County Appraisal District. <http://www.hcad.org/> [Accessed May 15, 2011].

"Hispanic activist Marron honored in park renaming." Houston Chronicle, Monday, 03/30/1998. Section: A, Page 13, 3 Star Edition.

2. Ibid.

3. Schwartz, Matt. "City, county squabble over pavilion, park bathrooms." Houston Chronicle, Friday, 08/01/2003. Section: A, Page 44, 3 Star Edition.

4. "Proler Southwest LP, 5557A9, 5557A5, 5557C1, Account number 0371890000048." Harris County Appraisal District. <http://www.hcad.org/> [Accessed December 20, 2007].

5. "Dan-Loc Bolt and Gasket." Laud Collier and Company. <http://www.lccap.com/pdf/danloc_march_1_release.pdf/> [Accessed June 17, 2011].

6. "Boyer, Inc., Appellant v. Texan Land and Cattle Company, Appellee." Opinion. Fourteenth Court of Appeals. State of Texas. December 13, 2001.

Nunn, Chanti. "Dr. DeBakey, Medical Pioneer, Honored." Texas Medical Center News. Volume 24, No. 10 (June 1, 2002). <http://www.tmc.edu/tmcnews/tmcnews/06_01_02/page_03.html> [Accessed December 21, 2007].

"Lockwood Drive, 5557C2." Harris County Appraisal District. <http://www.hcad.org/> [Accessed December 23, 2007].

"Ira Street, Account number 0371890000052." Harris County Appraisal District. <http://www.hcad.org/> [Accessed June 17, 2011].

7. "[Adams Street New Bridge Views.]" Houston Chronicle, December 9, 1928.

8. Burklin, Raymond. Personal communication, January 17, 2008.

"Drawbridge Operating Regulation; Buffalo Bayou, TX. October 14, 1998 - 63 FR 55029." OpenRegs.com. <http://openregs.com/regulations/view/69155/drawbridge_operating_regulation_buffalo_bayou_tx> [Accessed September 15, 2011].

9. Russell, Marie. 1850 Census Harris County, Texas with added genealogical notes. Baytown: n.p., 1981.

"Ingraham, Robert, 1870 Census, Series M593, Roll 1589, Page 627." Heritage Quest Online. ProQuest Information and Learning Company. <http://www.heritagequestonline.com/> [Accessed June 9, 2011].

Murray's City Directory for 1870-71. Houston: W. Murray, 1870. Page 40.

"Public meeting." Houston Telegraph, November 10, 1860, page 2.

10. "Japhet, Isadore, 1870 Census, Series M593, Roll 1589, Page 579." Heritage Quest Online.

Murray's City Directory for 1870-71. Pages 59, 97.

Mooney & Morrison's directory of the city of Houston for 1877-78. Houston: Mooney & Morrison, 1877. Page 88.

11. Ibid. Pages xi, 88.

12. Morrison & Co.'s general directory of the city of Houston for 1879-80. Houston: C. D. Morrison & Co., 1879.

Page xix, 86, 203.

13. Morrison & Fourmy's general directory of the city of Houston for 1880-81. Houston: Morrison & Fourmy, 1880. Page 173.

Morrison & Fourmy's general directory of the city of Houston for 1882-83. Houston: Morrison & Fourmy, 1882. Page 25.

Morrison & Fourmy's general directory of the city of Houston for 1884-85. Houston: Morrison & Fourmy, 1884. Page 178.

"Houston, August, 1885. Sheet 11." Sanborn maps, 1867-1970: Texas. [Ann Arbor, Mich.?]: Bell & Howell Information and Learning, c2001.

14. Mooney & Morrison's directory of the city of Houston for 1877-78. Page 45.

"Day at Houston." Galveston Daily News, December 25, 1895, page 3, Issue 276, column A.

Morrison & Fourmy's general directory of the city of Houston, 1889-90. Galveston: Morrison & Fourmy, 1889. Page 48.

"Southern Culture." A History in Progress. <http://trojanowski.no-frills.net/index.html> [Accessed December 7, 2003].

15. "Late Houston Locals." Galveston Daily News, March 25, 1890, page 2, Issue 332, column B.

"Houston Happenings." Galveston Daily News, April 6, 1890, page 3, Issue 344, column A.

16. "Wipprecht, Rudolph, 1860 Census, Series M653, Roll 1291, Page 183." Heritage Quest Online.

"Mrs. Pullen to be buried Saturday." Daily Court Review, September 22, 1934. Page 4.

Morrison & Fourmy's general directory of the city of Houston, 1892-93. Galveston: Morrison & Fourmy, 1892. Page 273.

17. Morrison & Fourmy's general directory of the city of Houston for 1894-95. Galveston: Morrison & Fourmy, 1894. Page 305.

18. "Day at Houston." Galveston Daily News, December 25, 1895, page 3, Issue 276, column A.

"Japhet." Glenwood Cemetery. <http://www.glenwoodcemetery.org/search/> [Accessed June 19, 2011].

19. "Day at Houston." Galveston Daily News, January 19, 1896, page 3, Issue 301, column A.

"Day at Houston." Galveston Daily News, March 6, 1896, page 3, Issue 348, column D.

20. Morrison & Fourmy's general directory of the city of Houston, 1899. Galveston: Morrison & Fourmy, 1898. Page 153.

Morrison & Fourmy's general directory of the city of Houston, 1902-03. Galveston: Morrison & Fourmy, 1902. Page 238.

Morrison & Fourmy Directory of the City of Houston, 1910-11. Houston: Morrison & Fourmy, 1910. Page 51.

21. Morrison & Fourmy Directory Co. Houston City Directory, 1918. Houston: R. L. Polk & Co., 1918. Page 580.

Morrison & Fourmy Directory Co. Houston City Directory, 1919. Houston: R. L. Polk & Co., 1919. Page 649.

Morrison & Fourmy's general directory of the city of Houston, 1900-01. Galveston: Morrison & Fourmy, 1900. Page 171.

Morrison & Fourmy Directory Co. Houston City Directory, 1922. Houston: R. L. Polk & Co., July, 1922. Page 810.

Morrison & Fourmy Directory Co. Houston City Directory, 1923-1924. Houston: R. L. Polk & Co., 1924. Page 885.

Morrison & Fourmy Directory Co. Houston City Directory, 1918. Houston: R. L. Polk & Co., 1918. Page 580.

"Japhet, Alfred K., 1920 Census, Series T625, Roll 1814, Page 255." Heritage Quest Online.

"Houston, 1924-1951. Volume 8, Sheet 845." Sanborn maps, 1867-1970: Texas.

22. "Mrs. Pullen to be buried Saturday." Daily Court Review, September 22, 1934. Page 4.

"Real Estate Transfers." Daily Court Review, March 21, 1921. Page 1.

23. "Japhet, Ida, 1930 Census, Series T626, Roll 2352, Page 267." Heritage Quest Online.

"Lecture, plus more on old Houston hospitals." Bayou City History. Houston Chronicle. <http://blogs.chron.com/bayoucityhistory/2011/01/a-lecture-plus-more-on-old-Houston-hospitals/> [Accessed June 12, 2011].

Morrison & Fourmy Directory Co. Houston City Directory, 1917. Houston: R. L. Polk & Co., 1917. Page 480.

"Japhet." Glenwood Cemetery.

24. "125 Emile Street, Account number 0212280000003." Harris County Appraisal District. <http://www.hcad.org/> [Accessed June 12, 2011].

25. Britt, Douglas. "On the waterfront." Houston Chronicle, June 13, 2007. <http://www.chron.com/disp/story.mpl/nb/east/news/4883981.html> [Accessed June 13, 2011].

26. "Day at Houston." Galveston Daily News, Sunday, July 7, 1895, page 3, Issue 105, Column A.

City of Houston and environs. Houston: Whitty & Stott, 1895. <http://lcweb2.loc.gov/cgi-bin/map_item.pl> [Accessed June 12, 2011].

27. "Over the state." Galveston Daily News, Friday, August 10, 1883, Issue 141, Column E.

Morrison & Fourmy's general directory of the city of Houston, 1895-96. Galveston: Morrison & Fourmy, 1895. Page 204.

"Day at Houston." Galveston Daily News, Sunday, July 7, 1895, page 3, Issue 105, Column A.

28. "Multiple News Items." Galveston Daily News, September 1, 1896, page 8, column E.

"Houston, 1924. Volume 8, Sheet 845." Sanborn maps, 1867-1970: Texas.

29. "New charters filed." Galveston Daily News, March 25, 1910, page 10.

"Exporters Compress & Warehouse Company vs William P. Harris, et. al." Daily Court Review, December 5, 1936. Page 3.

30. Ibid.

"Merchants Compress is divided into companies." Galveston Daily News, July 4, 1923, page 3.

31. "[Advertisement]." Houston Port Book, Volume 11, Number 2 (1933). Houston: Houston Port Authority. Page 48.

"[Advertisement]." Dallas Morning News. March 17, 1949, Section 2, page 19.

32. "Upper Channel Industrial Development." Houston Port Book, Volume 35 (Spring), 1957, page 71.

33. Darwin, Jennifer. "Prolers sell family business to scrap metals consolidator." Houston Business Journal, Friday, March 24, 1997. <http://houston.bizjournals.com/houston/stories/1997/03/24/story7.html> [Accessed December 20, 2007].

"Proler International Corp." Business Week. <http://investing.businessweek.com/research/stocks/private/snapshot.asp?privcapID=298175> [Accessed May 17, 2011].

"Metal Management announces completion of Proler Southwest and Proler Steelworks merger." HighBeam Research. <http://www.highbeam.com/doc/1G1-19721736.html> [Accessed December 20, 2007].

"Sims Metal Management History." Sims Metal Management Limited. <http://www.mtlm.com/about/history/> [Accessed on June 15, 2011].

34. "Exporters Compress & Warehouse Company vs William P. Harris, et. al." Daily Court Review, December 5, 1936. Page 3.

"Houston, 1924. Volume 8, Sheet 845." Sanborn maps, 1867-1970: Texas.

"Kelley Industries, Inc. business records (MS102)." Woodson Research Center. Rice University. <http://library.rice.edu/collections/WRC/finding-aids/manuscripts/0102/> [Accessed June 16, 2011].

35. Ibid.

36. Ibid.

37. "North Side Wastewater Treatment Plant, 5557A10, 5557B9." Harris County Appraisal District. <http://www.hcad.org/> [Accessed December 20, 2007].

"A&A Plastics." Employer Contacts. Socrates. <http://socrates.cdr.state.tx.us/Socrates/> [Accessed December 20, 2007].

"It's in the bag." American Bag Manufacturing, Inc. <http://american-bag.com/> [Accessed December 20, 2007].

38. Smyer, Susan. "City of Houston Wastewater History." City of Houston. Public Works and Engineering Department. <http://documents.publicworks.houstontx.gov/documents/utilities/history_waste_water_operations.pdf/> [Accessed June 18, 2011].

Melosi, Martin V. Effluent America: Cities, Industry, Energy and the Environment. Pittsburgh: Univ of Pittsburgh Press, 2001. Page 169.

39. O'Kane, Elisabeth. "To lift the City out of the Mud: Health, sanitation and sewerage in Houston, 1840-1920." Houston Review. Volume 17, No. 1 (1995). Houston: Houston Library Board, 1995.

Smyer, Susan. "City of Houston Wastewater History."

"Needed sanitation for Houston." Galveston Daily News, May 4, 1881, Issue 36, column B.

40. Melosi, Martin V. Effluent America: Cities, Industry, Energy and the Environment. Pages 170-171.

41. Smyer, Susan. "City of Houston Wastewater History."

42. Ibid.

McComb, David G. Houston: A History. Austin: University of Texas, 1981. Page 90.

Melosi, Martin V. Effluent America: Cities, Industry, Energy and the Environment. Page 174.

43. Smyer, Susan. "City of Houston Wastewater History."

44. "City's inattention to surroundings augments Houston's housing problem." Dallas Morning News. 12/10/1912, page 4.

Smyer, Susan. "City of Houston Wastewater History."

45. Ibid.

Freese, Simon W. and D. L. Sizemore. "A century in the works." Freese and Nichols. <http://www.freese.com/sites/default/files/Century.pdf/> [Accessed June 18, 2011]. Page 44.

46. "Houston, 1924. Volume 8, Sheet 845." Sanborn maps, 1867-1970: Texas.

47. Fugate, G. L. and W. S. Stanley. Experiences and experiments at the Houston Activated Sludge Plants. Sewage Works Journal, Volume 1, Number 1 (October, 1928), pages 70-76.

"Houston, 1924. Volume 8, Sheet 845." Sanborn maps, 1867-1970: Texas.

Smyer, Susan. "City of Houston Wastewater History."

Turney, J. G. "Sludge disposal study at Houston, Texas." Sewage Works Journal, Sewage Works Journal, Volume 21, Number 5 (September, 1949), pages 807-810.

48. Final Environmental Impact Statement for Northwest Regional Wastewater Facilities, City of Houston. Dallas: U. S. Environmental Protection Agency, 1975.

Mueller, Barbara and Dan Jones. "Conference Feature: Wastewater Treatmenet Parallels Growth of Houston." Journal (Water Pollution Control Federation), Volume 51, Number 9 (September, 1979), pages 2219-2223.

"Booming Economy (1970-1980)." Houston History. <http://www.houstonhistory.com/decades/history5q.htm> [Accessed June 21, 2011].

49. "69th St. Wastewater Treatment Plant." Water and Wastewater Plant Directory. <http://www.waterandwastewater.com/plant_directory/Detailed/503.html> [Accessed June 21, 2011].

50. Smyer, Susan. "City of Houston Wastewater History."

51. "Map of Houston, Texas." Fantham & Fantham, [March, 1928].

Ashburn, J. Foster. Ashburn's Map of Houston, Texas. 1942.

52. "Houston, 1924-1951. Volume 8, Sheet 849." Sanborn maps, 1867-1970: Texas.

"Turkey Bend, 5557C3, 5557A11." Harris County Appraisal District. <http://www.hcad.org/> [Accessed December 21, 2007].

53. "Lafarge forms asphalt firm in Texas." HighBeam Research. <http://www.highbeam.com/doc/1P2-1130479.html> [Accessed December 21, 2007].

"Company News; Cemex Unit to Buy Some Lafarge Assets for $100 Million." New York Times. May 19, 1994. <http://query.nytimes.com/> [Accessed December 21, 2007].

"Lockwood Drive, 5557C2." Harris County Appraisal District. <http://www.hcad.org/> [Accessed December 23, 2007].

Tuley, Aaron. "Presentation of Buffalo Bayou Master Plan to Houston Canoe Club meeting, 7/10/2002." Buffalo Bayou Partnership. Houston, TX.

54. "Turkey Bend, 5557C3, 5557A11." Harris County Appraisal District.

"Company Profile." General Stevedores, LP. <http://www.genstev.com/> [Accessed December 21, 2007].

"H. B. Fuller, 5557C4, 5557A12." Harris County Appraisal District.

55. Ibid.

"About H. B. Fuller. Our History." H. B. Fuller. <http://www.hbfuller.com/About_Us/History/> [Accessed December 22, 2007].

56. "H. B. Fuller, 5557C4, 5557A12." Harris County Appraisal District.

"Gulf Coast Portland Cement Co (Transenergy Grinding." Company Profiles. Manta. <http://www.manta.com/> [Accessed December 22, 2007].

57. "Drawbridge Operating Regulation; Buffalo Bayou, TX. October 14, 1998 - 63 FR 55029."

58. García, María-Cristina. "García, Macario," Handbook of Texas Online <http://www.tshaonline.org/handbook/online/articles/fga76> [Accessed July 19, 2011].

59. Ibid.

60. Ibid.

61. "Green secures $700,000 for the acquisition og Buffalo Bend." Congressman Gene Green. United States. House of Representatives. <http://www.house.gov/apps/list/press/tx29_green/nr112603.html> [Accessed August 3, 2004].

62. "2300 SSgt Macario Garcia Drive, Account number 037770000010." Harris County Appraisal District.

63. Murphy, Bill. "Plans for East End nature park get boost." Houston Chronicle, Thursday, 12/09/2004. Section: B, Page 3, 2 Star Edition.

"Green secures $700,000 for the acquisition og Buffalo Bend."

64. Walker, Ronald Boyce. "Ceremony marks new chapter for East End." Houston Chronicle, Thursday, 12/16/2004. Section: This Week Z11, Page 15, 2 Star Edition.

Chapter 14: Magnolia Park

1. Henson, Margaret Swett. The History of Galveston Bay Resource Utilization. Publication GBNEF-39. Galveston: Galveston Bay National Estuary Program, 1993. Page 35.

McComb, David G. Houston: A History. Austin: University of Texas, 1981. Pages 32-33.

2. Flachmeier, Jeanette H. "Brady, John Thomas." The Handbook of Texas Online. <http://www.tshaonline.org/handbook/online/articles/fbr17> [Accessed September 16, 2011].

Cases Adjudged in the Supreme Court Prior to July 1903, Volume 96. Austin: Gammel-Statesman Publishing Co., 1904. Pages 364ff.

3. History of Texas Together with a Biographical History of the Cities of Houston and Galveston. Chicago: Lewis Publishing Co, 1895. Page 377.

4. Ibid.

Flachmeier, Jeanette H. "Brady, John Thomas."

"Brady, J T, 1860 Census, Series M653, Roll 1296, Page 416." Heritage Quest Online. ProQuest Information and Learning Company. <http://www.heritagequestonline.com/> [Accessed July 16, 2011].

5. Flachmeier, Jeanette H. "Brady, John Thomas."

History of Texas Together with a Biographical History of the Cities of Houston and Galveston. Page 377.

6. "[Advertisement]." Houston Telegraph, July 28, 1865, page 1.

"[Wm. Brady, Esq.]" Houston Telegraph, September 29, 1865, page 2.

History of Texas Together with a Biographical History of the Cities of Houston and Galveston. Pages 377-378.

"Brady, John T, 1870 Census, Series M593, Roll 1589, Page 547." Heritage Quest On-line. ProQuest Information and Learning Company. <http://www.heritagequestonline.com/> [Accessed July 16, 2011].

Morrison & Fourmy's general directory of the city of Houston for 1882-83. Houston: Morrison & Fourmy, 1882. Page 73.

7. Cases Adjudged in the Supreme Court Prior to July 1903, Volume 96.

8. Werner, George C. "Texas Transportation Company." Handbook of Texas Online. <http://www.tshaonline.org/handbook/online/articles/eqt17> [Accessed July 19, 2011].

Farrar, R. M. The Story of Buffalo Bayou and the Houston Ship Channel. Houston: Chamber of Commerce, 1926.

"Houston and Galveston." Galveston Daily News, January 30, 1875, page 2.

9. Farrar, R. M. The Story of Buffalo Bayou and the Houston Ship Channel.

Werner, George C. "Texas Transportation Company."

10. Claudia Hazlewood. "Morgan's Point, TX." Handbook of Texas Online. <http://www.tshaonline.org/handbook/online/articles/hlm89> [Accessed September 17, 2011].

Marilyn M. Sibley. "Clopper, Nicholas." Handbook of Texas Online. <http://www.tshaonline.org/handbook/online/articles/fcl31> [Accessed September 17, 2011].

Brunson, B. R. and Andrew Forest Muir. "Morgan, James." Handbook of Texas Online. <http://www.tshaonline.org/handbook/online/articles/fmo50> [Accessed September 17, 2011].

11. Farrar, R. M. The Story of Buffalo Bayou and the Houston Ship Channel.

Houston, A History and A Guide. Houston: Anson Jones Press, 1942. Page 135.

Lyon, Lonnie N. "Morgan - the Pioneer." Houston Port and City, Volume 10, Number 2 (November 1932), page 45ff.

"Ship Channel." Galveston Daily News, February 6, 1875, page 4.

12. Ibid.

Sibley, Marilyn M. "Houston Ship Channel." The Handbook of Texas Online. <http://www.tsha.utexas.edu/handbook/online/articles/rhh11.html> [Accessed December 2, 2010].

13. "Ship Channel." Galveston Daily News, February 6, 1875, page 4.

Houston, A History and A Guide. Page 131.

"Proposal for piles." Galveston Daily News, May 7, 1875, page 2.

14. Lyon, Lonnie N. "Morgan - the Pioneer."

15. Werner, George C. "Texas Transportation Company."

"Morgan's Ship Channel." Galveston Daily News, April 21, 1876, page 8.

16. Baughman, James P., "Morgan, Charles." Handbook of Texas Online. <http://www.tshaonline.org/handbook/online/articles/fmogm> [Accessed July 22, 2011].

Farrar, R. M. The Story of Buffalo Bayou and the Houston Ship Channel.

Lyon, Lonnie N. "Morgan - the Pioneer."

17. Houghton, Dorothy K. H. Houston's Forgotten Heritage. Houston: Rice University Press, 1991. Page 93.

"Bayou City Budget." Galveston Daily News, July 2, 1891, page 6.

Kleiner, Diana J. "Magnolia Park, Texas." The Handbook of Texas Online. <http://www.tshaonline.org/handbook/online/articles/hvm06> [Accessed September 17, 2011].

18. "Magnolia Park Picnic." Galveston Daily News, May 23, 1889, page 5.

Morrison & Fourmy's general directory of the city of Houston, 1890-91. Galveston: Morrison & Fourmy, 1890. Page 4.

E-Newsletter. Historic Neighborhoods Council. November, 2004. Greater Houston Preservation Alliance. <http://www.ghpa.org/>.

Houghton, Dorothy K. H. Houston's Forgotten Heritage. Page 158.

19. "Charters filed." Galveston Daily News, April 3, 1889, page 9.

Morrison & Fourmy's general directory of the city of Houston, 1889-90. Galveston: Morrison & Fourmy, 1889. Page 60.

"Bayou City Budget." Galveston Daily News, August 20, 1890, page 5.

Houston, A History and A Guide. Pages 97-98.

Werner, George C. "Houston Belt and Magnolia Park Railway." The Handbook of Texas Online. <http://www.tshaonline.org/handbook/online/articles/eqh10> [Accessed September 17, 2011].

20. Houston, A History and A Guide. Pages 97-98.

History of Texas Together with a Biographical History of the Cities of Houston and Galveston. Page 379.

"Overcome by heat." Galveston Daily News, June 26, 1891, page 5.

"Large funeral." Galveston Daily News, June 30, 1891, page 5.

21. Ibid.

22. " Bayou City Budget." Galveston Daily News, July 2, 1891, page 6.

"Wheelmen's Race." Galveston Daily News, July 16, 1893, page 3.

"Concert at Magnolia Park." Galveston Daily News, July 16, 1893, page 3.

23. Werner, George C. "Houston Belt and Magnolia Park Railway."

"[Advertisement]." Galveston Daily News, September 15, 1895, page 9.

Cases Argued and Adjudged in the Courts of Civil Appeals of the State of Texas During the First Half of the Year 1903, Volume 32. Austin: Gammel-Statesman Publishing Co., 1904. Pages 466ff.

"Austin News." Galveston Daily News, March 26, 1896, page 4.

24. Werner, George C. "Houston Belt and Magnolia Park Railway."

Cravens, Chris. "Houston, Oaklawn and Magnolia Park Railway." The Handbook of Texas Online. <http://www.tshaonline.org/handbook/online/articles/eqh15> [Accessed September 17, 2011].

25. Sibley, Marilyn M. "Houston Ship Channel."

Farrar, R. M. The Story of Buffalo Bayou and the Houston Ship Channel.

Houston, A History and A Guide. Pages 136.

Antrobus, Sally. Galveston Bay. College Station: Texas A&M University Press, 2005. Page 58.

"Fleet of yachts." Galveston Daily News, November 29, 1907, page 3.

26. "Not wharf property." Galveston Daily News, August 4, 1907, page 9.

"[Advertisement]." Galveston Daily News, July 22, 1906, page 1.

"Editorial." Galveston Daily News, June 27, 1909, page 24.

27. "[Advertisement]." Galveston Daily News, June 26, 1909, page 3.

"Magnolia Park." Galveston Daily News. August 8, 1909. p. 16-1.

Houghton, Dorothy K. H. Houston's Forgotten Heritage. Pages 48, 163.

28. "[Advertisement]." Galveston Daily News, June 26, 1909, page 3.

"Magnolia Park News." Galveston Daily News, July 11, 1909, page 24.

29. "Magnolia Park." Galveston Daily News. August 8, 1909. p. 16-1.

Kleiner, Diana J. "Magnolia Park, Texas."

"For new school district." Galveston Daily News, August 2, 1911, page 8.

30. "Reception to Brigade Officers" Galveston Daily News, May 31, 1911, page 4.

"Beaumont & Great Northern Changes." Galveston Daily News, June 25, 1909, page 8.

"Texas Bankers' Attitude to the Texas Railroads." Galveston Daily News, April 9, 1911, page 53.

"Offer Maneuver Grounds." Galveston Daily News, May 20, 1911, page 12.

"Troops parade through Houston." Galveston Daily News, May 28, 1911, page 19.

"City of Houston sees First Brigade." Galveston Daily News, June 2, 1911, page 5.

31. "Day's Charters." Galveston Daily News, December 19, 1911, page 4.

"Streets to be improved." Galveston Daily News, June 2, 1912, page 19.

"[Advertisement]." Galveston Daily News, May 1, 1912, page 9.

32. Kleiner, Diana J. "Magnolia Park, Texas."

Bivins, Ralph. "Developers moving in at old hotel / Tennison being turned into apartments, offices." Houston Chronicle, Wednesday, 11/04/98. Business Section, Page 1, 3 Star Edition.

Rosales, F. Arturo. "Mexicans in Houston: The struggle to survive, 1908-1975." Houston Review. Volume 3, No. 2 (Summer 1981). Houston: Houston Library Board, 1981. Pages 224-248.

33. Melville, Margarita B. "The Mexicans in Houston Today." Houston History. <http://www.houstonhistory.com/> [Accessed January 27, 2005].

Kleiner, Diana J. "Magnolia Park, Texas."

34. Ibid.

Varela, Christopher. "Hidalgo Park Quiosco." Application for an Official Texas Historical Marker. Harris County Historical Commission. September 24, 2010. On file at the Harris County Archives.

"Parks." Buffalo Bayou Partnership. Houston, TX. <http://www.buffalobayou.org/parks.html> [Accessed August 19, 2005].

35. Varela, Christopher. "Hidalgo Park Quiosco."

36. Ibid.

37. Ibid.

38. Rosales, F. Arturo. "Mexicans in Houston: The struggle to survive, 1908-1975."

Kleiner, Diana J. "Magnolia Park, Texas."

39. Beck, Bill. At your service: an illustrated history of Houston Lighting & Power Company. Houston: Gulf Publishing Co., 1990. Page 83.

Henson, Margaret Swett. "Harris County." The Handbook of Texas Online. <http://www.tshaonline.org/handbook/online/articles/hch07> [Accessed September 17, 2011].

Tamborello, Charles J. "Reconstruction of Franklin Street Bridge at Buffalo Bayou." Tamborello Engineering Corporation. [1996?].

40. "Park Place Quadrangle, Texas - Harris Co. 7.5 Minute Series (Topographic)." Denver: U. S. Geological Survey, 1922.

Moreno, Jenalia. "Nonunion stevedores establish presence." Houston Chronicle, Thursday, 05/17/2001. Section C, Page 1, 3 Star Edition.
Houston, A History and A Guide. Page: inside back cover.
41. Moreno, Jenalia. "Nonunion stevedores establish presence."
42. Ibid.

Chapter 15: Harrisburg

1. "13 Wharf St, Account number 1281340010001." Harris County Appraisal District. <http://www.hcad.org/> [Accessed July 27, 2011].
"Profile." Derichebourg S. A. <http://www.derichebourg.com/pages_uk/groupe/profil_g.php/> [Accessed July 27, 2011].
Antrobus, Sally. Galveston Bay. College Station: Texas A&M University Press, 2005. Page 58.
2. Rust, Carol. "How Buffalo Speedway got its name ... and other street stories." Houston Chronicle, Sunday, 03/02/97. Lifestyle Section, Page 1, 2 Star Edition.
Brown, John Henry. History of Texas from 1685 to 1892. Volume 1. St. Louis: L. S. Daniell, 1892. Pages 94-95.
Smith, Daisey Lauretta. The history of Harrisburg, Texas, 1822-1927. [Houston, TX: s.n.], 1981. Page 52.
3. Beazley, Julia. "Harris, John Richardson." The Handbook of Texas Online. <http://www.tshaonline.org/handbook/online/articles/fha85> [Accessed July 27, 2011].
Walker, L. L., Jr. "The story of old Harrisburg." Houston: Harrisburg Bank, nd.
Fulmore, Z. T. The History and Geography of Texas as Told in County Names. Austin: E. L. Steck, 1915. Pages 77-78.
4. Houston, A History and A Guide. Houston: Anson Jones Press, 1942. Page 295.
Beazley, Julia. "Harris, John Richardson."
Houghton, Dorothy K. H. Houston's Forgotten Heritage. Houston: Rice University Press, 1991. Page 1.
Henson, Margaret Swett. "Harris County." The Handbook of Texas Online. <http://www.tshaonline.org/handbook/online/articles/hch07> [Accessed September 17, 2011].
5. Ibid.
Walker, L. L., Jr. "The story of old Harrisburg."
6. Hutton, Jim and Jim Henderson. Houston, a history of a giant. Tulsa: Continental Heritage, Inc., 1976. Page 9.
Houghton, Dorothy K. H. Houston's Forgotten Heritage. Page 17.
7. Muir, Andrew Forest. "The Municipality of Harrisburg, 1835-1836." Southwestern Historical Quarterly Online, Vol. 056, No. 1, Page 050. <http://texashistory.unt.edu/ark:/67531/metapth101145/m1/54/> [Accessed September 17, 2011].
Muir, Andrew Forest. "Harrisburg, TX (Harris County)." Handbook of Texas Online. <http://www.tshaonline.org/handbook/online/articles/hvh27> [Accessed September 17, 2011].
8. Fulmore, Z. T. The History and Geography of Texas as Told in County Names.
Houston, A History and A Guide. Pages 23, 139, 259.
Southwick, Leslie H. "Wilson, Robert." The Handbook of Texas Online. <http://www.tshaonline.org/handbook/online/articles/fwi56> [Accessed September 17, 2011].
9. Houghton, Dorothy K. H. Houston's Forgotten Heritage. Page 289.
Muir, Andrew Forest. "The Municipality of Harrisburg, 1835-1836."
10. Houghton, Dorothy K. H. Houston's Forgotten Heritage. Page 3.
Houston, A History and A Guide. Page 24.
11. Maxwell, Robert S. "Lumber Industry." The Handbook of Texas Online. <http://www.tshaonline.org/handbook/online/articles/drl02> [Accessed September 17, 2011].

"Harris, William Plunkett. Papers. MC065." San Jacinto Museum. <http://www.sanjacinto-museum.org/Herzstein_Library/Manuscripts/> [Accessed April 12, 2005].

Beazley, Julia. "Harris, John Richardson." The Handbook of Texas Online.

Muir, Andrew Forest. "Harris, Jane Birdsall." The Handbook of Texas Online. <http://www.tshaonline.org/handbook/online/articles/fha83> [Accessed September 17, 2011].

12. Southwick, Leslie H. "Wilson, Robert."

Houston, A History and A Guide. Page 36.

Muir, Andrew Forest. "Harrisburg, TX (Harris County)."

13. Muir, Andrew Forest. "Harris, Jane Birdsall."

"Harris, William Plunkett. Papers. MC065."

Muir, Andrew Forest. "Harrisburg, TX (Harris County)."

Jones, C. Anson. "Early history of Harris County, Texas." Genealogical Record. Houston. December, 1984. p. 141-144. and March, 1985. p. 17-21.

Houghton, Dorothy K. H. Houston's Forgotten Heritage. Page 6.

14. Muir, Andrew Forest. "Harris, Jane Birdsall."

Newton, Lewis W. "Briscoe, Andrew." The Handbook of Texas Online. <http://www.tshaonline.org/handbook/online/articles/fbr58> [Accessed September 17, 2011].

15. Houston, A History and A Guide. Page 140.

Sibley, Marilyn McAdams. Port of Houston: a history. Austin: Univ of Texas Press, 1968. Page 62.

Reed, S. G. "Harrisburg Railroad and Trading Company." The Handbook of Texas Online. <http://www.tshaonline.org/handbook/online/articles/eqh03> [Accessed September 17, 2011].

16. "Buffalo Bayou, Brazos." Texas Historical Commission. Atlas. <http://atlas.thc.state.tx.us/scripts/>. [Accessed January 12, 2001].

Newton, Lewis W. "Briscoe, Andrew."

Hurley, Marvin. "The Formative Years. Houston History, 1840-1850." Houston History. <http://www.houstonhistory.com/decades/history5a.htm>.

"History Timeline." Fort Bend Model Railroad Club. <http://www.fbmrrc.com/history_timeline.html> [Accessed June 18, 2004].

"Buffalo Bayou, Brazos." Texas Historical Commission. Atlas.

Spellman, Paul N. Forgotten Texas Leader: Hugh McLeod and the Texan Santa Fe Expedition. College Station: Texas A&M Univ. Press, 1999. Pages 142-143.

Houston, A History and A Guide. Page 141.

17. Henson, Margaret Swett. "Harris County."

Houston, A History and A Guide. Pages 142, 297.

18. Ibid. Page 297.

Muir, Andrew Forest. "Harris, Jane Birdsall."

19. Beazley, Julia. "Sherman, Sidney." The Handbook of Texas Online. <http://www.tshaonline.org/handbook/online/articles/fsh27> [Accessed September 17, 2011].

20. "Buffalo Bayou, Brazos." Texas Historical Commission. Atlas.

Houghton, Dorothy K. H. Houston's Forgotten Heritage. Page 9.

Houston, A History and A Guide. Page 295.

"Houston Local Items." Galveston Daily News, December 29, 1876, Issue 240, column F.

21. Seiler, Leslie Carl. "Buffalo Bayou and the Houston Ship Channel." Around Town Houston Through Postcards. <http://home.sprynet.com/~lcseiler/houarnd5.htm> [Accessed August 30, 2001].

Muir, Andrew Forest. "Harrisburg, TX (Harris County)."

22. Winkler, E. W. "The 'Twin Sisters' Cannon, 1836-1865." Southwestern Historical Quarterly Online. Vol. 21, No. 1, Page 61. Texas State Historical Association. <http://texashistory.unt.edu/ark:/67531/metapth101073/m1/67/> [Accessed September 17, 2011].

Hammond, Ken. "The mystery of the Twin Sisters." Houston Chronicle, Sunday, 12/07/1986. Section Texas Magazine, Page 10, 2 Star Edition.

Hunt, Jeffrey William. "Twin Sisters." The Handbook of Texas Online. <http://www.tshaonline.org/handbook/online/articles/qvt01> [Accessed September 17, 2011].

23. Hammond, Ken. "The mystery of the Twin Sisters."

Hunt, Jeffrey William. "Twin Sisters."

24. Ibid.

25. Ibid.

Tutt, Bob. "Long lost 'Twin Sisters' cannons coming back in form of reproductions." Houston Chronicle, Sunday, 02/09/1986. Section: 3, Page 1, 2 Star Edition.

Winkler, E. W. "The 'Twin Sisters' Cannon, 1836-1865."

Hammond, Ken. "The mystery of the Twin Sisters."

26. Ibid.

"Twin Sisters." Dallas Morning News. 4/15/1893.

"Lost Twin Sisters." Dallas Morning News. 4/21/1893.

Cox, Mamie Wynne. "Famous old 'Twin Sisters' cannon may be found and Graves' desire realized." Houston Chronicle, 07/03/1921.

Cox, Mamie Wynne. "Gift Guns from Cincinnati Declared Buried in Woods." Dallas Morning News. 4/5/1936.

27. Hammond, Ken. "Digging for the Twin Sisters cannons." Houston Chronicle, Sunday, 12/07/1988. Section Texas Magazine, Page 8, 2 Star Edition.

28. "Search for secrets of a sunken cannon." Richard Geldhof's Blog. <http://richardgeldhof.blogspot.com/2010/02/search-for-secrets-of-sunken-cannon.html/> [Accessed May 15, 2010].

Carroll, H. Bailey, "Texas Collection." The Southwestern Historical Quarterly, Vol. 55, No. 4 (Apr., 1952), p. 503-505.

Hayes, Robert M. "Will 'Twin Sisters' Ever Be Located?" Dallas Morning News. 4/19/1953.

Tolbert, Frank X. "Why Mr. Mitchell Posted a Reward." Dallas Morning News. 7/3/1961, page 1.

"History of NUMA. Project 22. Search for Sam Houston's Twin Sisters..." National Underwater & Marine Agency. <http://www.numa.net/history/project22/project22.html> [Accessed March 30, 2003].

Hammond, Ken. "Digging for the Twin Sisters cannons."

29. Houston, A History and A Guide. Pages 297-298.

Muir, Andrew Forest. "Harris, Jane Birdsall." The Handbook of Texas Online.

30. "Sidney Sherman Bridge." Wikipedia. <http://en.wikipedia.org/wiki/Sidney_Sherman_Bridge> [Accessed July 29, 2011].

Index

Biographical note

Louis F. Aulbach is the author of five best selling river guides to the rivers of West Texas, including three guides to the Rio Grande, a guide to the Pecos River and a guide to the Devils River. His first river guide, called the Lower Canyons of the Rio Grande, was first published in 1987 and is now in its fourth edition.

Aulbach, a native Houstonian, is a graduate of St. Thomas High School, Rice University and the University of Chicago. He recently retired after over 17 years as the Records Management Officer for the City of Houston. He served on the Harris County Historical Commission in the 2009-2010 term. The Commission is charged with promoting, preserving and protecting the history of Harris County.

Updated information to his published guides and excerpts from his current projects can be found on Aulbach's website: http://users.hal-pc.org/~lfa/

20952434R30402

Made in the USA
Charleston, SC
03 August 2013